Health care in the United Kingdom

Its organisation and management

Edited by
N.W. Chaplin
for The Institute of Health Service Administrators

Kluwer Medical **London**

ISBN 0 903393 54 9

First published in Great Britain by
Kluwer Publishing Limited, 1 Harlequin Avenue, Great West Road, Brentford, Middlesex TW8 9EW

Printed in Great Britain

Health care in the United Kingdom

Richard Piper. 30.4.82

Contents

Foreword

The Institute of Health Service Administrators has produced this book in the belief that managers working in the health service, members of health authorities and community health councils and other people both in the UK and overseas with an active interest in the health services will welcome a reliable factual account of current practice in the organisation and management of health care in the United Kingdom which also discusses current problems and the issues that arise from them.

The subject is a large and complicated one — the more so in that practice varies in the four countries of the UK — and this book, though large, is not comprehensive. It is not a resumé of the large and growing literature on the provision of health care, nor is it a manual for health service managers. The aim rather has been to describe the main features of both the public and the independent sectors in sufficient detail to be useful. Since all but a small part of the personal health care in the UK is provided through the national health service, the foundation of the book is necessarily the official literature: statements of government policy, circulars from the health departments, the reports of official committees and so on. This literature is the necessary working material of NHS authorities and their managers. To assist readers, the lists at the ends of chapters give the main statutory instruments, circulars and official reports. Contributors have also made use of the increasing number of academic studies which in recent years have brought new insights into health service policy and performance. The reading lists include some academic publications, and also some of the valuable contributions made by such bodies as the King's Fund and various professional associations and pressure groups.

In 1969 the Institute, then the Institute of Hospital Administrators, published *Modern Hospital Management,* to which the present volume is in a sense a successor. There is, however, a considerable difference. The earlier book was primarily a textbook for students of the Institute's examinations whereas the present one has been designed for a broader purpose, although it will undoubtedly be of great value to Institute students and to others interested in the study of health services.

When *Modern Hospital Management* went out of print some three years after publication it was clear that a revision was inappropriate in view of the then forthcoming reorganisation of the NHS. The Council of the Institute therefore decided to consider its replacement when the reorganised service was functioning. In 1978 the decision was taken to produce a work on the present lines rather than a replacement. The book was planned when the report of the Royal Commission on the National Health Service was awaited but not yet published. Following the publication of the Royal Commission's report, the government's plans for a further reorganisation of the NHS have gone ahead. The government's ideas of how the NHS will be organised and managed in future could be set out quite briefly, and in fact are outlined in the last chapter, but an account on the lines of this book of how it works in practice, including an account of the difficulties experienced, will be possible only after it has been functioning for several years, and then only if it is spared further upheaval. In this field change is always impending yet the underlying continuity is usually extensive. Thus, while some parts of this book will have to be read in the light of subsequent changes, most of it will remain valid, and a full understanding of future developments will hardly be possible except in the light of the arrangements described in this book.

The detailed planning of the book was entrusted by the Council to a steering committee on new publications comprising W.M. Naylor (chairman), B.G. Bush and B. Edwards. The steering committee outlined the contents of the book and drew up synopses. It then invited contributors to submit fuller synopses and when these were agreed to submit draft chapters.

A work such as this would not have been possible if the Institute had not been able to call on the expertise of its members. The Council is most grateful to the members of the steering group and to the contributors. The latter were: the late A.J. Brooking, and N.W. Chaplin, M.J. Fairey, J. Hallas, D.M. Hands, C.R. Hayton, R.C. Maingay, W.M. Naylor, D.K. Nichol, B. le G. Petfield, F.R. Reeves, M.S. Rigden, M. Schofield, C.G. Taylor, A.J. Wall, C.R. West and D. Woolley. Some of them wish to acknowledge the help they have received from colleagues. In editing the drafts the editor has been greatly assisted by the members of the steering committee and J.H. Button and G.G. Savage. If the diversity of origins has not been altogether disguised, or duplication altogether avoided, it must nevertheless be stressed that the editor has, to a greater or lesser extent, altered all the original drafts, for the most part without consulting the contributors, and it is he not they who must carry responsibility for the final result.

Official documents are reproduced by permission of the Controller of Her Majesty's Stationery Office. These include extracts from the HMSO publications *Better Services for the Mentally Handicapped, Management Arrangements for the Reorganised National Health Service, Priorities for Health and Personal Social Services in England, The Way Forward, Sharing Resources for Health in England, The Government's Expenditure Plans 1979-80 to 1982-83, DHSS Annual Report 1976, NHS Accounts 1977-78* and *Report of the Royal Commission on the National Health Service,* and also extracts from circulars and other publications of the DHSS.

1
Health services — historical background

In nearly all societies there are men and women to whom people turn for treatment and advice when they are ill. In our society that role is played by the doctor, particularly the general practitioner. It was in the nineteenth century that the medical profession as we know it evolved. At the beginning of that century there were three long-established professions with different functions and social standing: an elite of university-educated physicians, mainly in London and Edinburgh, the surgeons and the apothecaries. Most of the rank and file general practitioners were apothecaries, often also qualified as surgeons, but they were outnumbered by people practising medicine without qualification. The Medical Act 1858 established what is now the General Medical Council with the duty of registering the medical practitioners it considered suitably qualified. The unregistered were not debarred from practising medicine, except in public employment, though their scope for doing so became increasingly limited. Registration was through the approval of qualifications, which was possible because over the preceding fifty years the traditional method of training by apprenticeship had gradually been replaced by more formal teaching in medical schools, and examinations. The Act and the amending Act of 1886, brought order and new standards of education, ethics and practice to the medical profession.

In the nineteenth century and later the general practitioner was a private practitioner. Like other professional men he depended for his livelihood on the supply of people willing to pay for his services. General practitioners were therefore more numerous and more prosperous in the more prosperous parts of the country, not where there was most sickness.

Voluntary hospitals

General practitioners attended people in their homes. Then, as for centuries before, the natural place for a man to be ill was in his own bed, cared for by his family and servants, with visits from the doctor. For people who could be cared for in that way, hospitals did not become desirable until they had developed medical and nursing skills and technical facilities which provided a standard of care, and particularly of treatment, that not even the prosperous could obtain at home.

'Hospital' was originally a general term for institutions caring for people away from home — the aged, the poor, the orphaned and travellers, as well as the sick. After the Reformation, London had two endowed hospitals for the sick and one for the insane. The need for more does not appear to have been felt until early in the eighteenth century when, first in London and then in Edinburgh, Dublin and the main provincial cities, prominent citizens established voluntary hospitals or infirmaries. They were financed by subscription and gift and broadly speaking catered for the respectable poor, treating most types of short-term illness, though by modern standards the length of stay was very long and many patients were not confined to bed. A parallel movement, associated with the appearance of the man-midwife, was the establishment of lying-in or maternity hospitals, catering for women who could not be delivered at home.

At the beginning of the nineteenth century the number of hospital beds was still small, and comparatively few of the sick received hospital care. Throughout the century existing hospitals expanded, similar ones were founded in the new and growing cities, special hospitals were established treating particular types of patient, disease or parts of the body, and outside the cities cottage hospitals were developed to take paying patients cared for by their general practitioners. This expansion and renewal of the voluntary hospitals continued almost until the inception of the national health service.

Voluntary hospitals provided free treatment for the poor, often through the patronage of subscribers. When, by the last quarter of the nineteenth century, hospitals were beginning to provide a level of care attractive to people who could not expect to receive it as charity, equivalent care might have been made available in non-charitable institutions, and to some extent that happened, but on the whole the non-poor took to using the voluntary hospitals, which had a high reputation and the necessary facilities and were attended by the leading members of the medical profession. The voluntary hospitals met this demand in two ways, most of the change occurring in the twentieth century. They provided private accommodation for the fee-paying patients of their honorary staff and, in response to rising costs as well as to the wider social range of patients treated, they began in England and Wales, though not in Scotland, to charge all non-private patients who could pay. Payments were often made through contributory schemes and patients were charged what they could pay rather than what their treatment cost. Medical staff continued to serve unpaid. Thus, while no longer generally giving free treatment, hospitals continued to have a charitable rather than a commercial ethos.

Hospital doctors and general practitioners

In the early voluntary hospitals local physicians gave their services just as local benefactors gave their money. They made little demands on their time, most of the work being done by their apprentices and the apothecary. In the nineteenth century hospitals became central to their interests for they provided access to patients both for teaching (which earned high fees) and for research, and while hospital appointments were honorary they gave the reputation and contacts necessary for a flourishing private practice. From the early nineteenth century doctors increasingly took the lead in founding new hospitals; several were founded specifically for teaching, and many of the special hospitals reflected the medical interests of their founders. Medical schools developed in association with the leading hospitals and, particularly in London, were much closer to the hospitals than to the university.

Thus despite the formal unification of the profession it was divided into an elite holding hospital posts and the general practitioners. (In places where there was not enough private practice to support a full-time specialist, general practitioners served as part-time specialists in the local hospital.) In the later nineteenth century there were conflicts between GPs and hospital doctors, particularly over the retention of patients referred for consultation and the treatment in out-patient departments of patients who could have afforded a general practitioner. They were eventually resolved by the establishment of the convention that a consultant saw patients only by referral from a GP. The general practitioners, it has been said, retained the patients but the consultants retained the hospitals. The convention, though dating from a time when many consultants were still generalists, established a clear relationship between generalists and specialists which was to be important not only for the organisation of the profession but also for the structure of the national health service.

It is a debated question whether the activities of general practitioners and voluntary hospitals had any measurable effect on the nation's health in the nineteenth century and even later. It is certain, however, that they met a need in that they provided the type of care and treatment expected — though expectations, particularly of the poor, were low. What they could not do was provide a comprehensive health service for the country. Comprehensive care would require the intervention of the state.

Intervention of the state in the nineteenth century

At least until the last years of the nineteenth century the state had neither the finance nor the administrative machinery to provide health care for the population in general, and there was no expectation that it should do so. The state's personal health care responsibilities were limited to those associated with its traditional activities such as the criminal law and waging war. This was the century in which prisons and barracks were built through the country and, as a corollary, the state also built a hospital for the criminally insane and military hospitals. The latter had some general influence because Florence Nightingale was involved.

Yet despite the general assumption that health care was the individual's own responsibility, a general distrust of state action and reluctance to increase public expenditure, the state undertook three types of hospital provision through the Poor Law and provisions relating to lunacy and infectious diseases which together provided more beds than the voluntary sector. Voluntary hospitals and other charitable bodies made some provision for the same types of patients as those cared for by public hospitals, but to nothing like the extent necessary to meet all needs. It was to meet the general need that public provision was necessary, though the motive was not so much charity to the individuals in need as the protection of society. In the broad sense of the term the aim was the policing of society, and it is no coincidence that in one form or another compulsion was associated with all three types of provision. State provision does not mean provision by the central government. Although the three types of hospital were provided under statutory powers they were financed and administered by existing or *ad hoc* local authorities, so that government control was limited and conditions varied greatly from place to place.

The Poor Law, which had existed since the beginning of the seventeenth century, was radically reformed in 1834 in England and Wales and in 1845 in Scotland, with much more emphasis on relief being given in the workhouse. Since illness, poverty and old age were closely associated, many of those having resort to Poor Law care were the sick, particularly the elderly chronic sick, rather than the workless, and the punitive or at least deterrent approach was inappropriate. Nevertheless much workhouse provision for the sick was very poor by the standards of the time, but in the last third of the century many boards of guardians built infirmaries separate from the main workhouses and in due course, particularly in the first decades of this century, developed some of them as acute hospitals, and treated patients not strictly eligible for care under the Poor Law.

The interest in emulating the voluntary hospitals, rather than devoting more attention to the chronic sick whom the voluntary hospitals did not provide for, has been considered an unfortunate development, and it is true that much provision for the chronic sick was poor up to 1948. However, geriatrics was not a known specialty before the advent of the national health service so that the possibilities of better care were not appreciated, whereas the need to supplement voluntary provision for acute illness in some places was clear.

Special public provision for pauper lunatics dates back to an Act of 1808, under which the first county asylums were built. There were subsequent important Acts in 1845, 1853 and 1890, the last of which moved administrative responsibility from Justices of the Peace to the new local authorities. A feature of provision for lunatics was that it was subject to central oversight by, in turn, Metropolitan Commissioners, Lunacy Commissioners and the Board of Control. The responsibility of these bodies extended to private madhouses as well as public asylums; they owed their existence to scandals, particularly in private madhouses, and also to fears of wrongful detention. All admissions to public asylums were compulsory, under a Justice's order on medical advice, and as patients usually remained in an asylum for life it is not surprising that much of the legislation was concerned with confinement and protection against it. Throughout the nineteenth century asylums grew in number and, strikingly, in size. They were usually situated in the country and if these locations genuinely provided asylum they also conveniently removed the mentally ill from the sight of most of the population.

In Scotland there was less development of public mental hospitals because much of the need was met by seven royal, or chartered, mental asylums and because many insane paupers were boarded out.

The third form of public hospital provision was for infectious diseases mainly, in England and Wales, under the Sanitary Act 1866 — somewhat before the nature of these diseases was understood though centuries after the benefits of isolation had been noticed. In most places the powers were placed on 'sanitary authorities', small local government bodies which, even when several combined for the purpose, produced numerous small hospitals, many of them inefficient.

These various forms of public provision provided much necessary care, even if often of a standard regarded as unsatisfactory at the time. As with other forms of health care, their positive contribution to improving the health of the nation was slight. For that we must turn to public health.

A report on Scottish health services in 1936 remarked:

> In Scotland, as elsewhere, the beginnings of health services can be traced to fear of pestilence; and it can be said that, up to a period a little over a generation ago, this fear supplied the leading motive for nearly all organised health care effort in Scotland.

That is as true of public health measures as of provision for dealing with infectious diseases.

A concern for public health is a traditional responsibility of local government; the cities of the ancient world were provided with water and cleaned. The problems of the nineteenth century derived from the unprecedented growth of population and of cities, combined with the century's distrust of government. Also, despite much study and theories, some of which were eventually to prove correct, doctors did not have the knowledge to justify the compulsion and the expenditure so disliked by ratepayers. The heroic period of the early medical officers of health belongs to the middle decades of the century, but it was not until the last third that clean water, proper sewerage and other public health measures revealed their effects in improved mortality statistics.

The early twentieth century

The twentieth century in the UK as in other countries has seen an enormous increase in the role of government; in what it is considered proper or necessary for it to do, particularly in economic and social matters, in its means of raising the finance for its enlarged role and in achieving the necessary administrative control.

Before 1914 the state machine was remarkably small by modern standards, or even those of 1939. Although there were in Edwardian Britain a few people, including some senior civil servants, who could envisage such things as a state medical service, the Liberal government of 1906-16, which did much to lay the foundation of the welfare state, had limited aims, and limited means. It should be remembered that the need to finance the old age pensions introduced in 1908 led to the innovatory budget of 1909 which in turn led to the 1911 constitutional crisis. There was, however, one important development in government. The gradual working out after 1870 of the effects of compulsory, and subsequently free, education meant both that the state of health of the country's children was visible and that there was the administrative machinery through which a school health service could be provided. There was also, in the Edwardian years, a Board of Education anxious to foster such a service. In 1888 there was established for the first time a comprehensive elected system of local government for the whole country; it took over education in 1902, and was not radically changed until 1974. With this new local government machinery in existence it was possible to place on it various responsibilities which developed into what are now called the community health services. Unfortunately from the early years, and in fact following Victorian precedent, powers or responsibilities for different services were placed on different tiers of government, which proved one of the weaknesses of local authority services before 1948.

For various reasons, including the unexpected difficulties of the Boer War and the realisation that the industrial lead was being taken by the USA and Germany, the country was much concerned in the early years of the century about national efficiency, physical degeneration and the problems of poverty, and these worries affected the development of the welfare services. Thus the provision of medical inspection in schools derived from the poor physical condition of many volunteers for the Boer War, and the Mental Deficiency Act of 1913, the first important legislation concerned with people whose previous institutional care had been in Poor Law institutions, lunatic asylums or voluntary institutions, was as much the result of eugenic worries as concern for the interests of the handicapped.

The obvious way of extending public provision of health care would have been through the Poor Law. It suffered, however, from a great disadvantage: the fundamental principle of deterrence or lesser eligibility intentionally made the Poor Law unpopular and was very difficult to reconcile with the provision of care according to need. A Royal Commission was appointed to examine the Poor Law but although it produced majority and minority reports in 1909, no action was taken on either for twenty years. The Liberal government turned in other directions: the development of various local authority services and, most important, Lloyd George's Part I of the National Insurance Act 1911. (Part II, the responsibility of Winston Churchill, was concerned with unemployment insurance.)

The poor had always had access to various forms of care apart from admission to voluntary hospitals and Poor Law infirmaries. In the big cities, particularly London, they made extensive use of the out-patient departments of the voluntary hospitals — a tradition which survived the introduction of the NHS. Various voluntary dispensaries, some dating from the eighteenth century, provided out-patient care. Many working people, particularly the better off, contributed to friendly societies or sick clubs which contracted with a general practitioner to provide services to their members. From the later nineteenth century there were various voluntary organisations of district nurses, some of which were to provide services for local authorities on a contractual basis until 1948. And in the end, however grudgingly, the Poor Law provided home care. In total, however, the provision was inadequate.

The National Insurance Act covered manual workers, and other workers up to a certain income. It provided free care by general practitioners and free drugs for insured persons, cash payment sickness and disablement benefits, a maternity benefit for the wives of insured persons and, until 1921, sanatorium treatment for those suffering from tuberculosis. It was financed by contributions from employee, employer and the state. An incidental consequence of the Act was that the provision for a small levy for medical research led to the establishment of what is now the Medical Research Council.

The Act, like other arrangements for health care before and since, had to build on existing arrangements. The friendly societies and industrial insurance companies were powerful interests and were incorporated in the arrangements as 'approved societies'. Each insured person had to belong to such a society, and the society paid the financial benefits. Societies with sufficient funds were free to provide supplementary benefits; the most common were for dental treatment and spectacles. Nationally the system was administered by national insurance commissioners and subsequently the central health departments, and locally by insurance committees on which approved societies, doctors and local authorities were represented. All general practitioners were entitled to be on the panel of those providing care under the Act. They were normally paid on a per caput system.

As a system of providing personal health care the arrangements were obviously inadequate; they did not provide for hospital treatment, though that was available in other ways, and they did not cover the families of insured persons. It would be a mistake, however, to see the scheme as aiming at providing personal health care to citizens as a right; the aim was rather national well-being in a general sense, particularly improved efficiency — which justified a contribution by the employer — and an attack on poverty; it was the sickness of the breadwinner, not of his dependants, which drove a family into poverty.

The Act had a wider significance than simply that of providing general practitioner care for more of the population. In the first place it marked the adoption, from the Prussian example, of national insurance in social legislation. National insurance was to have its apotheosis in the Beveridge Report, and to this day remains an element in financing the NHS.

In the second place the Act, despite intense opposition from the British Medical Association, was the making of general practice. The rank and file of the profession, who did not have a well-to-do clientele, had had to accept the unfavourable terms offered by the friendly societies to look after their members. Part-time employment by Poor Law guardians was also ill-paid, and the development of professional midwifery and of local authority health services increased their anxieties. Henceforth practitioners with a fair number of panel patients had a secure and reasonable if not large income, were free from the control of the friendly societies and worked under administrative arrangements which they found sufficiently congenial not to want greatly changed at the introduction of the NHS. To this day the medical record used by most general practitioners is in the form laid down under the 1911 Act. The administrative and financial arrangements for general practice, established in 1911 and reinforced in 1948, combined with the established convention about the relationship between generalists and specialists, have served to preserve general practice in this country when it has declined in most others.

Between the wars

In 1919 a Ministry of Health was established. Though part of the short-lived post-war reconstruction period it was the culmination of the work of the pre-war reform movement. The new ministry was responsible until 1948 for the Poor Law and until 1951 for general local government matters including housing which, from the post-war period onwards, became an important part of local government activity. Amongst other things it took over the responsibilities of the insurance commissioners established under the 1911 Act and various health responsibilities of the Board of Education, and the Board of Control, which was responsible for the oversight of the care of lunatics and mental defectives, came within its ambit. The Minister was to establish a Board of Health for Wales. The Scottish Board of Health was established in the same year, becoming the Department of Health for Scotland in 1929.

The Ministry of Health Act 1919 proposed the appointment of a Minister of Health 'for the purpose of promoting the health of the people throughout England and Wales, and for the purpose of the exercise of the powers transferred or conferred by this Act'. The Minister was required to take all such steps as might be desirable to secure the preparation, effective carrying out and co-ordination of measures conducive to the health of the people, including measures for the prevention and cure of diseases, the avoidance of fraud in connection with alleged remedies therefor, the treatment of physical and mental defects, the treatment and care of the blind, the initiation and direction of research, the collection, preparation, publication, and dissemination of information and statistics relating thereto, and the training of persons for health services. Those pressing for the establishment of the Ministry had hoped that it would lead to the establishment of a national medical service. They must have been disappointed with the result, for it was only in the war and post-war years that it was active in this respect. Nevertheless the Ministry was responsible for a good deal of legislation on health matters between the wars.

The most important was the Local Government Act 1929, which transferred the administration of the Poor Law from the boards of guardians to the county councils and county boroughs. These authorities were to continue the provision of Poor Law infirmaries through their public assistance committees but were also empowered, though not obliged, to provide general hospitals, not associated with the Poor Law, by transferring Poor Law hospitals, by building new ones and by making agency arrangements with voluntary hospitals. The Local Government (Scotland) Act 1929 made provisions similar to those for England and Wales.

Another important Act was the Mental Treatment Act 1930, which followed the report of a Royal Commission in 1926. Lunatic asylums had been administered by quasi-independent visiting committees appointed by the county and county borough councils since the Lunacy Act 1890 and the new Act renamed them mental hospitals, removed the Poor Law stigma previously attached to all patients admitted to them and, with a view to encouraging early treatment, for the first time made provision for the admission of temporary and voluntary patients without certification. Although, as with most legislation, developments were uneven and disappointing, the mental health services, administered after 1948 by the national health service, evolved sufficiently under this Act for the 1959 Act to represent a codification of what had been achieved as much as a new departure.

Two other Acts may be mentioned, one from each end of the period. Although tuberculosis had been one of the most serious nineteenth-century diseases it was only after 1912 that much public provision was made for its treatment, and the main development was under the Public Health (Tuberculosis) Act 1921, which required county and county borough councils to make adequate provision for clinics and sanatoria. The Cancer Act 1939 envisaged somewhat similar provision for this disease, but the outbreak of war prevented the service from materialising.

The inter-war years were on the whole, despite economic difficulties and political strains, a period of economic growth, and accordingly saw a rise both in standards of health and in expenditure on health care, though the effects of these, like the economic growth, were felt very unevenly throughout the country. The legislation of the period is an indication, but not an exact measure, of the increasing provision of personal health care. Thus, though there was a remarkable development of provision for the treatment of tuberculosis, there was a shortage of hospital beds for the disease even in the early years of the NHS. The development of municipal hospitals under the 1929 Act was less than expected, partly because the legislation was only permissive and partly because economic recession coincided with the Act. Nevertheless a number of local authorities, including the London and Middlesex County Councils, developed extensive services, with acute hospitals providing care of a standard comparable with the best voluntary hospitals. The London County Council controlled some 100 hospitals with 70,000 beds, about one seventh of all hospital facilities in England and Wales.

The voluntary hospitals were in great financial difficulties in the post-war years and an official committee under Lord Cave in 1921 asked for an exchequer grant of £1 million. The government gave half this sum and was not prepared to recognise a regular obligation to assist these hospitals. In the 1930s the financial position of the voluntary hospitals improved, thanks to the policy (except in Scotland) of encouraging contributory schemes and charging patients who were not members of schemes. (Municipal hospitals also charged patients.) A report of 1937, the Sankey Report, was able to say that the voluntary hospitals in Great Britain as a whole were solvent, though many individual hospitals had serious annual deficits. The financial difficulties were caused not by a drying up of sources of income but by increasing expense as medicine became more sophisticated and more staff were needed.

The hospitals as a whole carried out building work between the wars at a higher level than was achieved by the NHS during its first fifteen years.

The considerable increase in the public provision of health care during these years was achieved without the political controversy which marked the developments of 1911, 1946 and 1974; the most important politician involved in health care in the period, Neville Chamberlain, was concerned more with administrative efficiency than with social reform. If the politicians for the most part had few radical thoughts on the future of health care provision, and were content with *ad hoc* developments, the period was marked by a great deal of radical thinking by doctors and others professionally involved.

The Act establishing the Ministry of Health had provided for a Consultative Council on Medical and Allied Services which, under the chairmanship of Lord Dawson of Penn, in 1920 produced an interim report outlining a scheme of primary and secondary health centres. No final report was issued, the interim report had no immediate influence and in retrospect it is difficult to believe that the recommendations could have been implemented even if the reformist mood of the immediate post-war period had lasted. Nevertheless its comprehensive thinking influenced all future discussions of the health services, and it gave currency to the concept of the primary health centre.

The title of a report published by the British Medical Association in 1929, and revised in 1938, is an indication of the broader terms in which people thought in this period: *Proposals for a General Medical Service for the Nation*. The fullest official report of the period, the report of the Committee on Scottish Health Services, published in 1936 was equally comprehensive in scope, as was the survey of British health services published in 1937 by Political and Economic Planning (PEP).

Even reports on narrower subjects had tended to think in these broader terms. The official Cave Committee in 1921 had argued for permanent machinery to co-ordinate the work and finances of voluntary hospitals and the Sankey Commission of 1937, established by the British Hospitals Association, repeated the recommendations, regretting that the voluntary hospitals had not accepted the Cave advice. The need for planning and organisation on the basis of regions in place of local authority and individual hospital independence was one of the constant themes of the period. Large scale organisation was not unknown. The Metropolitan Asylums Board had provided a service on a large scale and its successor, the London County Council, an even larger one, though unco-ordinated with the many voluntary hospitals in London. The King Edward's Hospital Fund for London from its establishment in 1897 endeavoured to bring some co-ordination into the work of the latter. In Wales most of the provision of tuberculosis services was undertaken for local authorities by the King Edward VII Welsh National Memorial Association. The Local Government Act of 1929 provided for local committees representative of voluntary hospitals to be consulted by local authorities, but effective co-operation was rarely achieved. A quite different sort of regional service had been provided in Scotland since 1913 when the Highlands and Islands Medical Services Board provided what amounted to a complete medical service, mainly by subsidising general practice, in an area where no adequate services were otherwise possible. In a few places, joint hospital boards for the local co-operation of voluntary and local authorities were successfully established, and in some schemes of collaboration an amalgamation of voluntary hospitals was effected. In 1939 a new voluntary organisation, the

Nuffield Provincial Hospitals Trust, was established to promote the co-ordination of hospitals on a regional basis.

If the co-ordination of hospitals on a regional basis was one of the needs generally agreed by 1939, others were equally clear: the extension of provision to those not covered by the National Insurance arrangements, more and better hospitals and a better geographical distribution of services. The pre-war services were fairly summed up in the 1944 white paper:

> In general terms, the result is a complicated patchwork pattern of health resources, a mass of particular and individual services evolved at intervals over a century or more — but particularly during the last thirty or forty years — and for the most part coming into being one by one to meet particular problems, to provide for particular diseases or particular aspects of health or particular sections of the community. Each, as it emerged, was shaped by the conditions of its time, by the limited purposes for which it was designed, and perhaps by the fashions of administrative and political thought current when it was designed. Most of these services, though progressively expanded and adapted as the years have gone on, are still broadly running on the lines laid down for them at the start and are administered largely, or partly, as separate and independent entities. The patchwork, however, contains some very good pieces — well established and by now rich in experience.

The war years

War was expected to make a heavy demand on the country's hospital services and plans had been made accordingly. If, as so often in war, the impact was not exactly what had been expected, the hospitals did eventually carry a heavy burden both in the numbers of patients treated and in damage from air raids. In the long term it was the organisational arrangements which had the greatest impact.

The Emergency Medical Service was organised on a regional basis. Voluntary hospitals were paid grants originally for providing for air raid casualties and later for wider groups of patients. Considerable sums were spent on improving their premises and facilities, and a large number of hutted wards — some of them still in use — were provided at various hospitals throughout the country. Although the voluntary bodies and local authorities continued to be responsible for their hospitals they were working within an unprecedented amount of oversight and guidance as a national system. It was through the Emergency Medical Service that there developed three national organisations which have continued ever since: the public health laboratory service, the hospital laboratory service and the blood transfusion service. Local authorities were also required to provide civil defence ambulance services. Previously they had been empowered, but not obliged, to provide ambulance services and various arrangements had existed for their provision by local authorities, voluntary bodies, individual hospitals, etc.

The Emergency Medical Service brought specialists from the leading hospitals in touch with hospitals outside the main centres, and the poor impression they gained was confirmed by full and systematic official surveys carried out for the whole of Great Britain between 1942 and 1945.

If the medical profession was increasingly aware of the need for major improvements in the health services, public enthusiasm had stemmed from the publication of the Beveridge Report in 1942. The report, though received tepidly by both the main parties in the coalition government, was remarkably popular with the public, who saw it as a promise of a better post-war world. The subject of the report was the extension of national insurance, but one of its assumptions was that there would be comprehensive health and rehabilitation services.

In February 1943 the government announced its acceptance of the assumptions of the Beveridge Report, including a comprehensive medical service. A white paper outlining the proposals was published in February 1944. The basic objectives were to ensure that everybody in the country should have equal opportunity to benefit from the best and most up-to-date medical and allied services available, to provide, for all who wanted it, a comprehensive service covering every branch of medical and allied activity, and to divorce the care of health from questions of personal means. The general aim was to make the maximum use of good existing facilities and experience, adapting and adding to them. While local organisation should be based on the county and county borough councils, generally joint authorities would be needed for the organisation of hospital services, and these joint authorities would also make contractual arrangements with voluntary hospitals. The services would be free to all, costs being met from both local and public funds.

The advent of the national health service

The ministers of health in the coalition and caretaker Conservative governments pursued negotiations with the various interests with a view to implementing the proposals of the white paper. With the advent of the Labour government of 1945 the task fell to a new minister, Aneurin Bevan, who was unencumbered by the previous negotiations. The National Health Service Act was enacted in 1946. With one major exception there was little effective opposition because the voluntary hospitals, while disliking the scheme, had no prospect of continuing without financial assistance from the government, and the local authorities, though reluctant to lose services, were at the time, when various of their other services were being nationalised, not in a strong position to resist. The exception was the medical profession, led by the British Medical Association. Accommodation was reached, partly because the profession was itself divided, in time for the service to come into being on the appointed day, 5 July 1948.

Like all previous and subsequent reforms, the national health service built on existing services. It did, however, make three important innovations. In the first place the government, despite considerable pressure, kept to the white paper principle that the service should be available to the whole of the population and not, as with the National Insurance scheme, and many present-day insurance schemes on the Continent, limited to people below a certain income. Secondly, in contrast to the white paper, the service was, for the most part, to be financed from general taxation. Thirdly, all voluntary hospitals (with certain exceptions) and all local authority hospitals were vested in the minister. This made possible a far simpler system that that envisaged by the white paper under which both types of hospital would have continued.

Clause 1 of the Act laid down that:

> It shall be the duty of the Minister of Health to promote the establishment in England and Wales of a comprehensive health service designed to secure improvement in the physical and mental health of the people of England and

> Wales and the prevention, diagnosis and treatment of illness, and for that purpose to provide or secure the effective provision of services in accordance with the following provisions of this Act.

Services were to be provided in three ways.

The basic services were to be provided by independent contractors. As far as the general medical and general pharmaceutical services were concerned, the arrangements were in many ways a continuation of those established in 1911, although there was a great difference between general practice divided between paying and panel patients and one in which nearly all were NHS patients. The insurance committees were replaced by executive councils with similar functions but a rather different membership, as the 'approved societies' no longer had a role. Two new services were added: the general dental and the supplementary ophthalmic. It was envisaged that in time the latter would be replaced by the hospital eye service. For these two services, unlike general practice, members of the public did not have to register with a practitioner but, subject to rules about frequency of use, could attend any practitioner they wished. Payment was accordingly by item of service, not per caput. Expenditure on all these executive council services was 'open ended', i.e. it was not to be confined within a budget. Fees were agreed with the various professions and what was due to be paid depended on the numbers of patients presenting themselves and the treatment prescribed. Within broad limits, however, the expenditure was predictable in the short term, the main fluctuation being the effect of an epidemic on drug expenditure. The pattern of expenditure changed over the years. From 1958 the general pharmaceutical services cost more than the general medical services, i.e. the drugs prescribed by general practitioners cost more than the services of the practitioners themselves.

Other services, often called the community services, were to be provided by local health authorities. This was very much on the lines of previous legislation, and most of the services were already provided by local authorities, though some of them under Acts which empowered rather than required them to do so. An important change was that only county councils and county borough councils were to be local health authorities, and the confusing and irrational distribution of powers between different tiers of local government was brought to an end. The duties falling to local authorities included the provision of maternity and child welfare services, health visitors and home nursing, vaccination and immunisation, health centres and ambulance services. The old Poor Law was finally brought to an end on the same day that the NHS came into being. The National Assistance Act 1948, part of the legislation making the change, placed various welfare responsibilities on local authorities, including such things as residential care for the elderly, infirm and handicapped and provision of meals for old people in their homes. Many of these welfare duties catered for the same people as did the local authority health services, and often the two services were administered together under the medical officer of health. Local authority health services, unlike the other parts of the NHS, were not financed from general taxation, but in the same way as other local authority services, by rates supplemented by central government grants.

An entirely new structure was introduced for the hospital and specialist services, which were much the most expensive part of the NHS. In accordance with the ideas of the previous ten years, they were to be regionally organised. There were thirteen regional hospital boards (RHBs) for England and one for Wales; the number was determined by the wish to have a teaching hospital in each. The boards, appointed by the minister, in turn appointed hospital management commitees (HMCs). Broadly speaking, RHBs were responsible for the planning of hospital services, including the employment of consultants, and HMCs for the day-to-day management of the hospitals in their charge. Most HMCs were responsible for a group of hospitals in a locality, but some managed only one hospital, usually a large mental hospital or a hospital of special character. The two principal officers of RHBs were the senior administrative medical officer and the secretary. HMCs followed the administrative pattern of voluntary rather than local authority hospitals, and the chief officer was the secretary. The teaching hospitals, including in London the postgraduate hospitals, were administered by boards of governors quite separate from the main structure. As far as their own hospitals were concerned, they combined the functions of RHB and HMC. Nearly all teaching groups contained not only the original teaching hospital but also a number of others. The hospital and specialist services were financed by the Ministry, which made allocations to regional boards and boards of governors.

In addition to these three services, which were available throughout the country, there were a number of national organisations, with functions ranging from advising the minister to checking and paying the claims of dental practitioner contractors.

The tripartite structure of the NHS was subsequently much criticised, and in fact the main purpose of the 1974 reorganisation was to do away with it. The arrangements were, however, far simpler and more rational than anything that had existed before. They probably represented as much change as was acceptable at the time, and in any case, given the very different types of service provided by the three parts, were not unreasonable in themselves.

The National Health Service (Scotland) Act 1947 applied the same arrangements to a country with a much smaller population, so that of the five regional hospital boards only one served a population comparable with the English regions, and many of the second tier hospital authorities, known as boards of management, were also small. It would have been impossible to abstract the Scottish teaching hospitals from the main organisation of hospital services, so there was no equivalent of the boards of governors. Following a Scottish tradition boards of management as well as regional hospital boards had a medical administrative officer as well as a non-medical secretary. The provision of ambulance services was laid not on local authorities but on the Secretary of State, and was carried out for him by the St Andrew's Ambulance Association.

In Northern Ireland health services were one of the responsibilities of the Stormont, not the Westminster, parliament. In accordance with its policy of providing social and related services on the same lines as Great Britain, the Northern Ireland government established a national health service in the province at the same time and on a similar pattern. A distinctive feature was that the hospital services were put under the Northern Ireland Hospitals Authority, which was the equivalent of a single regional hospital board serving the whole province. Hospital management committees were numerous and small. A pre-existing Tuberculosis Authority was retained, but with the decline of the disease the administration of its hospitals was subsequently merged with the general system.

A national service

The NHS so quickly established itself as an accepted part of the country's life that it is easy to overlook what a new departure it was. The novelty did not lie in the purpose of the service; the state's involvement in health care had steadily grown and it was only a further step to the view that the well-being of society demanded the provision by the state of personal health care to all its members — or, what was sometimes seen as the obverse, that all citizens had the right to such care. A somewhat similar development of attitudes can be seen in relation to education and housing. Nor was there any novelty in the central government undertaking responsibility for a large-scale enterprise; states have traditionally done such things, particularly in connection with war. The new departure lay in the central government taking direct responsibility for a service of a type which had previously always been laid on local authorities or *ad hoc* bodies. It was a sensible solution to the particular administrative problems and may have been politically more acceptable than it would have been earlier because the same government was nationalising various industries, though the 'nationalisation' of hospitals was not the same thing. The extent of the new departure was disguised by the fact that the new hospital service was not administered directly by the civil service but by committees of voluntary members in the usual British fashion. Hospital authorities, however, unlike local authorities, Poor Law guardians or school boards, were agents of the ministers, and without power to raise their own revenue.

The establishment of a national service entailed three things, particularly from the hospital service.

First, the service had to accept the consequences of government financing. On the technical side — standard forms of accounts, subjection to audit and parliamentary scrutiny, the financing of capital works by annual allocations instead of loans, and so on — adjustment was soon made, and without great difficulty. The more profound effects were to be appreciated only gradually. It was long before it was fully accepted that the government must decide what should be spent on the service and that its decisions were unlikely to coincide with what people working in the service thought ought to be spent.

Secondly, the new service became one of the largest employers in the country. The logical consequence of national financing was national salary scales, and the obvious model for negotiation was the Whitley system already well established in the civil service. Joint negotiation had been growing in the various services before 1948 and the staff organisations involved in them became members of the new Whitley councils, which were established by the end of 1950. As with finance, the deeper consequences of being a very large employer were appreciated only gradually. Although many hospitals had been training institutions, and had indeed used trainees to reduce staffing costs, awareness of the need for national policies on staff training, and more generally for manpower planning, took some time to develop. And although the influence of the medical profession on health services was always evident, only later was it appreciated that all staff groups had their interests and influence and that there was a touch of truth in the cynical view that the service existed for the sake of the staff. The wording of the terms of reference for the Royal Commission appointed in 1976 practically recognised this.

Thirdly, not only the new hospital authorities but also the central departments had to learn new roles, and to adjust to each other. Many of the first members of hospital authorities, and most of their senior officers, had had previous experience with voluntary or local authority hospitals, and had to adjust to the new circumstances. The central departments, for their part, despite their experience with the Emergency Medical Service, had little experience in the type of work they now had to undertake. Existing civil service practices, such as the issue of circulars, were available, but were not enough. The 1944 white paper had envisaged strong consultative councils to advise ministers, and accordingly the Acts established the Central Health Services Council, which lasted until 1980, and the Scottish Health Services Council, which was discontinued in 1974. These large councils, though responsible through committees for some important reports, were not the sorts of bodies which could regularly advise on and influence the development of the service. For advice on difficult or contentious matters ministers looked to committees either appointed by the councils or *ad hoc,* with some or most members drawn from the service. For day-to-day advice the departments built up large professional staffs drawn from most of the professions working in the service. The other approach was regular meetings between ministers and civil servants and chairmen and senior officers of hospital authorities. In this context hospital authorities were, among other things, pressure groups, but they were not the only such; the professions (particularly the medical profession), associations of authorities, voluntary organisations, members of parliament and others interested in the service attempted to influence ministers and departments, and were often consulted on matters affecting them.

The outcome of much of this activity was policy statements or 'guidance' to authorities by ministers. Despite the form of direction from above, it would be a mistake to suppose that it always represented initiative or leadership from the centre, for it was sometimes the result of pressure from the service. It would also be a mistake to assume that the policy or guidance was always translated into action, for there were matters on which ministers found it difficult to persuade authorities and their staffs to follow the spirit or even the letter of national policies.

Evolution of the service

The national health service reflected experience of the inter-war years. It was destined to function in a very different world.

The history of the service has coincided with remarkable advances in medical science, the nature and consequences of which are now familiar: the production of a wide range of effective drug therapies, advances in surgical techniques and the development of procedures such as renal dialysis; increasing specialisation in medicine, the development of acute hospitals as centres of expensive high technology and, in contrast with the pre-war period, greater numbers of hospital doctors than general practitioners; a rapid decline in the incidence and mortality of tuberculosis and the infectious diseases and an increasing incidence of degenerative diseases and the illnesses of old age. There were also important developments in the treatment of non-acute illness: the development of geriatric medicine encouraged the rehabilitation of many elderly patients who would previously have been consigned to chronic sick care; a more active approach to psychiatric care led to a decline in the number of psychiatric patients in hospitals; and in recent years there has been a more optimistic and active approach to the care of mentally handicapped, coupled often with a belief that their needs are educational rather than medical.

Like development in non-medical technology, such as computers, which have had an important impact on the health service, most of the developments in medicine have been a worldwide phenomenon and neither the achievements nor the disadvantages can be ascribed to the national health service, though the way they were applied in the UK was influenced by the character of the NHS.

The character of a health service depends as much on the nature of the society it serves as on the state of medical knowledge, and British society, no less than medical knowledge, has changed greatly since 1946. One of the factors determining both the demand for care and the supply of people available to provide it is the population structure, and there have been important demographic changes since the early years of the NHS: an ageing population, fluctuations in the birth rate and for some years until recently a decline, the establishment of new towns, the drift of population towards the south-east and in recent years the decay of inner cities, and large-scale immigration. A country's economy is equally important in shaping the nature of its health service. In common with the rest of western Europe, the country embarked on a long period of economic growth in the early 1950s thus permitting levels of health expenditure which we now take for granted. British economic performance, however, was uneven and recurrent crises led to changes in policy, particularly in public expenditure, which had a damaging effect on health service management and planning, while countries with more flourishing economies set standards in health expenditure which it was not possible for the NHS to emulate. Social values and expectations also shape the character of a health service. Here the changes have been so many, and of such different types, that only a few examples can be given: increasing acceptance of birth control and, more recently, abortion; the shorter working week and longer holidays; the movement for sex equality in employment; the consumer movement.

Statutory change

On the whole the NHS adapted itself successfully to these changing conditions. It was not until 1968 that major organisational change was seriously proposed, and another six years before it was accomplished. Much of the credit for the adaptability must go to the merits of the original structure, combined with the fact that the detailed arrangements were laid down by regulations, which could be amended to meet changing circumstances.

A number of amending Acts altered the original legislation, though only a few of the changes were of major importance. The National Health Service (Amendment) Act 1949 had as its main purpose the prohibition of full-time salaried practitioner service, thus fulfilling a promise made to the profession in settlement of the dispute before the inception of the service. Acts of 1951, 1952 and 1961 were mainly concerned with charges of various sorts although the first also provided for the treatment outside Great Britain of persons suffering from pulmonary tuberculosis — fortunately a provision that soon ceased to be needed. An Act of 1957 concerned local authority ambulance services, the NHS (Hospital Boards) Act 1964 achieved its purpose in enabling the Welsh Regional Hospital Board to drop 'Regional' from its title, and an Act of 1966 established the General Practice Finance Corporation as part of the 'Doctors' Charter' to make loans for the improvement of practice premises. The following year another Act empowered local authorities in England and Wales to provide family planning services.

The most substantial Act was the Health Services and Public Health Act 1968, which was designed to enact various desirable changes but not to initiate radical new policies. It acknowledged the permanence of the supplementary ophthalmic service, converting it to the general ophthalmic service. Various changes were made in provisions about private beds, providing that numbers rather than specific beds should be designated. At the same time, under existing powers, the approved number of beds was reduced. Provision was made for the establishment of university hospital management committees on which universities would be represented. This permitted the establishment of new medical schools in England and Wales, and the extension of teaching by existing schools, without putting more hospitals under boards of governors. RHBs rather than ministers were to approve the expenditure of HMCs and BoMs. The local authority family planning service was extended to Scotland, and various other minor changes were made.

Various other Acts of Parliament had more impact on the service than some of the rather technical changes in the NHS Acts. Of those directly concerned with the service, the most important were the Mental Health Act 1959 and the Mental Health (Scotland) Act 1960. The national health service, by incorporating mental hospitals in the service, had accepted them as part of the general provision for health care, though for the most part they remained administratively rather separate. The main effect of the new Acts, which replaced previous legislation relating to mental illness and mental deficiency, was to abolish any legal distinction between psychiatric and other hospitals and to allow admission to any hospital for psychiatric treatment without formality. Compulsory admission which was already used in only a minority of cases, was to be regarded as the exception not the norm, and it was to be authorised by doctors, not the courts. In England and Wales, though not Scotland, the Board of Control was abolished, and mental health review tribunals were established to examine appeals against compulsory detention. The statutory responsibility of the medical superintendent for all patients in a mental hospital ceased, and in due course the post generally disappeared as consultants' responsibilities were assimilated to those in other hospitals. These changes accompanied and facilitated but were not responsible for the changes in the treatment of psychiatric patients, including the discontinuance of almost all locked wards and the encouragement of early discharge, with readmission if necessary, which in time led to a remarkable drop in the numbers of in-patients. The changes were due rather to changes in attitudes to and understanding of mental illness, and to developments in drug therapy.

Organisational change

Apart from some rearrangement of councils following the reorganisation of local government in London, there was very little organisational change in executive council services between 1948 and 1974 although, as mentioned above, the supplementary ophthalmic service was formally accepted in 1968 as being a permanent feature. The main function of executive councils was to administer contracts, and the revised contract for general practitioners negotiated in 1966 — the 'Doctors' Charter' — greatly improved the general medical services. It replaced what was basically a system of simple per caput payments with one which recompensed heavier work, such as the care of the elderly, and provided incentives rather than disincentives for the improvement of practice premises and the employment of ancillary staff.

Local health authorities also saw little organisational change until near the end of the period. In 1968 the Seebohm Committee on local authority and allied personal social services reported and with remarkable speed, and despite the pending reorganisation of local government, its recommendations were implemented two years later in the Local Authority Social Services Act, which applied to England and Wales. The Act provided that authorities should establish comprehensive social services departments under directors of social services, and among the existing services taken over by the new departments were the welfare services until then usually administered with the health services under the medical officer of health. Changes came earlier in Scotland, under the Social Work (Scotland) Act 1968.

There was considerably more change in the hospital services, which were organised on a new and therefore experimental system, accounted for the largest share of NHS expenditure and were the direct responsibility of ministers.

The only change in regional organisation was the formation of the Wessex Regional Hospital Board in 1959; it had previously had a semi-autonomous existence within the South West Metropolitan region. For a few years it was unique in having no teaching hospital within its territory until the Southampton University Medical School was established. There was a good deal of regrouping of hospital management committees and boards of management, the general tendencies being to establish larger groups and to incorporate psychiatric hospitals and small special groups within general groups. As the London teaching hospitals took on district responsibilities, and also needed more beds for teaching, the hospitals of various HMCs in inner London were merged with boards of governors. After the 1968 Act several University HMCs were established, two of them — in Cardiff and Newcastle — replacing boards of governors.

Over the years the general tendency in the organisation of the hospital service was an increase in centralisation. In 1948 most HMCs and BoMs found themselves in charge of a number of hospitals which had previously been managed independently or as parts of local government systems, and it was only gradually that they came to think of and organise their services on a group rather than on an individual unit basis. With this went an increase in the number of group rather than individual hospital management posts, the development of functional management — which was to be much criticised as it further developed after 1974 — and a fundamental change in nursing. Following the recommendations of the Salmon Report (1966) nursing services, hitherto the responsibility of the matron of each hospital, were organised on a group basis under a chief nursing officer. Implementation took several years and had not been achieved in some groups when overtaken by the 1974 reorganisation. For some management purposes the group was considered insufficiently big, and in 1969 supplies in England and Wales were organised on an area basis, each area supplies officer serving several HMCs and BGs. There was also some reorganisation of pharmaceutical services in larger units.

The move towards group organisation and management, though a natural consequence of the decision to form hospital groups, was often criticised by hospitals as removing decision-making to too remote a level. HMCs and BoMs in their turn were critical of the increasing activity of regional boards, which proved to have a bigger role than had been expected in 1948. There were several reasons for expansion of the regional role. The central departments dealt with HMCs and

BoMs through the RHBs and as the emphasis turned on the development rather than the simple maintenance of services they looked to the regions to oversee and report on developments. This more active approach led to the establishment of activities such as staff training and development, and the development of management services, which were thought to require a basis bigger than the group and therefore management or co-ordination at region; and the growth of the building programme after 1961 required the expansion of regional works departments. Relations between RHBs and HMCs were occasionally strained and their different roles were never fully clarified despite the issue of a circular on the subject (HM (69) 59).

Both parties were, however, agreed in deploring the extent to which the central departments involved themselves in matters concerning the management of the hospital service. The involvement was not unnatural given the national character of the service, the wide powers placed on ministers, the pressure on the departments by all bodies interested in changing the service and, not least, the fact that expenditure was growing rather than steady, so that governments had a strong incentive to direct and control the activities of hospital authorities. Nevertheless ministers and the central departments, no less than the members and staff of hospitals authorities, deplored the tendency for decision-making to move upwards, and when the time came to consider NHS reorganisation the various schemes proposed by the governments were to stress the importance of keeping as much decision-making as possible at the local level.

Needless to say, organisational matters had been the subject of reports before then. The Bradbeer Report of 1954, on the internal administration of hospitals in England and Wales, which covered most aspects of administration at HMC and hospital level, took a middle-of-the-road line on a number of issues, some of which have remained contentious, whereas others have ceased to be relevant, or have been decided in a different way. The Farquharson-Lang report of 1966, on administrative practice of hospital boards in Scotland, was more radical. Its emphasis on boards' concentrating on policy, leaving its execution and day-to-day management to officers, if it had little immediate effect, foreshadowed the future, though its advocacy of a chief executive post has not subsequently found official support.

Development of services

The development of services is recorded in official statistics over the years: increases in all categories of staff, increases in expenditure, increases in the numbers of patients treated. The exception to this story of expansion, and one which would have surprised the authors of the pre-war and wartime reports, was a decline in the number of hospital beds despite the growth in population. It happened partly because many infectious diseases and tuberculosis beds soon ceased to be needed, partly because of a drop in the number of psychiatric beds, and partly because in the acute sector beds were used more intensively, the average length of stay dropping steadily over the years. Some forms of hospital provision, particularly maternity, were expanded.

The main developments in medicine have already been briefly referred to. Advances in medical care brought enormous changes in acute hospital work between 1948 and 1974. Some of the most encouraging developments were in the care of the elderly, the mentally ill and the mentally handicapped yet it was agreed in 1974 and even in 1980 that they were still the 'Cinderella services'.

In the early years of the service there was little hospital building except in Northern Ireland. In 1962 the government announced Hospital Plans for England and Wales and for Scotland. They were ambitious ten-year building programmes, subsequently revised, and if they proved to be excessively optimistic both about costs and about the speed of building they at least launched a much needed programme of redevelopment. They were based on the concept of the district general hospital, which would provide all hospital services except some forms of long-stay care, and envisaged the closure or change of use of many existing hospitals.

Equally important was the development of health centres in which both general practitioner and local authority community services were provided. It had originally been envisaged that they would form a basic part of the NHS but early experience suggested that building costs would be high and that GPs would be reluctant to practice from local authority premises. In the late 1960s, after the 'Doctors' Charter' had given GPs an incentive to improve their premises, there was a renewed interest in health centres, encouraged by the government, and they were provided in increasing numbers, with Scotland in the lead.

Dissatisfaction with the service

Inevitably the national health service has not given complete satisfaction to everyone, and it has been criticised in many ways. From the standpoint of recent years there are two main criticisms to be made of the service as it was established in 1948. The first is that it was based on a serious misconception. Dr David Owen, Minister of State for Health 1974-7, has written:

> The two assumptions underlying the then philosophy were that health need was finite and that, once identified, society would be willing to divert sufficient resources from other uses — for example, private consumption, education, housing to meet the need. This philosophy has subsequently been shown to have been hopelessly wrong , and demand, far from being finite, is now seen to be close to being infinite.

The development of forms of treatment which not even the wealthiest countries could afford to provide for all who might benefit from them is only a striking example of a more fundamental difficulty: that as medical skills increase more people are successfully treated, and survive to require more medical treatment later in their lives. Furthermore there is no clear-cut distinction between good and bad health, but rather a graduation, and the more successful medical science is the more there will be a demand for treatment for conditions which would once simply have been endured because there was no point in taking them to the doctor. Some critics would see much of this as the 'medicalisation' of life, and at the very least it seems clear that some doctors, particularly GPs, spend some of their time dealing with the results of the problems of life which previous generations would not have regarded as medical. The prospect of an almost infinite demand for health care is not, of course, a problem peculiar to the NHS, for it faces any health care system, but it is difficult to reconcile with the assumptions on which the service was founded.

The problem was discerned by the Guillebaud Committee — which is described below — when it considered what was meant by an 'adequate service'. If that meant that the service should be able to meet every demand which was justifiable on medical grounds, it said, then clearly the service was inadequate; to make it fully adequate in such terms would require a greatly increased share of the nation's human and material resources, and even then it might require continually increasing expenditure. The committee concluded that the aim must be to provide the best service possible within the limits of the available resources, and that the amount of national resources to be allocated to it must be determined by the government, having regard to the competing claims of other social services and national commitments and to the total amount of resource available. The full significance of this analysis was not to be appreciated for another ten or more years, by which time health service expenditure in all developed countries was rising faster than national income.

The second criticism is of execution rather than conception: the service failed to implement the egalitarian principles on which it was based. While hospital and consultant services, and the contractor services, were made available to all the population they were not made equally available when measured in terms of expenditure, staffing, usage or accessibility. The service started with a very uneven distribution of general practitioners, and the Medical Practices Committee had only limited success in persuading practitioners to work in the less popular areas. The extent of local health authority provision varied according to the interest and resources of individual authorities, and many people argued that uneven services were an inevitable consequence of relying on local government. Disconcertingly it was eventually appreciated that despite national and regional management hospital provision was hardly less uneven, not only between regions but also within them. The reason why this unevenness was recognised so late — at least sufficiently recognised to lead to effective action — was partly that before 1974 hospital authorities did not have responsibilities for defined populations against which to measure financial allocations, and partly the policy of generally maintaining existing services, and supplementing them as resources became available, because this inevitably led to the perpetuation of inherited inequalities.

These criticisms however were not those heard in the early years of the service. An early and frequent criticism was that the service was extravagant, and cost more than the country could afford. The government also was concerned at the cost of the service. In 1950 a ceiling on expenditure was imposed, various charges were introduced in 1951 and 1952, and in 1953 a committee under the chairmanship of C.W. Guillebaud was set up to enquire into the cost of the service and to suggest how an adequate service could be maintained without increasing costs.

The committee reported in 1956 and on the basis of a study by B. Abel-Smith and R.M. Titmuss into costs in England and Wales was able to show that there was little cause for alarm. Estimates of costs made before the service was introduced had been unrealistically low, and in the early days there had been an unexpectedly high demand for spectacles and dentures (the only examples of the arrears or pools of sickness which early discussion of the service had assumed) but as a proportion of the gross national product current expenditure had fallen from 3¾ per cent in 1949-50 to 3¼ per cent in 1953-4. At constant prices, taking account of the increase in population, cost per head was almost the same in the two years. Capital expenditure, in the view of the committee, had been too low.

The committee also examined the organisation of the service and, while making recommendations on detail, rejected the various radical changes which had been proposed: unification, the transfer of some or all hospitals to local authorities, the transfer of the work of executive councils to local authorities or RHBs, or the appointment of a national board or corporation. The general structure, the committee believed, was framed on broadly sound lines, it was too premature to propose any fundamental change and the prospect of a period of stability was needed. Reorganisation was not to be considered seriously again for another twelve years.

The findings of the Guillebaud Committee did not entirely put an end to criticisms about the cost of the service. The rising expenditure on drugs was particularly criticised, and caused the government much concern. In subsequent years a much more frequent criticism, sometimes based on international comparisons, was that expenditure on the service was too low. Some critics argued that that was an inevitable consequence of state financing, and that a market-oriented system would increase expenditure. The economic theories on which the argument was based were not in fashion at the time, and most people thought they had little to offer a service where the greatest need was in the long-stay sectors. Much more commonly it was argued that the principles of the NHS were sound, but that it was under-financed. Enoch Powell, writing after his term as Minister of Health, regarded this as a consequence of the structure of the hospital service, by which those working in it were divorced from the responsibility for raising funds. They were remote from those considerations which guided governments on what could be allocated to health care but well aware of the benefits which could be achieved by more funds, so that everyone, from RHB chairmen down, had an interest in 'denigrating' the service with the aim of persuading or shaming the government into providing more. The belief that the service was under-funded persisted for many years.

Another common criticism was that the service should be divorced from politics; it was often suggested that this could be achieved through a national board. Despite parliamentary scrutiny and certain differences of emphasis between the parties, the service was not much subject to political controversy between 1948 and the discussions on reorganisation, and an escape from politics seems to have been envisaged as a way of avoiding two consequences of government financing: changes in public expenditure policies and the involvement of the Treasury in salary negotiations.

Criticism of a different sort came from official reports, for there were few services or professions which escaped examination by a committee drawn partly or wholly from health service staff. The committees invariably made criticisms of existing arrangements, and suggestions for improvement. They would not have been appointed if it had not been thought that improvements were desirable, and such reports should be regarded not as hostile criticism but rather as one of the normal ways in which the service improved its performance. Detailed studies of a different sort became available from the 1960s as people from a variety of disciplines in the universities took an interest in health services. Although their studies did not carry the weight of official reports, and were not always welcome within the service, they added to a more critical approach.

In 1967 a body called Aid for the Elderly in Government Institutions published *Sans Everything — A Case to Answer,* which alleged that ill-treatment of patients in long-stay hospitals was not uncommon. The official investigation which followed was generally, and excessively, reassuring, for in subsequent years there were a number of official investigations into long-stay hospitals which showed that ill-treatment sometimes did occur. It was usually the consequence of a deep malaise in the hospital and after the publication in 1969 of the report on Ely Hospital, Cardiff, the Secretaries of State established the Hospital Advisory Service and the Scottish Hospital Advisory Service to advise and encourage psychiatric, mental handicap and geriatric hospitals. There were also in fact, though not in name, inspectorates, reporting direct to the Secretaries of State.

None of these various sorts of criticism, not even the investigations into particular hospitals, which were widely and sensationally reported, appears to have shaken the popularity of the NHS with the public as it was measured in opinion polls, etc. It may be that this record of popularity should be treated with caution, for consumer movement attitudes were late in coming to the health service, and it is unlikely that the matters complained of in recent years worried no one earlier. Also, an element in the popularity of the service was its success in relieving people of most of the financial burden of illness. It appears, however, that the public did also value the NHS for the services it provided. Various patient surveys were carried out in individual hospitals; while a few aspects of hospital life were frequently criticised, there was great appreciation of the care received and a reluctance to criticise at all.

Attitudes of the staff were more complex. There was satisfaction and sometimes complacency in working for a service both necessary and popular. On the other hand disputes over pay claims sometimes led to criticism of the service, if only that it was under-financed. This was particularly true of doctors; a legacy of the disputes of 1946-8 was that the profession was less committed to the NHS than most other staff, and dissatisfaction about particular matters surprisingly often led to assertions that the service was collapsing. More fruitfully, staff were better able than the public to assess particular shortcomings of the service, and where improvements were possible. A lot of the criticism turned on the tripartite structure. The basic argument was that hospital treatment was only an episode in the course of an illness, and that the necessary continuity of care was difficult to achieve when staff worked in three different systems. The Guillebaud Committee had not thought the difficulties great enough to justify reorganisation, though its concern at the lack of continuity in maternity care led to the appointment of the Cranbrook and Montgomery Committees on the subject. In later years the difficulties were felt, particularly in the care of psychiatric and geriatric patients, as increasing value was put on short in-patient care and a return of the patient to the community whenever possible.

The solution, it was argued, was a unified rather than a tripartite service, and it appeared that there was considerable medical support for this approach when an unofficial committee under Lord Porritt issued a report in 1962. Although the report was mainly about the future of the specialties it suggested that the various health authorities, other than the teaching hospitals, should be replaced by area boards.

Reorganisation of the NHS

The arguments for unifying the service, however cogent, would hardly in themselves have persuaded a government into action. It must have seemed, even before actual experience, that a major restructuring of the NHS would be expensive in political effort and parliamentary time, and for long ministers limited themselves to urging better collaboration. The motive for action came from the quite independent decision to appoint Royal Commissions on local government in England and Wales (outside London) and in Scotland. Any major reform of local government would impinge on the NHS and there was the possibility — confirmed by events — that the commission for England and Wales would recommend the transfer of the NHS as a whole to a reformed and strengthened local government.

To anticipate the report of the commission the Minister of Health, Kenneth Robinson, issued his own 'tentative proposals' — the first green paper — in July 1968. While it left open the possibility that the new health authorities might be committees of new local authorities, the paper clearly favoured specially constituted boards directly accountable to the minister. The great significance of this paper was that it firmly committed the government to the view that the tripartite character of the NHS was unsatisfactory and that a unified administrative structure was necessary; there could be no going back on that. The arrangement proposed was to replace executive councils and hospital authorities with some 40 to 50 new area authorities which would also take over the personal health services of local authorities. The proposals were put forward for discussion.

By the time comments had been received and digested the Ministry of Health had been amalgamated with the Ministry of Social Security to form the Department of Health and Social Security (November 1968) and the NHS in Wales had become the responsibility of the Secretary of State for Wales (April 1969). Henceforth proposals for the two countries developed separately, but on parallel lines.

The second green paper for England, issued by the new Secretary of State for Social Services, Richard Crossman, in February 1970, took into account the government's white paper on local government reorganisation, following the report of the Royal Commission. This second green paper set out more fully than the first the case for unification. Full co-ordination of the NHS could not be achieved in a service run by 168 bodies which were agents of or regulated by the Secretary of State, 299 agents of the regional hospital boards and 158 local authorities with only limited responsibility to him. Joint planning was obstructed by the sheer number of administrative authorities of varying size and the fact that populations served by hospital authorities and local authorities rarely coincided. The problems of co-ordination could be eased but not solved by liaison committees. This multiplicity of authorities impeded the aim of meeting the needs of individual patients and limited resources were at risk of being wasted or used to less than full advantage. Local authorities were responsible for other services and did not always give priority to health services, with the consequence that the hospital service had to look after people who could have been discharged for home care. The administrative divisions made it difficult to secure the flexible use of staff or continuity of relationships for users of the health service. The tripartite division gave administrative reinforcement to the evolving trend of separation between general practice and hospital practice, whereas greater mutual confidence and closer co-operation between consultants and family doctors were needed. Unification was needed to secure the co-ordinated planning of the services of each district and the more effective deployment of local resources, and also to improve teamwork and ease the problem of communication. 'All decisions on staffing, planning and the deployment of resources must be governed by the total health needs of each area. One authority must be responsible for the national health service in each area and it must administer the services of each district as a whole. Only if there is a total merger of hospital and community services in the administration of both district and area services will resources be efficiently deployed to meet the needs of each patient.'

The paper announced three firm decisions. Because the professions believed clinical freedom would be possible only in a service administered by special bodies, and because of the financial difficulties of placing it under local government, the service would be administered by about 90 area health authorities directly responsible to the Secretary of State; the personal health service responsibilities of local authorities would be transferred to the new authorities but local government would continue to be responsible for public health and personal social services; in general the number and areas of the new health authorities must match those of the new local authorities. The other proposals were open to further consultation. Area health authorities would have 20 – 25 members, a third appointed by local authorities, a third by the professions and the rest by the Secretary of State. Although there would be no other statutory tier, there would be district committees and regional health councils.

A change of government a few months later produced different plans for local government reorganisation and a different approach to the NHS. A short consultative document was issued in May 1971. The main changes were the emphasis placed on effective management, with maximum delegation downwards matched by accountability upwards, the establishment of a strong regional tier, the membership of authorities limited to about 14, with the main criterion for selection being management ability, and the establishment of community health councils as a consequence of rejecting representation as the principle for selecting authority members. A white paper in August 1972 set out in detail the government's firm proposals.

The parallel Welsh documents — green paper, consultative document and white paper — applied the same principles to Wales. The main difference was that none proposed a regional tier for the country; some regional functions would be taken over by the Welsh Office and others by a common services agency.

Confusing though these various proposals were, they did not amount to mere changes of mind. There was both continuity and development of proposals, and at no stage were previous schemes entirely abandoned.

The arrangements set out in the English and Welsh white papers were incorporated in the National Health Service Reorganisation Act 1973.

The course of developments in Scotland was rather smoother. A green paper was issued only in December 1968 after informal consultations. It proposed some ten to 15 boards, with no second tier. The next government took account of the green paper, the comments received on it and its own plans for local government reorganisation, and issued a white paper which proposed 14 boards, a planning council and a common services agency. The Bill based on the white paper proceeded through Parliament a year earlier than that for England and Wales emerging as the National Health Service (Scotland) Act 1972.

The Government of Northern Ireland issued a green paper in July 1969, which was followed by a consultative document in March 1971. The distinctive feature in the Province was the proposal to integrate the personal social services with the health service. It was possible because the new local authorities would be too small to provide an adequate basis. There were to be four health and social service boards, all but one of which would be small by comparison with the new English authorities, and under them would be districts, which would also be smaller than in Great Britain. As in Wales and Scotland there would be a common services agency, and no tier above area. Boards were to have from 26 to 34 members. The proposals were duly enacted, and came into operation on 1 October 1973.

During the later stages of the protracted discussions on reorganisation, when actual change was in prospect, two other activities were in progress: planning the management of the new service within the statutory framework and carrying out the necessary work to implement the new arrangements. The latter inevitably demanded most attention: the appointment of chairmen and members, the determination of districts, the appointment of staff to the new authorities, negotiations on salaries and protection arrangements, the provision of information and courses for staff, the maintenance of existing services while many senior staff were already involved in the problems of the new, and so on. Most of this was transitional work which, though placing a very heavy burden on the staff at the time, had no lasting importance except that it left most staff with a strong distaste for reorganisation. At the same time the foundations for the reorganised service were being laid, and typically the series of reorganisation circulars issued by all the departments both dealt with transitional matters and set out policy guidance which is still valid.

A working party of health service and DHSS staff, assisted by the Organisation Research Unit of Brunel University and a firm of management consultants was set up in 1971 to advise on management arrangements. Its report, known as the 'Grey Book', proposed the 'district' as the key operational unit (which implied AHAs with one to six districts) and the principle of multidisciplinary management teams at each level. The same management consultants advised a Welsh study group and in Northern Ireland a report was produced jointly with a different firm of consultants. There was no equivalent study in Scotland. Broadly speaking the management arrangements agreed on were very similar in all four countries, though with interesting variations. They are the subject of much of this book.

Also in 1971 the DHSS and the Welsh Office jointly established a working party on collaboration between the NHS and local government. It produced three reports, and some of its early recommendations were incorporated in the 1973 Act. A Scottish working party was set up only in 1975, and it produced a short report two years later.

Somewhat earlier, in 1970, a working party under Dr R.B. Hunter had been established to consider medical administrators. The concept of the specialist in community medicine which it expounded in its 1972 report was not new, but had a new relevance as the demise of local health authorities would bring an end to the long established office of medical officer of health. There was a Scottish report, *The Organisation of a Medical Advisory Service* (the Hendry Report), in 1973.

After 1974

The history of the NHS, or even of reorganisation, did not stop at 1 April 1974. It took years rather than months to implement the new arrangements, including the appointment of officers to all the posts in the new service, and the establishment of community and local health councils.

In May 1974 the DHSS and the Welsh Office published *Democracy in the National Health Service: Membership of Health Authorities* and *Making Welsh Health Authorities More Democratic,* which were designed to give effect to the new government's rejection of the distinction between management and representation of the consumer interest. They proposed to provide that a third of the membership of AHAs should be nominated by local authorities and that there should be two members elected from staff other than doctors and nurses, and accepted the consequence of larger membership. The first of these changes was carried out but the second, although provided for in regulations, was never implemented because of the difficulty in finding a method of selecting representatives. Other proposals in the documents concerned strengthening the role of CHCs. A proposal to allow simultaneous membership of AHA and CHC was dropped after the majority of CHCs rejected the idea. There were no equivalent changes in Scotland or Northern Ireland.

An essential element in the thinking behind reorganisation, though not part of the legislation or formal structure, was that there should be more effective planning. After some delay because of the change of government, a planning system was introduced and is discussed in Chapter 8.

A necessary ingredient of planning is agreement on priorities and in 1976 all four health departments issued proposals. At long last an attempt was made to tackle the problem of the uneven distribution of resources and therefore of facilities. Proposals for England (RAWP) were published in 1976, followed in the next two years by comparable documents for Wales, Scotland (SHARE) and Northern Ireland (PARR). There were no proposals for equalising resources between the four countries.

An event unconnected with reorganisation but involving much political activity was action by certain unions against private patients in NHS hospitals. It led to the passing of the Health Services Act 1976 which reduced the authorised number of pay beds and established the Health Services Board to oversee the withdrawal of the remainder over the following years. It applied to the whole of Great Britain.

Another new Act, also applying to the whole of Great Britain, was the National Health Service (Vocational Training) Act 1976, which provided that future practitioners in the general medical service must be 'suitably experienced'. The National Health Service Act 1977 was a consolidating Act incorporating most of the previous NHS Acts 1946-76 for England and Wales. The National Health Service (Scotland) Act 1978 similarly incorporated most of the Scottish Acts 1947-76.

Dissatisfaction with the reorganised NHS

The reorganised national health service came into operation in Great Britain on 1 April 1974, having been preceded by six months in Northern Ireland. The timing could not have been more unfortunate.

Some of the problems were intrinsic to reorganisation. The prolonged discussions had produced many different and incompatible ideas within the service as to what shape the reorganised service should take and while the outcome may have represented as much consensus as could be achieved in the circumstances few people regarded it as ideal, and were more inclined to be critical than they were of established and familiar arrangements. The reorganisation had meant changes of post, or retirement, for all senior managers in the service, who had thus had anxiety about their careers at a time when they were both maintaining the existing service and planning for the new. Despite the years during which reorganisation had been discussed, time for implementation was too short, and could not be extended because the new local authorities and water authorities in England and Wales were to come into being on the same day. (In Scotland local authorities were reorganised a year later.) Various decisions had therefore had to be taken by the Secretaries of State unilaterally rather than by agreement, and various transitional arrangements for staff not yet appointed to new posts had to be made.

A further complication was a change in government in February 1974 which meant that the transition was presided over not by ministers committed to the new arrangements but by ministers who had been very critical of some aspects of them while in opposition and who made it clear that they were allowing the change to go ahead only because it was too late to postpone it. Another difficulty, with more serious long-term consequences, was that the change followed shortly after the oil crisis which led to a world economic recession and particular economic difficulties for the UK. Reorganisation had been expansionist in mood, even though it had been found financially impractical to establish all the posts originally envisaged for the new management arrangements. The new government, despite early attempts to protect the service from the effects of inflation, had to restrain public expenditure and it was clear that planning based on the assumption of a reliable supply of growth money each year would not be possible.

National health service reorganisation was only part of the 1974 upheaval and in the first years the new local authorities, which were also larger organisations than before, were as much criticised as the new health authorities, and criticism of the one tended to reinforce criticism of the other. The health service developed its own particular problems. Until 1973 the service had had very little experience of strikes and other industrial action; from then on they became fairly common and sometimes serious. While a somewhat more distant, larger-scale management might have increased the problems of personnel relations, the main reasons for this new development — which was usually about pay and conditions of service, but also political in action against the treatment of private patients in NHS hospitals — were nothing to do with reorganisation. One of the consequences however was that action, usually well publicised, demonstrated that the health service had difficulties — difficulties which it had not previously experienced. Other difficulties were a consequences of reorganisation. The new arrangements, it might be said, institutionalised criticism; local authority appointments to health authorities politicised the behaviour of authorities in a way not previously experienced, it was a function of CHCs to criticise the service publicly and although not all councils were very critical it was naturally the most belligerent councils which received most publicity, and with the establishment of the Health Service Commissioner reports were periodically issued detailing particular shortcomings of the service. The reports on the redistribution of resources, particularly the English RAWP report, increased dissatisfaction; the 'over-provided' regions feared a reduction in resources while the 'under-provided', having been shown that they were not receiving their fair share, resented the delay in getting it. Reorganisation was intended to facilitate better planning and the more efficient use of resources. A rational use of resources entails on occasion the closure or change of use of a hospital. Closures have always been unpopular and politically difficult; their occurrence during the post-1974 years, sometimes as a consequence of the restraint on, and redistribution of, resources, was a further cause of criticism of the service.

Thus dissatisfaction with the NHS was much greater after 1974 than anything experienced earlier. The reasons, as we have seen, were mixed: the inevitable difficulties of bringing the new arrangements into working order, industrial action, financial restraint and a reduction in the rate of growth, and the inevitable (and intended) consequences of integration. But criticism, which was strongest among, but by no means confined to, doctors, concentrated on the real and supposed defects of NHS reorganisation, particuarly the management arrangements. Complaints were frequent about the remoteness of the new authorities, delays in decision-making, the excessive amount of time spent on consultations, the administration of hospitals being left to young and inexperienced administrators without adequate authority. The NHS, it was said, was worse administered than before 1974 yet had seen a vast, expensive and scandalous growth in the number of administrators.

Spokesmen for the medical profession called for the appointment of a Royal Commission on the NHS which, they believed, would support both their criticisms of the reorganised structure and their belief that the service was seriously under-financed. The Secretary of State, Barbara Castle, at first resisted the proposal on the ground that it would serve no useful purpose, but eventually conceded the point. In 1976 a Royal Commission under the chairmanship of Sir Alec Merrison was appointed, 'To consider in the interests both of the patients and of those who work in the national health service the best use and management of the financial and manpower resources of the national health service'. It was to cover the whole of the UK.

If a willingness to give evidence is an indication of dissatisfaction with existing arrangements, the appointment of the commission was justified, for about 820 individuals, and about 1,600 organisations with an interest in the NHS, gave the commission their views.

The Royal Commission reported in July 1979 and its findings are discussed in some of the following chapters, and summarised in Chapter 17. Although it was critical of many matters, including some aspects of the reorganisation arrangements, it did not on the whole uphold the criticisms of administrators or managers which had been so frequent since 1974 and it disappointed the hopes of those who expected it would call for large additional funds.

Meanwhile the commission, like so many initiatives since 1968, had been overtaken by events. After 1974 the opposition party was at first reluctant to criticise the results of the reorganisation for which their own party had been responsible while in office, but eventually the opposition spokesmen on health came to the conclusion that the management structure must be simplified and local management strengthened. Thus when the party was returned to office two months before the Royal Commission report was published the new Secretary of State for Social Services, Patrick Jenkin, had already committed himself to definite views about the future of the service. He soon rejected or cast doubts on some of the recommendations of the commission, but his views on restructuring and on the importance of local management were broadly in line with those of the commission. How the government set about implementing the changes is discussed in Chapter 17.

The national health service in context

The national health service is sometimes criticised as being only an illness service. While its purpose is, in the words of the 1977 Act for England and Wales, to provide a comprehensive health service designed to secure improvement in the physical and mental health of the people and in the prevention, diagnosis and treatment of illness, its main purpose is, and always must be, to provide treatment and care for the sick. Making the nation healthy is a more difficult and more elusive matter. The service contributes when it restores the sick to health, and it has responsibilities in health education. Local authorities responsible for environmental health also contribute, and their contribution might be increased by further control of pollution and other environmental hazards. In the end, however, good health depends on personal values and habits, education, income and housing more than on health services. Moreover, as the Royal Commission has remarked, health itself is not a precise or simple concept. Thus there is no way of measuring whether the country is getting value for the money it spends on the NHS. The immediate output can be measured, in terms of patients treated, etc., as can a variety of other things from cost per case to patient satisfaction, but there does not appear to be any way in which the health of the population, and the contribution of the NHS towards changes in it, can be measured. This uncertainty about ultimate achievements is not peculiar to the NHS, for it must be true of other social services.

The remote origins of the NHS, whether medieval hospitals or the Poor Law, were in bodies concerned generally with people in need, not exclusively with the sick. With expansion and development has come specialisation; health care is now administratively separate, and it is only with difficulty that the various special interests in health care are kept together. But health care has not entirely gone its separate way. National health insurance was associated with unemployment insurance in 1911 and followed soon after the introduction of old age pensions; one of the earlier forms of community health care was provided by education authorities; the National Assistance Act came into force on the same day as the national health service; and one of the greatest needs today is for close collaboration between health authority and local authority services. Thus the NHS must be seen as part of the social services. Health and personal social services together cost rather less than education and hardly more than half the cost of social security. The various social services are in competition with one another for their share of public expenditure as well as with other sectors of the economy for their share of the GNP. The government is bound for some financial purposes to consider them together, and although they are financed and organised in a variety of different ways it is likely that they will be subject to the same broad influences, whether the emphasis is on economy, better management, local involvement or consumer participation.

In sketching the history of the health services in the UK this chapter has made scarcely any reference to countries outside. Medicine itself is for the most part international but the evolution of our arrangements for providing health care have been almost entirely insular apart from the example of national insurance in Prussia and the use of overseas experience in technical matters such as hospital design. The result is a system which is more or less unique; it is not really to be compared with the state-run systems of the socialist world, and most other developed countries have systems which combine insurance with considerable state financing, though one or two have recently shown interest in developing services on NHS lines, one of its great attractions being its greater success in containing expenditure. Taking the broad view, however, all developed countries face similar problems in the provision of health services, and while there are good reasons for thinking that the NHS is particularly well designed to tackle them, it would be a mistake to think that it is the only form in which a satisfactory health service can be provided, and it must be recognised that its advantages also entail disadvantages when compared with the practices of other countries. What is certain is that it is closely bound in with the way the country manages its affairs in general, and must be seen in that context.

Health care outside the NHS

Nearly the whole of the population makes use of the NHS and for the majority it must be the only source of professional personal health care. However, it is far from having a monopoly.

The state continues with those functions which long pre-date the NHS. The Ministry of Defence is responsible for medical services for the armed forces and maintains a number of hospitals both at home and overseas, though with the reduction in the size of the services they are declining in number, and most of those in Great Britain also treat NHS patients. The Home Office runs a prison medical service. The DHSS and the SHHD are directly responsible for the management of the three 'special hospitals' and the 'state hospital' for patients needing treatment under conditions of special security on account of their dangerous, violent or criminal propensities.

State provision of this kind is for special circumstances. The independent sector exists in competition, or at least in parallel with the NHS, though the image is misleading; the independent sector is as much intertwined with as alongside the NHS. There are still private beds in NHS hospitals, while many of the small voluntary hospitals treat NHS patients, mainly the elderly and the mentally handicapped, under contractual arrangements with health authorities. Many consultants in the acute specialties also treat private patients whether in private beds in NHS hospitals or elsewhere, some general practitioners have private as well as NHS patients (and a few only private patients), and it is common for dentists to provide both NHS and private treatment. In recent years there has been some growth in the number of hospitals for fee-paying patients, particularly for patients from overseas (who are not eligible for NHS treatment) but despite this the independent sector remains small.

If local authorities are responsible for environmental health and the NHS for personal health care, there is another form of health care, part environmental, part personal, which falls partly on employers and partly on the state. The provision of occupational health services depends to a great extent on the size, resources and interests of individual employers. In the NHS itself these services are patchy and inadequate, and are unlikely to be expanded during the next few years. Another factor in the provision of occupational health services is the nature of the work; some occupations are dangerous, and since the industrial revolution the state has increasingly required employers to protect their workers. The Employment Medical Advisory Service, established in 1973 as part of the Department of Employment, can trace its history back to the factory inspectorate of the early nineteenth century. Under the Health and Safety at Work, etc. Act

1974 it is now part of the Health and Safety Executive and its main functions are helping to prevent ill health caused by work, and advising people with health problems about the type of work which suits them or which they should avoid on health grounds.

Health and safety at work depend on the attitudes and behaviour of workers as well as on providing the right environment. Much the same is true of health and safety elsewhere. Hence the need for health education. The provision of health education is one of the responsibilities laid on health authorities and in a different way is a responsibility of doctors, dentists, nurses and others providing direct patient care. Nationally, except in Scotland, it is the responsibility of the Health Education Council, established in 1968, which is outside the NHS and financed by a government grant. There is a Scottish council within the Common Services Agency.

The many authorities and organisations and their numerous staffs responsible for health care constitute, if much more than the tip of the iceberg, at least less than the complete picture. Health care is part of the economy of the country, from which it draws its resources through taxes, rates and fees. It constitutes an important market for such different products as drugs and dressings, X-ray equipment and bedding; and it is also an important client of the construction industry. Even more importantly, it is closely involved with the educational world. The NHS itself is responsible for a great deal of staff education and training; it trains nurses, for example, as do a few of the larger independent hospitals. For some skills, such as architecture or accountancy, it depends on the general educational system of the country. Medical education is essentially a partnership. The university medical schools, financed through the University Grants Committee, are responsible for providing undergraduate medical eduation to standards approved by the General Medical Council but they can do it only with the collaboration of teaching hospitals provided by the NHS. The most striking example is the dental hospitals which provide an NHS service for patients but would not exist but for the need to train dentists. In their postgraduate years doctors in training form an essential part of hospital staffing. The numerous professions in the health service are represented by even more numerous professional organisations, and most of these to a greater or lesser extent are involved in professional education.

With education goes research. Much that the health service does is the application of received knowledge and standard practice; there are critics who say that some practices have no warrant except that they are established. The universal application of the best standard practices would in itself improve the general level of health care. However, medicine as we know it is committed to the advancement of knowledge and the development of new treatments. The primary body responsible for sponsoring research is the Medical Research Council. The DHSS also makes grants, with the emphasis on practical rather than fundamental research. Research is undertaken by medical schools and other university departments, research institutes, health service staff and some of the larger professional organisations.

It is not only in medicine and the allied professions that research is needed. Hospitals and health services are complex institutions not only of interest to social scientists of different disciplines, but also able to learn from them, not least in management. In the earlier years of the NHS most research in organisation and management and related topics was sponsored by the Nuffield Provincial

Hospitals Trusts and the King's Fund. While these bodies have continued their interest, the DHSS is now the biggest provider of research funds.

At the beginning of the nineteenth century health care was a matter for the private individual or for charity; it had little importance for the economy and little interest for politicians. Nowadays the NHS absorbs some 5½ per cent of the gross national product and, as we have seen, involvement in health care extends beyond the NHS. This remarkable transformation is the result of the growth of medical knowledge and medical effectiveness, and the consequent growth in cost. Such an explanation, however, is incomplete, and a better one can be found in the interplay of supply and demand. In a general sense the demand for medical care is as old as mankind; it has become much stronger in the last 180 years because the country has become far richer and has therefore been able to afford to devote more resources to health care, and it has chosen to use its resources in that way because increasingly medicine and health care have appeared to offer something worth having. The demand has stimulated the provision not only of services and of the administrative skills necessary to provide them, but also advances in medicine itself, and in turn new services and new treatments have further stimulated demand. The particular form which demand has taken, leading to a predominantly public rather than voluntary or commercial provision of health care, can be fully explained only by the political and social history of the country. The consequences are familiar: a society in which the government is closely involved in the management of the economy and in the provision of social services. Considering the importance of the health services, their dependence on the state of the economy and the way they affect nearly all members of the population at times of great need, it is not surprising that their organisation and management are a matter of public and political interest.

Further reading

Official reports

Committee on Scottish Health Services. *Report,* Department of Health for Scotland. HMSO 1936

DHSS. *The Future Structure of the National Health Service* (Second Green Paper). HMSO 1970

DHSS. *National Health Service Reorganisation: England* (White paper. Cmnd 5055). HMSO 1972

Ministry of Health. *Interim Report on the Future Provision of Medical and Allied Services* (Dawson Report). HMSO 1920

Ministry of Health. *National Health Service: The administrative structure of the medical and related services in England and Wales* (First Green Paper). HMSO 1968

Ministry of Health and Department of Health for Scotland. *A National Health Service* (White paper. Cmnd 6502). HMSO 1944

Report of the Committee of Enquiry into the Cost of the National Health Service (Guillebaud Report. Cmnd 9663). HMSO 1956

SHHD. *Administrative Reorganisation of the Scottish Health Services* (Green Paper). HMSO 1968

SHHD. *Reorganisation of the Scottish Health Services* (White Paper. Cmnd 4734). HMSO 1971

Welsh Office. *National Health Service Reorganisation in Wales: Consultative document*. 1971

Welsh Office. *National Health Service Reorganisation in Wales* (White paper. Cmnd 5057). HMSO 1972

Welsh Office. *The Reorganisation of the Health Service in Wales* (Green paper). HMSO 1970

Other publications

Abel-Smith, B. *The Hospitals 1800-1948: A study in social administration in England and Wales*. Heinemann 1964

Abel-Smith, B. *National Health Service: The first thirty years*. DHSS. HMSO 1978

Brown, R.G.S. *The Changing National Health Service*. Routledge 1973

Brown, R.G.S. *Reorganising the National Health Service: A case study of administrative change*. Blackwell and Martin Robertson 1979

Honigsbaum, F. *The Division in British Medicine: A history of the separation of general practice from hospital care 1911-1968*. Kogan Page 1979

Levitt, R. *The Reorganised National Health Service*. Croom Helm 1976

Lindsey, A. *Socialized Medicine in England and Wales. The National Health Service 1948-61*. University of North Carolina Press/OUP 1962

Jones, K. *A History of the Mental Health Services*. Routledge 1972

Office of Health Economics. *The Reorganised NHS*. 1977

Pater, J.E. *The Making of the National Health Service*. King's Fund 1981

PEP. *Report on the British Health Services*. 1937

Powell, J.E. *A New Look at Medicine and Politics*. 2nd edition. Pitman Medical 1976

Scottish Home and Health Department. *The National Health Service in Scotland 1948-1978*. HMSO 1978

Smith, F.B. *The People's Health 1830-1910. Croom Helm 1979*

Stevens, R. *Medical Practice in Modern England*. Yale University Press 1966

Watkin, B.(Ed). *Documents on Health and Social Services 1834 to the Present Day*. Methuen 1975

Watkin, B. *The National Health Service: The first phase*. Allen & Unwin 1978

Willcocks, A.J. *The Creation of the National Health Service*. Routledge 1967

Woodward, J. *To Do the Sick No Harm: A study of the British voluntary hospital system to 1875*. Routledge 1974

2
Health care — clients and services

It has already been shown that the intention of the National Health Service Acts of 1946 and 1947 was to provide a comprehensive service for the people of the country and that the aim of the service was to prevent, diagnose and treat illness. It is significant that at its beginning the service's objectives were defined in terms of sickness. Thirty years later commentators continue to point out that the demands of a sickness service are insatiable.

Does this mean that the national health service has failed in its task? To answer that question, it is necessary to explore in more detail what its task is in terms of the types of service it provides, the clients it serves and its effectiveness.

But what is the nature of sickness? The World Health Organisation, in an often quoted and somewhat grandiose statement, has said: 'Health is a state of complete physical, mental and social well-being, not merely the absence of disease and infirmity'. This implies that 'well-being' is definable in objective terms; all evidence suggests the contrary. It has been shown that people's perception about how well they feel varies enormously and certainly there is often little relationship between a doctor's view of the seriousness of an illness and the patient's readiness to seek help.

In a study undertaken in the London borough of Southwark, Wadsworth *et al.* showed that people's own definition of sickness was markedly different from that defined by a screening exercise undertaken by the medical officer of health. Coughs and colds, headaches, tiredness, and low back pains were common symptoms but difficult to demonstrate medically. On the other hand digestive, nervous or circulatory disorders were frequently identified in screening but gave rise to fewer complaints from the patients.

An interesting enquiry by the Office of Population Censuses and Surveys (OPCS) in their Household Survey of 1972, asked people to say whether they had suffered any symptoms during the last two weeks, and to what extent these were incapacitating and what they had done about them. The result showed that while over 90 per cent of people had had symptoms during the period, less than 10 per cent of them had gone to their own doctor. It is clear therefore that while access to the NHS is open to all the population, the great majority do not use it whenever they feel ill, albeit a great deal of that illness will be of a self-limiting and minor nature.

The extent to which people do refer themselves to the NHS is said to be conditioned by who they are and where they live. To take the latter point first: it has been sometimes assumed that access to the NHS varies geographically, and there are undoubtedly geographical variations in the provision of services. However, one interesting conclusion in Research Paper No. 6 for the Royal Commission was that (despite the very small sample) patients, whether in urban Stoke Newington or largely rural West Cumbria, on the whole did not have very great difficulties in getting to see their doctor and from that it was concluded that the proximity of health facilities was not a significant factor in establishing whether patients use the NHS or not. This is not to say that regional variations in access do not exist, but the reasons for them are probably more to do with class than geography.

Certainly class differences are significant. Various studies have observed that working-class people (socio-economic groups IV and V) use the NHS less even though they have a higher rate of morbidity and die earlier. It would be simplistic however to assume that *because* the working class use the NHS less they die earlier; as will be discussed later tentative conclusions suggest that environment and other social factors are equally significant.

Townsend's study on poverty has shown how slowly economic adversity and environmental hardship are being eradicated from typical working-class life. A sense of well-being has not therefore been expected as either usual or indeed a personal right. Cockerham has pointed out that there exists a 'cultural lag' so that the working class persists in its traditional attitudes to sickness even though a greatly improved health service is available largely free of charge.

Before examining in much greater detail the services which are available to the population of the UK it is worth attempting to define what health is, so that there is some standard, however relative, by which the NHS can be judged.

Ivan Illich has said, 'Health, after all, is simply an everyday word that is used to designate the intensity with which individuals cope with their internal states and their environmental conditions'. But if this were all, there would be little need for a health service. Other writers are more realistic, if less inspired. McCormick wrote, 'Health depends upon having enough (of the right sort) to eat, protection from infectious disease by immunisation and proper hygiene; protection from accidents by legislation; the provision of clean air and water, and the early diagnosis of pre-symptomatic disease in health populations. Health depends upon a job, a house and being loved!' In other words, 'Health is the ability to live autonomously; health is successful coping'.

But to cope successfully it is necessary to understand how the NHS works. Broadly speaking health care is offered at three levels: *primary care,* that is care within the community; *secondary care,* specialist care usually within hospitals; and what is rather vaguely called *tertiary care,* which might be described as ultra-specialist care, only available in highly developed departments in hospitals and usually after previous medical investigation has been undertaken.

It is worth reminding ourselves here that someone who feels the need of health care does not *have* to turn to the NHS. Those people mentioned above who were found to have had symptoms but had not consulted their doctor will have ignored them, or consulted their family, who may have suggested traditional remedies, or consulted their local chemist. Pharmacists spend a lot of their time giving advice to customers and, with or without their advice, many patent medicines are bought. Even when patients feel the need of medical advice they are not obliged to turn to the NHS, for they may make use of the private sector if they can afford it. However this sector, which is described in Chapter 14, is small, and the majority even of people insured for hospital care will use the NHS for primary care. There are also people who are not entitled to use the NHS; visitors to the country are given emergency treatment if they need it, but if they come to the country for medical treatment they must look to the private sector. The generous treatment of visitors who fall ill is sometimes criticised; the policy has been defended on the grounds that special arrangements for charging would entail disproportionate administrative costs. UK citizens who travel abroad are unlikely to do as well despite EEC regulations and reciprocal arrangements between the UK and various other countries, and most travellers consider it prudent to take out insurance.

Primary care

The general practitioner

The importance of the general practitioner as family doctor is what makes the NHS unique among health care systems. Few other health systems (with the possible exception of Denmark's) have a GP service as extensive and, in terms of patients' access, as crucial as ours. As we saw in Chapter 1, the strength of the GP service derives from the National Insurance scheme of 1911, but the historical reasons for a comprehensive GP service inadequately describe the quality of the relationship between the GP and his patients, the overriding characteristic of which is that the relationship is a continuing one, unlike the relationship of hospital doctor to patient which is episodic.

Any person can ask a GP to accept him or her, although the GP is not obliged to take the patient on. Reasons given for refusal are usually that he is too busy or that the patient lives too far from his surgery. If the GP does accept the patient he is responsible for arranging, if not actually undertaking, all the treatment the patient requires. As GPs are in part paid according to the number of patients they have, the accepting of a patient has to be documented and this is arranged through the family practitioner committee in England and Wales or the health authority in Scotland and Northern Ireland.

If the GP is willing to accept the patient, a medical card issued by the FPC or health authority confirms the arrangement. This also allows the FPC to keep a record of the number and characteristics of patients on a GP's list, which is essential both for controlling the size of the list, and the remuneration of the GP.

The freedom of both the patient and the doctor to choose each other and the freedom to discontinue the relationship, although a comparatively rare event except when patients move locality, might well account for a high level of satisfaction with the GP service.

But what exactly are the duties of a GP? According to Schedule 1 of the General Medical and Pharmaceutical Services Regulations 1974, they are to 'render to his patients all necessary and appropriate personal medical service'. A more comprehensive description was submitted by the Royal College of General Practitioners to the Royal Commission, which included in its report:

> The general practitioner is a licensed medical graduate, who gives personal, primary and continuing care to individuals, families and a practice population, irrespective of age, sex and illness. It is the synthesis of these functions which is unique. He will attend his patients in his consulting room and in their homes and sometimes in a clinic or hospital. His aim is to make early diagnoses. He will include and intergrate physical, psychological and social factors in his consideration about health and illness. This will be expressed in the care of his patients. He will make an initial decision about every problem which is presented to him as a doctor. He will undertake the continuing management of his patients with chronic, recurrent or terminal illnesses. Prolonged contact means that he can use repeated opportunities to gather information at a pace appropriate to each patient and build up a relationship of trust which he can use professionally. He will practise in co-operation with other colleagues, medical and non-medical. He will know how and when to intervene through treatment, prevention and education to promote the health of his patients and

> their families. He will recognise that he also has a professional responsibility to the community.

Such a range of responsibility would seem to require not only highly trained people but those possessing human qualities not always ascribed to professionals. Horrobin in his reply to Illich has stated baldly, 'My own belief is that most doctors are neither particularly humane nor particularly perceptive of the needs of society in general or of patients in particular'. Such a view would not appear to be general and most patients would prefer to support McCormick when he says:

> There is a course which the profession can follow which lies between human plumbing and paternalism. It is possible to combine technical competence with knowledge of its limitations, possible to recognise human needs and to allow everyman his autonomy and his right to human dignity. The doctor can still aspire, as his forefathers did, to mediate between the patient and his illness. He can enhance the prospects of care, diminish unreasonable fear and assist in the process of adaptation.

Certainly the GP has a strong cultural position in English society and despite considerable changes in his way of working over the last twenty years, his patients generally hold him in respect. It would however, be misleading to imply that general practice gives universal satisfaction. It is often criticised by patients, the profession and observers of the service. The Royal College of General Practitioners said, in what the Royal Commission described as an admirably candid view, that, 'our picture of the assets of good general practice must be balanced by the frank recognition that care by some doctors is mediocre, and by a minority is of an unacceptably low standard'. The level of primary care is thought to be generally poor in inner city areas. The Royal Commission considered there were three main reasons for the weakness of general practice: the absence hitherto of adequate previous training for work in the community, though this is now being met; the absence of national standards in the selection of principals in general practice; and isolation and a lack of close contact with professional colleagues.

The conditions of general practice have changed considerably, not only the conditions of service, but the typical working arrangements. The average GP in England and Wales has 2,300 patients on his list. In Scotland the average is 1,900 and Northern Ireland 2,100. Only 17 per cent of doctors now work in a single-handed practice, most preferring to work with others and about 37 per cent of these are in groups of four or more. Although it has been claimed that a GP could handle a personal list of 4,500 patients quite easily, this in fact is the top limit allowable for a doctor in a group practice and then only if the average within that practice is 3,500 per doctor. As we have seen, the average is considerably lower and it has been suggested it should fall to well below 2,000 if GPs are to devote more time to consultation and also have reasonable time off.

It had been envisaged in 1948 that most GPs would work from health centres. In the event fewer than 20 per cent practise from health centres, nearly all of these established in the last ten years. There are proportionately more centres in Scotland and Northern Ireland than elsewhere, and in England the conurbations, particularly London, have relatively few.

The advantages of the health centre are largely those of team working, though it would be wrong to assume that a well-organised group practice in the doctor's own premises cannot get the same results. During the last ten years there has also been an increasing tendency to attach nurses, midwives, and health visitors to particular doctors or group of doctors, forming what is sometimes called the 'primary care team'. This helps make the best use of skill, it improves communication between professionals and encourages a more positive approach to health education and general preventive care.

A health centre will be a focus for primary care and is likely to be staffed all day and in the early evening during which time at least one doctor and other skilled staff are likely to be available. This may be particularly important where there is no readily accessible hospital to undertake minor casualty work. Apart from usual surgery periods, doctors, nurses, midwives and health visitors may also arrange regular clinics for minor treatments, antenatal and mother and baby care, and family planning. In a few cases consultant doctors from the district general hospital may have regular out-patient sessions in the health centre. Reception and other clerical and secretarial staff are likely to be more organised in a health centre than in a small practice, and most health centres have an administrator, either as a practice manager employed directly by the practice or an out-posted administrator from the AHA.

Since the changes brought about by the Seebohm reorganisation of social work in 1971, relationships between GPs and social workers have in some places become more strained. Attachment to a health centre or group practice has sometimes helped to overcome difficulties; in others, GPs are tempted to use the health visitors in lieu of social workers.

In future it may be assumed that GPs will continue increasingly to work together in groups, although not necessarily in NHS health centres. The days when a GP can be expected by his patients to be on duty 24 hours a day are passing. Without giving up the important personal nature of the GP's relationship with his patient, some form of deputising by another partner or, particularly in large urban centres, by a deputising service, is becoming normal practice. The deputising services, often staffed by junior hospital doctors, are probably the least liked aspect of general practice from the patient's point of view.

A GP may wish to have more time available not only for his leisure, but also to increase his skill and develop some degree of specialised clinical knowledge. Some work as clinical assistants, on a sessional basis, under the supervision of consultants in district general hospitals. Many are contracted to undertake children's developmental assessment clinics and family planning clinics. This area of work is a natural extension of their work as family doctors. Similarly, becoming a doctor for a private school or for a local factory also contributes to a GP's experience of primary care.

In many parts of the country small local hospitals, often originally established by private donation, have provided a service to the community for many years. These hospitals are called 'cottage' hospitals and provide the GP with facilities which can extend his capacity to look after his patients without referral to the district general hospital. Such hospitals usually undertake out-patient clinics as well as in-patient care and can be a useful meeting place of consultants and GPs. The extent to which surgery and radiological examinations should be conducted in a GP hospital which has no resident medical staff has been hotly debated, not least in the circular HSC(IS)75 on community hospitals issued in 1979, although a somewhat rigid view was modified by *The Way Forward* and the government is further considering its policy. Increasing financial pressure in the acute sector of care has led to suggestions that local GP hospitals are uneconomic and should be closed. Although some hospitals have been closed local opposition is often strong, and the present government is generally averse to such closures.

Many of these developments in the role of the GP have happened since the mid-1960s, and the decline of general practice that was then being predicted appears to have been halted. In this the UK is untypical of the western world. It is an interesting development because the GP is a generalist yet in medicine, as in many other occupations, specialist skills are much valued and carry high status. Earnings are a good rough indication of status, and from the time of the 1965 Doctors' Charter, GPs have achieved higher remuneration reflecting their extended role. It is based on a complicated system which supplements the basic capitation payment with a range of payments recognising particular responsibilities and providing incentives to good practice. While GPs, like the rest of the profession, often express dissatisfaction with their remuneration their relative position within the profession seems secure and indeed a few years ago the provincial consultants were complaining that they were underpaid in relation to GPs.

We now turn to three other primary care services provided by independent contractors and administered by FPCs or their equivalent: the general dental, pharmaceutical and ophthalmic services.

The dental service

Dental services are not exclusively administered by the FPC; practitioners in hospital oral surgery and orthodontic departments and practitioners providing the school dental service are directly employed by regional and area health authorities.

The majority of dentists however work in general practice. Although it might be better for the dental care of the nation if the relationship between dentist and patient were made as formal as that between doctor and patient by some form of registration, the present arrangements allow patients to choose dentists when and where they like and, as a result, the relationship may only last for one course of treatment. It is not known how many patients change dentists but provided they are happy with the service it is likely that there is some loyalty to one practitioner. Many dentists endeavour to build up relationships with their patients and will remind them of the need to have regular check-ups.

The distribution of dentists is uneven, with marked regional variations, and the proportion of the population seeking regular dental care varies by region and social class. The FPC does not have the power to control the distribution of general dental practitioners. Recently there has been criticism that dentists are increasingly refusing to take on other than private patients.

Charges have been a characteristic of the NHS dental service from the early days, with maxima laid down for courses of routine treatment and for treatments requiring dentures, bridges, crowns, gold fillings, etc. The Dental Estimates Board determines the exact charge for more complicated treatments. Exemptions exist for children, pregnant and nursing mothers and pensioners.

As dentists' incomes are related to the number of treatments, it could be said that quantity rather than quality of work is encouraged. However, as a consequence of the fee-for-service method of payment, the Dental Estimates

Board monitors dentists' work, and its prior approval is required for more expensive courses of treatment. Some practitioners argue that the method of payment militates against good dentistry, but a satisfactory alternative method is difficult to find. The Royal Commission was seriously disturbed at the state of the dental health of the population despite the considerable improvements since 1948. Perhaps the basic difficulty is that the demand for dental care is much less than the need; if the demand in all places and among all classes were as great as in south-east England, the supply of dental practitioners would be quite inadequate. It is therefore disturbing that the current charges for dental treatment are said to be a serious deterrent.

The pharmaceutical service

Increased charges for prescriptions also have a deterrent effect, at least in the short run, although the effect was less marked in 1979 than in 1968. Against this, there has been an increase in the number of people exempt from charges; in 1979 65 per cent of prescriptions were free. Amongst the groups of people exempt from charges for drugs and appliances, the elderly are by far the heaviest users of the pharmaceutical services.

Charges apart, the general pharmaceutical services are easy for both the patient and the GP to use. The family doctor makes out a prescription as he sees fit in the interests of his patient and the patient then presents it to the pharmacist (universally referred to as the chemist), who supplies the drug. The pharmacist obtains his drugs direct from suppliers and is reimbursed monthly by the FPC which is advised by the Prescription Pricing Authority (or its equivalent outside England — see Chapter 3) of payments due for drugs dispensed.

Pharmacists must seek approval to practise from the FPC, which legislates as to hours of opening, at least for dispensing purposes. However, pharmacists could not survive on the money they receive for prescribing alone, and are dependent on the sale of other medicines and toiletries, etc. to remain in business. A considerable number of pharmacies have gone out of business over the years, so that in some places patients have to go some way to find one. Since many patients use the pharmacist nearest their GP, the establishment of a health centre may affect business, and sometimes local pharmacists form a consortium to open a dispensary in the centre. In certain circumstances general practitioners remote from a pharmacy are authorised to dispense drugs themselves.

Despite any deterrent effect of charges, expenditure on drugs has on the whole continued to increase and has frequently been a matter of concern. The prescribing habits of GPs vary remarkably, not only between areas but also within an area. Their expenditure on drugs is known from the records of the Prescription Pricing Authority, etc. and those whose expenditure is remarkably above the local average are visited by regional medical officers of the Department in England and Wales or through the area medical committee in Scotland. While this monitoring may affect the prescribing habits of individual GPs, it appears to have had little effect on the overall cost of the general pharmaceutical service. The Royal Commission recommended the introduction of a limited list of drugs available through the NHS and further steps to encourage prescribing by generic rather than proprietary names. The government has preferred to continue to rely on educating practitioners in more economical prescribing. In this it faces the efforts of the drug companies, which spend large sums on advertising and otherwise promoting the sales of their products. The increasing NHS expenditure on drugs, which is almost as difficult to control in hospitals as in the family practitioner services, has long caused many, particularly on the political left, to regard the drug companies with suspicion. While there are arguments for and against the commercial practices of the industry, it is generally accepted that the benefits of developments in drugs have been accompanied by some unfortunate concomitants, particularly unnecessary or excessive prescribing and sometimes adverse reactions to drugs. It also appears that many patients do not in fact take the drugs prescribed for them by their GPs.

The ophthalmic service

Another service under the control of the FPC is the general ophthalmic service which, more that the dental and pharmaceutical services, appears to give general satisfaction both to patients and to those responsible for managing and financing the NHS. This may be because of a happy compromise between public and private practice, and an emphasis on a service to customers rather than patients.

Anyone wanting his sight tested for the first time must obtain a medical certificate from a doctor; no certificate is required for subsequent tests. He may be tested by any ophthalmic optician on an FPC list, and spectacles will be provided if necessary. Lenses are provided at a standard charge, and there is a range of NHS frames at limited cost. Most people prefer to pay for alternative frames, which sometimes require lenses not available through the NHS.

There are three professions involved in the service. An ophthalmologist is a doctor specialising in the treatment of eye disease, including testing sight and prescribing lenses. An ophthalmic optician tests sight and prescribes and supplies spectacles, whereas a dispensing optician may only supply spectacles on prescription. All three groups of ophthalmic practitioners are entitled to fees from the FPC in return for their NHS work.

Other services

A review of primary care is not complete without reference to public and environmental health and school health services. However, it is more logical to discuss these within the analysis of care groups which follow. Before that, brief reference should be made to what is meant by secondary and tertiary care.

Secondary care

There are many aspects of care and treatment which the primary care service is unable to carry out. A patient requiring intensive care and treatment with regular supervision 24 hours a day will be beyond the resources of the community nursing service. A patient who needs the full range of diagnostic facilities, such as radiology, endoscopy or the pathology laboratory, can get these services only at a hospital. Treatment requiring the combination of several skills can only effectively be concentrated in a hospital, and it is only there normally that specialist, as distinct from generalist doctors, are available.

The hospital has assumed the principal place in the NHS and indeed in the health care provision of all developed countries, and absorbs a large proportion of the resources available, both financial and professional. Recently, however, the paramount position of the hospital has been challenged. So far as long-stay hospitals are concerned, it is said that institutional care robs a patient of his independence and his individuality; hospitals may cause as many problems as they cure. Against acute hospitals it is held that they absorb most of the resources of the NHS yet treat only a small minority of episodes of illness. In its crude form the argument is untenable unless it is held that all illnesses, from the trivial to the near-fatal, need the same resources. It is however true that hospitals are tending to take a larger rather than smaller proportion of resources, and this is particuarly discouraging to those who believe that more expenditure on preventive medicine and primary care would reduce the need for hospital treatment.

Except in the case of emergency a patient cannot be admitted into hospital, other than a general practitioner hospital, until he has been referred to a consultant by his GP. When a choice is practical the GP will decide, taking the patient's wishes into account, which hospital to refer him to. Except that some psychiatric and mental handicap hospitals serve specific catchment areas, access to hospital is not limited by administrative boundaries, and in fact many patients are treated outside the area or region in which they live. The consultant will normally see the patient first in the out-patient department (or sometimes on a domiciliary visit to the patient's own home) before contemplating admission to hospital. Only 20 per cent of out-patients become in-patients.

Many patients are admitted as a result of an emergency; in fact most general medical as opposed to surgical patients come into hospital in that way. The other main reason for emergency admission is as a result of an accident at work, at home or in the street. Accident and emergency departments, although intended for serious cases, still in many places provide the means whereby people present themselves for hospital treatment, even though their needs might be better met by their GP.

One other form of direct access to hospital treatment is commonly available. Clinics for sexually transmitted diseases or 'special clinics', usually though not invariably provided on hospital premises, do not require a GP's referral, which might deter many patients. In places where there is a dental hospital that, too, is available to patients without referral by their GP or dentist.

Compulsory admission to hospital is sometimes necessary. Most commonly this is done under the Mental Health Acts, but there is also provision under the Public Health Act 1936, as amended, for notifiable infectious diseases, and under the National Assistance Act 1948, for chronic incapacity to manage at home.

At least since 1962, when the Hospital Plan was published, NHS planning has been based on the assumptions that each district should have a district general hospital providing nearly all the hospital care in the district. The evolution of this concept is described in Chapter 10. Its realisation in terms of new hospital building is very far from complete and will probably be abandoned as an aim, though the concept of a district general hospital service, often based on a number of separate hospitals, is likely to be retained.

Even if the replacement of old hospital buildings has been disappointing, expansion of hospital activity, despite a decline in the total number of beds, has been dramatic. There have been big increases in staff, although not all groups of staff have increased in the same proportion, and the intensity of labour has allowed a much greater throughput of patients: discharges and deaths overall in Great Britain rose from 4,554,000 in 1959 to 6,294,000 in 1976. This increased productivity should not be seen as a sign either of worse health (more treatment needed) or better health (more treatment given). It reflects rather changes in what medical care can do and correspondingly higher expectations on the part of patients and their GPs.

Tertiary care

One of the ways that expectations have been raised is by the development of 'super' medicine, often supported by a demonstration of considerable skill allied to high technology. Patients receiving this level of care only do so after careful selection, hence the term tertiary care, meaning that patients have already been screened twice before being presented for treatment, first by their family doctor, second by the hospital specialist.

The development of tertiary care, while being exciting to professionals and public alike, is expensive in terms of manpower and money, though not as expensive as long-term care. Such developments should not be seen as a manifestation of public demand; rather they represent the ability of professionals and technologists to extend the frontiers of knowledge. Particular examples of tertiary care now being given may be found in specialties such as radiotherapy, neurology, endocrinology, oncology, neurosurgery, plastic surgery, cardiac surgery.

An attempt has been made to draw broad distinctions between primary, secondary and tertiary care and give some indication as to how patients gain access to the NHS. It is now intended to look more closely at the patients themselves and to do this they will be broadly classified into care groups as follows: maternity, children, the younger disabled, the elderly, the mentally ill, the mentally handicapped and the acutely ill.

Maternity

It could be said that one of the foundations of a satisfactory health service is good maternity care. If this care is lacking not only is the risk to babies greatly increased but the mother also is put in peril and this will lead to a progressively deteriorating state of general health.

Satisfactory care of mothers and their babies has become one of the main indices of the civilising effect of modern medicine. In many primitive societies many babies will die shortly after birth, as will their mothers. Although the UK perinatal mortality rate (babies stillborn or dying within the first week of life) is not yet as good as many of our European neighbours and varies between counties in the UK, the situation has improved dramatically since the beginning of the century. In the early 1900s in England and Wales about 130 babies in every 1,000 were stillborn or died within the first week of life. Many more were to die in infancy, particularly from infectious diseases. Mothers were not exempt from risk whereas now the death of a newly delivered mother is a rarity (45 cases in 1978). So rare are maternal deaths today that there is a national procedure for enquiring into the reason for them known as the Confidential Enquiry into Maternal Deaths. The reports from this enquiry show that even amongst the very limited number of maternal deaths about half of the mothers need not have died as there were avoidable factors which, with more care, could have been overcome.

This attention to detail is typical of maternity care today. The specific timetable of pregnancy and after-care renders it more suitable for close supervision than any other specialty. Because of the ease with which maternity can be supervised, significant changes in practice have been made relatively easily. In particular the marked developments during the last 15 years were a response to the 1959 reports of the Cranbrook and Montgomery Committees which said categorically that maternity services must be improved by greater supervision of mothers by specialist obstetricians. This inevitably led to a higher demand for institutional confinement so that whereas in the later 1950s, only about 60 per cent of mothers were delivered in hospital, by 1978 hospital confinement was almost total. Such a change in policy over such a short period is remarkable. To a certain extent it was accelerated by the publication of the 1971 Peel Report which advocated a unified midwifery service which did not draw distinctions between hospital and community midwifery. This change in practice has been brought about by the high level of professional supervision of mothers once pregnancy has been acknowledged. Unfortunately there remains a small number of mothers who conceal their pregnancy and do not as a result benefit from antenatal care. The risks they face during delivery are consequently much higher.

Normally, however, a woman thinking herself pregnant will present herself to her GP early in pregnancy, preferably before the end of the first trimester (three months). A decision will be made as to whether the delivery is to take place under the supervision of a consultant obstetrician or under the GP. If under the GP he must be on the obstetric list of the FPC and this usually means that he would have had special training in obstetrics probably holding the postgraduate diploma in obstetrics, DRCOG.

Indications for delivery under a consultant will include mothers having their first, fourth or more babies, previous obstetric complications such as miscarriage, high blood pressure and other medical conditions which pregnancy might exacerbate. Normally, the doctor will review the mother's condition at least twice during pregnancy. During the rest of the time the mother will be kept under surveillance by the midwife at antenatal clinics and routine checks of urine, blood pressure, weight and so on will be undertaken.

As medicine has become more sophisticated it has been possible to screen the foetus for abnormality. If this is found therapeutic abortion can be carried out but should be done as early as possible and certainly will very seldom be attempted after the eighteenth week.

Concern about the number of 'back street' abortions led to the passing of the Abortion Act 1967, which allowed therapeutic abortions within time limits, for the following reasons:

1. Risk to the pregnant woman's life
2. Risk of injury to her physical and mental health
3. Risk to life (or physical or mental health) of existing children of the woman's family
4. Substantial risk of the expected child being born with severe physical or mental abnormality.

Despite the passing of the Act access to abortion in the NHS differs greatly up and down the country and voluntary agencies have been set up to advise and, in some cases, to make arrangements for women who are unable or unwilling to obtain an abortion through their GP or obstetrician. These organisations must be registered and approved by the DHSS.

Mothers about to be delivered will have clear directions from the midwife how to proceed, but in the cases of sudden emergency each health district will have an obstetric flying squad, an obstetrician, anaesthetist and midwife who can go out from the hospital.

Once in the hospital the mother will normally stay up to eight days unless she has been booked as a patient suitable for return home with her baby within 48 hours. Some hospitals also have units where the mother is only delivered in the hospital, returning home very shortly afterwards. Most district general hospitals now have a GP unit attached and in addition some districts will have separate general practitioner units to serve local sectors of population.

The midwife has a statutory responsibility for the mother for the first ten days. After this the health visitor will renew her links made with the mother during pregnancy and help her on matters of baby care, including feeding. She will also be able to check during this period that the development of the baby is satisfactory and to encourage the mother and baby to attend mother and baby clinics.

It can be seen that the maternity service is highly organised both clinically and administratively, and the return for this organisation has seen greatly improved standards. Inevitably such a high degree of organisation has its critics. The system it is sometimes said is insensitive, too like a factory production line. A common cause of complaint is the increasing practice of inducing labour which, it is alleged, is often done for staff convenience rather than medical reasons. There is now increasing pressure on professionals to give mothers more choice. This may centre on home or hospital confinements or on the manner in which the birth is conducted. Childbirth, though calling for medical attention, is not an illness, and it is not surprising that some mothers have strong views about it, and that their values are not always the same as those of the professionals. Although the service often goes to considerable lengths to meet the wishes of mothers, the emphasis has rightly been on safe delivery. Yet obstetricians are not happy at the present perinatal mortality rate and its improvement is a national priority.

Services for children

It has already been pointed out that one of the foundations of a satisfactory health service must be effective services for mothers and their children. Although parents' rights to look after and provide for their children are constantly reiterated the state does interfere considerably to ensure children's needs are met, and that they have a chance of growing up healthy.

A comprehensive review of child health services in England and Wales was conducted by the Committee on Child Health Services under the chairmanship of Professor S.D.M. Court which reported in 1976. This report, entitled *Fit for the Future,* made many significant recommendations (several of which are unlikely to be accepted). The Committee summarised its objectives as follows:

> We want to see a child and family centred service; in which skilled help is readily available and accessible; which is integrated in as much as it sees the child as a whole, and as a continuously developing person. We want to see a service which assures that paediatric skill and knowledge are applied in the care of every child whatever his age or disability, and wherever he lives, and we want a service which is increasingly orientated to prevention.

Just before the Court Report was published, the DHSS issued its own Priorities document which listed the following areas of concern: improvement in special care for babies in hospital; expansion of the health visiting service; development of day facilities; development of services for children in trouble and with special problems. From these two documents it might be supposed that health and social services for children were grossly deficient, so it is worth noting that the Court Committee's own belief was that 'all industrial countries have achieved high standards of child health; standards scarcely even envisaged before the second world war'.

In 1973 there were just over 11½ million children under 16 in England of whom 3½ million were under five. It says much for the comprehensive nature of the child health services that none of these children would have been entirely unknown to the NHS. Such a degree of surveillance could only come about after years of organisation.

Broadly speaking the services for children and young people can be divided into three main bands: the under fives, those at school and, overlapping somewhat, young people.

First the under fives. Ten days after birth a health visitor will take over from the midwife the responsibility for the young baby and its mother. Every mother discharged from hospital or having been delivered at home will receive an early visit from the health visitor who will check that both the mother and baby are progressing satisfactorily. Where there are difficulties the number of visits will be increased. Such problems may be related to the mother and her adjustment to the new baby, to establishing and maintaining satisfactory feeding or to ensuring proper weight gain of the baby. Subsequently the mother is encouraged to attend mother and baby clinics where not only will health visitors check the development of the baby but also a doctor trained in developmental paediatrics will see the baby and ensure that there are no impediments to development.

Child health clinics are held in health centres where they are available, otherwise in special or rented accommodation. They also serve as a point for distributing welfare foods, carrying out vaccination and immunisation, arranging discussion groups for mothers when this is felt to be valuable, and occasionally providing crèche or playgroup facilities.

It has been estimated that 60 per cent of all women are now in employment and very many will be younger women with children. There has been an ever-increasing demand for child care facilities for working mothers. Day nurseries are usually set up by the local authority's social service department but voluntary agencies and some employers also provide facilities. Nursery schools and pre-school playgroups are set up by many (although by no means all) education authorities and help to prepare children for school. Some education authorities take in children about to be five years old, known as the 'rising-fives', while others wait until the child has had his birthday.

It is hoped that by the time children are ready for school their health will have been well-documented and suitable preventive measures taken. Many children will have been immunised against diphtheria, measles, polio, TB, whooping cough and tetanus. From time to time concern is expressed about the possible harmful effects of one or other of these vaccinations. Professionals are somewhat divided but the risk of not undertaking vaccination is felt by many to be as great or greater.

Despite the fact that all children are known to the NHS at birth, some will have bypassed the regular screenings by health visitors and general practitioners during the pre-school phase. Indeed less than half the child population under five attended child health clinics during the period 1964-73. Mobile parents may not have registered with a GP and their children may for a while be 'lost'. This can be a particular problem for children at risk due to handicap — physical or mental — or for those who suffer from unexplained injuries, popularly called 'battered babies'. Class also affects this situation and it has been shown that children in social classes IV or V are less likely to be presented for vaccination and immunisation and similarly so are those living in the north compared with those living in the south.

The child's attendance at school is therefore an important milestone not only in his education but also in his health history. The school child is a captive patient who is under regular surveillance by teachers, school nurses and doctors and can be well documented.

The Court Report suggests that even at school the level of concern could be greater and would like to see the medical examination of every child at entry to school made statutory, with every child seen by the school nurse annually thereafter. The report sums up the present service saying, 'the school health service has become primarily a health advisory service and an ascertainment service for handicapped pupils'. One of the current problems is that the school health service is not sufficiently integrated with family general practitioners although at least some AHAs have attempted to overcome this by using general practitioners to undertake some of the school doctor's duties. Records, which ideally might be said to be better held with the GP records, are in fact held sometimes at school but normally in community health offices where they can be systematically maintained.

Another criticism that Court makes is that for those children with special needs the at-risk registers are not sufficiently integrated with other records. Furthermore the whole idea of the child 'at-risk' tends to highlight 'problem' children and possibly ignore others. Despite the administrative attempts to keep track of all children there have been some notable scandals where children have suffered injury and abuse, mainly from their parents or foster parents, despite attempts by health and social services to keep the situation under review.

Nevertheless for the most part children can be said to be receiving what help they need. This extends also to dental care where, despite the somewhat unsatisfactory nature of provision of dental care under the NHS, it is still possible for children to receive reasonably satisfactory treatment and remedial care.

Some children have handicaps which do not permit them to attend ordinary schools. For them local education authorities have set up special schools which may be residential. Some of these will be in hospitals and are run either by the local education authority or by boards of governors as private schools providing, on an agency basis, a service to local education authorities and charging accordingly.

Children are healthier nowadays and less likely to experience hospital care. One aspect of this is the steep decline in the incidence of many infectious diseases, so that admission to a fever hospital is no longer a common childhood experience. Nevertheless, each year some 6 per cent of children are admitted as in-patients, and they are between a quarter and a third of the patients attending emergency and accident departments.

There has been a revolution over the last thirty years in how children are treated in hospital. It was shown in the 1950s what harm young children suffer by being separated from their parents by admission to hospital and, prompted by the recommendation of the 1959 Platt Report on the Welfare of Children in Hospital, most hospitals allow open visiting, and some actively encourage parents to come into hospital with their children. The National Association for the Welfare of Children (NAWCH) is a voluntary body which has actively encouraged this policy. Today children are admitted to hospital only when absolutely necessary and as far as possible well separated from adult patients. Local education authorities have a duty to continue the education of children while they are in hospital. The Court Committee thought that in the treatment of children in hospital, as in many other matters, there is still room for much improvement.

Some children require psychiatric care for behavioural and emotional problems, although seldom as in-patients. Where that is necessary there are special children's units. The child psychiatric service organised by health authorities works closely with the child guidance service organised by local education authorities, but there are sometimes problems of co-ordination.

One of the Court Committee's recommendations was that all children on the threshold of adolescence, say at the age of 13, should be seen by the school doctor. It is increasingly being recognised that young people have their own special needs, which the traditional school health service is not particularly geared to meet. Some of the problems are straightforward, for instance the need to check that all girls have had the opportunity to have a vaccination against rubella (german measles) to ensure that if they become pregnant their babies are protected. Other problems are more complex and may particularly concern sexual development.

As with many other groups, a satisfactory provision of child health services relies on the successful integration of all the people concerned. It was felt by Court and others that much more yet needs to be done to ensure that health, social and education services are not only clear about their own particular responsibilities but also know how and when to get together to ensure that children grow up as healthy as possible.

The younger disabled

One group of people whose needs have been increasingly acknowledged, particularly during the last ten years, are the younger disabled. The term 'young' means under 65, i.e. not geriatric, and the disablement in this context is generally considered to be physical not mental.

The causes of physical disablement vary considerably. Poliomyelitis was, until the early 1950s, a significant cause of physical disability, particularly in the young, as its popular name 'infantile paralysis' suggests. The last significant outbreak, nearly 8,000 cases, was in 1947. Not until vaccination became widespread in the late 1950s did the risk decrease. By 1978 the number of recorded cases was 32. Similarly the early 1950s saw the rapid decline of tuberculosis from 8,653 cases in 1949 to 897 cases in 1978. Road, work and home accidents, diseases of the nervous system such as multiple sclerosis, and rheumatoid diseases, all contribute to the level of disablement in younger people.

Provision for the rehabilitation and care of the younger disabled was ill-distributed for the first decade or more of the NHS. Whereas Stoke Mandeville Hospital and the Nuffield Orthopaedic Centre, Oxford, did pioneering work, many other parts of the country had no other provision than general hospital wards for those requiring comprehensive care.

That such facilities are scarcely adequate may be seen by contrasting the care of a patient with head injury on a general ward with that provided by a specialist neuro-surgical unit with full rehabilitation backup. A study undertaken in the 1960s showed that staff in the general ward tend to be unduly pessimistic about the outcome of such cases and this fatalism may remove the patient from the acute ward where he is 'blocking a bed' to a chronic ward far too early on. Specialist units provide a more optimistic approach, appreciating that recovery will be very slow and that some patients will only regain reasonable capacity after some years rather than months.

Two groups of patients, however, have long benefited from special treatment, the war disabled and miners. The war disabled needing long-term hospital care are accommodated in special units or hospitals. Their interests are well looked after by a variety of voluntary bodies, notably the British Legion. Miners have also benefited from specialist units known as Miners' Rehabilitation Units. Whether these hospitals will survive now that most district general hospitals have comprehensive departments of physical medicine must be doubted.

Excluding these two groups, the younger disabled person requiring regular or permanent hospital care will be fortunate if he is accommodated in a special unit designed for his needs. There are still only about 1,900 places in such units and at least another 4,000 people are accommodated in geriatric wards. Progress in developing new units is slow. Even when they exist, priority goes to younger people leaving a difficult gap for those patients over 50, particularly for those who have suffered from stroke for whom progress is slow, or for those with a degenerative disease such as multiple sclerosis.

Despite slow progress in the provision of general hospital units, the overall level of awareness of the problems facing the disabled was much increased by the passing of the Chronically Sick and Disabled Persons Act 1970 which promoted concern for all disabled people including the deaf and the blind. Local authorities are now obliged to establish the number of disabled in their area and publicise the facilities available. These facilities include practical assistance in the home, including aids and adaptations. All public authorities (and private too) are obliged to make suitable provision for the disabled in their buildings particularly to improve access and provide special lavatories. Parking concessions are also available to disabled people on application to their GP.

The DHSS document, *Priorities for Health and Personal Social Services in England* of 1976, stresses the need for a high rate of expansion of facilities for the younger disabled. This continuing emphasis has been in large measure stimulated by the many voluntary bodies devoted to the care and welfare of the younger disabled, such as the Disabled Living Foundation, the Disabled Drivers' Association and the Disablement Income Group.

Registering as a disabled person under the Disabled Persons (Employment) Acts of 1944 and 1958 will help to obtain various facilities and not least the services of the Disablement Resettlement Officer (DRO) who has a duty to help find work for disabled people, although some people who would qualify for registration believe they do better without.

The elderly

By far the largest care category are the elderly. By this is meant those over retirement age, 60 for women, 65 for men. In health service terms geriatric medicine usually starts at 65 whether in men or women. Such a demarcation line is significant in allocating patients to a geriatrician rather than another doctor and consequently the placing of the 'young elderly' can be a problem.

It is characteristic of western society that the number of elderly people has grown during the last century. Paradoxically this is not so much due to the improvement in the health of the elderly themselves but to the very significant increase in the survival rate of children and young people. 'In 1911 a man aged 65 could expect to live a further 11 years compared with just over 12 years now; a woman aged 65 could expect to live 12 more years as opposed to over 16 years now. However, life expectancy at *birth* has improved from 49 years in 1911 to 70 years now in the case of men and 52 to 76 years for women.' *(A Happier Old Age.)*

Such a change has considerably altered the age structure of our society. About 14 per cent of the population of England and Wales is 65 or over, the actual numbers having increased considerably in the decade 1966-76. While the rate of increase will be much less in the next decade, there will be a marked increase in people of 75 and over. In 1976 1 in 104 of our population was aged 85 and over; by the end of the century the figure will have increased to 1 in 65. This has considerable implications for all those agencies concerned with the care of the elderly.

About a third of the total public expenditure on the main social programmes is attributable to the elderly, most of it in retirement pensions and other cash and indirect benefits. It would be wrong to assume, however, that except in cash terms the elderly are heavily dependent on the state. Most of them in fact continue to live at home. In 1976, in England, 41 per cent were living with their spouse in a two-person household, 12 per cent were living with children and 28 per cent were living alone. Of the rest, 13 per cent were in other types of household, and only 6 per cent were in residential or hospital accommodation. Living alone brings its problems and is particularly the fate of women, since they generally live longer than men. Over the age of 75 there are twice as many women as men.

There is a common belief that the rise of the nuclear family makes it more difficult for modern society to care for the elderly. In fact the nuclear or two-generation family has been the norm in this country for centuries and the great change, as we have seen, is that many more people live into old age. Another, rather more arguable difference is that society is more mobile, so that many more people do not live near their elderly parents and so cannot look after them. It is a common assumption among doctors, nurses and social workers, who are in a position to know the stfain it can entail, that people should support their parents. The assumption is shared by the population at large and despite many exceptions people on the whole live up to it. But a third of the elderly are either childless or have outlived their children.

If the elderly need support and that cannot be provided by their children then the task must fall on the state through professionals. Yet there can never be enough professionals to supervise all elderly people and in any case it could be argued that where possible the emphasis should be on independence and that the state does not have the automatic right to supervise the lives of its elderly citizens.

Undoubtedly elderly people do suffer from a host of maladies which drive them more and more often to seek the help of their doctor. In old age it becomes increasingly likely that the person will suffer from more than one ailment at a time and indeed in some instances the situation may be said to have got out of hand when elderly people have to take so many drugs that they are not aware what treatment is for what condition. Approximately a quarter of all prescriptions are given to the elderly age group. The most common conditions are arthritis and rheumatism leading to considerable physical handicap, heart disease and hypertension, and bronchitis. Mental illness, including senile dementia, is becoming an ever increasing problem and is dealt with in more detail later in the chapter.

Many elderly people suffer from a variety of problems, which react on one another. A particular health service cannot in such circumstances meet their needs. That is one of the reasons why such stress is laid on their collaboration with local authority services. That in many cases these services have failed to respond adequately is inevitable, particularly as the elderly as a group are rather less likely than some other care groups to campaign for improvements in the services for themselves. This is understandable given the gradual nature of increasing disability in old age. Many people take a somewhat fatalistic view and the average GP's remark 'remember that you are getting on a bit' will seem to them to be fair comment.

Positive policies are needed however if only to sort out which agency is responsible for what. At what point do housing and social services confer in providing special accommodation for the elderly? Is there any truth in the statement that many elderly people would not be in hospital care if social services departments increased their provision? Such questions are constantly being posed and need answers if the inevitably limited resources are to be used to the best advantage.

We have already noted that about 94 per cent of all old people are living at home either alone or with others. This is not to say that they do not need help. GPs' increased involvement with their elderly patients is recognised by a higher capitation fee and there may well be a much greater need to visit the patient in his own home rather than to conduct a consultation in the surgery. Health visitors are somewhat slowly reorientating themselves to work more with the elderly as opposed to their traditional role of involvement with children. Home nurses will spend a certain amount of time giving care at home, such as applying dressings and giving injections. Social workers and health staff will continue to discuss the individual needs of particular elderly people and between them arrange for such matters as meals-on-wheels and bath attendants, special aids and appliances. Health workers also arrange for chiropodists, sight testing, hearing testing and dental treatment. Provision of chiropody services is inadequate in many places at present.

Given the British system of general practice and community health care, the chances of supporting the elderly at home are high, but there will always be a small minority of people who are not accounted for, who do not appear on a GP's list and who may escape attention until circumstances or even death brings them to the general notice.

Many elderly people will eventually require more than care at home but increasingly there is a reluctance to admit them into hospital if they can receive the necessary care as a day patient. Hospital admission can be disturbing for many reasons, not least that many geriatric hospitals are still in old workhouse buildings with their unfortunate associations for a generation of people for whom the workhouse (officially a discontinued term since 1929) still generates fear, not perhaps so much of the conditions inside, but for the loss of independence that the workhouse symbolised.

The half-way house between treatment at home and that as a patient in hospital, is the day hospital, which provides rehabilitation, maintenance treatment, social care and medical and nursing investigation and treatment. The day hospital has a staff of physiotherapists and occupational therapists and is visited by therapeutic staff all under the supervision of a consultant geriatrician. Few patients attend every day but some will come as many as three times a week. Transporting patients to day hospitals has placed a heavy workload on the ambulance service. Social service departments also provide day centres but the emphasis is more on resocialising elderly people rather than treating them. Insofar as social therapy is an important part of maintaining a person's ability to cope, the health and social services overlap.

Day hospitals do not eliminate the need for more formal out-patient sessions or for particular courses of treatment in physio/occupational therapy departments. The services of the dietitian, the speech therapist, the chiropodist, the dentist, the ENT department, the eye department, may all be required.

Many elderly people go to a hospital out-patient department to see a consultant in a particular specialty and are never referred to the geriatrician. Indeed 50 per cent of all hospital beds other than maternity and psychiatric are at any one time occupied by people of 65 and over, though few of them will be under the care of the geriatrician. Some of those treated by other specialists may be transferred to the geriatrician if they cannot be discharged and are therefore blocking an acute bed.

The present DHSS guidance is that the number of geriatric beds in hospital should not be more than 10 per 1,000 of the population over 65. Present provision is less than this, and it may be that a lower figure will be found adequate. Scotland has worked to a different figure, and in 1970 the Scottish Health Services Planning Council suggested that planning should be related to the 75 and over age group: 40 beds per 1,000. In any case bed numbers by themselves are an inadequate guide; an effective department with a good record for rehabilitation and discharge may be under less pressure than a much larger department with a low discharge rate which is unable to admit except from a waiting list. Current policy is that 50 per cent of the beds should be in a district general hospital, thus ensuring full access to diagnostic, therapeutic and rehabilitation facilities, with the remaining provision in community hospitals. In 1980 the DHSS suggested that only 30 per cent of the beds need be in the DGH, and it seems likely that this will become official policy. It is certainly doubtful whether the more ambitious plans for geriatric provision can be realised within the foreseeable future.

The geriatrician has many more beds under his charge than most consultants. In 1977 in England the average number of beds available to hospital medical staff (not just consultants) was 13.2 each; the figure for general medicine was 8.2 and for geriatrics 48.4. This shows a remarkable change from 1963, when the average for all specialties was 25.8, for general medicine 12.3 and for geriatrics as high as 165.7. Against these figures should be put those for discharges. The average per doctor for all specialties in 1977 was 188, for general medicine 216 and for geriatrics only 196. In other words, if geriatrics have larger numbers of beds than other consultants, it is because many of them are occupied by long-stay patients requiring less medical attention than acute patients. Nevertheless it is commonly held that geriatric medical staffing is too low, and certainly it is one of the least popular specialties with doctors looking for a hospital career. That is not altogether surprising given the size of geriatric departments, the fact that many are still housed in former 'chronic sick' accommodation (though usually much upgraded) and that geriatric medicine is less glamorous than much of the acute medicine practiced in teaching hospitals. Moreover, one school of thought in the profession still holds that geriatrics is not a true specialty, and should be the responsibility of general physicians with an interest in the elderly. According to the British Geriatric Society, 'geriatrics is a branch of general medicine concerned with the clinical, preventive, remedial and social aspects of illness in the elderly'. In other words it is the awareness of the combination of factors in treating illness in the elderly which is significant. An effective geriatrician has to be able to look at the patient as a whole and, much more than most hospital doctors, to be aware of the interrelation of medical and social problems.

There can be little doubt that the care of the elderly has greatly improved in the last 30 years, yet standards and practices still vary remarkably from place to place and improved provision for the elderly has a high place in official programmes of priorities. Geriatric services have come within the purview of the Hospital (now Health) Advisory Service since its establishment, and this is an indication that the services, particularly for long-stay patients, have given cause for anxiety, even though the main function of the service is advisory rather than inspection.

The HAS has among other things given valuable guidance on the environment in which patients have to live and which can do so much to support or weaken their individualism and personal dignity. The quality of life in hospitals has improved although there is still a gap between what is desirable and what has been achieved. Voluntary bodies such as Age Concern have done much to create awareness of the problems facing the elderly. Central to improvement has been the recognition of the need for adequate financial support. This, of course, though very relevant to the health of the elderly is a matter not for the NHS but for social security or perhaps even for some radical change in our social arrangements.

Finally it should be noted that whatever the hardships of increasing disability and reduced income brought on by old age, an OPCS survey has shown that elderly people express more satisfaction about their life than do younger people. It would be too optimistic to assume that this is because their level of care and support is satisfactory; it is more likely that the elderly person is more realistic about the limitations of what life has to offer.

The mentally ill

The term 'psychiatric' tends to be used sometimes to refer to mental illness and sometimes to both mental illness and mental handicap. Since these are quite different conditions — or groups of conditions — it is better that they should be considered quite separately.

Jane Gibbons points out that:

> There is at present very little consensus on the nature of mental illness; at one extreme are writers who argue forcibly for a purely physical conception of

> mental illness and pay little attention to the role of social factors either in their causation or treatment; at the other extreme are those who explain all so-called mental illness as a result of social and intimate personal processes. *(The Social Context of Health Care.)*

Faced with this disparity of views, those responsible for providing the resources may find it difficult to know where to place their priorities, and in 1972 Kathleen Jones pointed out that there could be said to be no fewer than five models for the future (although the last two are unlikely to get the support of ministers, planners or psychiatrists):

1. A pluralist provision model such as has been suggested by the WHO Expert Committee. (This would appear to be what we have.)
2. A medical model based on hospitals which emphasises the sickness element of mental illness and therefore is devoted to treatment and cure.
3. The social care model which suggests that it is society rather than patients which needs treatment and whose most advanced protagonists such as Szasz suggest that mental illness is a 'myth'.
4. The conspiratorial model in which mental illness is 'so to speak in the eye of the beholder'.
5. Closely related to this view is the no-model school which seems to say that mental illness is other people — a conspiracy which makes the so-called patient a scapegoat for society.

So the definition of mental illness is difficult. The term itself is fairly recent, and before this century the terms madness, lunacy and insanity were the ones normally used, though they did not necessarily apply to exactly the same conditions now referred to as mental illness, and still less imply present views about cause or treatment. It might seem safest to define mental illness as those conditions treated by psychiatrists, but that too brings problems. Ian Kennedy began his 1980 Reith Lectures by saying: 'Six years ago the American Psychiatric Association took a vote and decided homosexuality was not an illness. So, since 1974 it hasn't been an illness.' The problems which people bring to psychiatrists, or which psychiatrists profess to treat, cannot always reasonably be regarded as illnesses and, without at all committing ourselves to the conspiratorial theory of mental illness, we can see that in extreme cases it is possible for the politically or socially deviant to be regarded as mentally ill.

These uncertainties do not usually have much bearing on day-to-day practice. Despite confusions of concept, most staff concerned with mental illness accept that it can be treated. Furthermore they find the broad classification into neurotic and psychotic disorders useful. Neurosis may be described as disorders which invoke in the patient feelings of fear, panic, anxiety but without involving a loss of contact with reality. Psychosis, however, is typically characterised by loss of contact with reality and the patient enters a world of his own; his delusions may involve him in considerable unhappiness but on occasions he may feel confident that he is right and the rest of the world is wrong. Psychotic patients appear to be 'mad' to society in general.

The prevalence of mental illness has been the subject of a considerable amount of study but the results are by no means conclusive. One of the problems is again the uncertainty of definitions, which makes any attempt at study over time very difficult. Also it appears that psychiatrists in different countries tend to diagnose differently when using the same International Classification of Diseases.

However, it does appear that psychosis is fairly uniform in incidence throughout the world, irrespective of class or culture. Some studies have suggested that schizophrenia, one of the most commonly diagnosed psychotic conditions, is more prevalent in social classes IV and V, but the explanation of that could be that the schizophrenic sink in the social scale. The incidence of psychosis does not appear to have altered much in time, but it is widely assumed that neurosis was never more prevalent than now, particularly in western industrial societies. Whether this is the case is open to question, given the uncertainties of definition and the willingness these days of people to consult psychiatrists about matters for which at one time they would have sought help elsewhere, or would not have thought help necessary.

A National Morbidity Study carried out by the OPCS in 1970-1 indicated that on average one in 14 males and one in seven females in England and Wales consulted their GPs for some form of mental illness. This may be an underestimate for it seems that GPs do not always detect psychiatric symptoms. The proportion of those referred by their GP to the specialist services is about 12 per cent.

The statutory basis for the mental health services, insofar as one is needed over and above the NHS legislation is, as we saw in Chapter 1, the Mental Health Act 1959 and the 1960 Act for Scotland. Well over 95 per cent of patients are admitted to hospital informally. The others are detained under one or other of the appropriate sections of the Act. Those most frequently used in the 1959 Act are Section 25 which allows a patient to be detained in hospital for a period of 28 days for observation on the basis of two medical opinions, following an application from the patient's nearest relative or an approved social worker; Section 29 which allows for emergency detention for up to three days on the same grounds as Section 25 but with only one medical recommendation; Section 26 which allows the patient to be detained for treatment for up to one year, but this can be reviewed. Patients can appeal against detention through the Mental Health Review Tribunal. In Scotland appeal is to the Mental Welfare Commission.

The 1959 Act has had its critics, and in 1975 the government announced its intention to review it. Following consultations, a white paper was published in 1978 which proposed amending legislation. The subject is difficult because on the one hand there is pressure to strengthen the rights and liberties of the mentally ill and on the other hand to protect the public and staff, and so far no change has been made.

The institutional core of the service remains the large mental hospitals inherited from the nineteenth century. These often remote and forbidding hospitals, built to meet nineteenth century needs, are not very suitable for modern care. They are liable to be traditional in outlook, their patients, like the inmates of most institutions, are liable to become 'institutionalised' — dependent on the institution and its routines, and unwilling to leave it — and, it is said, the staff too become institutionalised. It is not really surprising that there have been unfavourable reports on several such hospitals following enquiries into alleged scandals. It would be misleading, however, to suggest that they are altogether unsatisfactory. They have been responsible for many of the developments in psychiatric care over the past 30 years and, as the various enquiry reports have shown, even hospitals with serious shortcomings also have good features. The 1962 Hospital Plan predicted, on the basis of existing trends, that there would be a rapid fall in the number of patients in these hospitals, and that many of them could be closed. The trend has been slower than expected, and so far only one large hospital has been closed. In 1955 the 101 large mental illness hospitals in England had nearly 140,000 patients, and in 1979 the figure had fallen to 64,000. More than half these hospitals now have under 600 patients, and are thus hardly large in the traditional sense. More closures can be expected, but it is likely that 70 or so of these hospitals will continue to provide in-patient care for a district.

Except sometimes in an emergency, these mental illness hospitals are now unlikely to be the first contact of a patient with the specialist services. For at least 20 years the emphasis has been on the development of community rather than in-patient care, though there is still a long way to go. The GP who thinks a patient needs specialist treatment will generally refer him to an out-patient department, often in a district general hospital. Out-patient treatment may be sufficient, or may be supplemented with attendance at one of the day hospitals which now exist in considerable numbers. These may also be used after a patient has received in-patient care. If the consultant decides that in-patient care is needed, admission will often be to a psychiatric unit in a district general hospital. These units are more conveniently situated and, it is hoped, avoid the stigma traditionally attached to admission to a mental hospital. Their design, equipment and staffing usually compare favourably with the old mental hospitals. They are intended for short-term care and in 1978 in England half in-patient stays were under a month, and 84 per cent were under three months.

If most patients need only short-term or mid-term care, a minority become long-term patients and it is probably the existence of these which has made the decline in the need for the old mental hospitals slower than was expected in 1962. The long-stay patient will normally be transferred to such a hospital, though it is recognised that there will be problems of morale and staffing if the hospitals treat only such cases, and that links with the short-stay unit must be close. Long-stay care is expensive even if the costs per week are much lower than for patients receiving active treatment, so that the relatively small number of patients requiring it place a disproportionate burden on the service.

Although there have been several reports on various aspects of the psychiatric services over the years, it was only in 1975 that the government issued a comprehensive survey of needs and programme for the future in a white paper entitled *Better Services for the Mentally Ill.* This white paper first tried to define the nature of the problem and it reviewed what had so far been achieved. It faced considerable difficulty when exploring what should be done in the future. Recognising the limitation of resources it said, 'we thus see the next three or four years as a time for Health and Local Authorities firstly to do whatever is possible within the very limited resources available'. The white paper accepted that existing mental hospitals would continue for the foreseeable future. The priorities promoted by the DHSS were the continued development of community care within the context of a district or a sub-district organisation. In practical terms this meant allocating psychiatric teams to particular areas so that the relationships between professionals, particularly health staff and social workers, could be combined in the interest of the patient. A normal team responsibility was seen as being a population of approximately 60,000 people.

The white paper was conscious of the relatively poor staffing levels and besought authorities to try and improve these. One way of doing this in the hospitals was to reduce the number of beds and indeed such reductions have been considerable during the last few years. This has put increased pressure on the community, and the white paper emphasised the need to set up adequate day hospital and community nursing support.

The particular need of mentally ill offenders often left in prison because no hospital facilities were available other than those in the state hospitals of Broadmoor, Rampton and Moss Side, was to be met by the setting up of secure units, one for each region. Considerable opposition from staff and some of their unions, and also from local communities, has made this difficult to achieve.

Drug misusers and alcoholics also need special care and health authorities were asked to consider setting up special units.

For a variety of reasons the services for the mentally ill have received a lot of criticism. Relative to some parts of the service they have been underfunded, as is acknowledged by the high priority they now receive in official plans; the various 'scandal' enquiries have shown reason for concern; the use of compulsory powers in connection with both NHS and special hospital patients has sometimes provoked controversy; and laymen are much more likely to have theories about mental than about physical illness. When hospitals adopted a policy of discharging patients as early as possible it was alleged that this meant a 'revolving door' policy, i.e. that discharge was frequently followed by readmission. It was also said, sometimes with reason, that the health, and particularly the local authority, services were inadequate to support discharged patients in the community. Yet despite the acknowledged shortcomings, developments over the past 20 years have been encouraging and the implementation of present policies, slow though it may be, should lead to further progress. There are indications, however, that the service is facing an intractable problem.

Many of the long-stay patients are old, and of those many have grown old in hospital. It is to be hoped that in future there will be fewer of them now that most patients are discharged after weeks or months, though it is likely that there will still be some. There are other people who develop mental illness only in old age, and it is usually combined then with various physical impairments. These psychogeriatric patients present difficult problems and though their condition can sometimes if not always be improved it needs a combination of psychiatric and geriatric skills. With the large increase in the numbers of very elderly in the population during the next decades there will be a growing problem in making provision for this type of patient. As we have seen, large mental hospitals providing mainly for long-stay and elderly patients are undesirable, and patients with psychiatric problems are usually difficult to accommodate in geriatric units. The DHSS has seen catering for these patients as one of the main roles of the community hospital, but the idea has not proved popular and seems unlikely to be pursued. A report of the Scottish Health Services Council in 1970 made some positive proposals, including proper assessment to determine exactly the nature of the disorder so that no opportunity for rehabilitation is lost. In 1979 a later Scottish report, *Services for the Elderly with Mental Disability in Scotland,* came back to the subject. Among other things it called for urgent action to develop psychiatric day hospital places for old people and said that a new type of continuing care unit for the elderly confused should become the main form of health service provision for the long-term care of elderly persons with dementia. It estimated that about 5,500 new and replacement beds would be needed.

The mentally handicapped

As we saw in Chapter 1, it was not until this century that the state made provision specifically for the mentally handicapped. The services for this relatively small group of people have always been somewhat isolated and neglected. In the last 15 years or so their needs have received much more attention, and there is more optimism about what can be achieved. In practice they have not fared well despite the fact that providing care for the mentally handicapped has become almost a symbol for the alternative to the high technology style of medicine.

Professor Kathleen Jones in a review of current policies and subsequent action concluded that, 'there are two long-standing problems in the services for the mentally handicapped; stigma and inertia'. (*Opening the Door.)*

It is likely that in past centuries, when infant mortality rates were high, not many of the severely handicapped survived early childhood, and it may be that the mildly handicapped found it easier to cope in a rural society which did not require literacy or technical skills. Nevertheless the mentally handicapped have always been known and, as Joanna Ryan has shown, society has always been puzzled to define how they are different. At one time it could be debated whether they were really human; now the discussion tends to turn on how near they are to normal, with reformers stressing that they are not so very different from other people, and should not be treated very differently, while others have emphasised the differences and argued for a more segregated life.

Eugenic fears about breeding a degenerate race, prevalent at the beginning of the century, may have disappeared, but fears about violence and promiscuity, though unjustified, are still common, and difficult to combat. Perhaps reformers underestimate another, less specific fear; the behaviour of the mentally handicapped (and of the mentally ill) can be unpredictable by normal standards, and that makes many people uncomfortable. Moreover mentally handicapped children, who these days are much more likely than adults to be living in the community, do undoubtedly give their parents great problems and that may increase society's feelings that the handicapped should be cared for away from the community by professionals. Yet it has been shown that the staff of hospitals for the handicapped themselves underestimate and sometimes look down on their charges; treating mentally handicapped adults as 'children', however kindly meant, hinders the development of their capacities.

Terminology is revealing. Nineteenth-century legislation used robust traditional words such as idiot and imbecile. In this century the official terms have been successively mentally deficient, mentally subnormal and mentally handicapped. Mental handicap is now the usual term, although mental deficiency is still used for some official purposes in Scotland. Other terms have been tried: in England 'developmentally young' and in North America 'mentally retarded' and even 'exceptional child'. The search for a term which is descriptive without carrying a stigma may be futile while the public's attitude is ambiguous.

When care for the handicapped came to be provided on a large scale it was based on the medical model, and this has persisted. In 1969 Dr Pauline Morris published in *Put Away* a study of 35 hospitals. She found that the usual mode of running them was in a clinical rather than a socio-therapeutic style. Thus, the effect of the environment, of the need to develop interpersonal relationships and train for particular tasks, were all undervalued and custody and treatment by drugs were correspondingly overvalued. Yet, although doctors are among those who have done valuable work in the study of mental handicap and the improvement of services, the specialty carries little prestige in the profession and does not attract many young doctors of good calibre.

Ironically, the most usual method of assessing mental handicap is by IQ, which is an educational rather than medical test. It is commonly accepted that those having an IQ of 50 – 70 are mildly mentally handicapped and those under 50 severely handicapped. In recent years the scientific validity of IQ measurements has been questioned, and it seems that class, cultural values, housing and poverty can affect a child's IQ attainment level. Since the condition is not precisely defined there can be only rough estimates of its prevalence. Severe handicap appears to occur irrespective of class or the other factors which affect IQ performance, and since in the end virtually all such cases come to the attention of the health service estimates can be made. In 1971 about four persons per 1,000 in the age group 15 – 19 came into this category in England and Wales. Because they do not live as long as the population as a whole, the figure in relation to the total population was between two and three per 1,000. A considerable number of them also suffered from severe physical handicaps.

The definition of mild handicap is so uncertain that official reports seldom offer estimates, and it may be more useful to attempt to assess the numbers likely to need help rather than incidence. There were until recently, and perhaps still are in some hospitals, people committed to them before the war on account of some sexual or other misdemeanor. They would not now be considered in need of hospital care, but do not necessarily benefit from discharge after 30 or 40 years of institutional life.

In some respects services for the mentally handicapped are like those for the mentally ill. The core of the service is still long-established hospitals, many of them large and many of them remote from patients' families. They suffer from the same institutional defects as the mental illness hospitals and have been the subject of several enquiries following 'scandal' allegations. As with mental illness, the emphasis has moved towards care in the community, with provision of a range of facilities such as day hospitals, hostels, day centres and so on by health and local authorities — facilities increasingly provided but so far unevenly and on an inadequate scale.

If, as is generally accepted, the handicapped are not ill and their primary need is education and training, their services should probably be more different than they are from those for the mentally ill. (These two client groups are still sometimes considered together and both are covered by the provisions of the Mental Health Acts, which lay down the circumstances in which the handicapped as well as the mentally ill may be compulsorily detained.)

The main differences in arrangements do in fact derive from differences in the conditions. Severe mental handicap usually reveals itself at birth or in early childhood, so that maternity and paediatric departments have a part in diagnosis and parental guidance. Many handicapped children are cared for in hospitals, though this is now considered undesirable and the number has declined. Since handicap is not a condition calling for only short-term treatment, there is no equivalent to the psychiatric department of the district general hospital.

What the services ought to be was outlined in a white paper, *Better Services for the Mentally Handicapped,* published by the DHSS and the Welsh Office in 1971. The following is its summary of basic principles.

1. A family with a handicapped member has the same needs for general social services as all other families. The family and the handicapped child or adult also need special additional help, which varies according to the severity of the handicap, whether there are associated physical handicaps or behaviour problems, the age of the handicapped person and his family situation.
2. Mentally handicapped children and adults should not be segregated unnecessarily from other people of similar age, nor from the general life of the local community.
3. Full use should be made of available knowledge which can help to prevent mental handicap or to reduce the severity of its effects.
4. There should be a comprehensive initial assessment and periodic reassessment of the needs of each handicapped person and his family.
5. Each handicapped person needs stimulation, social training and education and purposeful occupation of employment in order to develop to his maximum capacity and to exercise all the skills he acquires, however limited they may be.
6. Each handicapped person should live with his own family as long as this does not impose an undue burden on them or him, and he and his family should receive full advice and support. If he has to leave home for a foster home, residential home or hospital, temporarily or permanently, links with his own family should normally be maintained.
7. The range of services in every area should be such that the family can be sure that their handicapped member will be properly cared for when it becomes necessary for him to leave the family home.
8. When a handicapped person has to leave his family home, temporarily or permanently, the substitute home should be as homelike as possible, even if it is also a hospital. It should provide sympathetic and constant human relationships.
9. There should be proper co-ordination in the application of relevant professional skills for the benefit of individual handicapped people and their families, and in the planning and administration of relevant services, whether or not these cross administrative frontiers.
10. Local authority personal social services for the mentally handicapped should develop as an integral part of the services recently brought together under the Local Authority Social Services Act 1970.
11. There should be close collaboration between these services and those provided by other local authority departments (e.g. child health services and education), and with general practitioners, hospitals and other services for the disabled.
12. Hospital services for the mentally handicapped should be easily accessible to the population they serve. They should be associated with other hospital services, so that a full range of specialist skills is easily available when needed for assessment or treatment.
13. Hospital and local authority services should be planned and operated in partnership.
14. Voluntary service can make a contribution to the welfare of mentally handicapped people and their families at all stages of their lives and wherever they are living.
15. Understanding and help from friends and neighbours and from the community at large are needed to help the family to maintain a normal

social life and to give the handicapped member as nearly normal a life as his handicap or handicaps permit.

In 1975 the Secretary of State set up the National Development Group for the Mentally Handicapped as an independent body to advise on the development and implementation of better services. Before its disbandment in 1980 it produced a number of valuable reports and in 1980, too late for summary here, a review of services in England since the 1971 white paper.

In Scotland a paper on services for the mentally handicapped was issued in 1972, and it was followed in 1979 by a report of the Scottish Health Service Planning Council and the Advisory Council on Social Work.

The 1976 DHSS Priorities document upheld the principles of *Better Services* and attempted to set objectives in financial terms. Yet progress continues to be slow and it has been estimated that even in a region which has done more than most to promote better provision, Wessex, less money proportionately was allocated in 1978 than in 1968. To try to overcome this inertia the region stated in its 1979-80 annual plan that it intended to reach the target of 100 per cent provision for those mentally handicapped people needing hospital/hostel type care by 1989. While the declaration is to be welcomed in principle, its implementation will present severe problems to authorities faced also with demands for more expenditure on the services for the elderly and the mentally ill, and for acute care.

One of the reasons for under-achievement is the conflict of opinion about appropriate care models. Should the handicapped be looked after in hospitals at all? If so, what size should these hospitals be and how should they be run? A leader of the non-hospital school of thought is Dr Albert Kushlick of the Wessex region, who maintains that hostels of not more than 26 people not segregated according to level of attainment and placed in a community not on a hospital site provide the most promising environment. Several such hostels have been provided in the region. However, they have their critics, who maintain that the hostels can become ghettos, isolated from the community yet without the facilities of a hospital. The National Development Group said in 1978 that the model should not automatically be assumed as the only way to effective care.

The DHSS has been experimenting with other types of provision and two centres at Sheffield and Peterborough provide large hospitals (up to 200 places) but in smaller living units than the Kushlick hostel, i.e. not more than eight to a group, which are considered to create a family atmosphere. This move towards individualism has been considerably influenced by Scandinavian models.

Differences of opinion were strikingly shown over the Jay Report, published in 1979. The committee was set up to explore a suggestion of the Briggs Committee on Nursing that a new caring profession for the mentally handicapped should emerge gradually. The Jay Committee reasonably felt that it could not make recommendations about the caring profession without first positing the type of care that should be provided. It assumed a model based on small, local residential units in the community and recommended a new profession trained for a Certificate in Social Service. It might seem logical that if the mentally handicapped are not ill their main need is not for nurses, although initially the new profession would have been drawn from mental handicap nurses. In fact the recommendations were vehemently opposed by nurses, who wished neither to lose their existing professional role and status nor to see much of the responsibility for the handicapped transferred from NHS hospitals to local authority provision. In face of this opposition, and even more the financial implications of the care model, the Government rejected the recommendations of the report, though hoping for some common training in nursing and social work.

The acutely ill

In looking at those care groups that it is easy to categorise generically, it should not be forgotten that the greater part of the resources of the NHS are spent on what are loosely called the acute services, that is those services which look after people who have illness characterised by sudden onset or severity of symptoms.

If the architects of the NHS expected the cost of treating sickness to stabilise, this has certainly not proved to be the case. The 1976 Priorities document pointed out that in the period 1970-3 in-patient admissions to acute specialties in England rose by over 1 per cent a year and out-patient attendances by nearly 2 per cent. The cost of acute services during the same period rose by 3 per cent a year as did the overall staff numbers. This led to an increase of about 2 per cent in the average cost of in-patient treatment per year. Against these increases, there was a reduction in the number of acute beds available and the length of time patients remained in hospital. There is no reason to suppose that those years were in any way untypical. Indeed it is the experience of all western industrial countries that the cost of care is escalating, with a corresponding difficulty in meeting those costs.

Provision for acute care is defined here negatively as care for people not falling into the special group discussed above (though it is provided for many people over 65), and as the preceding paragraph implies, discussion of acute care normally turns on hospital care. It should not be forgotten however, that most cases of acute illness are initially treated by GPs, and that most require care from GPs and the community services after hospital treatment. Another point to be made is that until about 25 years ago a discussion such as this would have had a separate section on provision for infectious diseases. In 1952 there were 15,371 beds for infectious diseases in England and Wales, and 33,787 for tuberculosis; in 1978 there were 2,109 beds for infectious diseases and 6,274 for diseases of the chest.

As acute care is all the care provided in the district general hospital, other than in any maternity, psychiatric and geriatric unit, a very rough indication of provision can be found in official figures for bed allocations (e.g. the tables in *The Hospitals and Health Services Year Book).* A more detailed picture can be obtained from morbidity and mortality statistics. Morbidity statistics are a better indication of the burden on the NHS — and on patients — since there are some very disturbing illnesses, such as rheumatism and arthritis, some skin conditions (and most forms of mental illness) which do not lead to death. However, while comprehensive mortality statistics exist, since the cause of death is registered, there are no comparable morbidity figures, though there are many studies related to particular diseases or particular communities. Causes of death vary by sex, age and part of the country, and the same will be true of morbidity.

Circulatory diseases and cancers are the main causes of illness and death from middle age on. These, and a number of others, are sometimes referred to as 'degenerative diseases', though the term does not indicate very much. If some of the cancers can be effectively treated, others lead to a fairly long illness, often marked by periods of acute care before death, whereas other degenerative diseases, such as rheumatism and arthritis, are more chronic than acute and may entail frequent attendance at hospital out-patient departments but not in-patient treatment. In a different category are the victims of accidents, who form an important part of the work-load of acute wards and come from all groups of the population. Certainly road accidents affect all groups, though young men who ride motorcycles are particularly strongly represented. The main victims of accidents in the home are children and the elderly, whereas accidents at work particularly affect men in certain industries.

The interest of patients, and of their clinicians, is in effective treatment. Most cases treated are, by definition, for common conditions and in that sense run-of-the-mill. Although they are much the same sorts of cases that were treated 20 or 30 years ago, for many there has been steady though not revolutionary improvement, made possible by new techniques and new drugs. Possibly the clearest indication of this is the much shorter in-patient stay for nearly all types of treatment. It is the more revolutionary developments in medicine which attract public attention. One such, which has accelerated demand on the acute services, is joint replacement, particularly of hips but increasingly of other joints, which has benefited many sufferers from arthritic degeneration. Others, though very remarkable medical developments, can benefit only a few. A striking and much publicised example is heart transplants. These operations have given a new lease of life to some who have received them, but their impact on the incidence of heart disease is negligible. It is understandable that nevertheless they should have captured the public imagination. In other things too the public's interest is captured by developments which may not be central to medical need. The whole body scanner is an advanced technological development for the diagnosis (not treatment) of some cancers and other diseases, and the public has contributed large sums for the purchase of such machines for NHS hospitals, but some would say that it is arguable whether the benefits justify devoting resources to it. *(The Image and the Reality.)*

Many patients receiving acute care must wonder whether they could have avoided the need for it, and clinicians certainly are very conscious of what prevention could have done; if the patient had not smoked, or had been wearing a seat belt, he would not be in hospital. Prevention, it hardly needs saying, is important not only to individuals as potential beneficiaries but to the community as a whole both in terms of a healthier population and in terms of avoiding the heavy financial burden on the NHS, and thus on the community, of treating preventible accidents and illnesses.

Some forms of prevention are for the individual. Not to smoke, to drink only moderately, to eat sensibly and to take moderate exercise will not guarantee perpetual good health but will greatly reduce liability to suffer from heart disease, lung cancer, bronchitis and other illnesses. However, changing people's habits is not easy and health education, although important and receiving greater emphasis, is not likely to produce dramatic changes in the morbidity and mortality statistics. Other forms of prevention call for community action: measures to reduce accidents on the roads, at work and at home, reduction of pollution and so on. Most of such measures cost money and call for political action, and are often controversial. To take one example, if all people in cars wore seat belts the number of serious injuries from car accidents would be greatly reduced, and there has therefore been strong pressure within the service for making wearing them compulsory. There was opposition to legislation, partly because of doubts about how far it is right to require people to do things for their own protection as distinct from that of other people, and even more because of doubts about the wisdom of enacting a law which would be very difficult to enforce.

Between prevention and treatment for acute illness comes screening, i.e. the testing of whole populations, or groups known to be at risk, for diseases at the pre-symptomatic stage. It seems common sense to discover and treat illnesses as early as possible, yet the whole subject is controversial. In the first place screening costs money and it is not the best use of resources to undertake an expensive programme which reveals very few cases of the disease being tested for. That is why with the heavy decline in the incidence of tuberculosis, the mass miniature radiography service has been discontinued. Secondly, it is apparently not always the case that early diagnosis benefits final outcome. Thirdly, as the study mentioned early in this chapter showed, a screening programme can reveal much illness which the people screened are not aware of. While sometimes that may be beneficial, it may be that people above a certain age tolerate a certain amount of pre-symptomatic and mild illness and it would certainly not be beneficial to carry out screening programmes which revealed a lot of illness apparently calling for treatment but which the NHS did not have the resources to treat. Thus, although some forms of screening are desirable, it cannot be regarded as a universal approach to health care. Some cases remain controversial, and public pressure seems sometimes to have been misguided.

To revert to the subject of acute care, we should repeat here that nowadays the patient's experience of hospital is short. In 1977 average length of stay for the acute specialties in England was 9.5 days, compared with 16.3 in 1959. Some patients, as we have seen, are transferred to long-stay hospital accommodation, but most will return home. While they may subsequently visit the hospital out-patient department to check on progress or for out-patient treatment, their care henceforth lies with the GPs and the community health services. This makes it important that there should be good communications between consultants, GPs and the community services.

In the end we all die, and the health service is much involved with death. Although it is more usual nowadays to die in hospital than at home, it is said — not only in this country — that hospitals are not good at caring for the dying. Doctors, it is argued, are so conditioned to saving life that when they can no longer do that the patient is regarded as a failure, or at least is no longer of interest; that skills in curing are not accompanied by skills in enabling patients to die in dignity and peace, with the minimum of pain. While it would be quite wrong to regard these criticisms as commonly applicable, there has in recent years been a marked interest in improving care for the dying. One facet of this has been the establishment of hospices, which are described in Chapter 14.

Team work

The popular view is that doctors and nurses provide health care. Certainly it is inconceivable to have a health service without them, but the increasing sophistication of treatment and the development of alternative regimes for care make it very difficult for doctors and nurses to manage on their own. The management of patients has become a multiprofessional activity, as is the planning of new facilities.

An example of multidisciplinary management of a patient's needs may be seen in the continuing care of a mentally ill or mentally handicapped patient. Patients with acute illnesses also need the skill and experience provided by a team. A patient undergoing surgery will need the skills not only of doctors and nurses, but also those of the laboratory scientific officer, the operating department assistant, the physiotherapist and possibly the occupational therapist and the social worker. When the patient is discharged, careful co-ordination is necessary for his further care outside hospital. Whereas the care of the patient with an acute episode of illness can be reasonably easy to manage because the time span is short, care of the chronically ill disabled patient may offer more problems and a case conference where professionals all contribute their perception of what should be done for the patient may have to be held. However, as the 1975 white paper, *Better Services for the Mentally Ill,* observed:

> Multiprofessional team work, adequate assessment and consultation and arrangements of after-care and sound social work support are as yet sadly all too often theoretical ideas which bear scant relation to the practical realities. Inevitably patients and their families do not always receive the standards of care and support they should.

Team work is difficult, perhaps particularly so when it involves the co-operation of people in different professions and therefore different outlooks and some of the professions are new or expanding while others are old-established and concerned about the claims of the newcomers. This is a problem which is discussed in Chapter 15.

Patients, particularly hospital patients, are dependent not only on the many health care professions, but also on a wide range of other staff, from the managers to the support service staff. Patients come into contact with some of these — out-patient department receptionists, porters or cleaners, but may have no awareness of others such as engineers or central sterile supply department staff. It is for the skills of the health care professions that patients enter hospital and in that sense they are the most important. Nevertheless the support service staff are also essential as they have demonstrated in recent years when taking industrial action. Indeed it appeared that sometimes one of the factors behind industrial action by ancillary staff was a feeling that their importance was not sufficiently appreciated and acknowledged by patients and more particularly by professional staff.

Providing health care, and particularly hospital care, is now a complicated and expensive business, and in that lies a great paradox. It is only because patients can be classified by sex, age, condition, treatment and so on, and processed accordingly, that they can be provided with modern health care at a tolerable cost. Yet there are few if any circumstances in which a patient can be treated like a machine needing repair; all patients have their individual needs, fears and anxieties. There are few things they dislike more than feeling that they are being processed on a conveyor belt, or treated simply as cases. Inevitably these things sometimes happen yet it is remarkable how successful staff are on the whole in treating patients as individuals while at the same time 'processing' them as fast as possible.

Comprehensiveness

The discussion so far has shown the wide range of demands made upon the NHS and the comprehensive way in which attempts are made to meet these demands. Does it add up to the comprehensive provision envisaged when the NHS was founded? We have already seen, in this and the previous chapter, that the NHS is not the exclusive provider of personal health services. Care is also provided by a variety of other agencies, public and private, and someone feeling ill has a range of alternatives to the NHS, extending from taking patent medicines to admission to a private hospital. In addition to the possibilities already mentioned, he may have recourse to one of the practitioners of 'fringe medicine'. Furthermore we have seen that the potential demand for medical care is apparently unlimited, and that the possibilities of medical technology have extended beyond what any economy could support. Our account of the services for the various client groups pointed to shortcomings and plans for improvement, but if the service were really comprehensive plans would not be needed except to meet changes in population and in medical knowledge. However, that near perfection does not exist in the real world, and it may be pointless to try to measure the NHS against some unreal measure of comprehensiveness.

It might be more useful to use some such measure as whether adequate provision is made for all reasonable need to a standard the country can afford. Such a formula gives scope for endless debate. What, for instance, constitutes need, and who determines it, and how does it differ from demand? All the same it may be that the hopes and idealism of 1946, if expressed as a specific programme, would have been more on these lines than some wider and unrealisable comprehensiveness.

Certainly one of the strongest sentiments in the post-war years was the need for fairness, including geographical fairness. In this respect the NHS has remarkable achievements to its credit. To quote one example, Swindon, a largely industrial town in a rural setting, had only one doctor of consultant status in 1947 and its hospitals were a small voluntary hospital, a hospital in a poor state of repair built for the employees of the Great Western Railway, an isolation hospital, a small maternity nursing home and a public assistance institution. By 1978 the number of consultants had increased to over 50 and they were practising from one of the first purpose-built district general hospitals, the first phase of which opened its doors in 1961.

The many achievements like that have been overshadowed in the past few years by the publication of the various reports on the allocation of resources, particularly the English one (RAWP). For these have revealed in precise terms how uneven the allocation of money to health authorities still is. By this measure fairness has not been achieved, and whatever we may mean by comprehensive it must at least entail a similar availability of services to people in all parts of the country. When Buxton and Klein made a study of RAWP for the Royal Commission they stressed that, 'the variations in resources can only be used as a very rough and ready definition of variations in provisions and availability of care'. The authors of the RAWP report would not have claimed any more, if only because much must depend on how efficiently resources are used locally, but Buxton and Klein went on to make a more disconcerting point: 'what little evidence we have suggests that the link between resource level and satisfaction is tenuous'. Thus satisfaction and a sense of fairness have apparently little to do with measurable factors such as expenditure and staffing levels.

If fairness and comprehensiveness must be national in a national service, for most people most of the time the importance of the service is local. The establishment in 1974 of health authorities responsible for all the health services of specified areas has intensified the issues of comprehensiveness at local level. If a comprehensive range of services must be available to the population, it is natural that each authority or district should wish, acknowledged regional specialties apart, to provide them for its own population itself. Self-sufficiency may not prove the most economic approach, particularly at district level. That aside, any authority and district or area management team will find it is spending a great deal of time balancing the distribution of resources at local level, and the unenviable task of deciding between, say, appointing a consultant in psycho-geriatric medicine and one with an interest in renal medicine may only be resolved by a recourse to arguments on balance and comprehensiveness of care. Moreover, despite elaborate area and regional plans, local management teams will continue to be subject to local pressures based on the assumption that the provision of care is a political matter where fairness is ultimately not a demonstration by statistics so much as a consensus of local aspirations.

Effectiveness

Comprehensiveness is not in itself enough. Health authorities, clinicians and administrators alike are concerned with the difficulty of ensuring that what they are doing is effective.

To the individual patient, what counts is the result of the medical and nursing care he receives. He knows the outcome, but unless he accepts a simple *post hoc ergo propter hoc* argument he cannot be sure that it is the result of the treatment. Still less can he know whether some other treatment would have served him better. In his influential book, *Effectiveness and Efficiency,* published in 1972, A.L. Cochrane pointed out how little evidence there is for the effectiveness of many medical procedures, and argued for the wider use of randomised controlled trials. Their results can be striking. Several studies, for example, have suggested that coronary care units do not reduce deaths from heart disease. A whole variety of other diagnostic and therapeutic procedures have been questioned, though not many of them have been abandoned in consequence. The Royal Commission wrote in this context:

> Medicine is still an inexact science, and many of the procedures used by doctors, nurses and the remedial professions have never been tested for effectiveness. They are used because they have always been used and the patients seem to get better. The patients get better anyway in most cases and a particular procedure or treatment hallowed by time and use may have little to do with it; certainly, the fact that one procedure helps does not mean that another procedure does not help more.

If doctors limited themselves to proven diagnostic and therapeutic procedures, the effects of the NHS would be drastic, and probably unpopular. While that is hardly to be expected, there is more room for assessing work done, whether by professional audit on the peer group principle, or by other means. One of the things that merits attention is the marked variations between consultants on how long they keep patients in hospital for various common conditions.

To look at effectiveness in that way is to remove attention from the individual patient to the statistical group; the same is true of randomised controlled trials. It is at that level, probably, that medical effectiveness is best measured, but once the picture is broadened further, it becomes more difficult. It ought to be possible to measure the effectiveness of the national health service as a whole in terms of the state of the nation's health, but as we have already said, health depends on so many other things besides personal health care that it is not a promising approach. When comparisons can be made they produce curious results. The Royal Commission looked at some international comparisons of expenditure on health as a proportion of the gross domestic product and compared them with life expectancy figures and perinatal and maternal mortality rates. The UK's low rating in expenditure was not correspondingly low in these measures of outcome, though the only safe conclusion from this is a negative one: that more expenditure on health care does not necessarily bring higher standards of health.

The future

What is the future of the patient services described in this chapter? Clearly provision will continue to have to be made for all the various client groups, and primary, secondary and tertiary care will continue to be needed. Few services, on the face of it, are likely to prove unnecessary, and nearly all would benefit from further development. Considering the remarkable changes over the past 30 years, most of which it would have been difficult to foresee in 1948, it would be rash to make predictions about the next 30. So far as the next ten years are concerned the answer ought to be clear. The NHS is now committed to planning and therefore to making decisions about priorities. Planning so far has given priority to prevention, the development of services for the disadvantaged groups (the elderly, the mentally ill, the mentally handicapped) and community services. While priorities are subject to revision it is unlikely that there will be a change in the values implied by these priorities. Since resources are likely to allow at best only modest expansion of the NHS for some years, giving priority to these services implies that others, particularly acute hospital care, will have less resources for expansion, or may have to achieve any developments through economies elsewhere within their own sector.

Such is the future as envisaged by current planning, but some people argue that there is little sign so far of such a switch of resources and that it is inherently unlikely despite planning intentions. The doctors, it is said, have a preponderant influence on the development of the service and the number and standing of those concerned with the acute services will ensure that those services do not lose in the competition for resources. While there is force in this argument, there are other factors at work: medical science develops a momentum of its own and its discoveries lead to a demand for implementation, most often in the acute sector; the acute is always more urgent than the long-stay and therefore its demands are difficult to deny; and the disadvantaged groups, with the possible exception of the elderly, are minorities whose needs may evoke sympathy but are unlikely to receive the public support which is given to services likely to be needed by the majority of the population at some time or other.

Whether the service develops on the lines envisaged in current plans, or whether it develops on scientific lines with more resources spent on highly sophisticated methods of diagnosis or treatment, it will certainly feel constrained by the limitations on resources. There will therefore be more emphasis on avoiding the need for health care, though it may depend on the course of politics whether the emphasis is more on the individual's responsibility to lead a healthy life or on the state's responsibility to achieve a healthy and safe environment. Both things are necessary, and while hardly an alternative to expenditure on health care should enable the best use to be made of the resources that are available for health care. That brings us back to the point that the health of the population depends as much if not more on housing, diet, style of life and so on as on the personal health services. At a time when public expenditure is being cut, changes of policy in social services, housing or education not only impinge on the NHS but might have more effect on the nation's health than constraints on NHS expenditure. As the Royal Commission said, 'No health system can be looked at in isolation from the society it serves or the way that that society chooses to behave'.

Further reading

Circulars

England and Wales

HM(61)96. Immunisation in childhood
HM(70)52. Chronically Sick and Disabled Persons Act 1970
HM(71)97. Hospital services for the mentally ill
HM(72)71. Services for mental illness related to old age
HRC(74)27, WHRC(74)22. Health education
HSC(IS)75, WHSC(IS)66. Community hospitals
HC(78)5, WHC(78)4. Court Report on child health services
HC(80)6. Health centre policy

Scotland

SHM23/1973. Young chronic sick
HSR(74)C9. Health education

Official Reports

Central Health Services Council. *Domiciliary Midwifery and Maternity Bed Needs* (Peel Report). HMSO 1970

Central Health Services Council. *Report of the Committee on the Welfare of Children in Hospital.* HMSO 1959

Committee of Enquiry into Mental Handicap Nursing and Care. *Report* (Jay Report. Cmnd 7468). HMSO 1979

Committee on Child Health Services. *Fit for the Future* (Court Report. Cmnd 6684). HMSO 1977

DHSS. *Better Services for the Mentally Ill* (Cmnd 6233). HMSO 1975

DHSS. *Care in Action: A handbook of policies and priorities for the health and personal social services in England.* HMSO 1981

DHSS. *Health and Personal Social Services Statistics.* HMSO Annual.

DHSS. *Inequalities in Health.* Report of a Research Working Group (Black Report). 1980

DHSS. *Mental Handicap: Progress, problems and priorities.* 1980

DHSS. *Prevention and Health: Everybody's business.* 1976. *Prevention and Health: Occupational health services — the way ahead.* 1977. *Prevention and Health: Reducing the risk — safer pregnancy and childbirth.* 1977. *Prevention and Health: Eating for health.* 1978 HMSO

DHSS. *Priorities for Health and Personal Social Services in England: A consultative document.* HMSO 1976

DHSS. *Sharing Resources for Health in England.* Report of the Resource Allocation Working Party (RAWP Report). HMSO 1976

DHSS. *The Way Forward: Priorities in the health and social services.* HMSO 1977

DHSS and Welsh Office. *Better Services for the Mentally Handicapped* (Cmnd. 4683). HMSO 1971

DHSS and Welsh Office. *A Happier Old Age: A discussion document on elderly people in our society.* HMSO 1978

DHSS, Home Office, Welsh Office, Lord Chancellor's Department. *Review of the Mental Health Act 1959* (Cmnd 7320). HMSO 1978

Development Team for the Mentally Handicapped. *First Report: 1976-77. Second Report: 1978-79.* DHSS

Health Service Commissioner. *Annual Reports.* HMSO

Ministry of Health. *Report of the Maternity Services Committee* (Cranbrook Report). HMSO 1959

Office of Population Censuses and Surveys. *General Household Survey 1973.* HMSO

Royal Commission on the Law Relating to Mental Illness and Mental Deficiency. *Report.* HMSO 1957

Royal Commission on the National Health Service. *Report* (Cmnd 7615). 1979. Research Paper Number 3: *Allocating Health Resources: A commentary on the Report of the Resource Allocation Working Party* (R. Klein and M. Buxton). 1978. Research Paper Number 6: *Access to Primary Care.* (National Consumer Council). 1979 HMSO

Scottish Health Services Council. *Maternity Services in Scotland* (Montgomery Report). HMSO 1959

Scottish Health Services Council. *Services for Elderly with Mental Disorder.* HMSO 1970

Scottish Home and Health Department. *Scottish Health Authorities Priorities for the Eighties.* HMSO 1980

Scottish Home and Health Department and Scottish Education Department. *A Better Life: Report on services for the mentally handicapped in Scotland.* 1979. *Changing Patterns of Care: Report on services for the elderly in Scotland.* 1980. *Services for the Elderly with Mental Disability in Scotland.* 1979. *Towards Better Health Care for School Children in Scotland.* 1980 HMSO

Other Publications

Abel-Smith, B. *Value for Money in Health Services.* Heinemann 1976

Age Concern. *Profiles of the Elderly.* 1977

Brearley, P., Gibbons, J. *et al. The Social Context of Health Care.* Blackwell and Robertson 1978

Brocklehurst, J.C. (Ed). *Geriatric Care in Advanced Societies.* MTP 1976

Cartwright, A. *Human Relations and Hospital Care.* Routledge and Kegan Paul 1964

Cartwright, A. *Patients and Their Doctors.* Routledge and Kegan Paul 1967

Cochrane, A. *Effectiveness and Efficiency.* Nuffield Provincial Hospitals Trust 1972

Cockerham, W.C. *Medical Sociology.* Prentice Hall 1978

Cooper, M.H. *Rationing Health Care.* Croom Helm 1975

Goffman, E. *Asylums.* Penguin 1968

Hazell, K. *et al. Social and Medical Problems of the Elderly.* Hutchinson 1973

Horrobin, O.F. *Medical Hubris.* Churchill Livingstone 1977

Illich, I. *Limits to Medicine.* Penguin 1977

Jones, K. *History of the Mental Health Services.* Routledge and Kegan Paul 1972

Jones, K. *Opening the Door.* Routledge and Kegan Paul 1975

King's Fund. *Management of Chronic Illness.* 1979

King's Fund. *Management of Minor Illness.* 1979

Lee, K. (Ed). *Economics and Health Planning.* Croom Helm 1979

McCormick, J. *The Doctor — Father-figure or plumber?* Croom Helm 1979

McKeown, T. *The Role of Medicine: Dream, mirage or nemesis?* Blackwell 1979

Meredith Davies, J.B. *Community Health, Preventive Medicine and Social Services.* 4th edition. Balliere Tindall 1979

Morris, P. *Put Away.* Routledge and Kegan Paul 1969

Office of Health Economics. *Compendium of Health Statistics.* 3rd edition 1979

Office of Health Economics. Studies of Current Health Problems, e.g. 51 *Parkinson's Disease* 1974, 52 *Multiple Sclerosis* 1975, 57 *Asthma* 1976, 62 *Renal Failure: a priority for health?* 1978, 64 *Scarce Resources in Health Care* 1979, 66 *Dementia in Old Age* 1979.

Pritchard, P. *Manual of Primary Health Care.* OUP 1978

Rhodes, P. *The Value of Medicine.* Allen and Unwin 1976

Ryan J. *The Politics of Mental Handicap.* Penguin 1980

Stocking, B. and Morrison, S. *The Image and the Reality.* OUP for Nuffield Provincial Hospitals Trust 1978

Susser, M.W. and Watson W. *Sociology in Medicine.* OUP 1971

Townsend, P. *The Last Refuge,* Routledge and Kegan Paul 1962

Townsend, P. *Poverty.* Penguin 1979

Wadsworth, M.E.J. *et al. Health and Sickness — The choice of treatment.* Tavistock 1971

3
Organisational structure of the national health service

In this chapter the legislative basis and the principal features of the organisational structure of the national health service in the UK are described. Only the broad constitutional arrangements are dealt with here. The management arrangements at each level of the service are considered in greater detail in later chapters.

During 1973 and 1974 the organisational structure of the national health service was radically changed for the first time since its inception. The purpose of this reorganisation was to replace the tripartite administrative structure, which had existed since 1948, with a network of new statutory health authorities, each based on a defined geographical area, and each responsible for every aspect of the planning and administration of a comprehensive health service for the population within its geographical boundaries.

The reasons for the reorganisation, and the principles upon which it was based, were the same in England, Scotland, Wales and Northern Ireland. The organisational structure and administrative arrangements in each country are broadly similar. However, each of the constituent countries of the UK has its own constitutional position, so that the legislation which governs the NHS in each country is specific to that country. Legislation for England and Wales is usually incorporated within the same Acts of Parliament or Statutory Instruments. Scottish and Northern Irish legislation is almost always separate. The result is that legislation, organisational structure, administrative arrangements and terminology vary between different parts of the UK. The major differences between the structure of the service in different parts of the UK are summarised in Table 2 (page 103) and are elaborated in the following sections of this chapter.

The present organisational structure of the NHS was established in England and Wales under the National Health Service Reorganisation Act 1973. The equivalent legislation for Scotland was the National Health Service (Scotland) Act 1972. The institution of direct rule from Westminster following civil disturbance in Northern Ireland, and the consequent prorogation of the Northern Ireland Parliament in 1972, meant that the reorganisation of the Health Service in Northern Ireland was brought about by Order in Council. This was the Health and Personal Social Services (Northern Ireland) Order 1972 (SI72/1265(NI14) made under Section 1(3) of the Northern Ireland (Temporary Provisions) Act 1972.

Detailed administrative arrangements are prescribed for each country by regulations made under the enabling legislation. Consolidating legislation was passed after reorganisation which repealed and consolidated a variety of health service enactments passed between 1946 and 1976 including most of the provisions of the legislation which created the reorganised structure. These Acts were the National Health Service Act 1977 (for England and Wales) and the National Health Service (Scotland) Act 1978. Further changes were enacted in the Health Services Act 1980, but those relating to the restructuring of the service will not apply until 1 April 1982 and are not discussed in this chapter.

The general effect of the reorganisation legislation was to establish on 1 April

1974 new integrated health authorities in England and Wales, health boards in Scotland and, on 1 October 1973, health and social service boards in Northern Ireland. Each of the new authorities is now charged with responsibility for providing a comprehensive health service and for ensuring a proper balance of preventive services, primary care, domiciliary, community and hospital services appropriate to the needs of the communities it serves.

The reorganisation legislation abolished most of the hospital authorities (hospital boards, hospital management committees, boards of governors, and boards of management) which were established under the original legislation (see Chapter 1). Some boards of governors of postgraduate teaching hospitals in London were temporarily retained pending further review of the relationship of their specialised functions to the rest of the service. The functions of executive councils in England, Scotland and Wales, and of the general health services board in Northern Ireland, were transferred, in England and Wales, to family practitioner committees which cover the same geographical area as the new area health authorities. In Scotland, the contracts of independent contractors are now held by area health boards. In Northern Ireland they are held by health and social services boards.

The community health services administered by local government (the health committees of local authorities) were simultaneously transferred to the new health authorities. Local government in Wales and England (except for London) was also reorganised on 1 April 1974, under the provisions of the Local Government Reorganisation Act 1972. A two-tier structure of 53 county and 369 district councils was created. (London local government had been reorganised earlier on a two-tier basis — the Greater London Council and 32 London boroughs (plus the Corporation of the City of London) under the provisions of the London Government Act 1963.)

Scottish local government was reorganised under the Local Government (Scotland) Act 1973 on 15 May 1975 creating nine regional councils divided into 56 districts and three island councils. In Northern Ireland 26 district councils now administer local environmental and other services. Area boards similar to area health and social service boards and responsible to appropriate central departments, administer local education and other local services. The Northern Ireland Housing Executive, responsible to the Department of the Environment for Northern Ireland, administers housing.

One effect of the legislation was to make the boundaries of the new health authorities in all parts of the UK are broadly conterminous with the boundaries of the new local authorities. However, it should be emphasised that the health authorities are not part of the locally elected local government structure, and health and local authorities are statutorily independent bodies. Within the new NHS structure, the responsibility of the new health authorities for the planning and management of the service was clearly distinguished from responsibility for representing the interests of the patient and the community at large. Entirely new local bodies were specially established to perform the representative function. These are called community health councils in England and Wales, local health councils in Scotland and district committees in Northern Ireland.

The political context

The present structure of the NHS can only be fully understood and properly assessed against the constitutional framework and the political, economic and social background against which the reorganisation of the service took place. Before the revised organisational arrangements are described in detail, it may therefore be useful to pick up the main threads of the political debate about reorganisation described in Chapter 1, to emphasise those features which most influenced the present design of the service, and to indicate the circumstances which are most likely to govern the evolution of the structure in the future.

The reorganisation of 1973-4 is a major landmark in the development of the NHS. It marks the transition of the service from the fragmented organisational structure born in the political compromises of wartime negotiations to a new structure which, for the first time in the UK, brings together in each country the former three divisions of the service under a single administrative framework.

It will be clear, from the historical account in Chapter 1 of the development of the proposals for reorganisation between 1948 and 1974, that reorganisation was itself embedded in the political process. The aims of reorganisation were not achieved by the mere act of reorganisation in 1974. The legislation created a new statutory organisational framework which changes the context and perspective against which future developments of the service can evolve. Reorganisation exposed inequalities, imbalance between services, and opportunities for change and redeployment of resources, which were obscured by the old tripartite structure. These new perspectives and the reorganised structures have themselves stimulated proposals for further change including modification of the structure itself. The debate about the best organisational structure for the service continues. The 1979 report of the Royal Commission on the National Health Service while endorsing the broad principles and form of the reorganised service, proposed a number of changes, and subsequently the government announced, and set about implementing, its own proposals for change. These developments are described in Chapter 17.

During the 1960s there was a widespread consensus that a new unified structure for the service was required. Although there was a large measure of agreement about the fundamental purpose of reorganisation — the integration of the service — there were differences of opinion about the exact form which an integrated administrative structure should take. The green papers and consultative documents of the 1960s were consecutive attempts by succeeding governments of different political complexions to put flesh on the philosophy of integration, to incorporate the best features of the then tripartite structure and to reconcile the new structure with the simultaneous proposals for the reorganisation of local government. Local government reorganisation had itself been prompted by a desire to unify and rationalise a structure which had not substantially changed since the end of the previous century.

One fundamental dilemma, which was present in the debates which preceded the creation of the NHS in 1948, and which is still a source of a major tension within the health-care system, is whether the service should be a truly *national* service, controlled and wholly funded by central government but administered locally by agents of the Health Minister (who is in turn, accountable to Parliament), or whether it should primarily be a nationally co-ordinated, *local* service accountable locally to locally elected people and drawing at least a proportion of its income from local sources. Delegation of powers by the UK Parliament for the operation of health services in England, Wales, Scotland and Northern Ireland varies in practice because of the differences in the constitutional relationships of each of these countries to Parliament. The extent of the pressure for delegation to each country at any particular time varies according to the current state of the debate about constitutional devolution to Scotland and Wales, direct rule in Northern Ireland, regionalism in England, and the possibilities of moving towards a federal system of government in the UK. Similarly, the arguments for making the health service primarily the responsibility of national or local government within each of the countries are part of the continuing debate about the proper functions of local authorities and their relationship with central government.

The early consultation documents on reorganisation, such as the first green paper on reorganisation in England and Wales, published by a Labour government, did not rule out the possibility of control of the NHS by local government, and this possibility was suggested in 1969 by the Royal Commission on Local Government. However, the 1970 green paper accepted the separation of health authorities from local authorities and the notion of health authorities as nationally appointed corporate local agents of a national minister responsible for the local administration of part of a *national* service. Nevertheless, the desire for 'coterminosity' of boundaries of local and health authorities, based on belief in the importance of providing a framework for effective joint planning for interdependent local services, coupled with the parallel reorganisation of local government, resulted in a health service structure very much influenced, particularly in England and Wales, by the decisions finally reached on local government reform.

The Conservative government, in its 1971-2 consultative documents and white papers on health service reorganisation had emphasised the *national* nature of the service and strongly emphasised the managerial responsibilities of health authorities as the centrally appointed corporate agents of ministers and the UK government. The change of government which occurred very shortly before the reorganised structure was implemented, meant that a Labour government found itself unexpectedly implementing a structure about which it had publicly expressed reservations while in opposition. It was impossible either to prevent the implementation of the Conservative legislation or to introduce new legislation in the short term. However, the new government announced its intention, shortly after taking up office, to review the new structure. This action slowed the impetus towards implementation and decreased commitment to the new arrangements within the service. The effect was to prolong the period of uncertainty about the future structure of the service. The reorganisation arrangements of 1974, which had become widely accepted as better than the previous arrangements, and probably the best that could be achieved at the time, were again questioned and the old debates were reopened. The accompanying economic crisis and consequent squeeze on public expenditure led even Conservative spokesmen to criticise the new organisational structure. A structure which had seemed reasonable such a short time ago was widely criticised, particularly within England, for being over-elaborate.

In 1975 the Labour government made a number of relatively small, but significant changes to the structure of health authorities in England and Wales. The proportion of local authority nominated or appointed members of authorities was increased and the inclusion of a wider range of staff groups in the membership of authorities was made possible. The powers of community health councils were also strengthened. These measures were designed to strengthen local control without actually transferring responsibility to local government or changing the methods of central funding. The changes had the effect of increasing local influence but not local accountability. The national agency principle, emphasised in the 1972 white papers, was weakened and the central/local tension became more obvious. This, coupled with an economic recession and industrial unrest within the service contributed towards the pressures which forced the establishment of the Royal Commission on the National Health Service in 1976.

Party politics are, of course, only one of the many factors influencing the evolution of the service. Professional politics are of at least equal (but probably greater) importance. At each stage in the development of the service, the influence of the medical profession has been particularly important. The preference of most doctors for national rather than local control of the service was the most important single factor influencing the decision against local government control. The importance of the protection of clinical autonomy was written into the reorganisation documents. The independent contractor position of general practitioners was retained within the reorganised structure, and, in England and Wales, special family practitioner committees were created to hold and administer independent practitioner contracts.

Many other staff groups were influential in shaping the reorganised structure. Each of the professional groups in the service took the opportunity which reorganisation offered to strengthen its own position. The recommendations of the various working parties established in each country to consider the detailed management arrangements within the new structure and the subsequent circulars and regulations which modified and implemented these proposals show clearly the influence of professional groups and the desire of each profession to improve the service from the perspectives both of its own professional values and of its own position in the structure. In particular, the concept of the multidisciplinary team, responsible for the management of the service at each level of the organisation (described later) may be considered, to some extent, to be a reconciliation, within a constitutional framework, of the relative power of the health professions. The principal professions concerned with the management of the service achieved representation in the multidisciplinary management teams. Other professions established specialised professional hierarchies with direct access to the health authority itself. There are statutory requirements for all health authorities to establish a wide range of professional advisory mechanisms to ensure that specialised professional advice is available.

The organisational position of some of the professions, particularly the paramedical professions, in relation to the health authority and the other professions represented within management teams, was not satisfactorily resolved during reorganisation and the precise organisational position of several staff groups remains uncertain. It is likely that the dynamics of professionalisation and professional politics will continue to be a major force shaping the future structure and reorganisation of the service.

In summary, therefore, it can be seen that the present structure of the NHS evolved through a series of political initiatives which were strongly influenced by professional ambitions. A number of aspects of the 1974 reorganisation were either not fully implemented or were subtly, but significantly, changed as a result of the unexpected change of government in 1973-4 and by the subsequent issue of central guidance, influenced by professional groups, on the implementation of detailed management arrangements. The further change to a Conservative government in May 1979 has led to a policy which emphasises the local rather than the national aspect of the service but at the same time aims to reduce the influence of local authorities in its management.

Key features of the reorganised structure

The aim of reorganisation was to bring together, within a single administrative framework, the fragmented authorities responsible for different parts of the NHS. As the white paper on NHS reorganisation in England, published in 1972, put it:

> The national health service should be a single service. Its separate parts are intended to complement one another, and not to function as self-sufficient entities. In practice, however, the fragmented administration ... throws barriers in the way of efforts to organise a proper balance of services — hospital and community — throughout the country. The administrative unification of these services will make a firmer reality of the concept of a single service. (Para. 1.)

Similar sentiments were expressed in the white papers for Wales, and Scotland and the consultative documents in Northern Ireland. In England, a management study was undertaken to make recommendations about the detailed management arrangements for the reorganised services within the broad statutory framework proposed in the 1971 consultative document. A study group of DHSS and NHS officers advised by management consultants from McKinsey & Co. Inc. and the Health Services Organisation Research Unit of Brunel University reported to a steering committee representative of a wide range of NHS interests chaired by the Permanent Secretary of the DHSS. The report of the study, *Management Arrangements for the Reorganised National Health Service* ('The Grey Book'), was published in 1972. In the same year, a similar report ('The Red Book') was produced by a similar steering committee and study group established in Wales and advised by McKinseys; it proposed similar management arrangements.

The responsibility for the reorganisation of health services in Northern Ireland passed from the government of Northern Ireland to the Secretary of State for Northern Ireland following the introduction of direct rule. The management consultants, Booz Allen and Hamilton, were commissioned to undertake a study of the management arrangements for the reorganised service in the province and their report, *An Integrated Service: The reorganisation of health and personal social services in Northern Ireland* ('The Black Book'), was published by the Ministry of Health and Social Services for Northern Ireland in 1972.

In Scotland, a series of studies and consultations was undertaken but recommendations about detailed management arrangements were not published in one comprehensive report. However, the Scottish Home and Health Department began a series of circulars (the HSR series) which gave guidance to health authorities. Similar series of circulars were introduced in England (the HRC – Health Reorganisation Circular – and HSC(IS) – Health Service Circular (Interim Series) – series) and in Wales (the WHRC and WHSC(IS) series). Some of the more important circulars are listed in the reading list at the end of this chapter but, for complete information, reference should be made to the complete list of circulars given in the *Hospitals and Health Services Year Book*.

Information about development thinking was cross-fertilised between each of the study-groups. The proposals for detailed management arrangements in each of the reports — particularly the concept of the management team — were broadly similar in each country. There are differences in job titles and other terminology. Accountability relationships also vary. These will be described in greater detail in the next section of this chapter and in Chapters 5 and 6.

The starting point of each of the reorganisation studies was the identification of the fundamental reasons for reorganisation and an examination of the features which would have to be built into the new structure in order to obtain the benefits which reorganisation was expected to bring. Within the general aim of reorganisation to provide a fully integrated administrative structure which would be better able to perceive and respond to the health needs of the community as a whole, a number of specific objectives were identified. The following objectives, extracted from the English 'Grey Book' (para. 1.4, page 10) are typical of those which the studies felt should be promoted by the management arrangements.

(a) Co-ordination of the planning and provision of all personal health services (including heath education, prevention, diagnosis, treatment and rehabilitation) with each other and with local government services.
(b) Planning of services in relation to needs of the people to be served (e.g. the elderly, the mentally ill, the physically handicapped) irrespective of whether the services are provided in the home, in the doctor's surgery or in hospital.
(c) The more effective working of professional practitioners through the provision of a structure and systems to support them administratively.
(d) Means whereby doctors and dentists can contribute more effectively to NHS decision-making.
(e) More uniform national standards of care.
(f) Innovation and the rapid implementation of improved approaches to health care.
(g) Clear, but flexible career structures for staff.
(h) Effective education and training of health service personnel.

The 'Grey Book', like the other studies, went on to establish general organisational principles in the context both of the legislation proposed in the consultative documents and 'from reflection on the nature of the NHS'. (para. 1.5 page 10):

(a) The health care professions should be integrally involved in planning and management at all levels. This involvement must be achieved without infringing the clinical autonomy of medical and dental consultants and general practitioners and without interfering with the professional standards of the health care professions or inhibiting the exercise of professional judgement by members of those professions.
(b) Responsibilities must be clearly defined and allocated. This applies both to the responsibilities of regional health authorities and area health authorities and the relationships between them and to the responsibilities of officers of RHAs and AHAs and their decision-making discretion. It should be clearly established for what duties an officer will be accountable and to whom.

(c) There should be maximum decentralisation and delegation of decision making, but within policies established at national, regional and area levels.
(d) Higher organisation must be designed to provide policies within which local services can be managed effectively. Higher levels of management should therefore agree objectives with lower levels as the basis for delegating authority and for monitoring performance.
(e) Delegation downwards should be matched with accountability upwards.

The recommendations of the working parties on management arrangements were broadly implemented although several modifications were subsequently introduced. The main distinguishing features of the organisation of the NHS in each of the countries of the UK, introduced as a result of the legislation and the implementation of the recommendations of the management studies, are best considered in turn. Each level of the structure will then be analysed in greater detail in the next section.

England

England is by far the largest of the countries of the UK both geographically and in terms of population (approximately 46 million). The reorganised structure was introduced on 1 April 1974 under the 1973 Act. The service is the responsibility of a government minister, the Secretary of State for Social Services. He is a member of the Cabinet and is responsible for health and personal social services in England and for social security in Great Britain. He is supported by ministers of state and parliamentary under-secretaries; their number, titles and responsibilities vary with governments. It is laid down in SI(1) of the 1977 Act that it is the duty of the Secretary of State:

To continue the promotion in England and Wales of a comprehensive health service designed to secure improvement:
(a) in the physical and mental health of the people of England and Wales and
(b) in the prevention, diagnosis and treatment of illness, and for that purpose to provide or secure the effective provision of services in accordance with this Act.

Sections 2, 3, 4 and 5 continue to prescribe in greater detail the general powers and duties of the Secretary of State in relation to the NHS. The Secretary of State and junior ministers are supported by the Department of Health and Social Security which is staffed by permanent civil servants.

Responsibility for the operational planning and management of the NHS in England is delegated by the Secretary of State to 14 regional health authorities and 90 area health authorities. Regional and area health authorities are corporate bodies with appointed members. The authorities are supported by regional and area teams of officers. The populations of the regions vary between 1.8 million (East Anglia) and 5.2 million (West Midlands) and the areas from less than 250,000 to more than one million (see Table 1). There are between three and 11 areas in a region. Area health authorities are accountable to regional health authorities. Their areas have boundaries which are mostly coterminous with those of local authorities. Each area health authority is required to establish a family practitioner committee, which administers the contracts of general practitioners and other family practitioners within the area.

Table 1. Numerical summary of NHS regions, areas and districts

	Population (millions)	No. of areas	No. of areas with 1	2	3	4	5	6 districts
ENGLAND (regional health authorities)								
Northern	3.1	9	6	—	2	1	—	—
Yorkshire	3.6	7	1	4	—	2	—	—
Trent	4.5	8	3	2	2	1	—	—
East Anglia	1.8	3	—	2	1	—	—	—
N W Thames	3.5	7	1	3	1	2	—	—
N E Thames	3.7	6	—	3	2	—	1	—
S E Thames	3.5	5	1	1	1	1	—	1
S W Thames	3.0	5	2	—	2	—	—	1
Wessex	2.7	4	1	1	1	1	—	—
Oxford	2.3	4	1	3	—	—	—	—
S Western	3.0	5	3	—	1	1	—	—
W Midlands	5.2	11	7	—	2	1	1	—
Mersey	2.5	5	3	1	—	—	1	—
N Western	4.1	11	9	—	1	—	—	1
Totals	46.5	90	38	20	16	10	3	3
WALES (health authorities)	2.7	8	3	3	—	2	—	—
Totals	49.0	98	41	23	16	12	3	3
SCOTLAND (health boards)	5.2	15	5	4	4	1	1	—
Totals	54.2	113	46	27	20	13	4	3
N IRELAND (health and social services boards)	1.5	4	—	—	2	—	1	1
TOTALS	55.7	117	46	27	22	13	5	4

Most of the areas are subdivided geographically into districts. Districts have a population of approximately 230,000 people on average although the range varies from under 100,000 to about 500,000. There are between one and six districts in each area (see Table 1). There is no statutory authority at district level. The responsibility for the day-to-day operation of a district's services lies with a multidisciplinary district management team accountable to the AHA. There are community health councils in each district which are responsible for the representation of the public in relation to the health services in the district.

Wales

The organisation structure of the NHS in Wales was established under the 1973 Act and follows the same broad structure as England. However, both in terms of population (2.7 million) and geography, Wales approximates to one of the regions of England. There are two main structural differences in the organisation. The first is that central administration of the service is undertaken through the Welsh Office based in Cardiff. The accountable minister is the Secretary of State for Wales. Secondly, there is no regional health authority in Wales. The eight area health authorities are directly accountable to the Secretary of State. Their boundaries are coterminous with those of the Welsh County Councils and their populations range from under 100,000 up to 550,000. They are supported by area teams of officers. Some of the functions of the regions in England are carried out by the Welsh Health Technical Services Organisation which serves both the area health authorities and the Welsh Office.

Some of the area health authority areas are divided into two, three or four districts (each with a district team) as in England. There is a family practitioner committee for each area and a community health council for each district.

Scotland

Scotland is much larger geographically than Wales or any of the English regions although the population (5.2 million) is similar to that of the largest English region, the West Midlands. The service in Scotland was established under separate legislation from that for England and Wales (the 1972 Act). There are a number of differences, particularly in terminology, between Scotland and England and Wales.

The NHS in Scotland is the responsibility of the Secretary of State for Scotland. He has a wide range of other responsibilities and much of his NHS work falls to a minister of state. They are assisted by the Scottish Home and Health Department based in Edinburgh. The general duty of the Secretary of State in relation to the NHS in Scotland, as set out in SI(1) of the 1978 Act, is almost identical to that of the Secretary of State in England and Wales. The responsibility for ensuring the provision of services is delegated by the Secretary of State to 15 health boards the boundaries of which follow the regional and district local government structure and which have populations of between 17,000 (Orkney) and 1,106,000 (Greater Glasgow). The boards are supported by an area executive group. There are no family practitioner committees in Scotland. The general practitioners and other independent contractors are in direct contract with the health boards. There is a Common Services Agency for the Scottish Health Service which fulfils a similar function to the Welsh Health Technical Services Organisation providing common services which can be more effectively provided centrally for the whole of Scotland and in fact has a considerably wider range of responsibilities than WHTSO. The Secretary of State for Scotland is advised on the planning and development of the service by the Scottish Health Service Planning Council.

The 15 health board areas are divided into a total of 34 districts with a district executive group for each. There are between one and five districts in each board area. Local health councils represent the public and fulfil a similar function to community health councils in England and Wales.

Northern Ireland

The structure of the service in Northern Ireland (population 1.5 million) has a number of interesting distinctive features. These differences are largely due to geographical separation and to the existence, until relatively recently, of a separate legislature (Stormont) for the province. Legislation on health and welfare matters was until 1972, delegated to the province and, historically, the pattern of health services has evolved in a different way from the rest of the UK. The present structure was established under the 1972 order and is the responsibility of the Secretary of State for Northern Ireland assisted by a minister of state responsible for the Department of Health and Social Services based in Belfast. Under the 1972 Order (S.4) the duty is laid upon the Department (formerly called the Ministry):

(a) to provide or secure the provision of integrated health services in Northern Ireland designed to promote the physical and mental health of the people of Northern Ireland through the prevention, diagnosis and treatment of illness;
(b) to provide or secure the provision of personal social services in Northern Ireland designed to promote the social welfare of the people of Northern Ireland.

The major difference between the structure of the service in Northern Ireland and that in the rest of the UK is that personal social services are integrated with the health service as part of the responsibility of Health and Social Service Boards.

The structure resembles those of Scotland and Wales in that there is no regional tier. The health and social service boards are responsible directly to a government department. There are four boards. Three of them have populations of between 235,000 and 345,000 divided into districts of between 50,000 to 100,000 people. The eastern board area includes the Belfast conurbation and has a population of approximately 700,000. It is divided into three districts. The boards are supported by area executive teams. The management of districts is delegated to district executive teams.

There are district committees which fulfil a similar function to community health councils in England and Wales and local health councils in Scotland. A central services agency, a consortium of the boards, handles certain matters of common concern and there is a health and social services council for Northern Ireland to advise the Minister.

It can be seen, therefore, that although there are certain detailed differences between the organisation of the NHS in different parts of the UK, the structure of the service has certain common key features:

1. It is *population-based*. Regions, areas and districts have defined geographical boundaries (although the geographical boundaries are not rigid barriers to the movement of patients for treatment).
2. It is a *national* (UK) and *nationally financed* service organised hierarchically with ultimate accountability to the UK government.
3. Local management is the responsibility of *appointed corporate bodies* separate from the elected local government authorities.
4. Day-to-day running of each level of the service is in the hands of *management teams*.
5. *Public representation* is separated from responsibility for managing the service and is institutionalised in district-based councils and committees specially established for the purpose.

An analysis of the structure

Following this description of the main features of the organisation of the NHS in each country, each level of the structure will now be analysed in greater detail. In order to avoid confusion, the framework and terminology of the English service will be used as a basis for the analysis, but the parallel institutions in Scotland, Wales and Northern Ireland will be considered together with those which exist in England.

The central departments

Each country has its own central government department responsible for policy development and central co-ordination of the service. In England this is the Department of Health and Social Security (DHSS), in Wales the Welsh Office (WO), in Scotland the Scottish Home and Health Department (SHHD), and in Northern Ireland the Department of Health and Social Services (DHSS – NI). These departments are staffed by permanent civil servants. Occasionally, staff are seconded from the NHS to the central departments or from the central departments to the NHS, but those staff who work in the central departments are essentially part of the central civil service machinery and are liable to be transferred to other departments of state during the course of their careers. The staff of health authorities, although public (i.e. Crown) employees are employed by individual health authorities and are not civil servants. The organisation structure of the central departments is considered in greater detail in relation to the NHS in Chapter 5. Only an outline of their function will be covered here.

The principal function of the departments, in relation to the NHS, is to help ministers to provide central leadership in the health and social services, to advise them on ultimate choices about the nature and scale of the NHS, to take decisions on the development of national policies, objectives and priorities and to make decisions on matters of public concern.

Much of the work of the central departments, particularly that work performed by the most senior staff ('the top of the office') is concerned with supporting and advising ministers in relation to government policy on health matters and on health service development. A major preoccupation is supporting the Minister in his relations with Parliament and, in particular, handling parliamentary questions and enquiries from Members of Parliament. Although ministers have a permanent civil service to advise them, they sometimes appoint further political advisers and advisers on special subjects drawn from outside the civil service.

The detailed organisation of each of the four central departments varies but the general function is the same. The DHSS is by far the largest and therefore the most elaborately organised, but the main division of its functions into groups indicates the activities which all four must undertake: regional, services development, NHS personnel, finance and support services. In addition it has three large professional divisions: medical, nursing and works.

The civil service staff of the central departments consist of both administrators and a wide range of other professionals. Separate organisational hierarchies are preserved for the different disciplines (professional and administrative), but each hierarchy is related closely to a common work structure so that the disciplines can work in partnership.

On many matters ministers obtain advice from their professional civil servants and there is frequent informal contact between ministers and civil servants in a department and chairmen and senior officers in the NHS. Sometimes ministers appoint a formal committee or an informal working group to advise them on a particular topic; these bodies are supported by civil servants but some or all their members are drawn from the NHS. In addition there are statutory bodies charged with advising ministers.

From 1946 until 1980 one such body was the Central Health Services Council, which advised both the Secretary of State for Social Services and the Secretary of State for Wales. The Council was dissolved by the Health Services Act 1980 but its standing advisory (medical, nursing and midwifery, dental, pharmaceutical and ophthalmic) committees were to continue in being. They were to consist in future wholly of members appointed by the Secretary of State after consultation with such representative organisations as he recognised for the purpose. The ministers decided to wind up the CHSC in the interests of reducing the number of separate and overlapping channels through which they received advice, and to achieve administrative economies. The standing committees were retained because ministers saw a continued need, on professional matters, to balance the advice that was received from special interests within the separate professions.

In Scotland, the Secretary of State for Scotland is advised on the planning and development of the Scottish service by the Scottish Health Services Planning Council. This Council is now established under Section 5(1) and the third schedule of the 1978 Act. It consists of a chairman appointed by the Secretary of State and other members including one member appointed by each health board, one member appointed by each university in Scotland which has a medical school, not more than six officers of the Secretary of State appointed by him, and such other members, not being officers of the Secretary of State, as may be appointed by him.

In Scotland, provision is also made in the 1978 Act (Section 6) for the establishment of representative committees of any, some or all of the professions engaged in the provision of care or treatment. The general function of the national consultative committees is to advise the Planning Council on the provision of health services in Scotland.

In Northern Ireland, Section 22 and the second schedule of the 1972 Order establishes the Northern Ireland Health and Social Services Council. The function of the Council is to advise the Department of Health and Social Services on the provision of integrated health and personal social services. The Council consists of a chairman and vice-chairman appointed by the Minister and the following other members: the chairman of, and one other person nominated by, each health and social services board, the chairman of each central advisory committee, a person or persons appointed after consultation with any university appearing to the Minister to have an interest in the provision of health or personal social services and such other persons as may be appointed after consultation with such other interests as appear to the Minister to be concerned.

In addition to these central advisory agencies established to advise ministers on any aspect of the general development of the NHS in the countries with which they are concerned, there are a variety of other central executive and advisory agencies which exist independently of the central departments. These are considered at the end of this chapter.

The regional level

It has already been mentioned that Wales, Scotland and Northern Ireland resemble one of the 14 English regions in terms of population if not in geographical size. Although the central departments in Wales, Scotland and Northern Ireland are part of the civil service machinery supporting and advising ministers, they also, to some extent, perform the functions of regional health authorities in England in helping to shape UK health policy to the special needs and circumstances of their countries. They are assisted in this function by the advisory councils.

Because of the much larger population and geographical size of England, it was felt necessary during reorganisation to continue a regional level in the English structure. It had been suggested in the 1970 green paper that regional strategic planning could be undertaken by consortia of area health authorities (regional health councils) but the 1973 Act hardened the regional concept and introduced regional health authorities as corporately accountable *management* bodies in a hierarchical position between the Secretary of State and area health authorities. The regional boundaries are similar to those of the regional hospital boards established in 1948 although the names of the regions were changed and several significant boundary changes were made.

The functions of regional health authorities are prescribed by regulations (SI74/24 and SI74/36) now made under Section 13 of the 1977 Act. The regulations specify the functions of regional health authorities and require them to issue written directions allocating functions to area health authorities. The general principles underlying the directions to authorities regulations were stated in HRC(74)18 as:

(a) maximum delegation with matching accountability of area to region and region to centre;
(b) sufficient flexibility to take account of local circumstances and changing patterns of health care.

The distribution of functions between regions and areas varies but, broadly speaking, the regional health authorities are responsible for strategic planning and resource allocation for their regions. They also provide certain specialised services which can be more rationally or economically organised on a regional basis.

In HRC(74)18 there is a list of the following main activities undertaken at region. The list is a combination of strategic-planning and service-giving functions.

1. Regional planning and policy making.
2. Allocation of resources between area health authorities.
3. Monitoring performances of AHAs.
4. Developing and implementing regional personnel (including education and training) policies.
5. Developing regional supply policies and making regional contracts.
6. Implementing a major capital building programme and providing to AHAs a design service and professional advice on works matters.
7. Property management.
8. Managing ambulance services in metropolitan counties.

9. Managing the blood transfusion service.
10. Providing management services (including computer services, operational research, statistical and information services) to areas and districts.
11. Employment of regional staff and of medical and dental consultants and senior registrars (except in teaching areas).
12. Managing the research programme for the region.
13. Determination of matters reserved to RHAs (e.g. approval of schemes of management, directions on extra-territorial management).
14. Public relations services.
15. Legal services.

Regional health authorities are constituted by regulations (SI75/1100) now made under Section 8 and the fifth schedule of the 1977 Act. The chairman and members of regional health authorities are appointed (SI73/1286 as amended by SI77/1103 and SI78/228) by the Secretary of State for Social Services normally for a four year period. No maximum number is prescribed for the membership of a regional health authority, but the current membership ranges from 17 to 23. The fifth schedule of the 1977 Act provides that, except in prescribed cases, it is the Secretary of State's duty, before he appoints a member of a regional health authority other than the chairman, to consult:

(a) the local authorities within the region of the authority, namely, county councils, metropolitan district councils, the Greater London Council, London borough councils, and the Common Council of the City of London (since 1975 at least one-third of the total number of members have been drawn from the nominations of local authorities);
(b) the university or universities with which the provision of health services in that region is associated (usually one member);
(c) such bodies as the Secretary of State may recognise as being, either in that region or generally, representative respectively of medical practitioners, dental practitioners, nurses, midwives, registered pharmacists and ophthalmic and dispensing opticians, or representatives of such other professions as appear to him to be concerned (usually at least one consultant, one GP and one nurse or midwife serve on each RHA);
(d) any federation of workers' organisations which appears to the Secretary of State to be concerned and any voluntary organisation or any other body which appear to him to be concerned; and
(e) the existing members of the regional health authority in question.

Following the decisions taken by the Secretary of State after the publication of the 1974 consultative document *Democracy in the National Health Service* and under the 1975 regulations, it is possible for further changes in the total membership of RHAs to be made by administrative action without further subordinate legislation (HSC(IS)194).

Each authority exercises its functions as a corporate body, the decisions being made by the members collectively. The main duties of the members are, first, to settle policies (in accordance with national policy) to be carried into plans for the provision of health services within the region; and, second, to ensure implementation of approved policies and plans by the officers and area health authorities. The regulations give regional (and area) authorities power to establish committees to exercise functions on their behalf but it was considered undesirable, following reorganisation, for standing committees to be appointed to deal with parts of an authority's functions (HRC(73)22).

Day-to-day responsibility is delegated to a regional team of officers (RTO) consisting of a regional administrator, a regional medical officer, a regional treasurer, a regional nursing officer, and a regional works officer. The details of management structure at regional level are discussed further in Chapter 5.

The central services supplied by regional health authorities to area health authorities in England are supplied by common services agencies in Wales, Scotland and Northern Ireland. In Wales the common services agency is called the Welsh Technical Services Organisation (WHTSO) now established under Section 11 of the 1977 Act (WHRC(73)29 and SI73/1624). The services offered by WHTSO include the design and construction of major capital works; certain specialised management services, such as computers; the central supply function; printing; and prescription pricing. The services provided from WHTSO are under the direction of a board which is appointed by, and accountable to, the Secretary of State. The chairman and three members are appointed by the Secretary of State, three are nominated by area health authorities and up to two members may be appointed by the Secretary of State after consultation with area health authorities. Members appointed by the Secretary of State include senior civil servants employed at the Welsh Office.

The Common Services Agency for the Scottish Health Service provides, on behalf of the Secretary of State or health boards, a number of important services which can be more effectively administered nationally. These services include the ambulance service; the blood transfusion service; the design and management of major building projects; dental estimates; the pricing of prescriptions; health education; legal advice to the service; and certain aspects of supplies, of management education and training, and of information services. Responsibility for the efficient administration of the agency rests with the management committee now appointed by the Secretary of State under Section 10 and the fifth schedule of the 1978 Act. The Management Committee (HSR(73)C38 and SI75/196 S15) consists of the chairman and five other members appointed by the Secretary of State, six members appointed by the Secretary of State on the nomination of the health boards acting jointly; and such other members as may be appointed by the Secretary of State after consultation with the health boards acting jointly.

In Northern Ireland, the Central Services Agency for the Health and Social Services is established under Section 26 and part 1 of the third schedule of the 1972 Order. The chairman and vice-chairman of the Agency are appointed by the Minister and other members are also appointed after consultation with the health and social services boards and any other interests which appear to the Minister to be concerned. The Northern Ireland Agency, unlike its counterparts in Scotland and Wales, services the contracts of independent contractors such as family doctors and makes appropriate payments to them on behalf of the health and social services board with whom they are in contract. Appointment procedures for senior hospital doctors are also organised through the Agency. The Agency supplies legal services and places central contracts for supplies. However, unlike its Scottish and Welsh equivalents the Agency does not execute the works programme nor does it provide computer services. These services are undertaken by the Department through a Works Unit and Research Intelligence Unit. There is a separate Staffs Council which develops and operates appointments procedures, provides some common personnel systems, and organises administrative and management training.

In summary, therefore, it can be seen that, although there is variation in the actual services which are provided centrally, it has been found necessary in Wales, Scotland and Northern Ireland, and in each of the regions of England, to organise and offer central services on a 'regional' basis to the area authorities responsible for the operational management of the service. In England, the RHAs offer these services to AHAs but the regional authority is also in a line management relationship to the area authorities. This is in contrast with the consortium arrangements evidenced in the constitution of the common services agencies.

The area level

Area health authorities in England and Wales are now constituted, like RHAs, under regulations made under Section 8 and the fifth schedule of the 1977 Act (see previous section). The Secretary of State appoints the chairman of each area health authority. There are between 18 and 33 other members. The majority of the members are appointed by the appropriate regional health authority in England, and the Secretary of State in Wales:

(a) after consultation with local bodies representative of the health professions (doctors, dentists, nurses, midwives, pharmacists and opticians) and the existing members of the AHA itself; and
(b) upon the nomination of the university or universities associated with the provision of health services in the region (at least one member but more where the authority is an AHA(T).

In addition to the members appointed by the regional health authority up to one third of the total number of members are *appointed* by the corresponding local authority or authorities (i.e. the councils of non-metropolitan counties, metropolitan districts, London boroughs, the Inner London Education Authority, the Common Council of the City of London, and the Council of the Isles of Scilly).

The legislation provides that not fewer than four members of each area health authority should be appointed to serve on the AHA by the corresponding local authorities. Originally, the regulations made under this section provided that the local authority should appoint four members. Now, following the decisions made by the Secretaries of State in relation to the 'Democracy' consultative papers the regulations on the constitution of AHAs (SI75/1099) provide for an increase in size of each AHA so that at least one third of all members of area health authorities are drawn from local government, (HSC(IS)194 and WHSC(IS)188). Provision is also made for the appointment of members nominated by non-metropolitan district councils (who cannot themselves directly appoint members of AHAs) by regional health authorities. Local authorities are not obliged to nominate elected councillors although they are normally expected to do so. The 1975 regulations also provide for the attendance of one representative of each community health council within the area to act as a non-voting but speaking observer at AHA meetings.

This change in the constitution of AHAs was a subtle but significant change in the strength of central direction in the service. As indicated earlier, it tends to increase local authority and other local influence within the AHA and dilutes the original principle of the 1972 white paper that members of authorities should be appointed primarily for their management abilities. The district health authorities which will replace AHAs under the 1980 Act will be smaller bodies and have fewer local authority members.

Some area authorities have responsibility for providing teaching facilities for a related medical school. It is provided under Section 9(1) of the 1977 Act that an area health authority, 'may be called an Area Health Authority (Teaching) if and only if the Secretary of State is satisfied that the Authority is to provide for a university or universities substantial facilities for undergraduate and postgraduate clinical teaching'. These teaching authorities — designated AHA(T) — have taken over the functions of boards of governors of teaching hospitals originally established under the 1946 Act (except for the 'preserved' boards). The members of an AHA(T) must contain up to three people who have knowledge of, and experience in, the administration of a hospital providing substantial facilities for undergraduate or postgraduate clinical teaching. University liaison committees may be established in the area.

In Scotland, health boards are now constituted according to Section 2 and the first schedule of the 1978 Act. A health board consists of a chairman appointed by the Secretary of State and such number of other members so appointed as the Secretary of State thinks fit. Appointments are made after consultation with each local authority in the area of the health board concerned, any university appearing to the Secretary of State to have an interest in the provision of health services in that area, such other organisations as the Secretary of State may recognise as representative of the health professions and any other organisations that appear to the Secretary of State to be concerned. The current regulations determining the areas, constitution, functions, and membership of health boards (SI74/267; 74/466; 75/197) provide that the maximum size of each of the 15 boards shall be 22 members. Unlike the situation in England, local authorities have the right to be consulted but they do not appoint any members of health boards. All members are appointed by the Secretary of State. In the consultative document *The National Health Service and the Community in Scotland* (the equivalent of the 'Democracy' papers in England and Wales) the Secretary of State reaffirmed the principle, which has always applied in Scotland, that all members of health boards should be appointed by him. The justification given for this is that, in Scotland, area health boards fulfil some of the functions of regonal health authorities in England. RHAs in England are entirely appointed by the Secretary of State and it was therefore decided that the same principle of appointment should be applied to area health boards in Scotland.

In Northern Ireland, health and social services boards are constituted under Section 16 and the first schedule of the 1972 Order. The chairman and vice-chairman, and such number of other members as the Minister thinks fit, are appointed by the Minister as follows:

(a) at least one person nominated by each of the district councils in the area of the health and social services board;
(b) persons appointed after consultation with such organisations as appear to the Minister to be representative of such professions as the Minister considers appropriate;

(c) any university appearing to the Minister to have an interest in the provision of health or personal social services;
(d) such other bodies as appear to the Minister to be concerned.

The term of office of members of a health board is two years. Each health and social services board is required to appoint a health services committee and a personal social services committee. As in Scotland, local authorities do not have the right to appoint members to health and social services boards but they are consulted before appointments are made by the Minister. One reason for this is that district councils in Northern Ireland have considerably reduced responsibilities compared with district councils in the rest of the UK. In particular, they do not administer personal social services or housing.

In Scotland and Northern Ireland, the contracts of independent practitioners (such as general practitioners) are held by health boards and health and social service boards respectively. In England and Wales, such contracts are held by specially constituted family practitioner committees (FPCs) established in each area to hold and administer family practitioner contracts. The geographical boundaries of the family practitioner committees are the same as those of the area health authorities. Family practitioner committees are now established under Section 10 and the fifth schedule of the 1977 Act (SI79/739). It is the duty of the AHA to establish the family practitioner committee for its area but the committee is not a sub-committee of the AHA. It is the duty of each family practitioner committee (Section 15(1) of the 1977 Act), 'to administer, on behalf of the area health authority by which the committee was established, the arrangements for the provision of general medical services, general dental services, general ophthalmic services, and pharmaceutical services for the area of the authority'. A family practitioner committee consists of 30 members of whom 11 are appointed by the area health authority responsible for establishing the committee (one of whom must be a member of the authority); four are appointed by the local authority entitled to appoint members of the area health authority; eight are appointed by the local medical committee for the area; three are appointed by the local dental committee; two are appointed by the local pharmaceutical committee. One must be an ophthalmic optician appointed by members of the local optical committee and one must be a dispensing optician appointed by the local optical committee.

Each family practitioner committee administers an 'open ended' budget allocated directly to the committee by the DHSS. It is not subject to the financial control of its corresponding area health authority. The separate existence of FPCs has been criticised because they perpetuate the divisions which existed before reorganisation. The Royal Commission recommended that FPCs should be abolished and the functions transferred to AHAs, but the government did not accept this.

Because of the single tier structure in Wales, Scotland and Northern Ireland, the area health authorities, health boards, and health and social services boards in these countries combine the functions (with the exception of the functions performed by the common services agencies or the central departments) of the area health authorities and the regional health authorities in England.

The following list of functions of area health authorities in England and Wales, taken from HRC(74)18, may be contrasted with the functions of the regional health authority listed in the previous section:

1. Area planning and policy making.
2. Allocation of resources between districts.
3. Monitoring performance of districts.
4. Developing and implementing area personnel (including education and training) policies; formal employment of all AHA staff.
5. Developing area supply policies and making area contracts.
6. Undertaking selected capital building works delegated by RHAs; a programme of minor works; specialised maintenance and day-to-day property management.
7. Managing ambulance services in non-metropolitan counties.
8. Collaboration with local authorities including arranging for certain staff to be made available to local authorities.
9. Managing community dental and hospital pharmaceutical services.
10. Child health (including school health) services.
11. Determining financial policies and those financial services to be provided from area headquarters.
12. Managing health education.
13. In teaching areas, the provision of substantial clinical teaching facilities and the appointment of consultants and senior registrars.

It has already been mentioned that, in all parts of the UK, the boundaries which were finally fixed for all of the area-level authorities were very much influenced by the parallel reorganisation of local government, because the principle of coterminosity of health and local authority boundaries, in order to facilitate joint planning of services, has become enshrined in the consultative process which preceded reorganisation. In Northern Ireland the HSSB boundaries follow groups of district council boundaries. The principle of coterminosity is perhaps less important in the province because personal social services — the main area where overlap of services is likely to be important — are incorporated into the health service structure and because local authorities provide a narrower range of services than in the rest of the UK. In Scotland, the health boards are coterminous either with the local authority regions or with groups of local government districts within local government regions. In Wales the AHA boundaries are coterminous with the Welsh county councils.

In England the picture is more complicated because of the differences in function between the district and county councils in metropolitan and non-metropolitan counties. In non-metropolitan counties, the county councils are responsible for social services and the district councils for housing. In metropolitan counties the district councils are responsible for both social services and housing. It was therefore decided that the boundaries of AHAs in England were to be made coterminous with non-metropolitan county councils and with metropolitan district councils. In England and Wales there is a statutory requirement (Section 22 of the 1977 Act) to establish joint consultative committees between health and local authorities. The Scottish Act (Section 13) requires health boards, local authorities and education authorities to co-operate with one another, but does not lay down that committees shall be established.

In London the boundaries of the new health authorities were contorted even more than in the rest of the country to match the boundaries of the existing London boroughs. Local government in London was reorganised much earlier than in the rest of the country and the London borough boundaries were already well established when reorganisation of the health service occurred. The boundaries of London area health authorities broadly coincide with the boundaries of between one and four London local authorities. The planning and administration of health care within the capital is further complicated by the division from north to south and from east to west of the area of the Greater London Council into four regional quadrants. This makes the planning of services in inner London an inter-regional as well as an inter-area exercise. However, the quadrant arrangement does make it easier to relate the planning of services within inner London to the wider hinterland stretching down to the south and south-east coast and northwards into the commuter counties of the north west and the north east. A London health planning consortium has acted as a liaison mechanism between the London health authorities. In addition, one of the regional liaison divisions of the DHSS has particular responsibility in connection with the planning of health services in London. In 1980 the government appointed a London advisory group to advise it on matters relating to the development of health services and on the restructuring of health authorities in London.

In addition to the statutory requirements for health and local authorities to establish joint planning mechanisms, each authority provides services to the other. Local authorities provide social work support to the health service (except in Northern Ireland). In turn health authorities supply services to local authorities. The most important of these are related to port and environmental health and institutional support services. The local authorities are the environmental health authorities under the Public Health Acts but the health authority provides medical advice as required to the chief environmental health officer and the environmental health department of the local authority. The adviser is usually a community physician designated as 'proper officer' under the regulations. Institutional support services include catering, laundry and other services where economies of scale can be achieved within the health service and the benefits shared between health and local authorities. A number of further recommendations for collaborative arrangements between health and local authorities were suggested in the series of reports of the Working Party on Collaboration Between Health and Local Authorities published shortly before reorganisation.

Despite broad coterminosity of boundaries, collaboration in practice has not always been easy to achieve. The effectiveness of joint planning depends considerably upon local attitudes and willingness to work together. Health and local authorities operate under different constitutions and different political structures, health authorities being appointed bodies and local authorities locally elected. The financial arrangements are different and, although boundaries may coincide, the detailed management arrangements within local authority and health authority departments at operational level do not always match (for example, the population of a social services fieldwork area (from 30,000 to 100,000) is frequently smaller than that of a health service district). The difficulties of collaboration have persisted despite incentives to work and plan together, such as joint financing.

Area level authorities are supported in all countries by teams of officers. The structure of these teams is essentially the same in each of the countries although the terminology varies. The titles of each of these officers are listed in Table 2. In England, Scotland and Wales, the team consists of four people: an administrator, a nursing officer, a medical officer (community physician) and a treasurer, with the addition, in single-district areas, of clinical representatives and, in single-district teaching areas, of a medical school representative. In Northern Ireland the area executive team has, in addition, the director of social services, and the chairman of the area medical advisory committee (either a consultant or a general practitioner). In Northern Ireland, the administrator is accountable for the accounting function and there is therefore no treasurer on the team. In addition to team members, there are other chief professional officers at area level who, in most cases, are directly accountable to the area authority. These are also listed in Table 2.

The district level

Although the population covered by area level authorities varies between different parts of the UK, it has been shown that the boundaries of these authorities were determined to a large extent by the parallel reorganisation of local government. In most cases, the optimum population which was felt at reorganisation to be able to justify the creation of a management unit which could be charged with the task of providing a comprehensive range of health services locally is smaller than the population of most of the health areas. The optimum population size was felt to be in the region of 250,000 but most area-level authorities cover a larger population than this. Therefore, most of the areas are divided for operational management purposes into districts. In England, approximately two-thirds of the areas are divided into between two and six districts. In Wales five of the eight areas are divided into two to four districts. In Scotland ten of the 15 health boards are divided into between two and five districts. In Northern Ireland two of the four health and social services boards have three districts each and the other two have five and six districts.

The figure of 250,000 for the size of a population required to justify a comprehensive range of health services is based on the population (and therefore the incidence and prevalence of illness) felt to justify the provision of one district general hospital offering a basic but comprehensive range of specialist services (excluding regional specialties) linked with a complementary range of community, primary care and preventive services. This population size was mentioned in the 1969 Bonham-Carter Report *The Functions of the District General Hospital* which recommended that, 'most district general hospitals should be planned to serve at least 200,000 and up to 300,000 or more in the major concentrations of population'. Although the Bonham-Carter concept of the district general hospital has since been modified it was influential in determining the size of districts in 1973-4. Nevertheless, where populations are more dispersed (as in Scotland, Wales and Northern Ireland), districts tend to be based on smaller populations. The other important factor in determining where district boundaries should be drawn in 1973 and 1974 was the prior existence of district general hospitals and teaching hospitals in particular localities. Many districts' boundaries, particulary in large cities like London, were drawn around existing institutions rather than catchment areas or local authority administrative boundaries.

This distinction between the population appropriate for operational management of the service and the (larger) population for which area authorities are responsible has undoubtedly created tensions within the structure (particularly between the area and district officers) and given rise to the widespread feeling within the service that the so-called single district areas (where the area is not divided into districts and where the functions of area and district officers are combined into individual members of one team) are less complicated and confusing to administer. This view was endorsed by the Royal Commission.

Responsibility for the operational management of districts is delegated to a team or group of officers. Detailed job titles and a complete list of the members of the district teams are listed in Table 2.

In England and Wales, the district management team consists of four full-time officers and two clinical representatives, one consultant and one general practitioner. The clinical representatives are elected by their peers in the district medical committee. The full-time officers are the district administrator, the district nursing officer, the district community physician and the district finance officer. In England the non-clinical team members are accountable directly to the area health authority and not to their counterparts on the area team. Individual officers are personally responsible for the management of their own discipline but share a joint accountability with other members of the team for the management of the total service within the district. Each DMT officer is monitored and co-ordinated by his or her professional equivalent on the area team of officers. In Wales although the structure of the district management team is the same, the team as a whole is responsible to the area team for specific delegated functions. Individual non-clinical team members are accountable to the equivalent area team officer.

In Scotland, the district executive group consists of an administrator, a nursing officer, an administrative medical officer and a finance officer. There are no clinical representatives. Group members are accountable as a team for team functions. Individuals are accountable to the equivalent area officer. The district executive team officers in Northern Ireland are similar except that, as with the area executive team, there is no separate finance officer on the team and the district social services officer is included. Clinical representation is achieved through the membership in the district executive team of the chairman of the district medical advisory committee. The district executive team is corporately accountable for team functions and, as in Wales and Scotland, individual non-clinical team members are accountable to the area equivalent officer on the area executive team.

The basic function of the district team is the organisation of comprehensive health services for the population of the district for which it is responsible. This task was represented diagrammatically in the 'Grey' and 'Red' Books in terms of the reconciliation of three dimensions of the district. This diagram is reproduced in Figure 1. The district team's function is, first of all, to analyse the *needs* of the various health care groups which comprise its total population. This is essentially the first part of the planning process described in Chapter 8 and consists of an analysis of the absolute and relative morbidity and mortality within that population. Having analysed the need, the district team must mobilise the right combination of skills (mainly professional staff) in the most appropriate places (hospitals, clinics, health centres or the patient's own home). This concept of 'the comprehensive health district' was fundamental to the thinking about reorganisation and, although now modified, is likely to endure and perhaps override the sometimes competing requirements of coterminosity with local

Figure 1. Organisation of a NHS health district

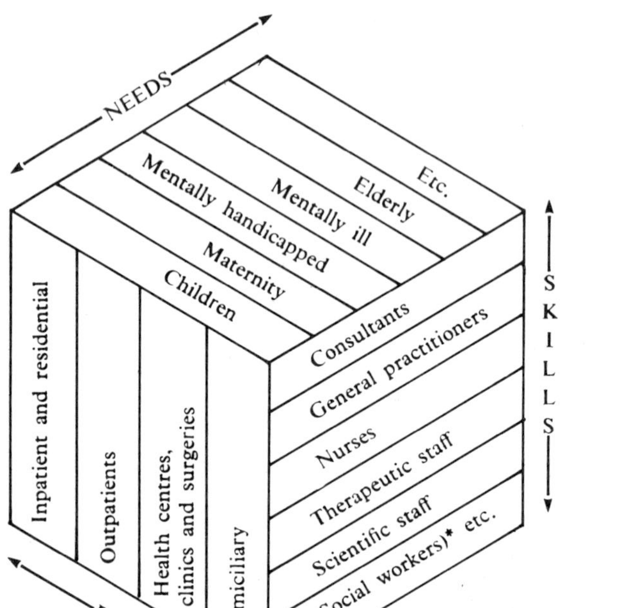

authorities (unless local government is again reorganised) as the service develops in the future.

Finally, each district has its own mechanism for representing the users of health care provided by the area authority and by the district team. These are the community health councils in England and Wales, the local health councils in Scotland and the district committees in Northern Ireland. They are discussed in Chapter 17.

Preserved boards of governors

The functions of most of the former boards of governors of teaching hospitals in England were taken over by area health authorities (teaching) during reorganisation. However, 12 boards of governors of the London specialist postgraduate teaching hospitals were preserved under Section 15 of the 1973 Act, and SI74/281 made under that section. The effect of this is that the constitution and appointment of members of the boards of governors of these hospitals is governed by the 1947 Regulations (SI47/1298) made under Section 11 and the third schedule of the 1946 Act. This provides that the board of governors of a teaching hospital shall consist of a chairman appointed by the Secretary of State and such number of other members appointed as the Minister thinks fit. Not more than one-fifth are nominated by the university with which the hospital is associated; not more than one-fifth are nominated by the regional health authority; not more than one-fifth are nominated by the medical and dental teaching staff of the hospital. The remainder are appointed after consultation with health authorities and other organisations which appear to the Secretary of State to be concerned.

These hospitals and their associated teaching institutes had, despite a distinguished record, been a matter of concern for some years before reorganisation. Most badly needed rebuilding but general opinion was against the continuance of single specialty hospitals and single faculty academic institutes. The alternatives were to bring them together in a consortium or consortia, or to associate them with undergraduate teaching hospitals and their medical schools. Neither policy won general acceptance and therefore the 1972 white paper, while accepting that each of these hospitals should become closely associated with other hospitals and health services in the vicinity, announced their retention for a transitional period. Their life is now extended by regulation until 1982. In 1978 the DHSS issued a consultative document which proposed that a new authority should be set up to administer them to prepare for their full integration into the NHS structure. The Royal Commission expressed doubts about this solution, and their future remained undecided at the end of 1980.

Central advisory and executive agencies

The constitution of the main general advisory agencies in the central departments has already been described. There are a number of other advisory and executive agencies which perform specific specialised functions in relation to the principal health authorities in all or part of the UK. In addition to these described below, a new body, the Health Service Supply Council, has recently been established. (See Chapter 11.)

The Public Health Laboratory Service Board

The Public Health Laboratory Service was originally established under Section 17 of the National Health Service Act 1946 to provide for the surveillance and control of infective disease in England and Wales. A principal function of the service is the monitoring of the microbial disease prevalent in the country. The PHLS Board was established on 1 August 1961 under the Public Health Laboratory Service Act 1960. The Act provides that the Board is to consist of a chairman and not less than eight members (the present number is 15). Members are appointed by the Secretary of State for Social Services, after consultation with relevant bodies and organisations in the fields of microbiology and community medicine. The service carries out its function by providing specialist diagnostic services for hospitals, general practitioners and environmental health officers from its 54 regional and area laboratories, by providing specialist diagnostic facilities in its hospital laboratories and producing the weekly communicable disease report. Other functions of the PHLS include the provision of a quality control service for microbiology, and research and development in both epidemiology and technology, most of the work being based at the Central Public Health Laboratory at Colindale in North London. In Scotland and Northern Ireland public health laboratory services are provided by health boards and some university departments.

The Medical Practices Committees

The constitution of the Medical Practices Committee for England and Wales is now governed by Section 7 of the 1977 Act. The Scottish Medical Practices Committee is governed by Section 3 of the 1978 Act. The Committee consists of a chairman (who is a medical practitioner) and eight (in Scotland, five) other members (6 (3) of whom are medical practitioners). The Committee is appointed by the Secretary of State. The function of the MPC is to consider and determine applications made by medical practitioners for inclusion on national health service family practitioner committee lists of medical practitioners and the need to fill vacancies on such lists, with a view to securing that the services in the areas of different family practitioner committees or in different parts of those areas is adequate. There is no equivalent committee in Northern Ireland.

The Prescription Pricing Authority

The Prescription Pricing Authority is involved principally in pricing prescriptions and calculating the amounts due to chemists and dispensing doctors for reimbursement through family practitioner committees in England. There are offices of the authority in London, Birmingham, Durham, Liverpool, Manchester, Preston, Sheffield, Wakefield and Bolton. The authority replaces the Joint Pricing Committee and the Joint Pricing Bureaux which existed before reorganisation. The authority was reconstituted (SI78/331 and 332) in 1978. The membership of the new authority, appointed by the Secretary of State, consists of a chairman plus registered pharmacists, general medical practitioners, family practitioner committee members or administrators, employees of the authority, one lay member, one DHSS representative and a representative of academic and research interests in the field. The functions of the PPA are fulfilled in Wales by the Welsh Health Technical Services Organisation and by the Common and Central Services Agencies in Scotland and Northern Ireland.

The Dental Estimates Board

The Board is now established in England under Section 37 of the 1977 Act (SI73/1468 as amended by SI74/53). It consists of a chairman and vice-chairman (both of whom are dentists) and seven other members (five of whom are dentists). Members are appointed by the Secretary of State for Social Services and the Secretary of State for Wales. The function of the Board is to consider all dental estimate forms for prior approval of treatment or for approval of payment and to carry out other duties imposed on them by the regulations. The Board is constituted for England and Wales. In Scotland and Northern Ireland its functions are performed by the Common and Central Services Agencies.

The Health Advisory Service

The Health Advisory Service in England and Wales (originally Hospital Advisory Service) was set up in 1969 following public disquiet about conditions in a number of long-stay hospitals. The Hospital Advisory Service for Scotland was established in 1970. At present there is no Health or Hospital Advisory Service in Northern Ireland. Originally the remit of the Hospital Advisory Services was confined to long-stay hospitals but, in 1976, the HAS in England and Wales was renamed the Health Advisory Service and its remit extended to cover community services, including those provided in collaboration with local authorities. The needs of the mentally handicapped are dealt with separately in England by the Development Team for the Mentally Handicapped (see below). In Scotland and Wales the advisory services have retained responsibility for the mentally handicapped. The services consist of a director for England and Wales and for Scotland who report directly to the Secretary of State, together with teams of doctors, nurses, administrators and other staff who are seconded to work with the service from the NHS and who visit and evaluate mental illness, geriatric and (in Wales and Scotland) mental handicap services. The HAS is, in a sense, an inspectorate for long-term care services although in its style of operations, it stresses its advisory rather than its inspectorial functions. It has been suggested that the role of inspectorates should be extended in relation to the NHS but the Royal Commission concluded that further inspectorates would be costly and unlikely to be effective outside the management system of the NHS.

The Development Team for the Mentally Handicapped

In 1975 the Secretary of State for Social Services set up the National Development Group for the Mentally Handicapped, which subsequently prepared a series of valuable reports covering a wide range of health and personal social services for mentally handicapped people. At the end of 1979 it was announced that the group would be wound up but that the Development Team for the Mentally Handicapped, which had been associated with the group, would continue in being. The team consists of a director, and three associate directors assisted by a panel of specialists in psychiatry, paediatrics, administration, nursing, psychology, social services, etc. It offers advice and assistance to individual health and social services authorities in England on the planning and operation of services in their locality. It visits authorities either by their invitation or, in the case of health authorities, by decision of the Secretary of State, and it makes follow-up visits.

Other bodies

For the sake of completeness, various other bodies should be mentioned here. The first are those forming part of the NHS machinery: the NHS Whitley Councils and the various national staff committees and training councils. They are described in Chapter 13. In the same category comes the NHS Supply Council described in Chapter 11.

The professional regulating bodies, such as the General Medical Council, the General Nursing Councils and the Council for the Professions Supplementary to Medicine are not part of the NHS, but the work of these independent bodies has an important influence on the way the service develops. They are described in Chapter 15.

The Medical Research Council is another body outside the NHS which collaborates with it and has a long-term influence on its activities. The council was incorporated under royal charter in 1920, succeeding the Medical Research Committee established in 1913. A new charter was granted in 1966. Under the Science and Technology Act 1965, it is responsible to the Secretary of State for

Education and Science. The council consists of a chairman, a deputy chairman and from 14 to 18 other members, four of whom are nominated by, and represent, other government departments. Not less than three-quarters of its members must be appointed on account of their qualifications in science. All appointments are made by the Secretary of State for Education and Science. The chief medical officer of the DHSS is a member of the council.

The object of the MRC is to promote research into all aspects of health and disease. It conducts research in its own establishments (including the National Institute for Medical Research, the Clinical Research Centre and more than 60 other research units), and supports research workers in universities and elsewhere by long-term and short-term grants for specific programmes or projects. The council also provides training awards and fellowships, some tenable abroad. It is assisted in its work by four advisory boards and by numerous specialist committees and working parties. In 1973 some aspects of its work were taken over by the chief scientists of the central health departments following the implementation of the recommendations of the 1971 report of the Rothschild Committee, *A Framework for Government Research and Development*. This arrangement was reversed in 1980, but the council undertook to meet the needs and priorities of the health departments in its programme of biomedical research and to mount and manage, in partnership with the DHSS, additional health services research.

Further reading

Statutory instruments and circulars

England and Wales

SI47/1298. The NHS (Regional Hospital Boards, etc.) Regulations 1947 (as amended)
SI73/1191. The NHS (Determination of Regions) Order 1973 (as amended)
SI73/1275. The NHS (Determination of Areas) Order 1973
SI73/1286. The NHS (Regional and Area Health Authorities: Membership and Procedure) Regulations 1973 (as amended)
SI73/1624. The Welsh Health Technical Services Organisation (Establishment and Constitution) Order 1973
SI74/24. The NHS Functions (Directions to Authorities) Regulations 1974
SI74/190. The Health Authorities and Local Authorities Joint Consultative Committees Order 1974
SI75/1099. The NHS (Constitution of Area Health Authorities) Order 1975
SI75/1100. The NHS (Constitution of Regional Health Authorities) Order 1975
SI78/331. The Prescription Pricing Authority Constitution Order 1978.
SI78/332. The Prescription Pricing Authority Regulations 1978
SI79/51. The NHS (Preservation of Boards of Governors) Order 1979
SI79/738. The NHS (Health Authorities: Membership) Regulations 1979
SI79/739. The NHS (Family Practitioner Committees: Membership and Procedure) Regulations 1979
SI80/796. The Health Service Supply Council (Establishment and Constitution) Order 1980
SI80/987. The Health Service Supply Council Regulations 1980

HRC(73)3, WHRC(73)7. Management arrangements for the reorganised NHS
HRC(73)4. Defining districts
HRC(73)22. Membership and procedure of regional and area health authorities
HRC(73)24, WHRC(73)22. Area health authorities: determination of boundaries and constitution
HRC(74)14. The work of family practitioner committees
HRC(74)18, WHRC(74)19. Functions of regional and area health authorities
HRC(74)23,38. Management arrangements: health districts
WHRC(73)25. Statutory framework of the NHS in Wales after reorganisation
WHRC(73)28. Establishing family practitioner committees
WHRC(73)29. WHTSO
HSC(IS)80, WHSC(IS)72. Social work support for the health service
HSC(IS)194, WHSC(IS)188. Democracy in the national health service
HC(76)8, WHC(76)9. Family practitioner committees: membership and procedure
HC(76)21, WHC(76)19. Health Advisory Service
HC(77)27, WHC(77)37. The NHS (Health Authorities: Membership) Regulations 1977
HC(79)1. Appointments to area health authorities

Scotland

SI74/266 (S15). The NHS (Determination of Areas of Health Boards) (Scotland) Order 1974
SI74/267 (S16). The NHS (Constitution of Health Boards) (Scotland) Order 1974
SI74/466 (S27). The NHS (Functions of Health Boards) (Scotland) Order 1974
SI74/467 (S28). The NHS (Functions of the Common Services Agency) (Scotland) Order 1974
SI75/196 (S15). The NHS (Common Services Agency: Membership and Procedure) (Scotland) Regulations 1975
SI75/197 (S16). The NHS (Health Boards: Membership, Procedure and Payment of Subscriptions) (Scotland) Regulations 1975
HSR(72)C2. Common Services Agency
HSR(72)C3. The administrative structure of health boards
HSR(73)C6. Advance studies in areas
HSR(73)C7, C31. Health board districts
HSR(73)C9. Health board areas
HSR(73)C38. Appointment of management committee of the Common Services Agency
NHS Circular 1974(GEN)28. Management committee of Common Services Agency
NHS Circular 1974(GEN)97. Scottish Hospital Advisory Service

Northern Ireland

SI72/1265 (NI14) The Health and Personal Social Services (Northern Ireland) Order 1972

Official reports

DHSS. *National Health Service Reorganisation: England* (Cmnd 5055). HMSO 1972

DHSS. *Management Arrangements for the Reorganised National Health Service* (The Grey Book). HMSO 1972

DHSS. *Democracy in the NHS: Membership of Health Authorities.* HMSO 1974

DHSS and Welsh Office. *A Report from the Working Party on Collaboration between the NHS and Local Government on its activities to the end of 1972.* HMSO 1973

Ministry of Health and Social Services. *An Integrated Service: The Reorganisation of Health and Personal Social Services in Northern Ireland.* Booz Allen and Hamilton 1972

Royal Commission on the National Health Service. Research Report No. 1 *The Working of the National Health Service* (M. Kogan). HMSO 1978

Royal Commission on the National Health Service. *Report* (Cmnd 7615). HMSO 1979

SHHD. *Reorganisation of the Scottish Health Services* (Cmdn 4734) HMSO 1971

SHHD. *The National Health Service and the Community in Scotland.* HMSO 1974

Welsh Office. *National Health Service Reorganisation in Wales* (Cmnd 5057). HMSO 1972

Welsh Office. *Management Arrangements for the Reorganised National Health Service in Wales.* HMSO 1972

Other publications

Association of Chief Administrators of Health Authorities. *A Review of the Management of the Reorganised NHS.* 1976

Brown, R.G.S. *The Changing National Health Service.* Routledge 1973

Brown, R.G.S. *Reorganisation of the National Health Service: A case study of administrative change.* Basil Blackwell, Martin Robertson 1979

Brunel University. Health Services Organisation Research Unit. *Working Papers on the Reorganisation of the National Health Service.* 1973

Edwards, B. and Walker, P.R. *Si Vis Pacem ... Preparation for Change in the National Health Service.* OUP for Nuffield Provincial Hospitals Trust 1973

Jacques, E. (Ed). *Health Services: Their nature and organisation and the role of patients, doctors, nurses and the complementary professions.* Heinemann 1978

Levitt, Ruth. *The Reorganised Health Service* Croom Helm 1977

Medical Services Review Committee. *A Review of the Medical Services in Great Britain.* (Porritt Report) Social Assay 1962

Naylor, W.M. *Organisation and Management of a Unified Health Service: Organisation of Area Health Services.* Institute of Health Service Administrators 1971

Office of Health Economics. *The Reorganised National Health Service* 1976

Table 2. Principal differences between the organisation structure of the national health service in England, Wales, Scotland and Northern Ireland

	England	Wales	Scotland	Northern Ireland
1. Principal legislation	National Health Service Reorganisation Act 1973. National Health Service Act 1977	National Health Service Reorganisation Act 1973. National Health Service Act 1977	National Health Service (Scotland) Act 1972 National Health Service (Scotland) Act 1978	The Health and Personal Social Services (Northern Ireland) Order 1972 — SI72/1265 (NI 14)
2. Date of introduction of organisation	1 April 1974	1 April 1974	1 April 1974	1 October 1973
3. Responsible government department/minister	Department of Health and Social Security/Secretary of State for Social Services	Welsh Office/Secretary of State for Wales	Scottish Home and Health Department/Secretary of State for Scotland	Department of Health and Social Services/Secretary of State for Northern Ireland
4. National advisory structure	Standing Advisory Committees	Standing Advisory Committees	Scottish Health Services Planning Council National Consultative Committees	Health and Social Services Council. Central Advisory Committees
5. Regional tier	14 Regional health authorities accountable to Secretary of State	No regional authority	No regional authority	No regional authority
6. Central services	RHA provides central services to areas but some services delegated to AHAs	A central Welsh Health Technical Services Organisation to serve AHAs and Welsh Office. Services include: — major building and engineering design — computer service — central supplies — some management services	A central Common Services Agency to serve both Scottish Home and Health Department and area boards. Services include: — major capital works — ambulance service — information services — management services — central supplies — blood transfusion	A Central Services Agency to serve area boards and DHSS (NI) Services include: — legal services — central supplies — advice on catering domestic, laundry services

Table 2. Principal differences between the organisation structure of the national health service in England, Wales, Scotland and Northern Ireland *(Continued)*

	England	Wales	Scotland	Northern Ireland
7. Team structure at regional level	Regional administrator Regional medical officer Regional nursing officer Regional treasurer Regional works officer	Not applicable	Not applicable	Not applicable
8. Area level health authority	90 area health authorities accountable to RHAs. (12 boards of governors for London postgraduate teaching hospitals)	8 area health authorities accountable to Secretary of State for Wales	15 health boards accountable to Secretary of State for Scotland	4 area health and social service boards accountable to Department of Health and Social Services
9. Family practitioner contracts	Family practitioner committee for each area	Family practitioner committee for each area	Family practitioner contracts with area health boards	Family practitioner contracts with area boards. Central Services Agency services contracts and makes payments for the boards
10. Social services	Under local authority management	Under local authority management	Under local authority management	Personal social services and health services unified under HSSBs
11. Team structure at area level	Area team of officers: — Area administrator — Area nursing officer — Area medical officer — Area treasurer (Area management team in single district areas includes 2 clinical representatives)	Area team: — Area administrator — Area nursing officer — Area medical officer — Area treasurer (plus 2 clinical representatives in single district areas)	Area executive group: — Secretary — Chief area nursing officer — Chief administrative medical officer — Treasurer	Area executive team: — Chief administrative officer — Chief administrative nursing officer — Chief administrative medical officer — Director of social services — Chairman, area medical advisory committee (either consultant or GP)

	England	Wales	Scotland	Northern Ireland
12. Other chief professional officers at area level	Area dental officer Area pharmaceutical officer Area works officer	Area dental officer Area pharmaceutical officer Area works officer	Chief area dental officer Chief area pharmaceutical officer	Chief dental officer Area pharmacist
13. Employment of consultant and senior hospital medical and dental staff	Consultants and senior medical and dental staff in contract with RHA or AHA(T)	AHAs hold contracts of consultants and senior medical and dental staff	Health boards hold contracts of consultants and senior medical and dental staff	Consultants and senior medical and dental staff in contract with area boards. Central Services Agency organises appointments procedures for grades above house officer
14. Team structure at district level	District management team: — District administrator — District nursing officer — District community physician — District finance officer — 2 clinical representatives: 1 consultant, 1 GP Non-clinical team members accountable to AHA; monitored and co-ordinated by professional equivalent on area team of officers	Distric team: — District administrator — District nursing officer — District community physician — District finance officer — 2 clinical representatives: 1 consultant, 1 GP Team as a whole responsible for specific delegated functions. Individual non-clinical team members accountable to equivalent area team officer	District executive group: — District administrator — District nursing officer — District administrative medical officer — District finance officer Group members accountable as a team for team functions. Individuals accountable to equivalent area executive team officer	District executive team: — District administrative officer — District administrative nursing officer — District administrative medical officer — District social services officer — Chairman, district medical advisory committee Team corporately accountable for team functions. Individual non-clinical team members accountable to area executive team officer
15. Community participation	Community health councils at district level	Community health councils at district level	Local health councils at district level	District committees at district level

4
Health authority administration

As we have seen, the 1974 reorganisation of the NHS was based on the concept of the district as the basic operational unit for management but responsibility for the provision of health services was placed on statutory authorities only a minority of which are responsible for a single health district. In Scotland and Northern Ireland there is only one type of statutory authority — the health boards and the health and social services boards respectively. In England and Wales there are also family practitioner committees which, although appointed by area authorities, must be regarded as statutory authorities. In England there are also regional health authorities.

The main responsibilities of these bodies were set out in Chapter 3, and how they set about performing them is described in more detail in Chapters 5 to 7. Here we are concerned mainly with the way they function as statutory authorities.

The legal relationship between the DHSS, health authorities and family practitioner committees must be sought in the National Health Service Act 1977. Section 1(1) of the Act makes it quite clear that the overall responsibility for the health service lies with the Secretary of State: 'It is the Secretary of State's duty to continue the promotion in England and Wales of a comprehensive health service'. However, Section 13 of the Act allows the Secretary of State to 'direct a regional health authority ... to exercise on his behalf such of his functions relating to the health service as are specified in the directions'. In turn Section 14 of the Act permits regional health authorities to 'direct any area health authority in its region, to exercise such of the functions exercisable by the regional health authority by virtue of Section 13 as are specified in the directions'.

The Secretary of State may however direct a 'regional health authority that any of its functions are or are not exercisable by an area health authority'. This clearly reflects the pattern proposed by the Grey Book, that of 'delegation downwards matched with accountability upwards'. It is clear thus far that regional and area health authorities have no original statutory responsibilities of their own in respect of hospital and community services, but are simply agents of the Secretary of State. In Scotland the position is if anything even clearer; Section 2(1) of the 1978 Act provides that, 'the Secretary of State shall by order constitute ... boards for such areas as he may by order determine, for the purpose of exercising functions with respect to the administration of such health services provided by him as he may so determine'.

The relationship is somewhat complicated by paragraph 15(1) of Schedule 5 of the Act for England and Wales which provides that:

> An authority shall, notwithstanding that it is exercising any function on behalf of the Secretary of State or another authority, be entitled to enforce any rights acquired in the exercise of that function, and be liable in respect of any liabilities in the exercise of that function.

Put in the simplest terms this means that an area or regional health authority can sue or be sued in its own name just as if it were acting as a principal. The first schedule of the Scottish Act achieves the same effect in providing that 'A health board shall be a body corporate and shall have a common seal'.

The provision for family practitioner committees in England and Wales produces a further complication. Although in respect of hospital and community health services area health authorities act as agents of the Secretary of State, in respect of family practitioner services Section 10 of the 1977 Act places a duty directly on AHAs 'to establish for its area a body called a family practitioner committee' and Sections 29, 35, 38 and 41 require them specifically to make arrangements in respect of general medical, dental, ophthalmic and pharmaceutical services for the people in their areas. Section 15 of the Act places on FPCs the duty 'to administer on behalf of the area health authority by which the committee was established, the arrangements made in pursuance of this Act for the provision of general medical services, general dental services, general ophthalmic services and pharmaceutical services for the area of authority'. To this extent the AHA is acting as a principal with the FPC as its agent. However, the FPC is not a sub-committee of the AHA and once the FPC has been established the AHA's formal relationship is limited to nominating 11 of the 30 members of the FPC and providing accommodation, staff and certain services. (The FPC is not an employing authority.) The FPC deals directly with the DHSS on matters concerning the administration of the contractor services. The administrator (family practitioner services), although an employee of the AHA, is seconded to the FPC and accountable to it for work done on its behalf. There is provision in circular HRC (73)3 for agreement to be reached under which part of his time he works for the AHA in contributing to the planning of primary health care services and in this role he is accountable to the area administrator. The FPC itself is responsible for the general efficiency and management of its business, but through its responsibility to provide the FPC with staff the AHA has the right to satisfy itself that its staff are being used effectively. It can be seen that there is scope for more than one interpretation of the precise relations between AHA and FPC.

Sections 84 to 86 of the 1977 Act contain provisions about inquiries, and default and emergency powers — very broadly steps which the Secretary of State may take when he considers that an authority, one of his agents, is not performing satisfactorily. Section 85 provides that when the Secretary of State is of the opinion that any body has failed to carry out any function conferred or imposed on it under the Act he may make an order declaring it to be in default. The order will provide for the appointment of new members and may authorise a person to act in the place of the body pending the appointment of new members. The bodies listed in this section include not only RHAs, AHAs and such bodies as the Medical Practices Committee but also family practitioner committees. This makes it clear that in this respect the Secretary of State maintains direct control of FPCs, not through AHAs.

It hardly needs saying that the default powers will be rarely, if ever, used. Normally if the Secretary of State believes that a health authority is not performing satisfactorily in some respect he will use persuasion. He will not reappoint a chairman if he believes that the chairman's performance has been disappointing (though this is certainly not the usual reason for a failure to reappoint). Similarly it is open to him, or in the case of AHAs to the RHA, not to reappoint individual members. It should be noted however that the RHA does not have such powers in respect of members of AHAs appointed by local authorities.

Section 86 of the 1977 Act gives the Secretary of State powers to replace a body or person if he considers that there is an emergency. In 1979, using this section, the Secretary of State replaced the Lambeth, Southwark and Lewisham AHA(T) on the grounds that it was refusing to limit its expenditure to its budget allocation, and appointed three commissioners to perform its functions. The direction was disputed in the courts and ruled invalid. The AHA was restored and the National Health Service (Invalid Direction) Act 1980 was passed 'to give temporary effect to an instrument purporting to be a direction given by the Secretary of State for Social Services'.

Chairman and members

A health authority comprises the members and chairman. Their numbers and methods of appointment were described in Chapter 3.

Chairman

Chairmen of health authorities are appointed by the Secretary of State, usually for a term of four years though appointments are sometimes for a shorter period, such as two years. Since 1974 there has been a greater tendency than was the case with regional hospital boards for secretaries of state to appoint active members of their own political party as chairmen — and sometimes not to reappoint chairmen who belong to another party. However, there is no general relationship between the political allegiance, if any, of chairmen and the party which is in office. Chairmen may be and frequently are reappointed, and some present chairmen were chairmen of authorities before 1974. It is unusual to retain chairmen in office after the age of 65, and sometimes chairmen approaching that age are appointed for a shorter period. Secretaries of state do not, of course, state publicly their reasons for appointing, reappointing or not reappointing. Whatever the reasons for particular decisions, the general need is to achieve the advantages of experience and continuity but on each occasion to make a number of new appointments. Unless this is done the time will come when a large proportion of chairmen have to be replaced at the same time, with a consequent loss of experience in the body of chairmen as a group. If a chairman dies or resigns during his term of office, the Secretary of State will make an appointment to complete the term.

Chairmen receive remuneration plus an allowance. In England and Wales these were originally fixed at £2,000 and £750 respectively and although following inflation the figures have been substantially increased the purpose remains the same: not to pay a full-time salary but to acknowledge responsibilities undertaken by the chairman and the demands on his time. In Scotland payment varies according to the size of the board.

Expenditure of the allowance is at the chairman's discretion but it is commonly used for such things as hospitality for visitors, staff retirement presentations and so on.

The original expectation was that a chairman should not need to spend more than a few hours a week in carrying out his duties. In practice many chairmen give much more time than this. Although the number of official committee meetings is generally fewer than in the former hospital authorities because of the discontinuance of standing sub-committees and house committees, there are more informal meetings with groups of authority members to discuss particular problems, meetings with officers, appointments committees to be chaired and so on. Even in the smaller authorities going round hospitals, clinics and so on to keep in touch may also take more time than it did with HMCs. In England regional chairmen have regular meetings with ministers, as do the chairmen of authorities and boards in other parts of the UK. In addition to their responsibilities for their own authority chairmen are often called upon to serve on national bodies such as the Supplies Council, or the Scottish Health Service Planning Council.

The post of chairman of a health authority is demanding not only in terms of time spent but also in terms of the pressure of responsibility which the post entails. In an organisation as complicated as the health service, it is virtually impossible for even the most capable chairman to be confident of always being in close touch with events. And yet if things should go wrong, it is usually to the chairman that the Secretary of State and the public turn for explanations. The health service is a regular focus of public interest and the chairman is frequently approached by the media for comment or opinion. He has a difficult position as a layman at the head of a service which is highly professional and which exists for a multiplicity of individual personal contacts between patient and doctor. The successes of the health service, the medical breakthroughs and the individual patients cured, are naturally seen by the public as primarily to the credit of the individual doctors concerned. It is when the service fails on a bigger scale that the authority is called to account, for example if there are deficiencies in services for the elderly or the mentally ill, or when waiting lists grow too long.

A chairman has to represent the members of his authority, both to outside interests, such as the press, and also within the authority, to the senior officers and the staff. He is a vital bridge between members and officers, being a sounding-board for officers' ideas and presenting to the officers a distillation of the members' expectations for the health service locally. Conversely, at times he will find himself assisting the management team or an individual officer in presenting proposals to the authority. Put simply the chairman is often an interpreter between the laymen and the professionals in the health service. His leadership or figurehead role is a vital one and successful chairmanship calls for considerable personal qualities.

One of the most demanding responsibilities of a chairman is the monitoring of the management team and the individual chief officers. He exercises this responsibility on behalf of the health authority, to whom the team and the officers are formally responsible. On major matters, for example, on strategic planning, the authority may itself be able to exercise a monitoring role but by and large a chairman would be expected to do this and to alert the authority if anything was seriously wrong. Some chairmen attend meetings of their management team on a regular basis, but the most common practice is to attend occasionally, either to discuss a topic of major importance or just periodically to keep in touch. The monitoring of chief officers is carried out on a more personal basis. There are, of course, requirements laid down in the chief officers' job descriptions and these are supplemented by more specific directives from the health authority in the course of business. The chairman will monitor officers' performance against these requirements by keeping in touch with them on a regular, informal basis and by being available to them to discuss any particularly difficult problem.

Members

Members of health authorities, although they may have been nominated by a body with a particular sectional interest, are nevetheless expected to contribute to the whole work of the authority and not concentrate only on a narrow field. They naturally use their special skills and experience where these are relevant but accept corporate and collective responsibility for decisions of the authority.

The role of individual members in practice shows many variations not only between individual members but also between different health authorities. There is obviously a basic obligation to attend and contribute to the full authority meetings, but most members give time to the health service between these meetings in various ways. It is rare for health authorities to have standing sub-committees, and indeed, these were actively discouraged in the reorganised health service in 1974. The reasoning has been that authorities should concentrate on policy matters at the monthly meetings and should leave day-to-day management to their officer teams. Nevertheless some authorities have found it valuable to establish small groups of members, sometimes called panels, which focus on certain broad areas, such as planning or financial affairs. This enables authority members to make more of a contribution to policy making and to discuss issues at greater length than they are usually able to do when the matter in question goes before the full authority as only one item among many. There are also sometimes *ad hoc* groups of members brought together to study a particular issue to which they may have some special or local knowledge to contribute. Members are involved from time to time in appointments committees for senior staff or in staff disciplinary hearings. Many authorities also have visiting rotas, to enable small groups of members to visit hospitals and clinics on a regular basis. This serves a dual purpose of enabling members to see things at first hand and also of letting staff and patients have the opportunity of talking personally with members. Obviously this is very much easier in a small compact health authority than in a large one. Personal visiting is much more difficult at the level of the English regional authorities but some regions do have members' visiting arrangements. If a health authority member is to keep reasonably well informed there is also a good deal of reading to be done and there is no doubt that in total this can be a very demanding public responsibility.

Some members take on additional responsibilities such as vice-chairmanship of the authority, or chairing a group or *ad hoc* committees. Another responsibility falling on some members is to serve on the management side of one of the Whitley Councils. It is often from such active and experienced members of authorities that new chairmen are recruited.

It is sometimes said that members of health authorities find their role uncertain and unsatisfactory. While they are expected to concentrate on policy matters their scope in this is restricted by the need to conform to national policies. The day-to-day activity of the authority and its hospitals, etc. is the responsibility of the officers and the medical staff and is in any case too complex for a body of members to manage in any direct way. Yet the 1974 reorganisation envisaged members as being responsible for management, and placed responsibility for consumer representation elsewhere. If some members have continued to see this representation as part of their role, the changes made following the 'Democracy' documents were only a slight shift of emphasis in that direction, while CHCs have succeeded in developing their role as spokesmen for the public. There was perhaps some acknowledgement of these difficulties in the 'Patients First' document issued in December 1979, proposing a restructuring of the service in England and Wales. 'In future', it said, 'authority members will be less remote from local services than many necessarily are today, and will be more closely in touch with the needs of the community. The need for separate consumer representation in these circumstances is less clear.' However, although it may be that the role of member of a health authority is less clear cut and less satisfying than that of a member of a local authority (and possibly, as implied by 'Patients First', particularly in a multi-district area) the role of a voluntary part-time member of a large and complex authority dependent on a large staff for day-to-day running is always difficult, whether members are appointed or elected. Nevertheless members of health authorities, like members of local authorities have an important role and although attitudes, like practices, vary, it appears that the majority find it a rewarding responsibility.

Functioning of health authorities

The detailed workings of health authorities vary to some extent according to local traditions and the personal wishes of those most closely involved. There are, however, several key features which are common to all.

Standing orders

Each health authority is required to have agreed standing orders for the conduct of business. These provide for the authority to agree on the frequency of meetings, which is usually monthly, and the time and place where they are to be held. There is also provision for special meetings to be called at any time either by the chairman or by requisition from a proportion of the authority members. There is a specified period of notice which members are required to be given, usually at least three clear days, giving details of the business to be transacted. Health authorities also publicise their meetings, perhaps in the local press or by posting a notice outside headquarters. The press and public are admitted to health authority meetings, unless the authority resolves, under Section 1(2) of the Public Bodies (Admission to Meetings) Act 1960 that publicity would be prejudicial to the public interest by reason of the confidential nature of the business to be transacted, or for other special reasons stated in the resolution. The community health council or councils in an area send an observer, often their chairman, to health authority meetings and he normally remains for the private as well as the public business, except where there is some particularly personal and confidential issue when he is expected to withdraw. There will be a stated quorum, or minimum number of members, necessarily present before business can be transacted and a record of attendance of members is kept. Membership can be called into question if attendance is not sufficiently regular. The standing orders also provide for the conduct of the meeting, for the proposal of motions and amendments and for voting.

Health authorities, as is usual in all public bodies, stipulate that a member must declare if he has any pecuniary interest, direct or indirect, in the matter under discussion. The member is required to declare this interest at the commencement of discussion, to take no part in the deliberations and refrain from voting. He may also be required to retire while the matter is under consideration.

The standing orders will also provide for the appointment of committees of the authority or joint committees with other bodies. Conditions for the use of the common seal of the authority for the sealing of documents, such as contracts, will also be specified. There will be procedures for competitive tendering and for inviting quotations for supplies or building and engineering work. There will also be a requirement of officers to declare any pecuniary interest, similarly to members. Associated with the standing orders are the standing financial instructions. These are described in Chapter 9.

Agendas

The business to be transacted by the authority at any meeting will be summarised by the administrator in the form of an agenda. This lists the items of business, usually with a brief reference to previous discussions, or to particular correspondence, or to a relevant written report which accompanies the agenda. Some of these agenda items appear each month as a matter of routine, for example, the approval of the minutes of the previous meeting, the receipt of minutes of other committees, for example the family practitioner committee, the joint consultative committee with the local authority, etc. There are routine items regarding the receipt of tenders and the placing of contracts. There is also customarily a financial statement showing the revenue position at the end of each month and whether the authority is overspending or underspending, with a breakdown of the expenditure under separate headings. These include the various staff salaries and wages groups, medical and surgical appliances, drugs, provisions, domestic repairs and renewals, uniforms, heating and lighting and so on. The financial statement for RHAs will provide information about the AHAs in the region.

In addition to such recurrent subjects as these, there will be each month a range of topical items for discussion and decision. Some of these are at the initiation of DHSS or region or some other outside body, for example the local authority or community health council. Some will have been initiated by the authority at an earlier meeting. Items are sometimes placed on the agenda by the chairman, either at his own request or after an approach by individual authority members. Other items will have been submitted by the management team or by individual officers. Once the agenda has been prepared by the administrator, it will usually be discussed with the chairman and with the other chief officers, either individually or at a more formal officer meeting. It will then be sent to the authority members usually four or five days before the meeting to enable members to digest the various reports and discussion documents and to prepare themselves for the meeting.

Planning cycle

The planning cycle provides a backbone and a timetable to much of the authority's work. The major policy decisions are taken as part of the strategic plan, which covers the next decade and is updated every fourth year. Detailed planning of developments and changes in services come within the scope of the operational plan, which covers three years, the first being in some detail. For example, the strategic plan would show the authority's intentions for the relocation of a specialist service such as the accident service. If a new accident department were actually to be opening within the next 12 months, the detailed staffing arrangements and costs would then be found in the operational plan. It is the administrator's responsibility to co-ordinate the planning activities of the various other specialists, to ensure that comprehensive plans are prepared and discussed by the management team and authority members in due time.

Conduct of the meeting

In the conduct of the meeting the chairman plays a prominent role. He opens the discussion of each item, and subsequent discussion is addressed through the chair in the usual way. At the end of the discussion it will often be apparent that there is one course of action which the members favour and the chairman will sum up the consensus feeling. Where there is no such consensus, a vote will be taken. Practice in respect of moving and seconding motions, and the consideration of amendments, follows the usual pattern. Before 1974 matters considered by hospital authorities were seldom put to a vote, but voting is now fairly common. One reason for this in AHAs is the presence of more members appointed by local authorities combined with the greater local authority interest now that health authorities have territorial responsibilities coterminous with those of local authorities. It is normal for local authorities to reach decisions by voting on party lines, and that practice has at least in some places been adopted. A hardly less important reason is that in recent years authorities have had to take more difficult and controversial decisions than was the usual experience of HMCs. An additional factor is that whereas before 1974 many topics received their main discussion in committee, with the meeting of the authority little but a formality (and not open to the public except in the case of RHBs) the main discussion is now at a full meeting open to the press and public. In these circumstances it is natural that on controversial topics the minority should wish to record their dissent rather than acquiesce in the majority view.

Minutes

A record of the meeting is kept in the form of minutes, which are the responsibility of the administrator in his capacity as secretary to the authority. The minutes record the attendance of members, a list of the matters which were discussed and, after each, a brief record of the discussion and of the decision taken. At the commencement of the next meeting the authority is asked to approve these minutes as a correct record and they are then signed by the chairman. The administrator ensures that the minutes are circulated to officers who need to have them and with the chairman he ensures that the various decisions are carried out, if not by himself then by one of the other chief officers. He must also ensure that, if the authority has asked for a progress report or a further discussion at some later date, it appears on the agenda at the appropriate time.

Delegation arrangements

Most health authorities have a formalised schedule which sets out the extent to which the authority reserves some decisions to itself, while delegating others to the chairman, the management team and the chief officers as individuals. For example, the power to incur expenditure on the authority's behalf will be clarified, with major orders needing the full authority's approval and so down, in descending order, through the chairman and the management team. With regard to staff appointments, there will be some senior appointments which the authority will wish to be involved in, usually by means of a sub-committee. On others the chairman will normally represent the authority while most will be delegated to chief officers or their subordinates.

Disciplinary procedures will be similarly codified, as will other personnel matters, such as the approval of special leave, for example to attend courses and conferences. Major capital schemes will require the approval of the full authority, while approval of lesser schemes might be delegated. Whatever the guidelines, however, the most important ingredient, without which no delegation scheme can work, is mutual trust. Delegation of authority must imply that the decisions are sometimes taken which, if they had been taken at a higher level, might have been different. If this is not generally accepted, decision-making can tend to drift to the top of the organisation, depriving staff directly involved with patients of the quick decisions they are usually entitled to expect.

Officers

For advice on policy and for the day-to-day management of services the authority members look to their chief officers.

The administrator

The administrator has a key role to play, with three principal responsibilities. First he acts as secretary to the authority and is responsible for the efficient conduct of business and for official communications on behalf of the authority. Secondly, he is the co-ordinator of the consensus management team of chief officers and is again responsible for the efficient conduct of business, for ensuring that his colleagues are properly informed, that the team works well together and tackles the problems within its compass. Thirdly, the administrator carries direct responsibility for a number of services. These include personnel services, management services, supplies, support services such as laundry, domestic, catering and medical records services and so on. He will need to give leadership to a substantial proportion of the authority's staff and there are few aspects of a health authority's business in which the administrator does not have some involvement, if not personally then through one of his subordinate staff. Because of the range of his responsibilities and particularly his role as secretary to the authority the administrator has a close working relationship with the chairman.

The medical officer

All health authorities also have a chief medical adviser, a full-time medical administrator. He has a particular responsibility for the planning of patients' services and the establishment of health care policies, for advising on the special needs of his region or area and seeing that there is a balanced development of all the medical specialties. This involves a knowledge of the local characteristics and historical background of a region or area, together with an understanding of epidemiology, which is the study of the health of whole communities rather than of individual patients. The full-time medical administrative staff at the various levels of the health service are collectively regarded as forming the specialty of community medicine, which embraces the pre-1974 medical administrators in the hospital service, together with the former medical officers of health and their staff. Within this specialty there is a wide variety of responsibilities, from health service planning to the giving of specialist advice to local authorities on environmental health, housing, education and social services. Medical staffing is a major responsibility and in England there is a two-tier system. Teaching areas appoint all their medical staff, from consultant downwards, whereas non-teaching areas appoint only up to the level of registrar, grades of senior registrar and above being appointed by the regional health authority. In addition to their responsibilities for medical staff, medical officers often have responsibility for the paramedical professions, i.e. radiography, physiotherapy, occupational therapy, speech therapy, dietetics, etc. There is no standard organisational pattern for these professions and in some authorities they come under the wing of the administrator, sometimes under the medical officer and occasionally a combination of both.

The nursing officer

Nursing staff form numerically the largest group of health service employees, almost half of all employees. They are managed by the nursing officer and the supporting nursing administrative staff. At the English regional level the number of nurses directly managed is very small, but there is a substantial responsibility for nurse manpower planning, for the development of the profession within the region and for specialist professional advice on a wide range of subjects, particularly on major planning matters. At the operational levels personnel work, in its broadest sense, is a major. responsibility and professional leadership and management of large numbers of nurses is a very demanding task. Health authorities also provide schools of nursing, indeed often several different schools within the same area. There is also a need for substantial nursing input to the planning of future developments. The inspection and registration of nursing homes is a responsibility of health authorities under the Nursing Homes Act 1975 and this is usually exercised by the area medical officer and area nursing officer, or by their senior subordinate staff. In an area with many such homes this can present quite a few problems.

The treasurer

Financial advice is provided by the treasurer who advises the authority on the financial implications of policy issues and guides his colleagues on the mangement team in the allocation of money and management of financial affairs. A financial service to the family practitioner committee is provided by the area treasurer in England and Wales. The treasurer is also responsible for the basic functions of salaries and wages, accounts, internal audit and management accountancy. He keeps all the necessary records and provides financial information and advice to the authority and fellow officers on a routine basis in some instances and also for *ad hoc* purposes if there is a particular problem under discussion. In Northern Ireland there is no treasurer in the area executive team.

The works officer

Having regard to the large stock of buildings in the health service, the building and engineering function is extremely important. In the English regions the regional works officer is a member of the regional team of officers and not only participates in the planning process but is also responsible for the execution of a substantial part of the capital programme and for architectural, engineering and surveying advice. At area level the works officer carries out small capital schemes and such larger schemes as are delegated. He is also responsible for the maintenance of the buildings and engineering plant and provides professional advice to the authority and to the management team, which he attends when matters crucial to the works function are being discussed.

The dental officer

A similar arrangement regarding team meetings applies to the area dental officer and the area pharmaceutical officer. The area dental officer is the chief adviser to the authority on dental matters and is responsible for planning and managing the salaried dental service, for promoting co-ordination of this service with that provided by general dental practitioners and for monitoring the overall standard of dental care. He advises the local authority on dental matters, being particularly involved in the school dental service. At regional level there is no post of regional dental officer but some regions have made *ad hoc* arrangements to obtain advice on the planning of these services, drawing on the expertise of the area dental officers.

The pharmaceutical officer

The area pharmaceutical officer is responsible for the planning and management of pharmaceutical services and for co-ordinating hospital services with those of chemist contractors. In some cases health authorities have combined to appoint an area pharmaceutical officer who then divides his time between his employing authorities. Sometimes one area also provides a specialised pharmaceutical service, such as quality control or sterile fluids, to the other areas in the region. The planning and monitoring of pharmaceutical services throughout the region is the responsibility of the regional pharmaceutical officer.

All these chief officers have access to the health authority, the right and the duty to report to it and to seek guidance on the services for which they are responsible. Some of the chief officers, those who are members of the management team, will customarily attend all meetings of the authority. Others attend when they consider that matters particularly relevant to their profession are under consideration.

Districts

Any description of health authority administration must take account of the complications produced by the existence of district management, though only a brief reference is made here. Chapter 3 described the arrangements, including the numbers of districts and the different arrangements for team membership and terminology in the four countries, and Chapter 6 will describe some of the implications for management of dividing responsibility between area and district.

The complications were of course recognised by the authors of the 1974 arrangements. While it was seen that there were advantages in large areas for certain services, such as ambulances and supplies, the rationale of the arrangement was coterminosity with local authorities. It was believed that the advantages of this would outweigh the complications of multi-district areas. Experience of the arrangements led many people to believe that the advantages of coterminosity had been exaggerated and the difficulties of management in multi-district areas underestimated, though experience varied and not everyone agreed with this assessment. In England several multi-district areas were with the agreement of the Secretary of State — though not without local controversy — converted to single-district areas. These rearrangements retained coterminosity; what was sacrificed was the concept of the district as the population served by a single district general hospital.

As was pointed out in Chapter 3, the principles of NHS reorganisation were the same in all parts of the UK but there was a good deal of variation in detail, and arrangements for districts are an example of this. A particularly important difference is that in England, but not elsewhere, district team officers are not in a line relationship with area team officers, but are directly accountable to the AHA. One consequence of this is that at least some members of district teams attend AHA meetings. Yet although district team members are chief officers it is inevitable that authority chairmen and members should be in less close touch with them than with members of the area team. Two other aspects of the arrangements in England may account for the greater volume of criticism of the 1974 arrangements there. First, the existence of regions led to the argument that three tiers was one too many. Similar arguments did not have such a force elsewhere. Secondly, most English districts were larger than most districts elsewhere and could therefore have made claims to self-sufficiency but for the constraints of coterminosity.

To sum up, the main problems encountered in some of the English multi-district areas were the greater difficulties of communication and difficulties over the relative responsibilities of area and district officers. They were also criticised for entailing greater management costs. One of the arguments used in some cases to justify conversion to single district was an expected savings in these costs.

The Royal Commission endorsed the view that a three tier system was unsatisfactory and following the publication of its report the government took steps, with the Health Services Act 1980 and the 'Patients First' consultative document, towards a reorganisation which will put an end to multi-district arrangements. Ministers in the other countries also made proposals for simplification. More is said about the proposals in Chapter 17.

Liaison and consultation

In planning, developing and managing services for their area, an important duty of health authorities is one of consultation and liaison with matching FPCs, local authorities, community health councils, professional advisory committees and staff organisations. RHAs have comparable duties, sometimes in relation to the same bodies, but the emphasis in what follows is on area authorities and boards.

Family practitioner committees

Something was said earlier in this chapter about the relationship between AHA and FPC. The fact that the AHA appoints 11 members of the FPC should contribute towards good liaison. The AHA provides the FPC with staff and premises and the control of management costs throughout the service applies equally to the FPC.

In its day-to-day activities the family practitioner committee has direct and frequent dealings with the DHSS, Dental Estimates Board, Prescription Pricing Authority and Medical Practices Committee rather than with, or through, the AHA. There are various matters on which joint consultation or action between the AHA and FPC are necessary. They are mainly though not exclusively concerned with the general practitioner services and in relation to these services, as distinct from administrative arrangements, the interest of the Scottish and Northern Ireland boards is similar to that of the English and Welsh authorities. Such matters include the planning of new health centres, the development of primary care teams and the investigation of complaints which involve both the family practitioner and the hospital service. Day-to-day co-operation is necessary in such matters as the transport of specimens from doctors' surgeries to the hospital pathology department. Wherever possible AHAs should make arrangements for general practitioners to have direct access to the hospital diagnostic departments, such as radiography. Close liaison between AHA and the FPC is particularly important in areas where there are GP hospital units. The FPC should be kept fully informed about the general and detailed policies of the AHA for the development of services in the area, and in the exercise of its functions the FPC must have due regard to these policies.

Local authorities

Section 22(1) of the National Health Service Act 1977 provides that, 'In exercising their respective functions health authorities and local authorities shall co-operate with one another in order to secure and advance the health and welfare of the people of England and Wales', and Section 13 of the 1978 Act makes a similar requirement for health boards, local authorities and education authorities in Scotland. In Northern Ireland, where boards are also responsible for social services, the need for co-operation is less pressing.

The interdependence between the services provided by local and health authorities is the reason why health authority boundaries were made largely coterminous with those of local authorities and why, since coterminosity would not in itself ensure close co-operation, other provisions were also made.

The most obvious area for collaboration is between the health and social services but co-ordination of planning and day-to-day work is also important in the fields of environmental health, housing and education. Sometimes, for example, one authority is required to provide services on the other's premises. Thus the education of children in hospital is the responsibility of the local authority, while the health authority goes into schools to provide a health service for children. Some AHAs provide a dental service for pupils in schools for the handicapped by means of a mobile dental surgery which visits the schools regularly and avoids the necessity of transporting children to dental surgeries. An important aspect of collaboration is the provision by the local authority social services department of social workers in hospital and their attachment to primary health care teams in general practitioners' premises or health centres.

The possibilities for co-operation and collaboration are not limited to the services for patients/clients. There is considerable scope for joint purchasing, and there may be collaboration in the joint use of vehicles and the sharing of mortuary facilities. The hospital laundry service is sometimes used to provide a laundry service for the local authority either wholly or to deal with a particular relevant group, such as incontinent people living at home.

Each health authority includes in its membership members of the corresponding local authority, and it is open to local authorities to co-opt health authority members on to committees such as those for environmental health, social services, housing and education.

In England and Wales joint consultative committees formed by members of each authority are a statutory requirement and meet regularly to deal with matters relating to the planning, development and operation of services of common concern.

The normal pattern of these committees is that in metropolitan districts there should be one joint consultative committee for all services, but in non-metropolitan counties the collaboration arrangements are rather more complex with two joint consultative committees being advised: one with the county council to deal with the social service, education and other county functions; and the other with the district councils for environmental health, housing and their other functions. In practice some county authorities have not set up two committees but have managed by having appropriate representatives on one joint consultative committee.

It has been left to the health authorities and their matching local authorities to determine the level of representation on the committee. Although members of the committee are expected to be members of the appointing authority, it is permissible for other persons to be nominated, such as a member of the regional health authority which has no formal machinery for consultation with the local authorities in its region. In any case, area health authorities are expected to keep their regional health authority informed on the activities of the joint consultative committee. Authorities are allowed considerable flexibility in operating their joint collaborative and consultation arrangements. The normal pattern for most areas in metropolitan districts appears to be six to nine members from each authority with support from the appropriate senior officers. In the case of county authorities the size of the committee may tend to be somewhat larger with at least one representative being appointed by each local authority district. In cases when an area health authority provides services for a substantial population outside its boundaries it is normal for a local authority representative from that district to be a member of the joint consultative committee.

Although proceedings at meetings of these committees are expected to be as informal as possible it is clear that some procedural rules are necessary and hence some committees have their own standing orders. The frequency of meetings has also been left to the discretion of the authorities involved and experience has shown that a meeting every quarter or thereabouts is the most usual arrangement. Meetings are not held in public, though arrangements are made for publicity to be given to achievements in joint collaboration arrived at through the committee. In some areas an observer from the local community health council is invited to attend meetings of the joint consultative committee.

The secretarial support for the committee will be provided jointly by the two authorities and sometimes the most convenient way of achieving this is for each authority to provide the secretarial services in alternate committee years. The participating authorities will also have to ensure that the joint consultative committee is supported by the appropriate chief officers. For the AHA these officers are likely to be the area team of officers supplemented from time to time by the area dental officer, area pharmaçeutical officer and area works officer. Some other officers also play an important part, particularly area nurses or area specialists in community medicine with local authority liaison roles.

Officer support from the local authority would be likely to include the heads of administration, finance, social services, education, environmental health, housing and planning.

In addition to these meetings regular contact must be maintained between officers of each authority both on an informal day-to-day basis and in the context of care planning teams.

Clearly it is important for the services provided in some groups of people such as the elderly, mentally or physically handicapped and children to be closely co-ordinated and service developments need to be planned jointly. The joint planning is achieved through multidisciplinary care planning teams whose membership should include representatives of all those professions who are involved in the care of any particular group of patient. Sometimes representatives of the community health council are also invited to participate in these planning teams.

The joint financing arrangements are important in encouraging collaboration and joint planning between the health and local authorities. Under these arrangements money is made available, via area health authorities, for the corresponding local authority to spend on schemes, either capital or revenue, which by agreement of both authorities are of greater benefit to the health service than if the money were to be spent directly by the health authority. Originally the schemes which could be undertaken with joint finance support were restricted to social services schemes. Subsequently, however, the scope of the joint finance schemes has been somewhat broadened and many of the schemes now being undertaken demonstrate great ingenuity on the part of the planners.

Agreement on financial arrangements can nevertheless present problems, since local authorities are understandably cautious about being committed to large sums on a recurring basis when the joint financing support runs out. Other difficulties are in the complexity of the collaboration arrangements between the county area health authorities and their corresponding local authorities, since the health authority will often have to relate to a multiplicity of district councils. Another area of possible difficulty occurs because the catchment area of health authorities for their hospital patients often does not correspond with the geographical boundaries of the local authority and this can create problems for the continuing care of discharged patients, particularly in the area of social services.

The financial aspect of these arrangements is discussed in Chapter 9. It should be noted that regardless of the level of support for both capital and revenue schemes the responsibility for managing the project lies with the local authority.

The types of schemes which can be suppported through joint finance monies are many and varied. The following are examples:

— An alarm system for elderly people living at home.
— A new home for the elderly to benefit the health authority by relieving pressure on geriatric beds.
— An alcoholism counselling and consultation service.
— Hostels for all types of people, such as recently discharged mental patients and severely handicapped young adults.
— Vehicles of many kinds, such as ambulances for the handicapped and vans for the meals on wheels service.
— Day centres for many types of clients, such as the elderly, mentally handicapped, mentally ill and severely handicapped young adults.
— A 'fighting hypothermia' campaign.
— A fork lift truck for an adult training centre.
— A centre for issuing aids and appliances, such as wheelchairs, both to patients discharged from hospital and to handicapped people in the community.
— A luncheon club for elderly and disabled people.
— Teaching accommodation at a children's hospital school.
— All kinds of staff including educational psychologists, night care assistants, chiropody aides, clerical staff, home helps, home wardens, occupational therapists, physiotherapists, drivers and social workers.

The Royal Commission remarked that, 'It is clear from our evidence that relations between health and local authorities range from indifferent to excellent'. After reviewing the evidence and comments received it said:

> There is no doubting the importance of effective collaboration between health and local authority services. While eventually the integration of these services may become possible, there is little in the present administrative arrangements to prevent or even hamper such collaboration, though its success depends on the attitude of the parties to it. If there is determination on both sides to work together, many of the problems . . . could be solved. If, however, authorities or professions are at loggerheads, coterminous boundaries, overlapping membership and joint committees will be ineffective. Post-reorganisation experience shows that effective collaboration requires that those involved should have appropriate training and sufficient authority within their own organisations to carry out the task which is to be performed jointly.

If successful collaboration is possible, there are important differences between the two types of authority which mean that it is rarely easy. The differences in financial arrangements are an example, but more important is the fact that local authorities are responsible for a wide range of services. In their choice of priorities they may not attach as much weight as the health authority would wish to those services most related to health care, and while for those services collaboration with the health authority is important, it is less central to their activities as a whole. Health authorities, it may be said, have greater need of collaboration.

While health authorities are the agents of the Secretary of State, local authorities are elected political bodies, some of them politically opposed to the government of the day. With the advent of territorial responsibilities for health authorities and coterminosity, local authorities have taken a more active interest in health care provision, and some councillors believe that as locally elected representatives they are also the community's spokesmen on health matters. Although unlikely to affect day-to-day collaboration of staff, this greater political interest in the health service may make for difficulties in policy and planning at a time when health authorities sometimes have to take unpopular decisions.

Community health councils

Community health councils and their Scottish and Northern Ireland equivalents, the local health councils and district councils, are discussed in Chapter 16, but must be considered here in connection with their relationships with health authorities.

With very few exceptions, councils are related to health districts, and, again with few exceptions, there is a single council for each district. This is because the district, not the area, is the basic unit for the provision of services and therefore the natural unit for local consumer representation. In multi-district areas, therefore, the main interest of the CHC will be district services and its dealings will be with the district management team rather than the AHA. Even in these areas, however, councils also have important relations with authorities.

In England councils receive their budget from the region, but AHAs generally administer arrangements for accommodation and provide an accounting service including payment of the salaries of staff. Councils are required to publish annual reports and AHAs are required to respond to them. AHAs are also required to hold a formal meeting with each CHC in their area at least once a year. Authorities must also grant reasonable facilities to community health councils to visit health premises, having due regard to the privacy of patients.

In addition to providing basic information about the authority's service, AHAs are expected to respond promptly to requests from councils for other information. AHAs have a duty to consult the CHC on developments of the health service in the council's district, including the establishment of new services and variations such as relocation or termination of existing services. If the community health council agrees with a proposal of an AHA to close a hospital the closure may go ahead, but if the council disagrees and formulates alternative proposals the matter must be referred to the Secretary of State. Discussion with the community health council also forms an essential element in the NHS planning system. As we have already said, CHCs send observers to AHA meetings; they may participate in the discussions, but not vote.

The position of community health councils is based on statute and regulations but apart from that it is clear that if health authorities are to carry out their responsibilities satisfactorily they must have good communications with the public. Close liaison with CHCs, and not only where it is a requirement, is a good means to this, although not all relations with sections of the public will be through the CHC.

Professional advisory committees

The 1977 Act makes provision for the establishment of regional and area advisory committees representative of the various professions and the 1978 Act makes somewhat similar provision for local consultative committees in Scotland. Health authorities need the advice of such bodies to keep them informed of the needs and developments of the various professions, but the professional advisory machinery has been one of the most criticised aspects of the reorganised health service, particularly because of its complexity. The problems are discussed in detail elsewhere in this book, particularly in Chapter 15, and all that needs saying here is that while in some places professional advisory committees work well and are very influential, on the whole both the professions and health authorities have found them disappointing.

Staff consultation

The health service is one of the country's largest employers. A great deal of administrative time and effort by the senior officers of authorities is therefore taken up with personnel management in its broadest sense. As the health service is so labour intensive it is dependent on successful team work by a wide range of staff with a variety of skills. In particular, it is important for staff to be involved at an early stage in the planning of the new services or the curtailment of existing services. The aim of this consultation is to ensure that once a set of proposals has been agreed between management and staff there will be a great degree of commitment from both sides.

In order that effective liaison between management and staff can be achieved joint consultative staff committees have been set up at area and district level and in the English regions. The membership of the committee on the management side is composed of chief officers and sometimes members of the authority while the staff side comprises representatives drawn from the whole range of staff. As the number of staff organisations is so large the staff side membership is appointed through a system of panels representing particular groups of staff, on which all the relevant bodies are represented. These panels may be arranged by discipline, e.g. administrative staff, nursing staff, etc., or by place of employment, e.g. hospital, clinic, health centre. The panels may also raise matters direct with management or can refer them through the joint consultative staff committee. One problem that has arisen is that many of the staff organisations, particularly the professional bodies, are not affiliated to the TUC with the result that in some places some of the unions that are affiliated have refused to take part in the joint consultative process.

Consensus management

One of the key elements in the 1974 reorganisation was consensus management. It was not entirely an innovation, for it had often been practised informally, but it was formalised and built into the structure. The membership of the teams at different levels in the various countries was set out in Chapter 3.

Circular HRC(73)3 gave the Department's guidance on district management teams, and what it said applies equally to other teams: 'The DMT will take decisions jointly on matters which are not exclusively the responsibility of any one of them and which are not provided for in approved plans nor regulated by established policies of the AHA'. They are small multidisciplinary teams charged with managing and co-ordinating the operation of the service and formulating policies and plans for future development.

The team members are officers. Additionally, except in Scotland, district teams (including area teams in single-district areas) have two clinicians — a consultant and a general practitioner. The involvement of clinicians is regarded as very important because of their direct expression of the views of hospital consultant staff and family practitioners and the commitment of the medical profession to management decisions, which it is hoped they will secure. Their presence, however, brings additional complications to consensus management. Unlike the officer members who, as heads of hierarchically organised services, can commit those services to team decisions, the clinicians are representatives of their colleagues and have no authority to commit them. They can only express what they hope is a course of action which most of their colleagues would endorse. They therefore have a difficult task; if they enter fully into team thinking they may cease to be representative of their clinical colleagues but if they reserve their position too often the team may become ineffective. Theirs is a difficult role which needs considerable qualities of statesmanship, not only from the clinical representatives themselves but also from their team colleagues.

Consensus management is an essential part of management in the reorganised health service, and will be more fully discussed in Chapter 6. It is not, of course, the whole of management. While team members share joint accountability to the health authority for the work of the team, officer members are individually responsible as chief officers for particular functional services.

Although, as we have said, team management was not something entirely new in 1974, its systematic adoption in 1974 was. It is not surprising, therefore, that it has provoked a good deal of discussion, and varying judgements of its effectiveness. There has been one well-publicised failure, but Professor M. Kogan in his research study for the Royal Commission reported that 'support for consensus management was wide-ranging, and only a small minority of respondents thought that it could never be successful'. The Royal Commission accepted it, limiting itself to the recommendation that the health departments should give further guidance about the role of members of teams. What it had in mind was that individual team members should have a firm grasp of the distinction between their personal responsibility and those of the team.

Communications and leadership

Clearly there is a very complicated communications network within health authorities. The authority chairman and members, the family practitioner committee, the management teams, the professional advisory committees, trade unions and staff organisations, the local authorities and community health councils, all have important roles to play in the delivery of health care. On any major issue, such as the siting of a new hospital or the closure of an old one, all these component parts of the health service have something to contribute to the debate.

Effective communications are, therefore, absolutely vital. It is primarily the administrator's task to see that the lines of communication are working properly and that advice is sought and obtained from those who have a right to be consulted. Sometimes this right is explicit, as in the case of hospital closures, where there is a specified list of those to be contacted. In most cases, however, the right is implicit and a judgement is required, on commonsense grounds, as to which bodies should be consulted and how this is to be undertaken. This decision is usually influenced by the administrator but is not always his alone and often the management team or the health authority itself will agree on some specific process of consultation. Indeed the whole of the management structure of an authority is involved, from the authority through the team and the chief officers to their subordinate staff. For example, the area nursing officer will take a particular interest in the quality of communication with the area nursing committee and with the nursing professional organisations, such as the Royal College of Nursing. The area medical officer will similarly be closely involved with the area medical committee and the British Medical Association. The list of possibilities is endless and each health authority is better seen as a living organism than as a replica of some standard organisation model. How it functions is subject to some extent to national specifications, which have been summarised briefly in this chapter. Overlying this, however, is a metaphysical mixture of local tradition, geography and individual personalities. The lifeblood of this living organism is communications and proper functioning depends on teamwork of a very high order. But perhaps most of all, to enable this organism to know where it is going, there is a need for leadership. This may come from the chairman, the health authority, the management team or the chief officers, or most probably from some combination of these. This is the paradox of the health service, that its complexity and the diffusion of power makes leadership extremely difficult and, by the same token, absolutely essential.

Further reading

See also the lists for Chapters 3 and 6.

Statutory instruments and circulars

England and Wales

SI73/1286. The NHS (Regional and Area Health Authorities: Membership and Procedure) Regulations 1973

SI79/738. The NHS (Health Authorities: Membership) Regulations 1979

HRC(73)22. Membership and procedure of regional and area health authorities

Scotland

SI74/267(S16). The NHS (Constitution of Health Boards) (Scotland) Order 1974

SI75/197(S16). The NHS (Health Boards: Membership, Procedure and Payment of Subscriptions) Regulations 1975

Official publications

Royal Commission on the National Health Service. *Report* (Cmnd 7615). HMSO 1979

Other publication

Hall, W.E. and Hunt, P.A. *The Authority Member*. National Association of Health Authorities in England and Wales 1979

5
Management at national and regional level

Health care and central government

Because the bulk of health care in the UK is provided and delivered through state financing the central government naturally has an important and powerful role. Within the UK four ministers have overall responsibility for health — the Secretary of State for Social Services in England and the Secretaries of State for Scotland, Wales and Northern Ireland. This responsibility is exercised through the central government health departments — the Department of Health and Social Security in England, the Scottish Home and Health Department, the Welsh Office, and the Northern Ireland Department of Health and Social Services. (In Northern Ireland responsibility for health services and personal social services rests with the Department of Health and Social Services which exercises its functions under the direction and control of the Secretary of State for Northern Ireland. References to the Secretary of State for Northern Ireland throughout this chapter should be read in this context.)

The statutory provisions governing the powers and duties of the Secretaries of State in relation to the NHS are the National Health Service Act 1977 in respect of England and Wales and the National Health Service (Scotland) Act 1978 for Scotland which consolidate previous NHS legislation. In Northern Ireland the relevant statutes are the Health and Personal Social Services (Northern Ireland) Order 1972 and the Northern Ireland Act 1974.

The structure of the NHS in all four countries is designed to enable comprehensive health services to be planned, organised and run in a manner consistent both with the Secretaries of State's accountability to Parliament and with the need for the local management of the services. Apart from a small range of centrally provided services, the powers and duties of the Secretaries of State in relation to the service are exercised on their behalf by health authorities; health authorities are accountable to the Secretaries of State for the proper and efficient administration of the services they provide.

Not all health care functions of the central health departments, however, come within the scope of the National Health Service Acts. Other statutory provisions apply to activities which contribute directly or indirectly to health. One example is the Medicines Act 1968, the main purpose of which is to ensure the quality, safety and efficiency of medicines supplied to the public.

The central departments also advise on the health implications of various government activities such as the toxicological and nutritional aspects of food policy. Much of these responsibilities centre on the special position of the chief medical officer as adviser to other departments and to government on health matters generally. Finally the DHSS has a major role in international health matters, in the promotion of health industries and health exports.

The Secretaries of State

The National Health Service Act 1977 lays a duty on the Secretary of State to 'promote the establishment in England and Wales of a comprehensive health service designed to secure improvement in the physical and mental health of the people of England and Wales and the prevention, diagnosis and treatment of illness, and for that purpose to provide or secure the effective provision of services'. The Act states that the services so provided shall be free of charge except where it expressly provides for the making and recovery of charges. There are similar provisions for Scotland and Northern Ireland.

The Secretaries of State's responsibilities are for providing or securing the provision of services and facilities, not for providing diagnosis and treatment. At the inception of the NHS, the government made clear that its intention was to provide a framework within which the health professions could provide treatment and care for patients according to their own independent professional judgement of the patient's needs. This independence and clinical freedom remains a central feature of the organisation and management of health services. For the family practitioner services the duty is to 'make arrangements' with practitioners who provide services as independent contractors.

The Secretaries of State, as well as having wide general powers, also have specific duties to provide certain services: these include hospital and other accommodation; medical, dental, nursing and ambulance services; facilities for the care of expectant and nursing mothers and young children; facilities for the prevention of illness; other facilities required for the diagnosis or treatment of illness; and facilities for family planning. The duty to provide these services is qualified by the phrase 'to such extent as he considers necessary to meet all reasonable requirements'.

Most of the powers and duties of the Secretaries of State are exercised on their behalf by health authorities. In England the Secretary of State directs regional and area health authorities to perform his functions through the NHS Functions Regulations 1974. Nevertheless the Secretary of State retains some important powers and places some restrictions upon the freedom of health authorities in the exercise of their delegated functions. For example under the 1977 Act (Part III of Schedule 5) each health authority is free to decide whom it will employ but under the NHS Remuneration Regulations 1974 no authority may pay more or less than rates of pay agreed by national negotiating machinery and applied by direction of the Secretary of State.

Moreover the Secretary of State has the power to give directions to health authorities with respect to the exercise of any functions exercisable by regional and area health authorities and it is the duty of those authorities to comply with any such direction. (Regional health authorities in England also have power to issue directions to area health authorities.)

Under Section 6 of the Health Services Act 1980 health authorities are required to ensure that their annual expenditure does not exceed the amounts allotted to them (plus any other income) and the Secretary of State has power to give them directions which he may consider necessary to this end.

Under Section 84 of the NHS Act 1977 the Secretary of State in England and Wales has power to order an inquiry into any matter arising under the NHS Acts. This power is used sparingly and is normally reserved for serious incidents or shortcomings which give rise to national concern. Unlike inquiries set up by health authorities, statutory inquiries under Section 84 have power to summon witnesses and examine them on oath and the Secretary of State has powers to order costs. There are similar powers in Scotland and Northern Ireland.

Under Section 85 of the NHS Act the Secretary of State has power after inquiry to declare a health service body in default if it has failed to carry out any of its statutory functions or failed to comply with any regulations or directions relating to those functions. When such a body is declared in default the members of the body concerned vacate office immediately and the Secretary of State may appoint new members in their place and make arrangements for the carrying out of the functions by some other body or person in the meantime. The Secretary of State also has powers under Section 86 to make special arrangements to deal with emergency situations.

In England the Secretary of State appoints the chairmen and all the members of regional health authorities and the chairmen of area health authorities. So far as members of RHAs are concerned he is required to consult with a number of organisations including local authorities in the region, the main health professions and workers' organisations and any university in the region with a medical or dental teaching school. Members are, however, appointed as individuals for their personal qualities and are not representatives. There is no statutory requirement to consult on the appointment of chairmen of either regional or area authorities.

In Wales, the Secretary of State appoints the chairmen and those members of health authorities not appointed directly by the local authorities. He also appoints the members of the Welsh Health Technical Services Organisation.

In Scotland the Secretary of State appoints the chairmen and members of the 15 health boards.

In Northern Ireland the responsibility rests statutorily on the Department but in practice all appointments are approved by the responsible Minister and in the case of chairmen by the Secretary of State.

The accounting officers

The national health service is funded by votes approved by Parliament under the annual Appropriation Act. In relation to the votes for health and personal social services the permanent secretaries of the appropriate central department are the accounting officers personally accountable to Parliament and they can personally be surcharged for the misapplication of funds. The accounting officer in England is the first permanent secretary at the DHSS.

Parliament has long laid it down as a principle that for each parliamentary vote, one specified individual shall be personally responsible and that responsibility cannot be delegated. The effect of this principle on the NHS and the central department is considerable. The parliamentary 'watchdog' over this principle is the Committee of Public Accounts and its agent, the comptroller and auditor-general. Accounting officers have to appear personally before this committee to account for their vote and for any irregularities, or apparent misuse of funds or any wastefulness recorded in the report of the comptroller and auditor-general. Consequently much detailed work has to be undertaken to brief the permanent secretary for his appearances before the Committee of Public Accounts. In 1979 the House of Commons established the Select Committee on Social Services, as part of the arrangements to replace the Estimates Committee and its sub-committees.

Suggestions have been made from time to time (notably by RHA chairmen in 1976) that the NHS vote might be sub-divided into (say) 14 regional votes — one for each of the English regions — so that more personal accountability could be devolved. Alternatively or as an interim measure it was suggested that regional chairmen should accompany the permanent secretary to answer for the performance of their own region if this is called in question. So far nothing has come of either suggestion. The Royal Commission on the NHS recommended that formal responsibility, including accountability to Parliament, for the delivering of services should be transferred to RHAs, but the government rejected the idea. However, in 1981 for the first time two RHA chairmen, accompanied by two officers, were examined for the first time by the Public Accounts Committee, and the committee expects to continue the practice.

The central departments

Although the statutory responsibilities for the NHS and the wider health responsibilities of the government rest ultimately upon the Secretaries of State, most of the functions of the Secretaries of State are exercised on their behalf by the central departments. As the situation varies in detail each country is dealt with separately.

As we have seen, the NHS in the four countries of the UK is based on the same principles and, despite considerable differences in detail, structures and management arrangements are on the same lines. Since each Secretary of State and health department is responsible for only one country, co-ordination is required at the UK level to maintain this unity with diversity. Politically it is achieved by the fact that all four Secretaries of State are members of the cabinet, committed to the same government policies. A further factor making for consistency is that all the health departments like other government departments are subject to the same Treasury oversight and conduct their business in much the same way. In addition the departments, particularly those in Great Britain, maintain close liaison, and make use of each other's work. Because it is by far the largest, the DHSS plays the preponderant part in this co-ordination. As an example, it is the DHSS which provides the management side staffing for the Whitley Councils serving the whole of Great Britain.

England

The DHSS was created in 1968 by the merger of the Ministry of Health and Ministry of Social Security; these two major spheres of activity are still largely separated organisationally in the DHSS although linked at the top and by some common administrative services.

The social security side of the Department is far and away the larger in terms of staff employed: of the total staff of 97,000 about 87,000 are engaged in the complex and wide ranging systems for collecting and recording contributions and awarding and delivering benefits. About 15,000 are employed in the central offices at Newcastle upon Tyne and North Fylde and the remainder are scattered over regional and local offices throughout Great Britain. All these staff are civil servants employed directly by the Crown. The social security functions also cover Wales and Scotland, but not Northern Ireland which has its own arrangements.

The health and personal social services side of the Department (HPSS) is responsible for government functions relating to the national health service, general health matters and personal social services. The total staff engaged on these functions is about 9,300, of whom 3,160 are engaged in the direct provision of services in the special hospitals and artificial limb and appliance centres and the remainder in central administration. Again, these staff are civil servants employed directly by the Crown.

The Department's task in the HPSS sector is different in important respects from that in the social security field. As with social security the Secretary of State, and therefore the Department, has a wide range of statutory responsibilities and duties; but in the HPSS sector these have to be discharged through a large number of authorities and bodies, which are linked to the Department by statute, regulations, financial arrangements, or in other less formal ways. In general the HPSS sector is less concerned with implementing policies directly and much more concerned to ensure that external authorities deliver health and social care on the basis of Departmental guidelines relating to policy and management, with which this sector is concerned.

Personal social services (PSS) in England are administered by 108 local authorities who are answerable to their electorates for the quantity and quality of the services provided. They have however, under statute, to act under the 'general guidance' of the Secretary of State although the latter has no general powers of direction and little by way of formal sanctions (short of default powers). The main funding mechanism, the rate support grant, does not provide the Department with direct financial control. The Department's relationship with local authorities for PSS is therefore similar to that of other departments such as Environment and Education and Science in respect of their relationships with local authorities. The Department's role reflects an amalgam of duties arising from a number of statutes. It includes responsibilities for negotiating, within government, revenue and capital funds; and for co-operation with voluntary associations. Because of its limited power, the Department must rely primarily on consultation for disseminating national priorities and policies. The close rapport needed with local authority social services depends for its effectiveness on the experience of the professional staff of the Department; this capacity is provided by the Department's Social Work Service (SWS), whose regional offices provide a two-way channel of information and guidance.

The Secretary of State has much more direct responsibility for the NHS. The health authorities are accountable to the Secretary of State. There are also several central executive agencies or bodies to which reference is made later and 12 boards of governors each of which manages a London specialist postgraduate teaching hospital.

Wales

In Wales the Welsh Office through its Health and Social Work Department is responsible for health; the Secretary of State for Wales is the responsible Minister. There are eight area health authorities. The Welsh Health Technical Services Organisation, directly accountable to the Secretary of State, provides certain central services. There is a family practitioner committee for each area, as in England.

Scotland

The central department responsible for health in Scotland is the Scottish Home and Health Department, one of five departments forming the Scottish Office under the Secretary of State for Scotland. The Scottish Home and Health Department is responsible, in addition to the NHS and miscellaneous health functions, for police and fire services, civil law and criminal justice and prisons.

Below the Secretary of State are the 15 health boards appointed by him, and a Common Services Agency provides a range of central services.

Northern Ireland

The Department of Health and Social Services is the central government department in Northern Ireland. Accountability lies through the Secretary of State for Northern Ireland to the Parliament of the United Kingdom. Article 4 of the Health and Personal Social Services (Northern Ireland) Order 1972 imposes upon the Department the duty of providing, or securing the provision, of integrated health services and of providing or securing the provision of personal social services. The Department is required to discharge its duties so as to secure the effective co-ordination of health and personal social services. There are four health and social services boards.

The relationship of the central departments to the NHS

The relationship of central departments with health authorities is in many respects unique. The NHS is a centrally financed service for which Secretaries of State have wide statutory duties and responsibilities for which they are accountable to Parliament. However this service is provided to each person individually by a wide range of professionals exercising independent clinical judgement. Health care is such that a large degree of delegation is needed to the health authorities set up by statute. This involves the professional bodies and individual practitioners in policy making, determination of priorities and management generally at the national level as well as at the regional and operational levels.

In practice the Departments have a number of different roles to perform in relation to the NHS: they are both a department of state and a national tier of the NHS; they relate both to the management structure of the NHS and to a wide range of professional bodies and individuals. Their organisation needs to reflect the complex organisational, contractual and personal relationships which exist, and to be responsive to changing political, economic and social pressures.

Despite, however, the different nature of the Department's functions in relation to personal social services (except in Northern Ireland), to the NHS and to wider health responsibilities, all these functions are closely interrelated. In broad terms the major tasks of the Departments are to formulate policies in relation to the general health and welfare of the nation: to assess needs, to balance needs with resources and to determine priorities. These tasks are directed to the same groups of clients — for example children or the mentally ill — and it is essential to look at the total health and welfare needs of each client group.

More specifically the main tasks of the Departments are

— to assist the Secretaries of State in meeting their responsibility to Parliament

and in securing an adequate share of public expenditure for the NHS;
- to advise on the overall shape and size of national policies on health matters and on the allocation of resources, approved by government for the health services;
- to allocate capital and revenue resources, and joint finance, to health authorities and to prevent maldistribution of scarce medical manpower;
- to set objectives for the service, by formulating policies and declaring priorities for the use of resources and the provision of services;
- to oversee the total working of the NHS and to satisfy themselves that health authorities are carrying out their functions effectively — in terms of financial rectitude, national policy objectives, and the quality of health care provision;
- to provide centrally some services which, by statute or because it proves economic, should be provided by the central departments;
- to ensure that national machinery exists, within a system of Whitley Councils, to negotiate the pay and conditions of service for NHS staff; and
- to provide professional advice and support to the NHS not only on medical and nursing matters but on aspects such as the design and maintenance of buildings, supplies and computers.

In translating these crucial central tasks in terms of the NHS the Departments not only issue general guidance based on the policies determined by the Secretaries of State and the government, but also allocate funds, monitor the use of those funds and are accountable for them to Parliament. The monitoring role of the Departments, supporting as they do the personal accountability of the Secretaries of State and the accounting officers to Parliament, has substantial implications for the role and organisation of the Departments and their relationships with the health authorities.

Three chairmen's report

The relationship of the Department of Health and Social Security to the English health authorities came in for particular scrutiny in the period 1975-8. A series of studies was undertaken by the Department and regional health authority chairmen into the relationships between the Department and the NHS, and more particularly in relation to regional health authorities.

The series of studies began at the end of 1975 when the then Minister of State (Health), Dr David Owen, invited regional chairmen to examine the functions of the Department in its relationship with RHAs and to recommend whether there should be a transfer or reduction of departmental functions. The review was carried out by three of the regional health authority chairmen and their report *(Regional Chairmen's enquiry into the working of the DHSS in relation to Regional Health Authorities* known as The Three Chairmen's Report) was presented to the Secretary of State, David Ennals, in May 1976. The report made a large number of recommendations for the clarification of the Department's functions in relation to the NHS, for the devolution of functions to health authorities and for the reorganisation of that part of the DHSS dealing with health and personal social services.

The organisation of the Department as it stood in 1976 was largely determined as a result of a study in 1972 which was carried out by a team which included outside management consultants working under a steering committee with members from the Civil Service Department, the NHS and local authorities as well as the Department itself. This study had recommended that the administrative element of the HPSS sector of the Department should be reorganised into three main groups — one dealing with 'NHS Personnel' matters, another a 'Services Development Group' concerned with policy formulation, and the third a 'Regional Group' concerned with the Department's relationships with the NHS and with other matters such as supply. A primary object of this 1972 reorganisation was to strengthen the geographical element in the department and links with the new health authorities about to be brought into operation by the 1974 reorganisation of the NHS.

In their 1976 report the RHA chairmen criticised the way this organisation worked and especially its complexity. They argued that the structure of the Department had become over-complicated partly because of the centralising tendencies of successive governments and partly because of the confusion over the years between its executive and its advisory responsibilities. Moreover the complication of functions unconnected with the NHS had made the lines of responsibility even more diffuse. The Department had in consequence grown steadily in size to the detriment of its effectiveness, ability to make decisions and capacity to manage the service as it should. This had resulted in considerable duplication of effort between the Department and regions with consequent duplications of staff and hence of cost.

To remedy these deficiencies the Three Chairmen's Report recommended that there should be a separate grouping of staff concerned with the NHS and personal social services leaving other separate groupings for all the advisory responsibilities and for executive functions not directly concerned with the health and personal social services. The report particularly criticised the failure of the Department to link policy formulation with the availability of resources and argued that this failure stemmed from the separation of policy making in the Services Development Group from implementation and relationships with the NHS in the Regional Group. It therefore recommended that the Department should be structured to bring together the essential functions of determining policy, allocating resources, setting objectives and monitoring performance. It proposed a much smaller policy-making and operational 'spine', consisting of a central office which would be the main management organisation of the Department.

The report also proposed a drastic curtailment of the work of the policy-making branches in the Services Development Group with a substantially greater involvement of the NHS itself in the formulation of major departmental policy. Much work within the Services Development Group, it was argued, was abortive, many activities never came to fruition because of lack of resources, while others, although desirable, were of low priority; there appeared to be a very limited mechanism for authorising work on new projects or for cutting off work which had little or no prospect of being translated into practical activity. The report recommended a reduction of the staff involved in policy making to match a much smaller number of attainable projects, the establishment of a strict mechanism for authorising, monitoring and cutting off projects in the light of changing circumstances and a leaner Regional Liaison Division to transmit these policies to regions and to receive back their reactions.

Finally the report suggested as one of its major recommendations that those services provided centrally for the NHS by the Department because it was considered economic and prudent to do so ('agency services') should be separated from the central stream of the Department and managed by consortia, composed of users (the health authorities), the users being required to pay for the services used. The role of the Department would be to organise and supervise these agency services. It was crucial to this recommendation that the health authorities should be involved in the policy and operation of the services concerned.

These then were the major policy recommendations put forward by the RHA chairmen in 1976. They also made a number of detailed recommendations about the devolution of functions from the Department to health authorities mainly in relation to building, personnel, supplies, research and development work. One particularly important recommendation led to the establishment of the NHS Supply Council referred to in Chapter 11.

Joint steering group of the DHSS/NHS

The Three Chairmen's Report was published in July 1976. In his foreword the Secretary of State announced that a more detailed study was to be carried out within the Department by a joint team from the Department and regional health authorities. This study would take account of the other responsibilities of the Department which had not come within the scope of the chairmen's review. A joint steering group, chaired by the permanent secretary and including the three chairmen who had written the report, was set up to supervise this new study.

This new study had two major tasks: first to look at the detailed recommendations about the devolution of functions to health authorities and the proposals about agency services; secondly to consider the major organisational changes proposed. So far as the first task was concerned some of the recommendations were accepted wholly or in part and subsequently implemented; others, for a variety of reasons, did not find favour.

On the major organisational issues the steering group made proposals for a new structure for HPSS which more fully reflected the Department's top management role for the NHS as well as its other duties. These proposals, although different in detail from the RHA chairmen's suggestions, largely endorsed their proposals in that it was proposed that the main policy and operational responsibilities for the NHS and PSS were to be brought together in one group, while other health matters and functions, such as supplies, were placed in another group. The NHS Personnel Group was to be largely unaltered.

However, another development prevented the implementation of these proposals. Early in the work of the joint steering group a 'management review' of the DHSS was proposed. The management review of the DHSS was one of a series of reviews of major government departments, the primary purpose of which was to help the top management of the Department to improve the effectiveness and efficiency of its organisation and management, including the planning and control of its resources.

The management review of DHSS 1976-8

Whereas the joint steering group which looked at the RHA Chairmen's Report had consisted of departmental and NHS representatives, the management review of the DHSS carried out between 1976 and 1978 was conducted by a steering committee which included not only members of the Department but also members from another Department and the Civil Service Department and an outside businessman. One of the three chairmen who conducted the RHA chairmen's study was also a member. The management review was concerned with the Department as a whole, both its health and personal social services duties, its responsibilities for social security and for the development of government health and social policy more generally.

The management review analysed in detail the Department's complex and interrelated responsibilities for personal social services, the NHS and the health of the nation more generally. Although they noted weaknesses in the way the 1972 reorganisation was working and made some proposals for remedying these weaknesses, they came down firmly in favour of maintaining the 1972 structure. Although they recognised that the proposals put forward by the joint steering group would simplify and strengthen the Department's oversight of NHS planning and might help on more general health matters, they noted that the suggested structure would break up the Services Development Group and might weaken the Department's handling of HPSS policy as a whole, which went beyond the NHS and the PSS. Moreover they believed that the combination of policy work with operational duties for the NHS and PSS might cause an imbalance in the work-load of senior officials, particularly at deputy secretary level.

Pointing out recent experience of the high cost of making major changes, the review concluded 'that there was both *insufficient* evidence to show that the gains from structural change would justify the cost and *sufficient* evidence to show that there was more which could be effectively done to improve the organisation as it is'. This conclusion was accepted by the government and consequently no radical structural changes were made. While regional chairmen were not happy about the rejection of their recommendations about major organisational changes, they recognised that in the end it was for the Department to decide on the organisation it needed to carry out its duties and there the matter rested.

One recommendation however emerged from the review which recognised the need for closer co-ordination of the work of the HPSS side of the DHSS below permanent secretary level. The review concluded that 'there is a need for an effective top-level body to bring together HPSS strategy as a whole' and suggested the establishment of an 'HPSS Strategy Committee' chaired by the permanent secretary whose terms of reference generally should be to assist in formulating new policy and keeping existing policy under review in the field of health and personal social services. This committee was seen as a top level advisory body to assist permanent secretaries in preparation of advice to ministers on major strategic issues in the HPSS sector. The recommendation was accepted and the committee was set up in 1978, together with a parallel 'Social Security Strategy Committee'. A multi-professional Policy Planning Unit (PPU) was also set up in support of the HPSS Strategy Committee.

Organisation and staffing of central departments

Department of Health and Social Security (England)

The organisation of the DHSS headquarters is illustrated in Figure 1.

The work of the Department in relation to health and personal social services is divided into five administrative groups which provide the basis for the formal

Figure 1. Organisation of Department of Health and Social Security (Headquarters)

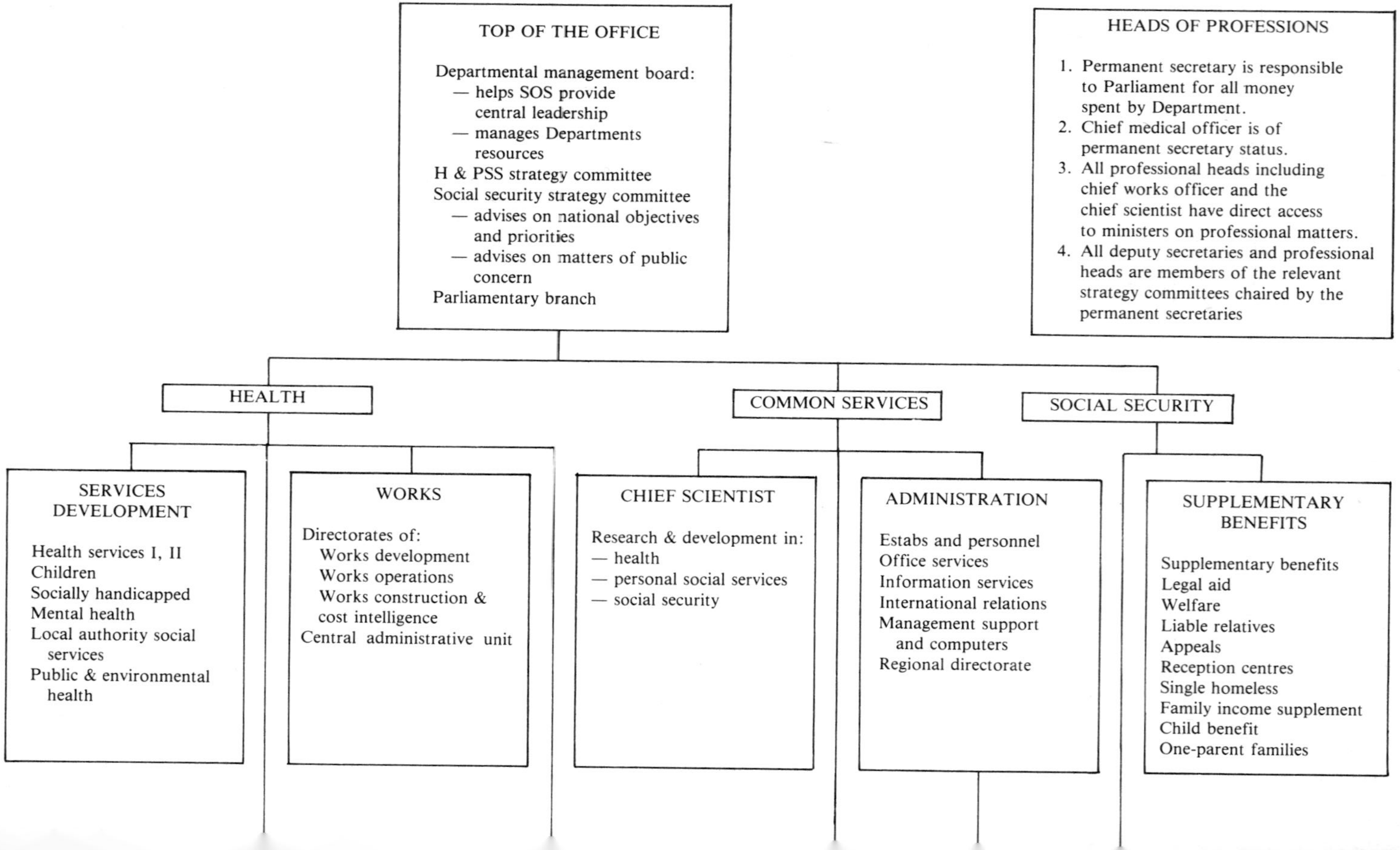

TOP OF THE OFFICE

Departmental management board:
— helps SOS provide central leadership
— manages Departments resources
H & PSS strategy committee
Social security strategy committee
— advises on national objectives and priorities
— advises on matters of public concern
Parliamentary branch

HEADS OF PROFESSIONS

1. Permanent secretary is responsible to Parliament for all money spent by Department.
2. Chief medical officer is of permanent secretary status.
3. All professional heads including chief works officer and the chief scientist have direct access to ministers on professional matters.
4. All deputy secretaries and professional heads are members of the relevant strategy committees chaired by the permanent secretaries

HEALTH

SERVICES DEVELOPMENT

Health services I, II
Children
Socially handicapped
Mental health
Local authority social services
Public & environmental health

WORKS

Directorates of:
Works development
Works operations
Works construction & cost intelligence
Central administrative unit

COMMON SERVICES

CHIEF SCIENTIST

Research & development in:
— health
— personal social services
— social security

ADMINISTRATION

Estabs and personnel
Office services
Information services
International relations
Management support and computers
Regional directorate

SOCIAL SECURITY

SUPPLEMENTARY BENEFITS

Supplementary benefits
Legal aid
Welfare
Liable relatives
Appeals
Reception centres
Single homeless
Family income supplement
Child benefit
One-parent families

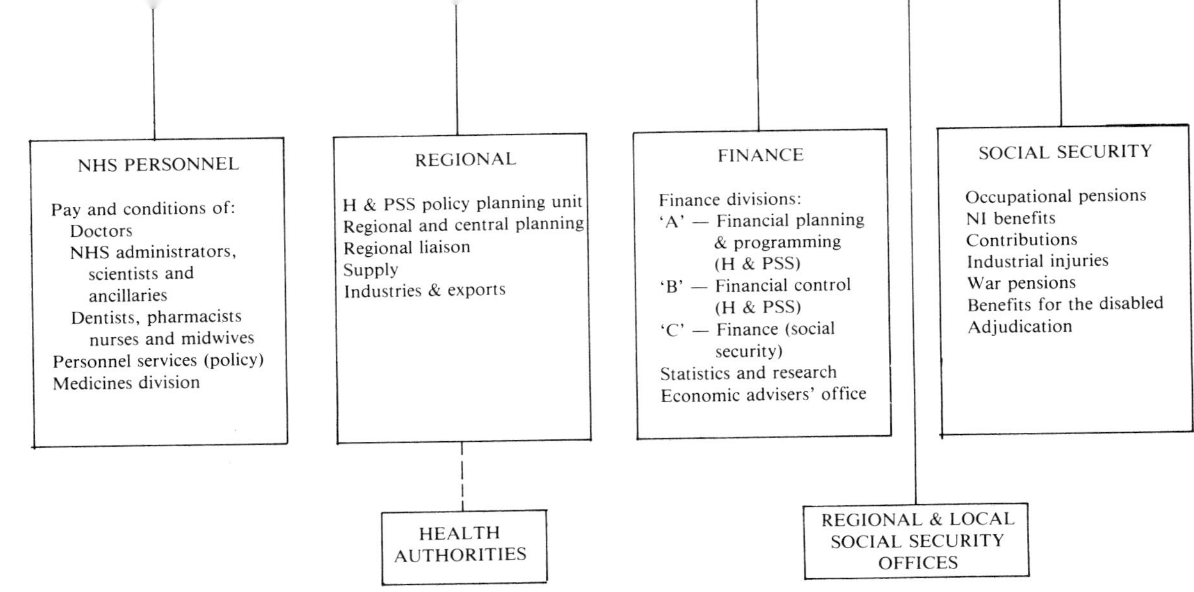

NHS PERSONNEL
Pay and conditions of:
Doctors
NHS administrators, scientists and ancillaries
Dentists, pharmacists nurses and midwives
Personnel services (policy)
Medicines division
REGIONAL
H & PSS policy planning unit
Regional and central planning
Regional liaison
Supply
Industries & exports
HEALTH AUTHORITIES
FINANCE
Finance divisions:
'A' — Financial planning & programming (H & PSS)
'B' — Financial control (H & PSS)
'C' — Finance (social security)
Statistics and research
Economic advisers' office
SOCIAL SECURITY
Occupational pensions
NI benefits
Contributions
Industrial injuries
War pensions
Benefits for the disabled
Adjudication
REGIONAL & LOCAL SOCIAL SECURITY OFFICES

structure of the Department. Table 1 gives the groups, the number of administrative staff working within them involved in health and personal social service work, the annual salary costs as at 31 March 1976 and the total costs, i.e. the salary costs plus additions to cover common services and on-costs.

Table 1

	Administrative staff	*Salary cost*	*Total costs*
Regional Group	485	£2.450m.	£3.792m.
Services Development Group	302	£1.682m.	£2.604m.
Personnel Group	446	£2.193m.	£3.395m.
Finance Group	398	£1,860m.	£2.879m.
Support Services (part of the Administration Group)	300	£1.355m.	£2.097m.
TOTAL	1,931	£9.540m.	£14.767m.

(Source: *Three Chairmen's Report,* paragraph 37)

These administrative groups are directly concerned with health and personal social services. They are supported by other branches of the Department responsible for services common to both health and social security.

In addition there are other divisions or branches of the Department whose functions are concerned with health but not directly with the NHS; these include Industries and Export Division, International Relations Division, Medicines Division, Public and Environmental Health and the Mental Health Review Tribunals. The five administrative groups are also supported by a wide range of professional officers — doctors, nurses, dentists, professional works staff and others, and these professional divisions have some administrative and support services.

Table 2 shows the total staff and annual costs of the DHSS in 1976 in relation to health and personal social services.

Table 2

	Staff	*Salary cost*	*Total costs*
Administrative Groups — HPSS	1,931	£9.540m.	£14.767m.
Common Services — proportion on HPSS	910	£2.911m.	£ 4.506m.
Health (non-NHS divisions/branches)	212	£1.020m.	£ 1.579m.
Professional Divisions	998	£7.981m.	£12.354m.
Administrative & Support Services to Professional Divisions	820	£2.500m.	£ 3.870m.
TOTAL	4,871	£23.952m.	£37.076m.

(Source: *Three Chairmen's Report,* paragraph 42)

Although the five administrative groups, together with the professional support, provide the basis for the formal structure of the Department it has to be realised that the Department is a dynamic organisation. Few, if any, major problems can be handled in isolation by particular groups. In the policy field the NHS, PSS and wider health policies have to be considered together; planning and monitoring of the implementation of policies for the NHS have to be linked to the policies for personal social services; policies and priorities have to be linked with the total resources available. Co-ordination of the work of several different groups has to be achieved below permanent secretary level while still recognising that ultimate responsibilty under Ministers can only come together at that level. A substantial proportion of the Department's business is conducted by the interplay of multiprofessional, multidivisional working groups or working parties or meetings concerned with particular subjects. The informal relationships are therefore just as important as the formal structure in the actual operational activities of the Department.

The paragraphs which follow briefly describe the work and organisation of the five administrative groups and the three main professional divisions — medical, nursing and works. They conclude with a brief outline of the 'Top of the Office' and the 'Private Offices' which support ministers and the permanent secretaries.

Regional Group

The Regional Group guides health and local authorities on national objectives and priorities and supports and monitors the planning and running of health services. The NHS planning process is one of the main means of achieving an effective balance between local planning and operational responsibilities and central strategic direction and control. The DHSS must be able to relate the totality of the Department's policies and priorities to the particular circumstances of individual regions; conversely in deciding national policies and priorities the Department must take account of their operational feasibility in the field. Through the Regional Liaison Division, the Group is responsible for being aware of policy changes, or impending changes (except in the personnel field) and for transmitting and interpreting those changes to the NHS. It is also concerned with organisational and management issues within the NHS.

This Division fulfils the principal liaison functions with the NHS and has a duty to keep the rest of the DHSS informed about NHS conditions and problems.

Through the Regional and Central Planning Division, the Group allocates resources to health authorities and is responsible for the operation of the NHS planning process. The Division's task is therefore to bring together policy aspirations and resource constraints and translate them into achievable policies.

Of the other two Divisions within the Group one offers specialist services in supplies and the other (Industries and Exports Division) is responsible for promoting and co-ordinating export work of other divisions and for the general promotion of the health supplies industries of the UK.

The Supply Division has four main branches. The Hospital Services and Supply Branch is concerned with the general procurement of supplies in the NHS. For some commodities the Supply Division itself is the contracting party and is responsible for storing and issuing of goods. For others it negotiates call-off contracts, but with orders placed directly by health authorities. In others the health authorities place the contracts and the Supply Division is concerned with general oversight and advice on 'best buys'. These functions were the subject of review by the Joint NHS/DHSS Working Group under Brian Salmon which led to the establishment of the NHS Supply Council, with members drawn mainly from the NHS.

The Scientific and Technical Branch is mainly concerned with the professional management and evaluation of projects on development of equipment and new techniques. The Disablement Services Branch is concerned with the provision of various aids for the disabled. Artificial Limb and Appliance Centres which are run by the Department come under this branch. The Policy and Prices Branch is responsible for price negotiations with the pharmaceutical industry and others for drugs, etc.

The Group has by design the greatest contact with health authorities. At the same time, this task demands considerable contacts with the rest of DHSS, both to explain conditions in the field and to discern policy shifts which might affect health authorities.

Services Development Group

The Services Development Group is concerned with the creation of policies for specific services or clients. Its primary objective is to help the Secretary of State to decide national objectives, priorities, and standards for the health and social services. In particular, the Group advises on the nature and scale of the services; develops policies needed to improve health services; promotes local authority social services; and identifies and develops plans to meet the needs of selected client groups such as, for example, the elderly. The Group offers support — by encouragement or interpretation — both to health and local authorities, and to the Regional Group in the implementation of specific policies. The Group, through the Planning Policy Unit, is responsible for the Departmental planning process and NHS planning system, though responsibility for the actual operation of the latter falls to the Regional Group, the review of health information and the co-ordination of consideration of the report of the Royal Commission on the NHS.

The Group's relationships are very largely with other government departments, the local authority associations, and Groups within DHSS. There is some contact with NHS field authorities, mainly through a network of formal and informal contacts with individual specialists over particular topics. The main formal link with the health authorities is through the Regional Group.

Personnel Group

The Group deals with all matters concerning personnel employed in the NHS and with the administration of the family practitioner services. A primary objective of the Group is to service the Whitley machinery for determining the pay and conditions of service for all NHS personnel. It is also concerned to help the NHS recruit, train, retain and employ wisely sufficient staff of the required calibre and experience. The Group administers the National Health Superannuation Scheme. It is in addition responsible for the administration of the Medicines Acts, and related pharmaceutical work.

The Group has a wide range of relationships outside the Department. Through the Whitley Council machinery it has extensive contacts with all those staff organisations and trade unions concerned with pay and conditions of service of NHS staff. It also deals with regulatory bodies such as the General Medical

Council and the General Nursing Council. It has detailed contact with health authorities on the interpretation and variation of Whitley Council agreements; and, particularly through the personnel discipline, offers advice to the service on a whole range of personnel functions.

Within the Department there is considerable contact with the Finance Group on the financial implications of pay negotiations in progress or contemplated. There is also contact with the Regional Group on the effect upon the service of Whitley negotiations, particularly where national negotiations or difficulties in reaching agreement result in industrial action.

Finance Group

The Finance Group is responsible for broad financial planning for the Department, for operational control methods, and for advice to other Groups on the financial implications of policy, existing or proposed.

One of the two Divisions concerned with the health service (FDA) has a particular responsibility for negotiations with central government on the total financial resources to be made available to the Department, and the primary allocation of those total resources between social security, health, and the personal social services. It also advises the Personnel Group on the financial implication of impending wage settlements.

The other Division with health service responsibilities (FDB) prepares health service accounts for presentation to Parliament; devises accounting and reporting systems; and conducts the NHS Audit. This Division also supports the Regional and Central Planning Division (RCP) in the capital and revenue allocation to health authorities. RCP, with its responsibility for the NHS planning process and its knowledge of individual regional developments, settles the details of revenue and capital allocations. FDB is responsible for the vote and the cash limits and must ensure that health authorities do not in aggregate exceed the cash limits at the end of the year. However RCP is responsible for the initial monitoring of individual regions' cash limits. Both Divisions provide financial liaison with other Groups, and comment on the financial implications of proposed policies, particularly those emerging within the Services Development Group.

The major relationships of the Group are with central government, and within the Department. The notable exception to this lies through the NHS audit, dealt with in more detail in Chapter 9.

Administration Group (including Central Support Services)

The Administration Group supports the Top of the Office in personnel, organisation and efficiency matters, and in negotiations with the Civil Service Department and Treasury on these topics. It provides advice to the rest of the Department on organisation staffing, the efficient use of resources, and staff development. It offers to the Department specialist support in computing, the management of the major portion of the Departmental research and development programme, operational research, economic analysis and statistics. For health authorities, it represents Departmental interests in computing, management services, and research.

The Group is therefore mainly concerned with intra-Departmental matters, and negotiations with central government on matters ranging from Departmental establishments to computer procurement policy. Links with health authorities are mainly restricted to the application of the research and development programmes, computing and management services.

Medical Division

The Secretary of State looks to the chief medical officer for medico-administrative advice on a wide range of topics. In addition, the CMO is also chief medical officer to the Home Office and the Department of Education and Science and is responsible for medical advice to the Department of the Environment and the Ministry of Agriculture, Fisheries and Food, and occasionally to other Departments. Within the Department, his staff with the help of consultant advisers, and the professions, provide the medical viewpoint on all topics where this is required.

Under the chief medical officer the Division is divided into four branches each headed by a Deputy CMO. One DCMO, on operational services, is concerned with regional liaison and medical aspects of building, supplies and exports together with surveillance and control of communicable diseases. A second DCMO is responsible for health policy including medical and surgical specialties, primary care services and medical manpower and staffing of the NHS and medical education. A third DCMO is responsible for community policy including services for children, the physically handicapped, the mentally ill and handicapped and the elderly, and services on prevention and nutrition. The fourth DCMO is concerned with scientific services and medicines which include international health, toxicology, microbiology, research and scientific and technical services.

Nursing Division

The Nursing Division, under the chief nursing officer, provides the nursing viewpoint on those matters where it is felt necessary. The Division's effort is concerned mainly with the topics covered by the Services Development Group, the Regional Group, and the Personnel Group, and the Division is organised on that basis under three deputy chief nursing officers. The chief nursing officer maintains close contact with leaders of nursing in government service, professional, statutory and voluntary bodies, both national and international. She also maintains contact with the development of trends in the EEC.

Works Division

The Works Division, under the chief works officer reporting directly to the permanent secretary, incorporates both the administrative and professional branches concerned with health and personal social services building and works and land transactions.

The Division has three main directorates: the Directorate of Works Development is concerned with building and engineering standards, management and publication of guidance, determination of cost allowances, experimental building projects (e.g. Nucleus hospitals) and international liaison. The Directorate of Works Operations is concerned with building and engineering maintenance and operations, staff management and training, estate management and statutory regulations, engineering technology and safety. The Directorate of Works Construction and Cost Intelligence deals with case work on RHA building schemes, other non-RHA building schemes and local authority social services schemes, health building procedures, statistical and intelligence studies, NHS building procurement, land policy and land transactions.

Supporting the chief works officer and the three directorates is a central administrative unit which is an integral part of the works organisation incorporating administrators and works professionals but excluding doctors and nurses who remain in their separate hierarchies.

Top of the Office

The work of the various Divisions is knit together by 'The Top of the Office' — a shorthand description of the most senior staff of the Department individually or jointly responsible in varying combinations, according to the matter in hand, for advising ministers on matters of major importance.

In addition there has been established a HPSS Strategy Committee consisting of permanent secretary (chairman), chief medical officer, deputy secretaries for personnel, regional and services development groups, the four deputy chief medical officers, principal training officer, chief social work officer, chief scientists, chief works officer and chief nursing officer, with the Policy Planning Unit (PPU) providing the secretariat.

The Social Security Strategy Committee consists of the second permanent secretary (chairman), deputy secretaries for social security policy and adminstration, principal training officer, under secretaries for social security division and the controllers for Newcastle and North Fylde Central Offices, with the Management Support and Computers Division (Social Security) (MSC) providing the secretariat.

There is also a cross-sector and wider social policy Review Group consisting of the chief social work officer (chairman), deputy chief medical officer for community policy and the deputy secretaries for social security policy and the services development group, with the secretariat jointly provided by PPU and MSC (and with the under secretaries RCP, MSC, LASS/SH and the chief scientist in attendance as necessary).

Finally, a Planning Steering Committee (PSC) provides a general oversight of the DHSS (HPSS) and the NHS planning processes, and their interaction and aims to identify in good time major policy issues requiring decisions by the Top of the Office. It consists of the deputy secretaries for the regional and services development groups (joint chairmen), principal training officer, the first deputy chief medical officer, two deputy chief nursing officers, the deputy director of the social work service, the under secretaries for RCP, FDA, P4, LASS/SH, the director of statistics and research, the head of ORS and the head of EAO, with the secretariat provided by the PPU.

The private office

Each of the Ministers and the Permanent Secretaries has a small private office headed by a private secretary. The private office is the formal channel of communication between the Minister or permanent secretary and the Department, and vice versa. It is responsible for arranging the Ministers' or permanent secretaries' meetings and visits, for handling their correspondence, and for liaison with private offices in other departments.

Ministerial correspondence with Members of Parliament and certain bodies, much of which involves complaints or enquiries on behalf of individuals, is handled by the specialist private office correspondence sections in conjunction with the Division responsible.

The Welsh Office

The Health and Social Work Department of the Welsh Office is divided into several Divisions concerned with: health services policy and liaison with health authorities; health finance; health building supplies and supporting services; health service personnel; local authority social services; and research management. There is also a health professional group with sub-groups concerned with medical services, medical planning and research, nursing midwifery and health visiting and professional divisions concerned with dental services, pharmaceutical services and scientific services.

The Scottish Home and Health Department

The functions of the Department in relation to health cover all aspects of health care for the people of Scotland. The health service divisions are organised into two main groups — health care and resources. The health care group deals with health care services; the resources group with staffing, salaries and conditions of service, operational efficiency and central policy on building and supplies. The health care professional staff are organised to parallel the administrative structure.

A health service policy group of senior administrative and professional officers under the chairmanship of the secretary of the Department advises on policy and co-ordinates the work of the divisions. The secretary of the Department, together with the secretaries of the four other Departments which comprise the Scottish Office and the deputy secretary (common services) constitute a management group under the chairmanship of the permanent under secretary of state to ensure co-ordination of work and to consider common problems across the whole field of Scottish Office responsibilities.

The Scottish Home and Health Department employs a staff of about 1,000. It also employs about 2,800 people in prisons, borstals and the state hospital at Carstairs.

Department of Health and Social Services (Northern Ireland)

The functions undertaken by the Department are broadly similar to those of the central departments in the other parts of the UK especially Wales and Scotland where also there is no separate regional tier of administration. The main difference is the Department's direct responsibility for the provision of most of the personal social services and for their co-ordination with the health services. The Department also provides certain centralised services for the boards such as the planning and execution of the major part of the building programme, O&M and work study services, etc.

The Department is organised into functional divisions:

(a) a planning division responsible for objectives and priorities and co-ordination of planning for the health and personal social services;
(b) a group of operational services divisions responsible for policy, for the development of the various health and personal social services and for monitoring the services provided by boards;
(c) a number of other divisions responsible for finance, personnel, works and supplies management services, research and intelligence; and
(d) three professional divisions providing professional advice on the planning and provision of health and personal social services.

Services provided by central departments

The central departments provide a number of services centrally which contribute to, or are allied with, the development of health services.

Disablement services

In England and Wales disablement services are administered directly by the Departments. Most of the staff in England are employed at 27 artificial limb and appliance centres; these centres, which may be part of hospitals, provide wheelchairs, road vehicles and artificial limbs. Proposals were made in the Three Chairmen's Report for the transfer of these centres to the appropriate health authorities but so far no change has been implemented. In Wales there are two artificial limb and appliance centres and one appliance centre. The Disabled Services Branch of DHSS is also responsible for the procurement of hearing aids and batteries for them. The aids are prescribed and dispensed by health authorities in hospital clinics. Contracts arranged by DHSS cover Wales but the service is provided through the Welsh Office.

In Scotland there are five artificial limb and appliance centres, three of which also supply vehicles and wheelchairs, and one vehicle centre which also supplies wheelchairs. A basic difference compared with England is that these centres are an integral part of the NHS and not part of the central department. The arrangements for prescribing and dispensing hearing aids and batteries are similar to those in England. Northern Ireland is in a similar position to Scotland.

Special hospitals

Under Section 4 of the National Health Service Act 1977, the Secretary of State is responsible for providing and maintaining special hospitals 'for persons subject to detention under the Mental Health Act 1959 who in his opinion require treatment under conditions of special security on account of their dangerous, violent or criminal propensities'. The hospitals for England, Wales and Northern Ireland are provided directly by DHSS which also controls admission of patients. There are three such hospitals serving England, Wales and Northern Ireland: Broadmoor, Rampton and Moss Side. A fourth, Park Lane, is under construction on a site adjoining Moss Side Hospital.

In Scotland the state hospital, Carstairs, is managed on behalf of the Secretary of State for Scotland by a committee consisting partly of departmental and partly of non-departmental members; the Department does not control admissions.

Research and development

The office of the chief scientist advises DHSS (and the Welsh Office) on the organisation and promotion of research and development. A number of research liaison groups comprising professional and administrative officers of the Departments with some NHS representation have been established to define research requirements and priorities and to secure the promotion, supervision and application of research and development to meet them. Commissions for research are arranged by the Departments' research management organisation and the research is carried out by a number of external research units and teams.

In Scotland the chief scientist of the Scottish Home and Health Department has a separate structure. He is advised by a chief scientific committee whose membership includes a wide range of academic specialists in medicine and allied fields and the chief professional officers of the Department.

Management at regional level

This chapter has dealt so far with the functions and organisation of the central departments in England, Wales, Scotland and Northern Ireland. Between the central departments and the operational health authorities there are a number of bodies and organisations which undertake various functions and provide various services; because of its relative size England has significantly different arrangements from the rest of the UK.

Only in England are there authorities — regional health authorities — intermediate between the central departments and the operational health authorities. In Wales, Scotland and Northern Ireland many of the functions which are performed by RHAs in England are performed by common service agencies, by the AHAs or health boards, or by the central department itself.

The essential difference between the regional health authorities in England and the common service agencies elsewhere is that the RHAs not only provide common services for the operational health authorities, they allocate resources to the area authorities, resolve competing priority issues particularly in relation to major capital schemes, plan regionwide services and are directly accountable for the performance of the area health authorities in their regions.

The remainder of this chapter deals with the organisation and management of health functions at the regional level in England and towards the end of the chapter will be found a description of the functions and organisation of the Welsh Health Technical Services Organisation, the Scottish Common Services Agency, and the Northern Ireland Central Services Agency for Health and Social Services.

England — regional health authorities

The development of the regional organisation in England has been traced in Chapter 1. Regional hospital boards were set up in 1948 and were superseded in 1974 by the establishment of regional health authorities. In England there are 14 such RHAs. The regions vary considerably in area and population, and may be compared with the populations of Scotland, Wales and Northern Ireland. Within each region the number of area health authorities varies from three to 11. (See Table 1 in Chapter 3.)

Main functions and responsibilities of regional health authorities

The constitution and appointment of members of RHAs have been dealt with in Chapter 3. The principal functions of an RHA may be briefly described as responsibility in consultation with AHAs for the formulation within national guidelines of regional strategic plans for the health services in the region, the allocation of resources to AHAs, and monitoring the performance of AHAs in achieving agreed plans. The planning of some medical services has to be carried out on a regional basis because individual areas are not large enough to be self-sufficient for all services. Examples are neuro-surgery, cardio-thoracic surgery, radiotherapy and various specialist pathology services.

In addition RHAs have some direct executive functions which, for the sake of economy or other reason, are better exercised on a scale larger than that of the average AHA. The most important of these are the design and construction of major new building works, the running of the blood transfusion service and, in the case of six regions, the running of an ambulance service for the Metropolitan counties within their regions. The London Ambulance Service is administered on behalf of the four London regions by the South West Thames Regional Health Authority.

Common services provided by RHAs include management services such as computer services, O&M, work study and operational research, personnel services, particularly manpower planning and training, central purchasing and contracting, land transactions as well as various advisory services.

Senior medical and dental staff except in teaching areas are appointed and employed by RHAs. Regional authorities are also responsible for manpower planning for the whole region, including teaching areas.

Except for the chairmen of area health authorities and those members appointed directly by the local authority, the regional health authority appoints AHA members after consultations with a number of organisations including local authorities in the region, the main health professions and any university in the region with a medical or dental school.

Although Section 20 of the National Health Service Act 1977 lays a duty on the Secretary of State to establish for each area health authority one or more community health councils, the Secretary of State has delegated this duty to RHAs under the Functions (Directions to Authorities) Regulations 1974. Regional health authorities are therefore responsible for establishing community health councils within their region and appoint one-sixth of their membership, the remaining five-sixths being appointed by the relevant local authorities and voluntary organisations. As the 'establishing authorities' RHAs maintain contacts with CHCs and are available to resolve difficulties if they arise between them and the AHAs. The full-time paid staff of community health councils, although technically on the staff of the RHA, work to the instructions of the CHCs.

Regional health authorities are predominantly lay bodies of between 17 and 23 members with knowledge of the region. To assist them in their tasks the members require professional advice which is provided partly by their full-time officers and partly by professional advisory committees set up under the provisions of Section 19 of the National Health Service Act 1977. These are the Regional Medical Advisory Committee, the Regional Dental Advisory Committee, the Regional Nursing and Midwifery Advisory Committee, the

Regional Pharmaceutical Advisory Committee and the Regional Optical Advisory Committee. The detailed organisation of the statutory professional advisory machinery varies within regions but most regions have separate specialty sub-committees in support of the Regional Medical Committee. Although not required by statute, all regions have established a Postgraduate Medical Education Committee to advise on the postgraduate medical education of doctors within the region.

To assist with promoting liaison with universities with medical and dental schools each region is required to establish a Regional University Liaison Committee consisting of representatives of the universities with medical or dental schools, the area health authorities and the regional health authority.

Although not part of the RHA structure, there is also for each region a Regional Nurse Training Committee which consists of representatives of the health authorities and the nursing profession to advise the General Nursing Council on the requirements of nurse training within the region.

The management structure at regional level

The management structure of a regional health authority can be looked at from two points of view: that of the authority itself and that of its full-time officers. Because the RHA consists of unpaid voluntary members (other than the chairman) most of the detailed work has to be carried out on its behalf by officers. Members must concentrate on the important issues of policy, planning and resource allocation and reviewing the performance of its chief officers and of area health authorities. Most RHAs have accepted the advice given in HRC(73)22 not to appoint standing committees in order to carry out their main functions and most authorities meet on a monthly basis to deal with formal business. In addition members have to provide a considerable additional input to the work of the authority by membership of various *ad hoc* committees, chairmen of appointment committees for senior medical and dental staff, membership of joint consultative committees with staff representatives and various miscellaneous duties. Performance of these tasks requires a minimum of two or three days per month from each member, and some members do considerably more, particularly if they are appointed to national committees (e.g. Whitley Councils) concerned with national issues.

The authority iself is expected to review proposals on policies and priorities submitted to it by area health authorities and by the regional officers and decide on regional policies and priorities within the framework of national policy and guidelines. The authority must also approve planning guidelines for AHAs and allocate resources, both revenue and capital. Subsequently it must review the plans and budgets submitted annually by area health authorities and by the regional officers for regional services, resolving competing claims for resources between area authorities and for particular kinds of services. The authority itself must also review the performance of its AHAs and its regional officers in order to ensure that progress is according to plan and that services are being provided throughout the region with efficiency and economy.

In order to enable the RHA to perform these important major responsibilities it is essential that the authority should have strong advice and support from its regional staff. A typical organisation structure of a regional health authority is set out in Figure 2. Although individual regional authorities' organisations vary in detail the main features are similar and are provided for in HRC(73)3.

Figure 2

RHA

Regional team of officers

ADMINISTRATION	FINANCE	MEDICAL	NURSING	WORKS
Regional administrator	Regional treasurer	Regional medical officer	Regional nursing officer	Regional works officer
Administration	Allocations	Health care planning	Education personnel and development	Architecture
Planning and capital developments	Financial services	Medical information and research	Services planning	Engineering
Management services	Capital developments	Medical manpower and PGME	Capital developments	Quantity surveying
Personnel	Internal audit	Capital developments	Nursing information and research	
Supplies		Scientific services		
Ambulance services				
Legal services				

Blood transfusion service

Pharmaceutical services

Regional team of officers

Each regional authority has a regional team of officers which consists of the regional administrator, regional medical officer, regional nursing officer, regional treasurer, and regional works officer.

Regional health authorities are essentially organised on a professional departmental basis with a professional head responsible directly to the RHA for the individual responsibilities allocated to him. The Grey Book considered that it was inappropriate for the organisation of a RHA to be controlled in a single hierarchy with a chief executive. As in the case of the teams at area and district level the structure which has been devised requires the co-ordination of the professions at regional level by means of a multidisciplinary team to deal with issues which require joint decisions or recommendations to the RHA. Thus the regional team of officers is a consensus forming group of equals with a joint responsibility to the authority for preparing plans, making delegated planning and operational decisions and monitoring performance against plans (para. 1.25 of the Grey Book). Such decisions need the agreement of each of the team members, and failing agreement the issue is reported to the chairman of the regional authority for decision. The regional administrator provides the general administrative support and co-ordination for the team.

The main duties of the RTO are to recommend regional policies to the RHA and advise on its approval of area policies and to prepare strategic plans and, in the case of services managed directly by the authority, operational plans for those services, including proposals for the deployment of medical manpower, the selection of major capital projects, and the allocation of revenue and capital resources. The RTO also recommends planning guidelines for AHAs and subsequently reviews area strategic and operational plans and advises the regional authority whether or not to approve these plans.

In order to assist the regional authority in controlling the performance of area authorities, the team reviews information on the performance of area authorities and advises the regional authority on the issues which ought to be taken up.

Every RTO has a considerable measure of delegated authority. However it is not possible to generalise as it has been left to the discretion of each RHA to determine its own arrangements for delegation and control.

Apart from the five officers who comprise the RTO there are other officers directly accountable to the RHA who are not members of the team although they are entitled to attend and take part in its meetings when matters concerning their functions are being discussed. These officers are the regional pharmaceutical officer and the director of the blood transfusion service. Although there is provision in the relevant circular (HRC(73)3) there is no case so far of a RHA appointing a full-time regional dental officer, although most regions have a part-time regional dental adviser.

One of the major functions of the RTO is concerned with planning and in this respect there are two different planning roles: the first concerned with the planning and development of services and the second concerned with the planning of specific major capital building projects. The Grey Book (para 2.85) envisaged that the team itself should carry out the first of these planning activities and should delegate the second to a capital programme team. Most RTOs have in fact estabished a team concerned with capital programming and the control of specific capital building projects constituted on a multidisciplinary basis, including representatives of the five RTO members. Some regions have also established a service planning and monitoring team to advise the RTO on their service planning functions and to undertake the detailed work in preparation of the regional strategic plan and the review of area strategic plans.

Responsibilities of regional officers

Each of the members of the RTO has individual responsibilities as well as his joint responsibilities as a member of the team.

The *regional administrator* (RA) is also the secretary to the RHA. As such he acts as the formal channel of communication with the Department, AHAs and outside bodies and provides the secretariat services to the authority and its committees including professional advisory committees. In addition he is directly accountable to the authority for the management of administrative services provided by the region and for the general administrative co-ordination of the RTO. The administrative services for which he is responsible directly to the authority include the provision of personnel and management services, supplies services, public relations and information services and for any ambulance service run by the RHA. He is also responsible for the administrative aspects of the capital building programme and for providing the administrative support necessary for the regional services planning process.

The sub-structure within the regional administrator's department usually includes a number of divisions headed by a second-in-line officer responsible for the following functions: general administration (including public relations and information), personnel, supplies, management services, services planning, capital planning, and ambulance services. In the larger regions there are five or six divisions and in some of the smaller regions some of these may be combined.

The *regional medical officer* (RMO) has six main groups of activities:

(a) co-ordinating the formulation and advice to the RHA on policies and plans for the operational health care services;
(b) co-ordinating the development of postgraduate medical education and training throughout the region in liaison with the postgraduate dean, and medical manpower planning;
(c) providing personnel services for consultants and senior registrars;
(d) advising on the medical content and policies of major capital building projects;
(e) recommending priorities for the use of funds available for health care research and co-ordinating community medicine research in liaison with the departments of social medicine and of general practice of the associated medical school and university; and
(f) developing, in conjunction with other disciplines, adequate and effective health care information systems throughout the region.

To assist him in his responsibilities he usually has several specialists in community medicine, normally responsible for health care service planning and monitoring, capital building projects, information services and research, and personnel and postgraduate medical education. The regional medical officer is also accountable to the RHA for scientific and technical services and the regional scientific officer is accountable to him.

The *regional nursing officer* (RNO) provides nursing and midwifery advice to the RHA, supplies the nursing input into service and capital planning, provides personnel services and counselling advice for nursing staff within the region and plans programmes of nursing research and development in liaison with universities and educational establishments. As either a member or officer of the Regional Nurse Training Committee she advises that committee on nursing educational needs for the region and the implications of educational activities on service requirements. She co-ordinates the development of post-certificate nurse education and training throughout the region.

The RHA is the local supervising authority under the provisions of the Midwives Act 1957 and the RNO advises the RHA in relation to the administration of that Act.

The RNO is assisted in discharging her responsibilities by regional nurses as second-in-line officers whose work is usually organised in relation to capital planning, service planning, personnel and training, and research.

The *regional treasurer* is responsible for providing financial advice to the authority (e.g. in allocating finance to AHAs and reviewing their plans and budgets, monitoring their expenditure and their use of resources and in making decisions on the regional authority's own operations) and is also responsible for all financial services required by the RHA for the purpose of its own functions.

He is responsible for the preparation of the regional budget and accounts. The organisation of regional treasurers' departments varies but the regional treasurer usually has second-in-line officers concerned respectively with financial planning and allocations, financial services, and audit.

The *regional works officer* is responsible for providing advice to the RHA on works matters and is responsible for the architectural, engineering and quantity surveying aspects of all buildings, engineering, maintenance and property management matters within the region. He provides the single point of contact at the highest level on behalf of the works professionals with the user or client professions. His department is divided into three major divisions under respectively the regional architect, the regional engineer and the regional quantity surveyor.

Although the full time staff of an RHA is organised into five main professional departments it should not be thought that these departments operate in watertight compartments. Much of the essential work of the authority concerned with policy formulation, planning, resource allocation and monitoring requires multidisciplinary inputs and much of the work of the regional authorities, as in the case of the DHSS in relation to policy and planning, is carried through by informal working parties and *ad hoc* groups on a multidisciplinary basis. The outcome of this work is channelled through the RTO to the regional health authority.

Relationship of regional health authorities with other bodies

The main relationships of a regional authority are with the central department and with the AHAs. Area health authorities are accountable to the RHA for the efficient performance of their functions and the RHA is in turn similarly accountable to the DHSS.

Regional authorities also relate to other regional organisations outside the NHS, for example the Regional Committees of the Trades Union Congress and regional branches of central government departments.

Although there is no comparable local government organisation six regions have within their boundaries a metropolitan county council while in London the four Thames regions have to establish relationships with the Greater London Council.

Wales — Welsh Health Technical Services Organisation

The prime role of the Welsh Health Technical Services Organisation is to provide the Welsh Office and the eight AHAs in Wales with certain support functions. The constitution is described in Chapter 3.

There are four chief officers each responsible directly to the Organisation. The *chief administrator and chief financial officer* is responsible for providing the secretariat services for the board of the Organisation and he is the official correspondent of the Organisation. He is also responsible for providing personnel services, for public relations and for servicing the Welsh Pricing Committee. As chief financial officer he is responsible for the Organisation's finances. The *chief supplies officer* is responsible for the provision of an efficient supplies organisation to health authorities in Wales and for the provision of advice and consultancy on supplies to the Welsh Office and health authorities. As part of his work he is responsible for the negotiation of all Wales contracts and the management of nationally negotiated contracts, and also the management of a central printing section. The *computer services manager* is responsible for the provision of a central computer service to the NHS in Wales and for providing technical advice to area and district organisations on computer services. Responsibility for policy concerning computer services lies with the Welsh Office. The *director of works* is responsible for major capital building works in Wales. The Organisation also provides technical assistance to area health authorities on smaller schemes.

The Organisation had a staff of 642 (whole-time equivalent) in 1979.

Scotland — Common Services Agency

The purpose of the Common Services Agency is to provide health boards in Scotland and the Scottish Home and Health Department with a variety of executive and advisory services, which are better organised centrally rather than locally. Services provided by the Common Services Agency not only include some which were formerly provided by regional hospital boards but also services which had been carried out previously by voluntary bodies and various *ad hoc* agencies established under Part IV of the National Health Service (Scotland) Act of 1947, and by the SHHD itself.

The Agency is established under Section 10 of the NHS (Scotland) Act 1978 and the functions of the Agency are laid down in the National Health Service (Functions of the Common Services Agency) (Scotland) Order 1974. The constitution is described in Chapter 3. The Common Services Agency is a *service* agency and its existence does not detract from the authority of each health board in its own area and the direct accountability of that health board to the Secretary of State. Moreover the Agency is not a policy making body; the broad policies within which it operates are laid down by the Secretary of State. The Agency is jointly accountable to the Secretary of State and the health boards.

The function of the management committee is to keep under review the whole range of services provided by the Agency, and in order to carry out these functions it has established four standing sub-committees — finance and general purposes, personnel and accommodation, operations and resources, and blood transfusion service. There are two advisory committees, one for management, education and training, and the other for the Scottish ambulance service.

The services provided by the Agency are divided into four main groups:

1. Technical services in support of patient care
   - Blood transfusions service
   - Ambulance service.
2. Support services to health service management, research and development
   - Building and works
   - Supplies
   - Information services
   - Health education
   - Communicable diseases.
3. Accounting services
   - Dental Estimates Board
   - Prescription Pricing Service.

4. General management and advisory services
   - Management education and training
   - Legal services
   - Domestic, catering and laundry advisory services
   - Organisation and methods and work study services (though some health boards have their own work study departments)
   - Services and facilities for the Scottish Appeals Committee of the Whitley Council and Scottish Medical Practices Committee
   - Press and publicity services
   - Training facilities for catering and managerial staff.

The *secretary* is the chief administrative officer of the Agency and he is the official correspondent for the management committee. He is responsible for the provision of accommodation and internal services and supplies for all divisions and units of the Agency and is also responsible for co-ordinating the activities of the divisions and the deployment of administrative staff throughout the Agency. The *treasurer* is the financial adviser to the management committee and is responsible for the preparation of estimates and for the maintenance of proper budgetary control mechanisms. Each director, head of unit and adviser is responsible directly to the management committee for the day-to-day running of the particular service for which he is responsible.

The secretary and the treasurer have a joint responsibility for the total budget of the Agency. The directors of divisions and heads of units have responsibility to exercise control of those sections of the budget delegated to them by the secretary and the treasurer.

The Agency employed a staff of 4,346 (whole-time equivalent) in 1979.

The management committee does not concern itself with the detailed running of any of the services provided by the operational divisions and units. The main function of the management committee is to ensure that each service has sufficient resources to carry out its work effectively and efficiently and to monitor the various activities to ensure that the service they give is to the satisfaction of the users, i.e. the health boards and the SHHD.

Scottish Health Service Planning Council

The Scottish Health Service Planning Council advises the Secretary of State on the exercise of his functions under the Health Service Acts whether at his request or on its own initiative, and, for the purpose of performing this duty, is obliged to keep under review the development of the health service in Scotland as a whole and in the various parts of Scotland. In exercising its functions the Council is required to consult with national consultative committees representative of the main health care professions set up under the provisions of the NHS Act.

The Council normally meets about three times a year. It is an important part of the central administration of the NHS in Scotland because it brings together the central department, the universities with medical schools and the health boards. At its first meeting on 21 June 1974 the Council interpreted its role as being to advise the Secretary of State on:

(a) the identification of health care needs and of programmes of care, etc. to meet those needs and the assessment of priorities in relation to resource availability;

(b) the implementation, review and evaluation of health planning in the national health service in Scotland; and

(c) the integration of health care with other kinds of care to ensure an overall policy for the treatment and help of those in need.

The Council is essentially concerned with long range strategic planning of health care in Scotland and works through a series of programme planning groups and advisory groups for particular subjects. At present the programme planning groups are concerned with: care of the elderly, child health, mental disorder and cancer. The advisory groups are concerned with: information and computer services, scientific services, blood transfusion, epidemiological and other aspects of infections, medical and scientific equipment aids for the disabled and new developments in health care.

The Council employed a staff of 14 (whole-time equivalent) in 1979.

Northern Ireland — Central Services Agency

The Northern Ireland Central Services Agency for the Health and Personal Social Services undertakes, on behalf of the central department and of the four health and social services boards, activities best performed by a central body without detracting from the overall aim that each board should provide or secure the provision of a comprehensive and integrated service for its own area.

The Agency performs most of the functions for Northern Ireland which in England and Wales are performed by family practitioner committees, the dental estimates boards and the prescription pricing bodies. Thus it provides the central payments machinery, the register of patients and lists of general practitioners and the service committee procedures for the family practitioner services. It also provides personnel services and, though its medical committee, advisory services for the filling of general medical practitioner vacancies. However, to assist in the integrated planning of health services the contracts with general practitioners are with the four boards and not with the agency. In addition to this involvement with the family practitioner services it also provides personnel services for the appointment of hospital medical and dental staff down to, and including the registrar grade. Other services include the provision of legal services; the provision of advice on, and co-ordination of, supplies and the arrangements for central and regional contracts; the promotion of research on supplies matters; the provision of advice on catering, domestic and laundry services; and the operation of central banking arrangements.

The work of the Agency is organised through a series of committees as follows: dental, medical, extended study leave, loans and improvements grants, ophthalmic, pharmaceutical, services, drug and appliance testing, grading and grading appeals. Most of the members of the committees, apart from the chairman, who is usually a member of the Agency, are drawn from the appropriate professions within Northern Ireland. There are also other *ad hoc* committees concerned with the central supply of drugs, supplies, catering and domestic services, laundry and transport.

The Central Services Agency had a staff of 340 (whole-time equivalent) in 1979.

Further reading

Statutory instruments and circulars

England

SI74/24. The NHS Functions (Directions to Authorities) Regulations 1974
SI74/296. The NHS (Remuneration and Conditions of Service) Regulations 1974
HRC(73)3. Management arrangements for the reorganised NHS
HRC(73)22. Membership and procedure of regional and area health authorities
HSC(IS)85. Medical and dental teaching of university students and associated research: liaison between NHS authorities and universities

Official reports

DHSS. *Annual Report 1977* (Cmnd 7394). HMSO 1978
DHSS. *Regional Chairmen's Enquiry into the Working of the DHSS in relation to Regional Health Authorities* (Three Chairmen's Report). 1976

Acknowledgement

Management Review of the DHSS: Report of the Steering Committee. (Unpublished) February 1978. We are grateful for the permission of the DHSS to quote from this report, and also to reproduce the diagram of the organisation of the Department.

6
Management at area and district level

Whereas the principal responsibilities of the DHSS and the RHAs are concerned with strategic planning at the national and regional levels, AHAs have twin responsibilities for both planning and the day-to-day delivery of health care. The AHA is thus the lowest level of statutory authority charged with both planning and operational responsibility.

Outside England the health authorities and boards have similar responsibilities, and most of what is said in this chapter applies equally to them. The absence of a regional tier, however, makes important differences. If some of the 'regional' functions are performed by the central agencies, and others are assumed by the central departments, others fall to the single-tier authorities. They are, for example, responsible for the appointment of consultants which in England is a regional responsibility except for the AHA(T)s. One of the most important differences is that these single-tier authorities are in a direct relationship with the central departments, maintaining the same close contacts as do the RHAs with the DHSS. Another important difference is that most, though not all, of these health authorities and boards are smaller than the English AHAs, and in Scotland particularly there are remarkable variations in size. The management of health services in Greater Glasgow is obviously very different from the management of services in the Shetlands.

The basic planning task of the AHA is to provide a comprehensive health service to its residents and to those parts of the population of neighbouring authorities which flow naturally across its boundaries to receive hospital care. The service planning of an AHA should reflect national and regional guidance on priority developments and be prepared in consultation with its matching local authority. In preparing plans, the AHA will need to review its services regularly, identifying both over-provision and under-provision compared with national and regional norms and standards. For its planning and operational responsibilities it is held accountable to the RHA. In addition to these general responsibilities AHA(T)s also have the duty of providing undergraduate and postgraduate facilities to meet the requirements of the university medical schools in the field of teaching and research.

The operational responsibility for the day-to-day delivery of services is principally discharged at the district level. As we have seen in earlier chapters, the district is conceived as a natural community served by local community health services and supported by the specialist services of a district general hospital, and an AHA may be responsible for a single district, or for two or more.

Each AHA is statutorily required to establish an FPC. It is not a committee of the authority. Although AHAs have powers under the regulations to establish committees, they have been advised by the DHSS that they should avoid establishing standing committees to deal with particular functions, such as finance and planning, or adopt territorial responsibility for districts or sectors. However, it is clear that on an *ad hoc* basis it may be helpful for selected members of authorities to give more consideration in depth and detail to plans and proposals than would be possible in a full meeting of the AHA. This should not be allowed to detract from the collective responsibility of the authority in matters of major policy and resource allocation. An authority may need to establish committees to perform certain duties under the Mental Health Act (see circular HRC(74)7), to carry out programmes of visiting and in connection with appointments and appeals procedures.

Another statutory requirement in England and Wales (under Section 22 of the National Health Service Act 1977) is the establishment of joint consultative committees with local authorities. Their function is to advise the AHA and local authority or authorities on co-operation. Section 19 of the Act provides for the recognition of area advisory committees of the health professions, and it is the duty of the AHA to consult them on relevant matters. The AHA is also required to consult the CHC formed for each district.

The health boards in Scotland normally have a committee structure and it is within this structure that they perform the duties that are carried out in England and Wales by the FPC. The Northern Ireland boards are required to appoint a health service committee and a personal social services committee. In Scotland there is no formal committee structure on advising on collaboration with local authorities.

Circular HRC(73)22 sets out the main functions and responsibilities of authorities. The AHA is a statutory body corporate. It delegates executive responsibilities to its area team of officers, individual officers at area level, its district management teams and individual officers at district level. The authority should focus its attention on key policy and resource allocation issues. In deciding on area policies in the light of national and regional guidelines, it reviews policy recommendations submitted by the area team of officers and the district management teams and sets priority guidelines for the development of comprehensive health services within its area. Its critical tasks involve challenging plans and budget proposals prior to agreeing proposals for services against which performance can be monitored. In multi-district areas it resolves competing claims for resources between districts.

In order to monitor and control the performance of its team and directly accountable officers, it needs to establish effective reporting systems that allow a progress check to be made against plans and budgets and that allow scrutiny of efficiency and cost effective measures. A key responsibility is the appointment of its chief officers, and the degree of delegation to officers and teams. In monitoring the quality of services delivered it needs to arrange programmes of systematic visiting to all premises but particularly the longer-stay institutions where the emphasis should be as much on reviewing patient care systems and procedures as on the physical environment of the patient.

Area and district

Earlier chapters have explained how the concept of the health district combined with the principle of coterminosity led to the establishment of multi-district areas, and Chapter 4 mentioned the difficulties that had been experienced in the management of these multi-district areas. Although such arrangements are expected to disappear shortly, at least in England, with the further reorganisation of the service, it is worth expanding on them here both because the multi-district area is an essential part of the arrangements described in this book and because the new reorganisation is best understood in the light of what it is reacting against.

In order that authorities can delegate executive responsibilities to district management teams in multi-district areas while retaining the means of exercising overall control and co-ordinating plans and activities between districts, they need corporate advice from the area team of officers. The ATO recommends area-wide policies and reviews the proposals of districts. In proferring advice, the ATO has the sensitive task of interpreting guidelines emanating from the national and regional levels in a way that must demonstrate a local understanding of district circumstances. The ATO will therefore undertake the task of critically reviewing district planning proposals and comparing them with policy guidelines to advise the authority whether to challenge or amend its plans. In this context the ATO must necessarily advise on the distribution of resources between districts. In preparing overall area plans, the ATO is called upon to resolve basic planning issues with the RTO and to draw up plans jointly with the matching local authority.

In assisting the authority to control the performance of the DMTs, the ATO is responsible for presenting information that describes the performance of districts, providing a basis on which to select issues that need to be brought to the attention of the AHA. The ATO will advise on appropriate corrective courses of action.

It is a challenging task to undertake these responsibilities without being drawn into the detail of operational management which is the principal province of the DMT, but without knowledge in detail on some occasions it would be difficult to discuss plans with the RTO and local authority officers with the same commitment and understanding as DMTs. It is this kind of difficulty, perceived and sometimes exploited by area and district officers, which has led to criticisms of the duplication of tasks, undue interference by area officers, lack of co-operation by district officers, lack of clarity between area and district roles, allegations of insufficient delegation and delay in decision-making.

In the management relationship between the ATO and the DMT there is a major variation in structure between England and the other countries of the UK in that England provides the only situation where there is no line relationship between area and district officers. In England at the team level and at the level of individual officers, the area works through a monitoring and co-ordinating relationship. In this management relationship agreements have to be negotiated rather than imposed. It also follows that if area and district officers are on the same managerial level, the ATO cannot be held accountable for the work of the DMT, or individual area officers for the work of their district counterparts. The ATO must persuade the DMT to conform with its policy, arguing from the position of interpreting AHA policies and guidelines. If the ATO is not satisfied with the response or performance of a district, then the issue must be referred to the AHA. In practice this philosophy of equality has proved to be unrealistic. There has been competition to gain the upper hand, competiton that cannot always be described as constructive conflict. On the one hand some DMTs have felt impeded in their just rights to present their position direct to their authority and on the other hand area officers have felt that they do not possess the necessary authority to guarantee that the AHA's policies will be accepted and implemented. While it would be misleading to suggest that relations between area and district officers are always marked by strain or conflict, or that effective management cannot be achieved in a multi-district area, there has generally been greater satisfaction about the effectiveness of the management structure in single-district areas, where the dichotomy between policy and planning on the one hand and operational management on the other does not exist. Certainly there has been general welcome for the present government's proposed reorganisation, despite the disturbance it will cause and the prospect of losing the advantages as well as the disadvantages of multi-district areas.

Among the advantages, it may be claimed, is the provision of certain services on a larger scale than are provided by the district, although it must be acknowledged that these services are also provided by single-district areas, some of which are no larger than some health districts. Some of these services, such as supplies, are described in later chapters. Here we must briefly describe two — the family practitioner committee and the ambulance service — before turning to the districts.

The family practitioner committee

Each AHA in England and Wales appoints a family practitioner committee of 30 members, half of them lay and half members of the professions providing family practitioner services. Details of membership were given in Chapter 3, and Chapter 4 discussed the relationships between FPC and AHA. In Scotland and Northern Ireland, where there is no FPC, family practitioner services are provided in the same way as they are in England and Wales, and responsibilities described here fall on the health board.

The FPC is required to establish a number of sub-committees — a medical service committee, a dental service committee, a pharmaceutical service committee, an ophthalmic services committee, a joint services committee, an allocation committee, an hours of service committee, and an obstetric committee. A dental conciliation sub-committee and a dispensing sub-committee may also be established.

The principal functions of FPCs are:

- to enter into a contract of service with each doctor, whose application to practise in the area has been approved by the MPC and with each dentist, chemist, ophthalmic medical practitioner, ophthalmic and dispensing optician and surgical appliance supplier working in the area;
- to enter into a contract of service with any doctor whose obstetric experience has been recognised by the local obstetric committee to provide medical maternity services;
- to report to the MPC on matters concerning medical manpower and future developments in the area, including population movements. The committee is required to inform the MPC committee on receiving notice of a vacant practice, and to report about the need for filling any such vacancy;
- to advertise medical practice vacancies and to recommend appointments to the MPC;
- to arrange payment for doctors, dentists, chemists and other professions;
- to investigate complaints about alleged breaches in terms of service;
- to publicise lists of doctors, dentists, pharmacists and opticians;
- to inspect professional premises following a written request to visit;
- to ensure the general efficiency of the general medical, dental, pharmaceutical and ophthalmic services within an area;
- to set up chemists' rotas;

— to 'assign' patients on the list of a particular doctor who are considered not acceptable; and
— to consult local committees recognised by the Secretary of State representing medical practitioners, pharmacists and dental practitioners known as the local medical, pharmaceutical and dental committees respectively. The requirement to consult is a statutory requirement. Local representative committees of ophthalmic opticians and dispensing opticians are also recognised.

The FPC maintains close co-operation with the local authority in the planning of services for new development areas, and collaboration is particularly close with the housing committee, so that the FPC is kept fully informed of housing developments, particularly those likely to affect the size of populations in particular neighbourhoods. The local authority reserves surgery accommodation or land for the construction of a health centre or surgery premises, and often provides temporary premises to cover transitional arrangements.

Complaints

Reference has been made to the professional service committees and the duty of the FPC is to investigate complaints about alleged breaches of terms of service. This disciplinary responsibility, and the constitution and procedure of service committees through which it is undertaken, is now described in more detail. The medical, pharmaceutical and dental service committees each consist of a chairman and six members, three members appointed from the lay members of the FPC and three members appointed by the local medical, pharmaceutical and dental committees respectively. The ophthalmic service committee consists of a chairman and ten members, of which four members are appointed from the lay members of the FPC. The professional members consist of two ophthalmic medical practitioners, two ophthalmic opticians and two dispensing opticians. The joint services committee consists of a chairman and ten members, two members appointed from the lay members of the FPC and two professional members from each of the medical, pharmaceutical, dental and ophthalmic service committees. The duty of the joint services committee is to investigate complaints alleging failure to comply with terms of service where more than one profession is involved.

A complaint must relate to an allegation of failure to comply with the terms of service, and must be made within prescribed time-limits of eight weeks, except for complaints against dental practitioners where a time-limit of six months after completion of treatment is accepted. The complaint is confined to the person who is entitled to receive a service from the practitioner in question, or in certain circumstances the spouse of that person. Under these conditions, the FPC administrator is required to send the chairman of the appropriate service committee a copy of the complainant's statement so that the chairman can form an opinion about whether the complaint has any prima facie substance, or is frivolous or vexatious. If the chairman of the committee decides that a hearing of the case is unnecessary, the case will be brought before the service committee which has the power to dispense with the hearing. If the case is heard, the procedure follows a pattern of strict formality. The appropriate service committee reports to the FPC in cases where any findings of fact in the report are required to be accepted as conclusive. Based on recommendations from the service committee, the FPC may decide that one or more of the following actions are appropriate: a special limit on number of persons registered with a general medical practitioner; the withholding of an amount from the remuneration of the practitioner; the recovery of expenses reasonably incurred by the patient as a result of the failure of the practitioner to comply with the terms of service. A dental practitioner may be required to submit all his estimates for treatment, other than for emergency treatment, to the dental estimates board for approval.

If the FPC takes the view that the continued inclusion of the practitioner on the appropriate list would be prejudicial to the efficiency of the services in question, representation to that effect is made to the tribunal established under Section 42 of the National Health Act 1946.

There is the right of appeal to the Secretary of State against any decision other than a decision to make representation to the tribunal.

On receiving a complaint, the administrator, FPS, will sometimes attempt conciliation before embarking on the formal complaints procedure.

Responsibilities of the administrator, FPS

The Grey Book, in giving the role specification for the administrator, FPS, defined four principal responsibilities: to inform area and district staff of the FPC's views and proposals, particularly on the planning and development of health centres, on attachment schemes and on manpower planning; to ensure that the FPC is informed of AHA plans in general and in particular any AHA policies on the planning and organisation of the FPS manpower planning and all other relevant development, including proposals for health centres; to provide general secretariat service and advice to the FPC and its committees; and to advise on problems relating to individual contractors.

The third and fourth of these reflect the basic administrative responsibilities of the FPC which constitute the largest part of its day-to-day activities. These activities, as the description of functions given above suggests, are largely governed by regulations and the terms of contracts with practitioners. The remuneration of general medical practitioners is particularly complicated, comprising a variety of payments of three main sorts: capitation and other basic payments, payments for specific items of service, and reimbursement of expenses for ancillary staff and premises.

The first two of the responsibilities relate more to the management of services. Management is important because the FPS forms an essential part of a comprehensive health service, but it is controversial because there is room for debate on how far the contractual services can be managed and, to the extent that they can be managed, who should be responsible. One obvious limit to management in the usual sense is that except for administrative costs FPC expenditure is open ended. Another aspect is that very broadly speaking the FPC does not seek practitioners, as would an employing authority; the initiative to practise in an area comes from the practitioners themselves. This is the case with dentists and opticians, and FPCs are not under an obligation to provide their services to a particular scale. The case is rather different with general medical practitioners. The profession as a whole has undertaken to provide general medical services for the population 24 hours a day on 365 days of the year, and certain things follow from this. It is, for example, the reason why the FPC has powers to assign to a doctor a patient who has not been able to find a doctor willing to accept him, and why the FPC must take an interest in deputising services. The FPC is thus naturally interested in having an adequate number of GPs in its area, and there are certain arrangements designed to promote this: a doctor may not set up an NHS practice in an over-doctored area, and there are incentive payments to attract doctors to under-provided areas. Also, the FPC advertises medical practice vacancies, an arrangement for which there is no equivalent in the dental and ophthalmic services. But if the FPC, in liaison with the Medical Practices Committee, takes a continual active interest in the supply of GPs, normally valid applications for inclusion in the medical list are granted without question except in 'over-doctored' areas, i.e. those classified by the MPC as intermediate or restricted. Thus, the FPC is to only a limited extent in control of its 'staffing'. Equally, it does not control the supply of chemist contractors. The pharmaceutical services, like the general medical services, are guaranteed to all patients, and when chemists are not available, as in some remote areas, GPs may be authorised to dispense medicines.

Another aspect of FPC services which diverges from a normal management pattern is that obligations and standards are determined by regulations and contracts. This is seen in the handling of complaints, as it is in other matters. It can be argued that this means the FPC can do nothing to improve services beyond ensuring that minimum standards are maintained, and that the approach even to these is legalistic. Against this it may be said that general practice has in many respects greatly improved its standards since 1966.

Relationships with GPs

A straightforward management approach is also ruled out in matters entailing collaboration between AHA services and GPs , such as the provision of health centres or the attachment of community health staff to particular practices. It is the AHA's responsibility to provide health centres, and until recently they were strongly encouraged by the Department to do so. However, although negotiations may be conducted through the FPC, each scheme must in effect be negotiated with the two or three practices that will practise from it, and it is not unknown for some or all of the practices to back out after the scheme has developed into an advanced stage. Although advocates of health centres have been known to say that GPs should not have a veto on their provision, it is pointless and a waste of public money to provide centres at which GPs do not wish to practise, since they cannot be compelled to do so.

The peculiar character of management in the contractor services, or its absence, has led to proposals for change. The Royal Commission proposed that FPCs should be abolished, though the government has rejected the idea. Transferring their responsibilities to AHAs might facilitate liaison but would be unlikely to affect the various non-managerial aspects of the service indicated above, and a more radical approach advocated by some critics is a salaried general practitioner service. This implies more control, though the Royal Commission, which did not support it except as an option open to individual GPs, said:

> If the general practitioner service were to provide the same kind of cover as it does at present, then it seems to us likely that GPs would continue to be very much their own masters.

A change to a salaried service is most unlikely unless the majority of GPs come to favour the idea, for a government would not embark on such a measure against the opposition of the profession unless there were overwhelming reasons in its favour.

Both AHAs and FPCs are liable to stress the difference between the contractual services and the rest of the NHS. The resemblances should also be noted. One feature of FPC services is the uneven distribution of doctors and dentists, but it is not only in the contractual services that professionals are reluctant to practise in some part of the country; some RHAs have difficulty in filling some established consultant posts. Another feature is the large element of negotiation with practitioners, but some observers of the directly managed part of the NHS would describe it as negotiated order rather than management based on command and control. A fairly common criticism of FPCs is that, despite having a half lay membership, they are unduly under professional influence. This criticism too is sometimes made of health authorities.

A final point to be made about the FPC services is that since in so many respects the powers and duties of FPCs are laid down by regulation or determined by nationally negotiated contracts, much of the management and development of services, as distinct from their administration, depends on national decisions. Thus, the supply of practitioners depends on the number of medical and dental schools, their intake, and possibly their location as far as recruitment to particular parts of the country is concerned. (These considerations apply equally to the hospital service.) The attractiveness of general practice compared with hospital medicine depends to a certain extent on relative remuneration, and remuneration will affect even more such considerations as the attractiveness or otherwise of such things as practice from a health centre, or providing specific services. And it is the medical practices committee which, in co-operation with the FPCs, has the power to classify general practice areas in accordance with the supply of doctors and thus take the only effective steps towards a better distribution short of direction or a radical use of different rates of payment.

The ambulance service

Prior to 1974, the ambulance service was managed by 142 county borough and county council authorities in England and Wales. At reorganisation this responsibility passed to 45 health authorities in England and 8 area health authorities in Wales. In England the London ambulance service is administered by the South West Thames RHA on behalf of the four Thames regions. In the six metropolitan counties the service is administered by RHAs and the remaining 38 ambulance services by AHAs. In Scotland the service is a responsibility of the Common Services Agency, which has eight local operational centres. In Northern Ireland the service is run by the four health and social services boards.

Since 1974 the new authorities have enjoyed considerable success in integrating the previously fragmented services and reconciling differing operational policies and staff terms and conditions of service. Ambulance control centres and radio communications systems have been rationalised.

The service in England and Wales is accountable through the chief ambulance officer to regional and area administrators with a role for monitoring medically related issues undertaken by the regional and area medical officers.

The majority of ambulance journeys are for routine in-patient appointments and a typical workload would be: emergencies 5 per cent; out-patients 66 per cent; day patients 17 per cent; inter-hospital transfers and other journeys 12 per cent. Despite this apportionment, the emergency service can account for over 75 per cent of the total budget.

Organising an ambulance service is a complicated technical operation based on the control centre, which keeps closely in touch with ambulance crews by radio telephones, etc. The centre has to organise the planned pattern of work, i.e. the routine journeys booked in advance, but must always be able, in response to an emergency call, to send the nearest available ambulance to the scene. In circular HSC(IS)67 the DHSS recommended standards of performance for both emergency and non-emergency work in terms of time taken to respond to calls or early or late arrival for appointments at hospitals. Different standards were suggested for metropolitan and area services, since the latter normally have to cover greater distances.

A specialised technical service such as this depends on special equipment, particularly ambulances. Most ambulances can carry both lying and sitting patients, though in urban areas there are usually also ambulances for walking patients. The fleets of ambulances entail service and maintenance facilities.

Transporting patients by ambulance is expensive, and the growing demands on the service have therefore caused some concern. The decline in public transport in rural areas appears to have increased the demand, and some health authorities have conducted publicity campaigns to combat the view that patients have a right to transport by ambulance when they consider they need it and to stress the cost of the service and the need to ensure that ambulances are available for patients who need them for medical reasons. One cause of increasing demand has been the development of day hospitals for geriatric and psychiatric patients. A particular problem that these pose is that all the demand comes at two peaks or rush hours, i.e. about 9.30 a.m. and 3.30 p.m. To a certain extent a similar problem is encountered in transporting patients to out-patient clinics.

Including workshop staff, there are over 20,000 ambulance staff in the UK in some ten ranks rising from ambulanceman/woman to chief ambulance officer. Since NHS reorganisation, the pay of ambulancemen has been negotiated in the Ambulancemen's Whitley Council, whereas that of the various ranks of ambulance officer is negotiated in the Administrative and Clerical Staffs Council. There is a six-week training course for new entrants to the ambulance service, and various other courses of training are available. There is a National Staff Committee for Ambulance Staff.

In 1980, in view of the impending restructuring of the NHS and the increasing demands on the ambulance service, a patient transport service working party was established under the chairmanship of W.M. Naylor. The working party has issued a consultative document which addresses a number of fundamental issues related to the responsibility and organisation of the ambulance service. It is argued that there should be a more positive definition of patients eligible for NHS transport which fits strict medical, rather than social, criteria of need against the following definition:

- Patients requiring immediate transportation to hospital as a result of accident, emergency or serious illness.
- Patients who suffer from a physical or mental illness or disability that precludes them from making their own way to or from hospital, hospital clinic or hospital unit for necessary treatment or diagnosis.

In proposing this definition the working party recognises that there needs to be considerable scope for collaboration between health authorities, local authorities and voluntary agencies in the development of 'community transport services' to meet a wide range of public need, including patients who are not eligible for ambulance transport.

The working party also addresses the question of whether there is benefit in introducing a tiered ambulance service with non-emergency services becoming the responsibility of district health authorities. Although the separation of accident and emergency services from routine patient transport services might appear to present an attractive option, studies have shown that in general a single-tier ambulance service allows higher operational efficiency, particularly in urban areas. In large rural areas with a low frequency of calls, the arguments are more evenly balanced. The ambulance service itself argues that, in addition to economic disadvantages, a two-tiered system would create personnel problems in pay differentials and limited career and promotion opportunities and that the system would be less flexible in dealing with major accidents.

Districts

One of the basic concepts of reorganisation was the district, defined as the smallest population for which comprehensive health care can be planned and provided. Since the new service, unlike the pre-1974 hospital service, was to be based on responsibilities for defined populations and geographical areas, this entailed the drawing of district boundaries. There was no intention that the establishment of these should inhibit the freedom of GPs to refer patients across district — or area — boundaries to the hospital or consultant of their choice, although clearly the concept of welding effective working arrangements between primary and secondary care services was a fundamental objective of reorganisation.

Needless to say, the district as a population of around 250,000 served by a district general hospital was a somewhat theoretical concept, and it would not have been possible to divide the country up into self-contained health districts all roughly the same size. That indeed was not the exercise, for it was not the country as a whole but each of the larger areas separately which had to be divided into districts, and it might be on occasion that an area boundary, determined by the requirements of local government reorganisation, divided a 'natural' health district. Some areas were seen as appropriate for management as single districts even though their population might be well above — or below — the ideal norm. When areas had to be divided, the determination of boundaries depended mainly on the distribution of existing facilities, particularly hospitals, and on the catchment areas they served, which in turn often depended on the local pattern of transport. It was also considered desirable that districts should correspond with groups of social service 'areas' and with combinations of local authority districts. There were also political considerations; one or two of the smaller districts appear to owe their existence to the effective resistance of smaller communities to being associated with the nearest large city. Districts emerged therefore with no strict upper or lower population limits, but with the majority roughly around 250,000 in England and smaller elsewhere.

Circular HRC(73)4 set out the detailed procedures for defining districts. It recognised that 'natural' districts, i.e. districts defined in terms of facilities and catchment areas, would not always coincide with health authority boundaries and that about 40 per cent of natural districts had ten per cent or more of their population outside an area boundary. Two main types of overlap were possible: an area boundary might divide a group of hospitals which operated as a district hospital complex, or an overlap not affecting hospitals might affect community services. The circular recommended that the responsible district should be the one with the greatest number of the natural district's population resident within its boundary even though a district general hospital fell outside its boundary; that hospitals working together to form an integrated district general hospital should not be split; and that parts of a complex lying outside a boundary should be managed extra-territorially. In relation to the management of community services in an overlap zone, staff could be managed by the district in which they worked with co-ordinating links to the remaining part of the natural district, or could be managed by the natural district and permanently seconded to the neighbouring district. In the case of significant overlap where more than 25 per cent of the population of the natural district fell in an overlap zone, the AHA of the area should make an agency arrangement with the area of the 'natural' district to provide and manage the services.

The large mental hospitals serve large areas, often more than one health authority area, and they are often situated at some distance from the main population served. In deciding which AHA should be responsible, the criterion should be not the authority in whose territory the hospital was situated but the authority it mainly served, even though that might mean extra-territorial management. In a multi-district area management responsibility would be delegated to one DMT or to an area serving a district, and since each district is responsible for planning its psychiatric service, planning and policy proposals need to be co-ordinated at area level and often, in view of the wide catchment areas of many hospitals, between AHAs. By contrast, the circular considered that for the large mental handicap hospitals the balance of argument favoured assigning responsibility to the district in which the hospital was situated.

In London and the large conurbations it was recognised that the density of population was likely to produce overlapping catchment populations between several district general hospitals. In these circumstances it was considered that if the district general hospitals worked independently of each other it would be inappropriate to form outsize districts, and the geographical boundaries of districts should be drawn in relation to primary care and local authority factors, particularly social service 'areas', with each district managing a DGH providing a substantial part of the secondary care services to that district.

The district management team

The DMT is responsible for reviewing its community's needs for health care and for assessing over-provision and under-provision of health care in relation to these needs, identifying the opportunities for changing priorities.

The membership of teams was described in Chapter 3. It is interesting to note that in an English teaching district, where a representative of the medical school is also a member of the team, the DMT has four medical members out of seven. There is even at least one non-teaching district team with two consultants and two GPs. This reflects the importance attached at reorganisation to involving doctors in management. The difficulties of this, arising from the fact that medical members are representatives, not officers with management authority, were noted in Chapter 4. Scotland shows a different approach, for there the representatives of the district medical committee are not full members of the district executive group, although professional representatives do attend district executive group meetings. Thus, the doctors enjoy a degree of independence from the decision-making process, but their contribution and commitment to decision-making may be weakened.

The DMT is a group of equals with no member being the managerial superior of other members, and the main disciplines are thus brought together on an equal footing to participate jointly in decision-making. The team works as a consensus group to resolve inter-disciplinary issues, with any unresolved issues passing to the AHA for resolution. The permanent officers on the team have individual responsibility for the services they manage as well as collective responsibility as team members.

The working methods of DMTs vary considerably, some being relatively formally constituted with a chairman responsible for the conduct of meetings and even action between meetings, acting as spokesman for the team in discussion with other bodies. In these more formal circumstances, when the administrator is not the chairman of the team the relationship between the chairman and the administrator needs to be carefully considered in order to reflect the general co-ordinating responsibilities of the administrator. More often, the team works informally without a chairman, with subjects placed on the agenda and introduced by individual members of the team. The administrator is then usually expected to take the lead in helping the team to come to consensus decisions on key policy issues.

The district medical committee

The 1974 reorganisation arrangements envisaged the involvement of doctors in management not only through membership of management teams but also through representative committees. The district medical committee represents all general practitioners and hospital doctors with the object of co-ordinating medical matters across the district. Members are nominated from the local representative committee of general practitioners in equal number to hospital doctors who are usually nominated through the medical executive committee. Additionally, doctors working in community medicine, including the district community physician, are members, as are representatives of the medical academic body in teaching districts.

The principal function of the DMC is to arrive at a consensus view on medical policies and priorities, to consider opportunities for developing services, to review the recommendations of health care planning teams, to communicate policies to individual clinicians and to undertake an executive function in influencing expenditure across a number of budget heads, such as drugs, medical consumables and other services prescribed directly for the patient.

In practice, problems have emerged in the functioning of DMCs, and even more so in the functioning of area medical committees in multi-district areas. The bringing together of hospital doctors and general practitioners, although apparently the right approach in a comprehensive health service, has emphasised the heterogeneous nature of hospital medicine and the relatively homogeneous approach of general practitioners, and has led some people to believe that GPs have managed to obtain a position of influence in hospital matters without offering any reciprocal opportunities for hospital doctors. In some places hospital doctors have turned their attention back to those committees directly concerned with their work, and there has even been a resurgence of the importance of hospital medical advisory committees. General practitioners, on the other hand, have tended in multi-district areas, particularly urban ones, to be active at area rather than district level, for although the district is intended to be the main management unit the key committees for GPs — the local medical committee and the family practitioner committee — are area based.

Quite apart from the possible inadequacies of the DMC machinery, there are two reasons why the 1974 arrangements for involving doctors in management have led to disappointment. One is the basic difficulty facing clinical representatives on management teams, which was discussed in Chapter 4. They are expected to agree to management decisions but as they cannot commit the colleagues whom they represent they are therefore always liable to disappoint one party or the other. In addition to this basic dilemma they face a practical problem: much of the value of their contribution to the team stems from the fact that they are actually involved in medicine, but membership of a management team makes considerable demands on their time, particularly if, as is usually the case, they are also chairman of the medical executive committee and a member of various other committees. It is therefore difficult to keep up a busy clinical workload. There is a limit to which clinical responsibility can be delegated to colleagues, but it appears easier to share work in some specialties, such as anaesthetics, pathology and radiology, and clinical team members and medical executive committee chairmen have increasingly emerged from these specialties. They are not necessarily specialties representative of consultants as a whole.

The other difficulty, perhaps easier to overcome, is the sheer complexity of the medical advisory machinery, which has been one of the most criticised features of the reorganised service. It is discussed more fully in Chapter 15. There are various reasons for complexity, relating partly to the complexity of the NHS structure, particularly in multi-district areas, and partly to the complexity and diversity of the profession itself. While it should be possible to simplify the machinery, consultation will remain important since clinical autonomy precludes any other way of involving doctors in the management of the service.

Organisation of services at area and district

The officer and clinician members of area and district management teams, together with the three officers directly accountable to the authority although not members of the team (i.e. dental officer, pharmacist and works officer) are accountable for, or represent, all the services in the area or district, although in some of the professional services the relationship is not clearly defined and varies between authorities. From the following account of services the interests of two team members are excluded: the general practitioner services because they are not organised by the authority, and the responsibilities of the treasurer/finance officer because they are discussed in Chapter 9. It hardly needs saying that financial services, information and advice are needed by all these services.

The intention of establishing the district as the basic management unit was to ensure that operational services should be managed at a point as close as possible to the delivery of service to the patient. The great majority of operational services are therefore co-ordinated at the district level. Services provided directly for the patient in the clinical, nursing and paramedical diagnostic and therapeutic fields have their resources essentially managed within districts, with heads of service either accountable to the DMT or with heads of services who are members of the DMT. The majority of 'hotel' services managed by the administrator are similarly organised within districts, although there are some exceptions where the economic advantages of large-scale operation make management at area level preferable. This particularly applies to some commercial-type hotel services such as laundry, transport and supplies, although there are no firm patterns of organisation common to multi-district areas. Some compact urban areas centralise services more than is possible in rural areas.

Where a service provides essentially a 'staff' as opposed to a 'line' function the emphasis has been towards establishing an area-based organisation. Management services, financial services concerned with salaries, wages and accounts, audit, capital building and some aspects of personnel work fall into this category, although it should be emphasised again that there is no common blueprint.

At area level reciprocal services are provided between health authorities and their counterpart local authorities. Common to all health authorities is the statutory requirement to provide medical and nursing advice to local authorities in relation to social services, education and environmental health, and advice is extended to other local authority departments such as housing and recreation. Many health authorities provide an occupational health service to their local authorities. Reciprocal services provided by local authorities are less in evidence with the exception of the hospital social work service which is provided by all local authorities, but can include, for example, the provision of a statistical/information service to the health authority.

Hospital medical service

In one sense it is inappropriate to discuss medical services in an area/district context. The basis of organisation is the individual clinician and in hospitals, as in general practice, there is no hierarchy of authority and responsibility up to area/district. In another sense it is essential to consider the hospital medical service in this context, for it is a primary responsibility of the health authority to provide such a service: to provide, for example, an adequate geriatric service, including the employment of appropriate medical and other staff, and the necessary accommodation and facilities. The consultants themselves, despite their clinical autonomy, co-operate, have common interests and collectively constitute a very powerful pressure group.

In 1953 the Ministry of Health issued guidance about the role of medical advisory committees. It suggested the following areas of activity: developments in medicine, bed allocations, criteria for admission from waiting-lists, arrangements for emergency admissions, complaints procedures involving medical and dental staff, appointment procedures for the junior medical and dental staff, medical and dental equipment and supplies, medical records, economies in prescribing, control of infection, nomination of staff to serve as members of governing bodies, the medical library, and the organisation of clinical meetings. It also said that medical advisory committees should regularly review the performance of clinical work in order to maintain standards.

It can be seen from this list that the collective opinion or action of medical staff was being advocated on matters of several different types, and the same has been true of subsequent arrangements. First, there are matters on which medical staff have a common interest, such as the control of infection or the quality of the medical records service. Second, there are matters where there are conflicting interests that need resolution, such as the allocation of beds, or whether priority should be given to new equipment for one department rather than another. Third, there are matters, such as economies in prescribing, which interest management and the government but do not affect the *immediate* interests of medical staff. The last, expressed more generally in terms of economy and efficiency, has received increasing emphasis, and most medical staff are well aware of its importance. But while the economical and efficient use of resources is in the long-term interest of clinicians, there may be no immediate benefits except under arrangements where part of a budget saving is used for providing extra facilities for the department concerned.

An important change was initiated in 1967 with the publication of the first 'cogwheel' report — so named from the design on the cover. (A more detailed Scottish report appeared at the same time. It exemplified the same approach while taking account of the existence of medical superintendents in Scottish hospitals.) The 'cogwheel' reports are discussed in Chapter 15, but must be noted briefly here. The first significant thing about the 1967 report was that it advocated organising medical work on a wider base than the individual hospital — then the group and now the district. Even more significantly, it launched the often repeated theme that the doctor must take his place within the general management framework; as the initiator of considerable expenditure the clinician should not be divorced from the policy, planning and budgeting of governing authorities. Clinicians should undertake a continuous review of hospital activity and take part in co-ordinating and planning services both within hospitals and in liaison with community services. The report advocated the establishment of a small medical executive committee and the grouping of clinical specialties into divisions with each division sending a representative to the MEC. The MEC would appoint a chairman who would have time allocated in his contract for administrative duties. He should serve in this capacity for five or more years. The MEC was seen as a body receiving reports from divisions and considering major medical policy matters and particularly planning and co-ordinating medical work in hospitals without infringing the clinical freedom of individual doctors.

The recommendations of the report were widely though not universally adopted. The report expected variations to meet local circumstances, and this in fact happened. For example, divisions for the medical and for the surgical specialties are usual, but the other specialties have been grouped in a variety of ways.

The second 'cogwheel' report was published in 1972 with the aim of producing a progress report and of giving examples of the new system in action. The third report, published in 1974, was concerned to anticipate the medical advisory machinery that would be appropriate in the reorganised NHS, and at district level particularly to define the relationship between medical executive committee, district medical committee and district management team. The existence of both MEC and DMC contributes to the complexity of the advisory machinery already referred to. The case for the DMC is the need to bring representatives of all branches of the medical profession together for an integrated approach to the issues of health care covering the whole spectrum of patient need; it is not enough that there should be a representative of the general practitioners and of hospital medical staff on the DMT. The case for the continuance of the MEC and its divisions is that there is still a need to co-ordinate hospital work. It was never envisaged that all the business of MECs would pass through the DMC.

The 'cogwheel' system, though not intended to apply medical audit or peer review of the type common in the very different context of American hospitals, was intended to encourage the profession as a whole to look at the hospital medical service as a whole, including the review of variations in clinical practice. The Scottish report in fact discussed medical audit or 'patient care evaluation'. The Royal Commission of 1976 did go so far as to say that audit is a responsibility of the clinical divisions in hospitals, though it added that progress had been slow.

A more common achievement of 'cogwheel', noted by the second report, has been measures to control medical expenditure. Where this has been tackled, a medical expenditure sub-committee has been established, and appropriate budgets delegated to it. In addition to the more obvious budget heads of medical and dental staff salaries, drugs, dressings, medical and surgical equipment and patients' appliances, some expenditure sub-committees have assumed broad control of paramedical support service budgets, such as pathology, X-ray, central sterile supply and physiotherapy, with provision made for appropriate department heads to attend meetings. Sometimes there is an agreement on the part of clinicians not to introduce new drugs into the pharmacy without reference to the expenditure sub-committee, and items of medical equipment costing more than a prescribed figure may be scrutinised. However, this is a very difficult management area that depends heavily on persuading doctors to an attitude that accepts the need to scrutinise clinical requirements and assess them against competing demands from other departments on financial resources. Divisions have a fairly straightforward job in presenting their order of priorities, but it is a sensitive and difficult task for the MEC to weight priorities between specialties.

The Royal Commission expressed disappointment at the performance of divisions, though it saw no alternative to making the system work. There is perhaps a greater difficulty at MEC level. The office of chairman makes great demands on time, and we have already referred to it in relation to the consultant member of the DMT, since the two offices are frequently combined. It also makes great demands on the qualities of advocacy, tact and diplomacy.

The second 'cogwheel' report noted the advantage of having representatives of other professions attending meetings of the divisions and the MEC. It had become a feature with few exceptions that senior administrators attended meetings of the MEC, and this pattern has continued in the reorganised NHS, where the administrator is joined at MEC meetings by the chief nursing officer and the community physician. On the other hand it is felt generally that regular attendance at the DMC by non-medical disciplines would not be appropriate since this is the formal mechanism through which the medical professional channels its advice on medical policies and priorities, and it should be regarded essentially as a medical arena for debate between doctors.

Crucial to the effective working of the 'cogwheel' system is the administrative support available to the MEC and the divisions. The relationship needs to be one of mutual trust and sensitivity on the part of the administrator to the demands placed on the role of MEC chairman by doctors. At the same time the MEC chairman must safeguard his position of being able to maintain policies independent of and sometimes opposed to the administrator's.

It has been disappointing to see in general how little use has been made of the information services potentially available to 'cogwheel'. Many doctors mistrust the accuracy and usefulness of hospital activity analysis data, and limited application has been made of these and other similar data in the solving of clinical resource allocation problems and priorities. Further collaboration in this field between clinicians, administrators and community physicians is needed in the future to make the optimum use of resources.

The nursing service

In direct contrast to the medical services, the nursing service is completely hierarchical. The chief nursing officer is responsible for assessing the nursing needs, taking into account both service and education demands, for drawing up and managing detailed nursing plans and budgets, and for maintaining professional standards both in the community and in hospital. At area level the area nursing officer acts as head of the nursing profession in the area, providing professional nursing advice to the AHA, to the ATO and to the matching local authority, advising on the implications of district plans from the nursing viewpoint and monitoring and co-ordinating the performance of district nursing officers against agreed policies and plans. Senior nurses on the staff of the area nursing officer typically include a nurse with special advisory and co-ordinating responsibilities for child health, including the school nursing service, who can appoint and second nursing staff to work for which the local authority has statutory responsibility, e.g. residential accommodation for the elderly and mentally handicapped. In addition, there may be a nurse whose principal responsibilities will be in the field of capital and service planning and a nurse for personnel work who in some instances may be fully integrated within the area personnel officer's department.

The post of district nursing officer brings together the responsibility for the management of the hospital and community nursing services for the population within a district. As a member of the DMT she, or he, can represent nursing in a total way, sharing responsibility with other members of a team for the management of all the health services provided in the district and undertaking an integrated professional role of organising all the nursing needs of the district. A structure that provides for hospital and community nurses to belong to a single nursing team facilitates co-operation between the various branches of nursing and contributes to an integrated approach to nursing care. Many regard the post of district nursing officer as the most challenging and demanding nursing responsibility. It is concerned with the operational delivery of the nursing care service within a district, and a nurse manager at this level can be accountable for an establishment of 2,500 nurses or more and a budget exceeding £10,000,000.

It is inevitable that the nurse member of the DMT should appear remote from the wards and departments yet share the basic responsibility of the professional nurse to provide nursing care at the point of need at the highest possible standard. The way the district nursing officer contributes to this objective is by bidding for resources, deploying staff effectively and by managing the nursing budget, maintaining good industrial relations and developing training and research opportunities.

The DNO works through delegating to divisional nursing officers whose responsibilities may reflect a geographical or a functional organisation of service, but more commonly a mixture of both patterns. A glance at the directory pages of *The Hospitals and Health Services Year Book* will show the variety of arrangements that have been made.

In addition to the possible permutations of service divisions, there is an education division, with the education divisional nursing officer responsible for co-ordinating the educational and service needs within a district. At the time of reorganisation the DHSS issued advice on the arrangements for organising nursing, midwifery and health visiting training and recommended that all facilities should be grouped together in nurse education divisions based on districts, but in some cases on multi-district areas with the exception of health visitors and district nurse training. The education division is responsible for arranging basic and post-basic educational training and aspects of in-service training for nursing auxiliaries and assistants. Midwifery training is the responsibility of the area/district nursing officer, and authorities are responsible for sponsoring health visitors at appropriate training centres. Future developments in nurse education and training depend on official decisions about the recommendations of the 1972 Briggs Committee on the subject.

Nursing services have been hierarchical at least since the time of Florence Nightingale, and it is probably inevitable that they always should be. The way in which the hierarchy is arranged in the reorganised NHS, however, is fairly recent, dating from the Salmon Report, which is discussed in Chapter 15.

Administrative services

Both area and district administrators undertake three principal responsibilities: managing the institutional and other support services, which account for approximately 20 per cent of the total health services revenue expenditure; providing administrative services to authorities and professional colleagues; and general co-ordination. Specialist support is provided at area level by a supplies officer, a personnel officer and the administrator, family practitioner services. In the non-metropolitan counties there is also the chief ambulance officer.

The organisation of administrative services can take a variety of forms at second-in-line and below, although some broad patterns for dividing administrative responsibilities have emerged. Various titles of general administrator, assistant administrator (planning), assistant administrator (operational services), operational services administrator and support services manager are commonly used. Although the concept of deputies was frowned on at reorganisation, the title of deputy administrator is used occasionally, and associate administrator rather more frequently. Whatever the titles used, the second-in-line posts encompass the following functions:

— service and capital planning and the project management of capital schemes and the management of information services;

— the management of 'hotel' services organised on a functional basis across a district where lines of accountability and budgetary control channel to a district-based manager in such services as catering, domestic and laundry services;

— general administration including such duties as responsibility for complaints systems and the management secretariat in support of the authority, its management teams and also in many instances its professional advisory machinery;

— responsibility in a few cases for the day-to-day supervision of the management of major district general hospitals.

In most instances the second-in-line administrators, usually the one concerned with 'hotel' services management, have taken direct accountability for the performance of sector/unit administrators. In some instances the sector administrators are accountable to the district administrator, but such an arrangement tends to produce a span of control which many administrators argue cannot be sustained effectively.

The growth of functional management over the years focusing authority at the district level and away from the sector has been the most controversial issue affecting the management of administrative services. At the time of reorganisation the concept of functional management was reinforced by the management arrangements described in the Grey Book and by subsequent circulars proposing pyramidal structures not only in hotel services but also in paramedical services. The development of these management structures has undoubtedly provided enhanced career opportunities for a whole range of professional groups, and in some disciplines has enabled scarce management expertise to be concentrated at a higher level and spread more effectively across a wider geographical base. However, it seems inevitable that as the majority of the functional management posts established at district level are supervisory and not advisory in nature, management decisions get drawn up to the district level which previously were exercised within the hospital or the community services.

Budgets necessarily follow the management arrangements and are formulated for services across the district rather than within a hospital. As a consequence, the base against which expenditure and priorities are considered has shifted from the conflicting demands within a hospital and clinics towards conflicting demands within a service across hospital and clinics. The cross-over point for priorities moves to district level and away from the institutional level and the power of virement across budgets is exercised at district level. The Royal Commission has associated with a functional management organisation some of the problems of slowness of decision taking, the raising of the decision level away from the lowest effective point nearest to the patient, and the difficulty of those working in the hospitals and clinics, and particularly the clinicians, of identifying the decision point.

In the further reorganisation of the service now pending, the tide has turned against functional management, so it is more useful to emphasise the advantages that may be lost than the difficulties that have been experienced. Management pyramids within the different functional services have not been established solely to meet the aspirations of staff for career structures which then tempt the best managers away to a level that is remote from patient care. The NHS must be able to offer attractive career opportunities in terms of scale and content, and therefore the corresponding job satisfaction, if it is to attract its quota of able managers into the hotel services, particularly those services that are not the exclusive domain of the NHS. Many of these managers have been instrumental in improving professional standards, morale and efficiency to a level that otherwise would not have been possible. The question and dilemma is whether the best of functional management can be preserved in the process of reversing the level of decision taking back towards the level of the hospital and community services. In those authorities where functional managers have recognised their role as service-giving with a client orientation, divisive issues about who administers discipline or who controls budgets have been less contentious. A working partnership has been possible between the functional manager and the local administrator, who has been involved in the process of setting service budgets within his hospital. Within this working relationship it has been possible to negotiate, for example, the transfer of staff from one functional service to another in terms of the priorities of the institution.

The issue needs to be solved flexibly by each authority in a way suited to local circumstances. It is sensible to argue that services such as laundry, CSSD, transport and bulk cook-freeze operations will benefit in unit cost terms if they are provided from a base wider than the institution, and clearly the same argument will apply to ambulance services. The case for the large-scale organisation of supplies has been officially endorsed, and here the question is how effectively it can be combined with institution-based staff responsible for local distribution and handling systems, and with easily accessible professional advice. The catering and domestic services will continue to benefit from professional advice and inspiration provided on a wider than institutional basis whether or not the heads of such services work in an advisory or supervisory capacity. There is another activity where the trend is likely to be more district-level involvement; as medical records develop as an integrated part of a wider information service increasingly employing computer technology, within hospitals and clinics in pursuit of the benefits of record linkage across catchment populations as well as within institutions, professional expertise will need to be provided to co-ordinate this activity.

One of the most important administrative services is personnel management, and it is discussed in detail in Chapter 13.

Although the organisation of management services is essentially a regional activity, some organisation and method and work study resources are deployed in the larger areas, particularly in support of the maintenance of fully measured pay/productivity schemes. In addition, some areas have appointed management consultants in operational research to tackle specific projects relating to the distribution of clinical services, or more commonly to the efficiency of commercial-type services. However, a relatively significant investment at area and district level has been made to develop information services, sometimes with close professional links to a regional statistical unit. The development of information services has concentrated on obtaining the maximum benefit from applying to the solution of problems the data held in hospital activity analysis and related systems. These problems have tended to be more in the arena of medium-term and long-term planning, although a few authorities have worked at developing the relevance of the data for medical management purposes within MECs and 'cogwheel' divisions. Information support is particularly important in providing a quantitative base for the formalised NHS planning system. Second-in-line general administrators whose job responsibilities contain a substantial commitment to service planning, and community physicians with a special interest in service planning and information services, are particularly dependent on the support available from an information and statistical unit. Although the head of such a unit is a member of the administrator's staff, the unit is available to all members of a management team and other staff, and its policy direction and the broad deployment of resources within the unit is a management team concern rather than the sole prerogative of the administrator. In a few authorities the development of an information service has been closely linked with corresponding staff in the matching local authority, and in some cases even provided as an agency service by the local authority. The reorganised NHS has given considerable prominence to strengthening service planning and information resources in supporting the need to develop a more rational base for decision making and to priority choices within a system of cash limits.

Administrators are responsible for identifying the need for legal services and for co-ordinating the use of these services, which are usually provided by legal advisers at region on matters of potential litigation concerning the treatment of patients, general issues of employers' liability, conveyancing, trusts, and other legal aspects of estate management. Administrators are also responsible for co-ordinating public relations activities and may use the specialist support of a public relations officer at region.

Community medicine

There are four main aspects to the role of the community physician in management as reviewed by the Hunter working party on medical administrators. In planning, the community physician contributes epidemiological and medical statistical skills in reviewing overall community health care needs. He works alongside clinicians contributing to the formulation and discussion of plans through the professional medical advisory machinery, and in particular maintains a close oversight of the joint care planning teams constituted in collaboration with the local authority for patient care group services for the mentally handicapped, the mentally ill, the elderly and children. In the development of information systems and the interpretation of information, he plays a part in the design of information systems and in the quality control of data and undertakes an important role in interpreting information for team and clinical colleagues both within and outside the formal planning process. He reviews statistics to analyse need and to comment on performance and results within an authority and in comparison with other authorities, evaluating the different approaches to health care and the balance of provision between hospital and community services. He has specific responsibilities for co-ordinating preventive services, particularly vaccination and immunisation, screening and health education programmes, and in deploying clinical medical officers. Finally, he holds responsibilities in relation to the local authority in the fields of school health, social services and environmental health. Depending on the nature of the area, either the area medical officer or the district community physician or one of the specialists in community medicine at area level is appointed by the local authority as 'proper officer' responsible for environmental health. Also supporting the area medical officer at area level is a community physician who has special responsibilities for child and school health services, directly advising the local authority through its education committee, and a community physician who has responsibilities in the field of social services, directly advising the local authority through its social services committee. Especially in the larger areas, community physicians have been appointed who specialise in planning, information and in medical manpower.

The health education officer, the head chiropodist and the head speech therapist are directly accountable to community physicians, and in some areas the heads of the paramedical therapy departments, such as physiotherapy and occupational therapy, are accountable to management teams through the area medical officer and the district community physician. The AMO in a teaching authority provides the personnel services associated with the appointment of consultants and senior registrars, which outside teaching areas falls as a regional responsibility. Particularly in teaching areas, he also enjoys links with academic departments of social and community medicine.

The pharmacy service

In 1970 the Noel Hall Report, which was concerned with the whole of Great Britain, argued that the small-scale organisation of pharmacy services had resulted in inflexibility in the deployment of resources, producing uneconomical management of staff, materials and equipment. Despite the recommendations of the Linstead Committee in 1955 that the organisation of hospital pharmaceutical services should be on a group basis, in the main hospitals were independently organised, with the resulting duplication of services between hospitals in the same group, and with hospitals purchasing from outside when a nearby hospital could have assisted. With a small-scale organisation it was not possible to justify the division of pharmaceutical services into specialised sections. Nor was it possible to provide an economic base for the deployment of technicians and other supporting staff, which resulted in pharmacists undertaking work that could be carried out by technicians or unqualified assistants. The small department was also seen to be particularly vulnerable to staffing shortages and a small department in itself was a disincentive to staff recruitment, with pharmacists being unable to maintain and develop their professional skills.

Against this background the Noel Hall Report recommended that the basic unit of pharmaceutical organisation must be large enough to provide an area of work to ensure that pharmacists, technicians and other supporting staff could be fully used on the work appropriate to their training and skills. The scope and responsibility of the work would justify the employment of a top-grade pharmacist who would be able to ensure that pharmacists worked within a team, obviating the practice of pharmacists working single-handed in isolated departments. A wide range of work would give the opportunity for specialisation by some staff and also produce sufficient flexibility in staffing to absorb peaks and troughs in workload and to facilitate staff release for training purposes.

It was considered that a pharmaceutical area should be large enough to provide work for a team of at least eight pharmacists and their supporting staff. However, this was a minimum and it was argued that there should be many far larger pharmaceutical areas. A service covering an area of 4,000 to 6,000 beds of all types was recommended as respresentative of a cross section of the pharmaceutical work necessary to meet all requirements without the disadvantages of extended lines of communication. While there were no standard patterns of organisation, it was expected that in a pharmaceutical area of such a size in-patient and advisory services would be provided at all major hospitals, while bulk production would be concentrated on one site or even on a sub-regional basis.

The implementation of the Noel Hall recommendations anticipated in spirit the larger-scale organisation that was applied generally to the service in 1974, but the Noel Hall pharmaceutical areas by no means coincided with the new areas and districts, and in circular HRC(73)28 the DHSS set out the various possible management arrangements that would reconcile the two.

In a single district area broadly coterminous with a Noel Hall pharmaceutical area the services are managed by an area pharmaceutical officer appointed by and accountable to the AHA with services provided through departments managed by principal and staff pharmacists, themselves accountable to the area pharmaceutical officer. The APhO is responsible for all the pharmaceutical services, including local manufacture, quality control and deployment of staff. Similar arrangements apply in multi-district areas coterminous with a Noel Hall area, with the addition of district pharmaceutical officers. The latter are accountable to the APhO for co-ordinating the managed pharmaceutical services of the district, but are not the managers of the other heads of pharmaceutical departments in the district. Other arrangements have been made where areas do not broadly coincide: two or more smaller areas have jointly appointed an area pharmaceutical officer, and in large multi-district areas covering two or more Noel Hall areas the APhO manages one of these sub-areas and the others are managed by area pharmacists directly accountable to the AHA, the APhO having a co-ordinating role for the area as a whole.

In relation to the APhO's responsibility for co-ordinating services with general practice pharmacy and advising on all policy matters concerning pharmacy, there needs to be close consultation between the APhO and the FPC administrator, whose duties include keeping the adequacy of general practice pharmacy services under surveillance and conveying the views of the FPC on such matters affecting pharmacy as the planning and development of health centres.

Speech therapy

Before NHS reorganisation, speech therapy services were organised in two main categories. There was an education service and a hospital-based service, with approximately three times as many speech therapists employed by local authorities as by the hospital service. Those speech therapy services forming part of the school health service fell to the responsibility of the principal school medical officer, who was also the medical officer of health for the local authority. The three main categories of children seen by speech therapists in the education service were those at ordinary schools, those of pre-school age, and handicapped children in special schools. Speech therapists working in hospitals normally fell loosely under the supervision of a department headed by a consultant. The relevant department might be rehabilitation, paediatrics, ENT or neurology.

In 1972 the Quirk Committee reviewed the arguments for a unified structure for speech therapy to provide liaison and mutual help between therapists working on the one hand only with children and on the other hand primarily with adults. The Committee considered that there was a prima facie case for organising speech therapy services under local authorities as the major employer of speech therapists, regarding speech therapy more as a branch of remedial teaching. However, local authorities were not regarded as the appropriate bodies to organise services for adults, and the committee was more impressed by the evidence that the speech therapists' basic function was therapeutic, involving a large element of assessment and continuing observation. It was therefore resolved that AHAs should assume responsibility for a unified speech therapy service. Within each AHA therefore an area speech therapist is appointed, accountable to the area medical officer and responsible for the direction of the service and for overall planning. Some of the larger areas are split on a district basis for day-to-day management of speech therapy, but because of the comparatively small numbers of speech therapists employed, the co-ordination of scarce and limited resources in speech therapy has tended to be regarded as an area rather than a district function. The priority task of the area speech therapist has been to ensure the integration of the speech therapy services provided to local authorities with those provided in the NHS. The area speech therapist continues to provide a focal point to whom officers of the education committee and schools can turn and whom the community physician with responsibility for child health consults in providing advice to the local authority. Authorities are given the option of making a part-time or full-time appointment, or indeed of making a joint appointment between neighbouring AHAs.

Scientific and technical services

There are over twenty separate staff groups in the scientific and technical services, a fact that reflects the disparate nature of these services. The Zuckerman Report on hospital scientific and technical services was published in 1968. Its main objectives were to promote the better co-ordination of scientific and technical services and to integrate non-medically qualified scientists and technical staff into a new staffing structure that with appropriate improved training arrangements would facilitate the career progression of staff. It was foreseen that improved prospects of promotion and job satisfaction would attract an increased number of high-calibre non-medically qualified scientists and technical staff and provide a means of retaining them in the NHS. It was also recognised that there would be an increasing requirement for more medically qualified scientists in the light of the increasing scientific content of clinical work.

The government accepted the recommendations of the report in principle in 1970, but the recommendations were not liked by all the professions concerned, and progress towards implementation was slow. In April 1974 the DHSS issued circular HSC(IS)16, which was concerned mainly but not exclusively with diagnostic activities including pathology services, radiodiagnosis and radiotherapy, nuclear medicine, medical physics and bioengineering and physiological measurement. These are all services based on hospitals, and the circular suggested three different possible patterns of organisation: a departmental structure, a single-profession hierarchy, and a 'cogwheel' division structure. In multi-district areas there would be need for co-operation between districts in the organisation of scientific work, and the necessary co-ordination should be the concern of the area medical officer. Advice to the AHA should be provided by an area scientific committee, which should work in close liaison with the area medical committee. In practice, relatively few areas have established area scientific committees and informal links have emerged in multi-district areas between the heads of scientific departments, the ATO and the regional scientific officer. Regional scientific committees, however, have been established in all regions, making a considerable contribution to the development and co-ordination of scientific services.

The Zuckerman Committee attempted to bring together into a single staffing structure some twenty different staff groups, and HSC(IS)16 attempted to do the same thing organisationally, fitting these groups into the normal pattern of the 1974 reorganisation. However, most of these groups are employed in only small numbers in any area and they have different and potentially conflicting professional interests. In view of the difficulties in achieving integration, the DHSS appointed a departmental team which in 1977-8 reviewed some of the organisational issues. The team concluded that 'a single scientific service — in terms of organisation, management and staff structure and grading — is not practicable nor acceptable; rather we should recognise the present development of three main scientific services — medical laboratory services, radiological services, and clinical engineering and physical sciences services'.

It excluded from consideration some of the services that had been covered by the Zuckerman Report, such as pharmacy, psychology and dietetics. It seems certain therefore that a single scientific service, as envisaged by Zuckerman, will not now come about.

One of the difficulties of these services is inter-professional rivalry. Non-medical scientists feel that their prospects are limited by a preference for doctors in the scientific departments, while doctors feel that non-medical scientists want to take over some of their responsibilities. The medical laboratory scientific officers want a staff structure that would integrate them with the biochemists and physicists (who are opposed to such a change) and want to be responsible for the management of pathology laboratories. Both the 1977-8 review team and the Royal Commission considered some of these matters. The review team ruled out the idea of a dual head of department role as an unworkable management arrangement but argued for identifying those management activities which should be delegated by the head of the department and which should be regarded as the province of the departmental 'manager', a compromise the Royal Commission rejected. The Commission declined to rule that the head of a laboratory should always be medically qualified; the head should be the most able scientist available.

The remedial professions and linked therapies

The remedial professions and linked therapies have much in common with the scientific and technical professions: they are mostly among the smaller groups of staff; while they are a group with common interests they have not enough in common to be organised in a single structure and therefore do not fit easily into the 1974 organisational pattern; there are various patterns of accountability; and the aspirations of some of them have appeared to threaten the medical profession.

The Macmillan Report on the future structure of the remedial professions was published in 1973 and its recommendations were still under consideration at the time of reorganisation. Guidance on interim arrangements was therefore issued in circular HSC(IS)101, which was concerned with occupational therapy, physiotherapy and remedial gymnastics, and the linked industrial, art, drama and music therapies. Services would normally be organised on a district basis. AHAs should designate in districts a senior occupational therapist and a senior physiotherapist (and a remedial gymnast where appropriate) as having responsibility for advising DMTs. These therapists, in conjunction with medical advice, would advise district community physicians on the organisation of their services for the district and would be responsible for ensuring that professional standards were maintained. They would be accountable to the district community physician for these responsibilities, but for other duties would continue to be responsible to doctors. They would not relinquish all clinical responsibilities. It was not envisaged that arrangements for the linked therapies should be disturbed; a variety of arrangements would continue, with therapists accountable to the senior occupational therapist, a consultant, the district administrator or others, depending on local arrangements.

At the end of 1978 the DHSS circulated for comment a report on the organisation of the remedial professions in the NHS concerned with the implementation of the Macmillan Report and, following consultation on this Report, issued new guidance about the management of the remedial professions in circular HC(79)19. The DHSS circular takes as its main starting point the view recommended in the Macmillan Report that the remedial professions should be responsible for their own management, arguing that this is entirely consistent with the premise that the medical profession would continue to take the lead in guiding the optimum deployment of rehabilitation services and that the ultimate responsibility for the management of all rehabilitation services falls to the DMT. The Macmillan Report had recommended the establishment of a hierarchical structure of management for the remedial professions. The DHSS report debated the issue of appointing a manager therapist, which considerably extends the role of the district therapist designated under circular HSC(IS)101, or of appointing a co-ordinator therapist to represent the views of senior colleagues but who is not in a line-relationship to them. The report acknowledged the attraction of the concept of a co-ordinator therapist as ensuring consultation and collaboration and minimising the threat of intervention from a superior officer. However, it concluded that in practice the relationship was too weak to ensure that disagreements within a department were resolved and that the policies of the DMT are implemented.

Circular HC(79)19 asked AHAs to appoint district therapists to manage and plan services for their professions within a district, but stressed that there was no intention of grafting a hierarchical administrative structure on to the remedial professions. It was hoped that district therapists would retain some unit responsibilities which would enable them to keep in touch with clinical practice. At the same time the DHSS recognised that the time was not right for the imposition of a single solution in the light of widely varying circumstances across districts; in some situations one or other of the remedial professions might continue with the designation of a senior therapist to carry out the advisory functions recommended under the interim management arrangements.

Although earlier advice had recommended that district therapists should have links to the DMT on planning matters through the district community physician and on personnel and management matters through the district administrator, DHSS guidance rejected the idea that the district therapist should hold a dual accountability and recommended that the district therapist's accountability to the DMT should be entirely through either the district community physician or the district administrator. District therapists should be involved in strategic and operational planning matters. In relation to the requirement for medical advice in the formulation of plans for rehabilitation services, the DHSS strongly recommends the formation of a group of major users of rehabilitation services. The supply of remedial resources will continue to fall short of competing demands, and the major users group would play an important part in contributing to decisions on the deployment of resources and the protection of priority services by bringing together clinicians, therapists and other staff directly concerned with these issues.

Dietetics

Although at one time considered in the context of the Zuckerman Report, dietetics has emerged as an independent discipline with close working links with individual clinicians and with the general catering function. Dietetic services are organised on a district basis with a district dietitian responsible for advising the DMT on the provision of a nutrition and dietetic service and for managing services covering both the hospital and community requirements. The district dietitian is accountable to the district administrator, but works in a service-giving relationship to clinical doctors and community physicians.

Within 'cogwheel' arrangements the district dietitian may be attached to a particular division, such as the division of medicine, or may have access to the MEC when matters affecting dietetics are being discussed. The district dietitian is available as an adviser on nutrition to the local authority social service and education departments. The district dietitian should be a practising dietitian. Area appointments have not been considered justified.

Chiropody

Before NHS reorganisation chiropody services were provided by hospitals and by local authorities for education and social service departments. The main task at reorganisation was to merge these various services into a single co-ordinated service within each district and to maintain close working arrangements between health and local authorities. District chiropodists were appointed who were responsible for the organisation of chiropody services throughout a district, covering services provided in hospitals, health centres, clinics, patients' homes, schools and domiciliary services. District chiropodists are expected to undertake some clinical work. In multi-district areas, an area chiropodist accountable to the area medical officer or another community physician at area headquarters is necessary to plan the development of chiropody services for the area as a whole, to develop effective recruitment policies and in-service and post-basic training for qualified chiropodists, technicians and foot care assistants in order to make the best use of scarce resources, and to collaborate with social service and education departments in the provision of chirpody services, particularly for the school health service and for other priority groups, such as the elderly and the handicapped. An area chiropodist may be a full-time appointment or combined with some district responsibilities.

The principal task of the head chiropodist is to develop the more effective use of the skills of trained chiropodists, to improve levels of service which are generally inadequate even for the priority groups. The DHSS encourages chiropodists to explore measures for reducing the high proportion of domiciliary treatments other than those required for the housebound elderly, and to examine the possibilities of arranging transport for patients to travel to a clinic for chiropody treatment or to use local centres for chiropody sessions, such as old people's homes, day centres and day clubs where the elderly and the handicapped are brought together already. Mobile clinics have been introduced in some places, providing the chiropodist with the opportunity to visit centres over a wide area. In particular, encouragement has been given to training an increasing number of foot care assistants capable of carrying out simple foot care and hygiene in order to conserve the time of the trained chiropodist for work that requires his or her skills and expertise.

Psychology

A good deal of discussion has taken place in recent years about the development of the role of psychologists. The various issues relevant to the organisation of psychology services were considered by a sub-committee established by the former standing mental health advisory committee to the DHSS under the chairmanship of Professor Trethowan. The Trethowan Report concluded that the professional status of clinical psychologists in the NHS should be acknowledged. Psychology should not be regarded as subservient to any other profession. This has raised difficult questions regarding the ultimate responsibility of the medical profession for the treatment of patients which the Trethowan Report argues can only be reconciled satisfactorily through multi-disciplinary teamwork, implying the mutual recognition by different professions of a shared responsibility for patient care. The distinction is made, therefore, between the independent professional status of psychologists and full clinical responsibility that can only be exercised by consultants and general practitioners.

The organisation of psychology services is seen as an area-based function, although it is recognised that there must be scope for flexibility in the organisation of services within the larger multi-district areas. Within an area department of clinical psychology, ideally there would be sub-division into a number of specialist sections corresponding to the different clinical fields in which psychologists work. This organisation has the advantage of allowing the special expertise of psychologists in particular care areas to develop while retaining the opportunity for psychologists to meet so as to counter the dangers of working in isolation. The area psychologist is also in a position to make the optimum use of scarce resources and to protect an adequate level of service, particularly in the fields of mental illness and mental handicap in which psychologists are relatively well established. In a fully developed area the Trethowan Report recommends the following pattern of specialist groups: physical handicap, mental handicap, child health, neurological services, mental illness, geriatrics, adolescent services, and primary health care. The area psychologist is responsible to the management team but co-operates particularly with the area medical officer in the co-ordination of clinical psychology services. Each specialist psychology group is headed by a principal psychologist who is not expected to account to the area psychologist on matters of professional judgement. It is envisaged that there will continue to be a place for area psychology advisory committees, providing a means for the clinical psychologists as a whole to participate in advising AHAs and including representatives of occupational and educational psychologists. In relation to the 'cogwheel' arrangements, a representation by psychologists specialising in particular branches of psychology is suggested on such divisions as psychiatry, medicine and child health. It is emphasised that psychologists also have an important contribution to make to the work of joint care planning teams.

The works service

The works service is an important part of area and district management but not much need be said about it here since it is covered in Chapter 10. The execution of smaller-scale capital works is an area responsibility. Possibly more important at area and district level, and certainly a continuing responsibility, is estate management. Although the day-to-day maintenance aspects of the service are a responsibility principally undertaken within hospitals and community premises, extraordinary maintenance and the overall professional oversight of the works service are, like capital building, essentially area- and district-based functions.

Teaching areas and districts

It has always been a fundamental aim of medical education in the UK that teaching should be undertaken in an environment where the highest standards of patient care can be demonstrated, setting an example which it is hoped doctors will follow throughout their working lives. The distinctive character of teaching hospitals was recognised at the establishment of the NHS, when boards of governors were set up to manage them in England and Wales. In 1974 they were integrated into the main NHS organisational structure, as they had always been in Scotland and Northern Ireland.

Until fairly recently there was one university medical school and correspondingly one teaching hospital group in each region in England outside the south-east. In marked contrast, there was a concentration of teaching in London: fourteen undergraduate medical schools, one multi-specialty postgraduate school and twelve single specialty postgraduate schools, all associated with different hospitals. In the rest of the UK the pattern was similar to that of the English provinces, with four centres in Scotland and one each in Wales and Northern Ireland.

The recent policy of expanding the output from medical schools has somewhat modified this pattern. New medical schools have been established, so that there are now three in the Trent region instead of one. Much of the expansion, however, is by an increased output from existing schools, and that increases the need for clinical facilities in the associated hospitals. From the university's point of view it is desirable that these facilities should be available in reasonable proximity to the medical school, particularly in the early part of the undergraduate clinical course. Within this constraint, medical schools in recent years have sought to adapt to the increasing pressure on clinical facilties by seeking access to hospitals away from their immediate vicinity, and in the undergraduates' final clinical year increasing use has been made of hospitals throughout the region.

In London the problems posed by an expansion of medical education are compounded by another: the over-concentration of medical schools combined with a big fall in population and therefore in the need for hospital beds. In 1980 the London Health Planning Consortium, a body representing both NHS and university interests, estimated that over the succeeding ten years there should be a reduction of some 2,300 acute beds in the London teaching districts and 3,900 in the non-teaching districts to achieve a more equitable balance of health care provision throughout the four Thames regions. It represents a reduction by nearly a quarter of the existing acute bed stock.

The situation in London focuses starkly the dilemma faced to a greater or lesser degree by all teaching districts in striking an appropriate balance between their service commitment to offer a balanced and comprehensive range of health care services to their local community, their regional or sub-regional service commitment, and their research and teaching commitment.

The first of these elements can be controversial, at least in London. At one time the London hospitals preferred to admit cases suitable for undergraduate teaching or research, and they could be selective because there were other hospitals managed by HMCs. It is questionable how far this happens now that the teaching hospitals have district responsibilities, but it has left a legacy of some local hostility to these hospitals despite their high clinical reputation.

Research is a very important element of the work of teaching districts. In all university settings, teaching and research thrive together. The NHS is no exception, and teaching hospitals have fostered much of the research in the NHS. Research is supported by significant financial contributions from the DHSS and regions, although most academic and non-academic departments in teaching hospitals depend heavily on monies obtained through project grants from the major charitable research institutions and from industry. The medical staff recruited to teaching hospitals are appointed, therefore, not only for their clinical expertise and their teaching interests, but also on their demonstrated excellence and commitment to research.

A major proportion of regional specialty services has gravitated towards teaching districts, depending as the majority of them do on a high concentration of interdependent resources which can be provided only in a limited number of centres, although it should be emphasised that the provision of regional services is by no means confined to the teaching districts. It is not only the more clear-cut examples of regional specialties, such as radiotherapy, cardiothoracic surgery and renal dialysis, which are to be found in teaching hospitals, but also the more elusive 'hidden' centres of excellence serving a much wider population than the local district community and not formally delegated as regional specialties.

The provision of such a range of specialised facilities that are interrelated requires not only a high concentration of doctors but also specially trained and experienced nurses and paramedical staff. And high technology medicine, which tends to be concentrated in teaching hospitals, is very expensive. It is not surprising, therefore, that teaching hospital costs have always been higher than those of non-teaching hospitals, though there have been surprising variations, with the London hospitals considerably more expensive than the others. While the teaching hospitals in England and Wales were separately financed through boards of governors, and generally hospital allocations followed the same pattern from year to year, the high costs were on the whole accepted, despite some unfavourable comment from non-teaching hospitals. The integration of the teaching hospitals into the main organisational structure, combined with the policy of equitable allocation of resources through RAWP, etc., have brought their costs in question. The RAWP report, which is described in detail in Chapter 9, provides an element in its formula to cover the extra expenses necessarily incurred as a consequence of teaching responsibilities. It does not take account of the 'centre of excellence' element. However, it is very difficult to identify and demarcate the various cost variables inherent in the make-up of teaching hospital expenditure, and it will not be surprising if some teaching districts feel that RAWP does not adequately recognise their needs, particularly at a time of severe financial restraint and when official policy is to divert more resources to the non-acute services.

The organisational arrangements for achieving liaison between the NHS and the universities have been set out earlier in this book. There is a university nominee on each RHA and AHA, and the number is increased to two or three in the teaching areas. Not all districts in a teaching area are teaching districts; in the majority that are, it is usual for a representative of the medical school to be a member of the district management team. Circular HSC(IS)85 issued guidance on the establishment of area university liaison committees. These are advisory to authorities and universities over a wide range of issues of common concern. However, they are not concerned with postgraduate education, which continues to be the responsibility of regional postgraduate medical education committees, or with the locally organised research scheme, which provides monies for NHS research under the guidance of regional research committees.

Further reading

Statutory instruments and circulars

England and Wales

SI73/1275. The NHS (Determination of Areas) Order 1973
SI73/1286. The NHS (Regional and Area Health Authorities: Membership and Procedure) Regulations 1973
SI73/1468. The NHS (General Dental Services) Regulations 1973
SI74/160. The NHS (General Medical and Pharmaceutical Services) Regulations 1974
SI79/738. The NHS (Health Authorities: Membership) Regulations 1979
SI79/739. The NHS (Family Practitioner Committees: Membership and Procedure) Regulations 1979
HRC(73)4. Defining districts
HRC(73)10. Ambulance services
HRC(73)22. Membership and procedure of regional and area health authorities
HRC(73)32. Establishing family practitioner committees
HRC(74)32. Management arrangements: agency arrangements and extra-territorial management
HRC(74)37. Management arrangements: works staff organisation and preparation of substantive schemes
HSC(IS)85. Medical and dental teaching of university students and associated research — liaison between NHS authorities and universities
HSC(IS)101. The remedial professions and linked therapies
HC(79)19. Remedial professions management
WHRC(73)7. Management arrangements for the reorganised national health service in Wales
WHRC(73)8. Ambulance services
WHRC(73)19. Membership and procedure of area health authorities
WHRC(73)24. Management arrangements: district pattern and specialists in community medicine
WHRC(73)28. Establishing family practitioner committees
WHRC(73)34. Organisation of pharmaceutical services

WHRC(74)15. The work of family practitioner committees
WHRC(74)19. Functions of area health authorities
WHRC(74)38. Administrative management structure
WHSC(IS)81. Medical and dental teaching of university students and associated research — liaison between NHS authorities and universities
WHSC(IS)100. The remedial professions and linked therapies

Scotland

SI74/466. The NHS (Functions of Health Boards) (Scotland) Order 1974
SI74/505. The NHS (General Dental Services) (Scotland) Regulations 1974
SI74/506. The NHS (General Medical and Pharmaceutical Services) (Scotland) Regulations 1974
SI74/507. The NHS (General Ophthalmic Services) (Scotland) Regulations 1974
HSR(72)C3. The administrative structure of health boards
HSR(73)C7. Health board districts
HSR(73)C8. Overlap of services between health boards and extra territorial management of institutions
HSR(73)C19. Relations with universities: university liaison committees
HSR(73)C41. Relations between health boards and universities
HSR(74)C11. Structure of pharmaceutical services
NHS Circular 1974(GEN)9. Professional advisory structure

Official reports

DES, DHSS. Scottish Office and Welsh Office. *Report of the Committee of Enquiry into Speech Therapy Services* (Quirk Report). HMSO 1972
DHSS. *Management Arrangements for the Reorganised National Health Service* (The Grey Book). HMSO 1972
DHSS. *Report of the Working Party on Medical Administrators* (Hunter Report). HMSO 1972
DHSS. *Second Report of the Joint Working Party on the Organisation of Medical Work in Hospitals.* HMSO 1972
DHSS. *Third Report of the Joint Working Party on the Organisation of Medical Work in Hospitals.* HMSO 1974
DHSS. *The Role of Psychologists in the Health Services* (Trethowan Report). HMSO 1977
DHSS. *Scientific and Technical Services in the NHS.* A report following a review by a departmental team 1977-8. 1978
DHSS. *The Remedial Professions* (Macmillan Report). HMSO 1973
DHSS, SHHD and Welsh Office. *Report of the Working Party on the Hospital Pharmaceutical Service* (Noel Hall Report). HMSO 1970
DHSS, SHHD and Welsh Office. *Report of the Working Party on Management Structures in the Local Authority Nursing Services* (Mayston Report). HMSO 1969
Ministry of Health. *First Report of the Joint Working Party on the Organisation of Medical Work in Hospitals* (Cogwheel Report). HMSO 1967
Ministry of Health and SHHD. *Hospital Scientific and Technical Services.* (Zuckerman Report). HMSO 1968

Ministry of Health, SHHD. *Senior Nursing Staff Structure* (Salmon Report). HMSO 1966

SHHD. *Organisation of Medical Work in the Hospital Service in Scotland.* First Report of the Joint Working Party. HMSO 1967

SHHD. *The Organisation of a Medical Advisory Structure.* HMSO 1973

Welsh Office. *Management Arrangements for the Reorganised National Health Service in Wales.* HMSO 1972

Other publications

Association of Chief Administrators of Health Authorities. *A Review of the Management of the Reorganised NHS.* 1976

Kogan, M. *The Working of the National Health Service.* Research Paper No. 1 for the Royal Commission on the NHS. HMSO 1978

London Health Planning Consortium. *Towards a Balance: A framework for acute hospitals in London reconciling service with teaching needs.* 1980.

Stewart, Rosemary, *et al. The District Administrator in the National Health Service.* King's Fund 1980

7
Organisation and management below district level

The district is normally referred to as the operational level of the health service, but most operational activities are performed in the services and institutions below district level which together make up a comprehensive district service. The NHS is unusual in organisational terms in that it is at this operational or 'shop floor' level that there takes place the most crucial interaction in the service — that between doctors (and other professionals) and the individual patient. The staff who have the highest status in the organisation — consultant medical staff — work at the operational level, not in the higher tiers of administration. It is this which accounts for many of the peculiar features of health service organisation and management.

Administrative organisation below team level

At the time of reorganisation in 1974 it was left to the new health authorities to determine the management arrangements within their districts. The DHSS advised AHAs that they could subdivide their districts on a functional or a geographical basis, or a mixture of both, i.e. hospitals, health centres, clinics and other facilities could be linked administratively because they were of a particular specialty, e.g. acute, psychiatric, geriatric or mental handicap, or because they provided health services in a particular geographical area. A new term — sectors — was introduced to describe these subdivisions of districts. Most districts were said to be unlikely to have more than two or three sectors. Areas were asked to ensure that within these sectors satisfactory multidisciplinary working could take place, but it was emphasised that a sector was not to be a multidisciplinary management tier separate from the district.

In determining sectors, areas and districts were thus left with considerable choice. Large general or long-stay hospitals were obviously suitable as a single sector with or without the associated community services. More difficult decisions arose when there were several hospitals in a particular area but of different specialties, such as a medium-sized general hospital, two cottage hospitals and a mental handicap hospital. It was in some cases advantageous to gather as many hospitals as possible into the sector to attract a higher salary grading for the post of sector administrator. Some districts have found that a disparate mix of hospitals and other premises is inappropriate and have revised their arrangements.

A major decision to be taken in 1974 concerned the integration of hospital and former local authority health services. It could be argued that to link administratively a hospital with local health centres and clinics was a tangible step towards the full integration of health services at local level. Conversely it was sometimes feared that if they were linked the pressures and power groups within the hospitals would work to the detriment of the community services, which would therefore be best served if organised as a distinct sector. Some authorities chose one course and some the other.

A sector, therefore, may comprise a single large institution, whether a general or a single specialty hospital; or a large institution and a number of smaller hospitals; or a collection of small hospitals; or a collection of community staff and premises including health centres and clinics; or a hospital or group of hospitals and associated community premises. In an urban area the acute sector may include all hospital premises within the district, possibly on one site, whereas in rural areas a sector may consist of a number of small hospitals in small towns miles apart. In any generalisations about sector management arrangements these differences must be borne in mind.

Authorities' arrangements for sectors can be found in the directory sections of *The Hospitals and Health Services Year Book,* which also show how much, or how little, administrative sectors match nursing divisions. A complete matching might have been desirable, but different considerations affected the two organisations. Thus, while a midwifery division is nearly always called for in the nursing service, the maternity services would rarely if ever make an appropriate administrative sector. Arrangements in Wales and Scotland are similar to those in England.

Since a sector might comprise a number of hospitals with or without associated health centres and clinics, the term 'unit' was introduced in 1974 to describe a single, usually small, hospital and possibly associated community premises. It is not surprising that in a service with administrative levels of unit, sector, district, area and region there have been complaints of administrative complication.

Some districts have been reluctant to introduce the terms sector and unit, and pre-1974 titles such as house governor and hospital administrator are still sometimes used.

Hospital organisation

Hospital is a broad term covering institutions which vary greatly in size, age and function. If the 1962 Hospital Plans had worked out as originally expected that might no longer be the case, but a more realistic approach to the cost of hospital building, combined with a new belief in the merits of small hospitals, means that we can expect the variety to continue indefinitely, though new hospitals will be opened and some existing ones closed. Any short account of hospitals therefore makes generalisations which may not be applicable to many individual hospitals. To make an obvious example, a large psychiatric hospital is a complex organisation but is very different from a large general hospital in which there are patients needing a wide variety of different medical and other professional skills. A detailed comparison would show a large number of elements in common between the two and perhaps a larger number of differences.

A number of attempts have been made to conceptualise the complex web of relationships which make up a hospital. A common model is of a central triangle comprising doctor, nurse and patient surrounded by concentric rings of supporting services with the rings close to the central triangle representing staff dealing directly with the patient such as physiotherapists, social workers and occupational therapists, the next rings representing staff involved in patient-related activities such as pathology and radiography but with less of a one-to-one relationship and the outer rings representing supporting services such as catering, engineering, finance and housekeeping. Even this model is far too simple to reflect the different specialty groups and their different demands on services such as theatres, X-ray and rehabilitation, or the links between hospital services and community services. The different services involved have different organisational arrangements, different training and different statuses in the organisation. It has been argued that few organisations are as complex as hospitals and this complexity has significant implications for the role of the administrator. The remainder of this section will describe the organisation of the main staff groups within hospitals.

Doctors

The neat if complicated organisation structures of the NHS belie the complexity of relationships at operational level. It is misleading to speak of doctors as if they constitute a homogeneous group. Apart from general practitioners with part-time hospital appointments they are all specialists and therefore by definition have different professional interests. As medicine develops more specialties evolve. There are now 47 recognised specialties, some practiced by only a few consultants, mainly in teaching hospitals, others such as general medicine, general surgery, anaesthetics and mental illness (adult), practised in every general hospital. Within the profession different specialties have a different status. High status appears to be associated with high technology and high earning potential in the private sector. A measure of status is the career choice of newly qualified doctors; another, and a consequence of the first, is the amount of competition for consultant posts. If the ablest and most ambitious young doctors opt for the specialties with the highest status, that is likely to perpetuate that status. The specialties with higher status are more likely to be successful in the competition for resources.

The standing of the various specialties does not of course provide a comprehensive explanation of doctors' attitudes. The differences, though real, are not clearly defined, and although the long-stay specialties have low status there are nevertheless distinguished psychiatrists and geriatricians. There are other factors making for both groupings and differences. The various surgical specialties, for example, have interests in common. It is sometimes thought that doctors whose interests are centred on a department, such as pathologists and radiologists, have a different attitude from those involved in direct patient care. A further feature which increases the profession's heterogeneity is the proportion of doctors who were born overseas — 35 per cent in England in 1978.

A peculiar feature of hospital medical staffing is that the majority of staff are in training posts. In England in 1977 the total number was 28,397, of whom 10,115 were consultants; nearly all the rest were in the two registrar and two house officer grades. Whilst the numbers of training posts in the higher levels are controlled in the light of training needs, and the training role is recognised in such things as arrangements for study leave, the doctors in the training grades, generally referred to collectively as the junior doctors, constitute an essential part of hospital medical staffing. It is arguable that there are far too many doctors in training in relation to the number of permanent, i.e. consultant, posts and that the present system is radically unsound and owes its existence to staffing rather than training needs. The subject is discussed in Chapter 13.

After completing the undergraduate course newly qualified doctors spend one year in pre-registration posts — usually six months in medicine and six in surgery, before becoming eligible for full registration. Then as senior house officers they can apply for posts in whatever specialty they choose according to their career intentions. Increasingly rotational schemes are offered to SHOs in which they may spend successive six month periods in surgical and medical specialties to gain varied experience. For prospective general practitioners a series of rotations in surgical and medical specialties is being developed as part of an attempt to make the postgraduate training of GPs more systematic.

When a doctor has decided on his career intentions he will, if he wishes to specialise, seek a registrar post in his chosen specialty and study for the necessary qualification — fellowship of the appropriate royal college. The final step on the path to consultant status is a period of higher professional training as a senior registrar, possibly again involving rotation between different hospitals to gain experience. Such posts are tightly controlled both numerically, to ensure that the majority of senior registrars can become consultants, and in quality of experience so that the appropriate royal college is satisfied that adequate training is being given.

Doctors are organised in specialty groups known as firms: a consultant assisted by a team of juniors who are in some or all the grades described above. Normally the consultant has access to a specified number of beds in one or more wards. Assisted by his juniors he will also conduct out-patient sessions and, if a surgeon, theatre sessions. He will call on the assistance of the diagnostic specialists such as pathologists, and on the anaesthetist, as necessary, and also on the paramedical professions.

The consultant is not accountable to any superior authority in clinical matters, but he needs to collaborate with other professionals to carry out his task. Moreover the decisions he takes—and the decisions his juniors take on his behalf — account for a large part of hospital expenditure. Virtually the whole of the machinery of the hospital can be seen to be in support of the clinical decisions made by individual consultants about their patients. Arrangements are therefore needed which, while recognising the clinician's autonomy, relate his needs to those of other clinicians and to the resources available to the hospital so as to achieve the best use of them. The present elaborate arrangements derive from the 'cogwheel' reports, and are described in Chapters 6 and 15.

Nurses and midwives

Nurses constitute by far the largest group of hospital staff. While there were 28,397 hospital doctors in England in 1977, the number of nurses (whole time equivalent) was 286,040. The public is more inclined to think of hospital nurse staffing than of medical staffing as being dependent on trainees, but the picture is not as simple as that.

Doctor trainees and nurse trainees are trainees in rather different senses. Junior doctors are qualified, though they have not yet acquired the further experience and qualifications required for a substantive post, whereas student and pupil nurses are as yet unqualified and training for their basic qualification. Basically theirs is an apprenticeship system, though with increasing emphasis on periods of formal education in school or college rather than traditional learning on the job. If the recommendations of the Briggs Committee are accepted the apprenticeship element will be very slight. In recent years a number of university undergraduate courses in nursing have been introduced. Another difference between trainee doctors and trainee nurses is that most junior doctors plan to spend their whole working life in the profession whereas many nurses remain in the profession for only a few years. The problem with doctors is how to relate the number of training posts to career expectations and yet meet immediate staffing needs. Many nurses drop out before completing their training and, because it is a predominantly female profession, many leave it temporarily or permanently fairly soon after completing training. Thus many more trainees must be recruited to ensure an adequate supply of trained staff than would be the case if most of those trained remained in the profession. This benefits the service in that trainees make a very important contribution to staffing, but it does mean that a lot of the profession's energies must be directed to recruitment and training.

Nevertheless hospitals are somewhat less dependent for staffing on trainees than is sometimes supposed. Of the total staff for England quoted above, some 73,000 were 'other nursing staff' such as nursing assistants without a professional qualification and not training for one. Roughly the same number were trainees either as students (54,000) or pupils (20,000). The total of qualified staff, registered and enrolled, was 138,500, nearly as many as the other two groups together.

These total figures are no guide to the staffing patterns of individual hospitals. The traditional pattern is familiar: at one extreme the large acute hospital with large numbers of both registered and student nurses and at the other the long-stay geriatric hospital with far fewer nurses, most of them 'other nursing staff'. This pattern has been considerably modified. One factor contributing to change has been the implementation of the Salmon Report, bringing all the nurses in a hospital group and now a district within a single management structure, so that staffing needs can be considered as a whole. Whatever may appear the ideal staffing pattern and staffing levels there are a number of constraints — quite apart from financial constraints — on what can be achieved. In the first place decisions on staffing patterns and numbers will depend on how nursing management assesses needs — which may be affected by such different things as pressure from the medical staff affected and what has traditionally been regarded as appropriate. Long-stay wards have traditionally had fewer nurses despite the heavy burden of basic as distinct from technical nursing, and it may be that that is an aspect of the general attitude to the Cinderella services, though it might be argued that, given the total labour force and other needs, it represents the optimum. Training requirements are an important constraint. Nurses may be trained only in approved hospitals and they must be allocated to wards in accordance with their training needs, which may not always correspond with staffing needs. An even more important constraint is the numbers of staff who can be recruited. It is very questionable whether there is an overall shortage of nurses — and what would constitute such a shortage might be a matter for debate — but there are difficulties in recruiting nurses in some places or some hospitals or for certain times of the day or night or of the week. The increasing use of part-time nurses does not always meet the difficulty. A further constraint is the increasing specialisation in nursing. Specialisation has always existed; a registered general nurse and a registered mental nurse are not interchangeable, even though they are classed together in the broad statistics. Nowadays, however, a hospital may in general be adequately staffed but find it difficult to recruit enough nurses specialising in theatre work or intensive care.

There are two levels of qualified nurse — registered and enrolled — and consequently two types of trainee — students and pupils. Training arrangements are described in Chapter 15. After initial training a nurse may choose to take a postgraduate course in a specialised field such as cardiothoracic surgery, intensive care or community nursing. Some after qualifying for one part of the register choose to train for another part, e.g. to take general training after obtaining the RMN qualification. A popular choice is to become a pupil midwife. Midwifery is a separate profession from nursing though they are grouped together in the management structure and seem likely to come closer together. Most midwives have previously qualified in nursing; some spend the rest of their careers in midwifery while others revert to nursing after obtaining their midwifery qualification.

Normally after qualification a registered nurse becomes a staff nurse and may then proceed through the hierarchy of sister/charge nurse, nursing officer, senior nursing officer, divisional nursing officer or area nurse and district, area or regional nursing officer. These grades and titles derive from the Salmon Report on nursing, which is discussed in Chapter 15.

Wards are generally organised by specialty or sub-specialty into groups of three or four under a nursing officer. As Chapter 6 explained, within a district the nursing service is organised in divisions, either geographical or functional.

The paramedical professions

The training and qualifications of the professions supplementary to medicine are discussed in Chapter 15, and management arrangements at district level in Chapter 6. They are therefore only briefly discussed here.

The eight professions covered by the Council for Professions Supplementary to Medicine can be divided into the scientific group — dietitians, medical laboratory scientific officers and radiographers — the remedial group — occupational therapists, orthoptists, physiotherapists and remedial gymnasts — and chiropodists. Speech therapists, though not covered by the council, are normally grouped with the remedial professions; they have more in common with them than do the medical laboratory scientific officers who in this survey will be included in the scientific staff.

Dietetic departments consist of basic grade, senior and chief dietitians with a district dietitian in overall charge. Their role is to give advice on general nutritional matters to appropriate patients such as the elderly and expectant mothers, to ensure that patients' meals are nutritionally satisfactory and to advise on special diets for patients with special needs such as diabetics and patients with metabolic disorders. They have a special role in health education.

Diagnostic radiography is an essential service in all but very small hospitals and often also provides a service for GPs. Increasingly it is making use of sophisticated and expensive equipment. A typical radiography department will consist of student, basic grade and senior radiographers managed by a superintendent. Normally one of the consultant radiologists is designated a head of department and he is often in total managerial control of the department, its staff and budget — an arrangement that is not found between, say, consultants in physical medicine and physiotherapists. Radiographers are also employed in therapeutic radiography departments, which use radiation for treatment — especially for cancer. Because of the expense and sophistication of the equipment radiotherapy departments are provided only at regional or sub-regional centres.

Physical medicine is the term used to describe the departments of physiotherapy (including remedial gymnasts) and occupational therapy. Their purpose is to rehabilitate patients whose physical movement has been impaired by injury, disease, mental handicap or old age. The staffing structure within these departments comprises basic grade, senior occupational therapists/physiotherapists — so designated if they supervise junior staff or their work is of a specialised nature — and head occupational therapists/physiotherapists managerially responsible for the department. Untrained helpers are also employed. The previous chapter describes the confusion that has existed over the managerial responsibilities of these staff.

This is perhaps the best place to refer to medical social workers who, although not NHS staff, have an important role in hospitals. They are discussed in Chapter 15.

Orthoptists are employed particularly in subregional ophthalmic units to assist in the diagnosis and treatment of eye conditions.

Both speech therapists and chiropodists mainly practise outside the hospital. As Chapter 6 explained, before 1974 many speech therapists were employed by local authorities and they are now organised on an area basis. Many registered chiropodists are in private practice. The services of those employed in the NHS are available only to certain priority groups: the elderly, the handicapped, expectant mothers, schoolchildren and hospital patients. The main users are the elderly in the community and in many places the demand for the service appears to exceed the supply.

Pharmacists

As the previous chapter explained, since the Noel Hall Report pharmacy services are organised on an area basis. Nevertheless it is at hospital level that pharmaceutical products are prescribed and taken, and all but the smallest hospitals have a pharmacy for the acquisition, storage and dispensing of drugs and often dressings and other sundries. The district pharmaceutical officer may manage the pharmacy department in the main district general hospital; otherwise the hospital department, comprising staff and basic grade pharmacists, student, pharmacy technician and ancillary staff, will be managed by a principal pharmacist.

With the increasing range and complexity of drugs and the need to become aware of contraindications and reactions to drugs the role of pharmacist has developed from dispenser to specialist adviser on pharmaceutical matters which may involve consultation at ward level. The annual increase in drugs expenditure has also given the pharmacist a vital role in advising on the use of proprietary drugs and the availability of cheaper preparations under generic names.

Scientific and technical staff

The proposals of the Zuckerman Report for an integrated scientific service, and their failure to win favour, were described in Chapter 6. Of the three main scientific and technical services, the radiological and medical laboratory services are a basic element of all general hospitals, whereas the clinical engineering and physical sciences services comprise a variety of different professions usually represented in only small numbers in any one area, and some more often found only in regional or sub-regional centres.

Radiological services were discussed above, and here we are concerned with the medical laboratory services, which are staffed by medical laboratory scientific officers. Pathology departments are normally divided into four sections: chemical pathology or clinical chemistry, haematology, histopathology and bacteriology. Each section is normally headed by a medical consultant or by a graduate scientist. Non-medical scientists hold posts in the basic, senior and principal scientific officer grades. As in radiography departments a consultant head of department is usually in complete managerial control although, as Chapter 6 explained, there is some controversy about this.

The pathology laboratory provides a diagnostic service normally on a 24 hour basis. The work has become highly automated and equipment can process a large number of tests simultaneously, often with computer control and automatic print-outs of results. Pathology work has expanded remarkably over the years and the availability of a wide range of tests is thought to have encouraged excessive use of this diagnostic service, especially by junior medical staff. The Royal Commission urged the need for greater cost consciousness.

Medical records

Medical records staff provide a support service but one more directly related to patient care and it should therefore be described separately from the other support services.

The medical records department normally fulfils three main functions at hospital level: the documentation and safe keeping of medical records for all in-patients, out-patients and day patients, the organisation of out-patient services and the management of medical secretarial services. In larger hospitals these three functions may be separated.

The documentation role involves the production of a set of case notes for any patient in the hospital and the setting up of systems for the preparation of such case notes whether patients are admitted as emergencies or referred by GPs or transferred from other hospitals. There must be a master index from which basic details of any previous patient can be extracted and a library of case notes from which the notes of any individual patient can easily be recovered. Waiting lists for admission are also normally maintained within the medical records department, and statistics are extracted of all the main patient activities going on throughout the hospital. These data have to be supplied to the relevant central department on a regular basis, and more detailed computerised information is available from Hospital Activity Analysis — a computerised system which summarises the basic information of patients' admission, treatment and discharge and which should be a valuable tool for administrators and clinicians interested in the throughput of patients of particular kinds or in particular specialties, etc.

The basic function of the out-patient department is to bring together a patient and his consultant, or a member of the consultant's firm, together with the patient's medical records, at an agreed time on an agreed day. Each out-patient clinic comprises a considerable number of such arrangements. The organisation of the out-patient department is far from easy and has been a matter of concern for many years because of the frequently recurring complaints about the length of time patients have to wait in the department to see a doctor. There are various reasons why arrangements may go wrong: patients may arrive too early or too late, particularly if they are dependent on the ambulance service, some patients fail to keep appointments, a doctor may start his clinic late, or may be called to attend a patient on a ward in the the middle of it, or the layout of the department may militate against efficient functioning. There appear, however, to be two main reasons. First, surveys have shown that sometimes booking arrangements bear no resemblance to the method in which the medical staff actually work; if bookings are made at ten-minute intervals and consultations average a quarter of an hour, delays build up throughout the session, and if the doctor does not see patients in order in which they are booked some will be kept waiting a long time. The second main reason is a common assumption that doctors must never be kept waiting whereas patients' time is unimportant. Block bookings ensure that a patient is always available even if some fail to keep an appointment, but patients understandably dislike it when they find that several of them have an appointment for the same time. The out-patient department therefore needs regular management supervision to ensure not only that the arrangements are satisfactory but also that they are adjusted to meet changing circumstances.

The objective of the medical secretarial service is to ensure that the medical staff in the hospital can produce their letters, etc.; the main need is to ensure that reports of patients' treatment are sent promptly to patients' general practitioners. Medical secretaries are usually linked to a particular consultant but may be organised in small groups throughout the hospital or in a centralised pool. There may be a supervisor of typists who ensures that the workload is evenly distributed among staff, and trainees, who work with various secretaries before being allocated to a particular consultant, may be employed.

Support services

Most of the staff described above provide services that are essentially hospital-centred. When it comes to the support services the picture is rather more complicated. There are a number of ancillary services provided directly at hospital level, usually under the control of the hospital administrator, such as porters, switchboard operators, mortuary attendants and car park attendants. There are other services, particularly laundries and central sterile supply departments, which because of their industrial character are best organised on a larger scale. They are usually, though not invariably, sited at a hospital but they are essentially district services and some serve more than one district. There are two other services — works and supplies — that are also thought to require large scale organisation. They are fully described elsewhere in this book and there is no need here to rehearse the rationale. Finally there are two services — catering and domestic — which have to be provided at the individual hospital but which have been increasingly, and since 1974 generally, responsible to a district functional head. The results have in some respects been beneficial, but relating district-based functional management to effective sector management has proved difficult and controversial. The issues were discussed in the previous chapter and only two points need making here.

The first is that although we may speak of district services, most of the staff in some of these services in fact work at hospital level. Each hospital has its own catering department with a catering officer, head cook, cooks, porters and domestic staff and its own domestic department with domestic superintendent, supervisors and domestic assistants, even though they may all be ultimately responsible to a district functional head and not to the local administrator. At hospital level the works department may be represented by building officers and engineers according to the extent of the premises and the existence of specialised plant such as lifts, laundries and CSSDs. The various tradesmen such as plumbers, bricklayers, plasterers and painters in the building section and fitters and electricians in the engineering section report to the senior officers through foremen. These staff may be employed totally on maintenance duties or may be part of a larger directly employed workforce which engages in major upgrading schemes within hospitals. The benefits of having staff employed by the hospital are that they are familiar with the working arrangements within the NHS and can be used flexibly in patient areas, whereas it has been argued that the employment of outside contractors would be cheaper. The district works officer will also employ incinerator attendants and garden staff who may be allocated to individual hospitals.

The other point to make is that while there are good reasons why some services should be organised on a large scale, whether district, area or region, their purpose is to assist staff working at the hospital or at community level and they are subject to user assessment from that point of view. Thus, while there are strong arguments for large scale purchasing and storage of supplies, at hospital level there must be arrangements for requisitioning supplies, receiving them and distributing them and feeding back to the supplies officer information about their suitability. There may be two problems. The greater the distance between the user and the ultimate provider of the service the greater is the difficulty of communication and therefore the greater the need for the provider to achieve effective communication. The other problem is one of viewpoint. Large scale purchasing entails 'variety reduction', which is unwelcome to staff with strong views about particular products. The supplies officer may know more about many products than do individual users but the important thing is not so much the merit of the particular purchases but the fact that the service simply cannot afford to meet all the preferences of individual users. This has to be recognised at the user level, though it is part of the task of the supplies officer to make out the case. Similar considerations apply to works, that is the need to maintain effective communication between district or area organisation and individual hospitals and staff, and the need on both sides to balance the overall problems of maintaining the health service estate against the particular problem which seems most pressing to the hospital or department affected. Laundries also illustrate the problems of reconciling a district service with local needs, for it is fairly common for ward staff to complain either about irregularities in the supply of linen or about the quality of the laundering.

Summary

This short and inevitably superficial review of the main groups of staff within hospitals has indicated the range and variety of staff employed and the complexity and variety of organisational arrangements. The survey has not discussed ancillary staff despite the fact that they are the second most numerous group. This is not because their contribution is undervalued but because, as their title indicates, their contribution is made through other departments, particularly most of the service departments.

The range of hospital sizes must be borne in mind when considering even such a sketch as this of hospital activity, for the internal arrangements of a small cottage hospital with 50 beds will be vastly simpler than those of a 1,000-bed district general hospital employing perhaps 3,000 staff. Also the sketch has hardly acknowledged the existence of hospitals of a special character. There is no space to enlarge on these, but a list of just four of the ways in which a large psychiatric hospital differs from a large general hospital serves as a reminder of how different hospitals can be: all the medical staff practise the same specialty (though like most specialties it is developing sub-specialties), even the short-stay patients are in hospital much longer than patients in acute hospitals, most patients are not confined to bed, and many of the nursing staff live with their families in estates in the hospital grounds.

The problems of co-ordinating the complex range of hospital staff and departments will be considered later in this chapter. However, the single most unifying influence within the hospital and the focus through which the complex range of departments can be understood is the needs of the individual patient. Thus, while the large number of departments may seem very complicated, if the hospital is looked at in terms of a series of diagnostic, treatment or supporting departments all directed to making sure that the individual patient gets the range of services he requires, then some sense can be made of the links between departments and staff. Again, using the focus of the individual patient in his bed, the set of case notes brings together the various diagnostic departments and by looking through such a set of notes there can be seen the report forms from pathology, X-ray and other investigative departments and the notes of the doctors resulting from these investigations and their prescriptions for treatment. The nursing record gives a good indication of the day-to-day activities of the patient and the observations and treatment by nurses. Looking more widely than the case notes, the environment for the patient can be seen to be maintained by a range of supporting services — the building has to be heated, maintained and kept clean and the patient has to be fed and linen supplied to the bed. It is useful here to recall the model of the hospital referred to at the beginning of this chapter as a series of concentric circles surrounding the central triangular relationship between doctor, nurse and patient.

The second chapter of this book looked at the health service from the point of view of the wide range of services available to the patient. The next section of this one takes a closer look at the experience of the patient with one particular service, the hospital, with the emphasis on administrative aspects.

Patients and hospitals

Patients reach hospital by three main routes: as a result of accidents and emergencies (i.e. those who have suffered a serious injury or the sudden onset of severe symptoms); by referral by general practitioners; and by transfer from other hospitals. There may be some overlap between the categories since a GP may see an emergency case at home and telephone for direct admission.

Accident and emergency departments need the staffing and resources of a big hospital and are therefore provided only at designated hospitals. Most patients are brought by the ambulance service. In many places people with minor injuries or ailments present themselves at the A&E department; they are seen but may have to wait a long time if the staff are dealing with serious cases of the type for which the department is intended. When a patient is brought in the doctor in the department makes an initial assessment and if he considers that admission is indicated the patient will be seen by a doctor from the appropriate specialty. Sometimes a patient who is destitute or living alone may have to be admitted for social reasons even if the medical need is not great simply because there is insufficient support outside. Attempts have been made to strengthen accident and emergency work as a specialty in its own right by appointing consultants in accident and emergency work rather than attaching the department loosely to the orthopaedic or another department.

A bed bureau may be maintained by the medical records department showing how many beds are available by ward at any time so that medical staff can make a quick decision on whether admission is possible. The absence of such procedures can mean long and uncomfortable waiting in the accident and emergency department until a decision is made.

If a general practitioner considers that he needs the advice of a consultant on the treatment of a patient, or that the patient needs hospital treatment, he will, unless it is an emergency, arrange for the patient to be seen in the out-patient department. (Occasionally he will arrange instead for the consultant to visit the patient's home.) The patient may make more than one visit to the OPD; it may, for example, be necessary to have the results of X-rays and other diagnostic tests before the consultant can make a decision. Sometimes the consultant will prescribe out-patient treatment, or simply advise the GP on treatment. Sometimes he will decide that in-patient treatment is indicated and add the patient's name to the waiting list. Thus the consultant controls access to hospital beds — though many patients are admitted as emergencies rather than by the waiting list. The management of waiting lists has been frequently criticised and often studied. A growth in the numbers on lists is viewed with concern, but the important measure is not the length of lists but how long patients have to wait for admission. The DHSS has recommended that all 'urgent' cases should be admitted within one month and all non-urgent within 12 months, but often these standards are not achieved. The requirements for waiting list management are easy to state: patients should be admitted in accordance with the urgency of their medical need but weight must also be given to the social burden waiting places on them and their families, and the non-urgent cases must get a fair deal. They should not have to wait indefinitely while more and more urgent cases are put ahead of them in the queue. The extent to which a hospital achieves the requirements depends not merely on the management of the list but on the resources available to it and the efficiency with which it uses them. By efficiency we mean the minimum average length of stay and the minimum interval during which a bed is unoccupied. Resource difficulties may be of various sorts: some beds must always be kept in reserve for emergency admissions and the balance may not be enough to admit waiting list patients as fast as new names are added to the list; beds may be under-used because of a shortage of theatre or diagnostic facilities; there may be staff shortages. Some resource difficulties may be temporary, resulting from the closure of wards or theatres for cleaning, industrial action by staff, a reduction in staff numbers during holiday periods or exceptional numbers of emergency admissions in winter. Two other complicating factors should be mentioned. Consultants will wish to plan a suitable mix of cases for admission, e.g. a consultant would not admit on the same day a number of patients requiring very lengthy operations. Finally, the management of waiting lists is not a whole-hospital operation; it is the individual consultant who decides admissions, and even when there is some flexibility in bed allocations some consultants have much longer lists than others.

The other main way of admission — transfer between hospitals agreed by the consultants concerned — is to place the patient in a more suitable hospital. It takes various forms: from a general hospital to a regional or sub-regional centre with special facilities; between acute and psychiatric; from acute to long-stay or convalescent.

Some patients may be admitted to hospital for only a single day, particularly for minor surgery. Providing for day patients in this way is an economical use of resources. Another measure adopted by some hospitals for saving staffing and other costs is the provision of five-day wards.

Patients may under certain circumstances be admitted to hospital under compulsory order. If a patient is suffering from one of the infectious diseases, such as typhoid (which under the Public Health Act 1936 have to be notified to the district community physician/area medical officer as part of his 'proper officer' functions) and refuses to go to hospital when admission is thought essential to avoid spreading the infection, a Justice of the Peace may be asked to make a compulsory order for admission. Similarly under the National Assistance Act 1948 an order may be made, again on the recommendation of the 'proper officer' for the compulsory admission of a patient who is suffering from a serious chronic disease or is unable to look after himself properly because of age, infirmity or physical disability and is living in insanitary conditions.

Patients may be compulsorily admitted to mental illness hospitals or units or mental handicap hospitals under the Mental Health Act 1959 if in the opinion of two doctors they require observation (Section 25 of the Act) or treatment (Section 26). Section 29 of the Act allows compulsory detention on a single medical recommendation for 72 hours in case of emergency. The doctors must certify that the patient is suffering from mental disorder of a nature or degree which warrants his detention under observation or treatment and that he should be detained in his own interests or to protect others. There is similar provision in the Mental Health (Scotland) Act 1960.

It is vital that all admissions are properly documented and that in acute hospitals patients receive their unique hospital number as soon as possible. Case notes and other documents can be prepared in advance for waiting-list cases (pre-registration), but a system has to exist for accident and emergency cases. Batches of prepared case notes and series of registration numbers may be allocated to A&E departments and there may be clerks on duty during the evening and night to ensure that registration is carried out.

When patients are admitted the hospital takes on a duty of care towards them and their belongings. Patients are advised however that unless they hand over valuables for safe keeping the hospital can take no responsibility for them and patients are encouraged to hand over clothing and other items to relatives. A secure system must exist for the recording of any valuables handed over and for their safe custody. It is easy in the dramatic atmosphere of the accident and emergency department for items to be lost or mislaid and the hospital is likely to be held responsible unless it can be shown and documented that the patient was given every opportunity to hand over valuables. If the patient is unconscious any recording of valuables must be carried out by two staff who would list the items and sign the list. This kind of protection is also essential for patients who may not be fully in charge of their faculties, such as children and the elderly.

Discharges

The average length of stay for acute specialties is slightly more than a week. The trend towards shorter stay means that on discharge more support must be provided by social services and community staff and the general practitioner. The decision to discharge is made by the consultant or one of his staff, and the ward sister has a vital role in making sure that all necessary services are mobilised. This obviously cannot happen if a sudden decision is made on a Friday afternoon to discharge a patient needing heavy community support. The full range of community services — for example meals on wheels and home help from the social services department, district nursing and GP visits may take a little time to organise and liaison officers help to bring all the services together. Relatives must be informed, medication prescribed, valuables returned, transport ordered and the GP informed by a brief discharge note, to be followed as soon as practicable by a full discharge summary. Complaints can arise if some part of the complex machinery goes wrong.

Transfers

We have already seen that there are various reasons why patients are transferred from one hospital to another. The pressure on acute beds often encourages the transfer of patients as soon as possible. When a transfer is made in the same district the case notes will accompany the patient. Relatives must be informed and transport, and an escort if necessary, arranged. Sometimes the speedy transfer of a seriously ill patient to a regional unit for specialised treatment, e.g. for head injuries or burns is necessary. A police escort may be required and in cases where a long journey by ambulance is not advised helicopters may be used.

Births

Every birth and still-birth (after 28 weeks) in a hospital must be notified to the appropriate medical officer of the AHA within 36 hours after the birth. The responsibility normally lies on the midwife who was in attendance at the birth. The birth must be registered by the parents or, in default, by the 'occupier' within 42 days. The birth certificate is issued at the time of registration.

Deaths

When a patient dies it is a medical responsibility to certify that death has occurred. The death must be registered within five days of the date of death. The registrar may issue a certificate for the disposal of the body unless the cause of death is unknown or the death falls into one of the following categories: violent or unnatural or sudden death from an unknown cause, deaths on the operating table or under anaesthetic, deaths during labour or in a labour ward and deaths from notifiable diseases. In these cases the coroner will normally order a post mortem and must decide whether an inquest is necessary. The disposal order is issued only when the coroner is satisfied that the cause of death has been established. The hospital must not release a body for burial or cremation unless a disposal order has been issued.

If a patient dies in hospital and relatives do not arrange for burial the hospital must arrange for it and meet the cost, and can claim the death grant where appropriate. If the patient has been transferred to another hospital some distance from his home the hospital should pay the cost of transporting the body back.

Hospitals normally offer to arrange for the burial of still-births at their own expense unless parents seek to make their own arrangements. Bodies may be cremated unless the deceased is known to have directed that this should not occur; a second medical certificate is necessary. It is essential that these formalities are complied with and that proper systems exist for identifying the bodies of deceased patients — usually by labelling and marking the body with indelible pencil or some other fixed label — and for recording and identifying bodies in the mortuary. The system must ensure that the correct body is handed over and that the undertaker and mortuary attendant jointly identify the body to be handed over. Unless the system is strictly enforced it would be possible for post mortems to be performed on the wrong body and for bodies to be discovered in the mortuary without proper labelling. It causes great distress to relatives if the wrong body is handed over.

Post mortems may be requested by a doctor to ascertain more about the nature of the illness when the coroner is not involved. The relatives are asked to sign a consent form.

The certification of death and the removal of tissue from deceased patients has become a sensitive area with the increasing use of life support equipment which can maintain body functions although 'brain death' has occurred. A procedure must exist to ensure that all necessary steps have been taken if life support is to be discontinued and organs removed. Two doctors other than the transplant team, one of whom must have five years' experience since qualification, must certify that death has occurred; the coroner must be informed and his authorisation obtained and relatives' permission must be sought. If there are no relatives or they cannot be contacted despite the taking of reasonable steps to do so an officer of the AHA may give consent.

The property of deceased patients can normally be handed over to the next of kin, against a letter of indemnity. If the property is valuable often a limit is set at £500, or if there is any uncertainty about the next of kin the hospital can refuse to hand over property until letters of administration are provided. If a patient dies intestate and has no relatives the property is dealt with by the Treasury solicitor or the solicitor to the Duchy of Lancaster or the Duchy of Cornwall according to the place of death.

Detention of patients

It is illegal to detain a patient against his will even if he is seriously ill unless one of the following circumstances applies: he is temporarily delirious because of illness; he is subject to detention under the Mental Health Act, Public Health Act or National Assistance Act as described earlier in this chapter; he is to be charged with an 'offence' and is being detained until the police can be summoned; or he is in the custody of the police or the prison service. If a patient insists on discharging himself against medical advice he should be asked to sign a form certifying that he accepts responsibility for the consequences.

Patients and the law

Patients are particularly vulnerable as consumers of health services. Often the whole of the episode of illness is only superficially understood by the patient; he simply presents himself for diagnosis and treatment. The doctor tells him what the problem is and what treatment is necessary and probably how successful treatment has been. The patient of course knows if he feels substantially better or worse on discharge but he normally relies heavily on what the doctor tells him and the quality of patient/doctor communication is therefore important. Inevitably in such a huge organisation as the NHS mistakes occur and the source of redress for patients who have suffered as a result of a mistake is through the civil courts as an action for negligence.

Negligence can be regarded as having three elements: there must be a duty of care owed to the injured party, this duty of care must have been broken and that breach must have resulted in actual 'damage' to the injured party. It is the duty of the Secretary of State to provide a national health service and he fulfils his obligation through the statutory health authorities. These authorities have a duty of care to patients by providing safe premises and adequate equipment properly maintained, by ensuring that systems of work are safe and by employing competent staff.

The level of competence expected of staff is that they should exercise a degree of care which a normally skilful member of the profession would exercise in the circumstances. Thus not every slip or mistake can be regarded as negligence and the professional is not expected to be familiar with every piece of literature on a particular topic. The normal test is whether a particular action would find favour with a substantial proportion of professional colleagues.

Thus any member of staff whether doctor, nurse, radiographer, physiotherapist etc. has a direct duty of care to the patient and could find himself accused of negligence. However, the health authority which employs him also has a duty of care and is regarded as being 'vicariously liable' for the acts of its employees. In practice therefore if a nurse makes a mistake it is the health authority which is sued. Medical staff are more likely than other staff to be sued for negligence because of their primary role in diagnosis and treatment. All medical staff must be members of a medical defence organisation and if a doctor is sued for negligence it is normal for the health authority and the doctor to be sued jointly. If the plaintiff is successful the health authority's legal adviser and the defence organisation apportion the damages between them according to the nature of the case.

The extent of liability may be reduced if a patient failed to carry out instructions and this failure contributed directly to the injury; the patient can be argued to have contributed to the negligence.

Under the Limitations Acts, when a patient has suffered personal injuries the case for negligence must be brought within three years of the incident. This limit is waived if the plaintiff could not be expected to have known that he had suffered injuries as a result of negligence within that time. In such circumstances the plaintiff may bring an action within 12 months of discovering that negligence might have occurred.

Consent to treatment

It is an offence of trespass to the person to interfere with a patient's body without consent. Therefore if a surgeon performs an operation without consent he and the health authority may be sued for damages. Obtaining proper consent is essential. Patients who attend A&E and out-patient departments for treatment and are conscious and not anaesthetised can be assumed to be giving their consent to treatment. However, a specific written consent is necessary whenever a anaesthetic is to be administered or a special risk is involved. Consent is usually obtained on a consent form which gives the name of the operation to be performed and states that the nature and purpose of the operation have been explained by a doctor who countersigns the form. It is essential that this explanation is properly carried out in non-technical language since a consent is worthless if the patient could not be expected to have understood the explanation. Consent is equally worthless if the patient could not have been capable of understanding the significance, so there must be no last minute attempts to obtain a signature after premedication.

If a patient is unconscious and urgent treatment is necessary a relative's consent should be obtained if possible. If it cannot be obtained the surgeon may proceed with urgent treatment on the assumption that the patient would have consented. The nearest relative's consent should be obtained for operations on patients detained under the Mental Health Act and also for voluntary psychiatric patients who are unable to understand the significance of the operation. Parents' consent must be obtained for operations on children up to the age of 16 but the Family Law Reform Act 1969 makes it clear that the consent of a child of 16 or 17 can have the full force of adult consent. Parents can also consent for a 16 or 17 year old but not veto the child's consent.

Adults may refuse treatment for themselves and cannot be forced to accept treatment. It is usual for the patient to be asked to sign a form to say that despite the consequences being fully explained he refuses consent. A note to that effect should also be made in the case notes. Parents may refuse to give consent for treatment to their children for religious or other reasons. If urgent treatment is necessary it is reasonable for the doctor to do what is medically necessary without consent. If the treatment is not urgent a court application may be made through the social services department to have the child taken into care, when consent can be given by the social services department *in loco parentis*.

It is usual to obtain the spouse's consent for any procedure which may affect the ability to have children.

Identification of patients

It is part of the health authority's duty of care to patients to ensure that patients are properly identified and that the correct operation is carried out on the correct patient. Patients should be labelled with an identity bracelet giving usually surname, forenames and hospital number and sometimes date of birth. A system must exist in the accident and emergency department for ensuring that unconscious patients receive a bracelet and number even if their names are not known. The bracelet must only be subsequently changed or removed with the strictest supervision. It is not unusual for patients with the same name to be in the same ward and special care is required to ensure that case notes do not become linked with the wrong patient. The procedure for transferring a patient to theatre must include rigorous checks — that the correct patient is sent to the theatre, that the correct operation is identified and that changes to the operation list are notified to all concerned. Before administering the anaesthetic the doctor should check that it is the correct patient with the correct records and that the consent form is completed and operation identified.

Patients' complaints

In an organisation as huge and complex as the NHS it is inevitable that things go wrong; the NHS is labour intensive and however thoroughly staff are trained and procedures laid down staff are not infallible and mistakes will occur. In the same way the size and complexity of the NHS offer manifold opportunities for communications between different parts of the system to break down. It is equally inevitable that in a highly professionalised organisation some staff will be reluctant to acknowledge the right of patients to complain; patients tend to be seen as the passive recipients of care not expected to question or disapprove of the treatment they receive unless something is blatantly amiss. This tendency of all large organisations to be defensive has been the target of the consumer movement since the late 1960s.

Formal machinery exists for dealing with complaints about the family practitioner services, and it is described in Chapter 6. No similar formal machinery exists for the rest of the service. Official guidance has been issued on the handling of complaints in hospitals and the same principles should be applied as far as possible to the community services. What follows concerns England; Scotland has had separate guidance and a separate report, but broadly the principles are the same.

In 1966 the Ministry of Health issued general guidance on how complaints should be handled (HM(66)15); they should be dealt with as promptly as possible, they should be passed to a higher level of management if the complainant is not satisfied with the initial reply, all written complaints should be seen by the district/area administrator and members of authorities should be involved if officers are unable to deal with the complaint. Supplementary advice was issued in 1970: the information booklets issued to new in-patients should tell them how to make complaints, the complaints procedure should cover untoward events as well as complaints and staff in contact with patients should be told how to deal with complaints.

In 1971 a committee was set up under Sir Michael Davies to review the handling of complaints — 'to provide the hospital service with practical guidance in the form of a code of principles and practice for recording and investigating matters affecting patients which go wrong in hospitals; for receiving complaints or suggestions by patients, staff, or others about such matters; and for communicating the results of investigations'. Its appointment arose from the public enquiries into long-stay hospitals which had shown that complaints could be suppressed. The Davies Committee reported in 1973; it found that the principles set out in HM(66)15 had not been put into practice, that only 57 per cent of patient booklets referred to the complaints procedure and there was evidence of a substantial number of oral complaints not being investigated. The committee recommended a standard code of practice for handling complaints and the establishment of an external check for dissatisfied complainants in the form of independent investigating panels.

The DHSS was slow to react to the Davies Report. A draft code of practice was circulated to the service for comment in 1976; it was thought that investigating panels overlapped too much with the role of the Health Service Commissioner. General reaction was that the draft code was too complicated, and an amended draft was circulated in 1978 (HN(78)39). The draft emphasised the importance of good communications and pointed out that many complaints could be handled by junior staff immediately. If a complainant was not satisfied a more senior member of staff should be involved and the complaint put in writing if still not resolved. The draft reiterated the basic principles that the complainant should be informed of any reasons for delay in replying and that any member of staff complained about should be given full details and be given every opportunity to reply. The district administrator should see all written complaints and the AHA should set out what kinds of complaints it should itself see. Details of the complaints procedure should appear in patient booklets and be displayed in out-patient departments. In April 1981, too late for summary here, the Department issued HC(81)5 Health Service Complaints Procedure, which was an amplification, not replacement of HM(66)15.

This brief review demonstrates the difficulty in agreeing a complaints procedure nationally. In part this reflects the complexity of the service, but there is another reason. Some complaints, perhaps the most important, are about treatment, but the medical profession has proved very reluctant to agree to the external investigation of such complaints. The attitude is understandable. Doctors can be sued in the courts — and naturally do not wish to encourage arrangements which would facilitate this procedure; the upholding of complaints against them can be very damaging to their professional reputation and career; they attach great value to their clinical autonomy; and for their effectiveness they depend on the trust of patients, which might be damaged by a proliferation of successful complaints. Some people would argue that this defensiveness in fact works against good doctor/patient relations because it makes for mistrust; that the 'sue me or don't complain' attitude is mistaken because most complainants do not want damages but simply an acknowledgement that something went wrong.

The basic principles for dealing with complaints are easier to state than to put into practice all the time. That they are not always followed can be seen by looking at the reports of the Health Service Commissioner. A complainant who is not satisfied after a health authority has examined his complaint may refer it, if it is not about about a clinical matter, to the Commissioner, whose role is described in Chapter 15. The Commissioner publishes both annual reports and, from time to time, detailed accounts of some of his investigations. These deserve study, for many of them are accounts of things that have gone wrong administratively at sector level and below. The immediate point here is that it is quite common for the Commissioner to reject the substance of a complaint but to criticise the handling of it by the authority e.g. by slowness, by inadequate investigation or by failure to answer all the matters complained of. This is not altogether surprising, since it is only dissatisifed complainants who will refer their case to the Commissioner. Nevertheless it shows that authorities do have difficulties in dealing with complaints.

One of the difficulties in complaining about health services is the complexity of the machinery and the difficulty of knowing who to complain to. CHCs can advise patients on how to make complaints, though they are excluded from investigating individual complaints. CHCs may also ask for comments on services which appear to be the subject of a number of complaints and may draw the attention of authorities to areas where they feel complaints may arise.

Community health services

Some of the health care in the community is provided by general practitioners but here we are concerned only with the community health services now administered by the health authority and before 1974 by the local authority. At the risk of stating the obvious, one of the great differences between hospital and community care can be put this way: in hospital the patient receives total care, for he is housed, fed and constantly under staff surveillance whereas in the community care is partial and intermittent — limited to the particular needs of the patient and provided only when he visits or is visited. This does not mean that the community services are necessarily easier to administer, though the problems are certainly different: against the advantages and difficulties of organising a wide variety of professional and support services on a single site and under close management supervision there is the need to provide particular services where and when they are needed throughout the district and under much less supervision. Nor are the community services necessarily less expensive to provide. This is usually the case, but a patient needing a wide range of services, including some from the local authority, may cost more to care for than if he were in hospital.

Another important difference is that the community services are not concerned only with the sick. To a large extent that is their concern, which is why the hospital and community services are complementary, but they also have an important role in the oversight of the healthy. This is particularly the case with child-care services. And in a rather different way health education also is concerned with the healthy.

The 1974 reorganisation was designed to integrate the health services but while it brought community and hospital services together it led to some disintegration within the community services themselves. Previously managerial responsibility for all these services had lain with a single officer — the medical officer of health — but they were now split up, the nursing services for example being the responsibility of the district/area nursing officer.

We noted early in this chapter that in deciding on sectors some authorities established a separate community sector whereas others preferred to integrate hospital and community services on a geographical basis. Whichever option is chosen the disadvantages must be acknowledged and provided for; if community and hospitals are linked there must be a sufficient allocation of administrative time to community matters and if there is a separate sector, linking mechanisms such as district planning teams must be used to ensure that the links with hospitals are maintained.

Community health services comprise the following: health visiting, district nursing, domiciliary midwifery, chiropody, family planning, the school dental service, child health services including the school health service, health education, vaccination and immunisation, speech therapy and in some places occupational therapy, physiotherapy and dietetics. Day hospitals for the elderly and for the mentally ill are hospital services but their function is to help patients to continue to live in the community. The purposes of most of these services, and how they work, were described in Chapter 2.

Services are provided either in patients' homes or in a wide range of clinics, health centres and GP practices. Clinics may be in permanent facilities used daily, or may be in rented halls used only one or two sessions a week. It is important that clinics should be readily accessible particularly to 'at risk' groups, so that proximity to shopping centres and bus routes is vital. Although health visitors and district nurses may be based at clinics they are often attached to particular GP practices. GP attachment to form the 'primary care team' is a significant development towards integrated primary care services and makes it much more likely that a full range of community services can be successfully co-ordinated according to an individual patient's needs. Health centres, where GPs, community health service staff and social workers can be based, should make the best setting to encourage the team concept of community health care, though location in the same building does not guarantee team working and is not a necessary condition for it. It may be that the number of health centres will now increase less rapidly than in recent years for the present government attaches less priority to them than did its predecessors and the amount of money available for capital development of any sort is severely limited. In any case the provision of centres depends on the willingness of GPs to practise from them. Not all GPs wish to do so, and it may be that facilities have already been provided for the majority of those most in favour.

The development of community care was established as a priority in the DHSS priority documents of 1976 and 1977. This view is based on assumptions that patients would prefer to be treated outside hospital if possible, that pressures on hospital services will be relieved by an increase of community facilities and that the overall cost of care would be reduced; little work has been done to test these assumptions, but the priorities documents did recommend a greater relative increase in expenditure on community services than on hospital services. The other health departments have followed the same policy.

The Royal Commission found it difficult to measure whether there had in fact been a switch in emphasis to community. It found some indication of greater community care for the elderly, the mentally ill and the mentally handicapped but concluded that the important measure of staff numbers did not indicate a greater increase in community rather than hospital staff. It agreed however that community services should be developed, but considered that this should be achieved by channelling additional resources into the community rather than by expecting savings to be made in acute hospital services. Financial restrictions have become even tighter since the commission wrote its report, but it might be possible for those looking for an expansion of the community services to derive some comfort from a remark of the commission: 'expenditure on community health services is a relatively small proportion of total NHS expenditure'. It could be argued that a quite modest diversion of resources from other parts of the NHS could permit a worthwhile expansion in the community.

The commission found that communications between hospital and community were frequently criticised, for example that patients were referred to hospital without adequate documentation and that patients were discharged from hospital without adequate warning or information to GPs. Such difficulties could be alleviated if more staff had a dual role of working both in the community and in hospitals. The commission emphasised the need to co-ordinate the flow of information between hospital and community; this can be achieved for example by the appointment of district nurse liaison officers. The paper on rehabilitation included in the commission's report cited the problem of co-ordination for the rehabilitation of patients, pointing out that the consultant has access to paramedical staff, aids and appliances but only short-term responsibility for the patient and a limited knowledge of his home circumstances whilst the GP has long-term responsibility and potentially better local knowledge but is unsure of his responsibilities and has only limited access to rehabilitation services.

Community health services cannot be considered in isolation from other community services provided by local authorities such as housing and in particular social services which provide social work support, home helps, meals on wheels, home adaptations, aids and appliances, and residential accommodation for the elderly, the mentally and physically handicapped and the mentally ill. In addition, a wide range of voluntary organisations provide services for particular client groups such as the elderly, the mentally handicapped and patients suffering from cancer. Some impetus to co-ordination with local authorities was given by the introduction in 1976 of a system of joint financing. The financial arrangements are described in Chapter 9, and some examples of services that have been financed are given in Chapter 4.

Administration at sector and unit levels

Before 1974 hospital secretaries were responsible for the management of hospitals and administrative officers on the staff of the medical officer of health managed the administrative aspects of local authority community services. The importance of the hospital secretary's role was recognised in the 1954 Bradbeer Report on the internal administration of hospitals and the 1956 Guillebaud Report on the cost of the NHS, though these reports might have stressed the matter less if the importance had invariably been recognised in theory and practice.

At the time of the 1974 reorganisation the emphasis was on the integration of services and there was little comment for example in the 'Grey Book' on the management of hospitals. It was pointed out that the various institutional and support services must be co-ordinated with the clinical support and diagnostic services and with primary care and hospital services, and a specimen job description for a sector administrator was suggested. (See the appendix to this chapter.) The grading of posts in the reorganised service gave sector administrators at best the status of third-in-line officers. The retirement of many senior officers and the creation of new posts produced many promotions in 1974 and a shortage of experienced administrators at sector level. One of the common post-1974 criticisms which led to the establishment of the Royal Commission was the lack of administrators at hospital level with adequate experience and authority. The Royal Commission endorsed this criticism, and concluded that the management of institutions had suffered substantially. In line with the Bradbeer and Guillebaud Committees it considered that the administrator in charge of the hospital is a key figure and that his grading should reflect the substantial responsibilities he carried. The commission believed that the role should be expanded and the government, in its subsequent proposals for further reorganisation, supported this view.

Predicting the role

The concepts of organisation theory help to shed some light on the management role likely to be required in hospitals. It must again be emphasised that no single blueprint is likely to be successful for the NHS as a whole; there are major differences between teaching and non-teaching hospitals, hospitals in metropolitan and rural areas, acute hospitals and long-stay institutions, and developing and contracting authorities.

In determining the role these local circumstances must be taken into account. That is not to say that there are not a number of general principles to be observed. It is a commonplace that as an organisation increases in size there is a tendency for the attributes of Weberian bureaucracy to become more pronounced, rules and procedures are likely to be developed to deal with routine matters and a managerial hierarchy with defined areas of responsibility in specialised fields will appear. With increasing size communication problems intensify. Such bureaucratic trends conflict with the professional ethic that emphasises professional control of activities and individual autonomy, although the trend towards greater specialisation will be enhanced in a professional organisation as work groups seeking professional status try to define their own specific area of expertise. Organisation theorists have also demonstrated that the technology of an organisation should affect its management structure. Thus a rigid rule-bound structure will be inappropriate in a time of rapid technological change. Similarly a different role is required in an organisation facing severe external pressures — such as resource restraint or major redevelopment — from what is required in a stable situation.

Applying these principles to hospitals it can be seen that they are very complex organisations, often large, with some services showing strong bureaucratic tendencies such as the formal hierarchies in nursing and functional departments and with others, notably the medical staff, highly professionalised, with clinical freedom as a major concern. Hospitals face rapid technological change in medicine, and operate in relatively unstable environments, with pressure on public expenditure set against increasing demand, with increasing militancy of staff and with NHS organisation subject to externally-decided change. Since 1969 with little intermission NHS reorganisation has been on the agenda or in progress.

The complexity of hospitals puts them into the category of a highly 'differentiated' organisation — a term coined by Lawrence and Lorsch.[1] These authors argue that if an organisation displays this tendency, in which the multiplicity of component parts detracts from the organisation's functioning as a coherent whole, then strong integrating mechanisms are required to ensure that a balance is kept between the component parts and that a sense of direction is maintained. It may be argued that the sector administrator is the only person with a comprehensive view of all aspects of a hospital's activity and that the importance of his role derives from this central position. The variety of tasks through which he should fulfil this role will now be reviewed.

Management of administrative services

The sector administrator normally has direct managerial responsibilities for certain services within the hospital, usually including portering, switchboard and general office. He must ensure, often through an assistant administrator, that these services are properly controlled, that staff are allocated according to workload on satisfactory rotas, that supervision is adequate, that overtime is managed properly and that grievances and disciplinary matters are correctly handled. In the general office he will ensure that proper systems exist for dealing with such matters as petty cash, patients' property, private patient accounts and payment of wages.

He may also be responsible for medical records and medical secretarial services through a medical records officer and must ensure that the services described previously are managed efficiently.

As well as these staff the sector administrator is normally directly in control of a number of non-pay budgets such as patient clothing, bedding and linen, furniture and furnishings, printing and stationery, telephones and office equipment. He must prepare annual estimates for these services and, anticipating workload and incorporating changes in activity, must set priorities within the budget.

For these services the sector administrator is head of department and can be held directly accountable for their efficient organisation and management.

Support services

Enough has already been said in this and the previous chapter about the difficulties which the functional management of support services on a group basis makes for the sector administrator's co-ordinating role. Briefly, when budgets and ultimate responsibility for these services lie at district level it is there that difficulties have to be negotiated and resolved. This detracts from the role of the sector administrator and removes decision-making to a higher level than is desirable.

Personnel services

The personnel services are a special case of functional management. Sector administrators, and to some extent all managers, must have certain personnel responsibilities, but with the establishment of area/district personnel departments in 1974 a large proportion of the personnel work previously carried out by hospital secretaries was transferred to the area/district level. There is no doubt that in many ways the change has been beneficial. AHAs as employing authorities must have area-wide personnel policies, and the establishment of personnel departments permits the development of specialised skills and services which are not possible when all personnel work is performed by a number of general administrators who also have many other responsibilities. It may be argued however that matters concerned with staff are so important in such a labour-intensive service as the NHS that excessive centralisation can have serious disadvantages. As Chapter 13 makes clear, personnel management arrangements are not at present uniform throughout the service, and it would be rash to argue for a standard pattern placing the maximum responsibility on the sector administrator, particularly after what we have already said about the way hospitals and sectors vary in character. However, the case for greater sector responsibility should be made.

Consultation and negotiation should take place as close as possible to the workplace, and not at district level unless the issue has clear district-wide implications. Similarly grievance and disciplinary matters should be handled locally. The sector administrator should have a clearly defined role in them. He can be regarded as the local representative of the employing authority and could therefore be given authority to appoint and dismiss specified grades of staff after consulting with the district administrator and district personnel officer. The growth of legislation in the employment field makes it important that there should be a local source of advice for departmental heads on such matters and the sector administrator can fulfil this role, looking to the district personnel officer for help with difficult or unusual problems.

The growth in trade union membership and staff militancy since 1974 has created a need for strong local management able to deal with industrial relations problems at the lowest practicable level. It should be unnecessary for minor matters to be referred to the specialist personnel department and the sector administrator should be seen as the focus for negotiation with shop stewards for all matters which departmental heads cannot resolve. Similarly the joint staff consultation machinery should be sector-based since the majority of matters concerning staff representatives are likely to involve their workplace and local facilities.

None of this is to deny the case for a specialised personnel function. It is rather, as with other specialisations, a question of how best to combine those advantages with effective local management.

Finance

The sector administrator is directly responsible for his own budgets and should have a hospital-wide responsibility jointly with the finance officer or his representative to review expenditure patterns, to investigate over and underspendings and to agree corrective action with department heads. The sector administrator is concerned with all services within the hospital and since the 'output' of health services is so difficult to measure, the inputs in terms of staff and expenditure should be carefully monitored. He should receive copies of the budget statements for all departments within the hospital and a sector summary and no major adjustments should be made to hospital budgets unless he is involved. If development or non-recurring monies are available he should co-ordinate the proposals for expenditure and if cutbacks are necessary he should prepare proposals in consultation with department heads.

Monitoring

The sector administrator has a responsibility as the representative of the employing authority and as the 'generalist' among professionals to detect breakdowns or deficiencies in the services within the sector. He can monitor directly the cleanliness of areas, the appearance and demeanour of staff and the quality of food. He can rely on comments from department heads to ascertain if there are communication problems or a lack of co-ordination between departments. His contact with staff representatives and trade union officials can provide useful information on difficulties within departments.

In the medical and paramedical areas patients' complaints can give an indication of difficulties such as staff attitudes, waiting times and communication problems. The importance of detailed and thorough investigation of complaints has already been mentioned, and the sector administrator has a key role to ensure that the complaints procedure is properly implemented. Patient data on admission rates, waiting lists and bed usage may reveal where pressures or underuse of facilities exist. It is the sector administrator's responsibility to take the initiative and investigate whether any remedial action is necessary.

Co-ordination

There is a vital role of 'co-ordination' in hospitals. It is essential that all relevant disciplines are involved particularly in planning and implementing changes whether in support or patient services. In the hospital the administrator has this overall co-ordinating role, which can be facilitated if a mechanism exists for taking multidisciplinary decisions for the hospital as a whole. It can best be achieved through a 'sector team' with nursing and medical representatives. If the nursing management structure and the medical representative structure do not coincide with sector boundaries there may be difficulty in constituting an appropriate team. The sector team should agree relative priorities to development plans from departments in the light of the activities of the hospital as a whole, and should peruse requests for additional staff and capital developments. The sector team should be the focus for reconciling service needs, development plans and expenditure.

Planning teams

The sector administrator should make a major administrative contribution to district planning teams, especially if his sector is a single specialty such as mental illness or mental handicap. In a community service sector the focus will be more on the development of services than institutional co-ordination.

Health and safety, fire precautions and other hazards

The implementation of the Health and Safety at Work etc. Act 1974 has brought new responsibilities to department heads for safety matters. The sector administrator should be responsible for ensuring that the Act is implemented in his hospital, that departmental heads draw up and implement safety policies, that safety representatives are afforded the necessary facilities and that the safety committee is set up and enabled to carry out its responsibilities. He will be required to determine priorities for expenditure on safety items.

This duty has been added to the previous responsibility for ensuring in consultation with the fire prevention officer and local fire brigade that all necessary fire precautions are taken within the hospital and that staff are trained in firefighting and evacuation techniques and that fire drills are carried out.

Under this heading too falls the completion and monitoring of accident forms. They are prepared for possible future use in legal proceedings, but they can give valuable information on hazards to safety committees.

The DHSS regularly circulates 'hazard' letters about faults in equipment and unsafe practices. It is important that a clear policy should exist to identify who is responsible for investigating the local situation and implementing any necessary changes, and the sector administrator should identify what action is required and who should take it.

External relations

Hospitals are public institutions and the public and press take a close interest in developments and in particular matters of interest. The sector administrator is the hospital spokesman on such matters and should take the initiative in using the local press to make the public aware of activities within the hospital, especially if public response could relieve the pressure on the service, for example discouraging the use of ambulances or unnecessary attendances at accident departments.

Public involvement in health services is the main concern of CHCs and the sector administrator is likely to be involved with visiting CHC members and CHC investigations relating to his hospital.

Conclusion

As we have said more than once, this account is necessarily general. It applies particularly to the management of large general hospitals and needs adjustment for other sorts of sector. The extent to which the administrator carries out the functions described will in any case depend on the extent of delegation from district and the definition of roles at that level. It is important that roles should be clear so that those outside the administrative hierarchy, particularly medical staff, know where responsibility lies. People turn to the administrator when there is a problem — or when looking for someone to blame when things have gone wrong. At the working level it is the sector administrator they should look to — and he must have both the ability and the authority to take the necessary action.

Appendix

Role specification G3 from 'Management Arrangements for the Reorganised National Health Service'

Sector administrator

General characteristics

The sector administrator co-ordinates the various administrative support services in the hospitals, health centres and clinics in his sector with each other, and he ensures that they combine effectively with doctors, nurses, paramedical and social services staff working in the sector.

Principal responsibilities

1. Monitors and co-ordinates, and in some cases* manages directly, institutional support services in his sector.

* Two basic alternative organisation patterns are possible for institutional services within districts. Under the first alternative, the sector administrator manages all the support staff and is responsible for their budgets. Under the second, functional managers at district, e.g. catering and laundry manager, are responsible for the different services and, although they outpost staff to the sector, they remain responsible for the budget. Outposted staff, in this case, are subject to the monitoring and co-ordinating authority of the sector administrator.

1.1 Maintains medical records and financial records and pays wages and salaries, as necessary.
1.2 Carries out certain personnel functions for all staff, other than nursing or medical staff, including the maintenance of all personnel records.
1.3 Provides typing and office services.
1.4 Purchases and stores supplies and equipment.
1.5 Provides catering, laundry and CSSD services, where these are not made available on a district or area-wide basis.
1.6 Provides personal transport for sector staff and takes responsibility for administration of staff accommodation in the sector.

2. Sees that institutional services in the sector combine to meet the needs of patients and professional staff.
 2.1 Maintains contact with doctors (GPs and hospital doctors), nurses, paramedical and local social services staff in the sector to identify opportunities to improve institutional and support services.
 2.2 Contributes towards discussions within the sector on proposed changes in local services and takes necessary administrative action to implement agreed changes, e.g. to out-patient procedures, medical records systems.
 2.3 Provides a channel of communication between the district administrator and professional staff.
 2.4 Keeps in touch with local voluntary organisations, local press, etc., to ensure that local health services are sensitive to local needs and that local people are well informed about their health services.
 2.5 Initiates action to deal with complaints and decides which complaints need to be referred to the district administrator.

3. Participates, as appropriate, in district planning activities.
 3.1 Contributes to proposals for improving administrative services within the district.
 3.2 Participates in the work of health-care planning teams where he has a particular interest.
 3.3 Participates, as appropriate, in the work of planning and commissioning teams for new buildings in the sector.

Working relationships

Accountable to:	*either* district administrator *or* support services manager
Manages:	sector administrative staff not outposted by district functional managers (e.g. catering officer)
Monitors and co-ordinates:	administrative staff outposted from district

Reference

[1] Lawrence, P.R. and Lorsch, J.W. *Organisation and Environment.* Harvard 1967

Further reading

Most of the publications listed in Chapter 6 are relevant, and are not repeated here.

Official publications

Central Health Services Council. *The Organisation of the In-Patient's Day.* HMSO 1976

DHSS. Management Services (NHS)1. *Guide to Good Practices in Hospital Administration.* HMSO 1970

DHSS and Welsh Office. *Report of the Committee on Hospital Complaints Procedure.* (Davies Report). HMSO 1973

SHHD. *Suggestions and Complaints in Hospitals: Report of the Working Party.* (Elliott-Binns Report). HMSO 1969

Other publications

Benjamin B. (Ed). *Medical Records.* Heinemann Medical Books 1977

Davies, J.B. Meredith. *Community Health, Preventive Medicine and Social Services.* Ballière Tindall 1980

Essex-Cater, A.J. *A Manual of Public Health and Community Medicine.* J. Wright & Sons, Bristol 1980

Grant, C. *Hospital Management.* Churchill Livingstone 1973

Jacob, J. (Ed). *Speller's Law Relating to Hospitals and Kindred Institutions.* H.K. Lewis 1978

Revans, R.W. (Ed). *Hospitals: Communication, Choice and Change. The Hospital Internal Communications Project seen from within.* Tavistock 1972

Wieland, F. and Leigh, H. (Eds). *Changing Hospitals: A Report on the Hospital Internal Communications Project.* Tavistock 1971

The Role of Unit and Sector Administrators in the National Health Service. Report of a joint working party. IHSA 1976 (op)

8
Health care planning

Some chapters in this book give a history of their subject, and it is paradoxical that that is not possible for planning. The NHS was established to provide a comprehensive health service, and it was not supposed that this would be achieved simply by new administrative arrangements and the vesting of existing hospitals in the minister. Moreover the regional organisation of hospital services was a recognition that planning was required. Nevertheless planning as an integral part of health service management did not exist for many years.

It might be argued that in an informal sense management of health care planning is an integral part of the management of any health care organisation; that it is the task which any and every health services administrator undertakes, either occasionally or continually as part of his everyday work; and that it is in no sense a new development that merits special treatment, or particular techniques of management. To argue this way ignores the reality. The creation of a plan requires structure and form if it is to be anything other than a pious statement of objectives, relating only to a particular administrative unit, and unrelated to the resources of the service or the nation. We have only to regard the present distribution of health services throughout the UK to see that informal planning in this sense has little to commend it.

The history of health care planning in the NHS effectively begins with the 1962 Hospital Plans. It proved out of the question to realise them within the time originally envisaged, which may be taken as an illustration of the initial difficulties on planning. They were in any case related solely to capital development and perhaps for too long concentrated too much attention and effort on this aspect. Amongst the preliminary work for the 1974 reorganisation, however, was a concerted attempt to evolve a planning mechanism for the use of both capital and revenue in the reorganised service. That preliminary endeavour was consolidated and emphasised by the work of the Devolution Working Party in 1974-5. The draft NHS planning system for England was published in 1975 and only then did it become possible formally to plan revenue and capital expenditure together in a way which took account of national aspirations, and the possible course of national expenditure.

A discussion of the management of health care planning requires the capacity to distinguish between the conceptual base of health care planning — the whole uncomfortable process of thought about the future — and the external form given to express that thought process. In managing the planning process, it is deceptively easy to become obsessed with the external form, and with the completion of forms, rather than to consider the thought process behind it. For a variety of reasons, some of the forms of planning which this chapter will describe will change over time. The basic thought process however will remain the same, regardless of the formal expression given to it. For that reason some of this chapter is devoted to an examination of the conceptual problems inherent in planning. Whatever formal planning system is in existence at any given time, the conceptual problems will remain the same: and it is therefore to an examination of these problems that it is necessary to turn first.

Conceptual problems

It is possible to devise a deceptively simple statement of the aims of health care planning. The aim is to produce an arrangement of the resources available for health care in a way that produces the optimum results for the patient, and which is the most orderly possible in the circumstances of the day. But this simple sentence conceals within it the major dilemma for the health care planner. What is the optimum result for the patient? Can it be described, let alone defined, in any numerical, qualitative, or financial sense? The hard fact is that it cannot. And this difficulty lies at the heart of health care planning. It is one which cannot be avoided, but which remains an enigma central to the whole of the problem.

The inability to describe the final objective of health care plans — that is, the optimum result for the patient — is of course not restricted in its effects to health care planning. Its baleful influence extends also to health care information. The capacity to state accurately a comprehensive measure of health care outcome would of course be the lodestone of a health care information system. It would define what information it was necessary to collect, so as to determine whether a health organisation had achieved that which it had set out to achieve. Similarly, in creating a health plan — in determining how a health organisation might move from its present, imperfect, state to some more advanced, more nearly perfect, state — the capacity to define the objective precisely would make clear the gap between what was sought, and the present position: and thereby, define, if not the precise path to be followed, at least its general direction.

Such a measure, however, does not exist — and in the current state of knowledge is unlikely to be found. Health care planning has therefore to grapple with this central difficulty, and to devise methods by which it may be circumvented.

There is a second major area of imprecision that faces health planning. What does society require from its health care system? Who is to formulate that statement? In the absence of a precise measure of the achievements of health care, how can that statement be formulated? And above all, how is the resulting statement and its attendant expenditure to be ranked in comparison with all other competing social claims?

The creation of practicable methods by which to overcome the major conceptual difficulties that have been described is essential if health care planning is to be successful. Before 1974, the NHS signally failed to face up to the existence of the problems, let alone devise ways in which they might be overcome. Since then, however, the first major practical steps have been taken to enable planning in the health service to make a very real advance.

The method of approach to the first major problem — that of the absence of a measure of health care output — lies in the use of proxy measurements, not, in the main, of output, (that is, of results), but of input (that is, of resources). It is assumed that as it is not possible precisely to measure the result of health care, it is an adequate substitute to measure instead the effort employed in achieving it. And it follows that there has also to be a second, implicit, assumption: if more effort is deployed, the results achieved will be better.

These basic assumptions are of course open to criticism, but they act as a working hypothesis by which to progress. In terms also of resolving the basic problems, the assumptions are of value. They narrow the field of investigation to an examination of the relationship between input to health care and output, between effort and result. It may be objected that in thus limiting the scope of enquiry, the use of the assumptions that have been outlined may exclude from consideration certain other, possible, correct, solutions. It has to be remembered however that the results of health care are but one side of the equation: on the other, are society's expectations, however imprecisely formed or articulated. Those expectations, the way in which they change, and the degree to which society believes them to have been met, will continue to ensure that the measure of health care output (however it is finally formed) is a standard by which expectation and achievement may be adequately compared: and in so doing it will encourage those engaged upon the task to see that their search for the relationship between health input and output is responsive to the wider need of society.

There is one further difficulty which cannot be brushed aside. In accepting that measures of input can — for the purposes of planning and control — act as an adequate proxy for measures of output, it is necessary to accept measures that are diverse in character. Allocations, unit costs, number and type of employees, patients admitted as in-patients or seen as out-patients — all these differ from each other both in kind, and as units of measurement. But they all convey an impression of the effort which is being expended on, or in, the health machine, and, unless and until it is proved otherwise, it must be assumed that for all their diversity they help in some way to measure indirectly some aspect of achievement in the health care system. For those concerned with the control and planning of health care, the diversity of the measures used is a commonplace, and given the absence of a measure of health care output, is inevitable. It is also inevitable that without the unifying factor that a measure of output would provide, the precise relationship of the input measures must remain unclear. This lack of clarity makes for practical difficulty. Although the conceptual relationship of measures of input is unclear, it must obviously exist. In controlling a health care organisation, or planning for its future, those responsible have to cope with the problem of diversity. Unconsciously or consciously, they will form a judgement on the relative merits of the input measures which they regard as important in demonstrating the success of the institution. In planning, implicit judgements must be made explicit. If not, the perception will differ from group to group, from person to person.

Implicit assumptions also loom large in considering the question of society's expectations of the service. Public perception of medical performance is very much the sum of personal perceptions: and those perceptions are not necessarily of professional competence alone, but are often highly coloured by other, more human, considerations. Public perception of health care, and its results, suffers from the same difficulty; and public expectations of health care are formed, not only upon a view of health care that subsumes professional competence, but also on one which is centred — at least so far as overtly expressed expectations are concerned — on particular facets of care, almost without regard to the whole. Politicians and the health service are frequent victims to the same fault, and the planner must beware lest he too is lured on by the specific at the expense of the general. But behind the specific and overt expectations of particular areas of health, there lies an implicit general assumption about health provision: that when it is needed it will be there, and that it will embrace whatever advances medical science has achieved — or at least has been reported as having achieved by the popular press. It is the task of the health planner, at whatever level he may operate, to construct out of the broad spectrum of implicit expectation, a framework of explicit expectation that is internally coherent, and capable of rational examination. In short, it is his task to act as the midwife of ideas.

The planning process

Having rehearsed the basic conceptual difficulties of which the health planner must be aware as he embarks upon his tasks (and which will remain the same, whatever form the planning system might eventually take), it is now possible to turn to the practical planning process, and the various steps within it. The first step is to determine — within the constraints of time, available money, national policies and the heritage of the past — what the health organisation under review should achieve within the longer term, say, in ten to fifteen years. This process, the creation of a strategy, is a complex and time-consuming exercise with many strands; and is discussed in detail in the next section. The second step is to translate the longer-term objectives expressed in the strategy into a short-term programme of action for the immediate future, and this process — of operational planning — is epitomised by the oriental aphorism 'The journey of a thousand miles begins with but a single step'. Operational planning is discussed in detail in later sections, but its essence is to set out in simple programme terms the steps to be taken within the operational cycle.

The evolution of strategy

The evolution of a strategic plan may be regarded as the construction of an hypothesis — an hypothesis which best resolves the tensions between a number of factors. Those factors are the present position (whether it be one of strength or weakness); a statement of ideal objectives (whether those objectives are national, regional or local); and the availability of resources for the period which the plan is to cover.

With that concept in mind, it is now possible to examine the various components available for the preparation of a national, regional or local strategy. Those components — in addition to a statement of the present position — have until now consisted of the consultative document *Priorities for Health and Personal Social Services in England* and the subsequent paper *The Way Forward*, which — taken together — have formed the statement of health care objectives for the NHS in England, and the statement of government policy *Sharing Resources for Health in England*, and subsequent government pronouncements on the application of that policy, which together have formed the basis for deducing the funds available during the planning period. (In 1981 the government published *Care in Action*, a handbook of policies and priorities, but it is too early to judge how far its somewhat different approach to priorities will affect strategy.)

Components of strategy

The statement of objectives

It has already been observed that the 1974 reorganisation and the introduction of the planning system afforded an opportunity for the first time to spell out clearly detailed objectives for the NHS. The Report of the Devolution Working Party stated the problem clearly:

> The first requirement is a statement of broad national strategy indicating lines of change and development in the NHS, the interplay and interdependency of the services for particular client groups, policies for the utilisation of assets (manpower and physical) and the nature of links with other services, e.g. personal social services. The strategy should be related to estimates of resource availability. . . The initiative for this must properly lie with the Department. First the Department should produce a draft based upon consideration of current and developing ideas from whatever source. There would then be consultation with people at all levels inside and outside the National Health Service. At this preparatory stage when ideas are being considered participation by the NHS would be of a general nature seeking ideas where they are likely best to be found and not constrained by the organisation structure. . . Using the results of this, the Department should produce a draft of a strategy document including reference to the resource constraint and consult NHS and local government authorities formally. Thereafter the document should be widely published so as to provide the public and the NHS with a framework for the development of the NHS and personal social services.

The consultative document: *Priorities for Health and Personal Social Services in England* represents the culmination of the process outlined by the Devolution Working Party. It is a remarkable achievement since, for the first time, it sets out a comprehensive statement of the objectives of the national health service set against foreseen restraints upon expenditure. Further, it strikes a balance between the various competing claims of different health care groups, and advances a view as to how each of these health care groups should grow in relation, both to each other, and to overall growth of the service.

The major achievement of the document lies in its comprehensive nature. There have of course been many statements of government policy for various sectors of health care published in the years before 1974. Major examples of these policy pronouncements are *Better Services for the Mentally Handicapped* and *Better Services for the Mentally Ill.* Policy documents of this sort however — though providing a valuable initiative in the particular sector with which they were concerned — suffered from the major disadvantage that their recommendations were not set out against the backdrop of all NHS activity. The 'Priorities' document, on the other hand, draws together all the various strands of policy promulgated in earlier years and presents them as a comprehensive whole.

The document itself modestly recognises its pioneering status:

> This Consultative Document is a new departure. It is the first time an attempt has been made to establish rational and systematic priorities throughout the health and personal social services. Such an attempt is long overdue but it is given even greater urgency by the economic limitations outlined in the White Paper on Public Expenditure up to 1979-80 — the period on which this document also concentrates. The level of resources which will be available over the next few years means that difficult choices will have to be made. It is essential that they should be made in full knowledge of the facts facing the service as a whole: the likely changes in demand by different client groups; the areas where past neglect has led to serious deficiencies; the way in which the available resources can be used to get the best return; the vital importance of

> joint planning. It is essential too that Central Government and those who administer the service locally should work out together what the broad priorities should be.
>
> This document is only the first step in what will become a continuing process. Needs and the strategies for meeting them necessarily change and priorities must therefore be constantly modified. The proposed consultations may also point to better ways of presenting and discussing national strategies in the future but the need to establish a better framework for national and local planning is obvious.

The document begins by reviewing the changes anticipated by 1985 in the total population and in variations of the overall age structure. Of these changes perhaps the most notable are a projected reduction of some 17 per cent (from 8.1 million in 1973 to 6.8 million in 1985) of the number of children aged between 5 and 15. This reduction in the number of the young is accompanied by an increase of 25 per cent (from 2.3 million in 1973 to 2.8 million in 1985) of the very elderly (those aged over 75).

Attention is called to the considerable discrepancy in the level of services — as deduced from the costs which they incur — between various parts of the country. The costs quoted in the table which follows, relate to expenditure per head of population in 1972, and are illuminating:

	Highest region	*Lowest region*
Hospital services	£37.19	£21.09
Family practitioner services	£11.45	£9.20
Personal social services	£8.78	£5.12

The initial survey at the present state of the service is completed by a description of one of the major phenomena of the present day medical practice:

> Developments in medical science, innovations in methods of treatment and the development of new patterns of community care are all major influences on demand for resources. Pressures for improvements and expansion come from staff, professional bodies, the public and the Department itself. In the last few years there has been particular concern about standards of care for the elderly, the physically handicapped, the mentally ill and handicapped and children whose families cannot provide a satisfactory environment for them. These pressures are likely to increase the demands made on services.

This sketch of the outstanding features of the NHS and of the additional demands likely to fall upon it in coming years is followed by a brief statement of the economic climate within which these changes will take place. Although written in 1976, the description of the economic climate has about it a certain timeless charm:

> . . .two problems stand out in the management of total public spending:
>
> > The first has been with us for many years. Popular expectations for improved public services and welfare programmes have not been matched by the growth in output — or by willingness to forego improvements in

> private living standards in favour of those programmes. The oil crisis intensified this gap between expectations and available resources. The second problem is that of cost inflation which has become acute in the last few years and has added an extra dimension of difficulty.

This quotation from the then most recent white paper on public expenditure is followed by another:

> As soon as a sound economic base can be achieved, some growth in spending should again be possible but at least during the next three years or so no overall growth in public expenditure...is planned beyond the level now envisaged ...This means that in all programmes including the social programmes very strict tests of priority have had to be applied. The government's purpose in making these hard decisions was to ensure that the increase in national output in the next three or four years is not appropriated for use in the public sector but instead is available to put the balance of payments right, to provide increased productive investment, and to allow a modest rate of increase in private consumption.

From this general picture, the document draws out the consequences for the NHS:

> The challenge to those who plan, manage and work in the services is to find ways of developing them over the next few years so that the most urgent needs are met whether they arise from the increasing number of elderly people, or from the need to overcome past neglect by implementing new policies...or from pressures for the introduction of improved techniques and of patterns of providing care.

The document then proposes a solution for the problems inherent in the existing state of affairs:

> The first essential is to maintain the standard of service: to put people before buildings...the role of primary care in helping to relieve pressure on hospital and residential services by caring for more people in the community [is restated]. The family practitioner services will continue to expand at an average of 3.7 per cent a year; the health centre programme will be maintained and it is proposed that the growth of vital supporting services such as health visitors and home nursing should be given high priority. An expansion of 6 per cent a year in both these services is visualised ...There should be an increasing emphasis on preventive services...[The document] also highlights two problems: the extent of unsatisfied need in the provision for the mentally ill and the mentally handicapped and the pressure on services due to the rising numbers of elderly and of children needing help. It therefore suggests that unless the targets for meeting these needs are to be abandoned there must be a deliberate decision to give them priority over the development of the general and acute hospital services; and that there should be some reduction in expenditure on maternity services where in recent years costs have risen in spite of the falling birth rate. Differential growth rates are proposed for acute and long-stay services:

Services used mainly by the elderly	3.2 per cent per annum
— Services for the mentally ill	1.8 per cent per annum

— Services for the mentally handicapped	2.8 per cent per annum
— Services mainly for children and families with children	2.2 per cent per annum
— Acute and general hospital services	2.2 per cent per annum
— Hospital maternity services	a reduction of 1.8 per cent per annum

This overall distribution of proposed growth obviously creates severe problems for the acute sector; and the document recognises that these can only be overcome by a rationalisation of the service currently provided.

> The potential savings here are estimated at between £20m. and £40m. If the strategy suggested is to succeed all parts of the service must make their contribution to economies. Members of the medical profession while preserving their clinical freedom must be ready to seek more economical methods of providing health services which will enable available resources to be used more efficiently and in some cases freed for other purposes.

But the document also points out that the growth rates for services of first priority should be regarded as a minimum and that further efforts should be made to improve such services by exploiting fully the whole field of potential economies and rationalisation. In particular, the document recognises the need to:

> review the *level of provision* in all services with a view to finding particular elements which can be reduced in current circumstances. Some services may have been justified when they were first established but changes in the pattern of need and provision may mean that the resources could be used more efficiently elsewhere...No service should be exempt from this review...Of particular importance is the review of general and acute hospital and maternity services because this is the largest block of expenditure (some 40 per cent of the total) and because these services probably offer the greatest scope for redeployment of resources. There has already been a good deal of redeployment of resources in these fields largely due to scrutiny, by the medical profession in particular, of clinical priorities and methods. There is no question of interfering in clinical decisions but a realistic review of service priorities must involve discussion with the professions of the extent to which resources can be released by further developments of this kind.

Finally, the document tackles the difficult problem of the geographical reallocation of resources:

> There is also to be a shift of resources towards those regions and localities which historically have received less funds per head of population than others and where standards of service have suffered accordingly. Regions and localities which receive restricted allocations on this account will need to conduct a particularly searching review of their services so that those services which are relatively well provided with facilities and staff can yield resources to those which are underdeveloped.

It is of course possible to criticise the overall thrust of the strategy which the consultative document advances. It would, for example, be proper to examine the grounds upon which the document concludes that care within the community (i.e. using family practitioner services) is not only 'better', but also can be actually stimulated (in volume terms) given the present control mechanisms, and the role of the independent practitioner. It would be reasonable to enquire the basis upon which the document asserts that developments in medical science and innovations in methods of treatment can be achieved in the acute sector whilst still holding down the annual growth rate to slightly over 1 per cent. But a critique of the strategy is not within the scope of this chapter. In any case criticisms of this sort do not detract from the overall achievement which the document embodies. It is a turning point in the development of the health service, a keystone of health care planning in the UK — indeed in the world. It represents one of the major ingredients of the strategic hypothesis.

Of particular interest — in methodological terms — to the planner is the programme budget which is the basis of the document's division of resources between health care programmes. Though not a complex technical tool, it is nonetheless a method of costing policies based on past expenditure. The programme budget is neither a forecast nor plan but a way of examining possible strategies for development. It attempts to group expenditure into programmes which are more meaningful when considering possible lines of action than either the public expenditure survey breakdown or more traditional forms of estimating and accounting. Past expenditure trends are examined and an attempt made to analyse, where possible, how far these trends result from changes in the level of activity and how far from changes in unit cost. From this base, estimates were then made of the cost of policies for the development of each group of services. It has however to be noted that the projections advanced in the document are a quantitative illustration of the priorities which the document discusses but they do not in any way form a detailed plan. A methodological description in Annexe 2 of the document describes the method, and its advantages and disadvantages. Whatever the difficulties of method — the financial projections represent the first realistically costed comprehensive survey of the development of the service — and as such merit particularly careful study.

The statement of objectives revised

Following publication of the consultative document and the ensuing public discussions, the government considered in some detail the comments which it elicited. During the same period, RHAs were producing their first strategic plans, and these also were available to the Department in considering what alterations, if any, should be made to the formal statement of objectives embodied in the consultative document. The resulting exegesis is set out in a further document *The Way Forward* published in late 1977.

The Way Forward is a good example of the interactive nature of planning — a problem described in some detail later in this chapter. It demonstrates that the initial formulation of policy, however carefully performed, will always need adjustment in the light of the experience of those called upon to carry out the policy, and in the light of the existing situation. The Secretary of State, in his foreword, observed that:

> There has been little criticism of the long term aims set out in the consultative document but considerable doubt has been expressed on whether it is practicable to achieve them within the suggested time scale. While the government has ensured that there will continue to be at least a modest rate of increase in resources for these services in the country as a whole, I appreciate

> that we cannot hope to make significant and rapid changes in the desired directions without a more rapid growth of resources... It is not only the limited rate of growth of revenue which prevents us making rapid change. Much of what can be done is conditioned by what has already been achieved... Plans (particularly those involving major buildings) launched several years ago are coming to fruition and we must make the best possible use of them. Inevitably the capacity for change varies in different parts of the service and in different parts of the country. In view of all these constraints it would be easy for us to postpone the efforts involved in moving to new priorities until the impact of past plans has been absorbed and until it is possible to provide a more rapid growth of resources. But this would be wrong. We must be clear about the road we are all trying to take even though progress will be uneven. National policies must be clearly stated.

The Way Forward set out the minor changes in public expenditure expectations and in population projections that had taken place since the publication of the consultative document. It also described points of particular interest for this purpose which have emerged from the early RHA strategic plans. It re-emphasised the main future aims of health service policy: to lay stress on prevention; to remedy past neglect of services particularly for the mentally ill and the mentally handicapped; and the need to make provisions for the continuing increase in the elderly population and for the greater number of children in local authority care.

Amongst the short-term difficulties and pressures on resources facing the health service, *The Way Forward* instanced particularly the need to continue with the geographic redistribution of health resources; the need not to neglect training and education programmes for health and personal social services staff; the need to meet the revenue consequences of capital developments either at the expense of other developments or by saving through rationalisation, or by reductions in other services; and the continuing need arising from the relative gaps in services (particularly hospital acute services) and primary care facilities (especially in deprived areas), which there was a pressing need to fill at the earliest possible moment.

The document then reviewed the priorities set out in the consultative document and reaffirmed them with some minor amendments. On the major thrust of that document into the community and — if not necessarily away from the acute sector, at least proposing some curtailment of it — *The Way Forward* observes:

> The consultative document emphasised the importance of adjusting the balance of care to provide greater support in the community ... [this process] will be gradual and slow. It is clearly undesirable and often more expensive to admit, or to keep in district general hospitals, or long-stay hospitals, old or mentally ill or mentally handicapped people who could properly be looked after in the community. This will be avoided only if adequate progress can be made in developing community services including community hospitals. Progress will vary from place to place depending on economic constraints, local choice and differences in the existing level of provision.

For the acute services, the document accepts the problems brought out, not only in so many of the comments on the consultative document itself, but also made evident by early regional strategic plans:

> To enable priority needs to be met there has to be rationalisation and pursuit of economy in the acute sector by realising underused or less well used resources. This aspect of the strategy spelt out in the consultative document gave rise to more concern than any other. The requirement to restrain the growth of expenditure on acute services nonetheless remains, but the government recognise the importance of the acute sector in meeting the needs of priority groups, particularly elderly people. There can be no general formula for achieving the necessary degree of economy nationally upon which the rest of the national strategy depends but discussions of regional strategic plans against the background identified later in this document should enable agreement to be reached on the broad approach to follow in each region. It is clear that circumstances and timescales will differ both between and within the regions.

Finally, on the overall balance of service *The Way Forward* returns to the problems of the elderly:

> The consultative document reviewed demographic changes and estimated that a number of additional beds would be needed to match the increase in the numbers of elderly people. But it is not only beds that are needed, it is the additional staff, time and effort required to enable elderly patients to return home as quickly as possible. The appointment of additional medical, nursing or rehabilitation staff with skill in caring for the elderly may be a better investment than providing more beds with existing staff. It is likely that a higher rate of patients treated can be secured by all disciplines which deal with the acutely ill elderly and that the additional number of beds needed in England will be significantly lower than the total proposed in the consultative document. Health authorities should examine the scope for providing these beds by reassignment bearing in mind continued pressure on all those specialties which deal with elderly people.

The document acknowledged the practical constraints which authorities face, and accepts the limitations which ensue therefrom:

> Health authorities are being asked to restrict the services in the NHS as a whole to a slower rate of growth than in recent years. This policy is adopted deliberately with full awareness of the consequences, which will vary accordingly to local circumstances. The expectations both of the professions and of users will not be fully satisfied. . . This is the price which has to be paid if progress is to be made in those parts of the service which have been given priority for development. Much has already been done to increase the efficiency of acute services, but the further restraint required implies increased rationalisation, closure of some units, curtailment of some services in some places and more effective use of staff and facilities generally.
>
> Some authorities and professional bodies, individual doctors and nurses and others working in these services have been warned of the frustration they will feel at continued delay in achieving their long unfulfilled expectations. They are concerned that patients will suffer from real shortcomings in these services. The extent to which actual shortcomings in services can be reduced and therefore the extent to which the professions can be encouraged to participate fully will depend on:
>
> *first,* the vigorous pursuit of efficiency and economy not only in the acute services but wherever in the health and personal social services resources could

be better;
second, recognition of the priority pressures *within* the acute services;
third, the willingness of those concerned especially those in the professions to accept the policy and to join in planning for it;
fourth, the skill with which the planning is done and the timescale for changes. Planned measures tend to hurt less than hasty ones. It is not the intent of the government to rush acute services into sudden restraint.

The Way Forward then adumbrates the main priorities within the acute sector:

Concentrate acute services including those for the elderly in the newest and most suitable premises (closing if necessary less suitable facilities and those which are unduly expensive to maintain);
direct capital in the short term to small schemes designed to assist rationalisation — especially closures...
encourage local initiatives to make the most effective use of nursing and remedial staff...
develop day surgery, five day wards and programmed investigation unit;
pursue the possiblility of rationalising the provision of regional specialties.

Finally, having reviewed the DHSS planning effort and that for the personal social services *The Way Forward* has a few words of cheer for the NHS planner:

There must be real commitment at all levels to planning as a systematic approach to identifying needs, considering priorities, devising realistic ways of implementing those priorities and consulting and involving those whose interests are affected. It is worth emphasising the following points:

planning requires regular reviews of all services and resources, not simply the deployment of new money;
the RAWP report emphasised the importance of following through proposals for geographical redistribution of health resources effectively in the planning process;
while total self sufficiency in the area or district is not a necessary aim major imbalances in opportunity for access to services within a region need to be corrected over time in the planning and allocation process;
the planning process gives effect to one of the most important features of NHS reorganisation — the involvement of clinicians in management at all levels;
consultation is a vital element in planning, particularly with staff interests and CHCs;
priority selection through planning helps to show how resources can be deployed to meet changing patterns of need and to take advantage of changing medical technology;
the government needs to be able to draw on authorities' plans when developing national policies and priorities.

The Way Forward showed that government was prepared to adopt a flexible and realistic approach to the immensely difficult task of setting out the objectives of the health service. Taken together with the consultative document it represented that statement of objectives which the health service had for so long needed.

Resource allocation

The problem of resource allocation — one of the major elements in the formulation of a strategic plan — was also examined by the Devolution Working Party. Its report set out how that task might be approached.

> Revenue should continue to be allocated to RHAs on the basis of an objective formula designed to achieve broad parity between regions as soon as practicable. The main element in any such formula should be population, weighted by more appropriate factors than are used at present. The present factors (mainly weighted population, available facilities and case load and case mix) should be improved by refining the validity of the information upon which these factors are based. So far as the problem of incorporating better measures of relative need are concerned, if population weighting could be more closely aligned to needs, this factor itself could impart a sufficient recognition as between regions both of relative needs and of existing deprivation... The difficulty of measuring deprivation, particularly if defined in terms of states of health, is well known. A sophisticated approach to identifying deprived areas might well produce results little different from those of a weighted population formula, and it might be unwise to undertake any major exercise until a pilot study indicated that the results might be worth while. 'Deprivation' does not necessarily arise from financial shortage, and cannot always be remedied by the provision of extra funds. In some cases, accepted health 'need' arises from social or other causes, and the remedy may lie in other areas of social policy than health care. If and when an element can be introduced to take explicit account of deprivation, its basis should be clearly spelt out to all concerned — in the NHS and to the public as a whole.

The task which the Devolution Working Party sketched out was accepted as one which needed urgent attention. The Resource Allocation Working Party was appointed in May 1975 with the following terms of reference: 'To review the arrangements for distributing NHS capital and revenue to RHAs, AHAs and Districts respectively with a view to establishing a method of securing as soon as practicable a pattern of distribution responsive objectively, equitably and to relative need and to make recommendations'. The interim report of the working party was delivered in August 1975, and was intended to ease the transition from the existing basis of funding to that new equitable basis which the terms of reference required. Its final report, *Sharing Resources for Health in England*, was published in September 1976. Like the priorities documents, the RAWP report has already been discussed in previous chapters, and will be described in Chapter 9. Nevertheless, it must be discussed at length here from a different point of view since the principles on which it was based form an essential element of the planning process. The working party acknowledged the complex nature of the task before it:

> There is ample evidence to demonstrate that demand for health care throughout the world is rising inexorably. England has no immunity from this phenomenon and because it can also be shown that supply of health care actually fuels demand, it is inevitable that the supply of health care services can never keep pace with the rising demands placed upon them. Demand will always be one jump ahead...Supply of health facilities is in England as elsewhere also variable and very much influenced by history. The methods used

to distribute financial resources to the NHS have since its inception tended to reflect the inertia built into the system, by history. They have tended to increment the historic basis for the supply of real resources ... This led us in our Interim Report to interpret the underlying objective of our terms of reference as being to secure through resource allocation that there would eventually be equal opportunity of access of health care for people at equal risk... It has involved us in seeking criteria which are broadly responsive to relative need, not supply or demand, and to employ those criteria to establish and quantify in a relative way the differentials of need between different geographical locations ... In searching for criteria which are responsive in this way we have had perforce to consider only those criteria, the supporting statistical data for which are readily available and reliable... One of our main stumbling blocks has been the lack of relevant information in a suitable form ... We are conscious of the probability that any allocation method based upon the data available may be open to challenge on grounds which would be difficult either to substantiate or refute. Had better data been available we would have used them. In spite of these reservations however we are convinced that the data we have used are sufficiently reliable to support the conclusions and methods we propose... Not enough is known about the determinants of health needs. Even where particular factors can be seen to play a part in causing health need, it is often difficult to quantify the relationship and draw upon reliable information about when and where they occur.

The report then sets out the method which it has selected:

... formulae should be the chief determinants of allocation from the DHSS to RHAs. We recognise that limited use of central reserves may be unavoidable; this is acceptable so long as it is kept to a minimum. Application of a formula to the distribution of all but this fraction of the revenue available to services entails three distinct logical steps:

1. The application of measures of relative need to establish the share of available revenue to which each RHA would be entitled on the basis of need criteria alone. This share constitutes each RHA's 'revenue target' towards which it should be moving as fast as circumstances permit.

2. Establishing where each authority stands now in relation to its revenue target. For RHAs this means simply comparing the allocation actually received last year with the target allocation.

3. Determining how fast it is possible for each authority to move from its present position towards its revenue target bearing in mind practical constraints on the pace of change in whatever direction may be desirable.

Having described the method to be adopted, the report then tackles the major difficulty which faced the working party. It is of course possible — as the report suggests — to determine the population to be covered by the formula; to adjust that population by patient flows into and out of a particular region; and then to go further and attempt, for resource allocation purposes, to standardise the effect of different hospitalisation rates throughout the country. The major task however is to determine the measure of need — adjusted on the lines which have been described — to be used to modify the population figures.

It is in this field that the report breaks new ground:

Need for hospital in-patient services is not of course a function of age and sex alone. Many other factors are known to play a part... The difficulty is not in determining which factors are likely to be influential but in quantifying their influence and in eliminating overlap between them. Figures are available, for example, on relative population densities and on social class structure but we have not found it possible to relate this information quantitatively to the need for health care ...

But it would not be necessary to take account of causal factors such as those already mentioned if it were possible to measure health care need directly ... Whilst numbers of cases clearly reflect need they do so in terms of the available supply of services. Caseloads fail both to distinguish between degrees of need and to assess the extent to which need is unmet through lack of facilities. Waiting lists as one indicator of unmet need are also known to have questionable reliablility. Moreover there is ample evidence to support the view that the level of supply has a significant influence on the level of demand. Need must therefore be measured by an indicator that is far less dominated by supply.

Statistics relating to payment of sick benefit are more independent, in this sense, but do not apply to the whole of the population, important categories such as the elderly, children and many married women being excluded. There are also problems relating to the causes of incapacity as certified and regional differences may be partly attributable to industrial structure: the ability to work despite the presence of morbid conditions may, for example, be influenced by the nature of employment. Moreover sickness absence does not necessarily imply a need for health care over and above that which can be provided by a GP ...

The search for a reliable indicator as independent as possible of supply, which could be used to assess regional differences in needs led us to examine the possibility of using mortality statistics as a proxy indicator of morbidity. Mortality statistics cover the whole population, are readily available and permit compilation by place of usual residence. The quality of the statistics including analyses by cause of death is high. The crude death rate shows a considerable regional variation (maximum exceeds minimum by 38 per cent for both males and females). Even when allowance is made for age structure — which has a marked effect on comparative death rates — the residual variation is still as high as 28 per cent for males and 21 per cent for females ... The reasons for the pattern of differential regional mortality are not wholly understood but it is believed that regional differences in morbidity explain the greater part of it and that statistics of relative differences in regional morbidity, if they existed, would exhibit the same pattern as those for mortality.

Some support for this assumption is provided by a comparison of mortality rates adjusted to take account of age and sex differences with such regional morbidity-related data as exist similarly adjusted. The comparison reveals significant positive correlations ...

Mortality statistics also present an opportunity to relate differential morbidity to health care need by reference to conditions in a way that no other sources permit. It is possible to examine the variations in mortality between regions by diagnostic conditions — using the underlying not the associated causes of death — grouping the conditions according to the 17 chapter headings of the International Classification of Diseases (ICD). The statistic used is the Standardised Mortality Ratio (SMR) which compares the number of deaths actually occurring in a region with those which would be expected if the national mortality ratios by age and sex were applicable to the population of that region. In this way the unique pattern of mortality in each region can be established, calculated separately for each condition or group of conditions.

> Many of the commonest conditions — including some which lead to death — place relatively little demand on health care services. Others require expensive care, perhaps over a long period. This relationship can be established by reference to the national figures of hospital bed utilisation for each condition category considered, and incorporated in the calculation to provide the final link in the chain from mortality through morbidity to need for health services . . .
>
> As a result of the studies and analysis we have carried out supported by the findings of research in related fields and expert advice, we have come to the conclusion that SMRs — adjusted in the way we propose — are the best available indicators of geographical variations in morbidity. And to ignore the considerable variations which this analysis displays would be to ignore a crucial factor in determining the relative needs for health care of different localities.

The formula which results from this approach is set out in detail in the report and is described in the following chapter of this book. The method is complex and it is necessary to note here the particular allowance made for additional NHS service costs arising from the clinical teaching of medical and dental students (SIFT).

In one sense, the construction of a target allocation by the method which has been outlined above represents the easy part of the task. The greater problem is to devise a method by which to move present allocations towards targets — because it is a reasonable assumption that there will be very few cases where the target matches the allocation. The report devotes some considerable attention to this problem. It recognises that it is not possible for regions to lose revenue at too great a rate just as it is equally difficult for regions economically to absorb too much new revenue in a given span of time. On the other hand because, in the view of the working party, the process of reallocation should continue save in the harshest of economic climates, it proposes also methods by which the rate of reallocation can by geared to the national growth rate.

The pace of change in the reallocation of financial resources is perhaps the single most important feature of any attack on the problem. It is also the feature which excites the most political interest whether it be to urge the maintenance of the status quo, or to stress the need for more rapid change. The careful matrix in the report therefore — balancing change against growth, and even negative growth — has not commanded the acceptance of ministers to perhaps the same degree as the other recommendations. The reasons for this are complex, and are rooted far more in the evolution of political imperatives than in health care strategy. They are not therefore further discussed here, though the implications are examined later in the section on the problems encountered in the evolution of strategy.

The Resource Allocation Working Party was constrained in its work by the need to report in time to effect the preparation of the 1977-8 allocations. The report therefore indicated a number of topics where substantial future work was required. Those topics included a refinement of the calculation by which to determine the costs of teaching medical students; an examination of the costs of London, over and above those recognised by London weighting; and an examination of the interaction of health authority expenditure and family practitioner expenditure.

These further tasks were remitted to a new body, the Advisory Group on Resource Allocation, which was set up in 1978. Its terms of reference were 'To consider detailed improvements in the methodology recommended by RAWP of new data, as the result of research studies become available, and to advise on any practical and desirable changes which could improve the process of resource allocation for the hospital community services'. In its eighteen month existence, before it was discontinued, the group made substantial progress in its work on geographic cost variations, and went some way to improving, as a result of that work, the calculations made for the additional cost of London. Its progress in the extremely difficult field of the service increment for teaching was however discouraging; and its work was brought to a close before it could tackle the problem of the interaction of health authority expenditure and that incurred by family practitioner committees.

This is not the place to embark upon a detailed critique of the method of resource allocation advanced by the Resource Allocation Working Party and its successor. Detailed critiques may be consulted in many of the professional journals. There is no doubt that it is possible to critisise aspects of the report — though in evaluating those criticisms it would be as well to remember that much of the criticism is directed, not at the methodology of the report, but against the effects which flow from the application of the methodology. And it must also be remembered that much of the criticism comes from those who do not benefit from the formula's application. Whatever the strength of the criticisms, RAWP represents a major step forward in the creation of one of the most necessary elements in the formulation of any strategy for the health service. For the first time, the process of resource allocation from national sources has been given an overt, and cogently argued, basis. Gone are the days when the allocation process was a mysterious enigma and when it was impossible to determine logical bases for differential allocations of growth.

Resource allocation at sub-regional level

The development of strategy within a region obviously calls for a reasonable forecast of monies to be available to operational authorities during any given strategic planning period. The creation of a framework for this purpose is therefore of great importance, and the process is one which, in some respects, is more complex than the evolution of a formula at national level. At national level, the problem of resource allocation, and the attempt to relate it to health care needs was conducted, in one sense, in isolation; that is to say, it was conducted with a view to producing an equitable formula for the long-term distribution of funds. And deliberately — except through the medium of the transitional arrangements — it did not take into account the existing pattern of distribution of health care facilities. In the evolution of the formula, this was of course the correct course to pursue. Preceding formulae had relied heavily upon existing hospital utilisation and patient numbers. The effect was that which might have been anticipated, in that all attempts at redistribution followed the existing pattern of services, thereby giving to those that already had. One of the major successes of RAWP was that it broke away from this cycle of creeping incremental privilege.

At regional level, however, it is not possible to regard the construction of the resource allocation formula within so purely theoretical a light. While at national level, it is proper for target purposes that the existing distribution of resources should be ignored, within regions this is not practicable. At regional level, the objective must be the creation of a strategic plan which is achievable in the time available — and a plan, therefore, which it is possible to fund. In these circumstances it is not possible to maintain a strict separation between the theory of resource allocation and its practice, nor indeed between the practice of resource allocation and the execution of a plan. Despite the theory of resource allocation within regions is as vital as at a national level. The national working party devoted a section of its report to the problem — and stressed the importance that the work proposed at national level should find similar expression below regions:

> The criteria for establishing regional differentiation of need and the methods recommended for resolving the ensuing disparities would have no purpose unless applied to allocations below regional level. Indeed the only way in which our recommendations can have a real effect is to carry them through to the point where services are actually provided — the areas and districts.
>
> The problems are similar but with significant differences. Few areas and districts are entirely self-sufficient, nearly all provide services of one sort or another to others, and many will have to continue to do so for some considerable time. Movements of patients and services across area and district boundaries occur to a greater extent than across regional boundaries. Factors which can be largely ignored at regional level — e.g. seasonal demands and the effects of commuter traffic on services — assume far greater significance at sub-regional level. But the needs of populations served by areas and district remain and are assessable whatever the variations which occur in the delivery of services. And no matter whether these variations are unplanned and unacceptable or planned and acceptable they remain susceptible to treatment in much the same way as their regional counterparts.

It is possible to construct theoretical targets for operational authorities within a region, using a method similar to that used in the national method. The difficulty lies in making the necessary adjustments to take into account the special local factors which the national working party had in mind. Indeed, the RAWP report went on to list some of the factors which should be considered in making adjustment of this sort. Those factors were:

1. Special local factors such as the extent to which alternative facilities relieve or add pressure on the NHS.
2. Abnormal workloads which are not fully reflected in the estimates.
3. The revenue consequences of capital developments coming on stream.
4. Capacity to absorb revenue change in terms of capital stock and manpower. This may pose particular problems in RHAs where the need for change is concentrated in one or two AHAs.
5. Planning considerations — need to develop priority services, planned closures or changes of use, policy decisions whether or not to alter present patterns for delivery of care and the consequential patient flows, policy decisions on the extent to which it may be desirable to create or maintain 'centres of excellence'.
6. The need to hold reserves — though these should be kept to a minimum in order to secure the most equitable distribution possible and should be concentrated wherever possible at the AHA or district.

This list of exclusions allows very considerable amendment to be made to target allocations for operational authorities. But the major problem for those constructing the resource allocation element of the strategic plan is the need to determine the pace of change.

It has already been explained that, nationally, a formula for change was proposed, geared to the national growth rate of health. At regional level, the problem is more complex. Not only are regional allocations subject to variations in the national growth rate — which frequently do not correspond with those which have been projected — but also the achievement of change is frequently tied firmly to the achievement of positive physical events — the closure of hospitals, or the completion of new facilities. At regional level, therefore, the resource allocation formula, taken together with modifications appropriate for circumstances within the region, has to be a positive statement of the long term trend of the distribution of funds between operational authorities. The rate of change is not however a topic susceptible to a generalised formula, save one that is perhaps generalised to the point of platitude. Rather, the pace of change is a factor that forms an integral part of the plan — and it is for this reason therefore that further discussion on the matter is deferred until later in the section.

Distribution of regional specialties

One major feature which not only the funding formula, but also the regional plan, must take into account is the siting and extent of regional specialties and services. It is necessary to have, as an integral part of the formula, agreement on the extent to which specialties should be regarded as regional specialties; and — that extent having been determined — where those facilities are to be sited. Appropriate additions must then be made to the target allocation of the operational authority where such units are housed. At this point, it is necessary to enter a word of caution. The task of devising an allocation formula below regional level is complicated: the task of explaining it, whether to authority members, CHCs, or to clinicians is formidable. And it therefore becomes a popular misconception, particularly amongst clinicians, that for the purposes of resource allocation recognition as a regional specialty is, in some respect, a meal ticket for the future, which will provide a financial safeguard for the specialty concerned. This is an understandable hope, but misconceived.

The practice employed throughout the country for funding regional specialties varies. Some choose to fund directly, others choose to include an element thought to be adequate for the purpose of the specialty concerned, within a global allocation to the health authority. But whatever the practice so far as the allocation is concerned, the target allocation and its amendment to take account for any particular authority of the presence of regional specialties is not a method by which unlimited funds can be guaranteed for particular specialties. It merely represents an adjustment of an operational authority's target to take into account its agreed responsibilities within a region.

Similar alterations to target have to be made to take into account regional services, and — in particular — if these regional services are provided on an agency basis by operational authorities. The prudent planner will ensure that the quantum of money reserved for this purpose, or distributed amongst area targets, is agreed in advance with all those concerned.

The construction of a strategy

Preceding sections in this chapter have dealt at some length with the conceptual difficulties which lie behind the task of preparing a strategic plan. They have also discussed in detail the necessary constituent parts of national policy — in terms of objectives for health and resource allocation — which any strategic plan, be it at the level of a regional authority, or an operational authority, must take into account.

The view has also been expressed that the construction of a strategy is the construction of an hypothesis — an hypothesis which is the point of least tension between the demands of national policy (set out in the consultative document and *The Way Ahead*); the demands of national and regional resource allocation policy (as set out in the RAWP report and regional reports upon the problem so far as it applies to their particular authority); and the demands of the present — that is to say, the existing distribution of services, manpower and buildings which form the starting point of any planned progress towards the future.

The discussion so far therefore has been concerned with the fundamentals of the problem since these are crucial to the process, and will remain whatever changes are made to the external format of the planning system. This section relates to the process of creating a plan, and to the external form that the plan is required to follow. The process is described in detail in *The NHS Planning System* published in June 1976. The document is concise in its description of the task upon which authorities are to embark so far as strategy is concerned:

> Strategic planning is the means by which NHS authorities determine their long range objectives and priorities for the development of the full range of health services, and plot the course towards the achievement of those objectives. The purpose of such planning is to achieve in the foreseeable future a coherent pattern of service development and resource deployment designed to ensure the most cost effective use of all available resources for the benefit of those who use the services. Strategic planning must therefore be based on clear assumptions about resource availability and requires a willingness to recognise and accept the need for changes in conventional patterns of resource deployment.
>
> The strategic planning process following the pattern described in detail in [earlier parts of the manual] begins from an examination of the existing situation, including an assessment of the extent to which current policies are being achieved either generally or in particular localities. Taking account of this analysis, of the various policies for service development, and of any expected changes in population patterns the next stage is to draw up a list of objectives. Objectives may be expressed in a variety of ways including: results to be achieved (benefits to the patient or community); levels of service to be provided (in terms of quantity or quality); changes in service patterns; or particular developments (or stages of developments) to be undertaken. There will be both ultimate objectives and interim objectives — and possibly a mixture of the two, e.g. the achievement of a general long-term objective may be considered more urgent in one area than in others. Interim objectives will usually be positive but it is also possible for them to be negative in character. Given the comprehensive and long term nature of strategic planning it will sometimes be sensible deliberately to delay taking action in a particular field

whilst others are given emphasis and priority. In considering the future balance of services such negative choices (e.g. a decision not to seek self-sufficiency in an area in a particular specialty in the next ten years) may often be as important as positive choices, and should be clearly recognised as an important element in the planning process.

> The objectives decided upon will probably not all be capable of achievement. They will often be competing with one another for resources and some may well not be consistent with others. It is absolutely essential therefore that each objective should have a priority rating attached to it, so that there can eventually be produced a comprehensive statement of mutually compatible objectives for the plan period which would be seen as a statement of priorities. This statement of priorities may be regarded as marking out the route to be followed over the period of the plan with marker posts en route indicating the stages at which achievement or partial achievement of particular objectives is expected. It is essential that the strategy flowing from this must be consistent with the financial and other resource assumptions for the period of the plan.

The planning guide then stresses, as have earlier parts of this chapter, that the plans evolved have to be consistent with funds available both nationally and regionally, and also with a national expression of objectives for the health service. One interesting point to note is that, even in the planning guide, the struggle between idealism and reality has not been entirely resolved. 'The objectives decided upon will probably not all be capable of achievement...Some may well not be consistent with others...' But the realists win in the end. 'It is absolutely essential... that there can eventually be produced a comprehensive statement of mutually compatible objectives for the plan period which will be seen as a statement of priorities.' This is the major, and most important, feature of a strategic plan. Not only must it reconcile successfully the competing demands of national policy, existing circumstances and financial forecasts, but — from that reconciliation — it must produce a clear statement of action for the plan period — clear in that it can be understood by all those who are to take part in it, and clear in that it can be achieved within the timespan available. Plans which cannot be achieved in the timespan available are not worth the paper upon which they are written. The guide adds a further touch of modest realism:

> The first full strategic plans will be prepared in parallel with the first set of operational plans. It is recognised that this arrangement with the absence of any input from consultations on national strategy or from operational planning experience will inevitably result in strategic plans that are less comprehensive and polished and more tentative than authorities would wish. It is also likely in this initial phase that some operational plans will have strategic implications which do not fit in with strategies being developed at area and region...However as the planning arrangements develop these launching difficulties and deficiencies should progressively be eliminated.

The format for strategic plans is described in detail in the planning guide. It is not reproduced here since, as part of the process of eliminating launching difficulties and deficiences, it became evident that, detailed though the format might be, it did not afford an opportunity for a proper comparison of plans as between areas or as between regions; and subsequent amendments in the following cycle set out a much stricter format bringing together in the forms the effects of population changes, throughput and finance.

The planning guide contains some ingenious flow charts and diagrams to show the planning process, but maintains a silence as to quite how these processes might be achieved. In a subsequent section, this chapter discusses the problems of breaking into the process, which is essentially conceived as cyclical. It is necessary here, however, to set out the particular parts of the process which have to be performed in order to create a strategy which adequately reflects the needs and aspirations of operational and regional authorities.

The most important first step in the creation of a plan is the creation of an adequate set of guidelines, which should set out quite clearly what questions the strategic plan is endeavouring to answer. They must make quite clear to all those authorities taking part in the exercise, what the plan should contain, and what is expected from it. This process is one of considerable difficulty in the first instance, since the formulation of the correct questions requires a considerable understanding of the nature of the problem facing a particular group of authorities. The formulation of the wrong questions will justifiably cause a sense of frustration on the part of operational authorities and also produce a strategic plan which lacks coherence. The prudent planner will take particular care in ensuring that the guidelines are correctly and adequately framed. It is of particular value if they can be agreed by all the operational authorities involved before the planning process begins.

Experience has demonstrated that, amongst other things, strategic planning guidelines at regional level should contain a statement of geographical population for each operational authority; a statement — where this is different — of the planning population which an operational authority is required to plan for, together with estimates of those populations for both the mid point and the end point of the strategic planning period under review. In setting out this information, it is essential to quote the source of the population projections which have been used, together with an explanation of the reasons behind that particular choicc. Though this will not by any means reduce criticism during consultation from all those who are able to produce a different set of projections which is more advantageous to their own case, it will at least begin the argument from a basis of fact together with a rational explanation for it.

Guidelines should also state clearly which regional specialties are to be regarded as such, and the agreed siting for them. If there is doubt, the alternatives should be clearly stated.

Next, guidelines should state clearly what financial expectations each operational authority might justifiably entertain in the planning decade ahead. Particular features, which have been taken into account in making these assumptions, should be spelt out, including the provision of additional funding, where appropriate, for major new building, or — in other cases — expectation of revenue to be saved by closure programmes, or by rationalisation.

The construction of comprehensive guidelines is particularly worthwhile, since they sketch out the parameters within which operational authorities may plan. This reduces the possibility of frustration on the part of planning authorities, and sets out, from the very beginning, areas of potential difference which may be highlighted and, therefore, dealt with constructively.

Having constructed and issued guidelines, planners have next to consider how the various components of the plan are to be assembled. At operational level, this involves ensuring that all the components to be included are properly timetabled, and that the appropriate effort is being given to them early on in the process. At regional level, it involves considering with some care how to examine the strategic plans of operational authorities within the region when they are received: for example, the basis by which they are to be either compared, or checked, against regional guidelines. It is also valuable, at that early state in the exercise, to arrange to see draft plans as early as possible, and to prepare a provisional series of meetings with operational authorities so that the plans may be discussed — in draft if need be — as soon as possible, thereby reducing to a minimum unpleasant surprises finally revealed by the plans themselves.

The mechanism which each health authority will adopt to draw together the strands of the strategic plan, and to translate them into the plan itself will differ, but it should be made quite clear at the outset of the strategic planning cycle which group of people, or which person, has the responsibility of ensuring that the plan is indeed drawn together on time. The task of constructing the plan is one of very considerable ingenuity and complexity, and very time consuming and demanding. There is no point in compounding the difficulty by the failure to resolve internal problems between disciplines or between officers as to who is responsible for what. Experience demonstrates that a multidisciplinary planning team at the highest possible level is by far and away the most effective way of handling this problem.

One final point needs to be considered. After the plan has been prepared, and consulted upon, it needs to be accepted by the health authority. This is an exercise which needs to be undertaken with great care and after much preparatory thought. The document represents an authority's aspirations for a ten-year period. It will therefore generate much interest, some of which may seem factional and uninformed. Since the topic to be discussed is one of very considerable size it may well be that one meeting of an authority is insufficient to give adequate consideration to the document. There is some merit in attacking the problem in parts and inviting the authority to consider particular major issues as far in advance of its consideration of the full plan as possible. In this way not only will authority members have the opportunity to see particular problems exposed in detail, but they will also be aware of the background — and perhaps indeed already be committed to a certain course of action — when they come to consider the plan as a whole.

Problems and remedies

The overall description of the formal structure of strategic plans begs a number of questions — as does indeed the NHS planning manual itself. It will be apparent, however, that the formulation of an overall strategy is a cyclical affair with improvements and alterations achieved during successive reviews of the strategy. It is of course correct to view strategy in this light once it has been formed; but this approach ignores the difficulty of building the initial plan. Essentially, the creation of the initial plan makes it necessary to break into a process which is a cycle. Until that cycle is subsequently complete, there will be gaps and difficulties; and this point must not be overlooked.

Although we have now passed that stage it is worth noting both to complete the picture and perhaps to account for some of the early disappointments. Starting with the formulation of strategic guidelines centrally, without knowledge of the detailed problems of those who have to formulate strategic plans, may lack realism and lead to waste of effort. On the other hand to ask operational authorities to formulate their strategic plans and then aggregate them regionally and nationally will produce plans requiring more than the resources available and with different emphases and often the acute services over-represented. A middle course whereby the RHA issues guidelines may reduce both these difficulties but contain an element of both. In short, no starting point is satisfactory. Only after one complete cycle — guidelines, plans, an aggregated plan (whether regional or national) and a further set of guidelines amended in the light of the plan — will it be possible to ensure that the strategic planning process is responsive to the national expectations of the service and the capacity of health autorities to respond to those expectations.

There is another aspect of the initial creation of a strategic plan that needs to be carefully considered. If, as has already been explained, a strategic plan is an hypothesis which strikes a balance between potentially conflicting demands, and — from that balance — proposes a programme of action achievable over, say a ten year period, the plan acquires a synergy that at once subsumes and replaces its constituent parts. There is now no longer any necessity for a funding policy, or a statement of objectives, to stand on its own. As particular, and separate, statements of national or regional policy, they may be allowed to merge into the background. From the moment the strategic plan is accepted, the programme of action within it becomes the determinant of funding policy, and is an expression of the objectives of either the health service, or a particular part of it.

A major problem revolves around the timetable. It is of course considerable in the production of early versions of the strategic plan since the nature of the task to be accomplished then is more arduous than on later occasions. In some respects, the strict constraints of the planning cycle are beneficial, for they require the solution of problems which might otherwise be left unsolved. The prudent planner will begin by devising a firm timetable. It is of the utmost importance that the timetable for the various stages of the plan — guidelines, completion of draft plans, completion of final plan, the period of consultation, and final consideration by the appropriate health authority — is known right from the start so that all those who have a part to play can be aware of that part and the time when they will be expected to play it. This is particularly relevant for that part of the process which involves consultation, since one of the most common hazards of that process is the claim that insufficient time has been allowed.

A major hazard frequently encountered is the failure by many people to comprehend the task upon which they have embarked. Sometimes it is due to the failure of the planner to explain clearly what he needs, and why. Sometimes it is a failure to appreciate the sheer size of the task, and the intellectual effort required. Sometimes it is a failure to realise what an uncomfortable business it is. Nobody likes taking hard decisions, and to take those decisions in the light of a realistic appraisal of what is practically possible within a given time span, and with the funds which will actually be available, is a very disturbing experience.

This last point applies also to authorities and to all those people working in the service for whom a plan is being constructed. It is very natural that people should in general terms approve national policies but find unpalatable those which do not bring benefit to the institution or service where they have an interest. One of the major problems in managing the planning process is the capacity of people not to perceive that guidelines and national policies apply to them, and not just to everybody else.

Further difficulties on these lines are encountered in the consultation process, for the public too finds it difficult to accept the local application of national policies, particularly when it means no provision for a much desired and visible benefit, such as a new hospital. The public, like administrators and health service staff, is reluctant to accept that for some considerable time it will need to soldier on with existing resources, and is liable to think that if the new hospital has not materialised there is no point in thinking about health plans. The public must be persuaded — and staff no less — that the contrary is true, and it is the more positive side that should be emphasised in the consultation process.

There is more that needs to be said about consultation. As presently constituted the consultation process for strategic planning is cumbersome and time-consuming. It is perhaps right that it should be, since the strategic plan should cover all the really important topics that will affect health care within any given health authority over a ten or 15-year period and the public can therefore have its views on the future development of services, which will affect it radically, properly canvassed.

Mention has already been made of the need to provide a timetable for consultation from the start. Because of the overall structure of the timetable, time for consultation will almost inevitably be compressed. Some of the difficulty to which this could lead can be alleviated by alerting all those bodies who are to be consulted well in advance and telling them of the timetable. Health authorities can reasonably expect those whom they are consulting to work to a timetable which is no more demanding than their own. Bodies which are to be consulted in general appreciate advance notice of the timetable and, if a climate of co-operation has been engendered in the past, can be persuaded to organise special meetings of their respective committees in order to accommodate it.

Given the wide consultation that is required it is inevitable that some of the comments received will appear partial or parochial, and they will generally be recognised as such. The comments received will be bulky, and this presents a problem. It can be argued that the substance of the views received can be summarised for presentation to authority members and that to circulate them in full is wasteful and gives members an unmanageable amount of paper. Against this it must be stressed that consultation represents the major opportunity for public bodies with an interest in the health services to make their views known. To incur any suspicion that those views have been suppressed or lightly brushed aside is to set up barriers of ill-will against the future. Authority members must have the opportunity to judge for themselves the effect upon the outside world of the plans for which they are ultimately responsible.

Another point to take into account in determining how to prepare a strategic plan is the availability of the data which will be required. Nationally the initial stages of strategic planning were marked by some uncertainty on the part of central government about data which that required and this was understandable, not only because of the difficulties of any venture but also because of the deep-rooted problem, described at the beginning of this chapter, relating to the basic uncertainty about measures of health care output. It is now reasonably clear what data a plan will require and the point is to ensure that the data are available. This may seem self-evident, but many planners have discovered half way through the plan that the data which they require either do not exist or have not been collected for the year in question.

Even within a framework of national and regional guidelines and policies, the task of contemplating how all the health services within an authority's control might develop as a coherent whole over a ten-year period is both difficult and uncomfortable. In one sense, it brings to a head all the problems that political expediency might dictate should be shelved or put off. And to be called upon to bring those delicate issues out into the open, and to resolve them, not only in principle but also to set out a programme of action which will finally lay the matters involved to rest once and for all, requires very considerable moral courage. Worse than that, it will evoke a very considerable opposition from any entrenched interest that fears that in some way its future might be threatened. It is however not only the most honest way to proceed, but also in the long run the way forward which is most likely to achieve success. There is no point in making promises which cannot be fulfilled, or in having policies which are misunderstood. There is no point in attempting to conceal the course upon which any particular authority proposes to embark. The evolution of a strategy for health will produce strong opposition, sometimes virulent, but without such a strategy the health service will flounder. The working effort involved in producing a strategy is immense. Without it, however, the health service will not give the lead which the public has every right to expect.

Operational planning

> Properly developed strategic plans will provide a backcloth against which operational planning (that is, the development of specific proposals for change in the short term) may be undertaken. Operational planning will thus be given a sense of direction and a set of standards against which its achievements may be measured. It is the process by which decisions are reached on actual changes in patterns of service provision. Rolling three-year operation plans will propose what specific actions should be taken, in which locations, at what time, in order to achieve desired changes in the existing pattern of service provisions in keeping with agreed strategy.

This extract from the NHS planning guide exemplifies the need for the emphasis given in this chapter to wider planning problems, and to the formulation of the strategy. The operational planning task is entirely dependent for its success on sensible and rational answers to the overall strategic problem. Without such answers, the work of the operational planning cycle is unconstructive. If the strategic plan is primarily about direction of change, the operational plan must, within the strategy, be much more specific about time, cost and staff. The operational plan has three major objectives. They are:

1. To set out the steps to be taken in the forthcoming operational planning period (currently three years) towards the agreed long-term strategy.
2. To concentrate the mind of administrators (of all disciplines) to determine how progress towards the strategic aims may be achieved.
3. To impose a strong, financial discipline upon the entire process of allocation, and forward thinking.

The creation of a strategy is not an end in itself, and once objectives have been determined, positive steps must be taken to ensure that the health authority travels towards them, and within the time allotted by the plan. The operational planning cycle is an annual goad to that end: it affords also the opportunity in which to examine proposals for expenditure, for expansion, development or retrenchment. (The importance of the last of these should not by now need stressing.

Planning is not about spending development money but about the use of all resources and must include the search for economies and greater efficiency and sometimes the transfer or discontinuance of services.) Against the objectives which the health authority has agreed for its strategy, the annual planning cycle is the method by which to take practical steps to achieve the strategy, whilst guarding against the lure of transient objectives, no doubt highly desirable in themselves, which do not form part of the agreed strategy.

The annual operational planning cycle also has the advantage of concentrating the mind. The timetable is tight, and it is necessary to think out clearly well in advance what measures are needed in any given operational planning period to make progress towards the strategy, while at the same time meeting short-term local and frequently pressing needs. The preparation of the operational plan, therefore, is an occasion to think deeply about the various priorities with which every health authority is faced, and to examine yet again how best those priorities might be arranged in order to achieve them within a reasonable timespan. As a process it is overt, subject to public consultation, and debate at authority level. It is a method of making explicit the whole process of allocating funds. Though it is not obligatory under the terms of the NHS planning system, there is a great deal to be said for every regional operational plan to contain an additional section which sets out all those projects, advanced for inclusion in the plan, which it has not been possible so to include, and to give for each the reasons why it has not been possible. The value of this positive discipline is greatly enhanced if all sources of expenditure are channelled through the operational plan. Items such as scientific equipment are often omitted from the planning cycle, and run either on a separate timetable or employing different methods of selection. Discrepancies of this sort frequently present difficulties, and it is best to organise the activity of an authority so that the operational plan is a statement of the use of a comprehensive range of funds. Not only does this lead to administrative and financial tidiness, it also enables both members of authorities and officers to look in totality at their forthcoming proposed effort.

Methods in operational planning

As with strategic planning, guidelines play a crucial role in the operational planning process. Guidelines need to be drawn up to show health authorities what particular areas of activity should have priority in the forthcoming operational planning period. The guidelines should indicate the resources expected to be available in each of the years under review — and, if necessary, should indicate what range of variation might be expected in these allocations given sudden and unexpected changes in the national growth rate for health. Guidelines should also indicate the amount of capital money which might become available for each health authority for discretionary schemes, for scientific equipment, and for medium and major capital projects. In times of capital shortage, it is sometimes prudent to limit the numbers of schemes to be put forward by health authorities so as to reduce the amount of unnecessary preparatory work which might be involved, and — in particular — to reduce the degree of frustration felt by those whose pet scheme has not been included in the plan.

Timetabling for operational planning is perhaps of even greater importance than for strategic planning. The present annual cycle is tight; management teams therefore need to be very certain at the beginning of an operational planning cycle what the timetable involves, and what arrangements it is necessary to make. The guidelines should set out the overall timetable, but management teams, who will have the responsibility for the detailed execution of the timetable, should be prepared to do substantially more groundwork than that which the guidelines can possibly indicate. Particular problems which need to be examined are meeting dates for professional advisory committees, and for community health councils. As long as possible should be given to such bodies that the plan will be delivered for their comment by a particular date, and that their responses will be necessary by further particular dates in order to meet the overall programme.

The NHS planning system sets out in great detail the format of the operational plan. It is not intended in this chapter to examine that format in detail. All that is necessary to observe is that the format should have, as its intention, a method of setting out proposals in a clear and concise manner, so that competing claims may be compared and ranked in order of priority. Whether or not it is necessary to detail progress in each of the client groups year by year is debatable, and is perhaps one of the most contentious issues that the planning system has itself evoked. It is sufficient to observe here that although the format of operational plans is one which may vary from time to time, the principles behind them remain exactly the same. Whatever modifications to the format take place, either by evolutionary change, or as a result of administrative reorganisation, the operational plan is a method of drawing together the specific steps to be taken by any health authority in each year of the planning period, to cost them realistically, to rank them in priority order, and to set them against the overall objectives of the authority.

Some authorities use the medium of the operational plan to develop a detailed critique of progress in the past. This is a valuable exercise but it should not be allowed to develop into a witch hunt. The object of such a critique is purely constructive. It should point out those areas where the plan is weak, and where possible suggest other alternatives which might be explored.

Problems of operational planning

It is now possible to touch on some of the problems which may be encountered during the course of the operational planning cycle. Although in many respects these are very similar to those encountered in the strategic plan there are some respects where these are exacerbated. This is particularly so in the case of the timetable which, as had already been observed, is always very tight indeed, and with consultation. In the early stages of consultation operational plans are frequently either greeted with disbelief or lightly brushed aside by those consulted. It must be the aim of the planner so to structure his plan that those changes from plans submitted in previous years are easily visible. Not only is this good administrative practice, it also narrows down the field for discussion and brings down to particular points what might become a diffuse, wide ranging, and unconstructive discussion.

The other major difference in the problems encountered in operational planning by comparison with those encountered in strategic planning is that the discipline required is of a different order. Whereas in strategic planning the major discipline is one of intellectual rigour, in operational planning that discipline must be extended also to precision and care in the formulation of specific proposals.

Failure to do so at the operational planning stage may well cause a much needed project to be deferred since insufficient information is made available.

Conclusion

The planning system, although envisaged by the Conservative government responsible for the 1974 reorganisation, took shape under the Labour government that came into office that year, and it was under that government too that the essential elements of planning — priorities and a policy for the reallocation of resources — were formulated. It is to be expected therefore that all these things should be re-examined on a further change of government.

The present government's view of planning was given in 'Patients First':

> The discipline of planning in both the Department and the NHS has demonstrated its value and is to be retained. It provides the opportunity for the Government's policies and priorities to be reconciled with available resources. It also enables health authorities to appraise systematically their own services and to influence the Government. But existing planning arrangements are over-complicated and bureaucratic. A simpler planning system is being worked out and will be discussed with the Service.

Most people with experience of the planning system will welcome simplification and a reduction of bureaucratic features, though they will not suppose that planning can be made simple. Changes in this direction are unlikely to affect what has been said in this chapter because the emphasis has been on the principles — and on the difficulties of applying them — rather than on the formal procedures and on the details issued with the annual guidance. Similarly simplification is unlikely to affect the need for specific arrangements not discussed here, most of which however are referred to elsewhere, such as planning teams, health care planning teams for client groups and liaison with local authorities, particularly for joint financing schemes. Finally, any revisions of priorities which the government may undertake — and revisions will be necessary from time to time even without changes of government — are unlikely to affect the principles and methods of planning, though they may well alter the contents of plans. The priorities of *Care in Action* are broadly those of previous documents, though there is more emphasis on adjusting national priorities to local circumstances and less concern with precise targets.

The principles have always, of course, to be applied in a specific context and in a specified way. The discussion in this chapter has been based on the English context, but in general it applies also to the other parts of the NHS. In Wales and Northern Ireland a very similar system to the English is followed, the main difference being that important difference in context, the absence of the regional tier. In Scotland a somewhat different approach has been adopted. Whilst health boards, as an essential part of their functions, are involved in planning, and have established programme planning committees, usually as a sub-committee of the policy and resources committee, they do not have an annual comprehensive planning cycle. On the other hand the Scottish Health Services Planning Council, which is described in Chapter 5, provides a national forum for discussing plans and priorities which has no counterpart in England. It is concerned with strategic rather than operational planning, considering the planning of services for particular client groups and overall priorities.

Further Reading

Circulars

HRC(73)8, WHRC(73)11. Development of planning in the reorganised national health service
HSC(IS)126. NHS planning system: draft guide
HC(79)9. DHSS planning guidelines for 1979 – 80
HC(80)9. DHSS planning guidelines for 1980 – 81
HN(76)37. Report of a working party on devolution

Official reports

DHSS. *Better Services for the Mentally Handicapped.* HMSO 1971
DHSS. *Better Services for the Mentally Ill.* HMSO 1975
DHSS. *Care in Action. A Handbook of Policies and Priorities for the Health and Personal Social Services in England.* HMSO 1981
DHSS. *Priorities for Health and Personal Social Services in England: A Consultative Document.* HMSO 1976
DHSS. *Sharing Resources for Health in England* (Report of the Resource Allocation Working Party). HMSO 1976
DHSS. *The NHS Planning System.* 1976
DHSS. *Priorities in the Health and Social Services: The Way Ahead.* HMSO 1977
DHSS, Northern Ireland. *Strategy for the Development of Health and Personal Social Services in Northern Ireland.* HMSO Belfast 1975
DHSS, Northern Ireland. *Guide to Planning in the Health and Social Services.* HMSO Belfast 1980
SHHD. *The Health Service in Scotland: The Way Ahead.* HMSO 1976
Welsh Office. *Proposed All-Wales Policies and Priorities for the Planning and Provision of Health and Personal Social Services from 1976 – 77 to 1979 – 80* (Consultative document). 1976
Welsh Office. *Health Service Planning: A Short Guide.* nd

Other publications

Blum, H. (Ed). *Health Planning Methods: An International Perspective.* Department of Health, Education and Welfare, Washington DC 1979
Graham C. and Fairey, M. *Sharing Resources for Health in England through a Decentralised Planning System.* Department of Health, Education and Welfare, Washington DC 1980

9
Health service finance

It is tempting to think that because the health service is free at the time of treatment, all questions of money have been magically swept aside. If one believes that the state is committed to paying for whatever treatments are necessary, one may feel justified in criticising the government for the inadequacy of certain services, which results in delays in securing admission to hospital or failure to bring people with particular skills to one's home. Similarly, doctors and other health service staff may feel justified in asking that their particular specialties should be given more resources, because they know that there is an unsatisfied demand for the skills they are able to provide.

In Chapter 2 we saw who were the people who benefited from the national health service. Now we must ask ourselves who pays for all these benefits and whether, in practice, they can be expanded or improved. When the NHS was established, it was believed by some that the cost of providing this free service would not escalate, but eventually diminish; because people who were then sick and were made better would be able to return to work, thus increasing the total contributions to the National Health Insurance Fund and reducing the drawings from it. The general improvement in the standard of health throughout the country, which was expected to result from the availability of health care for thousands of people who had hitherto not been able to afford it, would mean that in ten or twenty years' time only the people with really inadequate bodies or minds and those unfortunate enough to be involved in accidents would need to receive hospital treatment. Looking back, it is easy to criticise that state of optimism, but at the time there were convincing arguments to support it. We now know that health is a relative term and that the more health care becomes available the more will be the demands made upon it. Illnesses and conditions, such as arthritic hips, which were formerly untreatable and known by the unfortunate term 'chronic diseases' are now operable, with great benefit to human comfort and length of life, but also at great expense to the NHS.

We looked, in Chapter 8, at the elaborate procedures which have been devised to plan the most effective use of the resources available to the NHS. It is arguable, in theory, that a state-controlled enterprise, such as the NHS, should be managed throughout the UK, in accordance with some great master plan, determined by parliament, through a regimented system of allocating and controlling funds and supervised by numerous teams of inspectors. Such a concept ignores many human factors and there is no public or private form of business which is more subject to the influence of human factors than the NHS. Even if there were a crock of gold from which all the demands made upon the health service could be met, there would still not be a uniform range of treatments or a uniform standard of care. It has been said that the business of those who control the finances of the NHS is to allow things to happen by providing the necessary resources. That is true, but what actually happens will always be a double compromise: first, between available resources and demands and then between national policy and local opinion.

To understand the financial aspects of the NHS, one needs the answers to a number of questions, such as:

— What does the NHS cost?
— Where does the money come from?
— Where does it go?
— Is it shared out fairly?
— How are changes in health services planned and implemented?
— How are the expenditure and income controlled?
— Do we get value for our money?
— Can financial management be improved?

Financial management is not, as some might suppose, an exact science. In some respects it may appear to be technical, but the principles behind it and the major factors affecting decisions can be readily understood by non-accountants. It used to be said that the standard arrangement which existed before 1974, whereby every hospital authority had a finance committee, was a distinct advantage to the public at large, as it ensured that financial matters were explained in laymen's terms. On the other hand, the corporate responsibility of mangement teams, under the current arrangements, also ensures that the treasurer (who is always an accountant) has to satisfy his colleagues on the team, in terms which they all understand, that his advice to the health authority has their full support and is presented in plain language.

What the NHS costs

In 1979-80 the UK government spent about £8,000 million on the provision of health services, and a further £1,400 million on personal social services (PSS). Except in Northern Ireland the two budgets are kept separate, but they are generally placed together in the broad categorisation of public expenditure.

Figures of this size are difficult to comprehend at the best of times, and when there is a high inflation rate they can seem practically meaningless, the more so because when comparisons between years are made they have to be adjusted to constant price levels. A different sort of comparison gives a better indication of the scale of NHS spending. Table 1 shows the breakdown of planned public expenditure in 1979-80. It can be seen that expenditure on health and PSS is exceeded only by education, etc. and by social security payments, which include retirement pensions (much the largest element), and supplementary, family, sickness and unemployment benefits.

Another way of looking at cost of health services is as a percentage of either the gross domestic product (GDP) or the gross national product (GNP), two somewhat different measurements of the economists. As we saw in Chapter 1, by these measures UK health care expenditure is low compared with that of most economically developed countries, and that is fairly often offered as a reason for increasing expenditure. However, international comparisons are difficult because when health services are so different it is not certain that the same elements are included in the calculations for each country, and in such labour-intensive services much depends on the relative price of labour. The figures may be more useful in comparing the expenditure of one country over time. To take the GNP, the NHS in the UK absorbed 3.93 per cent in 1949 and 5.51 per cent in 1978. Between 1957 and 1978 the GNP rose by 70 per cent in real terms, but NHS expenditure rose by 257 per cent. As in nearly all countries, health service expenditure has been rising faster than national incomes.

Table 2 takes a closer look at this growth in England and Wales over 20 years

Table 1. Summary of public expenditure in the UK. Forecast for 1979-80 at November 1978 prices

	£Billion
Social security payments and costs	16.3
Education, libraries, sciences and arts	9.1
Health (£7.4B) and PSS (£1.3B)	8.7
Defence	7.2
Housing	5.4
Trade, industry, energy and employment	3.4
Other environmental services	3.2
Roads and transport	3.0
Law, order and protection	2.3
Overseas aid and services	1.9
Loans to nationalised industries	1.4
All other programmes	4.0
	65.9
Debt interest	2.3
	68.2
42% of estimated value of Gross Domestic Product (£162 Billion)	

Source: *The Government's Expenditure Plans 1979-80 to 1982-83;* HMSO, Cmnd. 7439 adjusted for Northern Ireland programmes

the time when current financial restraints were beginning to be felt. Personal social services have grown much more rapidly than health services, though within the latter capital allocations grew almost as much.

Table 2. Growth of expenditure on NHS and PSS in England and Wales, 1955-6 to 1975-6 (all at 1975 pay and price levels)

	1955-6 £M	1975-6 £M	Increase %
Health authorities' revenue	1,654	3,272	98
Health authorities' capital	41	355	766
Family practitioner services	730	967	32
Other health services	132	226	71
NHS sub-total	2,557	4,820	89
Local authorities' personal social services	104	917	782
H & PSS total	2,661	5,737	116

Source: *DHSS Annual Report 1976*

Enormous though NHS expenditure is, there have always been people saying that the country should spend more, and the experience of other countries might indicate that it could. Within a given national income that would be possible only in one of two ways: by enlarging the public sector and reducing the private sector accordingly or by reducing some of the other elements in public expenditure listed in Table 1 to devote more to the NHS. There is a third way if the national income increases: the NHS share of the extra income might be greater than its share of the present income. In fact NHS growth since 1948 has been a combination of these factors; it has had an increasing share of a growing GNP. It is for the government of the day to decide whether more should be spent on health care; what it is deciding is whether the extra resources are better spent on health care than on something else, and in doing so it will consider among other things the political desirability and possible economic consequences of its decision.

The indications are that over the next few years at least the UK will not see the sort of economic growth that would make it fairly painless to provide extra resources for health care, and it would be unwise to expect a large diversion of resources from other forms of expenditure. For a few years at least the NHS must concentrate on getting better value from the money it now spends, rather than on planning to absorb a greater proportion of the nation's resources.

It is in any case unwise to attach too much significance to the share of the GNP. Between 1973 and 1975 the NHS share rose from 4.64 to 5.61 per cent and most of the increase was accounted for by higher salaries and wages, particularly for nurses and ancillary staff. Thus it did not represent a growth of services or of staff.

Where the money comes from

Almost all the money needed to run the national health service comes from exchequer funds. Not all treatment is entirely free, but the amount contributed by patients is only about 2 per cent of the total cost of the service.

Patient's payments include:

1. hospital services

—prescription charges to out-patients (unless exempt)
—charges for the supply and repair of non-standard appliances
—charges for amenity beds
—charges to private patients for the full cost of accommodation and treatment
—charges for the private treatment of some out-patients
—charges for emergency treatment made under the Road Traffic Act 1972

2. family practitioner services

—prescription charges
—charges for dental treatment and dentures (unless exempt)
—charges for glasses (unless exempt).

(Exemption is principally for children under 16, men over 65, women over 60 and sufferers from certain chronic conditions.)

About 98 per cent of the cost of the NHS is met from public funds. Towards that 98 per cent the National Health Insurance Fund contributes about 10 per cent leaving 88 per cent to be met from general taxation. The contribution from the so-called National Health Insurance Fund is in fact a fairly small, earmarked part of National Insurance, which is paid by employers and employees and collected by the Inland Revenue.

If one takes into account the personal social services as well as the health services, then local rates also play a part, but since 1974 no local authority money has gone towards the provision of hospital or community health services.

All the charges which are levied on patients are prescribed by regulations made under statute and are not therefore subject to any local discretion, which might otherwise allow some districts to provide a better standard of service than others, as happens in non-nationalised systems such as exist in the USA and elsewhere.

Outside the official funding arrangements, there are trust funds (mostly small) administered by health authorities and which are entirely at the discretion of those authorities. They originate in gifts and bequests to hospitals, many made before 1948. The older teaching hospitals tend to have fairly substantial trust funds, whose income can be used to supplement the government's allocations, though even the most wealthy would not be able to increase their total income by more than about 1 per cent through this means. In a few cases teaching hospital trust funds are administered by special trustees established under Section 95 of the National Health Services Act 1977.

Similarly, leagues of friends of hospitals, in addition to providing a valuable personal service to patients, tend to raise funds with which to purchase 'comforts', such as television sets, and items of equipment to be used for treatment and rehabilitation. Thus they, too, are, in a small way, supplementing public funds.

There is nothing to stop individuals or firms from making substantial gifts to health authorities and earmarking them for particular uses. The present tendency, however, is for employers who wish to benefit their staff in times of illness to pay subscriptions to one of the provident or insurance schemes which meet the cost of private treatment either within or outside NHS hospitals.

There is nothing to prevent a group of people from raising money for equipment, alterations or a new department for a local hospital either by appeals to the public or, less commonly, by a lottery. They need the agreement if not the active encouragement of the health authority, since it is for the authority to decide whether or not to accept a gift, but authorities have usually been happy to accept, even when it committed them to additional revenue expenditure. However, in recent years authorities have occasionally made it clear that they could accept a gift of expensive equipment such as a whole body scanner only if the campaigners also raised the money to meet the expensive running costs. Until recently health authorities were not themselves empowered to raise money by appeals, collections, etc. but they were given this power by Section 5 of the Health Services Act 1980, and the DHSS issued guidance on this in circular HC(80)11.

It remains to be seen whether fund raising activities, either by health authorities themselves or by others, can produce large extra funds for the health service. Even fairly small gifts to an individual authority or hospital work counter to the uniformity of financing which is the goal, if not yet the practice, of a centrally financed service. Against this, it could be argued that the central departments, and in England the RHAs, could take account of authorities' additional resources when allocating funds, and there might well be pressure for such measures if marked differences between authorities developed.

Lotteries and appeals are only two of the various suggestions that have been canvassed for increasing the funds available to the health service. As Chapter 17 explains, the Royal Commission examined the whole range of suggestions, and supported none of them.

In the end the method of raising NHS income is a question of public finance rather than health service management, and cannot be separated from political opinions and political practicalities. There is a strong belief in the Labour party that prescription charges are undesirable, yet is was a Labour government which introduced them and a subsequent Labour government which, after abolishing them, reimposed them as a means of economy.

The money required for capital expenditure (i.e. new buildings, extensions, and expensive equipment) comes from the same sources as the money required for running costs, commonly known as revenue expenditure. In the health service, unlike local government or commerce, there is no power to borrow money for capital purposes. Each year's allocation from the DHSS contains an earmarked sum to be spent only on capital purposes. While there is a little flexibility between the budgets for revenue and capital, the effect is that an area health authority with a tiny capital budget cannot engage in building works to improve the services provided, even though it may have the revenue required for the subsequent running costs. Nor can an AHA with large capital funds spend them on new accommodation if it is not guaranteed the future running costs by way of an enlarged revenue allocation. It can be argued that power to borrow capital or to lend it to another authority would be a very useful way for regions to smooth out their long-term plans for capital development. The effect would be to make future revenue and not the size of the current capital allocation the determining factor for future growth.

Where it goes

There are at least three ways of answering the question of where the money spent on the health service goes. One can analyse the expenditure between the different kinds of services provided (e.g. family practitioner services, hospitals, etc.) and the departmental functions within those services; one can analyse expenditure according to the type of resources consumed, i.e. 'subjectively' (e.g. labour, drugs, food, etc.); or one can look at the 'clients' who benefit from the service by saying how much is spent on different types of client (e.g. children, elderly persons, expectant mothers, etc.).

The following tables illustrate these various approaches. Tables 3 and 4 analyse expenditure by service and function, respectively, Table 5 by type of resource consumed (subjective analysis) and Table 6 by programme or client group.

Table 3. NHS expenditure (Great Britain only) — 1979-80 projection

	£M	%
Capital expenditure		
Hospitals and community health services	421	6.0
Other health services	14	0.2
Current expenditure (=revenue)		
Hospitals and community health services	4,912	70.4
Family practitioners	1,490	21.3
Other health services	143	2.1
	6,980	100.0

Source: Table 2.11, *The Government's Expenditure Plans, 1979-80 to 1982-3*, Cmnd. 7439

Table 4. NHS expenditure of NHS authorities — England only, 1977-8. Analysed by departmental functions within main services

Expenditure on revenue account	£000	£000
Headquarters administration		
Secretariat and finance	119,966	
Medical, dental and nursing administration	22,396	
Works and maintenance administration	12,828	
Other administrations	6,765	
Management services	10,761	
Training and education	4,780	
Office services and expenses	19,536	
Accommodation services, overheads, etc.	17,919	
Members' expenses	619	
Other expenditure	1,778	**217,348**
Hospital services		
Patient care services		
1 Direct treatment services and supplies:		
Medical staff services	281,836	
Dental staff services	7,034	
Nursing staff services	1,049,914	
Medical and surgical supplies, equipment and services	284,884	1,623,668
2 Medical and paramedical supporting services:		
Diagnostic departments	191,318	
Other	89,121	280,439
Administration and general services		
Administration in hospital departments	188,781	
Medical records	41,971	
Training and education	14,764	
Catering, domestic services, portering, transport, etc.	664,730	
Estate management	388,246	
Miscellaneous services and expenses	41,133	1,339,625
Less general services direct credits	*29,553*	**3,214,179**
Community health services		
Patient care services		
1 Direct treatment services and supplies:	22,074	
Medical staff services	11,064	
Dental staff services	172,291	
Nursing staff services	12,068	
Medical and surgical supplies, equipment and services		217,497
2 Medical and paramedical supporting services:		
Diagnostic departments	1,363	
Other	32,557	33,920
Administration and general services		
Administrative support services at local level	39,560	
Medical records	1,642	
Training and education	1,836	
Catering, domestic services, portering, transport, etc.	17,254	
Estate management	19,394	
Miscellaneous services and expenses	3,008	82,694
Less general services direct credits	*5,496*	**328,615**

	£000	£000
Family practitioner services		
General medical services		
Payments to general medical practitioners:		
Basic practice allowance and additions	84,458	
Standard capital fees	126,840	
Payments for out of hours responsibilities	26,160	
Direct payments for practice accommodation and ancillary staff	41,387	
Other payments, fees and allowances	41,099	
Superannuation contributions	13,672	
Payments to contractors for disposable sterile syringes	451	334,067
Pharmaceutical services		
Supply and dispensing of drugs and applicances by pharmacists	577,242	
Less charges to patients	*21,948*	
Supply and dispensing of drugs and appliances by medical and dental practitioners	35,632	
Superannuation contributions	1,047	
Other expenditure	1,661	593,634
General dental services		
Fees to dental practitioners	219,933	
Less charges to patients	*52,408*	
Salaries of dental practitioners practising at health centres	169	
Superannuation contributions	6,974	
Other expenditure	651	175,319
General ophthalmic services		
Fees for sight testing	25,346	
Supply and repair of glasses	40,664	
Less charges to patients	*23,116*	
Superannuation contributions	149	
Other expenditure	158	43,201
Total expenditure		**1,146,221**
Other services		
Ambulance services	115,497	
Blood transfusion services	19,539	
Mass radiography services	1,495	
Emergency bed services	381	
Contractual hospitals and homes	17,206	
Community health councils	3,089	
Other	13,753	**170,960**
Total expenditure on revenue account		**5,077,323**

Income on revenue account	£000	£000
Hospital and community health services		
From patients — supply and repair of appliances, drugs and medicines	1,454	
From patients — accommodation in single rooms and small wards	281	
From patients — private accommodation and treatment	28,869	
Under Road Traffic Act 1972	1,358	
Miscellaneous	1,470	33,432

	£000	£000
Family practitioner services		
Prescription charges	1;743	
From patients for dental treatment at health centres	45	
Repayment of group practice loans	139	
Other	*11*	1,916
Total income on revenue account		**35,348**
Net expenditure on revenue account		**5,041,975**

Expenditure on capital account	£000	£000
Hospitals		
New, replacement, virtual reconstruction	136,840	
Other	115,587	
Vehicles	1,041	
Acquisition of land and buildings	3,203	
Community health services	19,572	
Ambulance services	8,205	
Other services	15,852	
Staff services	15,702	
Total capital expenditure		**316,002**

Income on capital account		
Proceeds from sales of land and buildings	4,119	
Income from other sales	156	**4,275**
Net expenditure on capital account		**311,727**

Table 5. Expenditure of the Trent Region (4.5 million population) analysed subjectively (i.e. by type of employee and type of commodity) for the year 1977-8 (excluding the Family Practitioner Services)

	£000	£000
1 Salaries and wages		
Medical staff:		
Administrative grades	779	
Consultants	10,490	
Senior registrars, SHMOs, etc.	3,049	
Registrars	3,778	
House officers and juniors	5,906	
GP clinical assistants	1,291	25,293
Dental staff:		
Administrative grades	59	
Consultants	144	
Senior registrars, SHDOs, etc.	462	
Registrars	47	
Senior house officers	80	
General dental surgeons	331	
Part-time practitioners	116	1,239

	£000	£000
Nursing staff:		
Administrative grades	879	
Nursing officer and above:		
Nurses	3,793	
Midwives	494	
Health visitors	150	
Other trained staff:		
Nurses	48,673	
Midwives	6,415	
Health visitors	3,710	
Nursing assistants and auxiliaries	19,441	
Staff in training:		
Nurses	17,479	
Midwives	1,118	
Health visitors	337	102,489
Other NHS staff:		
Professional and technical	19,733	
Administrative and clerical	30,121	
Opticians	21	
Pharmaceutical	1,345	
Ancillary	51,662	
Ambulancemen	6,236	109,118
Non-NHS staff (agency, etc.):		
Nursing	23	
Professional and technical	208	
Administrative and clerical	84	
Opticians	1	
Pharmaceutical	9	
Ancillary	38	
Other	23	386
Total Staff		**238,525**

2 Other expenditure (abridged)		
Drugs and medical gases	8,584	
Dressings	1,788	
Medical and surgical equipment	9,245	
X-ray materials and equipment	1,659	
Patients' appliances	2,058	
Laboratory equipment and services	2,630	
Occupational therapy materials	295	
Fluoridation payments	122	26,381
Food		10,457
Staff uniforms and clothing	1,604	
Patients' clothing	842	2,446
Fuel, light and power	10,606	
Water	876	
Laundry	587	
Cleaning equipment, materials, etc.	1,510	13,579

	£000	£000
Furniture and furnishings	1,375	
Hardware and crockery	473	
Bedding and linen	2,189	4,037
Engineering maintenance	4,388	
Building maintenance	4,257	
Gardening and farming	555	9,200
Office equipment, stationery and postages	3,660	
Telephones	2,324	
Advertising	536	6,520
Transport (vehicles, maintenance and hire)		2,437
Travelling expenses and subsistence	4,654	
Removal expenses	583	5,237
Joint user agreements	228	
Contractual arrangements	708	936
Contributions in lieu of rates	4,727	
Rents	503	5,230
Patients' allowances		635
Student bursaries		291
All other expenses		2,875
Total non-staff expenditure		**90,261**
Grand Total		**328,786**

3 Direct credits		
From staff for accommodation	1,750	
From staff, etc. for meals	2,290	4,040
Recovery of silver and scrap	78	
Sale of therapy products	272	
Sale of farm and garden produce	23	
Sales from shops and canteens	634	1,007
Category II fees	29	
Students' fees	64	
All other direct credits	1,889	1,982
Total direct credits		**7,029**
Net regional expenditure		**321,757**

Note 1: After adjustment for the value of services provided to and by other health authorities the net regional expenditure amounted to £321,868,119, to which should be added the expenditure of the Family Practitioner Services, £105,237,418, making a grand regional total of £427,105,537. Against this total, income of £1,770,232 was received.

Note 2: HM Treasury make a distinction between 'direct credits' and 'income'. 'Direct credits' are receipts which reduce expenditure and are therefore retained by health authorities as an offset within the authorised budget. 'Income', because it arises from statutory charges or from sources outside the health authority's control, belongs to the DHSS.

Table 6. NHS and PSS expenditure (England only) by programme category (i.e. clients intended to benefit) 1975-6 and 1979-80

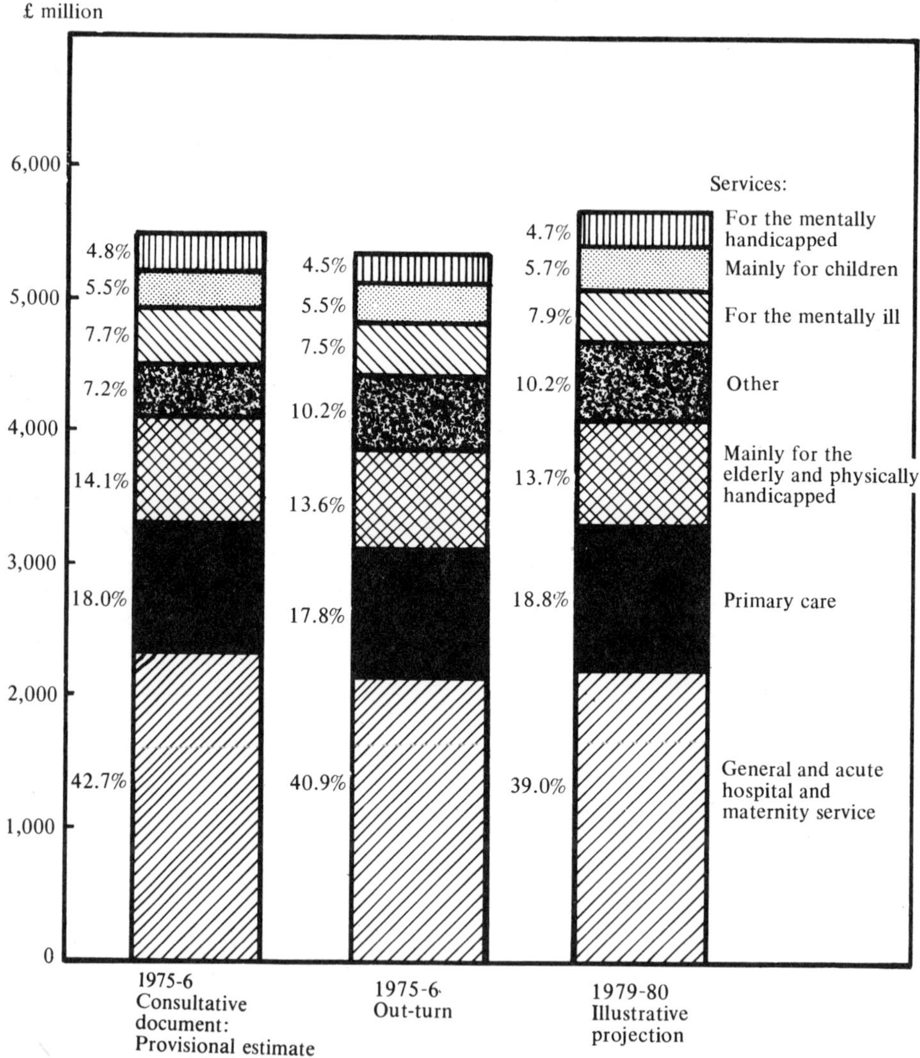

Source: *The Way Forward,* p.16, DHSS September 1977, from HMSO; a follow-up to *Priorities for Health and Personal Social Services in England — a Consultative Document,* 1976.

Note: The methodology for apportioning expenditure over client-based programmes was explained in Annex 2 to 'Priorities'. It is not a methodology which an accountant could use for day-to-day management, as it involves many assumptions and approximations. This type of analysis is therefore recommended only for the broader task of planning the use of resources at national and regional levels.

Summarised accounts of the NHS on the lines of Table 4, based on the published accounts, appear each year in *The Hospital and Health Services Year Book*.

Perhaps the most practical way of looking at the use of money for the health service is to see it in three parts, namely the money spent on maintaining the service as it is, the growth money which each year enables changes and improvements to take place, and, finally, the inflation money required to update rates of pay and the cost of materials and services for the developed facilities. Insofar as inflation money proves to be inadequate to meet real cost increases, growth money has to be raided, but if inflation money is more than is really necessary then additional growth can take place. To give the reader some idea of the relative size of these figures, a broad generalisation would be that while inflation has been hovering around ten to fifteen per cent per annum, growth has varied between one per cent and three per cent for some years past. Thus, in a typical budget, something like 85 per cent would be required to maintain the existing services, 2 per cent for growth and the remainder to meet changing values.

These three parts, it should be said, though applicable to recent history and the foreseeable future, are not immutable principles. Inflation at present levels is, we must hope, a temporary phenomenon. If it is reduced to a small and steady rate, there will be fewer problems with health service budgeting. As we have seen in earlier chapters, there is very strong pressure for growth because of demographic changes, advances in medicine and the desire to improve services. But we have also seen that in most countries health care expenditure has been growing faster than the GNP, and that cannot continue indefinitely. It can even be argued that there is no logical reason why as a minimum the service should have to be maintained at its existing level year after year, though that is to make a debating point rather than a practical approach.

Compared with other forms of public expenditure, the NHS has done well in recent years. Nevertheless with a growth rate of 2 per cent or less it will have difficulties in meeting the demands of an ageing population and also making some provision for medical advances and planning priorities, and it will have to use its resources more efficiently.

The advice issued annually by the Secretary of State for Social Services as to how the health service ought to be developed is helpful for planning purposes, but may well fail to be implemented because of economic pressures and insufficiency of total funds. Even so, substantial growth in health service provision and expenditure has taken place over the life of the NHS, particularly in the years before there was excessive annual inflation. Table 2 did not indicate only that the health service had become more expensive (though that is true), but also more intensive. Over those 20 years, for example, the average length of stay in an acute hospital was brought down from about 19 days to nine days.

How funds were shared out in the past

Until 1974 the central departments allocated funds only for the hospital service. The hospitals taken over by the NHS in 1948 were unevenly distributed throughout the country, and also varied considerably in their rates of expenditure. As hospital authorities were funded to enable them to maintain existing facilities and services the amount spent annually on health care per head of population continued to vary greatly from region to region.

Whilst various measures were introduced to encourage economies and to even out hospital running costs, the basic inequality would remain so long as hospital authorities were funded on the basis of the previous running costs and the distribution of hospitals remained uneven. The implementation of the 1962 hospital plans should in time have brought the remedy because hospital provision was to be related to population and annual allocations contained an earmarked amount known as RCCS (revenue consequences of capital schemes) to ensure that the revenue funds would be available to run the new hospitals.

The demands of RCCS on growth money proved very heavy and the hospital plans progressed much more slowly than had been expected. The uneven distribution of funds continued and in 1969 Richard Crossman, then Secretary of State, responded to pressure from some of the worse-off regions by devising a system for equalising the revenue expenditure of all English regions (excluding the boards of governors) over a period of ten years. He argued that if the revenue expenditure per head of population were equalised, capital expenditure would be applied in such a way that regions with gross deficiencies would spend all their capital on new facilities, whereas regions with surpluses in relation to the national average would spend such capital as they were allocated on renewals and improvements, but not on expansion. The Crossman formula for redistributing revenue began in 1971-2. It was decided that RCCS, as a separate item of allocation, should be phased out over six years. The formula continued to be applied for the next few years, though from 1974 provision had also to be made for the community services hitherto financed by local authorities. (In these services too expenditure per head of population varied considerably.) Mrs Barbara Castle, who became Secretary of State in 1974, made some changes in allocations in the hope of increasing the rate of redistribution and, much more importantly, in May 1975 she set up a Resource Allocation Working Party (RAWP) which produced an interim report in November 1975 and a final report in September 1976. The interim report enabled Mrs Castle to carry out her modifications to the Crossman formula; but the final report started some entirely new thinking and led to the present-day system of revenue allocations by the DHSS and to the principles on which RHAs are now expected to allocate funds to area health authorities. A similar approach was also evolved in the other three countries.

Sharing out today

At this point one ought to consider whether equalisation to a national average of expenditure per head of population is a justifiable policy. We noted in the first two chapters that RAWP contributed to the dissatisfactions with the NHS expressed since 1974, and that there is apparently no relation between the resources available to a health authority and local satisfaction with the services provided. Moreover, equal resources do not necessarily mean equal services; much depends on how the resources are used. However, equal distribution accords with the principles implicit in the NHS and it is therefore difficult to disagree in principle as distinct from disagreeing with the effectiveness of a particular formula in measuring inequality and remedying it. Moreover as Chapter 8 made clear it is an essential part of a planning system which aims at providing equal access to services.

A difficulty with equalisation has been its timing. Redistribution would have

Table 7. The Crossman formula for reallocating revenue between regions so as to reach parity in ten years (1971-81) — abridged

A: *Calculation of regional deficiencies (+) or surpluses (−)*

	£000
1 Population factor: Compare each region's fair share of the total revenue allocations for the previous year, based on that region's weighted population, with its actual allocation	$\pm$P
2 Beds factor: Compare each region's fair share, based on its occupied beds multiplied by national average costs per bed, specialty by specialty, and based on its out-patient attendances multiplied by national average costs per attendance, with its actual allocation	$\pm$B
3 Cases factor: Compare each region's fair share, based on the number of cases treated and the number of new out-patients, each multiplied by the appropriate national average costs, with its actual allocation	$\pm$C

B: *Method of application*

1 For each region, combine the above factors on the basis —

$$\frac{2P + B + C}{4}$$

to give a net deficiency or surplus.

2 Convert the cash deficiency or surplus to a percentage of the previous year's allocation, to show the desirable change over ten years.

3 Divide the results by 10 the first year, by 9 the next year and so on.

4 Adjust the national average percentage growth rate each year by the foregoing percentages, but only to the extent which will leave a minimum growth rate (provisionally ¼ per cent) for the regions which are in surplus.

been less painful when there had been a higher growth rate, for it could have been achieved by adjusting the growth of regions and areas. With a low overall growth rate it is necessary to reduce some authorities' growth rates to practically nothing, or even to cut allocations. Even the best financed health services are under pressure to expand, and authorities hurt by RAWP distribution undoubtedly face some problems in providing adequate services, so it is not surprising that RAWP redistribution is criticised as levelling down rather than levelling up. This criticism accepts the principle of equality but implies that the total resources of the NHS are inadequate. While this is a tenable point of view it is hardly realistic about the prospects for health service finance over the next few years at least. The choice appears to lie between levelling down and maintaining existing inequalities. Current low growth rates are in fact making the levelling process slower than had been expected.

Revenue equalisation

The fundamental problem for the Resource Allocation Working Party was to decide how to modify the crude population statistics of each region and area so as to reflect the true need of the future population for health care. They had to take account of factors such as the age and sex distribution, because, for example, those areas with a larger than average number of elderly persons would require more hospital beds, district nurses, etc. than those with a relatively younger population. Other important factors were the estimation of birth rate trends, any factors which indicated degrees of health and ill-health (morbidity), and the problem of services provided in one region or area for people living in a neighbouring region or area.

Table 8. Factors used by RAWP formula in arriving at theoretical revenue allocations for regional and area health authorities, i.e. 'revenue targets'

1. Resident population, forecast by OPCS
2. × age and sex banding
3. × standard mortality ratios
4. × other morbidity indicators, leading to 'weighted' population base
5. ± regional specialties (AHA targets only)
6. ± regionally managed services (AHA targets only)
7. ± cross-boundary flows, leading to 'served' population
8. + SIFT for medical and dental teaching
   leading to theoretical share of total resources

Note: The achievement of equality, resulting from the use of this formula, depends on the amount of 'growth money' available in each financial year and on the extent to which the government of the day is prepared to cut or restrict the allocations to the regions showing a surplus. In practice, no region has so far suffered a cut, even the best supplied being allowed a minimum growth. On the other hand, some regions, in applying the formula to their area authorities, have enforced quite drastic cuts in some areas in order to accelerate development in their worst funded areas.

The most difficult task for the RAWP proved to be the measurement of morbidity to assess the needs of populations for health care. Adequate morbidity statistics are not available and in the end the working party decided to use as a substitute standard mortality ratios (SMR), which are derived from an analysis of causes of death. Inadequate as such a measure of need may be, it was considered the best available and the recommendations of the RAWP represented a great step forward in arriving at the level of expenditure which each region was entitled to expect on the basis of equitable shares of available funds. The report of the RAWP was published in September 1976 under the title *Sharing Resources for Health in England.*

A somewhat similar report was published a little later by the Scottish Home and Health Department, following the work of a parallel working party, under the title *Scottish Health Authorities Revenue Equalisation* (SHARE). In Scotland there are no regional health authorities and so SHARE deals with allocations to health boards. The formula was originally calculated for use on a ten-year basis, but its implementation has varied and is currently adjusted to fulfilment over a 12-year period. The proposals do not involve an actual cut in expenditure by any area health board. In Wales a steering committee has taken the place of the original working party and has devised a similar formula to the English except that it excludes psychiatric services, and advises the Welsh Office annually on resource allocations with the long-term aim of bringing about reasonable access to all types of service across the country. In Northern Ireland a working party reported in March 1979, under the title *Proposals for the Allocation of Revenue Resources* (PARR). Fortunately, the variances in Northern Ireland were found to be not very great. In 1978-9, the Northern Board received 0.7 per cent less than its theoretical target allocation under the PARR formula and the other three boards received a little more than their fair shares. The method used by PARR was to identify the use made of health services by different population groups, such as the elderly, and to make allowances for people who were served from adjoining health areas without undue inconvenience. In essence, the report does not differ materially from either RAWP or SHARE.

A particular problem in making allocations is that teaching hospitals are almost always more expensive than non-teaching hospitals, and a problem facing RAWP was to make allowance for extra costs necessarily incurred by the presence of medical students undergoing clinical teaching. It was not concerned with other reasons why teaching hospital costs may be high, such as their providing regional specialties, being 'centres of excellence' or, as their critics have sometimes alleged, being extravagant; these factors must be provided for within the basic RAWP formula. The working party devised a 'service increment for teaching' (SIFT) based on the number of medical students. It is the estimated cost of teaching per student and is somewhat arbitrary because total teaching hospital costs vary greatly from one hospital to another and it is not easy to separate this element from other costs. The total SIFT allowance is deducted from the total sum available for distribution and after the balance has been allocated according to the basic RAWP formula the SIFT allowance is added to regional, and area, allocations in accordance with the number of medical students.

In Wales, Scotland and Northern Ireland the central agencies are funded each year according to their own budgeted pattern of operational costs before the balance of the national allocation is distributed to health authorities according to the national formula. In principle this is no different from the practice in English regions, where a sum must be allocated for regional services.

These measures towards equalising revenue expenditure do not affect the family practitioner services, where expenditure depends on the number of practitioners practising in an area and on the demands made on their services. Yet the level of provision of these services, particularly the number of GPs, may have a bearing on demand for budgeted services, even though the bearing may not be obvious. It may be that where there are fewer than average GPs serving the population more demands are made on the community and hospital services, but since demand is normally channelled through the GP it may be that an increase in the number of GPs would increase the pressure on these services. In any case a 'deprived' area building up its hospital and community services has no means of doing the same with the family practitioner services. By building health centres it may hope to attract more GPs, but this, like the financial incentives to attract practitioners to unpopular areas, may not be very effective.

To illustrate the working of the RAWP revenue formula the Table 9, based on a DHSS press notice, is quoted from the March 1979 issue of *Hospital and Health Services Review:*

A separate element in the funding of health authorities in England is a sum for joint financing of projects with local authorities. The arrangements are described later in this chapter.

Table 9. Application of RAWP principles to allocation of revenue increase of 2.0 per cent for 1979-80

Regional Health Authority	Starting figure (i.e. 1978-9 main revenue allocation) £000	Revenue 'target' £000	Distance from 'target' as % of starting figure	Revenue increase %	Main revenue allocation £000	Distance from 'target' after allocation as % of allocation	Capital allocation excluding joint finance £000
1	2	3	4	5	6	7	8
North Western	371,878	416,572	− 12.02	3.00	383,028	− 8.76	36,700
Northern	272,094	300,513	− 10.45	2.77	279,624	− 7.47	23,800
Trent	358,297	394,735	− 10.17	2.73	368,067	− 7.25	37,000
West Midlands	426,405	462,502	− 8.47	2.51	437,095	− 5.81	32,000
East Anglian	151,641	163,189	− 7.62	2.40	155,281	− 5.10	19,600
South Western	268,867	285,954	− 6.36	2.26	274,937	− 4.01	21,000
Wessex	217,847	230,906	− 6.00	2.22	222,677	− 3.70	20,700
Yorkshire	308,756	327,218	− 5.98	2.22	315,606	− 3.68	29,300
Mersey	231,069	237,808	− 2.92	1.90	235,459	− 1.00	22,400
Oxford	177,571	179,633	− 1.16	1.75	180,671	+ 0.58	12,900
SW Thames	296,993	283,218	+ 4.64	1.34	300,963	+ 5.90	18,400
SE Thames	372,052	338,462	+ 9.03	1.12	376,212	+ 10.03	22,700
NE Thames	389,333	348,358	+ 10.52	1.06	393,453	+ 11.46	24,700
NW Thames	351,236	308,751	+ 12.10	1.00	354,746	+ 12.98	18,500
	4,194,039	4,277,819	− 2.00	2.00	4,277,819		339,700

Revenue figures at November 1978 price levels: they exclude SIFT and other special additions. Capital at forecast 1978-9 out-turn prices.

Note 1: Unlike the Crossman formula, which set out to produce equality in ten years, the RAWP formula recognises that when there is overall national growth no region should be expected to manage with less than a growth rate of 1 per cent (needed to meet demographic changes common to all) and that no region can cope with a faster growth rate than 5 per cent because recruitment and capital works are both restricted by external factors. It follows that a definite date for equalisation cannot be predetermined; but it also follows that the national average (which is the basis of the target for equalisation) is rising steadily at the same time as the extremes are being brought closer together. Compare columns 4 and 7.
Note 2: RCCS no longer features as a separate element in revenue allocations at national level, but in regions and areas it is still important.

An element in funding which escapes the RAWP net is the money provided for the running cost of nurse training schools. This money goes from the DHSS to the General Nursing Council which, in discussion with regional nurse training committees, distributes it to schools of nursing. The payment of student and pupil nurses, however, falls on AHA budgets.

Finally, there are small exceptions to the sharing out principles whenever the DHSS decides to fund some activity specifically. Special allocations for such things as computer development or assistance to a region with abnormal problems still occur, though in theory they are contrary to the main policies of equalisation and delegation.

The RAWP report was not the last word on allocations. The working party recommended that research should be undertaken on various topics and an advisory group was subsequently appointed. The formula has been criticised and various studies have been carried out. Thus future amendments are possible, although some suggestions have been found to have too little practical effect to justify the added complication.

Detail apart, it seems likely that RAWP and the equivalent fomulae are here to stay, or rather until they have achieved equal distribution. They are not, however, the only way in which funds might be allocated. It might, for example, be possible to achieve a form of 'outcome orientated' costing based on measuring the cost and effectiveness of treatments, and to use that information for the distribution of funds. The difficulties, however, would be formidable, and any approach based on measured need rather than on relative need or priorities is probably unworkable when the total sum to be allocated depends on what the government decides can be afforded rather than is needed.

Capital equalisation

In England, the RAWP also attempted to draw up a new formula for the distribution of capital funds, using the concept of weighted population figures, five years ahead. But first they had to evaluate the existing stocks, which they did by a method wherein the values of beds in older hospitals were discounted as compared with beds in newer hospitals. Thus a relative surplus or deficiency against the average could be measured by using the method outlined in Table 10.

Table 10. RAWP formula for distributing capital funds

1. Evaluate each region's capital stock as at 1961 by counting all short-stay beds at £24,000 each and all long-stay beds at £12,000 each (being the 1975 cost allowances for such beds in new hospitals).
2. Depreciate the above values by the following factors depending on the age of the hospitals containing the beds:
   Built between 1949 and 1961 — 50 per cent
   Built between 1919 and 1948 — 65 per cent
   Built before 1919 — 70 per cent
3. To the resultant depreciated capital value of the stock at 1961, add actual expenditure since 1961, to give a current value (in 1977-8) on a 1975 price base.
4. Now add the regional capital values together to form the national capital stock value.
5. Apportion the national value (item 4) over the regions in proportion to their weighted population estimates five years ahead (arrived at on a somewhat similar basis to the revenue-weighted populations used in Table 8, but with less allowance for elements such as cross-boundary flow), to give 'target' values.
6. Compare the regional stock values (item 5) and extract the sums needed to bring all the regions with shortfalls up to their targets (i.e. the national average value), without recouping any of the excess values of those regions whose stock was above their target.
7. Distribute the available capital funds for each future year, partly on a fixed minimum basis and partly in proportion to the size of each deprived region's shortfall.

Note: The RAWP recommended that, for item 7 above, 90 per cent of the capital funding in 1977-8, 1985-6 and 1986-7; 80 per cent in 1978-9, 1982-3 – 1984-5; and 70 per cent in 1979-80 – 1981-2 should be distributed on a weighed population basis (except for safeguarding existing commitments in the first two years), that being the appropriate way to calculate the 'fixed minimum'.

As with revenue, objection can be made to the capital formula on the argument that it assumes that the present average is adequate. It should be noted that the RAWP did not recommend the use of the well-established bed norms for each type of specialty group in each district.

Table 11. The result of the RAWP exercise to compare existing regional capital stocks with 'fair shares' based on weighted population (i.e. target values)

Region (1)	Capital value (March 1977) (2) £000	Target value (3) £000	Shortfall (−) (4) £000	Excess (+) (5) £000
Northern	361,592	375,137	−13,545	
Yorkshire	407,956	429,393	−21,437	
Trent	490,584	526,051	−35,467	
East Anglian	218,509	208,078		+ 10,431
NW Thames	447,601	391,902		+ 55,699
NE Thames	481,036	430,160		+ 50,876
SE Thames	440,067	436,870		+ 3,197
SW Thames	376,716	351,353		+ 25,363
Wessex	285,836	317,515	−31,679	
Oxford	266,294	242,488		+ 23,806
S Western	361,000	364,705	− 3,705	
W Midlands	555,249	590,040	−34,791	
Mersey	350,491	303,969		+ 46,522
N Western	445,674	520,944	−75,270	
Totals	5,488,605	5,488,605	−215,894	+215,894

Source — Table D5 of Annex D, *Sharing Resources for Health in England.* HMSO 1976
Note: While the shortages shown in column 4 would gradually have to be made good from annual capital allocations, the report did not suggest any plans to reduce the excesses shown in column 5.

There are difficulties in distributing money for capital purposes on any formula. The practical difficulty is that a region's (or agency's) capacity to handle a bigger capital programme can only be built up gradually, so that it may be impossible to spend allocations. The other difficulty, in the broad sense political, is that capital funds cannot be shared out equally between areas or districts, except in the long run. Various alternative approaches have been discussed, most of them designed to avoid the consequences of the peculiar nature of capital funding in the NHS (and most public services other than local government). In a commercial system, capital developments are not funded separately but from loans which must be repaid from income over the ensuing years; a decision to invest, therefore, should only be made when the profit, taking account of loan charges, is greater than could be achieved by spending the money in some other way. While the commercial approach could not be applied straightforwardly in a service such as the NHS, it has been argued that capital money should not be regarded as an 'extra' and therefore highly desirable if it can be obtained, but rather one way of using part of total resources and a measure to be adopted only after being weighed against other uses of the money. One way of achieving this is suggested in Annex E to *Sharing Resources for Health In England.* It is a system of bidding by RHAs for capital and a reduction in revenue allocations to successful bidders.

How spending patterns are changed

The planning system (see Chapter 8) seeks to identify changes which ought to be made in the services provided by each district. Its objectives are to make up deficiencies, to redeploy surplus beds and surplus staff, to reduce waste and inefficiency and to achieve local self-sufficiency so far as that is consistent with the strategic plan for each region. The planning system cannot, however, be implemented without the use of a budgeting system based on estimates and approvals and followed up by monitoring of results.

From 1948 to 1962 the main changes which were made in hospital spending patterns were the result of capital expenditure, not in fact very large, followed by RCCS. From 1962 the amount available each year to each regional hospital board was made known in the previous autumn. Thus estimates were no longer bids for funds, but proposals for the use of funds which had been predetermined. Some RHBs made use of this advance information by setting spending targets for their hospital management committees, but many continued the old incremental basis of allocations and kept large reserves to cover such elements as wage awards, price rises and 'unforeseen contingencies'. RCCS continued to be the principal element in every budget plan. The availability of the capital allocation from the DHSS and the planning done at regional level for the use of that allocation determined the amount of RCCS which any hospital management committee would receive. While efforts were made in many quarters to reduce unnecessary expenditure and while ministers allocated special funds to benefit some of the long-stay categories, there was no overall plan to rearrange spending between one kind of hospital service and another. Community services were, in any case, outside the RHBs' control.

Reorganisation in 1974 brought about an entirely new situation in which area health authorities, now identified with a geographical area based on local government boundaries, demanded the independence which went with their new planning role. Regional health authorities therefore set about agreeing firm spending targets, projected several years ahead and rolled forward annually. Those spending targets are now arrived at after discussion of strategic and operational plans and are linked to firm estimates of the numbers of people to be treated in the foreseeable future and the numbers of staff required to treat them in each specialty and in the community. AHAs vary in the extent to which they delegate their planning function to district level. In Wales, Scotland and Northern Ireland the district teams are purely operational managers, all planning being done at area level and all financial reserves held there. In England the pattern varies between authorities.

Perhaps the most difficult part of the planning and budgeting system is the monitoring aspect. Insofar as financial allocations are associated with agreed work load targets and those targets do not materialise, there remains the temptation to withhold funds, by means of central reserves, until changes have been brought about. Past experience shows that the retention of central reserves in this way tends to inhibit local action to achieve change. If efforts have to be made to recruit additional staff or to move patients to new locations, there is nothing so helpful as 'money on the table'. Even if funds allocated recurrently to district level are not taken up on the intended developments immediately, they can be used temporarily to buy equipment or improve the patients' surroundings, but the funds are still there in the following year when the new staff actually arrive. If the funds were held at area or regional level, there might be some mistrust at district level or hospital level as to whether they would in fact be available when the necessary staff were recruited.

One aspect of the changes which the planning system is intended to bring about is priority development for certain client groups. Treasurers have difficulty in relating their budgetary system to planning guidelines because the accounting information in the health service comes out in terms not of client groups but of individual hospitals and the community services and the analysis of expenditure to departments by types of staff, materials, etc. To give an example of the problem, the planning system talks about the care of the elderly, but the elderly use the acute wards of hospitals as much as the geriatric units, although expenditure in acute wards does not form part of the budget for the 'elderly' in the planning system. Economists and treasurers, by working closely together, can produce estimated patterns of expenditure on client groups, but these cannot so far be built into a control system for expenditure. There is still a great deal of work for treasurers and their staffs to do in the provision of information to health care planning teams.

The limitations on capital funding are still a significant constraint in bringing about changes in the pattern of services. Another significant constraint is the availability of skilled manpower. No plan or budget to produce significant changes in service levels can be achieved without manpower planning, which may well require additional training facilities for doctors, nurses and other professional staff. Problems of manpower planning and determining staffing levels are discussed in Chapter 13. Uncertain though the whole exercise is, estimates of staffing needs and costs have to be made if planning is to go ahead.

Co-operation with local authorities is essential in developing health services. Joint funding arrangements were introduced in 1976 which permitted NHS funds to be used to support certain local authority responsibilities. The main criterion is that such expenditure must be accepted by the health authority as making a better contribution in total care than would the spending of the same money on direct health services. For example, homes for the elderly or the mentally handicapped, to enable them to be discharged from hospital, clearly benefit the health service, but are the responsibility of the local authority. The joint financing arrangement, put simply, is that the health authority will build or buy a facility and pay up to 60 per cent of the capital cost (100 per cent in exceptional circumstances), the local authority paying the balance. The local authority will take over the running cost in stages, meeting at least 40 per cent in the first year and building up to 100 per cent in six years or less. Even if no capital is required a health authority may agree to meet 60 per cent of the revenue costs, gradually reducing to nil as the local authority assumes full responsbility. Health service land may be used for such projects. The arrangements are set out in circulars HC(77)17 and HC(79)18. Similar arrangements were tentatively introduced in Wales in 1977. The Health Services Act 1980, Section 4, makes statutory provision for joint financing. The provision relates also to Scotland.

How the NHS controls expenditure

Within the NHS, the authorities and management teams at all levels operate a detailed system of budgetary control based on income and expenditure accounting.

Revenue expenditure

Revenue expenditure is controlled in two ways — by analysis of the expenditure according to the type of resources absorbed (known as subjective analysis — see Table 5) and by a parallel analysis of the expenditure according to the department or function using the resources (known as objective analysis — see Table 4). Since 1973 the emphasis has increasingly been upon functional management and therefore objective analysis has been the more useful. Systems vary as between a national functional analysis, and analyses which reflect more closely the actual pattern of management in each institution locally. The latter variant is sometimes referred to as responsibilty accounting. It must be said that, despite local variations and interpretations, the system of budgetary control in the NHS has been remarkably effective in keeping expenditure close to spending targets. Of all the decentralised public services it is said that the NHS has the best and most consistent record in this respect.

One big advantage of objective accounting over subjective accounting is that it requires estimates of levels of activity, such as turnover, throughput or workload, to be coupled with the estimates of spending, so that the cost of a department or function can be measured in terms of its planned and achieved levels of activity. Objective budgeting supplements at a very detailed level the intentions of the planning system in securing the best use of resources in relation to the desired patterns of activity.

One might think that such a detailed pattern of expenditure control left no room for reserves to be held. Unfortunately, the opposite is the case, in that the more sub-divisions one uses for dividing expenditure into manageable units, the more people become involved in the estimating and controlling processes and the greater is the number of variances from target that emerge.

Reserves have to be maintained for factors which are impossible to estimate in advance. One of these is inflation, i.e. changes in the level of wage rates and prices. There seems to be no best way of allocating inflation money in advance over departmental managers' budgets.

Some authorities keep a reserve to cover variances in the activity of clinical departments, but this is a negation of genuine planning and tends to inhibit the achievement of planned changes in activity. Nevertheless, major developments have a habit of not being ready on time and it would be foolish to give substantial additional funds to departmental managers to spend on, for example, staff who could not be recruited because they had nowhere to work.

Other authorities keep reserves for items of a non-recurring nature, but such reserves must be used up during the course of the year by forward planning. To leave a reserve in the expectation that someone might need it is to invite a last-minute scramble and almost certain underspending. An effective technique is to allocate a specific sum, say, to the medical staff of a hospital for the purchase of the more expensive items of medical equipment, the understanding being that the medical staff will keep a continuous register of equipment requested by any of their number and will at quarterly intervals decide which items from the list should be bought in the next but one quarter, at a cost exactly matching the available fund. Whatever pattern of reserves is decided upon by the authority or by the district team, it is essential that all reserves be committed early in the year, certainly by October/November.

There is an argument for what might be called activity-variable budgets. Such a budget would be at a unit cost for a given level of activity at a given price. This could be useful, for example, for the catering function. The amount to be spent on food would be determined at so much per head for all the patients fed. Each month the actual number of patients fed would be ascertained and the budget fixed, in arrears, according to the number fed. In addition the retail price index for food prices would be read every month and the food budget adjusted upwards or downwards according to the movements in the RPI.

Capital expenditure

There are two different types of budgetary control for capital expenditure, the one being the cost of each job and the other the total amount which may be spent in a financial year. Authorities cannot be certain how the work on each individual scheme will proceed from month to month and, even though the cost of individual jobs may be close to the estimate, the actual 'spend' in each month/quarter/year may be very different from the forecast, due to weather conditions, labour troubles and so on. The matching of capital expenditure to the annual budget is far more difficult than the similar revenue exercise.

Much attention has to be paid to the cost of variations to the content of schemes after they have been let to contractors. Additionally, there are price variances, which are generally permitted in the terms of the contract, except where fixed price contracts have been entered into, for schemes of less than two years' duration. RHAs employ quantity surveyors to help to ascertain the proper cost of building work and to monitor progress. On the engineering side, cost experts are needed for a similar purpose.

But neither of these procedures excuses the treasurer from his responsibility for ensuring that money is not spent unnecessarily. The DHSS has for some years published charts showing the probable 'rate of spend' from month to month on major works of various sizes and types. While these give a general indication of the timing of cash flow, they cannot possibly relate reliably to any particular job. Fortunately there are limited arrangements for underspending and overspending to be carried forward to the second year following the year of account. There is also a limited possibility of transferring funds to or from the revenue budget.

Family practitioner service expenditure

What has been said about budgetary control systems does not apply to the family practitioner services, other than for the budget for administrative costs, which is a very small proportion of total expenditure. Expenditure consists of payments to practitioners in accordance with contracts. A general practitioner remuneration may consist of 20 or more elements and whatever the total comes to must be paid by the FPC promptly at the end of the month. Payments to opticians, pharmacists and dentists may be described as 'piecework'. Pharmacists are reimbursed the cost of all the drugs they prescribe, together with a percentage addition to cover their overheads and profit. Opticians, similarly, are reimbursed their expenditure plus an allowance for overheads and profit. Dentists have to submit monthly claims to the Dental Estimates Board at Eastbourne and when the claims are approved they are returned to the local family practitioner committee for payment.

Because there are inevitably delays in agreeing the amounts due to some of the practitioners, particularly pharmacists, a system of payments on account at the end of each month has become the regular practice. There is at present no budgetary system applied to the payment of family practitioners, but in a very general sense an annual estimate could be made of the likely expenditure on all the various elements, against which out-turn could be compared and enquiries set up as to why variances had occurred.

Cash limits

From 1976 onwards, all the budgetary procedures which have been described above have been supplemented by a new system of government control known as cash limits. These came into being as a result of a crisis in public expenditure in 1975. With cash limits goes a financial information system known as FIS(HA). Put simply, the cash limits system means that no government department (and the NHS is financed from the DHSS vote) may spend in cash more than the authorised amount within the financial year from 1 April to 31 March. This control differs radically from income and expenditure accounting in that the latter allows for stocks in hand and debts due to and by the authority to be brought to account in a financial year if they relate to transactions taking place in that year. Cash limits apply only to the actual cash requisitioned from the Department of Health before 31 March to put a region's main bank account in funds, adjusted for certain transactions which are accounted for by book entries, i.e. non-cash transactions. While the system of cash limits has much to commend it from the parliamentarians' point of view, it has been described by accountants as an inconvenient excrescence on the more effective and more permanent income and expenditure budgetary control arrangements which have worked satisfactorily for 30 years. Heads of departments in a large and complex organisation cannot possibly know when bills are going to be paid and must therefore be free to work on the basis of goods and services they have received and staff they have employed, which means that income and expenditure accounting must apply at departmental level. Likewise, the total expenditure of a hospital is only meaningful in income and expenditure terms, because it should be related to the volume of activity which has occurred in the same accounting period as the expenditure. The reconciliation of the budgetary system with the cash limits system takes place at either district or area level and is consolidated at regional level. On top of this, family practitioner service payments, which remain outside the budgetary system, have to be brought into the cash limit system, because there is no other way of making the cash limit system cover the whole expenditure of the DHSS. The cash limit system has resulted in the need for the preparation, annually, of estimated quarterly receipts and payments and for the submission each month of the cumulative cash out-turn for revenue and capital payments. This information helps the Treasury to monitor the government's cash flow, minimising public borrowing and keeping down the interest on the national debt. At the end of the year every health authority has to add a supplementary statement to its annual accounts, showing, under separate columns for FPS, capital and revenue, the cash advances received from the DHSS (in England), the various agency payments and receipts (which are deemed to be settlements without cash transactions), transfers between health authorities, etc. leading to a total which is the amount chargeable against the cash limit for the authority.

Because of the tightness of Treasury control, and the fact that the NHS has no source of income other than from the DHSS and no power to borrow money, arrangements have been made to allow limited powers of carry forward and underspending. Currently, any health authority may underspend by not more than one per cent per annum its total cash budget for revenue purposes and carry that sum forward to the following year. Any greater underspending is lost and any overspending has to be repaid in the following year by a reduction of the cash limit for that year. There is also some flexibility between capital and revenue budgets, on the basis that not more than one per cent of the revenue budget could be switched to capital, if thought fit, and not more than ten per cent of the capital budget could be switched to revenue.

In Scotland an additional facility was introduced in 1978 whereby boards could borrow from or deposit funds with the SHHD for repayment or use in due course. As in England there is a facility to carry over one per cent on revenue account and from 1980-1 ordinary capital and revenue allocations have been notified as a composite figure within which virement would be allowed provided that no extreme adjustment to either subhead were made.

The Health Services Act 1980 places on health authorities the duty to restrict their expenditure in each financial year to the sum allotted to them plus any other income. Authorities have always been expected to behave in this way but the duty was not previously clearly spelt out by statute.

Making the system secure

Since the NHS is treated as a government department insofar as its expenditure is charged against the DHSS, Welsh Office and Scottish Office votes, it is subject to the usual parliamentary scrutiny of public expenditure as described in Chapter 5, i.e. through the Select Committee on Social Services and the Public Accounts Committee. The latter committee, on the basis of reports by the Comptroller and Auditor General and his staff in the Exchequer and Audit Department, examines accounting officers on topics brought to its attention, and subsequently issues reports. The PAC is constantly on the look out for the inefficient use of public funds and for any weaknesses in the system of control over expenditure. Its criticisms are taken very seriously by the central departments and, through them, by the NHS.

Within the DHSS in England there is a substantial team of auditors, answerable to the permanent secretary through the finance branch. Unlike district auditors to local authorities, these DHSS auditors have no power of surcharge and can only report their findings to the permanent secretary. They regularly visit all health authorities in England (and similar arrangements exist in Wales, Scotland and Northern Ireland) to audit the annual accounts and do such testing as they think fit of the systems of financial management. In particular they have to satisfy themselves that standing orders and standing financial instructions are being followed. The auditors in Scotland belong to a government audit department, not to the SHHD. By sharing information with each other, DHSS and government auditors can agree to follow particular lines of enquiry on a broad front, though their main duty remains to test and approve the annual accounts as submitted by each health authority. To a lesser extent Exchequer and Audit staff visit health authorities, either to follow up DHSS audit reports or to pursue lines of enquiry of their own.

Area health authorities and regional health authorities are under an obligation to approve standing orders and standing financial instructions, which are based on models or outlines approved by the Secretary of State. They employ internal auditors on the staff of the area or regional treasurer, as the case may be. Much has been written in recent years about the need to strengthen the internal audit function, particularly in the direction of computer accounting techniques and in the control of capital expenditure. Both these appear to justify more internal audit time and attention than they currently receive. Recommendations on the content and management of audit programmes have been published from time to time by such bodies as the Association of Health Service Treasurers and the Committee of RHA Treasurers. The general tendency today is for auditors to put as much emphasis on efficiency and economy as on probity and authorisation, though it remains inescapable that the prevention and detection of fraud and error are at the root of all audit work at any level. The task of area treasurers includes the supervision of the accountancy functions delegated to district treasurers/finance officers and therefore the internal audit staff are all answerable to the area treasurer, though some may be stationed in a particular district for the convenience of their work.

Standing orders and standing financial instructions must provide for at least the following matters to be regulated by decisions of the health authority:

— Rules for the conduct of the business of the authority
— Procedure for the appointment of staff
— Arrangements for the invitation of tenders and the letting of contracts for supplies and works
— Clarification of the roles of the various officers and teams
— Arrangements for adequate internal audit and routine internal checks
— Banking arrangements
— Routines for the approval of estimates and allocation of funds to budget holders
— Arrangements for the authorisation of payments to staff and to creditors
— Arrangements for the receipt of monies due to the authority and cash security in general
— Arrangements for the control and supervision of stores and of valuable items of equipment in use and
— Arrangements for the reporting and writing off of losses and for dealing with any unforeseen emergencies.

These rules and instructions will apply to trust funds as well as to the public funds of the authority, where appropriate.

Some health authorities go a step further and invite members of the authority to select one or two payments which have been made during the past month or months, for a report by internal audit staff of all the details leading up to the payment. This system has become known as The Cardiff Check System, as it originated in the City Hall at Cardiff many years ago. It has the merit of involving members personally in the process of testing the security of financial systems, at the same time limiting their responsibility to the selected items rather than to the whole field of financial management. It was customary, before the 1974 reorganisation, for every hospital authority to have a standing finance committee. Standing committees are now considered inappropriate by the DHSS and liable to cut across the responsibilities of management teams, but unless a system such as the Cardiff Check is employed, members may feel that they are unnecessarily excluded from detailed knowledge of the probity of expenditure.

It hardly needs saying that neither audit nor the existence of standing financial instructions are enough in themselves to ensure the security of the system. It is an essential part of the task of the treasurer and his staff to carry out those procedures laid down in the instructions. There is no space here to describe them, but there is a whole range of security measures concerned with receipts (e.g. banking arrangements, including the need to maintain low balances, recoveries by the sale of scrap and silver), payments (e.g. certification of goods and of travelling expenses) and stores and inventories control. Most of these are normal good financial practice, and on some matters guidance has been issued by the central departments. Guidance has also been issued on procedures for dealing with losses.

Perhaps this is the point to say that while, from the health service management point of view, the essential contribution of financial management is to contribute to the optimum use of resources, a large proportion of finance staff time is devoted to the no less essential task of routine financial administration. In particular, with over 70 per cent of NHS expenditure going on wages and salaries, the weekly and monthly payment of these, in accordance with increasingly complicated Whitley agreements, the payroll function is a very large one.

Getting value for money

One of the great dangers of allocating funds *en bloc* is that the money may be spent without due regard to efficiency. For every pound of public money spent on the health services, the public needs to know that the greatest possible amount of real service has been produced. It is not enough for the accounting system to demonstrate that budgets have been fully expended. It must also show what each item of service has cost. Comparisons can then be made between different hospitals or other centres of treatment to see whether the same item of service could have been provided more cheaply had the resources been managed differently.

One can look at health service costs in two ways, either broadly or narrowly. A broad 'macro costing' approach is to divide the total expenditure of a unit such as a hospital by the number of persons treated, to find out the average cost of treatment, whether as an in-patient, an out-patient or a day patient. 'Micro costing' on the other hand examines the detailed cost of a particular activity within the hospital, such as catering or pharmacy, and aims to measure the relative efficiency of that department rather than its contribution to the total care of all the patients.

The search for a macro costing unit began in 1949 and by 1951 the first national system of costing returns appeared. A costing return had to be prepared annually for every hospital. The total expenditure was shown, analysed over the various subjective headings, such as medical salaries, nursing salaries, food, drugs and dressings, etc. The figures on each line and the total were then divided by the total number of available bed-weeks, so as to show the itemised and the total cost per patient for an average week. The hospitals were classified into types, so that like could be compared with like. The classification into 19 different types has changed little over the years and is still employed for summarising cost accounts. Hospitals vary so much in the types and mixture of patients treated and in other ways, that they could be sub-divided or classified in a great variety of ways and in fact subsequent work in Scotland has resulted in something over 40 different types being identified.

This variety may be one reason why the use of the early costing system — and to some extent of later developments — was disappointing. Generally speaking it was left to the finance officers to take the initiative in enquiring why a particular hospital cost more than another or why a particular type of expenditure in that hospital was more expensive than in the other. Their enquiries sometimes showed that the information was unreliable, but even when such difficulties were sorted out enquiries tended to produce explanations for why the more expensive hospital was 'different' rather than action to reduce costs. This remains a problem. Very broadly the costs of one acute hospital should be similar to those of another acute hospital, and of one long-stay hospital to those of another long-stay. But the hospitals falling into these and other categories vary in character and the need is to recognise justifiable differences in cost but at the same time to recognise where resources are being used less effectively than elsewhere.

After research by the King's Fund and the Nuffield Provincial Hospitals Trust, a new costing system was launched in 1957 and revised in 1963. Unlike the previous system, this one estimated the actual cost of treating out-patients and day patients. In addition to the cost per patient-week (since 1973 this has been the cost per patient-day) attempts were also made from the beginning to identify a cost per case except for long-stay cases. Since the cases dealt with in an acute hospital vary so much from one hospital to another, the length of stay, when multiplied by the cost per day produces a vast range of different costs per case and makes cost comparisons even more difficult than those for a bed-week. It is, however, a more useful measure of cost.

In the 1960s research by M.S. Feldstein demonstrated that it was possible to estimate from the statistical returns of hospital activity (Form SH3) what the average cost per in-patient case ought to be, by taking each hospital's 'case-mix' and multiplying it by the national average costs per case for each type of patient in the mix. His research drew attention to the significance of measuring the length of stay of a patient and although his concept of setting target costs was not seen as a practical option, the thinking behind his theory contributed greatly to the subsequent measurement of workloads. What still remains to be developed in hospital costing is the recognition of different degrees of variability for different kinds of expenditure. Everything is ultimately variable except the shell of the building, but some costs vary rapidly with changes in length of stay whereas others vary much more slowly.

Although one or two hospitals had experimented earlier with departmental costing, it was not a national requirement until the 1957 scheme, when it was applied to larger hospitals. Departmental costings are essential for judging whether or not a manager is using his resources efficiently and economically. On the other hand, micro costing by itself is inadequate because it does not show the contribution which a particular department makes to the whole hospital. It is quite possible, for example, to have a physiotherapy department with such a large workload that it appears to be a very efficient department. Yet its total contribution to the hospital's costs makes the hospital expensive in terms of the patient-day or the out-patient attendance, because there is far more physiotherapy per average patient than in other hospitals. With both types of costing available, the governing body can consider whether a department is in itself efficient and also whether it makes a balanced contribution to the work of the hospital as a whole.

National summaries are now prepared annually to show the average costs of each hospital type per region and per area. Regions also prepare their own summaries of individual hospital costs. Attempts to extend the costing system outside the hospital range and into community services have not proved particularly successful or advantageous.

One use to which cost accounts have been put is to set standards of staffing and expenditure for new hospitals. Forty-five selected hospitals in England and Wales, all equivalent to a district general hospital, were chosen some years ago and their costs are each year aggregated and averaged to give RHAs and AHAs some idea of the running costs of existing hospitals, so that these can be applied in assessing the total budgets for new acute hospitals.

Some regional authorities have produced very detailed and useful analyses of costs for particular activities, such as the consumption of drugs or of food. Different types of drugs or food commodities have been identified and unit costs per patient or per day's feeding produced for each type of expenditure. Other authorities have concentrated on trying to ascertain the costs of each ward in a hospital, though here the case mix factor is a major difficulty. In recent years efforts have been made to produce specialty costs, identifying through the name of the consultant the cost of medication and surgical processes relevant to particular groups of patients with similar conditions. This type of costing is likely to be developed substantially within the next few years and may give a new insight into the need for funds associated with the setting up of new specialties and sub-specialties. Other facets of hospital costing have been some process costing, e.g. for laundries and sterile supply departments, and job costing for capital works and some of the more expensive maintenance works.

Before leaving costing, we should acknowledge the work done by the O and M department of the DHSS which, by work study techniques, has succeeded in producing a number of useful expenditure norms for different kinds of activities, particularly those involving a good deal of labour.

The next obvious stage is the integration of cost accounts with financial accounts. The 1973 accounting system, which was effective as from 1 April 1974, provides for expenditure to be analysed functionally, i.e. departmentally, and for the units of activity appropriate to each department to be measured at the same time, so that not only the annual but also the quarterly or monthly accounts can show unit costs as well as budgetary control information. In practice it has proved extremely difficult to get the workload statistics in time to prepare this type of integrated account without delaying the submission of the key information for the cash limits sytem. Hence work has been done to produce a computer program which will facilitate the regular and prompt production of integrated accounts. This is known as the Standard Accounting System (SAS), the West Midlands region being the centre of responsibility for its development. (Scotland has its own centres of responsibility for the development of standard computer systems.) The integrated accounting system, for which SAS provides the computer programs, is intended to show both hospital expenditure and community services expenditure divided between two main categories, namely patient care services and general services (see again Table 4). Patient care services are sub-divided to show medical staff services, nursing staff services, medical supplies and diagnostic and other paramedical services. The general services are divided to show the costs of administration, medical records, training and education, catering for staff and patients, domestic and cleaning services, portering, laundry, linen services, transport, estate management and miscellaneous expenses.

Alongside these basic sub-divisions of function, expenditure on hospital services is further sub-divided, by what is known as the secondary analysis, to show the expenditure on in-patients separately from that on out-patients, day patients, accident and emergency cases and day cases. The community health services are divided, by way of secondary analysis, between school health services, general community care, preventive services and family planning. Beside the primary and secondary analyses, the intention is to provide a tertiary analysis on the hospital side which enables expenditure to be grouped according to the type of client or group of patients receiving similar kinds of treatment. This area has not yet been properly developed.

The family practitioner service expenditure can only be divided for primary analysis between general medical services, general dental services, pharmaceutical services and ophthalmic services. No ideas for secondary or tertiary analysis have yet emerged for the family practitioner services.

To over-simplify all this stratified analysis, one might say that primary breakdown is into types of expenditure that can be controlled by each profession or by individual officers, secondary analysis indicates where the treatment takes place, either in a bed or in out-patient accommodation, etc. and tertiary analysis tries to identify expenditure according to the group of people benefiting from it rather than those who are managing the resources it absorbs. Specialty costing, if developed, would be an alternative way of using the tertiary part of the analysis structure.

It will be seen that although there is a common thread running through the analyses for hospital, community and family practitioner services, they really have very little in common. Also, alongside all this functional analysis is still the subjective breakdown of types of expenditure, very much as it was devised in 1948. Although the accountancy profession within the NHS has argued for the abolition of subjective analysis for many years, it remains a necessary activity for devising and monitoring a price index for materials and wages absorbed by the NHS.

None of this information, of course, guarantees that the service is giving value for money, for that depends on the information being read and acted upon. It does not always happen, and improvement is likely only if and when the SAS achieves a really high standard of accuracy and promptitude.

Improving financial mangement

The finance function within the NHS has never been static. From the early days, when the finance officer was very much a bookkeeper, there has been constant development of both the art of financial management and the demand for financial services. Particular boosts were given by the introduction and later development of departmental costing, the delegation of budgetary responsibility, the demands of the post-1974 planning system and, in 1976, the imposition of cash limits for revenue and capital. Treasurers and their senior assistants are now full members of management teams and working parties, except in Northern Ireland, and in England district finance officers/treasurers have independent responsibilty from area treasurers for the planning and managerial aspects of their work. Yet in many ways there is a need to increase the quality and quantity of the information and advice finance departments are able to offer.

Payroll

Payrolls and pay advices serve the purposes of managers as well as of employees. Employees expect their payslips to tell them how their remuneration has been earned and calculated, what deductions have been made and whether further voluntary deductions could be processed if demanded. Their staff organisations will speak for them when their expectations are disappointed. Heads of departments want an analysis of earnings which shows the effect of authorised overtime, shift working and other managerial decisions, as well as providing an up-to-date budget comparison for control purposes. The North Western region is responsible for developing and updating a standard payroll system (SPS) for the whole of England. Wales and Scotland have developed their own systems. Finance staffs need to work in close harmony with the staffs of personnel departments, particularly in the interpretation of Whitley agreements.

Budgets

Most managers would like more useful information on aspects of their departmental budgets, and they need it more quickly. Comparison statements, even if produced monthly, need to be accompanied by commentaries and suggestions. The detail, on the other hand, needs to be condensed so that only those items on which management action is both desirable and possible are highlighted. Information on price changes and on the reserves available to cover them needs to be shared between management teams and line managers, so that decisions to cut or to accelerate commitments can be taken with reasonable certainty. Individual managers may need additional information, peculiar to their particular functions, such as weekly food consumption statistics for a catering officer. Experiments are needed to find whether techniques such as standard cost control can be applied to the NHS budget.

Accounting and costing

The SAS is planned to have several later stages, once the basic accounting and budgeting processes have been generally adopted. These include the development of tertiary analyses, commitment accounting and full asset evaluation and depreciation. At the same time, the cost accounts derived from the SAS need to be made more relevant to the needs of managers and teams and linked to objectives derived from the planning system. More attention needs to be paid to the uncovering of wasteful procedures and unnecessary activities. In particular, the cost of the teaching function still needs to be thoroughly investigated and justified, so that the allocation of funds is seen to be fair to both teaching and non-teaching areas.

Planning and capital works

It is important that the use of money to bring about a change in services is fully justified in a 'case of need' and also that the best capital solution shall be found to the problem thrown up by the investigation. If capital schemes are needlessly expensive or even marginally unnecessary, funds are depleted and other possible developments are frustrated. It is important to balance the uses of capital and revenue funds, so as to secure the optimum service at the least combined cost. Techniques such as cost/benefit analysis and discounted cash flow can help to secure that objective.

Auditing and computing

Recent reports and the comments of DHSS auditors have emphasised that not enough manpower is invested in the internal audit function. In particular, computer auditing is a largely neglected field. Finance departments have done a great deal to create viable computer programs, but the daily operation of those programs is almost always in the hands of staff who are answerable to a management services officer. While that arrangement has some obvious advantages to non-financial managers, it does increase the need for the treasurer to test the security of the systems independently from the operators and to satisfy himself and the users that no risks are being taken with either the data, much of which is confidential, or with the computing. Auditing also needs to be intensified with regard to capital works.

Patients' funds and property

Finance departments have a duty to safeguard patients' property, issue pocket money, act as trustee for patients' allowances and, if necessary, invest surplus funds, either individually or collectively. On the whole the amount of staff time devoted to these activities tends to be minimal, as the Health Advisory Service has sometimes pointed out. Nursing staff are often involved in financial transactions which ought to be carried out by finance staff.

Trust funds

AHAs and special trustees need information to enable them to invest trust funds wisely and profitably. They also need expert advice on the best ways to spend either the capital or the income from those funds. Some trust bodies with very substantial funds have well-constituted advisory committees and employ their own accountants, but most health authority trusts rely on the authority's treasurer and the advice of a stockbroker.

Other financial services

Many outside bodies look to the AHA treasurer to provide accounting budgetary and advisory services. These include community health councils and regional nurse training committees. With teaching hospitals there needs to be continuous dialogue and cross-accounting with the matching university medical or dental school. Often the premises of a teaching hospital are so interwoven with those of the school that the true apportionment of expenditure and overheads becomes a very complicated matter. There is a further complication if both bodies have trust funds earmarked for teaching purposes. It is not only buildings that are shared; there also have to be financial arrangements for joint appointments.

Finance is no more exempt than other functions from changes in attitude which have affected the NHS in recent years. One of these is the expectation that decisions affecting the public should be seen to be arrived at in public, and this has statutuory support in that meetings of health authorities are open to the press and public under the Public Meetings Act. Treasurers, like other professionals have their own vocabulary, but if they are to be effective they must communicate clearly with many other professionals (and with members of health authorities) without financial expertise and must now also, like their team colleagues, explain themselves in public.

Further reading

Statutory instruments and circulars

England and Wales

SI74/541. The NHS Financial (No. 2) Regulations 1974
HRC(72)6, WHRC(73)4. Working party on financial administration
HRC(73)29, WHRC(73)26. Transfer of hospital trust property
HRC(73)30. Transfer of hospital trust property; appointment and functions of special trustees
HRC(74)34, WHRC(74)40. Financial management structures and preparation of substantive schemes
HSC(IS)28, WHSC(IS)21. Financial regulations
HSC(IS)74, WHSC(IS)89. Standing financial instructions for health authorities
HC(76)15, WHC(76)16. Financial information systems for health authorities
HC(76)20, WHC(76)25. Model standing orders for regional and area health authorities
HC(77)17, (79)18, WHC(77)21, (78)13, (79)1. Joint financing of local authority projects
HC(78)42, WHC(78)44. Losses and special payments
HC(80)11, WHC(80)15. Health Services Act 1980: fund raising by NHS authorities

Scotland

SI74/468. The NHS (Financial Provisions) (Scotland) Regulations 1974
NHS Circular 1974(GEN)60. Financial management structures and preparation of substantive plans
NHS Circular 1974(GEN)88. Standing financial instructions
NHS Circular 1976(GEN)31, 1980(GEN)11. Losses and special payments
NHS Circular 1980(GEN)5. Joint planning and support finance arrangements.

Official reports

DHSS. *Sharing Resources for England* (RAWP Report). HMSO 1976
DHSS, Northern Ireland. *Proposals for the Allocation of Revenue Resources for the Health and Personal Social Services* (PARR). 1978
Ministry of Health. *Report of the Working Party on Hospital Costing*. HMSO 1955
Ministry of Health. *Report of the Working Party on Hospital Allocations.* 1961
Royal Commission on the National Health Service. *Report,* Chapter 21 (Cmnd 7615) HMSO 1979. Research Paper No. 2 *Management of financial resources*

in the National Health Service (Perrin Report). HMSO 1978

SHHD. *Scottish Health Authorities Revenue Equalisation.* Report of the Working Party on Revenue Resource Allocation (SHARE). HMSO 1977

Welsh Office. *Report of the Steering Committee on Resource Allocation.* 1977, Fourth report 1980

The Government's Expenditure Plans 1979-80 to 1982-83 (Cmnd 7439). HMSO 1979, and later versions

Other publications

Abernethy, W.L. *Internal Audit in Local Authorities and Hospitals.* 3rd edn revised by D.R. Davies. Shaw 1971

Association of Health Service Treasurers. *Internal Audit in the National Health Service.* 1977

Association of Hospital Treasurers. *Free Monies.* 1966. *Patients' Property, Income and Allowances.* 1979

Chartered Institute of Public Finance and Accountancy. 'Financial Information Service.' *Health* Vol. 30. 1980

Feldstein, M.S. *Economic Analysis for Health Service Efficiency: Econometric Studies of the British National Health Service.* North Holland Publishing Co., Amsterdam 1968

King's Fund. *Accounting for Health.* 1973

10
Health building and estate management

In 1948 the NHS in England and Wales inherited some 2,800 hospitals with more than 500,000 beds, most of them in buildings which were old and unsuited to the provision of a modern hospital service. About 45 per cent had originally been built before 1891 and 21 per cent before 1861. Some of the general hospitals were inconveniently located for the population served and most mental hospitals were located away from, or on the periphery of, centres of population. The mental hospitals often had extensive estates, including farms. The Emergency Medical Service had left a legacy of hospitals in temporary brick or timber structures. Most of the building stock was therefore in need of replacement, and there was a backlog of maintenance. In the event, much of the stock was still in use in 1980.

One of the duties placed on the Minister by the 1946 Act was to provide hospital accommodation to the extent he considered necessary to meet all reasonable requirements. It would have been impractical in the post-war years, when there was a shortage of building materials, to have interpreted this as entailing a large building programme, and successive governments in fact chose to devote most of the public building programme to housing and schools. The Guillebaud Report of 1956 noted that in 1952-3 hospital capital expenditure had been at about a third of the 1938-9 level despite the fact that the capital assets had been unavoidably run down during the war years, and argued that the existing inadequate rate of capital expenditure could not be allowed to continue much longer without serious harm to the hospital service.

The amount spent on hospital building in England and Wales in 1949-50 was about £8.7 million and fluctuated a little in subsequent years, reaching £10.6 million in 1955-6, the year of the Guillebaud Report. In 1957-8 it was £17.2 million and then rose steadily to £23.7 million in 1960-1. These sums sufficed to produce a very few new hospitals and a considerable number of new departments and adaptations to existing hospitals. In addition local authorities spent modest sums on those services for which they were responsible under the 1946 Act, but the community services entail much smaller capital expenditure than hospitals and the original intention of building health centres was abandoned for many years. Overall the 1950s could be described as a period of 'patch and mend'.

The Hospital Plan

The increased capital sums available for hospital building in the late 1950s prompted a review of hospital building and the publication in 1962 of the *Hospital Plan for England and Wales,* which took a comprehensive look at hospital building needs and formulated a long-term national plan for meeting them. It set out to establish for the first time a planned pattern of hospital provision with building project starts identified for a period ten years ahead, bearing in mind the fact that it took several years to plan, design and build any major hospital development. The following year the Ministry published *Health & Welfare: The Development of Community Care* as a corollary, though it was a different type of document. Instead of a national plan it was a collection of the development plans of 146 local health and welfare authorities which varied considerably in ambition, and the emphasis was on the development of services rather than a building programme, although the plans did entail considerable capital development.

The Hospital Plan began by taking assessments provided by the Registrar General of the probable size and make-up of the population, region by region, area by area, in 1975 and set down ratios of beds required to population for acute, maternity, geriatric, mental illness and mental subnormality services. The ratios assumed continuing improvements in general practitioner and local authority health and social services.

Having established bed ratios, the Plan went on to consider how the beds and out-patient facilities ought to be arranged and located. Thus, the concept of the district general hospital (DGH) emerged. This was not an entirely new concept for the Ministry of Health had in the early days of the NHS advised HMCs to organise existing hospitals in a complementary manner to provide a full range of basic hospital services for their populations.

The DGH concept

The Plan recognised that there was a trend towards greater interdependence of the various branches of medicine and also a need to bring together a wide range of the facilities required for diagnosis and treatment. A network of district general hospitals was therefore proposed, each normally containing 600-800 beds and serving a population of 100,000-150,000. Some might be larger and some would be smaller, but none less than 300 beds. District general hospitals would provide treatment and diagnostic facilities both for in-patients and out-patients and include a maternity unit, a short-stay psychiatric unit, a geriatric unit and isolation facilities for infectious diseases. Regional specialties requiring a larger catchment area would be provided only at certain selected hospitals. Each DGH would be located in or near the centre of one of the centres of population of the area which it would serve.

Accident services were to be developed and organised on a regional basis ensuring continuous cover by expert medical staff. Most DGHs would contain full accident and emergency departments, linked to centres providing regional specialist services.

While a maternity unit would be a normal part of the DGH there would sometimes be justification on geographical grounds for providing maternity units in smaller towns. In all circumstances, however, potential abnormal deliveries should take place in the district general hospital.

It was implicit in the new pattern of hospital services that the great majority of beds needed would be contained in the DGHs and that as they were developed a large number of the existing small hospitals would no longer be needed.

The DGHs would contain short-stay psychiatric units, but long-stay mental illness hospitals would be retained and gradually reduced in size, and it was envisaged that separate and smaller units would be provided for mentally subnormal patients.

Teaching hospitals would continue to make an important contribution to general and specialist service needs, but their size, location and content would be largely determined by their function of providing facilities for clinical teaching.

The hospital building programme 1962

From these considerations an assessment was made of the hospitals needed for each hospital management committee area, and a long-term building programme for each region was outlined, which took account of the location and the condition of existing hospitals and whether these should be retained and modernised, redeveloped or replaced.

The rate at which the programme should be carried out would be determined by the availability of expert hospital planning teams, the capacity of the building industry, the state of the national economy and the amount of money made available to the hospital building programme against other claims on national resources. It was appreciated that the tentative estimates of cost of the developments programmed might have to be modified considerably in the light of detailed planning of the individual projects.

As regards the net additional running cost that the programme might generate, it was estimated that the real increase in running cost by the 1970s would be contained within a small annual increase of total expenditure. It was thought that new hospitals would be more economically maintained and operated.

The 1966 review of the hospital plan and building programme

The Hospital Building Programme published in 1966 acknowledged that the cost of the 1962 programme and the time periods required for planning and building new hospitals had been underestimated and that the expectations of the original Plan could not possibly have been fulfilled. It was not, however, suggested that the norms set out in the Hospital Plan needed revision, but the population projections were increased and the programme stretched. The concept of the DGH was endorsed and an attempt was made to relate building projects more realistically to total resources likely to be available. It was stressed that the capital programme and individual projects should be kept under continuous review and adjustments made as necessary to meet changes in need, priorities and resources available. It was also admitted that new hospital buildings required more staff and cost more to run because of the increased scale of provision and expansion of specialised services.

The report indicated how the services were expected to develop in each region and listed the major schemes then in progress and expected to start in the four year period 1966-70. Schemes expected to start after 1969-70 were also included in two broad classes of priority.

The Bonham-Carter Report

The building programme went through a second informal review when a committee of the Central Health Services Council reported in 1969 on the functions of the district general hospital (The Bonham-Carter Report). The concept of the district general hospital was further developed by this committee which stressed the desirability of providing a full range of services on one site, including provision for geriatric, mentally ill and mentally handicapped patients. This, it was claimed, would be beneficial to the patients, more economic and concentrate consultant manpower on one hospital, avoiding single-handed consultant appointments which were considered undesirable. The implication of the report was that DGHs could be as large as 1,500 beds serving a population of 300,000.

The conclusions of the Bonham-Carter Report were never formally accepted by the Department, but they influenced regions' development plans and some capital projects were started on the premise that a single district general hospital of the size envisaged in the report was the right solution. However, before too many such projects reached the point of no return, there was to be a change of policy caused by a reduction in public expenditure and a growing belief that very large hospitals were difficult to staff and manage, inaccessible to some patients and impersonal to both patients and staff. In addition, they took a long time to build, were potentially expensive and available sites were often too small or restricted.

Capital investment 1960-73

The amount of capital spent on hospital building continued to rise in real terms from 1960-1 to a peak in the period 1972-3 and the proportion spent on large schemes steadily increased.

Capital expenditure on hospitals in England rose from £32 million in 1961-2 (£143 million 1978 prices) to £197 million in 1972-3 (£536 million 1978 prices). Capital expenditure in the UK as a whole rose from £92 million in 1966-7 (£342 million 1978 prices) to £215 million in 1972-3 (£591 million 1978 prices). As a proportion of total NHS resources, capital expenditure was 4 per cent in 1948-9 and over 12 per cent in 1972-3. Local health authorities continued to develop health centres, clinics and ambulance service facilities at a modest rate.

NHS reorganisation 1974

From 1974 the regional health authorities were responsible for capital works, including the type previously the responsibility of local health authorities, and area health authorities for the maintenance and improvement of the existing capital stock and estate generally, but RHAs could delegate certain capital works to AHAs.

The community hospital concept

A DHSS paper entitled *Community Hospitals — their role and development in the National Health Service* published in August 1974 introduced a significant change of policy regarding the future of small hospitals. It was proposed that some suitably located small hospitals should be retained and developed or new hospitals built, to accommodate patients who did not require the highly specialised services provided by a DGH. The patients admitted to these hospitals were to satisfy three criteria. First, the medical and nursing care which they needed could not reasonably be provided in their homes; secondly, they were not expected to require highly specialised care or special investigation; and, thirdly, they would benefit from care nearer their homes where they could more easily be visited and maintain their links with the local community.

Community hospitals were expected to provide up to half the district geriatric beds plus the beds for the elderly severely mentally infirm, some general medical pre-convalescent and short-term admission beds and out-patient clinics. The size of the community hospitals would generally vary between 50 and 150 beds for a population of between 30,000 and 100,000. General practitioners would be responsible for the day-to-day medical care of all patients and certain services such as surgery, obstetrics, pathology and radiology were specifically excluded. This concept of the community hospital was subsequently modified by later planning guidance.

Capital investment 1974-8

NHS reorganisation coincided with a period of financial restraint and this is reflected in the reduction in real terms of capital expenditure on hospital and community health services in the UK from the peak in 1972-3 of £215 million (£591 million 1978 prices) to £338 million in 1977-8 (£362 million 1978 prices).

Post-1974 health services and building policies

The 1974-5 cuts in public expenditure and subsequent government policies to slow down the rate of expansion of public expenditure underlined the need to produce cost-effective health building programmes in keeping with the national and regional strategies and priorities for the development of comprehensive health care.

In a circular (DS 85/75) to health authorities on the planning tasks for 1975-6, the Department reviewed progress in implementing the Hospital Plan. While the concept of the DGH was again endorsed, the circular referred to the long time periods involved in fully implementing the DGH policy throughout the country and the limited progress made towards the objective. In particular, in view of the changed capital resource assumptions, there was a need to re-examine the assumption that DGH services should be on a single site. It was suggested that a single site policy was not achievable nationally in the foreseeable future. Instead, the creation of a DGH was to be seen as an organisational arrangement of all the appropriate hospital services in existing buildings in order to achieve in the short to medium term some of the service objectives underlying the DGH concept. This also involved the teaching hospitals in providing a full range of basic DGH services as well as the more specialised regional services and teaching and research facilities.

Similarly, a flexible approach to the creation of community hospitals was envisaged. It was hoped that most community hospitals could be provided through the change of use and adaptation of existing small hospitals at a significantly lower cost than DGH development. These hospitals should reduce pressures on DGHs and authorities were urged to include such developments in their plans.

This policy was restated in the consultative document *Priorities for Health and Personal Social Services in England* and later in *The Way Forward*. The policy was to maintain as the first priority the standard of services and to 'put people before buildings'. Capital expenditure would be cut back in order to allow current expenditure on health and personal social services to rise and the health capital programme for England would level out at about £235 million per year. This would still allow a modest number of major hospital schemes of high priority to proceed, in addition to improvements in existing buildings, but the importance of concentrating on low cost projects wherever possible and on innovations such as the 'nucleus' hospital was emphasised. The role of primary care in helping to relieve pressure on hospital and residential services by caring for more people in the community was re-stated. The health centre programme was to be maintained.

Previous guidance on community hospitals was not to stand in the way of practical solutions agreed locally. Services could be provided beyond the scale envisaged in the original concept if they were a logical and economic part of total district hospital provision. Up to a quarter of all in-patient beds and many day places might eventually be in community hospitals, and two-thirds of these should be for the elderly. It was hoped that four-fifths of community hospitals might be provided through the change of use and adaptations of existing small hospitals.

The future pattern of health services

Since 1974, therefore, there has been a broad affirmation of the 1962 DGH policy for the provision of hospital services for a health district but with flexibility in its application. Also, there has been much emphasis placed on the provision of comprehensive health care services for each district, ranging from primary care to district general hospital services, with support from selected centres by area and regional specialist hospital services, and more community-based services for the elderly, the mentally ill and the mentally handicapped.

In building terms the pattern of health services one would now expect to be provided or developing in a district would be health centres (or GP surgeries and community health clinics) serving as bases for primary care teams and providing first line medical service to the community. Patients requiring specialist hospital services will be referred by GPs or through the accident and emergency service to the district general hospital (or one of the general hospitals in the district organised on a complementary basis to provide a DGH service). For certain specialties, referrals still need to be to a hospital other than a local one where regional or sub-regional services are provided.

Each district general hospital or complementary DGHs will provide a full and balanced range of basic in-patient and out-patient, diagnostic, treatment and rehabilitation services, including a maternity unit with special care baby and paediatric facilities, a geriatric unit representing about half of the total district provision, a comprehensive psychiatric unit and assessment units for handicapped children and the elderly severely mentally infirm. The geriatric and psychiatric units include day hospitals for the rehabilitation of both in-patients and out-patients. The district acute services will be supplemented by area and regional hospital services at selected hospitals in the area and in the region. The balance of beds and day places for the elderly, roughly half of the total, will be provided in smaller peripheral units, those which are suitable to be retained in the long term being developed as community hospitals.

For mental illness, the policy is that in each district there would be a comprehensive psychiatric unit in a DGH plus one or more hostel-type units for long-stay patients and accommodation for continuing care for elderly severely mentally infirm patients, preferably in a community hospital setting. Nearly all the old mental hospitals will gradually be replaced by these facilities, but the existing large hospitals will need to continue to provide accommodation for their ageing long-stay population. The priority for the psychiatric service will be to provide a district based service to those districts not at present served by a mental illness hospital reasonably well sited within their own geographical area, but many of the existing mental illness hospitals are likely to continue to provide for some time most of the services for both short- and long-stay patients, including the elderly severely mentally infirm. Considerable expenditure will be necessary to improve standards in these hospitals.

For the mentally handicapped, the policy is to provide an integrated community-based and local service, including domiciliary support, local authority residential accommodation and small, domestic scale hospital units separate from DGHs and replacing the existing special hospitals for the mentally handicapped. Similarly, domestic-type hospital units are required for the younger disabled.

The pattern of health service provision outlined here is, of course, subject to changes in government economic and health care policies, and health authorities therefore need to be flexible in their forward planning. Perhaps in the long run health care policies are most likely to change in relation to mental illness and mental handicap, for these are the services about which opinions differ most. However, in May 1980 the DHSS issued a consultation paper, *The Future Pattern of Hospital Provision in England,* which appeared to some as a reversal of previous policies, though it can also be seen as a further evolution of policies as they have developed since 1974. It originated in ministers' doubts about the very large DGH and their dislike of closing small hospitals. At the time of its issue the Department called in plans for large developments, to re-examine them. The paper proposed to retain the basic concept of the DGH but with less emphasis on concentration of services on large hospitals, to accept the provision of DGH services on more than one site as a valid long-term policy, thus retaining many medium-sized hospitals in urban areas and enabling the main hospitals to be normally of no more than 600 beds, and to retain small and medium-sized hospitals wherever sensible and practicable, particularly in rural areas. One of the means of keeping down the size of the DGH would be to provide 70 per cent of geriatric beds elsewhere and to limit the size of the psychiatric unit.

NHS planning system — strategic plans and programmes

With the introduction of the NHS planning system following the reorganisation of the service in 1974, there was a fundamental change in the method of preparing the national health building programme. Instead of the new regional authorities continuing to implement and update the programmes inherited from the former regional hospital boards, and based on the earlier 1962 and 1966 hospital building programmes, the planning system demanded a total review by the new AHAs and RHAs of the hospital care needs of their populations; the setting of priorities and objectives to secure the required provision; and the preparation of related health building programmes. Under the NHS planning system, the area and regional authorities are required to prepare strategic plans for a ten-year period and the regional strategic plan includes the ten-year building programme.

A typical ten-year building programme will contain several major schemes for the development, usually in phases, of district general hospitals and community hospitals and many smaller schemes designed to improve existing buildings or to provide smaller scale new buildings, e.g. day hospitals and health centres. The programme will be derived from and reflect the service strategy and priorities and be contained within the capital resource assumption figures, i.e. the level of capital expenditure forecast for the ten-year period, given as part of the annual

DHSS planning guidelines. The programme will, therefore, be a manifestation of a determined policy of priority and selection acknowledging limited resources.

Because of the high priority given to primary care services, the Department for some years specified to each region a minimum capital sum to be spent on health centres and other primary care schemes, though this has now ceased. General medical practitioners can, in addition, obtain financial assistance to develop their own private surgery premises. However, much the greater proportion of available capital will still be spent on hospital building.

The national health building programme is now, therefore, the aggregate of the individual RHA programmes which are contained within a total annual capital sum determined by the government and projected forward for planning purposes.

Current priorities for capital investment 1978-9

Even allowing for a more flexible method of providing DHGs, current health care policies imply a considerable capital investment in new buildings to bring about the changes in the pattern of services envisaged, both in hospitals and in the community, and in the meantime to maintain and improve the existing building stock. As was the case in 1962 when the Hospital Plan was published, the rate at which the programme can be carried out will be largely determined by the state of the national economy and the amount of capital money available to the NHS. It is likely to be several decades before the pattern of services envisaged will be provided all over the country in adequate and correctly located buildings.

As always, priorities are necessary, and difficult choices have to be made. The post-1974 policy has been to give priority to the development of services for the mentally ill, the mentally handicapped and the elderly and primary care services, over the development of general and acute hospital services and to ensure that the limited foreseeable resources are not over-committed to relatively few large schemes and that 'health needs are met on as wide a front as possible using a modest scale of building giving the best possible value for money'. The Department's post-1974 guidelines required that proposals for whole hospital development should be questioned and that adaptation or improvement of, or addition to, existing buildings should first be considered for the achievement of policy objectives.

Capital programmes for the three years 1974-5 to 1976-7 were prepared by the new RHAs largely on the basis of the then contractual commitments and inherited plans, but taking into account as far as possible emerging national and regional priorities within the reorganised service. The capital programmes 1977-8 onwards have been directed to the achievement of the national policies and the regional and strategic planning objectives within the resource assumption figures, capital and revenue, given by the DHSS.

Planning and design of health buildings

The evolution of planning and design of health buildings in the first thirty years of the NHS is a subject deserving fuller treatment than is possible here, and indeed would need to be seen in an international context. Planning and design are multidisciplinary activities which lead to the interplay of sometimes conflicting professional values and have to be done in the context of changing philosophies (and sometimes fashion) in the delivery of health care, developments in science and technology, changing expectations amongst consumers (or changing professional conceptions of what the consumer requires), new building techniques and changing philosophies (or fashions) of designers. There is tension between the desire to keep within costs and the desire to get the design right, and both of these may conflict with the desire to build within the scheduled time.

The first new hospitals built for the NHS were 'one-off' jobs and although not built without regard to costs may seem in retrospect to have been somewhat generously financed and provided. In time the inevitable effects of public sector financing were felt; when a whole building programme is financed from a single source there is strong pressure to complete as many projects as possible with the money available and to discountenance schemes costing more than others apparently providing comparable facilities. The consequence was a more utilitarian and rationalised approach to the planning and design of health buildings.

A limited number of general building 'shapes' for hospitals emerged from the process. There is nothing unique to hospitals about these shapes, for one can build either vertically or horizontally, and most building shapes fall into a compromise between these two extremes. Traditionally the way in which in-patients are accommodated, that is the ward layout, influences more than any other feature the design of a hospital. In the fallow years before the Hospital Plan some research sponsored by the Nuffield Foundation produced the Nuffield ward: a combination of four-bed or six-bed bays and single-bed rooms to form the ward unit, and thus a compromise between the traditional open Nightingale ward and a collection of single or two-bed rooms. With many permutations it has been the normal approach to ward design in the NHS ever since. This design (or indeed the Nightingale or any other) is appropriate for most kinds of in-patient care, and a standard approach to ward layout leads naturally to the 'stacking' of ward accommodation in tower blocks. Such an arrangement permits the effective delivery of goods, services and people to each floor level and this design solution is to be found worldwide. Thus a tower block accommodating wards and possibly a few other departments placed on a podium block containing out-patient, diagnostic and support service departments tends to emerge as a natural shape for hospitals. It is economical in use of site but suffers from an inherent lack of flexibility.

Another factor in the evolution of hospital design has been 'on-costs'. The cost of any individual department in a hospital can be identified and measured within fairly well defined parameters, and so the cost of a range of departments making up a hospital can be readily identified. However, placing a given range of departments in particular configurations on a specified site entails on-costs, and it was not fully realised in the early days of the hospital building programme how high these can be. In extreme cases they can equal the total cost of the individual departments. Thus a high-rise hospital requiring special foundations can be very expensive. Furthermore running costs will be high, particularly when artificial environmental control is necessary, and that is normally the case at least for the podium block.

In contrast, a horizontal type of hospital development, say up to three storeys, permits a more domestic style of architecture, costs less to build and allows for natural lighting and ventilation. However, beyond a certain size communications become lengthy and might require more staff. Also such a hospital needs an extensive site not easily found within the large conurbations.

A compromise solution on shape emerges consisting of a series of medium rise (i.e. four/five storey) blocks with courtyards maximising the use of natural light and ventilation. It is suitable for development in phases and can often be used in the phased development of an existing hospital.

The essential features of a hospital are the in-patient and out-patient accommodation and the diagnostic and treatment facilities. There are also service departments but it is now realised that some which have traditionally formed part of a hospital complex are better provided on a larger scale with a more industrial approach and this development is potentially important for hospital design. It is even possible that factory-produced pre-cooked, frozen food will eliminate the need for large hospital kitchens.

One desideratum almost always claimed for hospital and health building design is flexibility to meet future change: it should be possible to extend buildings as well as adapt them internally. It may be questioned whether it is possible to provide for unknown future needs and, if it is, whether the cost is worth paying. Needs do change rapidly, so that the commissioning of a major new hospital has an element of making previous planning decisions work in changed circumstances, but hospitals built a century or more ago to meet quite different needs from today's still give a fairly satisfactory service. Fortunately people are flexible.

Hospital design and research

The *Hospital Building Programme* of 1966 referred to the lack of opportunity in the early years of the service to gain experience of the design of modern hospital buildings, and said that with the larger building programme postulated for the late 1960s and beyond, it would be possible to take advantage of the unity of the service and to make available the 'distilled experience of the hospital service in Britain and elsewhere'.

The DHSS has since at least 1960 made available the 'distilled experience' of the service and has also invested in significant research and development projects with a view to being able to give health authorities guidance on different aspects of building and investment programmes. Published documentation in the form of building notes, equipment notes, technical memoranda, building bulletins, etc., offers guidance on the planning, design and equipping of the various components and departments of the hospital and other health buildings, which now include health centres. Each guidance note is ultimately related to cost and area allowances within which the department should be capable of being built and equipped. The DHSS also has undertaken research into whole hospital and individual departmental operational policies and design problems and has itself built or sponsored several experimental approaches to hospital building and design. This has always been done with a view to cost effective standard hospital designs being made available for use within the service and thus ensuring that capital investment purchases an optimum amount of modern building and plant.

Work has also been undertaken on the application of industrialised building techniques and the national system of preferred dimensions, and standard building and engineering components have been introduced. Some projects have been more successful than others and it can be argued that the design of hospitals does not warrant so much investment of the Department's research and design resources. Nevertheless on balance the service has benefited from the experimentation and central co-ordination provided by the DHSS. Here it is worth quoting a recent author, a partner in Llewelyn-Davies Weeks and Partners, the architects who developed the Nuffield ward and have subsequently had a wide experience in hospital building both in the NHS and overseas. Speaking of how in the early days of the building programme several RHBs and private architects were solving the same problems simultaneously, he says:

> So the Ministry of Health co-ordinated the work of the public sector and began to produce standardised documentation for all aspects of a hospital brief (or programme). This work was exceptionally well done and has now resulted in the best and most comprehensive collection of technical hospital data available anywhere in the world. [1]

There has naturally been opposition to a rigid standardisation of design but as far ss possible the DHSS has adopted a fairly flexible attitude, allowing health authorities a degree of freedom in the application of central guidance to individual building projects. However any system which sets out to give general guidance and set basic standards is subject to the bureaucratising effect which turns philosophy into immutable laws. The building notes and cost allowances 'Capricode' — which figure largely later in this chapter — and so on were produced with a view to giving guidance but in practice they have become restrictions within which the service is required to operate. It is worth quoting the same author again:

> . . . few advanced nations regularly take a whole decade to complete a 500-bed hospital. In Britain, the reasons for this seem to be a combination of complex government procedures (some embodied in a document called Capricode); the labyrinthine tiers of an ever more complicated National Health Service; cumbersome town planning procedures and building regulations; and not least, the British desire to take decisions by a consensus of opinion.

The nucleus hospital concept

The DHSS requires authorities to consider the adaptation or improvement of, or addition to, existing buildings before entering into the field of totally new building projects. It is, of course, recognised that there will be places where new building is still necessary for a number of reasons, but such new buildings need to be of a modest scale and cost (both capital and revenue). The experience of hospital building obtained in the first 25 years of the service has shown that on balance they should be built in smaller and more manageable phases. The central view is held that a normal contract period should not exceed three years and, based on 1975 costs, not exceed £6 million in total.

In 1976 the DHSS announced its nucleus hospital concept consisting of a small general hospital of about 300 beds which was capable of subsequent expansion to 600-900 beds and which could be built in works modules at a cost below £6 million and within three-year contract periods. The concept was a development of earlier building research work undertaken by the Department exemplified by the Greenwich project, PGH 600, 'Best-Buy' and Harness hospital projects. It represents a response to a changed economic climate and it is intended to provide regional authorities with a standard whole hospital plan which is modest in scale, as well as bringing with it complete policies for operation and design, detailed co-ordinated room data and layouts and equipment schedules. Most important of all, the concept should be capable of being afforded within DHSS cost allowances.

The plans can be used to provide either a totally new development on a virgin site or can be adapted and used as a means of extending existing hospitals by adding departments, or groups of departments, thus realising the full potential of existing hospital buildings. This secondary use of nucleus is perhaps going to be the more important application in a period of severe financial restraint.

The briefing and design material is available as a tool to assist health authorities in carrying out building programmes effectively, efficiently and economically. The system is not mandatory, but represents a yardstick against which any non-nucleus hospital developments are undertaken, particularly in terms of space, finishes and services.

The building shape for nucleus hospitals is determined by seven basic principles which result in a building of up to three storeys of linked cruciform blocks which is flexible and relatively low cost in construction and use. The design employs maximum natural ventilation and light (thus minimising running costs) and the concept and design facilitate a phased development approach by a system of cruciform shaped buildings linked together by a main hospital street. The main communication routes, both vertical and horizontal, are kept separate from departmental accommodation. The overall effect is one of a low-rise but relatively high density solution which is 'open-ended' and therefore capable of further extension. The design incorporates the latest fire safety standards with particular emphasis on horizontal escape routes from one fire safety compartment to another.

The DHSS has designed wards and departments within the system and has overcome earlier problems of compatibility of floor area and services between departments which have to be placed one above the other. A relative space saving of about 25 per cent on other DHSS area guidance has been achieved, largely by the provision of 'shared use' accommodation and reductions in office, waiting and circulation areas.

The use of nucleus design requires, of course, acceptance by the client of standard policies, schedules and layouts with very limited scope for modifications. The advantages are that the planning and design time is reduced and the configuration is economical in terms of site cover. The disadvantage can be said to be that the client has to accept a standard solution with very little room for alterations. A full range of departments has yet to be made available and tested in use, particularly in ancillary areas, which have been reduced in size. The DHSS continues to add to the range of departments and no doubt the standard designs will be subject to the natural process of development through various 'marks' in the light of experience.

At the end of 1980 there were seven nucleus projects under construction and some 30 other schemes were using the nucleus design.

The organisation of the health building function

Capital planning and works functions exist at DHSS, region and area levels. Planning and designing health buildings is, as has already been observed, a multidisciplinary activity and the design building function at the three levels reflects this.

At DHSS level there is one multidisciplinary department under the direction of the chief works officer. At regional level there are separate medical, nursing, administrative and works functions with an interest in capital planning, co-ordinated by the RTO. The regional works officer is a member of the RTO and his role is to act as leader of the works professional team. He supervises the design of works and the execution of the region's capital building programme and also has ultimate responsibility for professional activities on estate management within the region. The RWO's department is usually split into divisions reflecting the three principal design professions, architecture, engineering and quantity surveying, each under its own chief officer who has professional autonomy but is accountable to the RWO for the work of his division.

The regional administrator has, as part of his co-ordinating role, an interest and responsibility for both service and capital planning activities. The distinction between these roles is sometimes not clear because they deal with interactive functions. Varying organisational structures at RHA and AHA level reflect the differing emphases and perceptions of the two types of planning which were held at (or have developed since) reorganisation. Whatever the structure, there is a need organisationally to co-ordinate policy and by this is meant the preparation of strategic and annual service plans from which priorities for capital investment programmes ought naturally to flow in terms of identified projects. There is also a need to co-ordinate the various disciplinary interests involved in preparing programmes and to ensure that programmes are adhered to in terms of time and cost parameters for particular projects.

Regional staff are responsible for progressing projects from conception to completion. The 'lead' responsibility for preparing the brief, including maintaining estimated costs within budget, for each project will usually rest with an administrator in collaboration with a medical officer. The responsibility for design and construction and maintaining costs within budget during these stages will rest with the regional architect, the regional engineer and the regional quantity surveyor — the 'lead' professional being either the architect or the engineer in terms of particular design elements and the quantity surveyor on overall costs.

Most RHAs have set up teams of appropriate senior officers below RTO level to draft the region's capital programme and to monitor its implementation. A typical team could comprise the regional architect, engineer, quantity surveyor, a specialist in community medicine, a nurse (planning), a treasurer's representative and the appropriate administrator.

The team is responsible to the RTO and also supervises the project teams which are set up for individual building projects and ensures that outline project policy is available for each project. This is the 'brief' to the project team which is then responsible for carrying the project forward. Nomenclature can be very misleading — 'brief' in this context needs to be distinguished from the 'design brief' which is the detailed brief to the design team leading to a completed design solution which has been agreed with the client.

At AHA level there are a variety of organisational practices, depending upon the size of the area, number of districts, etc. The area works officer is accountable to the AHA for the maintenance of buildings and plant and the estate generally. He prepares and supervises planned maintenance programmes for building, engineering plant and grounds for the area within budgets set by the AHA or DMTs. He may also be primarily responsible for the technical planning and implementation of delegated capital works. The regional works officer monitors the performance of area works officers. Administrative arrangements for service and project planning at AHA level are influenced by the same sort of considerations that affect the RHA organisation. Some areas have medical and nursing officers specifically identified for planning, others do not. Similarly, administrative and works responsibilities for various aspects of project planning can vary between AHAs. Works officers advise on planning appraisals and the feasibility of development proposals emanating from service planning activities. They have some responsibilities for estate records.

The constitution and role of a project team

The point at which a project team is set up varies between authorities. In some cases there will already have been a feasibility study and clear identification of the scope and content of the selected project (and perhaps, in the case of whole hospital development proposals, an identification of the scheme or phase with which the project team is concerned). A team may, however, be given a more limited brief simply stating the service plan intentions and a broad assessment of primary functional content, e.g. number of beds, out-patient sessions or day places needed. The project team is left to define more precisely a content for the project. It may need to carry out feasibility studies, including the consideration of development options and the identification of phases and capital and revenue costs. For smaller developments, the project team will usually have a basic statement calling for the provision of a building or adaptations to a building to provide for a defined service need.

In all cases, however, the project team will need to validate the content and feasibility of the proposed development and to complete a Capricode (Health Building Procedure) Stage 1 submission for approval by the DHSS and/or the RHA, or the AHA, as appropriate, before proceeding to prepare a detailed design brief, sketch plans and budget cost for the scheme. Schemes delegated to AHAs will generally need to be agreed in outline between the regional and area authorities.

The project team is concerned with the progressing, the planning and construction of the project through the building procedural stages set out in Capricode, including the initial arrangements for the commissioning of the building (usually through a separately constituted commissioning team). The Capricode Health Building Procedure Note 1 describes briefly the RHA and AHA capital project team arrangements that the DHSS expects to be made. There is a considerable degree of discretion left to individual authorities and practices vary, depending upon the nature and size of the project and the strength of 'professionalism' present. In some regions teams may be set up for individual projects. In others, they may be constituted on an area basis to deal with all schemes arising within an AHA.

The principles inherent in Capricode are applicable to all sizes of project. It is a mistake to suppose that because a scheme appears small and simple it does not need to go through at least the logic of the stages which apply to larger schemes. Problems and difficulties arise with small schemes as much as with large ones and there is less room to manoeuvre, particularly in terms of cost adjustments.

Project teams generally consist of a medical officer, nursing officer and administrator (the 'client group') and an architect, engineer and quantity surveyor (the 'design team'), with other officers and advisers co-opted or consulted as necessary. These six members form the permanent core of the team and will be supported by a treasurer on assessing revenue consequences and by a supplies officer on equipment matters. Because of the importance of revenue consequences, DHSS guidance has latterly suggested that the treasurer should be a core member. Not all members of the team need necessarily attend all its meetings, but they should receive all agenda and papers.

While Capricode recognises only the six core members as forming the permanent project team, most health authorities have had to come to terms with the demand for local participation and most regional project teams have representatives of the appropriate area and district and a representative of the users. The team also becomes larger if the design team comprises outside consultants, since their health service counterparts generally also attend. Projects for teaching hospitals also entail representation of the medical school.

Thus teams tend to become larger than desirable for effective working, and to show some of the familiar weaknesses of committees. They may devote much discussion to minutiae yet fail to deliberate on key issues so that major decisions fall to be taken by the design team unilaterally, or one of its members. There are two other difficulties: interprofessional conflicts and the fact that members of the client group are not always familiar with the intricacies of the design and construction industries. The unwieldiness of project teams can lead to the setting up of smaller working groups or sub-committees to tackle specific briefing or design problems.

The project team as a whole is corporately accountable to the RTO in the case of a regional scheme, or to the ATO or AMT in the case of an AHA scheme, but individual members of the team remain accountable to their own functional heads for their individual professional contributions. In the case of RHA projects, the area and district representatives on the team are generally responsible for keeping their own authority informed. Usually informal consultation is supported by more formal communication between the respective authorities, particularly on principles and policies. The project team should work on a consensus basis.

All this points to the importance of effective co-ordination of the work of the project team. The administrator member is generally regarded as the project co-ordinator and at region is responsible to the administrator (capital) for securing the progress of the project through each successive stage of the building procedures. He may also act as chairman of the team but another member, most often a medical representative, may take that responsibility and the possibility of conflict between the two roles then exists.

Neither the chairman nor the project co-ordinator is vested with any particular authority to direct and control the other members of the team, so that co-ordination and leadership depend very much upon the qualities of the chairman and/or co-ordinator. Capital schemes need to be driven along and since there is no clear authority to resolve difficulties, inadequate leadership produces expensive delays.

The case for a project manager has often been discussed but does not seem practical in a health service context. An alternative might be to place leadership on the administrator at the briefing sketch plan stage and on a works professional at the design stage.

While the client group is ultimately responsible for the preparation of the statement of the problem to be solved by the design team in spacial and cost terms, the point comes when its detailed involvement (particularly by the non-administrative members) decreases. The project team should remain active until the client group component is satisfied that it has a clear idea of the physical and spacial qualities and characteristics of the building that represent a solution to the problem it posed. Perhaps there is a tendency for the client group to withdraw too early so that some essential matters are decided by the design team who for their part may prefer to be left with these decisions. On the other hand it must be remembered that project teams are an expensive way of using professional people.

The design team is not a group that is capable of being held responsible for its corporate actions as if it were a body corporate. The team as such has not a defined existence in law and is not specifically mentioned in normal contracts. Outside professional design consultants are as a rule engaged separately by the client (i.e. the health authority), who reasonably expects them to act in concert in his interests. By custom the architect is usually leader of the team and it is the pace at which he works which sets the timing for the rest of the design team activities. However, it is well to remember that the design consultants do not have formal agreements with each other. It is through his management arrangements that the client must seek to ensure value for money.

To the layman the fees paid to outside consultants may seem high, but it is questionable whether employing more design staff within the health service would be cheaper or produce better designs.

The planning and design process and procedures

Capital investment programmes

Regional authorities prepare ten-year major capital investment programmes as part of their strategic planning function. Such programmes are updated annually and through such revisions, the estimates included in the early years of the programme are refined as projects go through various planning stages. Capital investment programmes ideally should represent, in terms of forward expenditure proposals, a statement of objectives in terms of 'start dates' for schemes. Each scheme has its peculiar financial profile in terms of expenditure pattern and, given the basic premise that once a scheme is started on site it continues through to completion, then the regulating mechanism for operating capital programmes is the use of the start date, hence the expression 'control by starts'. Projects can either be delayed or brought forward in order to maintain expenditure within approved resource limits.

Major schemes can take several years to plan and implement — up to as many as seven or eight years, depending upon size and complexity, although given sufficient staff and drive, much shorter periods can be achieved on particular projects.

Ultimately the management of capital investment programmes is a question of holding in balance expenditure arising from design costs (i.e. fees), building costs and furniture and equipment costs with cash limits for particular financial years. Programme management is a dynamic process which is influenced by a number of factors, principally relating to delays in planning or construction and variations in cost estimates. The key items being managed are cost and time.

AHAs also prepare capital programmes for smaller work schemes based on block capital grants made to them by their regional authority. Such grants are issued subject to a range of constraints and delegated financial limits and practices vary between regions. On the whole, however, the schemes delegated to area level are those involving modest extensions of existing plant, refurbishing of existing plant, refurbishing of existing building stock and equipment, specific building types, e.g. health centres.

Schemes should not normally be included in any programme until at least some outline planning appraisal and feasibility study work have been undertaken, so that broad cost parameters adequate for programming purposes can be established for the main components, viz., building and engineering works, fees, furniture and equipment. The latest point any scheme should enter the programme is two years before a start is expected on site. Ideally there should be a longer period so that by the time a scheme reaches the early years of the programme, it will have been well developed and its cost, planning profiles and characteristics defined.

It is wrongly assumed that schemes are or can be introduced into investment programmes in strict order of priority from established lists of desirable items which have been set out in order of importance. While this may be the aim, in practice, schemes can only be included in programmes if their practical planning position and estimated costs and planning date match the uncommitted money available, not only in the first year of expenditure, but in subsequent years. At the beginning of any financial year, the first charges against capital resources are the ongoing schemes from the previous year which may be subject to delay or cost increases. New starts of projects in the year in question obviously create commitments, not only for that year, but for the years which follow and, therefore, there has to be a 'viable mix' of schemes with differing expenditure characteristics.

RHAs have to operate more than one type of capital investment programme. Not only can funds be earmarked centrally, but even the normal capital resources made available to regional authorities have to be apportioned between funds earmarked for major schemes (over £2 million), small building and engineering schemes, capital equipment programmes, e.g. X-ray equipment, whole body scanners, block allocations for area authorities, etc. The salaries and wages of the works professionals and support staff employed particularly at regional level, whose duties are mainly connected with design and building work, are also a charge to capital funds. There is therefore a range of options which a regional authority can take up in the apportionment of its capital money. Also virement can be employment from capital to revenue or vice versa offering another potential choice.

Similar, albeit more limited, ranges of choice are open to area authorities and, particularly in teaching areas, there can be quite significant demands made upon capital allocations for the replacement of medical and surgical equipment. Equally at area level, virement can be employed to create non-recurring revenue for maintenance of building and plant and equipment replacement.

Preparation of costing information for a capital investment programme is provided by works professional officers, on occasions in consultation with private design consultants who have been retained for certain schemes.

An important factor in preparing and managing a capital investment programme is the planning of 'lead time', i.e. the time required to prepare the scheme for the contract stage and the start of works on site. As periods up to five years can be involved, depending upon the size and complexity of the project, planning (and managing) the briefing, design and approval of schemes is of utmost importance. Each project or scheme should have a timetable (management control plan) prepared at the outset, to establish the earliest practicable start date. Close monitoring of the progress of schemes in the planning stages is essential if the management of the capital programme is to be effective. It is notoriously difficult to control the rate of progress of a building contract once it has been let, and therefore the 'safety valve' in any programme where costs escalate is to delay the start of new works on site as well as to extend planning timetables for design and approval stages. Because of the interplay of cost and time for schemes or projects within the expenditure programme, 'domino effects' can be observed when there are particularly excessive variations in cost or time characteristics on projects which have started on site. Also there is a significant body of case law surrounding construction works and large claims can arise on contracts which have to be funded from the authority's capital resources.

Authorities are permitted to carry forward (to the next but one following year) any capital underspending on the cash limit for any financial year provided that this shall not exceed 10 per cent of the cash limit. All overspendings are similarly deducted from future years.

Apart from the capital programme *per se*, authorities have to be very conscious of staffing and recurring costs arising out of completed capital schemes. Indeed, additional revenue costs arising from new health building projects can be a limiting factor on committing new work.

Planning, design and construction of a health building

Projects and schemes for inclusion in investment programmes emerge as expressions of objectives identified in service planning activities by particular authorities. At a certain point in time, an outline policy for a project emerges and this forms the basis of the brief (in this sense meaning terms of reference) for the project team which will be established and charged with the responsibility for carrying the project through the various planning, design, construction and commissioning stages in accordance with DHSS and the relevant RHA or AHA policies and procedures.

The DHSS may well select projects and schemes for monitoring and control within regional programmes and similarly RHAs can select schemes within programmes operated at AHA level. All health authorities are required to follow DHSS health building procedures (Capricode). Such procedures are supplemented from time to time by other directions issued by the Secretary of State on building and engineering matters.

Capricode consists of Health Building Procedure Notes (HBPN Nos. 1-6) and was originally issued in the form of the first procedure note in 1967. In 1974, the reorganisation of the NHS, the Cruikshank Report recommendations, and the revised requirements of the restructured NHS, brought about a revision of Capricode. Appendix 2 of HPBN No. 1 describes in detail the work which is required to be done at each stage on a major project and indicates the executive responsibility and sources of guidance available to the project team. It is perhaps necessary to distinguish between project and scheme. Capricode defines the project as 'the completed development work envisaged in relation to any individual hospital or health service site . . . a project may comprise one or more schemes and one or more phases. A scheme and a phase will normally be identical in work content but in some circumstances a scheme may be broken down into two or more phases'. A scheme is usually recognised as work which is planned to proceed straight through design to construction in one continuous operation and will be normally the subject of a single contract.

Capricode originated as a philosophy but, as has already been mentioned, it has developed into a detailed bureaucratic procedure. The original concept was that, given the observance of generally accepted parameter indicators, schemes could proceed at regional level without the detailed and wasteful control from the centre which was the practice before 1964. A philosophy inherent in the code was that one should not normally set out to build a project without being sure (as far as this is possible) that one knew the outcome of one's actions. The principles were that decisions ought to be capable of being arrived at with the minimum of effort and therefore cost; that as a project moved through the process the focus of attention and accuracy sharpened from general approximations down to quite precise and measured costs and design; and that at a particular point in the building process the matter became a wholly technical issue for purposes of preparing working drawings and building the project, with the client interests being reactivated for commissioning purposes.

The original 1964 version of Capricode reflected these philosophies in the following way. Each stage of the process could be said to answer certain questions, viz:

Stage A: What do we want? Where do we put it? Are we likely to be able to afford it and is it to be phased?

Stage B: What is the management control plan? What are the 'on-costs' likely to be arising out of the particular site selected? What are the whole hospital policies, i.e. how will the components of a project relate one to another in terms of goods, people and things moving onto the site, into the building and within the building? What is the budget cost to be for the departments to be included, based on standard departmental cost and area guides? What are the on-costs based on the development control plan?

Stage C: This stage was concerned with the finalising of the detailed sketch plans and operational policies, room data sheets, furniture and equipment costs. At this stage the revenue implications would have been finally determined (as far as this was possible). The final cost for the project was established and at the end of this stage, theoretically the client disciplines (medical, nursing and administration) withdrew from direct involvement in the process having been satisfied that they understood precisely the nature and content and cost of the building they were seeking to provide and were eventually to receive.

Stages D and E (working drawings and contract stages) were seen as being wholly technical in content, implementing the decisions reached in Stage C. Planning of the commission stage could start at any time after Stage B. The various stages do not have to run sequentially, indeed, a maxim of project planning is that in order to prove one particular stage, outline work has to be undertaken in the subsequent stage. In practice this meant that Stage A approval was based on outline work from Stage B and, similarly Stage B budget costs were, in part, proved by Stage C outline design work.

The 1974 revision of Capricode produced the following, much more bureaucratic, designs stages:

Stage 1:
1A outline project policy
1B briefing of project team
1C outline management control plan
1D assessment of functional content
1E site appraisals
1F cost and phasing
1G approval

Stage 2:
2A management control plan
2B site selection
2C planning policies
2D building shape
2E development control plan
2F confirmation of functional content
2G budget cost
2H selection of contract method
2J approval

Stage 3:
3A notional cost plan
3B design brief
3C sketch plans
3D equipment schedules
3E check on design
3F detailed design
3G summary cost plan
3H approval
3J tender documentation

Stage 4:
4A contract
4B construction
4C engineering commissioning

Stage 5:
commissioning (to start any time after Stage 3E)

Stage 6:
evaluation.

There is no point in amplifying this since Capricode and other official guidance material is accessible and must in any case be used by people involved in a project.

Cost control

Control of costs properly begins long before any contract is let. Both the briefing and the design stages are subject to a series of cost checks. Cost control is vital irrespective of the size of the project.

HPBN 6 of Capricode deals comprehensively with the question of cost control.

A budget cost is established early in the planning process at Stage 2. From this budget cost, a notional cost plan is prepared, i.e. the elements of the building and services are apportioned appropriate amounts from the global cost.

The brief from the client should be regarded as being 'frozen' at the beginning of Stage 3, and thereafter, the closest scrutiny needs to be given by the project team to monitor proposed changes, either to the brief or the design, which have cost implications. Change usually means increased costs or delay. Sometimes a decision may be made to amend the design before the invitation of tenders, and sometimes to incorporate any change during the contract period. In general, the latter course of action should be avoided if at all possible because it tends to bring with it both time and cost penalties in the contract. Sometimes essential changes are better held until the contract is complete and then effected by means of post-contract alterations or additions.

Cost control needs to be applied not only to the building and engineering elements, but also to equipping and revenue headings of expenditure. Costs for these items should also be refined in parallel with mainstream design and building cost control.

In the public sector tenders should always be competitive (though it is sometimes better to negotiate) and it is preferable that tenders for the main sub-contractors (mechanical and engineering and lifts) should always be invited wherever possible prior to, or concurrently with, tenders for the main building contract. Building contracts are not usually entered into without knowledge of the effect of tendering on the principal sub-contracts involved. Unconventional methods of tendering require the prior approval of the DHSS. In any case any method of tendering other than by competitive tenders, even on small projects, will usually require a variation of standing orders by either the RHA or AHA. Standing orders generally provided for appropriate arrangements to be made in the case of other than the lowest tender being accepted. On large projects, the DHSS operates a system which requires RHAs to producc evidence that they are satisfied that the degree of preparation of the scheme is such that it can be brought to completion once the contract has been let without any foreseeable delay (DS(36)75).

The tender stage is a particularly crucial one in terms of cost control. Cost reductions may have to be effected to bring the cost of works within the approved sum and this usually requires the exercising of a value judgement as to whether the reductions in specification or omissions from the design necessary to bring costs down are acceptable.

Once the contract is let, there is a need to exercise continuing cost control. DHSS guidance (DS (43)75 and DS (184)75) refers to comments made by the Comptroller and Auditor General to weaknesses in the control of health building contracts. The Committee of Public Accounts has also dealt with the same subject. On very large schemes subject to DHSS control, RHAs are required to provide quarterly reports on the state of contracts.

Contract management is heavily cost orientated because in the contract stage, time (i.e. delays) ultimately can be expressed in terms of costs (claims on the client from the contractor for delay, or vice versa). It is therefore essential so far as possible to keep any variations in the contract stage to a minimum.

Commissioning of new health buildings

Capricode Stage 5 deals with the commissioning of new buildings, which is an activity that can start any time after Stage 3E. This means that once the final sketch plans have been agreed and all concerned are aware of the total cost implications (revenue and capital) then the client representatives can divert attention to the task of making arrangements for ultimately accepting the completed building and bringing it into use. Meantime the design professions can proceed with what is essentially a technical process of delivering a building against cost and time parameters which have been established.

Bringing into use a new health building of any size is a complex task, not only because health buildings are by nature complex but also because a large number of people with a wide range of disciplines and skills are making acquaintance with the building for the first time. They need to become familiar with it and absorb (and modify) the assumptions and planning intentions which went into it. There is a tension between the planning intention as expressed in the completed building and the customs, practices and attitudes of the staff who are coming into contact with it for the first time and will be expected to exercise their skills within it and give it a purpose. There is a need to develop good familiarisation techniques so that the intentions of the designers and planners are understood and potential frustration arising from misunderstanding or misuse of the new accommodation can be avoided.

The fundamental point about commissioning is that it is the transitional step from planning and construction to operational use. This is true of the building itself as well as of operational commissioning, for there can be a quite complex technical commissioning programme for testing the engineering system (ventilation, heating, lighting, lift installation, etc.). Within the commissioning period there is a potential conflict between the need to complete a technical construction process within the time and cost limits and the need for those taking over the building to be assured that it is suitable for the purpose for which it was intended.

Another point to be made about the building itself is that AHAs and commissioning teams need to be aware of the liabilities of the building contractor for defects in the building and the effect this might have on short-term alterations to new accommodation that commissioning organisations may suggest. Care needs to be exercised in order that the contractor/client relationship, which was brought into being to create the new building, is not in any way prejudiced or compromised by activities on commissioning. On the other hand the commissioning team must not be made to feel that the new building is sacrosanct and has to be made to work as it is when patently in some situations that is not possible.

In recent years changes in legislation relating to health and safety at work, and fire regulations, have necessitated adaptations and modifications at the commissioning stage.

Operational commissioning needs a management plan in which all the tasks are identified and their inter-relationship specified. Primary information for the commissioning organisation is the material produced during the planning stages (operational policies, room data sheets, etc.). These are not always produced with commissioning in mind, being geared to the furtherance of the design and construction stages, and they may not be up to date. The project team responsible for a scheme should see, as part of its remit, the need to secure an adequate corpus of documentation for commissioning purposes.

A team approach is required for commissioning, as for planning, and, particularly in the early stages, a strong co-ordination/management plan is necessary. With the passage of time and the build up of momentum this becomes less important as the new development takes on its own identity as a corporate entity. It may be considered necessary to appoint a full-time commissioning officer to manage or co-ordinate the programme of agreed activities. The co-ordinator and nucleus of officers reponsible for commissioning processes must have a clear relationship with the agency (AHA or RHA) responsible for the new building and also with existing services which may be transferring to new accommodation.

A King's Fund publication, *Commissioning Hospital Buildings,* provides a valuable guide to the whole range of commissioning activities. Most of them are to do with basic procedures and situations which most people will normally encounter at some time in their working lives. The commissioning process, however, tends to concentrate these experiences over a very short period in a way that highlights deficiencies that are not apparent in the normal tempo of working activity. Thus people coming into new departments may have to think for the first time how they are going to run a department, whereas previously they have followed a tradition without much question or critical analysis. Similarly, the question of procurement of large amounts of equipment or the need to appoint large numbers of new staff and organise recruitment campaigns tends to raise questions which in the normal course of events are not so pressing, e.g. standardisation of equipment, preparation of orderly procurement and requisition systems, staff appointment systems and policies, etc.

Part of the commissioning arrangements may be the organisation of an official opening ceremony, though it may fall to area or regional headquarters as a separate exercise. These occasions make such demands on time, staff and tact that their value has been questioned. At one level they can be justified as public relations exercises but it may be that they fulfil a deeper need as a social equivalent to a *rite de passage.*

Evaluation

Capricode calls for an evaluation or 'design in use study' to be undertaken as the last stage in the programme for new health buildings. Considering the effort, time and cost devoted to the planning, designing, construction and commissioning of such buildings, it seems logical that there should be a conscious effort made to find out how successful the building is in fulfilling the purpose for which it was constructed, i.e. in meeting the need which was originally identified and led to its construction. Yet there have been few such studies in the NHS, and those mostly in the early years of the building programme.

A King's Fund report on evaluating new hospital buildings suggests that the work should be undertaken by a multidisciplinary team. It asks four basic questions: Why evaluate? What to evaluate? When to evaluate? How to evaluate? Before undertaking evaluation, management will need to decide whether the study will provide useful information for future planners and designers; whether the information likely to be produced is worth the expenditure of time and money; whether there are any timing problems; whether the study is related to any existing design in use studies; how the results will be communicated to those most likely to be interested in them; how far the experience of the evaluators will affect the results that can be expected and the speed with which they can be produced; and whether the experience of taking part in the study will be useful to the evaluators. It may be that a consideration of these questions, taken with the knowledge that new health buildings are usually overtaken by changes in medical practice and technology, social expectations and changed economic circumstances, has discouraged evaluation.

Mistakes and omissions are bound to occur in new buildings, and most of them are discovered during the commissioning process. Health authorities should have a procedure for the identification of defects and deficiencies in new buildings and for their analysis and consideration with a view to rectifying them. This procedure should take account of the defects liability period in the contract. Some of the identified defects and deficiencies will be capable of rectification, but others will not and these will have to be overcome in use by changed operational procedures and noted for future planning. Some apparent deficiencies can be attributed to changes in operational policies or procedures since the building was briefed or designed.

Rectification at commissioning stage or later is, of course, no substitute for systematic evaluation but, desirable though the latter may be in principle, it is doubtful whether in most cases it justifies the cost.

Estate management

It could be argued that one of the weakest features of health service management has been in relation to the care of the estate, i.e. the land, buildings, grounds, plant and equipment which the service must have in order to deliver an acceptable level of service. Indeed it was not until the publication in 1970 of the Woodbine Parish Report on hospital building maintenance that the concept of the hospital estate and the comprehensive task of estate management gained currency in the service. Hospitals have, of course, always been concerned with building and engineering maintenance, but as the delivery of health care has become more technologically orientated, more dependent on sophisticated and controlled environment and equipment, its relative importance has increased.

The 1974 reorganisation of the NHS saw the advent of a more comprehensive works organisation at regional, area and district levels than had previously existed for the hospital service, with the introduction of the senior post of works officer at each level. The consequences of the new arrangements were the subject of frequent complaints from nurses and sector and unit administrators; urgent repairs, it was said, did not always receive prompt attention, and the works department might shut down a service for routine maintenance without the agreement of the hospital departments that would be affected. These difficulties were a consequence of the management arrangements whereby local works staff were accountable to the district and area works officers, the latter being a chief officer. The restructuring now pending, with its emphasis on local management and the accountability of functional managers to the unit administrator may overcome this difficulty. It would be a mistake in this context to overemphasise the difficulties and controversies arising from the arrangements for functional management; it is more important to emphasise that since 1974 the service has had a more comprehensive concept of estate management, and a works organisation more suitable for undertaking it.

In 1972 the DHSS issued the first draft sections of 'Estmancode' — Estate Management (Building, Engineering and Grounds) Practice Code, which will form a comprehensive guide. Much of this has yet to be published, but an outline produced by the Department gives a good idea of the scope of estate management:

Planning and controlled maintenance expenditure
Planned maintenance and inspection systems
Management of the maintenance programme (including a framework for reviewing performance)

Executing maintenance work
System of planned preventive engineering maintenance
System of planned preventive building maintenance
Use of directly employed labour
Staff aspects
Maintenance stores
Grounds and gardens maintenance
Relationship between hospital cleaning and maintenance

Relationship between design and maintenance
Maintenance manuals (feed forward)
Defect and performance data reporting (feed back)
Landscaping and maintenance

Published departmental guidance on maintenance
Staff recruitment
Training
Incentive bonus schemes
Shift, standby and call-out schemes
Maintenance research, including operational research and management by objectives.

Early in 1980 this scheme was revised, and it is now intended to issue the code in two volumes, one for estate management (development) and the other for maintenance and operations. The latter will be divided into six sections: planning and controlling maintenance expenditure; executing maintenance work; maintenance policy standards and efficiency; works department organisation; maintenance management information; estate management information directory.

The introduction to the code stresses the importance of the subject:

> Estate management is not an isolated, optional activity of a purely technical nature; it is an important, indispensable and integral part of the vital function of providing patients with the standard of care and treatment which the National Health Service is proud to sustain, and ensuring that all staff enjoy working conditions which will inspire them to give of their best in the interests of the patients.

This is a sound philosophy, perhaps even a statement of the obvious, and the production of the code is a welcome advance. Those sections of it which have been issued should be referred to for authoritative guidance, and it is hoped that the whole document will be available before long. It must be said, however, that it represents an ideal rather than a description of current practice, for the standards it advocates are well beyond the present financial or manpower capacity of the service. Moreover, before 1974 hospital authorities, when faced with financial difficulties, frequently chose to economise on maintenance expenditure rather than on direct patient service. This practice has by no means ceased in the reorganised service despite the strengthening of the works role. A further problem, in the view of some critics, arises from the distinction between capital and revenue budgets; since capital schemes must be kept within approved cost limits there is a tendency to make economies that eventually lead to excessive maintenance costs.

The maintenance of building, plant and grounds must be seen against the policy and procedures for disposal and acquisition of buildings and land. In 1977 the DHSS issued the NHS Handbook on Land Transactions, which had existed in draft form for nearly two decades previously. It gives a comprehensive treatment of all aspects of land and building transactions and could be seen as the administrative counterpart of Estmancode in that generally speaking it is the administrative function that co-ordinates and is reponsible for the management of the estate terrier and all legal aspects. Broadly speaking, it is regional authorities that ultimately control and make decisions on behalf of the Secretary of State in all matters relating to land and building ownership and disposal. The degree to which such duties and responsibilities are delegated to area and district levels varies by region.

For some considerable time it has been national policy not to hold more land, even to safeguard long-term developments, than is absolutely essential for the foreseeable future requirements of the service. In practice authorities have often been reluctant to dispose of land which they might possibly one day need, and for a long time there was no incentive for them to do so.

Another aspect of land and property which may not always be apparent as a function of health authorities is that of landlord. Most hospitals of any size have residential accommodation for staff, and some also have property let to other people. Estmancode would provide sound advice for the general maintenance of such properties, though some authorities are open to the criticism that they do not give such work adequate priority.

Finally mention should be made of legal arrangements about property with other parties. In teaching areas there may be arrangements entered into covering accommodation and services between health authorities and the university. (Arrangements are also necessary for capital expenditure when part of a teaching hospital development is financed by the University Grants Committee.) Particularly as a consequence of the 1974 reorganisation there are many agreements between health authorities and local authorities when property is shared. There are legal agreements with general practitioners who practise in health centres. These various arrangements, and also sometimes arrangements with housing associations and voluntary bodies, have increased the amount of administrative activity relating to the formal processes surrounding the holding and management of estate.

Wales, Scotland and Northern Ireland

The principles of planning and designing modern hospitals are much the same wherever such hospitals are built, and that is also true of other health care building and of estate management. Moreover, the management of a continuing health care building programme, as distinct from a single 'one-off' scheme, imposes its own disciplines and indeed principles. Thus, while this chapter has so far been concerned with English arrangements, most of it applies in broad terms to the other countries of the UK, the more so since the building programmes of the four countries are financed from the same source. Nevertheless there are considerable variations in the actual arrangements, particularly since 1974, and they are briefly noted here.

Before 1974 arrangements in Wales were exactly the same as in England, and for most of that time the service there was under the same Ministry. Wales was included in the 1962 Hospital Plan and its revisions. Arrangements in Scotland were separate but similar. The five regional hospital boards were responsible for capital works and the Scottish Home and Health Department performed the same functions as the Ministry of Health including some research into the design of health buildings, though on a smaller scale. The two central departments made use of each other's work. The Hospital Plan for Scotland, published in 1962 at the same time as that for England and Wales, was somewhat different in character, laying the main stress on the modernisation and rebuilding of certain key teaching hospitals and the provision of some ten new district hospitals in the other main centres of population. The Plan was revised in 1964 and reviewed in 1966. The most distinctive feature of Northern Ireland was that the Hospitals Authority undertook a major building programme some years earlier than Great Britain.

The absence of the equivalent to the English regional tier in the reorganised service in these three countries has entailed alternative arrangements for the execution of capital works. In Northern Ireland this is undertaken by the central Department itself. In Wales and Scotland it falls to the Welsh Health Technical Services Organisation and the Building Division of the Common Services Agency respectively. As previous chapters have stressed, these two bodies are not health authorities but agencies providing a service for health authorities and health boards. In this they are not in essence different from the regional works departments in England, for although the latter are departments of health authorities, and the regional works officer is a member of the RTO precisely because capital work is one of the main responsibilities of RHAs, the function of his department is to provide a service to area health authorities. This is far from saying that the agencies, or regional works departments, simply provide what the customer orders; as this chapter has made clear, hospital planning is a highly technical matter, and it is inevitable that the bodies with the expertise should have an influence on developments.

WHTSO and the CSA are responsible for the management of the major capital building programme, which will be mainly, though not entirely, hospital building. The Building Division of the CSA is also responsible for building work for other divisions of the agency, particularly the ambulance service and the blood transfusion service. The contents of building programmes are determined by the central departments in consultation with the health authorities. Health authorities and boards have their own capital allocations outside the major building programme, and for schemes above a certain cost they are expected to look to the agencies for technical assistance. In Scotland the Building Division has a number of local offices responsible for providing this assistance.

Both agencies have available to them the abundant technical advice, etc.

produced by the DHSS, though the Scottish Department has continued its practice of producing its own guidance material for authorities, and there is a Scottish Health Building Code, the equivalent of Capricode. Both agencies have to build within the national cost limits. Both follow the English practice in undertaking the full design work of some schemes themselves whilst others are entrusted to outside firms of architects and engineers. In both countries the supplies organisation is also based on the agency and therefore available, like a regional supplies department in England, for collaboration on the equipment of major schemes. Thus in all these matters there is a basic similarity of practice in England, Wales and Scotland, adapted to different administrative arrangements. Perhaps a more basic similarity should be stressed. The planning and design of health building is a complex matter calling, in each country, for collaboration between different parties and different professions; between central department, works organisation and the authority which will manage the institution when it is completed; between 'client' and 'design team'; and between the health authority and the doctors, nurses and other professional staff who will be the users of the building. And in all countries the key means of achieving most of this collaboration is the project team.

Reference

[1] Stone, P. (Ed). *British Hospital and Health-Care Buildings: Designs and Appraisals.* Architectural Press 1980

Further reading

Circulars

England and Wales

HM(71)67. Hospital building maintenance

HRC(74)37. Management arrangements: works staff organisation and preparation of substantive schemes

HSC(IS)75. Community hospitals

HC(77)6. Cash limits and the health capital programme; revised definition of capital expenditure; procedure for recovery of university share of cost of joint schemes

WHSC(IS)24. Building and engineering maintenance

WHSC(IS)66. Community hospitals

WHSC(IS)173. Works staff organisation and preparation of substantive schemes of management

Scotland

HSR(73)C37. Common Services Agency: Building Division

Official reports and guidance

Central Health Services Council. *The Functions of the District General Hospital.* HMSO 1969

Cruickshank, H.J. *Planning, Design and Construction of Hospital Buildings for the National Health Service.* DHSS 1973

DHSS. *Capricode* — Health Building Procedure Notes. 1969

DHSS. *Estmancode* — Estate Management Practices Code for the NHS. 1980

DHSS. *NHS Handbook on Land Transactions.* 1977

DHSS. *Building for the Health and Social Services: A Bibliography of Guidance Material.* 1974

DHSS. *Nucleus.* 1976

DHSS. *Hospital Services: The Future Pattern of Hospital Provision in England.* A consultation paper. 1980

DHSS, SHHD, Welsh Office. *Hospital Building Maintenance* (Woodbine Parish Report). HMSO 1970

Ministry of Health. *A Hospital Plan for England and Wales.* HMSO 1962. Revised 1963, 1964

Ministry of Health. *The Hospital Building Programme. A Revision of the Hospital Plan for England and Wales.* 1966

Ministry of Health/DHSS. *Hospital/Health Building Notes.* HMSO 1962 onwards

Ministry of Health/DHSS. *Hospital/Health Technical Memoranda.* HMSO 1962 onwards

Ministry of Health/DHSS. *Hospital/Health Equipment Notes.* HMSO 1962 onwards

SHHD. *Hospital Plan for Scotland.* HMSO 1962. Revised 1964, Reviewed 1966

SHHD. *Design Guide: Health Centres in Scotland.* HMSO 1973

SHHD. Scottish Health Building Code. 1 *Procedure for the Preparation and Approval of Individual Projects.* 1976. 2 *Cost Control.* 1977 *Land Transactions Procedure.* 1978

Other publications

King Edward's Hospital Fund for London. *Evaluating New Hospital Buildings.* 1969

Millard, G. *Commissioning Hospital Buildings.* King's Fund 1975

Pütsep, E. *Modern Hospital: International Planning Practices.* Lloyd-Luke 1979

Stone, P. (Ed). *British Hospital and Health-Care Buildings: Designs and Appraisals.* Architectural Press 1980

11
Health service supplies

The Royal Commission pointed out that the NHS spends over £900 million a year on a wide variety of equipment and supplies, including food, fuel, bed-linen, surgical dresings, surgical equipment and drugs as well as major items of scientific and medical equipment. With continuing inflation the actual figure will have increased since then, the scale remaining about the same. Supplies is not an aspect of health service management that attracts a great deal of attention except from those directly involved in it, and in fact it received less than two pages in the Royal Commission's report. Yet it is obvious that with expenditure on this scale supplies management is of vital importance, affecting practically everyone working in the service. At a minimum, the best value should be obtained for the money spent; if possible — and most people concerned with supplies believe it is — less money should be spent, the savings being diverted to other services.

Whether an organisation provides intangible services or manufactures nuts and bolts it needs a supply of goods, materials and services. Normally that supply comes mainly from other organisations, the responsibility for the arrangements resting with the supplies function. In nearly all large organisations supplies is the function or department responsible for correlating all the requirements for goods, materials and services coming from outside the organisation; for arranging the purchasing; for receipt and inspection; for storing and controlling stocks where appropriate and for delivering the goods to the user. The supplies function in the NHS has this responsibility, the only recognised exception being that the pharmacist normally orders stores and distributes drugs while the supplies officer arranges any contracts in close liaison with the pharmacist.

The establishment of a separate supplies function is an example of specialisation. It is the natural if not inevitable consequence of the growth of an organisation; the owner of a small business will personally deal with supplies as with the other functions which, with growth, are handed over to specialists. The advantages are that it concentrates in one place work which would otherwise be performed by all the managers, it allows those managers to concentrate on their responsibilities and permits a greater expertise in supplies management than would be possible if the tasks were diffused throughout the organisation. As with other specialisation it brings with it problems of communication and co-ordination.

In a factory the production managers will look for high stocks of components, materials and machinery spares to minimise the possibility of interrupted production. The accountant on the other hand will expect low stocks and a quick turnover to minimise the amount of money tied up unprofitably. Individual managers will disagree on the brand of commodities they need for essentially similar purposes. Also, users are often reluctant to commit themselves to individual products for long enough to permit economic purchases to be made. For these and similar reasons, the supplies function in industry and commerce is usually responsible directly to senior management, who can objectively balance and rule upon the various conflicting views. Equally in the NHS the supplies function is responsible to the area or regional administrator, the senior officer with an interest in the overall efficiency of the service.

There are three levels at which the supplies function operates within the NHS in England. At the national level the Health Service Supply Branch (HSSB) of the Supply Division of the DHSS is responsible for executing certain purchasing arrangements nationally, for advising the NHS on and for subsequently monitoring supplies policy. There is now also a national supply council which will take over some of these functions. At regional level there is a regional supplies officer (RSO) in each region with similar executive, advisory and monitoring roles. At area level, each AHA has an area supplies officer (ASO), occasionally one officer acting as ASO to two or more authorities. As with other functions of the NHS, there is no line relationship between officers of the HSSB and regional and area supplies officers.

Principles and methods of purchasing

There is no mystery about purchasing; everybody does it, though few people on the scale of a professional supplies officer. The principles and methods of purchasing in the NHS are basically common sense regulated by the discipline of standing orders and public accountability.

The main principles are: to establish what the user needs; to describe or specify that need in unambiguous terms familiar to the likely sellers; and to communicate that specification or description so as to achieve the supply of the required item to the user as economically as possible in the time available.

Putting these principles into practice is less easy than it sounds. If the user knows what he needs, why should it not be bought without question if he can afford it within his budget? For an isolated purchase that is sometimes possible, within the limits prescribed by standing orders. But there are very many users in the service each with their own idea of what is needed for the job. But there are fewer types of job than there are individuals; furthermore the types of job are often sufficiently alike for the same product to be appropriate for several. To put it another way, needs can and must be rationalised or standardised. The same conclusion will be reached by looking at it the other way. Brands of equipment and supplies on the market are legion and to avoid the expensive absurdity of buying small quantities of all of them in response to the preference of individual users, the choice of what to buy must be rationalised or standardised. Only in this way is it possible to use funds most effectively — which is not necessarily the same thing as buying cheaply.

The route to effective buying is via the right specification, and establishing the correct specification — which must be good enough for the purpose but not unnecessarily sophisticated — is the first basic principle of purchasing. The specification is the description, preferably written, of the item needed by the user in a form that enables the suppliers to visualise the item sufficiently clearly to be able to make or supply it consistently and in accordance with the user's expectations. The specification can be one of two kinds: either design, which describes prescisely the physical characteristics; or performance, which describes what the item is expected to do. In practice, specifications usually combine elements of both.

For a wide range of items there are published specifications, such as British Standards and Public Authority Standards, and often these may be used for NHS purchases. However, many needs are not so covered, and an original specification is needed. It is good practice to arrive at such specifications after thorough discussions not only with the users, including any processors, such as the laundry manager, but also with the trade for it would be a costly exercise to specify precisely what the user needed if by minor modifications the trade could provide it from its existing range at significantly lower cost.

The other main principle of purchasing is to ensure that the items specified are purchased and supplied as economically as possible. Purchasing costs money: the cost of ordering, the cost of receipt, inspection, storage and distribution to user and the cost of clearing and paying invoices. Estimates of these administrative costs vary. The marginal cost of each additional order is nominal, but the average cost of each order is some £3-£5. Clearly two orders should not be placed where one would do, and it is a task of the supplies department to ensure that that does not happen.

Essential to any purchase is the contract: the *offer* by the supplier of a *quantity* of goods or services at a *price or consideration* agreed and *accepted* by the buyer. How the buyer makes the contract ranges from a verbal offer and acceptance over the telephone to an official contract under seal. While the latter is seldom encountered nowadays, a written offer and acceptance are normal for all transactions of any size because unless the goods are available and delivered immediately it is only prudent to have the supplier committed in writing.

The methods of purchasing are: by individual or competitive, written or verbal, tenders or quotations; by orders against a call-off contract; by spot purchase against samples or catalogues; by repeat orders; by negotiation; from petty cash; by arranging manufacture within the NHS, e.g. in a CSSD department; or by variations or combinations of these.

Within the limits of what is permitted by local standing orders, the choice of purchasing method will depend mainly on the value of the purchase. Where values and/or usages are high or regular, and quantities can be agreed, the best method is to invite written tenders from approved suppliers for goods and/or services, clearly specifying quantities, delivery patterns and programmes and any other desired factors, and to award the contract to the tenderer offering the lowest price for the correct specification. Where the specification cannot be safely relied upon, samples should be requested as an essential part of tenders. Appropriate technical officers should be required to evaluate which samples are satisfactory for their purpose, the contract then being awarded to the lowest priced acceptable tender. If feasible a sample of, for example, the tea or the fabric being ordered should be retained for checking subsequent deliveries.

The term 'tender' is used here. For the most part terms such as tender, bid, offer and quotation are interchangeable.

Where quantities needed can only be estimated or where, because of limited storage space or the perishable nature of the goods, the quantities have to be called off from the supplier as required over a period, it will rarely be possible to have a fixed price for the whole period of the contract. Such contracts are not binding from the start; they are rather administratively convenient standing offers binding on the supplier only when an order has been placed and acknowledged.

It has already been pointed out that it costs money to place and administer an order. It is even more costly to invite tenders and subsequently schedule the offers, convene meetings to evaluate the samples and adjudicate the contract. The cost is well justified for bulk purchasing and when, as is often the case, it is a regional contract, the costs will be borne by the various authorities participating.

Other purchases call for something simpler, and at the far extreme from the regional or national contract, petty cash can be used to a limited extent for miscellaneous items below an agreed value, and is particularly useful at smaller isolated hospitals. Spot purchasing is another method for occasional use, for example where end of season sale quantities are available at favourable prices or where a small quantity is required for a trial of a new product. The method should be used with care since it deprives the purchaser of the advantage of competition by suppliers, and it should not be allowed to prejudice contractual commitments. Another method, using the supplies records, is to order by repeating a recent purchase. It is not indeed an order but rather the buyer's offer to purchase at a particular price; the supplier may choose not to accept it and the approach is naturally less effective in times of inflation. Suppliers' catalogues can be used as a basis for verbal or written competitive tenders. They may also be used for ordering by telephone. As we have said, most orders are written, and as an alternative to the telephone telex is increasingly being used since it combines the advantages of relative speed and written commitment.

Purchase by negotiation is perhaps the oldest of all ways of buying, though it is not normally a method considered appropriate to the public service. There are, however, circumstances when it is appropriate. For example, when a supplier has a monopoly of the product to be bought, or when a particular brand is strongly preferred so that its supplier has practically the advantage of a monopoly supplier, negotiation at a high level, probably national, is appropriate. Negotiation is also being used increasingly in call-off contracts incorporating price reviews. Negotiation of these requires a knowledge of price trends or neighbouring contracts.

Stores

No discussion of purchasing is possible without reference to stores; they are an integral part of buying. Only when stores are available is it possible to buy in sufficient bulk to obtain better prices, or to anticipate seasonal shortages. Stores are also an aid to minimising total supplying costs. It has already been said that the overall administrative cost of an order can be calculated. Equally, the cost of holding goods in stock can be calculated. From these two costs can be assessed the frequency of ordering and the level of stocks which will minimise total supplying costs. Third and perhaps of most importance, stores are the means of ensuring continuity of supply and consistent quality where delivery from the supplier is uncertain and where usage estimates are unreliable. Without stores, purchasing and supply to users would be at best expensive and at worst highly inefficient.

Although user departments hold a stock of the items they use regularly sufficient to last between agreed deliveries plus a small margin, these departmental holdings are serviced from the main accountable stores. They are usually part of the supplies organisation and thus the user is relieved of the responsibility for controlling the stocks and maintaining a continuous supply.

It would not be very helpful here to describe NHS stores as they exist at present, for the Salmon Report, which will be discussed later in this chapter, said in 1978 that 'it is the view of regional supplies officers that stores accommodation is generally inadequate both in size and in quality: it is often in make-shift or adapted accommodation, badly-sited, in basement or sub-basement rooms with poor access, and sometimes even unhygienic'. Ideally stores are housed in industrial-type purpose-built premises which combine sufficient storage facilities with suitable office accommodation for staff. They should be organised to provide a natural flow of work from the receiving bay through the storage and packing areas to the despatch dock. Dependent on the size of the stores and its throughput, it may be split into commodity sections or into palletised and shelved areas. The larger the store the more possible it is for staff to be specialised and the greater the need for good supervision and management. A lot of attention has been given to stores in recent years and HSSB has issued advice on a range of topics including staffing, layout, management and stock control.

Stores play an invaluable part in controlling supplies and it is preferable that all supplies should be initially delivered to them even if they are intended for the immediate use of an individual or department rather than to be put in store. All incoming goods can then be checked against a copy of the order to ensure that the correct quantity has been received, and inspected for quality and/or damage. The latter may mean calling in a technical expert. These checks ensure that any shortcomings are known to the buyer in supplies and no time is lost in contacting the supplier or carrier to put matters right.

Although deliveries are sometimes made by portering staff, stores staff are normally responsible for distributing stores to users. As such they play a key informal part for supplies in quality control and product evaluation because, as the department receiving requisitions and delivering the goods, stores is often seen as the supplies front line for communication with users.

This informal role is an extension of the more formal links between the user and the stores, which are the catalogue and the requisition. It takes longer to obtain items not in store, and may involve unnecessary expenditure, so it is important that users should know what is held in stores. A catalogue is therefore produced, in commodity sections, and the relevant sections are issued to all the main user departments. From the catalogue users select the items required. They make their orders on requisitions which, when properly authorised, are sent to stores for action. These forms are an important part of the financial as well as the supplies management system, as they provide the finance department with the necessary information to credit the stores account and debit the relevant user department's budget.

Relationships with other departments

Just as user departments depend on supplies for their needs, so does the supplies department in turn depend on other specialists. Sometimes the relationship is very like that of other departments to the specialist department concerned. Thus the personnel department will explain and advise on legislation relating to employment, etc.

Sometimes supplies has special needs. For example, the regional legal adviser is not often consulted because the supplies officer must have a working knowledge of mercantile law, but law often changes and interpretation is sometimes difficult, and sometimes his advice is essential.

From the point of view of management services there is probably nothing special about supplies, but it is a function particularly able to benefit from management services specialists. This is not only a matter of incentive bonus schemes, but also such things as advice on workplace layouts and procedures, the introduction of simple office routines or more sophisticated computerised stock control and supplies management systems. Operational research can give advice, sometimes regionally or nationally, on important policy matters such as stores and stock control.

As the department responsible for NHS funds which supplies commit, the finance department is that with which supplies relates most regularly on matters such as control of stocks and budgets, price trends, cash flow, invoice queries, payment conditions of contract, interdependent use of computers and accounting equipment and increasingly on decisions whether to buy or to lease.

Supplies departments can obtain valuable advice and information from other supplies departments either at different levels of the service or in different places.

Last and more generally, all specialist user departments have a two-sided relationship with supplies, both as recipients of a supplies service and as technical advisers on specifying, approving and inspecting commodities for which they have the necessary expertise.

The special relationships of the supplies function to the pharmacist have already been mentioned.

Suppliers

As the Royal Commission remarked, 'the suppliers of the NHS range from very large multinational companies to small local firms'. It is a duty of the supplies department to know its way round the maze of suppliers and potential suppliers. The discussion so far has assumed that the NHS deals only with reputable reliable firms. Normally this is true, and not by accident. Good purchasing and standing orders demand the conscious selection and adoption of suppliers to an 'approved list'. While much of this process depends on reference from other public authorities, it is not a finite process. It is rather a continuous evaluation carried out partly by gathering information from users, stores, colleagues and the trade, partly by visits to firms, and all supplemented by analysis of data on reject rates, standards of quality and delivery performance.

Market research is closely related to this. Existing approved lists of suppliers and ranges of products do not stand still. The supplies officer must be alert to this and take the initiative in examining new products and new suppliers. Discussions with colleagues and with trade representatives, visits to seminars, fairs and exhibitions, and regular reading of specialist trade and supplies literature all have their place.

Public accountability

The supplies department spends very large sums of money, and the scope for abuse therefore exists and must be guarded against. As in private industry, the auditor is a useful long-stop. (In passing it should be noted that at the highest level, the Comptroller and Auditor General and the Public Accounts Committee have from time to time had some harsh things to say about NHS purchasing, but they have been about the efficiency not the honesty of the service.) But if the supplies officer in the public service is to be, as he must, 'whiter than white', checks are not enough. Much more important are procedures and principles.

Health authorities are required by regulation (SI74/541) to make standing financial instructions for the regulation of the conduct of its members and officers in relation to all financial matters, and circular HC(76)20 circulated model standing orders as a guide to authorities in carrying out this requirement. Standing orders prescribe closely the procedures to be followed in arranging contracts according to a range of financial values.

Vital though standing orders are as a framework for purchasing, the doctrine of public accountability is even more important. This is not a question of honesty, for private industry no less that the public service requires that of its supplies officers. It is rather that no unfair advantage or disadvantage may be given to any supplier when business is being awarded. A company's obligations are to its shareholders, but the NHS is funded by the taxpayer and thus has an obligation to the public at large, which includes all potential suppliers. The other aspect of public accountability is the doctrine that the user, the buyer and the payer should be clearly separated to eliminate as far as possible the possibility of collusion, fraud or misappropriation of funds.

Thus public accountability requires fairness to suppliers and protection of the public's interest. It is because of this that the acceptance of gifts and hospitality, which is common enough in private business, is so frowned upon in the public service. The doctrine also accounts for the prevalence of purchasing by competitive tender even though, as we have seen, that is not always possible or appropriate. It often, of course, has the advantage of producing the best price, which is very much in the public interest, but it is also open, fair and objective.

Private industry sometimes prefers individual negotiations to the time and cost of competitive tendering, and generally the supplies officer in industry is permitted to use his discretion more freely to the benefit of his employer. However, supplies officers in the public and the private sectors are equally in a position of trust and must exercise that trust ethically and professionally.

Supplies officers in both the public and private sectors frequently belong to the Institute of Purchasing and Supply (IPS), for which membership is by examination. For the NHS there is the Association of National Health Service Supplies Officers.

The IPS has produced a code of ethics. To date the NHS has not done so, though guidance has been issued on the acceptance of gifts and hospitality. Given standing orders and public accountability it may be less necessary. Nevertheless a code would be helpful, at least in one respect. Favouritism for particular firms may start with the user, who may be swayed to believe that a particular product is the only suitable one. It is the supplies officer's task to ensure that other comparable products are fairly considered and that representatives are given no unnecessary, unjustified opportunities to press their products unreasonably to the detriment of others.

History of NHS supplies

So far we have outlined the principles of purchasing in the NHS, and the sort of organisation that that entails. But if the principles are clear, the organisation of supplies has a more complicated, and more reported on, history than many functions in the NHS, and that history must be sketched if the problems of supplies are to be understood. If there is a key to the history it is the interplay between the need for NHS management to be local and the need for supplies to be organised on the large scale which makes for the greatest efficiency and economy. Over time the emphasis has moved, though not without deviation, from the local to the large scale.

The supplies function existed, of course, before 1948, but the voluntary hospitals and the local authorities responsible for municipal hospitals were so varied in size and character that no generalisation is possible. The officer responsible was normally known as the steward. In mental hospitals the post was nearly always combined with that of clerk.

Circular RHB(48)2/BG(48)34 authorised the newly established HMCs and boards of governors to appoint a supplies officer to purchase all supplies and equipment (subject to any arrangements made centrally or for HMCs by an RHB with the Minister's consent), to maintain stocks to meet normal requirements and to distribute such stores and supplies to user departments. Authorities were not, however, required to make such an appointment. Some — on the whole the larger ones — appointed a supplies officer, some combined the post with that of secretary or finance officer, and some left supplies responsibilities with the secretary or other administrative officer without designation. It was left to individual hospital authorities to establish their supplies policy and practices, although the Minister of Health did decide to undertake central purchasing and contracting where it appeared to be advantageous. In the absence of a strong central policy, practice naturally varied; a limited range of useful central contracts were negotiated and authorities were encouraged to consider the economic advantages of joint contracting by several HMCs, but willingness to undertake these varied.

The diversity of purchasing practice was such that when in 1954 the Bradbeer Committee on the internal administration of hospitals reported it was unable even to decide the case between a supplies officer and departmental purchasing. Instead it recommended a more detailed investigation.

The Central Health Services Council accordingly set up a committee on hospital supplies under Sir Frederick Messer. Its final report was issued in 1958. The main recommendation of the committee was that joint contracting should be more actively pursued, and it issued an interim report to that effect in 1956. It considered that central contracting by the Ministry should remain on a limited scale, though at the other extreme buying should be by groups, not individual hospitals. The general approach was that no one pattern of supply would fit the requirements of all hospitals and groups and that this subject was a supreme example of the need to allow elasticity and natural evolution of the service. Whatever form of organisation was used it must remain subject to the authority of the responsible hospital group. Hence the emphasis on joint contracting, which was thought the only way of combining the advantages of large scale buying with the autonomy of hospital groups. The committee effectively restricted itself to recommending that RHBs and the Ministry should 'now take a more active part in encouraging individual authorities and their joint contracting committees by co-ordinating their activities and pooling information on matters of common interest to authorities engaged in buying supplies of the same kind'.

The committee considered that it was for the hospital authority concerned to decide whether a supplies officer was needed in any particular group. The absence of specialist supplies officers in many groups, combined with the usual reluctance of groups to surrender any of their autonomy in response to exhortation from Ministry or region, put a limit to the development of joint contracting, though some progress was made. In 1963 the Committee of Public Accounts commented on 'the wide variations in specifications used, and of prices paid by hospital authorities, for various items of furniture, equipment and household textiles which broadly serve the same basic function'. It regretted the delay in the preparation of standard specifications for these items, urging their early introduction. Hospital authorities, it suggested, might not fully realise how much money could be saved by a reduction in the range of specifications used.

As a result of these comments, commodity Specification Working Groups were set up by the Ministry and by a process of rationalisation produced useful specifications, some of which resulted in new central contracts. Of more importance, in 1964 the Minister appointed a committee on hospital supplies organisation to 'review the present organisation for the purchase and distribution of goods and equipment (other than items normally supplied as part of an initial building contract) for the hospital service in England and Wales on both capital and revenue accounts; and to make recommendations'. The chairman was J.F. Hunt, then assistant secretary in charge of the supply branch of the Ministry, and for the first time a committee on the subject included professional supplies officers.

The committee saw a number of difficulties in further developing joint contracting: a widespread reluctance by hospital groups to accept common specifications, a belief by some authorities that there was no financial advantage for themselves, a lack of specialist supplies staff in some regions and insufficient storage space in some groups. There had been comparatively little progress in the rationalisation of supplies and equipment since the inception of the NHS and one of the main reasons was the way the hospital service was organised. But unlike the Messer Committee the Hunt Committee saw no conflict between the rationalisation of supply and the responsibility of hospital authorities for the day-to-day management of hospitals. It did not accept the common belief that common specifications led to dull uniformity or to a reduction in quality.

The committee argued for a strong line of command and, seeing the need also to conform to government policy, urged the formation of an authoritative hospital service supply branch in the Supply Division of the Ministry, with compulsory powers to use if necessary. This was envisaged as an interim step towards a hospital service supply board separate from the Ministry. The Minister ruled this out, but it foreshadowed subsequent thinking. Basically the committee recommended that supplies should be organised with two contracting levels, one central and the other the area supplies unit serving a number of hospital groups, with RHBs assuming responsibility for supply activity in their regions and having power to implement policy.

Following consultations, the Minister announced his decisions in circular HM(67)95. A Hospital Service Supply Branch would be established, with at least a quarter of the staff seconded from the hospital service. It would deal with specifications, quality control, rationalisation of storage methods, national vocabulary and exchange of information, and would enter into contracts where this was financially or otherwise advantageous. Mandatory powers would be used if necessary.

RHBs were required to establish supplies committees composed of members of the RHB, HMCs and boards of governors in the region. Each RHB was to appoint a regional supplies officer (RSO) responsible directly to the secretary of the board. The RSO was to carry out such supply work as was done at regional level and to plan, co-ordinate and promote the efficiency of supply arrangements throughout the region. For supplies purposes HMCs and BGs were to be organised into area supplies units (between 3 and 8 per region). This was to meet the criteria of the Hunt Committee: units sufficiently large to justify the employment of specialist officers and to provide a viable purchasing unit, but not so large as to lose contact with users in hospitals. Supplies staff might be employed directly by HMCs or BGs, or the RHB might employ the staff direct, or there could be a combination of methods. This was a failure to insist on uniformity, and naturally resulted in a variety of different arrangements.

There was also a failure, or at least great reluctance, to use mandatory powers. For example a national uniform dress was developed for student nurses and others in full consultation with the nursing profession. It was introduced as mandatory but in wording so permissive that many authorities resisted, so that the administrative and purchase costs of nurses' dress provision is now higher than it need be.

Supplies organisation and activity greatly developed during the next few years. The newly appointed RSOs produced a paper on the economic criteria for purchasing as a guide to which contracting level was appropriate for individual commodities. The Specification Working Groups were re-formed as commodity Purchasing Advisory Groups (PAGs) which acted on the basis of the RSOs' paper and produced guidance on a still expanding range of commodities which were then purchased or contracted for at the level recommended by the PAGs. Work was started at HSSB on a national vocabulary as the cornerstone of a common supplies and stores management information system. The percentage of expenditure covered by central, regional and area contracts grew from less than 40 per cent in 1968 to nearly 60 per cent in 1974. Supplies now had a clear national structure and a stronger professional body of staff.

The Hunt Committee had acknowledged that the new system would need reviewing after a few years. That review was overtaken by events.

Organisation and management since 1974

With the reorganisation of the NHS in 1974 the hospitals supplies service took over responsibility for purchasing for community health services, in particular school health, community nursing and ambulance services. It might have been thought that the reorganised service, based as it was on areas not all that more numerous than the post-Hunt supplies areas, would have accorded fairly well with the recently established supplies arrangements. Things were not as simple as that, even though DHSS guidance stressed the need to build on progress made since 1968. The Department's advice was given in circulars HRC(73)5 and HSC(IS)73.

The first difference was that ASOs reverted to a line position with AHAs, being accountable to the area administrator. The RSO monitored them but the change somewhat weakened the relationships between RSO and ASOs. Moreover regional supplies committees were discontinued. Also in some places district supplies officers were appointed not directly accountable to the ASO, although subsequently circular HC(79)2, issued at the prompting of the Salmon Committee, required such district 'independence' in supplies matters to cease. The other great difference is that many AHAs are smaller than the former supplies areas. The Department had envisaged that smaller areas, not large enough to constitute viable supplies units, should combine to make joint appointments. It was envisaged that a grouping needed a total of not fewer than 5,000 hospital beds, particularly in geographically compact metropolitan counties. A few such arrangements were made but the Department's guidance was sufficiently loose to enable many smaller AHAs to exercise their natural preference for self-sufficiency.

Reorganisation did not make important changes at the national level. (More recent events will do so, but it is too early to describe their impact.) The HSSB, still including supplies staff seconded from the NHS, determines national supplies policy for the Secretary of State, in consultation with representatives of RHAs and AHAs. It arranges central contracts where this is agreed to be the proper level, provides advice where necessary to assist the NHS to implement supplies policy and monitors the performance of the supplies organisation.

The HSSB operates within the DHSS Supply Division and has itself nine sections each dealing with a particular range of commodities or other aspect of supplies practice such as training, equipping, stores and contracts procedure. These sections conduct the research necessary to arrive at policy decisions and, equally, put those decisions into effect, e.g. issue guidance following evaluation trials or arrange contracts and circulate the contract documents. They do not themselves make the policies. In this they act as back-up to and part of specialist advisory and working groups which include supplies and technical officers from regional and area authorities. These groups, with their closer links with the user, in turn pass their advice to the RSOs' committee. Although the HSSB on behalf of the Secretary of State has the power to decide policy and implement it, in practice decisions are normally taken only after detailed consultation, mainly through this mechanism.

As a link between areas and the HSSB, regional supplies officers meet informally every month to discuss specific and general supplies problems. Every other month, as the RSOs' committee, they meet the HSSB/DHSS officers for similar but formal discussions.

Each RSO is responsible to the regional administrator and has no right of access to the RHA, although generally he presents reports to the authority as required. He may have a department staffed with specialists, principally to enable him to negotiate regional contracts, acquire equipment for major new buildings and advise the RHA and AHAs on all aspects of supplies and storage policy, following thorough research and consultation. The consultation and much of the research is carried out via specialist commodity working groups which include supplies and technical officers from both regional and area levels. Most RSOs have regular meetings with their ASOs for general purpose and policy discussions. To a greater or lesser extent these arrangements provide some substitute for the pre-1974 line relationship. In some cases regional contracting is done by regional staff. Generally, however, staff are not concentrated at regional level as had been envisaged, and regional contracting is delegated to ASOs and their staff.

At area level the ASO is responsible to the area administrator with no right of access to the AHA, though in practice this access is made available by many authorities. In the few places where AHAs share an ASO, the ASO and his staff are paid by one AHA but are severally responsible to each for providing the supplies service. Whether serving one or several AHAs, the ASO is monitored by the RSO. His functions and means of operating are similar to those at the other two levels. It was envisaged in 1974 that any supplies activity at district level would be carried out by outposted staff working for the ASO although, as we have seen, actual arrangements were not always in line with this.

Supplies procedures and stores organisation

Supplies work starts on an individual transaction when a written requisition is received in the supplies office. After scrutiny to verify that it is properly authorised and contains all the necessary details, it is checked against the authority's stores catalogue. If the item is not stocked, a check is made to see if there is a contract against which it can be purchased. An order may have to be placed for an individaul item but before it is a check should be made to ensure that any similar items, or any which may be purchased from a common source, are processed on one order if possible. This is easier in larger supplies offices where the staff specialise in commodity ranges. Articles neither in stock nor on contract are purchased in accordance with the principles discussed in the first part of this chapter.

All orders should be priced to avoid the need for invoices to be referred to the buyer for checking and approval, and also as part of the process of controlling the transaction at the right price. How the price is established will depend on the value of the purchase and on the authority's standing orders. When prepared and typed, orders are signed and authorised by the ASO in all cases except orders for drugs which the pharmacist handles and for certain items which the ASO may delegate. It is unusual for this authority to be delegated other than to catering officers for perishable catering supplies on contract and to assistant ASOs for orders up to a specified value.

Copies of the order go to the treasurer for invoice and goods receipt note checking, budgetary control and possibly commitment accounting; to the requisitioning department as proof of ordering and as an aid to progressing the delivery where this is not done in the supplies office; to the receiving point, where this is not the requisitioning department, to enable the goods received note to be completed for the treasurer when the items are received; and to the supplies office records.

This latter copy is used for progressing the delivery and/or for entering on the purchase record card. This card should be checked regularly both as an aid to immediate buying and also for indications of possibilities of rationalisation or of the need to have the item available in the stores.

The purchasing record marks the end of each routine transaction. It is also, however, one approach to the supplies officer's constructive work of improving purchasing and supplies performance for his authority. Research on both existing and potential new products and suppliers depends on information and on its analysis in conjunction with users, the trade and other technical experts inside and outside the NHS. Through informal discussions and formal meetings of groups such as nursing procedure committees and supplies working parties, trials of new products are arranged, existing products rationalised and their performance monitored.

Activities such as these show the advantage of large supplies departments. When there are larger numbers of supplies staff they can specialise in particular ranges of commodities and their deeper knowledge provides a better service to technical officers, who in turn gain increasing confidence in the supplies staff.

At this point it may be appropriate to mention training. ASOs like all functional managers, are responsible for the specialist and professional training of their staff. Supplies staff, however, are relatively few in any one area and consequently most supplies training and development has been done at regional and national levels. A specialist working party at HSSB has initiated and developed various courses, some of which are necessarily national. Some, however, such as supplies foundation courses and courses for storekeepers, were designed as models or packages for local use.

Stores can best be understood if the stores is seen as both user and supplier. The general role and duties of stores were outlined earlier in this chapter. As a user, the stores must control its stocks, ensure that the goods received are correct in all ways, locate them correctly and ensure that the housekeeping is properly carried out.

When a stores requisition is received, the procedure is analogous to placing an order, except that stores receives all copies of the requisition except the one often retained by the requisitioning department. After the requisition is checked to ensure that it is complete and properly authorised, stores staff select the goods and marshal them ready for distribution. Stock records are adjusted from the requisition. Copies are used for confirming receipt and for passing to the treasurer to complete the cycle by crediting the stores ledger and debiting the user's or other appropriate budget.

It has already been said that at present a good deal of stores accommodation is unsatisfactory. That is not altogether surprising, for in the competition for limited capital expenditure, developments directly related to patient care are more attractive, and for long the supplies function did not speak with a strong voice. Yet purpose-built, properly designed stores undoubtedly increase efficiency and there is a strong economic case for large central stores. Although they entail extra distribution costs, and distribution points at the main hospitals served, they permit smaller stocks to be held and fewer staff to be employed than when stocks are spread over a number of stores, and they make it possible to buy in the largest and most economical quantities. They are in fact an essential element in the policy of large scale purchasing. It has been official policy since the Hunt Report to establish large central stores and some have been built, but progress is uneven.

Stores are managed by the ASO. The stores manager or controller may be responsible directly to the ASO or through an assistant ASO. Internally the main stores duties are stock control and recording, goods receipt, inspection and location, stock checking, materials handling, order packing and preparation for distribution, and internal housekeeping. A large store allows specialisation by commodity and by staff, though too much specialisation inhibits ready cover for absences.

Although not all features of supplies work can be described in this chapter, mention at least must be made of one other responsibility. It is summed up in the 'Grey Book' role specification for the area supplies officer: 'He arranges storage and, where necessary, operates condemning procedures and disposal of stores . . . Sees that all storekeepers in the Area understand the format and processes of stores documentation and procedures for losses, conversion, repair, condemnation and disposal of goods'. It is put rather differently for the RSO: 'In accordance with standing financial regulations, establishes procedures for conversion or repair, condemnation or disposal of goods and operates losses procedures'. In this context reference should also be made to inventory control.

Purchasing for capital schemes

The previous chapter dealt with the planning and building procedures for capital schemes. Here we are concerned with the purchasing and supplying of equipment for these schemes. Although an essential part of the supplies function, it is carried out separately from day-to-day supplies work. There are several reasons for this.

In the first place, this purchasing is charged to the capital not the revenue account and, for large schemes, is a regional responsibility. Secondly the two activities require different patterns and timescales, and if they are performed together one or the other is liable to suffer. Capital work on a particular project is intensive but relatively short, and if all the work is concentrated at region the problem of peaks and troughs is minimised. Finally, the range of supplies purchased for capital is different from that covered daily in the supplies office and calls for a different specialist knowledge. In capital schemes the emphasis is on durable furnishings, furniture and equipment as opposed to short-term consumables, which are the main concern of the average supplies office.

The equipment purchased for capital is grouped into four classes. Group I covers items supplied and fixed within the building contract; group II items fixed within the building contract but supplied under NHS supplies arrangements; group III items supplied and fixed where necessary under NHS supplies arrangements; and group IV items with no fixing or major space or engineering implications and likewise supplied by NHS supplies.

Although capital supplies work and revenue supplies work are carried out separately it is absolutely essential that they should be treated as related activities, for decisions taken at the capital stage have important revenue consequences. This is not least important for group I items, where the purchasing decision is often left to the consultant architect or engineer. Existing standards within the user authority must be examined and adhered to unless there are very good and accepted reasons to the contrary. The introduction of a new type of electric power socket could immediately double the number of plugs and spare sockets that need to be held for many years to come, and a change from washable to disposable bedpans and urinals increases vastly the revenue and storage requirements of the hospital.

Dealing with capital supply work at region may possibly reduce the attention given to revenue consequences. Another problem with the arrangement is that it increases the difficulty of reflecting user opinion when selecting equipment. This is normally resolved by close liaison through interdependent regional and area project teams including supplies staff at each level.

The supplies role in capital work is wider than merely purchasing, and embraces the full range of supplies responsibility, not least advice on supply, storage and distribution systems, and ensuring that regional colleagues in other disciplines are kept aware of supplies implications throughout. Capital schemes must adhere to regional and national policies, including supplies policies.

The regional supplies officer has on his staff an equipment officer who usually has the staff to carry out the full supplies equipping process, although the progressing of orders and the commissioning of equipment on site is normally done by the local ASO's staff. In some regions purchasing too is delegated.

To assist the equipping process the DHSS has issued a series of Health Equipment Notes, now available in computerised as well as the original printed form. This more recent computerised version gives a particularly helpful degree of control. It incorporates regular amendments of both equipment content and costs, permitting authorities readily to see very early in the project provisional equipment lists and costs which the DHSS accepts for budgetary purposes and which can be adopted and updated from the early stages specifically for each individual scheme. Periodically, each completed individual scheme is considered against the national standard lists which are then amended where appropriate for both cost and content.

A particular problem with capital equipment work is timing. On occasion building contractors complete a job ahead of schedule, and more often completion falls behind schedule. For some items of equipment it will take up to six months or more after the placing of the order for the supplier to deliver, so that a firm date for the handover of the building by the contractors needs to be known well in advance if some equipment is not to be ordered too soon or too late. The difficulty would be avoided if there were a longer period between handover and bringing the building into use, but from every other point of view it is desirable to complete commissioning as soon as possible. The supplies department is therefore likely to be faced with premature or late deliveries. The former though they do not have the disadvantage of risking a postponed opening, present particular difficulties for it is not easy to find enough suitable space to store much of the equipment needed for a large new hospital development. It may be possible for the AHA to find the space, and sometimes it is possible for the contractor to hand over part of the new building early so that it can be used for storage. Sometimes suppliers may be asked to defer delivery. In the end it may be necessary for the RHA to provide temporary storage for this purpose. It is however a solution to be used reluctantly. Wherever possible equipment should be ordered for delivery straight to its ultimate usage point. Every extra handling is an opportunity for loss or damage; storage itself costs money and furthermore storage and handling may damage the building as well as the equipment.

In theory a new capital development, including its equipment, should be evaluated in use after some six or 12 months, but as we saw in the last chapter that is not often done. There should at least be informal evaluation. Area supplies staff should be particularly attentive to requisitions for equipment for new buildings for some time after commissioning. Such requisitions are often indications that the original equipment was unsatisfactory. There may be a case for replacement by the supplier or the region, and they may point to the need to revise specifications or equipment content lists for future schemes. The equipment officer at region should canvass ASOs for comment at least on major equipment to assist with later schemes.

Although this section has concentrated on major capital schemes which are the responsibility of the RHA, smaller schemes delegated to AHAs are dealt with in the same way, though liaison is more straightforward.

Problems of supplies policy and practice

Since 1948 the supplies function has had more than its fair share of change, criticism and reports. These things have accompanied its evolution from an underdeveloped to a fully professional service, but the evolution has not been easy or altogether satisfactory. The basic difficulty has been that supplies has two different but essentially related functions. Operationally it exists to supply the local user and is to be judged by how well it meets the user's needs. It also has to buy, and is to be judged by how efficiently and economically it performs that operation. Savings of millions of pounds are in question. Economic buying entails national, regional and area contracts, a buying organisation organised correspondingly, area stores and staff who can specialise. From the time of the

Hunt Report, official reports and pronouncements have accepted that the scale of organisation required for economic buying is compatible with the provision of a service satisfactory to local users, and supplies officers agree. However, it is natural that health authorities should prefer self-sufficiency, to have their own rather than a shared ASO, and to buy without having to co-operate with other authorities. Their main concern is with the service rather than the buying aspect, and an individual authority will not always benefit from a larger contract even when that would save money for the service as a whole. It is perhaps no less natural that ministers and the departments have been reluctant to direct rather than advise authorities to adopt officially endorsed policies for that is their usual approach to the management of the NHS. But for supplies it has been an expensive policy.

It is fair to say that supplies officers have been disappointed by the 1974 developments. Under the post-Hunt arrangements, which brought supplies outside the administrative mainstream in a semi-autonomous structure organised regionally, the function made great progress. The return of supplies to the mainstream under the area administrator in 1974 weakened the regional coherence, and with the appointment of an individual supplies officer to nearly every AHA, even the smallest, lost some of the advantages of scale. If some people see an advantage for staff in the maximum number of top posts, it is offset by a disturbing lack of posts below the top grade. More will be said about post-1974 developments at the end of this section.

Information

A basic problem in determining NHS supply policies has been the lack of adequate information. In most supplies offices and stores, records have been maintained on all regularly used items, but mainly manually and to no common coding or vocabulary system. It has therefore been impracticable to obtain reliable supplies information in a form that can be combined for even neighbouring authorities, let alone nationally, for determining policies or for making buying decisions.

The replacement of manual records with computers would have been a great improvement, but until recently supplies have had access to computers only for the stores ledger, which is not appropriate for supplies management. Even if computer time had been available there was no common vocabulary system. The Hunt Committee recognised the need for this, and in 1971 work started on a national vocabulary for supplies, compatible with treasurers' requirements. The work is not yet complete, although it should be before long; the majority of sections are now issued and progressively coming into use. Its presentation and updating have been computerised and it is also available in convenient microfiche form. Furthermore, work is now well advanced in some regions on the introduction and use of mini-computers for supplies. Also, a national working party has been examining supplies management information needs.

Relationships with users

The service side of supplies is essentially one of relationships with users, and the relationship as a whole is not to be regarded as a problem. There are, however, problems. Administration generally is most noticed when things go wrong and that applies to supplies, whether it is a failure in service or in a product supplied. There are also in any organisation misunderstandings between one department and another, and perhaps a lack of tact, and supplies cannot be free of these. A more particular difficulty is that technical officers may doubt whether the supplies officer has the expertise to buy what they want. The feeling can be particularly strong in people who for long had their own stores and placed their own orders, such as works officers and catering officers, though it is not confined to them. The doubts may be justified in that the supplies officer may well not have the knowledge to write specifications or to assess quality on receipt, and the supplies officer will always need technical assistance from users and other appropriate experts, but that must be distinguished from his professional expertise in buying. Larger supply units, which permit specialisation by staff, facilitate liaison with technical users.

In 1974 what had previously been a hospital supply service also became responsible for supplying community health services. This naturally brought transitional problems both for supplies and for users. A more permanent matter may be mentioned. Even when the commodities used in hospitals and community services are the same, the supply, issue and delivery problems are not. A good example is incontinence pads, where delivery is now made to possibly hundreds of clinics and private homes instead of one or only a few hospital stores. Even the previous pack size is often too large.

Collaboration with local authorities

In 1974 it was envisaged that there would be scope for collaboration between the new AHAs and the new local authorities on supplies, but relatively little progress has been made. While the Department favoured collaboration it gave priority to the efficiency of NHS supplies and said that no arrangements should be made which would be detrimental to this.

There are several reasons why collaboration has proved difficult. First, NHS supplies are needed every day of the year whereas, particularly for schools, those of local authorities are not. Adding a local authority's fluctuating demand for say butcher's meat to NHS orders could even discourage suppliers. Second, and another factor which might discourage suppliers or increase prices to the NHS, local authority orders would entail many more delivery points for smaller quantities of goods. The third reason is organisational. Local authority buying arrangements are less standardised than those of the NHS, and sometimes there is no central supplies officer and no central store. In these circumstances joint buying is less easy and potentially less economical.

The NHS purchases relatively large quantities of provisions, medical supplies and certain textiles which local authorities buy on a lesser scale, while the position is the reverse for building and maintenance materials and equipment. There should therefore be advantages in joint buying if the difficulties can be overcome. AHAs are making some progress, but resources have so far prevented this being high on the list of NHS priorities.

Liaison with industry

The NHS deals with most UK industries to some degree, but large as it is, NHS business is a small proportion of the total of some industries, large for others.

With certain of the latter, particularly the manufacturers of X-ray and other technically complex equipment the NHS is very closely involved via HSSB and the Scientific and Technical Branch of the Supply Division of the DHSS. Generally, however, there is little effective liaison even where the industry has a co-ordinating association.

If industry and the NHS as buyer have conflicting interests in that the one wants the highest prices and the other the lowest, each needs the other. Despite the scale of NHS purchasing, supplies arrangements are not so organised as to allow the service to exercise the powers of a monopoly buyer. While that is in some ways an advantage to industry, it is also a disadvantage. Larger firm orders would enable equipment manufacturers to plan their production more economically, with benefit both to their NHS prices and their overseas sales prospects. A more co-ordinated evaluation of new and existing equipment by the NHS also has advantages for both the service and industry.

Government legislation and policies

Supplies policies in the NHS are expected to conform to government economic and financial policy. Also they are inevitably affected by a variety of legislation and by government policies that affect industry or the economy.

The Salmon Report set out the various functions of the Supply Division and the Industries and Exports Division of the DHSS which are not an essential part of the business of NHS procurement. One of them is: 'Interpreting and applying government policy to NHS procurement — e.g. as to suppliers in breach of the pay guide-lines, conformity with EEC directives, preference for UK manufacturers, encouragement of particular manufacturers in the national interest'.

The impact of these policies — which are liable to change — is variable. They are liable to generate administrative costs even when there is little other impact or benefit. Thus the EEC Supplies Directive has extended the programme for the larger contracts to ensure that EEC firms have the opportunity to quote, but so far little if any response has been forthcoming from the additional paperwork.

There can be more impact from legislation not directly related either to supplies or the NHS. Thus the Health and Safety at Work etc. Act imposes obligations on supplies as on other health service activities. It may even have the advantage of speeding the programme of building central stores, since some stores at present in use do not provide safe working conditions.

Direct policies over the years have included encouraging exports, buying British or EFTA, and supporting development areas. However, guidance on these has usually been qualified by a phrase such as 'all other factors being equal', and the effect has been minimal.

At least since 1945 governments have pursued a range of policies designed to encourage exports, but it was in the seventies that there developed a strong interest in exporting not only medical equipment and supplies but also hospital building and planning and organisational skills, particularly to the Middle East. The DHSS was given an important role in this but clearly the NHS can help only indirectly in an export drive, though it has been encouraged to allow senior staff to be seconded for short periods to assist with overseas schemes. The chief potential role of the NHS is as a major customer for the industries concerned, providing a sound basis of predictable orders for the home market.

This was the motive for a conference held at Sunningdale in 1971 on the supply of medical equipment. It led the DHSS to attempts to arrange bulk purchases of medical equipment, but these failed because authorities could not commit themselves in advance to the expenditure. There followed in 1976 the Collier Report *Buying for the National Health Service*. The committee had been asked to review existing policy for NHS procurement and to make recommendations as to the most cost effective policy and its implementation, bearing in mind the need to strengthen the home market as a basis for exports. It limited itself to medical equipment and while recognising the shortcomings of existing procurement arrangements declined to suggest a change other than strengthening the position of the ASO in relation to district supplies. Its chief concern was with the wide range of equipment on the market — e.g. over 53 different ECG monitors and over 32 blood pressure transducers — and its main recommendation was the development of a 'limited list' approach to medical equipment, associated with evaluation. A national evaluation programme has since been launched, but the report achieved nothing towards more co-ordinated buying.

Salmon and the Supply Council

In their report on the DHSS, which is described in Chapter 5, the regional chairmen pointed to the fragmented supplies organisation, and consequently the Secretary of State established a working group under the chairmanship of Brian Salmon, to 'examine the present arrangements for procuring NHS supplies ... and to make recommendations on how to make better use of resources by improving these arrangements, with particular regard to the proposal to set up a Supply Board'.

The group's report, issued in May 1978, contains a valuable account of previous and existing supplies arrangements, and also reproduces some of the key documents. The main recommendations were that all supplies and stores staff within areas and districts should be made directly responsible to ASOs; that strong operational organisations should be established, based where necessary on groups of AHAs to form viable professional units; that priority should be given to the development of information systems and central stores to permit those organisations to operate efficiently within the wider regional and national contexts; and that the Secretary of State should establish a Supply Council mainly composed of NHS officers to advise him on supplies policies, which should be mandatory if necessary. It was considered that the recommendations would be acceptable, having been formulated by this multidisciplinary NHS-staffed council. The working group considered that if the council was not set up, the only alternative would be direction by the Department.

Circular HC(79)2 required authorities to implement the recommendation on the line authority of ASOs. After consultation, the decision to establish a Supply Council was announced in circular HC(80)1. The Council would consist of an independent chairman, seven members nominated by regional chairmen, a doctor, a nurse, the DHSS Controller of Supply and a representative of the health care industries. The major responsibility for NHS supplies policies would be transferred to it from the Department's Supply Division.

> The Council will seek the views of users before making their recommendations. These recommendations should take account where appropriate of local needs

and local initiatives. On that basis the Secretary of State is sure that the Council's decisions will earn as well as command acceptance, and accordingly he is confident that they will be acted on throughout the NHS.

The functions of the Council are set out in an appendix to the circular. In consultation with health authorities, users and the supplies industries, it is to develop policies and introduce arrangements which will enable authorities to make the best use of their supplies resources while respecting the right of professional users to select what is appropriate to their local needs. In particular it is to arrange a co-ordinated system for the evaluation of equipment and supplies and to arrange for the introduction, as resources permit, of a comprehensive NHS supplies information system. It is to advise the Secretary of State and health authorities on the organisation of supplies work, having regard to the basic organisation of the NHS and the need for purchasing decisions to be taken at the lowest level with due regard to the need for efficiency and economy. It is also to encourage a strong and innovative UK health-care industry, capable of satisfying the needs of the NHS and building up a successful export market.

In carrying out functions such as making contracts, negotiating procurement arrangements, evaluating equipment, etc. the Council will look to the supplies staffs of the DHSS and health authorities. As soon as possible the use of these services will be put on a payment basis. The Council's expenses will be borne by RHAs.

The Council has now been set up, and has appointed a chief executive, but it is too early to describe, let alone assess, its activities. While the establishment of the Council is encouraging, to set against that there is another uncertainty.

The Collier Report remarked that:

> If those responsible for reorganising the NHS had given a top priority to creating the best possible procurement system they would certainly not have placed the Supply function into its existing structure within the Service. But their priorities were different, to give Authorities at each level the maximum overall responsibility and therefore the specific responsibility for all the functions of NHS management.

The further reorganisation now pending, with its even greater emphasis on local management and responsibility, seems even less likely to be ideal from the point of view of the supplies function. At the time of writing it is not known what arrangements the Secretary of State proposes to reconcile procurement needs with the general philosophy and arrangements of restructuring.

NHS supplies outside England

So far this chapter has been concerned only with England. The principles of purchasing and supply, and much of the practice, are the same in Wales, Scotland and Northern Ireland as in England. However, two of the themes of this chapter have been the importance of scale in purchasing and the effect of NHS organisation on supply arrangements. In countries with much smaller populations and generally smaller health authorities, and where the structure of the NHS is rather different, it is to be expected that there will be rather different arrangements for the supplies function.

The differences begin at the national level. As a natural consequence of its size, the DHSS takes the leading role on general purchasing policies. It has responsibility on a Great Britain basis for fostering developments of the medical and pharmaceutical supplies and equipment industries and it negotiates certain contracts for the NHS in the whole of Great Britain. In Scotland the SHHD has no executive responsibility for contracts and its role is confined to ensuring that government policy is followed, that resources are used efficiently and economically and in determining policy on equipment, research, development and evaluation. The Welsh Office monitors purchasing, and in most supplies matters follows the DHSS line as appropriate.

For most of the time before 1974 the Ministry of Health was responsible also for Wales and the history of supplies organisation followed the same course as in England, including the adoption of area arrangements after the Hunt Report. In Scotland things were rather different. Boards of management had no standard arrangements; there were very few designated supplies officers and a good deal of supplies work fell to hospital secretaries. On the other hand the regional hospital boards, particularly the two larger ones, played a larger part, arranging many contracts on behalf of boards of management. At BoM level the secretary and treasurer was the officer responsible for supplies.

The abolition of the regional tier in all three countries, and the establishment of service agencies, has led to a similar but not identical pattern. In Wales organisation at area level and below is the same as in England, under an ASO. Nationally the Supplies Department of WHTSO under a chief supplies officer is responsible for central contracting and the management of contracts and for computerised equipment scheduling through a centrally managed system for all new major building projects. WHTSO and its chief supplies officer are advised by a number of national committees.

In Scotland the SHHD handed over its executive supply functions to the Supplies Division of the Common Services Agency, which became responsible for determining, with the health boards, the level at which contracts should be let, making or organising some contracts, providing an information service, providing a specialised service for the selection, purchases and maintenance of complex X-ray and electromedical equipment, and so on. The Division also plays an important role in the equipping of major capital schemes. As in the other divisions of the CSA, the title of the chief officer is director.

In the reorganisation circular HSR(73)C20 the SHHD stressed that:

> the future pattern of responsibilities requires a new approach to staffing at health board level. At present, particularly at board of management and hospital levels, responsibility for purchasing may lie with a number of different individuals on a 'functional' or 'locational' basis but without any real co-ordination. For the future it is essential that each health board should have an officer — full time or part-time as appropriate, but with adequate supporting staff at area and district levels — with responsibility for supplies.

This was a move towards the development of a specialised supply function though not to the same extent as it has evolved in England and Wales.

In Northern Ireland arrangements are very similar to those in Scotland, central purchasing falling to the Central Services Agency, which has a chief supplies officer.

Further reading

Circulars

HM(67)95. Hospital supplies organisation
HRC(73)5. Joint liaison committees: supply matters
HSC(IS)73. Organisation of supply services
HC(78)21. Report of the Supply Board Working Group
HC(79)2. Organisation of supply services
HC(80)1. Supply Council
WHC(79)8. Organisation of supply services
HSR(73)C20. The supplies function
NHS Circular 1975 (GEN)1. Acceptance of gifts and hospitality: relationship with commercial interest

Official reports

Central Health Services Council. *Final Report of the Committee on Hospital Supplies* (Messer Report). HMSO 1958
DHSS. *Buying for the National Health Service* (Collier Report). HMSO 1976
DHSS. *Report of the Supply Board Working Group* (Salmon Report). HMSO 1978
Ministry of Health. *Report of the Committee on Hospital Supplies Organisation* (Hunt Report). HMSO 1966
SHHD. *Report of the Working Party on Hospital Supplies Organisation in Scotland.* HMSO 1969

Other publications

Baily, P.J.H. *Purchasing and Supply Management.* 3rd edn. Chapman and Hall 1973
Baily, P.J.H. and Farmer, D. *Purchasing Principles and Techniques.* Pitman 1968
Hyman, S. *Supplies Management for Health Services.* Croom Helm 1979
Ministry of Health/DHSS. *Hospital/Health Equipment Notes.* HMSO 1962 onwards
Morrison, A. *Storage and Stock Control.* 2nd edn revised. Pitman 1974

12
Management services

For the purpose of producing a definition of the term 'management services' appropriate to the health service, it is perhaps inevitable that one should look to the most recent DHSS circular on this topic. In HSC(IS)79, the term management services is used 'to cover management consultancy type work including management survey, organisation and methods study, work study, pay/productivity work, the provision of statistics and statistical advice, computer services, operation research (OR) commissioned within the NHS and related skills or services'. In examining each of these areas, one common theme is apparent; management services draws heavily on the discipline of structured methods or procedures and, through the use of quantitative techniques, attempts to ensure that available resources are used as economically and effectively as possible.

In the next sections a brief description of each of the activities listed in the circular is given.

Management survey

This technique, initially introduced to the hospital service in the late 1960s, involves a rapid review by a number of skilled management services officers of the services provided in a particular hospital. The purpose is to introduce simple improvements (often based on good practices in other institutions) quickly. The approach eliminates most of the high cost and time consuming task of basic data gathering and analysis undertaken in conventional O&M and work study projects by utilising data gathered from past studies on comparable functions. Unfortunately, it is not a technique that has gained wide use in the health service, mainly for one reason. The dominant pressure on O&M and work study officers in the 1970s has been to introduce and, to a much lesser extent, maintain bonus incentive schemes. Therefore, it has been difficult for management services divisions to bring together a large number of O&M and work study assignment officers, even for a relatively short period of time, in order to undertake a management survey of a district general hospital.

A further factor which has militated against the use of this particular approach by management services staff is that, as line managers and departmental managers have become more familiar with the relevant aspects of management survey techniques, they have been able themselves to introduce change leading to improvements and the more economical use of resources.

Organisation and method study

Organisation and methods are primarily concerned with advice on the structure of organisation, its control systems, procedures and methods. A typical O&M study will review organisational relationships, viz. functional versus sector organisation; centralisation versus de-centralisation; span of control; delegation and accountability and job evaluation. Organisation and methods work was the first area of management services to be introduced to the health service. Amongst the early applications of O&M work study were the introduction of simple financial control and accounting systems; improved clerical and secretarial reporting procedures in medical records, medical secretarial and paramedical departments; simple organisational studies in hospital administrative departments.

Work study

The British Standards Institution's definition of work study is probably the most widely accepted:

> A generic term for those techniques, particularly method study and work measurement, which are used in the examination of human work in all its contexts and which lead systematically to the investigation of all the factors which affect the efficiency and economy of the situation being reviewed in order to effect improvements.
> *Method study*
> The systematic recording and critical examination of existing and proposed ways of doing work as a means of developing and applying easier and more effective methods and reducing cost.
> *Work measurement*
> The application of techniques designed to establish the time for a qualified worker to carry out a specified job at a defined level of performance.

It is a popular belief that work study is either only applicable to factory-type processes or is more readily applicable to such processes rather than to administrative and office procedures. This is not true. Work study can be used with equal effect to examine alternative methods of procedures of work in the office environment as in the factory or ancillary staff environment. In the health service it does tend to be used more in relation to ancillary staff work, but that is for reasons explained later in this chapter and not because it is less suitable for office activities.

Pay/productivity work

With the health service, this term has become synonymous with incentive bonus schemes, even though in industrial organisations the term is used in a rather wider context. There are basically two types of bonus scheme and these are dealt with in detail in the section on work study.

The provision of statistics and statistical advice

There are a number of statistical returns made to the central Department by health authorities. Two data sets are of particular significance, those related to staff and those related to patients.

Each year, every health authority is required to submit a series of returns on the number of staff in post at a particular date (for most of the returns, this is the 30 September in the year in question). While the value of a once-a-year census is questionable, until it is replaced by a payroll-related computer-based system, such as the standard manpower planning system (STAMP) being developed by the Wessex RHA, it is the only manpower information that many health authorities have available.

The other significant area of data is the health services patient-related information. This ranges from the SH3 return to a number of returns giving details of individual departmental workloads. The SH3 is the basic annual return in England and Wales giving a breakdown by specialty of in-patient discharges and deaths, available beds and occupancy levels, together with an analysis of new and repeat out-patient attendances by specialty. There is, in addition, hospital activity analysis which is referred to separately.

Computer services

Computing in the health service falls into two basic categories: the first is computing for the purposes of planning and operational management (included in this definition are such systems as hospital activity analysis, payroll/accounts/supplies related systems and patient master indexes). The second category is scientific computing where a computer is operating in a dedicated capacity, that is, a computer system has been designed and is used for one very specific application. An example of a dedicated computer is a computer linked to an auto-analyser in a pathology laboratory. Since the prime focus of the section on computing is related to management information and this book deals primarily with issues of organisation and management, dedicated computers are not examined. A reader wishing to pursue this area of computer application will find some references in the reading list.

Operational research

Operational research is the application of mathematics to the solution of complex problems through the construction of a mathematical model which is usually manipulated on a computer. There are, in the main, four main techniques used by operational research staff: linear programming, waiting line models, simulation models and inventory models. Linear programming is the most complex of the four techniques. It has been used to help solve a number of problems in a variety of organisations. The one main application of linear programming in the health services is the 'balance of care model' developed under the auspices of the DHSS's Operational Research Services Section.

The other techniques used by operational research officers are in the main derived from probability theory. Amongst the uses made of these three techniques are studies of out-patient scheduling intervals for out-patient departments, studies of the siting of ambulance stations and the National Coal Board Operational Research Section studies on stores and stock operations. Perhaps the most ambitious study using simulation was the study undertaken by the Oxford RHB and IBM to determine the optimum size of a maternity hospital.

Development of management services

Before 1974, management services divisions were already emerging at several regional hospital boards (Sheffield, South-East Thames and Manchester in particular). Other regional hospital boards had embryonic management services divisions with O&M/work study units; computer bureaux; statistical units and, in a very few cases, operational research units. The 1974 reorganisation gave an opportunity for integration and consolidation to occur with, so far, 10 out of 14 regional health authorities creating management services divisions. In addition, in London, the London Teaching Hospitals Management Services Division has been established for some years.

The introduction of work study services in the health service dates from the 1950s when the Ministry of Health established a central O&M unit and experimental work study units were set up by the Board of Governors of Westminster Hospital and the Oxford RHB. HM(54)64, which announced the arrangements, makes interesting reading when one considers that management services, using the term in the widest context, now manages and deploys about 2,000 administrative and clerical staff. Twenty years ago, HM(59)13 was issued by the Ministry of Health, authorising each RHB to appoint at the grade of assistant secretary one officer specialising full-time on O&M work study activities. The circular referred to the benefits that had been achieved by the two experimental units and the unit at the Ministry and stated that the Minister's view was that all hospital authorities should seek to obtain the benefits arising from O&M and work study enquiries. The role of a permanent Ministry O&M unit was 'to assist in the development of O and M and work studies in the hospital field; training requirements; and to act as a pool for the collection and dissemination throughout the health service of information of interest and value to all hospitals regarding techniques of investigation and results achieved'. While not discouraging hospital authorities from appointing additional staff, the circular made it clear that if they did so, the cost would have to be met from non-Exchequer funds.

A year later HM(60)51 asked RHBs to increase the number of O&M and work study staff by appointing support staff, though only a very modest increase was envisaged. By 1963 there were still fewer than 120 O&M work study officers in the hospital service in England and Wales. That year saw the issue of the second report of the Advisory Council for Management Efficiency, a body established in 1959 under a chairman with industrial experience, which was converted into an advisory committee in 1963 and subsequently discontinued. While it issued some valuable advice during its existence, not only on matters coming within the scope of management services, perhaps its main significance was as an indication of the growing awareness of the need for greater efficiency. Circular HM(63)71, which accompanied the second report, urged hospital authorities to make greater use of O&M and work study and RHBs to increase their staff. It said that some of the additional staff should be drawn from people with experience of nursing and also, as suggested by the Council, that young administrators of high potential would benefit from spending two or three years in this area before returning to line management.

In 1968, following the Report No. 29 of the Price and Incomes Board, HM(68)23 announced the acceptance by the Minister of the introduction of bonus schemes for the health service. The implications of the circular and the acceptance of the report were clear. The circular stated that 'some hundreds of additional work study officers' would be required by the health service and that the costs of the additional staff should be more than offset by the lower running costs arising from their work.

By the time this broad development of O&M and work study in the health service had taken place, developments in other areas of management services had also occurred. A number of RHBs had established computer units operating on a bureau basis dealing with business system transactions such as payroll, accounts and stock control; in addition, within the area of computing some other developments were proceeding. Small dedicated machines were being introduced in laboratory areas and developments which formed the keystone of the DHSS experimental computer programme were taking place. Furthermore, by the late 1960s, significant developments in operational research and statistical services were under way. The Oxford and Sheffield RHBs were probably the first to realise the potential use of statistics in operational research to help plan and manage hospitals more efficiently. The Oxford RHB and IBM built the first operational research model of a total hospital system in planning the maternity unit for Princess Margaret Hospital, Swindon. Also, following the publication of HM(63)71 and the report it enclosed there was a growing awareness of the importance of monitoring and evaluating trends in waiting list management and hospital throughput.

In 1967, Dr R.A. Cunninghame-Green, the management services officer of the Sheffield RHB, wrote a paper[1], the principles of which were to be reflected seven years later in the 'Grey Book' and subsequently in the blueprint circular for integrated management services divisions (HSC(IS)79). Dr Cunninghame-Green argued for an integrated division encompassing O&M/work study, operational research, computing and statistics. These are the principles on which most RHAs have acted.

Development of O&M and work study services

Following the issue of HM(59)13, O&M and work study steadily developed. The number of staff grew throughout the country and the range of studies based on work measurement and method study steadily increased. Assignments were undertaken on administrative organisation and a wide range of administrative and clerical procedures, including admission and discharge procedures, forms for medical records, medical secretarial services (including centralised dictation systems), personnel department and establishment control procedures, stock control and supplies procedures, information systems for stores accounting and the whole range of financial procedures; a wide range of catering studies including studies of kitchen and catering department layouts, vending machines, frozen food systems, plated meal service, evaluating ward kitchens, meal trolley distribution systems to wards, the feasibility of using microwave cookers; the provision of central sterile supply department services (either on a disposable or re-usable equipment basis); the development and installation of patient master indexes; medical records departments; job assessment and job evaluation studies; studies covering the whole range of support services, including telephone organisation and management of central switchboards; laundry and linen services, including the development of group or area laundries, linen distribution systems, personal laundry systems for nurses; the organisation and management of domestic and portering services; the organisation of group pharmaceutical services and the standardisation of a wide range of procedures; studies of postal services; stores and supplies organisation; transport organisation; the organisation of management, clerical and administrative procedures for X-ray departments; staffing studies in all disciplines of staff — professional and technical nursing, medical, administrative and clerical and ancillary staff — and, finally, O&M and work study officers were often assigned to project teams to try and ensure that the layout and design of new hospital facilities recognised that staff needed to be used as economically as possible.

In 1968, with the issue of circulars HM(68)23 and 80 (in Scotland SHM78/1968) O&M and work study services received their biggest impetus since the inception of the NHS. The government's decision to implement the recommendations of Report No. 29 of the Prices and Incomes Board, published in March the previous year, had such significance in the context of labour relations, manpower control and management productivity and the development of management services, that it needs to be considered here. The consequences of its acceptance will be looked at again in Chapter 13 in the context of personnel management.

The Prices and Incomes Board existed as part of the government's attempt to maintain an incomes policy. Report No. 29 dealt with the pay not only of ancillary staff in the NHS but also the manual workers in the gas industry, the water supply industry and in local authority services; all these had been referred to the board because of the government's unwillingness to agree to the wage increases demanded by the unions. The board concluded that the average earnings of full-time male manual workers in the NHS (and local government) were low, a much higher proportion of the men being at the lowest level of earnings than in industry generally. Negotiated rates of pay compared favourably with other industries (as did holidays, sick benefit and pension arrangements), so that the reason for low earnings was limited earnings opportunities. The relative absence of overtime earnings was not materially offset by other elements in pay, such as incentive bonus schemes and shift allowances, although in the NHS shift allowances were important enough to constitute nearly 10 per cent of average earnings. Women full-time workers were better paid in relation to the average for all industries than their male counterparts. In fact three-quarters of the ancillary staff in the health service were women, half of them part-time workers.

The board considered that there was ample scope in all four industries for increasing labour productivity. It acknowledged that in a hospital there could be difficulties in applying too rigorously some of the normal techniques of management, but it noted remarkably different staffing levels in comparable hospitals and believed, after making full allowance for the special circumstances of the NHS, that there was still plenty of room for improvement in the utilisation of its manual labour force.

Faced with the problem of low pay, the board noted that the wage rate structures in the NHS and local government were so compressed that making a worthwhile increase at the bottom would swamp many differentials in the structure and thus lead to pressure to restore them. But a general increase in wage rates would be an unreasonable burden on the taxpayer as well as being incompatible with the current prices and incomes policy. There was thus no immediate answer to the problems of low pay; the root cause was low productivity and any remedy must cure low pay and low productivity at the same time. This entailed properly worked out and controlled schemes that would directly relate pay to improvements in productivity.

To achieve this, three things were required: higher standards of management, better supervision, perhaps by better pay to attract workers to take on the responsibilities, and work study in a much wider range of manual tasks. The board was very critical of management, seeing deficiencies both in organisation and in the use of modern labour management techniques. It suggested that improvements would be more easily achieved if individual HMCs were responsible for greater numbers of hospitals and could thus provide an adequate base for a full range of management services. Subsequent developments in this direction are probably a coincidence. The immediate effect of the report was to concentrate attention on work study, which in itself of course was an aspect of management.

In many respects the board's proposals were realistic. It appreciated that a vast number of fully work-measured schemes for ancillary staff could not be introduced quickly. Therefore it proposed that as a short-term measure productivity deals should be reached with groups of staff to pay up to a 10 per cent increase on basic rates of pay in return for a saving of 10 per cent in total labour costs. However, the long-term aim should be to provide incentive bonus schemes through which payment was not only related to performance, but also by an acceptance of flexibility in working methods.

A substantial number of interim schemes was quickly introduced throughout the health service. This was followed much more slowly by fully work-measured schemes. In some instances, the cause for slow progress was the reluctance of ancillary staff to expose themselves to a work study investigation. However, full-time trade union officials were keen to seize the opportunity and the real stumbling block to a rapid introduction of fully work-measured schemes was not apathy by the workers but a lack of work study staff, together with the unwillingness of some managers to understand and manage bonus schemes.

The basic approach on the interim bonus scheme is simple. A work specification is established for a particular department and the total labour costs over a reference period of thirteen weeks are examined. In full consultation with the staff, by changing shift arrangements, reducing overtime or manning levels and by increasing flexibility, costs are reduced in two stages each by 5 per cent. As each cost reduction is achieved, a 5 per cent bonus is payable to the staff operating the scheme. However, the interim scheme is only a stopgap measure until a fully work-measured bonus scheme is introduced.

The fundamental aim of either an O&M study or a work study is to improve productivity. A description of the issues explored in introducing a bonus scheme describes the approach adopted in most studies.

There are a number of reasons for poor productivity including an excessive range of activities required from individual employees, which do not permit them to develop skill, expertise and rhythm in their work; excessively high standards of work; poor quality control; poor equipment or inappropriate equipment; poor departmental layout and inefficient working methods; a lack of management control and information systems resulting in poor manpower and plant productivity coupled with material waste and idle labour; inadequate plant maintenance; poor working conditions and inadequate safety precautions; and a lack of control or motivation amongst both staff and management.

The basic approach in an O&M or work study project is very similar. There are a number of key sequences to be gone through. First, the organisation or department being studied can either be examined in a systematic manner arising from a preliminary survey or else the order in which the study takes place is geared to tackling the greatest problem areas first. In the survey a full examination is undertaken of the cost and productivity of labour, materials, machinery and plant as well as looking at management control, information and planning systems, plant layout and labour turnover. Second, a description is made of the way all staff think tasks are undertaken followed up by a process of recording how jobs are actually done. There are a number of ways in which records rather than written descriptions are made of the way tasks are undertaken. A description of the principal charts is set out below:

Process chart. Charts in which a sequence of events is portrayed diagrammatically by means of a process chart symbol.

Flow process chart. A process chart setting out the sequence of the flow of a product or a procedure by recording all events under review using chart symbols, e.g. 1. man type — a flow process chart which records what the worker does, 2. material type — a flow process chart which records what happens to material and 3. equipment type — a flow process chart which records how equipment is used.

Multiple activity chart. A chart on which the activities of more than one subject (worker, machine or equipment) are each recorded on a common timescale to show their interrelationship.

Flow diagram. A diagram or model substantially to scale which shows the location of specific activities carried out and the routes followed by workers' materials or equipment.

String diagram. A scale plan or model on which a thread is used to trace and measure the path a worker's materials or equipment travel during a specified sequence of events.

Once the existing patterns of work have been recorded, they are examined with the aim of eliminating unnecessary operations, identifiying the best location, sequence, employee and methods to undertake the work. Once the revised process and pattern of working has been agreed, then the following factors should be considered. First, it may be necessary to re-train operatives and managers. Secondly, it may be necessary to introduce new materials and improved methods of management control, and the agreed performance standards for the bonus scheme. Finally, in the context of method study, it is important to maintain schemes properly. Ideally, no scheme should go for more than two years before it is reviewed and, where necessary, adjusted.

It might seem that the easier part of a work study project is to record what is actually happening and that the more difficult part is to determine, through a process of measurement, the most efficient way of undertaking a particular task. Fortunately, the first steps to measure work and produce reliable indicators were taken at the beginning of this century. Therefore, most of the techniques are well tried and developed. The main techniques used to measure work are time study; synthesis; PMTs (predetermined measured times); rated activity sampling; and analytical estimating. The first work measurement technique, time study, is an approach which requires the work study officer to record the time taken to perform specific tasks by a competent operator operating an agreed procedure. The work study officer uses his professional judgement to 'rate' the speed at which the operative is working and to make adjustments to ensure that the values given to particular tasks are neither unrealistic in terms of setting impossible targets for workers nor are slack, thus permitting unfair productivity gain by the employees. Clearly, as a whole range of time studies on common procedures are taken, it is possible to use another technique known as synthesis. This is based on the approach that once standard times are agreed for a whole range of tasks, then all the O&M and work study officer need do is to simply record the tasks being undertaken. He can then refer to his standard data sheets for agreed work study values, add the appropriate allowances for the working conditions and then produce the final time required for each task. A further development of synthetic values is a whole range of systems including predetermined measured time systems; method time and measurement; clerical work data; basic work data; master standard data. All of these systems rely on predetermined values and the work study officer is simply required to record the movements or tasks undertaken. Another method of measuring work is rated activity sampling. It is a technique based on probability theory. The work study officer carries out a series of random observations of tasks being undertaken and, from these random observations and by using the rating factor, calculates the overall standard time for a task. Another way of calculating the time required to undertake tasks is simply by comparative estimating. That is, to determine time standards by comparing the work measured with a similar task for which the time values are known. Finally, one other method used is analytical estimating. This is a method that requires no observation by a work study officer. Agreement is made with a supervisor of the precise tasks to be undertaken. The tasks are then broken down into the basic elements and then time values from synthetic data (such as predetermined measured times) are applied to the tasks, building up an overall time for each task.

When constructing a bonus scheme, the management services officer needs to determine the basic activities and the system through which high performance will be rewarded. In addition, it is necessary to look at the relationship between bonus and overtime, whether there is to be any control on the total level of bonus to be earned, the amount of redeployment of manpower to introduce the scheme and the cost of such redeployment, whether the scheme will be group based or individual based and, if group based, what provisions will be made for individuals who do not wish to participate. Also, consideration needs to be given to what contingency allowances should be included, what dispute procedure will operate in the event of a disagreement about time values, what bonus payment will be made during sick leave or when operatives are unable to work at bonus levels through no fault of their own, and finally what arrangements will be made for both sides to withdraw from the agreement should it fail to operate to their satisfaction.

There are basically two categories of scheme in operation in the health service: measured day work schemes and variable schemes. There are two types of measured day work schemes: measured day work and graded measured day work. The procedure for a measured day work scheme is to establish a work specification, calculate the standard hours required to meet the work specification, set the performance levels (at anywhere between 75 per cent and 100 per cent) and then install the scheme. Under a measured day work scheme, the staff working within the scheme receive an unchanged bonus. With a graded measured day work scheme, the same procedure as for a measured day work scheme is followed, but the bonus earned is calculated from the actual manpower hours input to the scheme. Thus, if overtime increases or the gross level of manpower input to the work group increases over a bonus period, then the bonus could fall. The weakness of a measured day work scheme is that it presumes that the standard hour values are attained each week regardless of holidays, sickness and so on, so that workers can be working much harder than normal in order to meet the work specification but do not receive any increased bonus for their efforts. The graded measured day work scheme is better than a simple measured day work scheme because an allowance is made for the standard hours input by the work group. However, with this type of scheme, it is management which is liable to be at the disadvantage rather than the employees. Because in times of sickness and holidays, unless the work specification is tightly controlled (and in the health service it often is not), the employees may skimp their work and attract a higher bonus for what overall is the same level of output. For example, domestics may skimp cleaning and dusting in rooms; catering staff may serve the same total number of meals but reduce the choice and use more prepacked foods resulting in a higher overall cost to the organisation but ensuring that their bonus increases; portering staff may simply cut out the frequency with which they perform certain routine tasks such as mail rounds or by saying they are short staffed get other staff such as nurses to do some of them. Poor supervisory control of graded measured day work and measured schemes in the health service is compounded by the fact that supervisors receive a bonus.

The other type of scheme in use in the health service is a variable scheme. This type of scheme relates earnings directly to output and is of particular use in laundries, CSSDs and works departments. In that the scheme is output related, it should, if properly managed, be the best type of scheme to use and control, though effective monitoring is difficult.

Management services have put a great deal of effort into bonus schemes since 1968. Has it on balance been of benefit to the health service? The question is not easy to answer. Undoubtedly some benefits have arisen. In the late 1960s it was extremely difficult to attract ancillary staff of any quality in some big cities because take-home pay compared badly with that in other types of employment. Improvements in the recruitment and retention of staff since then must be at least partly due to bonus schemes. Another advantage is that there has been a substantial reduction in the total number of employees in health authorities where bonus schemes have been introduced on a wide scale, and overall the numbers of ancillary staff have not increased as much as other grades of staff in the service. However, there have certainly been disadvantages and many of them derive from the fact that while bonus schemes were envisaged as tackling jointly the problems of low pay and low productivity the main incentive for introducing them has been to deal with low pay. If they are to be judged from that point of view they are at least a partial success in that the staff involved have had more, sometimes considerably more, take-home pay. But the benefits of this have been uneven, with consequences pointed out in Chapter 13, and overall there does not appear to have been increased staff satisfaction. The unions have continued to complain of low pay.

Bonus schemes have to be negotiated with staff through the unions, and this appears to have been the main reason for the large increase in union membership since 1968. While it would be too simple to see this strengthening of the position of the unions as the direct cause of the industrial troubles which afflicted the service in the 1970s, it was at least a precondition. Leaving that aside, bonus schemes in themselves are a potential cause of industrial disputes when the expected earnings do not materialise or when efforts are made to correct a scheme that has got out of control.

The unions, despite their initial doubts, have been keen to press for bonus schemes as a means of improving pay. Unfortunately line management has not often shown a similar interest in them as a means to greater productivity. The initiative has normally come from a trade union officer on behalf of a particular group of staff and it has fallen to the work study officer to make a study, explain it to the staff and negotiate with the unions. All too often the line manager has left it to the management services department; he has not always understood the scheme fully, or been committed to it. He has, however, to live with it. After a time staff learn to manipulate a scheme; absenteeism rises, sickness rises, overtime earnings go up and bonus earnings geared to overtime increase take-home pay dramatically. Once a scheme is out of control it requires a monumental effort by both a committed line manager and management services staff to get it back under control. Not infrequently NHS auditors have drawn attention to schemes out of control, and the Committee of Public Accounts has also commented unfavourably.

It is salutary to note the remarks of the Advisory Council for Management Efficiency — remarks which went unheeded in 1968 but are still relevant.

> The introduction of formal incentive schemes cannot be recommended as a general practice without the most careful study. For lasting and effective results, they pose difficult problems even in the manufacturing industries; in the hospital service, the difficulties are far greater and managements as now organised are not well suited to the task. A few hospital activities such as laundry work, canteens or porterage might lend themselves to 'the measurement of work' and output incentives under work study control and an experiment is now being tried at Guy's Hospital. But even in such cases, a high level of management and supervisory control is necessary; far more needs to be done in training management in activity analysis, in organising work and planning generally, before embarking on incentive schemes. Unless incentive payments are properly used and adjusted systematically as conditions change, they can lead to disgruntlement rather than benefit. There is still the major problem where to stop; once the scheme has been started for one or more sections, others will naturally call for the opportunity to increase their earnings even though fair relation between results and rewards may be virtually impossible to determine. To grant them their request might involve all the bad features of 'lieu bonuses'. To refuse them may lead to dissatisfaction or worse. There is, too, the difficulty of drawing a line between the hourly paid and professional and technical staff.

If on balance the advantage of bonus schemes to the service is at least doubtful, what of the future? There seem to be three possibilities. One course would be a full drive to install proper work measured bonus schemes for all ancillary staff wherever possible. The schemes could be reviewed after intervals of two years and be subject to proper control by a competent, experienced and motivated line management. This might be the best course in terms of potential for improved efficiency but it would continue to make heavy demands on management services staff and it may be that they would be more profitably deployed in other ways. It would also make heavy demands on line management. Whether or not line managers can be persuaded to be more involved and committed than in the past, there will be other pressures on them at a time when management costs are being cut. Another course is simply to accept that after introduction and some initial control schemes are merely a device to permit staff to earn more money with some notional increase in productivity. If this pessimistic course is rejected, the third course is to try to find new ways forward. Some steps have been taken by the Oxford RHA O&M and productivity unit to do that. The approach is to take a bonus group on a district basis. Thus, for example, porters may be treated as a single bonus group throughout a district. An intensive study is done of their working practice and manning levels, overtime and shift payments, and then a productivity scheme is installed with elementary manpower controls and agreements from staff side to change patterns of work and redeploy staff from well established units to poorly established units, reduce overtime and sickness and change working practices in order to achieve a target saving of 20 per cent of the total costs. Simple controls are installed to ensure that the line managers can operate the scheme and a bonus of 20 per cent is paid to the staff.

It will be appreciated that this is little more than an updated version of the interim scheme. However, it does have an element of work measurement with a method study input coming from both staff and line managers. Hence they are more committed and more interested in making the scheme work. The demands made on management services staff are substantially fewer than with a conventional work study scheme and since there is no sophisticated work measurement the management services department has not built up a major maintenance problem for itself in the future.

Computers and information systems

What is a computer?

A computer can be regarded either as a very complex, advanced electronic and electromechanical device or simply a piece of equipment that can be used to carry out certain tasks. The latter view is the correct view for a manager to adopt, for the raw material of a computer is data and the end product is information which can be used either as part of a process, or to assist in the making of a decision.

The means of achieving the transition from raw, unstructured data to useful, well presented information is through the use of a system. This is a loose term covering actual computer programs, documented procedures, specially designed forms and training material. Such a system is developed by a systems analyst, and the detailed work of writing, testing and documenting the computer software is the work of a programmer.

A computer configuration must consist of essential elements:

1. a means of inputting data;
2. a processing unit;
3. a means of outputting information, and
4. a means of storing data for the longer term.

1. Data input

The process of converting raw data into a computer legible form is expensive, principally because most methods require a great deal of manpower. Consequently, as computing has developed, techniques have become available which aim to reduce or remove the two-stage transcription problem whereby data are written or coded, then keyed or punched on to some medium such as punched cards, paper tape or magnetic tape. Data captured 'at source' are cheaper and can be more accurate because of the reduction in handling. One technique for this are optical mark reading (OMR) which is used quite widely in the NHS. Data are directly coded in a series of marks on to specially preprinted forms which are directly scanned by an optical reader, the marks gauged, and computer output produced on a medium such as magnetic tape.

Visual display units (VDUs) are becoming increasingly used for direct data capture, particularly in relation to real-time systems. These devices are directly connected to a computer and can consequently be controlled by the programs in the processor.

Computer systems which cannot justify such techniques have to rely on a separate intervening process of keying. The vast bulk of data processed in the NHS now are transcribed via key-to-disc schemes, which are essentially purpose designed to stand alongside computer systems handling up to perhaps about 30 key stations. Each key station is controlled by an operator who, depending on the type of work being handled, can key 8,000 to 10,000 characters in each working hour. Needless to say, this task is highly repetitive and boring, so important data such as payroll are generally rekeyed and automatically verified against the original version. In this way, differences are detected and corrected. Once corrected, batches of data are accumulated on to a reel of magnetic tape, to be read on the main computer.

2. Processing

The central processor unit (CPU) is the heart of a computer configuration, controlling as it does all the data handling between the input and output devices or 'peripherals'. The feature of a computer which gives its main value is the ability to program the CPU with very large sequences of coded instructions which precisely dictate what is to be done with each piece of information, either in terms of comparing it with other items (e.g. is the patient over 65 years old?); of carrying out arithmetic operations (e.g. subtract total deductions from gross pay to give net pay) or of simply assembling data for presentation (e.g. take the patient identification details from the in-patient file, and the results from the clinical chemistry autoanalyser results file and print test results).

Each such program carries out a discrete process within a system. In a complex system such as the NHS Standard Payroll System, there may be 80 or 90 programs, some dealing with weekly paid staff, some for monthly staff, some for implementing pay awards, etc.

Each program is written in a language appropriate to the task and computer in use, with an almost exclusive use now of 'high level' languages such as COBOL, FORTRAN or MUMPS. These languages all have a highly structured form, requiring a strict adherence to a set of rules for the use of the various commands or instructions within the language. Each utilises what appears to the innocent observer a subset of pidgin English.

3. Data output

A clear, useable presentation of results is essential within any computer system. Information must be easily understood, relevant and available within the required timescale, if it is to be of value.

The printer has for a long time been the main data output device and is likely to continue to be so for some time. However, newer techniques have begun to make continuous stationery obsolete. Microfiche, which is a means of recording formulated output on postcard sized sheets of microfilm, offers enormous opportunities for space saving and cost reduction where large volumes of information have to be stored and referred to from time to time. A complete Patient Master Index (PMI) of 750,000 patients can be held in a postcard sized box no more than a few inches deep, on a desk. Equally valuable, multiple copies of that index are very cheap to produce and can be held in many sites, obviating the need for telephone calls from peripheral clinics and hospitals to a central hospital index.

VDUs were mentioned earlier as suitable devices for data capture in certain circumstances. They may also be used as output devices. They are particularly suited to the retrieval of limited volumes of information in response to an interrogation initiated from the VDU keyboard. A PMI system may have the facility to allow such interrogation to complement the microfiche production.

A clerk at a busy admission office may use a computer to search through the PMI selecting patients with similarly sounding names, using a techniques of soundex codes. The VDU can then present the clerk with a series of options, from which the correct patient can be selected by address or date of birth or sex, or a combination of any of these. The benefit of this is a greatly reduced likelihood of duplicating index entries and, consequently, a better chance of the correct notes following the correct patient.

4. Data storage

In any system, it is obvious that some data are transient, e.g. stock levels, while other data are required to be kept for a much longer time, e.g. stock item descriptions, units of issue. These 'master' data are generally held on magnetic backing store, such as magnetic tapes or magnetic discs, until required. The choice between the two is generally concerned with the question of the length of time which is acceptable before the data can be referred to when they are required. Tapes are cheap and relatively slow and discs are expensive but any item can be retrieved from an online disc in a very short time (one second) when it is required. Most computer systems of any size have both media available, with data stored on either medium according to the criteria above and controlled by a library system which prevents accidental erasure, identifies correct versions of files, and ensures that in the event of a disaster such as a fire in the computer centre, the system data can be recovered for operation at another site as quickly as possible.

How are computers used in the NHS?

For the purposes of examining this question, it is appropriate to categorise the main types of computer in use into three groups:

1. mainframe computers;
2. minicomputers;
3. microcomputers.

It must be emphasised at this stage that this grouping is by no means hard and fast; indeed, as the capabilities of machines change, the distinctions become increasingly unclear. However, for our purposes, these headings are best regarded as indicative of a type of equipment used for the solution to a group of problems.

1. Mainframe computers

These are generally regarded as the physically large, expensive, multipurpose machines which are found at regional level in the NHS. They require special buildings, with controlled environments, and frequently operate round the clock because their great cost limits the expansion which would enable them to cope with the work in a one or two shift operation. The regional computers are nearly all ICL machines, bought as part of the standardisation programme of the early seventies, and costing between £0.5 million and £0.75 million. Several of these 1900 series machines are now being replaced by 2900 series, with conversions for the whole of the UK likely to be completed by the mid-1980s. Machines in this latter series are likely to cost on average between £1.0 million and £1.5 million. Installation costs and system conversion costs will add to these figures. The revenue cost of running such a machine to provide the required service is around £0.75 million per annum, at current costs. Unsurprisingly, staff costs account for the bulk of this figure.

The greatest part of the work undertaken on these machines is batch processing, which as its name implies, involves processing of batches of data submitted to the machine as part of an overall process. A payroll is an obvious example of such a system, with batches of data for weekly staff being submitted on an area-by-area batched basis, at a particular predetermined time each week. Other applications which are typically processed on such computers are:

- Child Health systems, for maintaining records of vaccinations and immunisation programmes, and school health examinations;
- Financial accounts, now increasingly prepared using the Standard Accounting System;
- Payment of creditors, involving printing large numbers of cheques, remittance advices and schedules;
- Hospital Activity Analysis, which collects admission, discharge and diagnostic information about in-patient incidents.

2. Minicomputers

This is a generic term with as many definitions as there are manufacturers and models. Generally speaking, however, they are relatively small computers, typically occupying a normal single office space, requiring a less rigorously controlled environment, and costing much less than a mainframe (£20,000 to £150,000). It is usual to find them associated with real-time applications. These are computer systems which are generally available all or most of the work cycle, be it from 9 a.m. to 5 p.m. or a 24 hour, 7 day week, as in an admission area, and which are required to process information in a time cycle that directly influences the event or process occurring at that time.

A good example is the hospital admission procedure. Several large hospitals now have real-time in-patient systems, which have totally replaced the bed board principle and all related tasks associated with identifying patient locations, empty beds, etc. When a patient is admitted, either from a planned admission or an emergency, details about that person, his/her location, consultant, etc. are entered into the computer system. That bed is then instantly known to be occupied, obviating the need for a routine daily check of bed occupancy. The course of events in the admission section is thus controlled in ‘real-time’, as a subsequent patient would not be allocated to that bed.

This simple example can be taken a stage further to exemplify the wider benefits of having such a centrally held record. If the admitted patient has some tests, and requests for analysis are sent to the pathology laboratory, a common error in a non-computerised system is that the result is returned to the point of request, after the patient has been transferred to another ward. In such cases, tests might be wasted. In a study at one hospital, the incidence of such lost results was 12 per cent. By providing the pathology laboratory with a means of checking the *last known* location of the patient, this wastage was greatly reduced. This facility could be via a VDU to the in-patient computer system, or, as many laboratories themselves now have real-time computers, it is possible to have two minicomputers communicating with each other automatically.

In terms of their total cost and, even more dramatically, in terms of their cost performance, minicomputers are becoming cheaper and are consequently being used in an increasingly wide range of tasks. Programming languages and associated general purpose software have improved enormously during the 1970s to the point where they compare very favourably with the older mainframes.

Languages such as BASIC and MUMPS are sufficiently easy to learn and use for minicomputers to be no longer totally dependent on specialist computer staff to design and implement simple systems. Many users have learnt to define solutions for their own data handling problems and have acquired and applied minicomputers in the manner in which they should be used, i.e. as another type of aid to decision making, or to handle routine clerical chores.

By and large, the preceding examples of the uses of minicomputers relate to stand-alone machines. Increasingly, however, such machines are forming part of distributed networks, which are a means of associating the equipment configuration much more closely to the point when the data are available, or the information required, but without unnecessarily or wastefully duplicating system components. For example, the data-capturing process is one that is best done on-line, in order that validation and, if necessary, correction can be done when the source document is in front of the operator. Consequently, it may be that the cheapest solution to such a requirement is to locate a small minicomputer close to the source of data, with a number of VDUs connected to it. Its main work might then be no more than driving these VDUs in collecting, checking and organising the input data. The significant point, however, is that that computer would be linked, perhaps to another central minicomputer, but more probably to a mainframe, on which would be carried out the main processing, and the long term storage of such data as are required to be kept. By linking together a number of computers in this manner, radial pattern networks can be created, with the appropriate equipment at each physical site, as required.

3. *Microcomputers*

Such machines represent the latest step forward in the application of electronics technology. They are based on microprocessors, which are central processing units contained in a single component occupying no more than a square inch or two on a board. Assembled into complete systems with memory units, and VDUs, printers and discs similar to those used on mini systems, they represent a relatively low cost (£4,000 to £15,000) solution to data-handling problems where numbers of transactions, or total file volumes, are fairly small. However, this area of computing is changing rapidly and is well beyond the stage when a microcomputer could handle only one VDU. Their cost implies that they are best suited to dedicated applications and, for example, one might very reasonably consider purchasing such a system to maintain records in a GP group practice. From such a facility, a GP or his staff could acquire information to aid practice management, e.g. age/sex registers, practice administration, FPC claims, patient care, drug interactions, etc.

Microcomputers are also frequently encountered now as part of specialised pieces of equipment, particularly laboratory and monitoring devices. In this situation, they handle the data conversion and acquisition tasks, enabling machine results to be clearly and simply presented, e.g. detection of peaks on analogue signals from autoanalysers.

How does one set about computerising a system?

It is unusual for a manager or a clinician to have direct access to computer staff. Consequently, most people have to bid for a place in the queue for centrally allocated systems, programming and operational resources. It is, perhaps, worth dwelling on these terms for a moment to ensure an understanding of these functions.

The work commonly referred to as systems analysis covers the tasks of defining the data flows, document requirement, procedures, etc. of existing non-computer systems, and translating these into a design which can be based on some form of computer. It will also give at least the output of the pre-computer solution and usually the additional information that becomes available by computerising. This whole process must be overviewed by a project management mechanism such as a joint group, with appropriate commitment at a high level of management. Once the system has been defined in fine detail, the system specification is taken to the stage of a working computer application by programmers whose job it is to program, test and document the operational system.

Once the programs have been proved in system trials, the system can be implemented in the live environment, usually in parallel with the previous system for a time. This entails a variety of tasks, which could include staff training, physical reorganisation, managerial changes, changes of duties, etc. Obviously, such tasks, which are indirect results of computerisation, must be thought of in advance, planned for and solutions prepared in time for implementation. This requires the close co-operation of managers, their staff and staff-side organisations, as well as computer staff.

Once these steps have been completed, the system moves to full live operation. This will involve handing the application over to a separate computer operations section for a mainframe based solution, or handing over the responsibility for a mini or microcomputer to the user management. Computer sections at this stage should be removed from direct responsibility, but should continue to be available on a consultancy basis to correct any system faults that appear in live operation, and to maintain the computer systems in line with changing user needs.

Associated with all these stages of computerisation, there are tasks which ought to be pursued, but which are frequently skimped or ignored. Earlier, it was mentioned that a potential user had to justify the system being tackled from the outset. This process should involve analyses of cost benefits, as well as the qualitative aspects which are difficult or impossible to cost.

After a period of live operation, user management should appraise the change and attempt to judge the extent to which the original objectives and costs were met. It is unusual for a computer application to be withdrawn, with a reversion to manual methods, but in an organisation such as the NHS it is vital that the knowledge of other projects should be a basis for decision making on computer projects.

What of the future?

To say that the future in computing happened yesterday is remarkably true for our purposes if we are referring to technology. If we are referring to NHS policy and practice in relation to computers, what happened yesterday and before that is a poor guide to the future. It ought, however, to be briefly noted because the NHS has spent considerable sums on computers and the history has followed a rather different course from that of management services generally, with the DHSS for long playing a bigger role.

In the early years equipment from a variety of manufacturers was used, but as was mentioned earlier, since 1971 there has been a standardisation programme for regional computers. This is in accordance with policy for the whole of the public sector, intended to support the UK computer manufacturing industry and to obtain the benefits of large-scale purchasing. It is also thought to have the other advantages of standardisation. Based on the assumption that the information system requirements of all health authorities are the same, centres of responsibility (COR) have been charged with developing, for the whole of the NHS, a particular standard system. Thus one RHA was given the task of developing a particular system, such as the standard accounting standard payroll, standard hospital activity analysis, standard child health immunisation and vaccination and standard manpower planning systems.

In addition to these bread-and-butter activities based on the regional computer bureaux, the Department launched an experimental computer programme in 1967, and the policy was reviewed and revised a number of times in subsequent years. The aim was to establish where computers could assist in making decisions about the allocation of resources, in improving efficiency, and in improving the quality of care. There was a wide range of potential applications and the Department had to choose the most promising. The programme was envisaged in three stages: an experimental phase financed by the Department, a developmental phase financed jointly by the Department and the health authority, and an implementation phase when the health authority bore the full costs. A considerable programme developed and, as was to be expected, some experiments proved more valuable than others, but overall the programme turned out much more expensive than had been anticipated and in 1976 some aspects of it received severe criticism from the Public Accounts Committee. The Department subsequently ceased to support the experimental programme, the current view being that the development of computing should be done in a way that predominantly reflects the needs of users. This seems to be the best approach. There were obvious attractions in a national programme and a systematic thinking about priorities, and some benefits were obtained. On the other hand, although health authorities are generally willing to accept a special financial allocation from the Department for a project, they are not always as committed to it as they would be if it were their own choice and they were committing their own funds. Also, central funding is out of line with the general approach to allocating financial resources in the service.

If the experimental programme was terminated, it was not only because of the difficulties encountered. It was also a recognition of the implications in the developments in computer technology. This brings us back to the remark at the beginning of this section. By looking at current technological developments, we can speculate on the role that computers will play in the NHS in the next decade. With the cost and size reductions already discussed, it is quite clear that mini and microcomputers will be a major growth area, tackling data handling problems previously considered inappropriate, and doing so by locating the necessary equipment in the environment of the department or whatever, where the information is required. Proven applications, such as in pathology laboratories, will become much more widely used and were it not for the investment already made in software, and the standardisation programme, we would undoubtedly see a much more critical examination of the need for large bureau machines.

Developments in bubble memories and laser technology will downgrade the importance of magnetic tapes and discs, enabling very large files of data to be held in extremely compact forms, at the point of usage. Machines of this nature will form parts of extensive networks, linking, for example, the various main sections of a group of hospitals and associated administrative functions. Voice input and output from computers is already a reality and will become increasingly important in situations where time and hand-free operation is important.

Developing more slowly than the technology are the tools for software development for the computers of the future. Account must be taken of the current and likely future shortage of skilled personnel, for while the technological potential is infinite, the supply of skilled manpower is not.

If the NHS is to realise some of the potential benefits of computing, then managers in all disciplines should identify their information needs within the context of a total information framework for a district/area/region.

Integrated information systems

Traditionally, information systems are broadly of two types. Those related to the ongoing activities of clinics, wards and departments where the information system is an essential aspect of the operational duties of a particular department, and those systems that deal with management control and planning. In the NHS, the systems have not been related and major information systems, such as Hospital Activity Analysis, have been imposed on the NHS by the DHSS. Because the information systems in existence in 1974 have been developed on a functional basis, there is no cross-relationship between the major systems. Thus, any information linking between the major systems, such as Hospital Activity Analysis system and standard costing, has to be done manually. This particular approach is dominant because most of the information systems in the health service have been designed to gather data on the workload or activity levels in particular departments rather than to identify the causal unit of workload, e.g. the patient, and to identify those resources which are used by different departments in treating patients.

The implication behind a DHSS decision in 1974 in connection with the experimental computer programme, to give priority to patient administration and hospital organisation systems and to study the use of computers below regional level was that, for the first time, consideration was being given to a comprehensive information system for the health service. Certainly, this had been attempted before and the study undertaken by Scicon for the Scottish Home and Health Department[2] had attempted to describe an integrated information system for the health service in Scotland. Unfortunately, no similar attempt had been made to describe an integrated information system for the health service in England. Thus it has been inevitable that computing and information system developments have taken place in a piecemeal fashion, totally dependent on the initiatives of entrepreneurial individuals working within the service and operating within the general policy framework determined by the DHSS.

One or two small projects have attempted to provide a different approach to computing and information services and one of the most successful projects in this area has been at Guy's Hospital. The approach adopted by the project is to identify each patient from the moment he is entered on the in-patient waiting list (or is admitted direct through the accident and emergency department) and to tag a patient in such a way as to identify the variable resources consumed by each patient in the course of his treatment. Thus, it is possible to identify and link information detailing the individual consultant, the condition for which the patient is being treated, the length of stay (in order to apportion overhead costs) and all the individual tests, drugs and procedures undertaken in the course of the particular patient's treatment. The difference between the two approaches reflects the difference between the existing system prevailing throughout most of the health service (Figure 1) and the patient administration system (Figure 2). While there are deficiencies in the system in that it only deals with in-patients, it does represent a major step forward; and in any event, since in-patients account for approximately 90 per cent of the expenditure at that particular hospital, and a far smaller proportion of patient movements, it was sensible to try and capture data on the in-patients first.

Figure 1. Existing situation

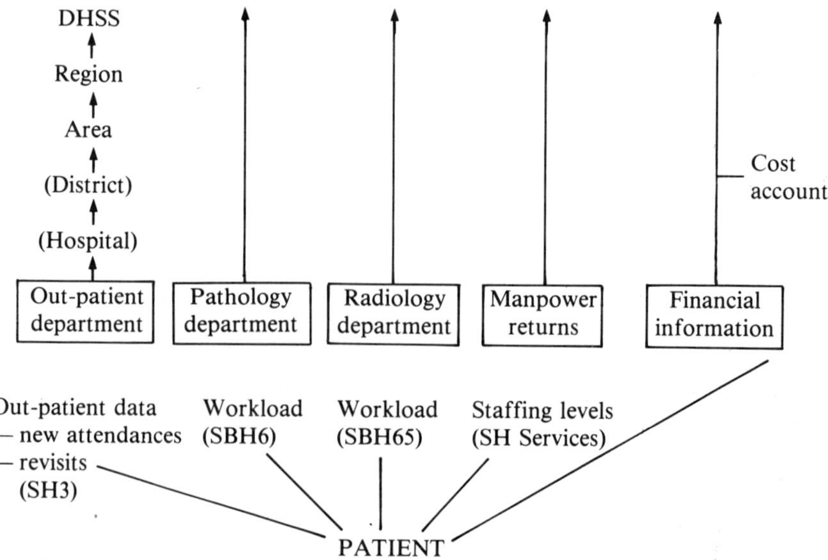

Figure 2. Patient information system

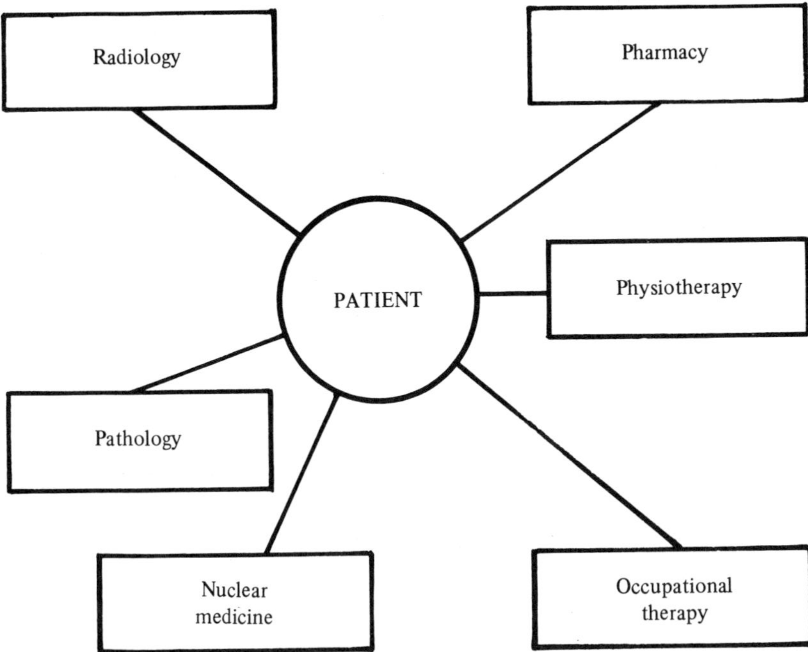

It is impossible to plan the proper use of computers and information systems in terms of the managerial needs of the organisation without first defining the total information network, seeing what is available now, then identifying a balance of the most important needs in a rank order of priority.

The complex features of an integrated information system covering health services can best be displayed diagrammatically. The diagram in Figure 3 is based in part on the Wessex RHA's monitoring programme structure. This classification is valid at each management decision level within a health region from clinic to hospital through to the RHA. At each level there are two things that differ:

— the time span of decisions between conception and implementation
— the indicator used to measure performance, for as the information centre moves away from a patient treatment area, a process of information aggregation occurs.

Figure 3 demonstrates the structure of health service information systems. The particular use of this structure is that the definition of management information required at each tier of the service can be agreed for the second level resource classification groups with manpower, buildings, stock, equipment. Those management information requirements can be applied validly to each of the services set out in the first level resource classification. Figure 4 demonstrates the relationship between the first level and the second level resource classifications and Figure 5 the relationship between the first level resource classification and care categories. It is an assumption in the framework that the definition of the management information for manpower in each level of the service will apply

Figure 3. Diagram of integrated health service information system

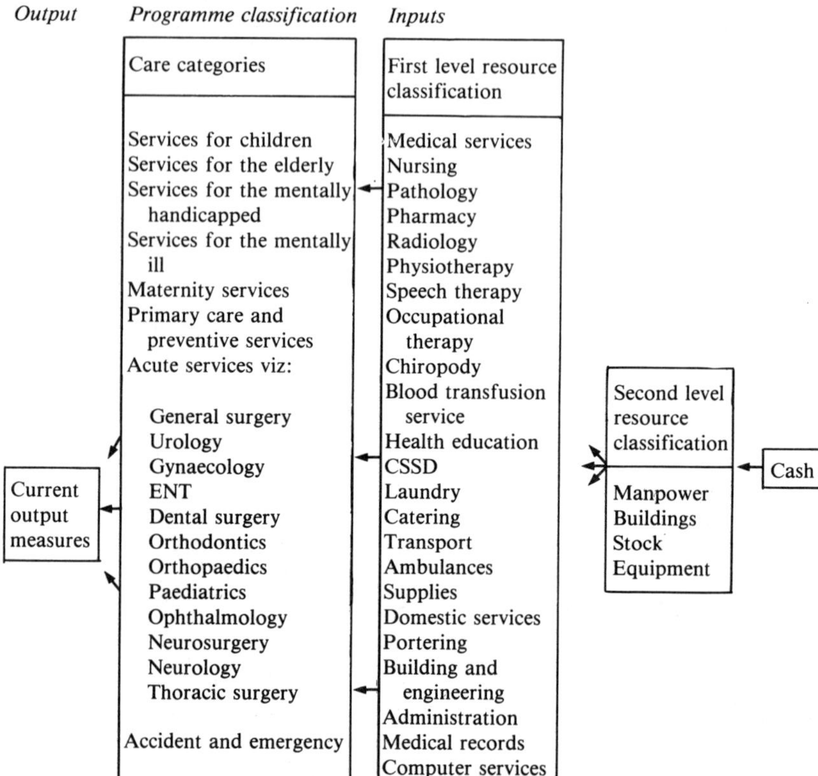

with broadly the same validity to the services classified in the first level classification of resources. This assumption enables a major part of the information requirements to be summarised in four tables. In each of these tables is arrayed the information required at the various levels, namely, ward, department, clinic, unit hospital, sector, district, area and region. These information requirements are scheduled in Figure 6 (manpower); Figure 7 (buildings); Figure 8 (stock) and Figure 9 (equipment). Against these analyses and inputs, it is necessary to array output. Figure 10 develops the information required.

Figure 4. Table relating first and second level classifications of resources

	Second level classification of resources			
First level classification of resources	Manpower	Buildings	Stock	Equipment
Medical services	●	●	●	●
Nursing	●	●	●	●
Pathology	●	●	●	●
Pharmacy	●	●	●	●
Radiology	●	●	●	●
Physiotherapy	●	●	●	●
Speech therapy	●	●		●
Occupational therapy	●	●	●	●
Chiropody	●		●	●
Blood transfusion service	●	●	●	●
Health education	●	●		●
CSSD	●	●	●	●
Laundry	●	●	●	●
Catering	●	●	●	●
Transport	●	●	●	●
Ambulances	●	●	●	●
Supplies	●	●	●	●
Domestic services	●		●	●
Portering	●		●	●
Building and engineering	●	●	●	●
Administration	●	●	●	●
Medical records	●	●	●	●
Computer services	●	●	●	●

Figure 5: Table relating first level of resource classification with care categories

First level resource classification	Services for children	Services for the elderly	Services for the mentally handi-capped	Services for the mentally ill	Maternity services	Primary care and preven-tion	Acute services	Accident and emergency
Medical services	●	●	●	●	●	●	●	●
Nursing services	●	●	●	●	●	●	●	●
Pathology	●	●		●	●		●	
Pharmacy	●	●	●	●	●		●	●
Radiology	●	●			●		●	●
Physiotherapy	●	●	●		●		●	●
Speech therapy	●	●	●				●	
Occupational therapy		●	●	●			●	
Chiropody		●	●			●		
Blood transfusion service	●	●			●		●	●
Health education						●		
CSSD	●				●		●	●

[contd.]

First level resource classification	Services for children	Services for the elderly	Services for the mentally handi-capped	Services for the mentally ill	Maternity services	Primary care and preven-tion	Acute services	Accident and emergency
Laundry	●	●	●	●	●	●	●	●
Catering	●	●	●	●	●	●	●	
Transport	●	●	●	●	●	●	●	●
Ambulances	●	●		●	●		●	●
Supplies	●	●	●	●	●	●	●	●
Domestic services	●	●	●	●	●	●	●	●
Portering	●	●	●	●	●	●	●	●
Building and engineering	●	●	●	●	●	●	●	●
Administration	●	●	●	●	●	●	●	●
Medical records	●	●	●	●	●	●	●	●
Computer services	●	●	●	●	●	●	●	●

Figure 6: Manpower management information system

	DECISION CENTRE							
	Ward	Dept.	Clinic/ Health Centre	Unit Hos.	Sector /Div.	District	Area	Region
Listing of staff by name	●	●	●	●				
Listing of staff by grade	●	●	●	●				
Comparison of staff in post against funded establishment				●	●	●	●	●
Premium hours worked (overtime, leads and bonus shown separately)	●	●	●	●	●	●		
Annual leave entitlement per employee	●	●	●	●				
Annual leave taken per employee	●	●	●	●				
Sickness taken per employee	●	●	●	●				
Length of service				●	●	●	●	●
Length of service in grade				●	●	●	●	●
Occupational coding				●	●	●	●	●
Age		●		●	●	●	●	●
Period to retirement		●		●	●	●	●	●
Qualifications	●	●	●	●				
Staff left by grade over past month, quarter, year		●		●	●	●	●	●
Staff by sex				●	●	●	●	●
Training Time lapse since last attendance on a course: Management				●	●	●		
Clinical/ operational				●	●	●		

Figure 7: Buildings and estate management information system

	DECISION CENTRE							
	Ward	Dept.	Clinic/ Health Centre	Unit Hos.	Sector /Div.	District	Area	Region
Identification of site			●	●	●	●	●	●
Area of site					●	●	●	
Schedule of buildings on site					●	●	●	
Schedule of rooms in each building on site by type/use				●	●	●		
by size				●	●			
by services within each				●	●			
Plan of site				●	●	●	●	
Plans of room-layout in all buildings on site				●	●			
Schedule of all electrical and mechanical systems, fixtures and fittings on site for the purpose of estate planning and planned preventive maintenance				●	●	●		

Figure 8: Stock management information system

	DECISION CENTRE							
	Ward	Dept.	Clinic/ Health Centre	Unit Hos.	Sector /Div.	District	Area	Region
Schedule of items of stock consumed by type classification	●	●	●					
Value per week	●	●	●	●	●			
Value per month				●	●	●	●	
Value per quarter				●	●	●	●	
Value per year				●	●	●	●	●

Figure 9: Equipment management information system

	DECISION CENTRE							
	Ward	Dept.	Clinic/ Health Centre	Unit Hos.	Sector /Div.	District	Area	Region
Identification of site				●	●	●	●	
Schedule of rooms on site				●	●			
Listing equipment in each room	●	●	●	●	●			
and giving name of equipment	●	●	●	●	●			
date bought				●	●			
life expectancy				●	●	●	●	

[*contd.*]

	DECISION CENTRE							
	Ward	Dept.	Clinic/ Health Centre	Unit Hos.	Sector /Div.	District	Area	Region
maintenance intervals	●	●	●	●	●			
cost at purchase				●	●			
cost of replacement					●	●	●	
name of custodian with managerial responsibility	●	●	●	●	●			

Figure 10: Units of patient treatment management information system

	DECISION CENTRE							
	Ward	Dept.	Clinic/ Health Centre	Unit Hos.	Sector /Div.	District	Area	Region
Unit of patient identification	●	●	●	●				
Age	●	●	●	●				
Sex	●	●	●	●				
Consultant	●	●	●	●				
Diagnosis	●	●	●					
Path. tests	●	●	●					
cost	●	●	●	●	●	●		
X-rays	●	●	●					
cost	●	●	●	●	●	●		
Drugs	●	●	●					
cost	●	●	●	●	●	●		
Physiotherapy	●	●	●					
cost	●	●	●	●	●	●		
Blood	●	●	●					
cost	●	●	●	●	●	●		●
Occupational therapy	●	●	●					
cost	●	●	●	●	●	●		
Operations	●	●	●	●				
Out-patient	●	●	●	●	●	●	●	
repeat attendances	●	●	●	●	●	●	●	
In-patient:								
date of admission	●	●	●	●				
date of discharge	●	●	●	●				
no. of moves in the hosp.	●	●	●	●				
Derived statistics throughput per bed	●	●		●	●	●	●	
percentage occupancy	●	●		●	●	●	●	
average length of stay	●	●		●	●	●	●	
turnover internal	●	●		●	●	●	●	
Nurse workload indicator	●	●	●	●	●	●	●	

Existing information systems

Nowhere in the NHS is there a comprehensive information system or set of information systems in existence. Thus, for the purpose of planning, management control and operational management, such systems as do exist are not related in a structural manner that permits the inter-system transfer of data. Some systems are extensive, such as those for finance, described in Chapter 9, but one major system used for both planning and management control which should be examined here is Hospital Activity Analysis (HAA).

Hospital Activity Analysis was introduced to the NHS following publication of HM(69)79. The system and data set were partly based on the Oxford Record Linkage Study, a project that began in 1962. The main purpose of HAA was stated in HM(69)79 as being:

> to provide for doctors and administrators both at hospital level and in the boards an information system in which details relating to individual patients are brought together for analysis; these include clinical data relating to diagnosis and operations, and patient characteristics such as sex, age, marital status and area of residence ... admission, stay and discharge.

On the discharge of each non-psychiatric in-patient, a form HMR1 is completed capturing personal, clinical and administrative information. The DHSS suggested that the following tables be produced:

1. Number of patients by age on admission and sex, by hospital, ward, and by consultant or firm.
2. Source of admission by hospital, ward, and by consultant or firm.
3. Time on waiting list — numbers and percentages of all patients according to time before admission to hospital; by sex and age; by specialty or diagnosis; by consultant or firm.
4. Average duration of stay by specialty or diagnosis for each hospital by sex of patient and age on admission.
5. Number of accident cases by type to show hospital and consultant or firm.
6. Number of discharges and deaths according to area of residence for each hospital, by sex and age; by specialty or diagnosis; by consultant or firm.
7. Disposal — home discharge, transfer to other hospitals, deaths with and without post mortem to show numbers and percentages of discharges and deaths.
8. Number of days after admission before first operation to show hospital, ward and consultant or firm.
9. Operations — patients having no operation, one operation, two or more operations to show numbers in each category and percentage of total discharges and deaths for each hospital.
10. List of operations performed and number of discharges and deaths for each type, showing age and sex.
11. Diagnostic index, i.e. listing under diagnostic headings of patients' case record numbers and other particulars as required, diagnoses being arranged alphabetically or in the order in which they appear in the ICD (International Statistical Classification of Diseases, Injuries and Causes of Death) by group, hospital and consultant, elaborated as required, e.g. to include summaries of throughput.

For the purpose of planning, the information in report (6) is probably most important. This particular report is used in RAWP to calculate the cross boundary flows and bed utilisation rates. For the purpose of management control reports (3), (4) and (8) are probably the most significant. HAA has provided important information in the past and some regions have extended the HMR1 data set to include additional information on X-ray procedures, blood transfusions and even nursing dependency levels. However, the system is not without its critics. It is expensive (estimated costs of between £3 million and £10 million); prone to error and an inefficient method of capturing data. Alternatives exist.

Reference has already been made to the patient administration system at Guy's Hospital; a system which completely replaced HAA and provides additional information facilities at a very small marginal cost. With the availability of minicomputers, microprocessors and high level program languages, there is a distinct possibility that by the end of the next decade, health authorities will have patient information which will replace HAA.

Whatever the alternative methods of data acquisition, one predominant factor will have to be satisfied if such systems are to retain the confidence of clinicians — the need to assume confidentiality. With most HAA systems a case note number and patient address are the only personal items of information completed on HMR1. However, the use of computer-based information systems for the provision of operational management and planning data will require important safeguards to be established to ensure that acceptable levels of confidentiality are maintained. National policy on the control and custody of data banks has been made clear in the recent white paper; but its provisions may not satisfy the medical profession, and each authority will need to make explicit a code governing such issues as physical access and system access.

Hospital information rooms

Reference has already been made to the use of HAA for influencing clinicians to reduce lengths of stay, waiting times and generally improve the efficiency with which resources, such as theatre time, are used.

Several studies have shown the value of presenting information on waiting lists, out-patient waiting times, bed states, occupancy levels, theatre utilisation and cost information in a central information room of a district general hospital. Clinicians respond to performance data presented in a simple, clear manner.

A particularly clear manner of presenting data either by consultant, ward/specialty, hospital or district is the Barber diagram. In the example shown in Figure 11 the performance of three districts is plotted over an 18 month period. The beauty of this diagrammatic method is that it is graphical, thus easy to understand; also, it captures in one picture factors used to evaluate the efficient use of beds. In terms of simple efficiency, the goal of each district should be to drive the graph line down towards the bottom left hand corner of the graph for this would minimise length of stay and turnover interval, while increasing the percentage occupancy and the annual throughput per bed.

It has already been demonstrated that it is within the grasp of available technology, using a minicomputer with a VDU to display not only the above information but also a wide range of cost and performance information on health service activities. Therefore, the hospital information room concept should be extended into a new dimension by interrelating hospital, community and general

Figure 11: Orthopaedic in-patients — diagram showing trends in hospital activity for each district between September 1977 and March 1979. (The diagram was developed by Dr B Barber, Regional Information Scientist, North East Thames RHA)

		Sept. 77 to March 79		
————————	District A	A	to	B
— — — — — —	District B	J	to	K
················	District C	R	to	S

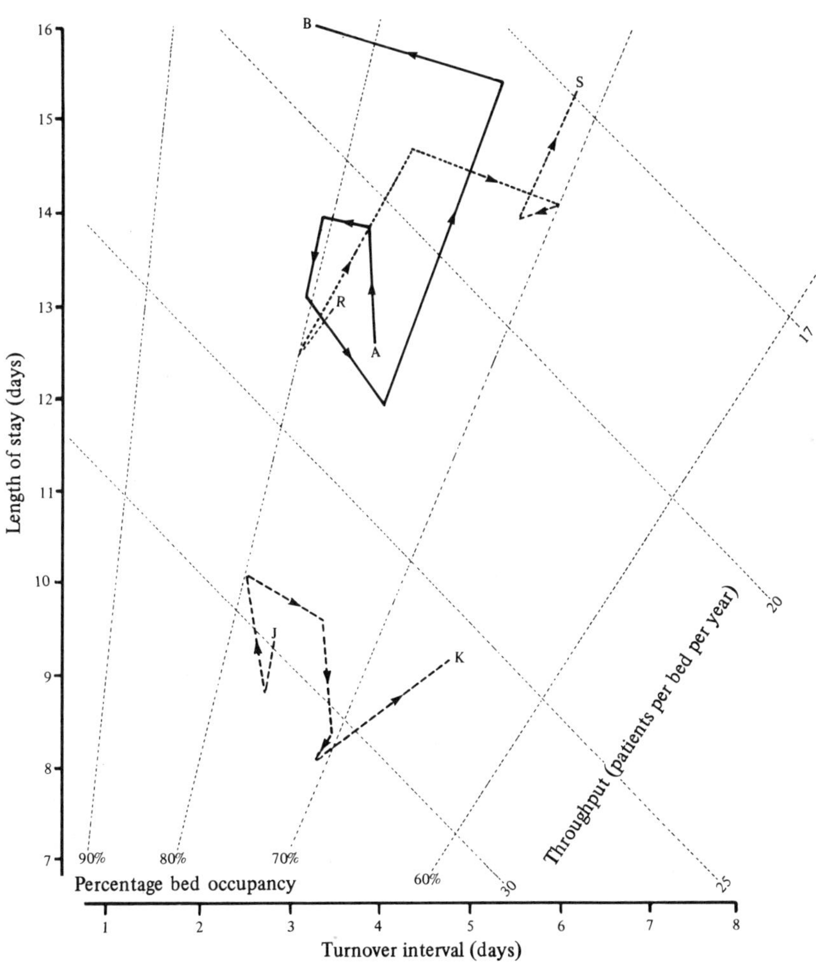

practitioner services with the purpose of delivering care quickly, and as economically as possible.

Operational research

The application of operational research to health service problems developed in the mid 1960s with the establishment of an operational research section in the DHSS and an involvement of a number of units in hospital operational research matters. Initial fieldwork studies were undertaken by the Institute of Operational Research on behalf of the DHSS (then the Ministry of Health). Subsequently, the Royal Institute of Public Administration's OR unit developed an interest in health service problems and several units were established within regional hospital boards. Two RHAs, West Midlands and North East Thames, have well established units. Two other regions, Trent and Wessex, have somewhat smaller units and Oxford possesses some semblance of an OR capability. In Scotland, work is done at Strathclyde University. Over the years, operational research has been used to solve a number of problems and its essential characteristic is that it is an analytical approach which usually leads to the creation of a model which management can use to select a particular option.

Operational research staff draw on a number of techniques in helping to analyse problems. Some of the principal techniques are as follows:

Simulation

Simulation involves the construction of a model that reflects the characteristics of a particular system. By varying the system inputs and manipulating key variables, assessments can be made on the way a 'live' situation will respond to change.

An example of a study using simulation is one in which management wishes to increase the output of a laundry at minimum cost. A model can be constructed to simulate the operation of plant and operatives within the laundry. By identifying places where bottlenecks occur, management can test the effect of increasing plant and operatives to the point at which the predicted production requirement can be satisfied at minimum additional cost.

Queueing theory

This technique, though mathematically more complex than simulation, is, in certain situations, quicker to use. Studies on ambulance stations and the number of vehicles needed at each station in order to meet the DHSS prescribed response time for emergency services (90 per cent of ambulances to arrive at the scene of the emergency call within 20 minutes) have used queueing theory.

Linear programming

This technique has been described as one of the most important, far reaching developments in management service methodology. Although it has been used extensively in commerce, particularly in chemical, petroleum and other process flow industries, it has been little used in the health service. The one major study using linear programming is the Balance of Care Model developed by the DHSS

Operational Research Section and Scicon Management Consultants, as an aid to inter-care category resource allocation.

Inventory models

Inventory models are used to determine stock levels and economic order quantities. The use of inventory models has been quite extensive in the health service following the work of the National Coal Board's Operational Research Executive on central stores within the NHS.

Network programs

There are two operational research techniques used for project control purposes: Critical Path Method (CPM) and Performance Evaluation and Review Technique (PERT). The techniques are similar and were both developed in the United States in the late 1950s to deal with the management and control of large and complex projects. They have been used extensively in the management of major capital projects; and the DHSS used PERT to manage the process of change in the period before and during the reorganisation of the health service in 1974.

It would be a fundamental mistake to consider that the application of operational research to problem solving simply requires the use of a given technique. The operational research officer will use a tried and tested technique as the starting point to assist in his analysis, but invariably he will need to develop a new model for the particular problem.

Operational research in the health service is primarily of use in planning, either at the tactical level or the strategic level. Since strategic planning has acquired such significance in the NHS, it might be useful to examine an application of operational research in the context of planning. A number of regions have used operational research in planning at the strategic level. The DHSS has also used models in this manner and has now commissioned work on the possibility of simplifying its main OR model — the Balance of Care Model — in order to make it available to area health authorities run on the standard ICL computer configuration. Although the model has only been used so far to plan the allocation of resources between health services and county social services, a pilot study is attempting to apply the model to optimise the allocation of resources between health, personal social services and the sheltered housing resource of district councils as shown below.

At the commencement of the study, it is vital to obtain agreement from professional staff (medical, nursing, social services and housing managers) on a range of classifications that can be applied to patients/clients for planning purposes. Then a census needs to be undertaken to identify the number of people actually receiving services, classified into the agreed planning categories. The next step is to classify the resources available (beds, staff — health visitors etc. — units of sheltered housing, etc.) together with the unit cost of providing those resources.

The additional data fed into the model are as follows:

1. Existing population — broken down on an age/sex basis;
2. Forecast population — broken down on an age/sex basis;
3. Assumptions about growth rates in the total sum of available resources;
4. Assumptions about achievable changes in different types of resources.

The model then iterates the data to find the solution that will provide the greatest range of services at least cost. If the proposed solution is either unacceptable or judged to be unattainable (e.g. the proposed solution may be dependent on an increase in community nursing staff that is beyond the capacity of the organisation to recruit), then the model can be constrained from developing a solution beyond a likely level of recruitment of community nursing staff. By a process of adjustment and reiterating the model, the most economical and acceptable solution can be identified.

The application of operational research to the problem of planning, particularly at the strategic level, has already been done on a small scale with benefit at national, regional and area levels. As the use of operational research becomes more extensive, it is in this area that the most effective contribution is likely to be made in order to achieve a balance and use the resources of revenue, capital and manpower to greatest effect.

Conclusions

There are several important points to make about management services in concluding this chapter. The most important is that no matter how well a management services project is done, it can never of itself be a substitute for good management. Any manager wishing to use management services must first define the problem and terms of reference for the study; second, the manager must agree the objectives and terms of reference with all staff likely to be involved in the project; third, the management services officer should meet all the staff with whom he will work.

When the project has been completed and the project report presented to the manager, then on acceptance of the report, the responsibility for the proposed change and for implementation passes to the manager, even though the assignment officer may assist this process. Thus, the manager has total control and total responsibility throughout the project.

The second point to consider is the development trends that are occurring in management services and which managers should seek to influence. There is a danger that the bulk of management services effort will continue to be spent on bonus schemes, whereas the more important tasks are efficiency studies into high cost areas, the development of operational research as an aid to planning, and the use of minicomputers and microprocessors to handle information for the purpose of better management and operational control.

The initiative for ensuring that the change in emphasis occurs lies as much with line managers and professional staff as it does with the management services staff themselves. Potential clients should make their expectations clear to enable management services staff to respond.

The last point to make is that generally the staff in management services have been recruited for their special skills so that, possibly even more than in other functional areas, their career runs separately from that of administrators in general administration. It should benefit both the staff and the service if there were more interchange.

References

[1] Cunninghame-Green, R. *The Scope for Management Services in a Hospital Region*. Sheffield Regional Hospital Board 1967

[2] Bodenham, K. and Wellman, F. *Foundations for Health Service Management: A Scicon report for the SHHD on the requirements for a health service information system*. OUP for Nuffield Provincial Hospitals Trust 1972

Further reading

Circulars

England and Wales

HM(54)64. Establishment of a hospital Organisation and Methods service
HM(60)14. Work study in the hospital service
HM(68)23. Development of O&M and work study
HM(68)80. Incentive bonus payment schemes and productivity agreements for ancillary and other manual staff
HM(72)55. Using computers to improve health services
HM(73)36. Measured day work incentive schemes for ancillary staff
HSC(IS)79. Organisation and development of management services
HC(77)11. A review of NHS computing needs
WHC(80)11. Computer services

Scotland

SHM78/1968. Linking pay with productivity for ancillary and other manual staff
SHM49/1969. Introduction and maintenance of pay/productivity schemes in the hospital service
SHM44/1970. Computer development in the hospital service
SHM51/1973. Measured day work incentive schemes for ancillary staff
HSR(73)C5. Information services in the reorganised health service: management of computers
NHS Circular 1975(GEN)75. Control of pay and productivity schemes

Official reports

DHSS. *Using computers to improve health services — A review for the National Health Service*. HMSO 1972
DHSS. *A Guide to Health and Social Services Statistics*. HMSO 1974
DHSS. *Annual review of National Health Service computing 1974*. (2 vols) HMSO 1975
DHSS. *Interim report on the evaluation of the National Health Service experimental computer programme*. HMSO 1977

Other publications

Abrahams, M.E.(Ed). *Medical Computing — Progress and Problems.* Chatto & Windus 1970

Acheson, E.D. *Medical Record Linkage.* OUP for Nuffield Provincial Hospitals Trust 1967

Buffa, E.S. *Operations Management.* John Wiley, New York 1968

Coles, E.C.A. *Guide to Medical Computing.* Butterworths 1973

Duncan, I.B. and Curnow, R.N. 'Operational Research in the Health and Social Services'. *Journal of the Royal Statistical Society.* Series A, Vol. 141, pp. 153-194. 1978

Lee, K. (Ed). *Economics and Health Planning.* Croom Helm 1979

Luck, G.M. *et al. Patients, Hospitals and Operational Research.* Tavistock 1971

13
Personnel management

It is a truism to say that health care in the western world is a labour intensive activity. It remains a basic fact that health services are largely dependent upon people to provide health education, care and treatment.

Technological advance within this century has led to a certain degree of mechanisation, but growth of the NHS since 1948 has resulted in a steady increase in both the amount and proportion of revenue consumed on manpower costs.

By the late 1970s the health service was employing directly almost a million people, about four per cent of the national work force as shown in Table 1 below. In addition, general practice doctors, dentists, opticians and pharmacists provided services in the community on an item of service basis. Staff costs accounted for over 70 per cent of the revenue budgets of health authorities. Table 1 illustrates the size and composition of the various staff groups. In all there were over 300 occupations employed within the service and this diverse and scattered work force operated from thousands of institutions and establishments within the UK.

Table 1: Total staff employed in the NHS in Great Britain as at 30 September 1978

Staff group	Number of staff (w.t.e.)*
Directly employed doctors	39,206
Directly employed dentists	3,103
Nurses and midwives	423,261
Professional and technical (excluding Works staff)	68,853
Ancillary	211,719
Ambulance	20,530
Administrative and clerical	118,716
Works and maintenance	30,777
Total	916,165

*whole time equivalent

Source: DHSS Official Statistics for England, Wales and Scotland

Hospital beds had decreased from nearly 470,000 to 407,000 over the period since the health service was established, whilst hospital treatments had doubled. The nature of health service provision had also changed considerably during the period. Developments in technology had led to increasing specialisation and more intensive treatments whilst the average length of stay in hospital had decreased.

The changes in the work had been reflected in changes in the work force. Increasing specialisation produced demands for different types of staff possessing the relevant skills and this in turn had led to increasing complexity in the organisation. The number of doctors and professional and technical workers had each tripled since 1949 while nearly twice as many nurses were employed.

The changes in size and composition of the work force took place against the background of social change which affected the NHS as much as any other employer. Educational patterns altered, particularly in the 1960s as higher education opportunities expanded, with the consequence that recruitment sources or basic education and training of health service staff also had to change. Successive incomes policies were reflected in the pressures exerted on the pay bargaining system. Major alterations in the law affecting employment and labour relations coincided with both the reorganisation of the NHS and the growth of trade union membership and changes in trade union attitudes within the NHS. By the mid-1970s the size, complexity and attitudes of the work force bore little resemblance to those of 1948 and at times the lay observer might be forgiven for concluding that health authorities were preoccupied with the problems arising from staff to the exclusion of almost any others. Indeed in 1975 the Secretary of State made it plain that the government's main priority in health at that time was to concentrate on the problems of staff morale.

The organisation of the NHS has a number of distinctive features which have implications for employers in relation to their personnel policies. The statutory position of the Secretary of State with his accountability direct to Parliament for the running of the service and, in particular, his responsibility for approving agreements on salaries, wages and terms and conditions of service, has been closely associated with the centralised nature of the bargaining machinery. This factor, together with the concept of a unified NHS, has resulted in standardised rates of pay across the country relieving local managements of the need to bargain in those areas, but presenting them with pay rates that are not necessarily sensitive to local labour market conditions.

A fundamental factor in managing health care provision is that the person who generates or undertakes the work at shop floor level is the clinician, with whom has traditionally been associated the highest status and highest earning power in the whole organisation. From this fact has flowed a number of consequences for the management of the service. The absence of any single role with overall managerial accountability derives from the principle of the doctor's clinical freedom. Clinical decisions by doctors commit resources yet cannot be countermanded by health authorities, other doctors or administrators and thus doctors cannot be managed in the conventional sense. The establishment of multidisciplinary management teams can be seen as one method of endeavouring to provide unified leadership. Team management, in turn, generates its own problems for the establishment of unified and consistent personnel policies and procedures.

Within hospitals, from the inception of the NHS, questions of recruitment, training and the application of pay rates and terms and conditions of service were largely the field of the administrator and the finance officer. In the case of nursing staff in most hospitals the matron and her senior colleagues were also involved, but in most cases day-to-day problems associated with pay and conditions were usually dealt with by hospital secretaries, establishment officers or salaries and wages officers and, generally speaking, management committees would look to the administrator for advice on the majority of staffing matters. During the mid 1960s changes began to occur in the nature of relationships between the staff and management at local level. Until that time matters for discussion between the two parties largely related to questions of individual grievance or well-being such as the grading of particular posts or the application of specific terms and conditions of service to individuals or small groups of staff. In 1967, in one of the Government's attempts to control inflation, the National Board for Prices and Incomes published a report recommending the introduction of incentive bonus schemes for ancillary workers in the NHS. While the implications of these recommendations were slow to take effect, their introduction brought managers and workers at local level into the arena of collective bargaining. In time many other issues besides bonus schemes came to be subject to this process.

By this time, too, managements in the NHS had come to recognise that the development and application of personnel policies and procedures was becoming a specialist field. The establishment officer responsible to the administrator, had traditionally dealt with such matters as well as the basic question of controlling numbers of staff in accordance with budget provision. The range of matters which now came to be referred to him, together with the increasing legislative complexity of personnel work, demanded an increased range of knowledge and skills. By the early 1970s, with some encouragement from the DHSS, posts of personnel officer began to be established within hospital management committees. Prior to reorganisation in 1974, the 'Grey Book' envisaged a much more significant role for the personnel officer. Each employing authority would need a personnel officer accountable directly to the administrator at district, area and regional levels, covering the whole range of functions commonly associated with the discipline. Detailed circulars were issued describing the organisation to be set up for both personnel and training and the appointments of regional and area personnel officers took place soon after the appointment of chief officers for the new authorities during late 1973 and early 1974.

The circular on personnel management issued in November 1973, HRC(73)37, described the general responsibility for personnel management, the aims of the function, the task at national, regional, area and district levels, relationships between personnel officers, teams and line managers and set out the main elements of the jobs of regional, area and district personnel officers. These were identified as the review or preparation of plans and budgets, the provision of specialist advice on personnel policies and practices, the support of subordinate personnel officers, undertaking establishment work and other personnel functions such as industrial relations and manpower planning, the development of training activities and the provision of personnel services for all staff employed. While there were differences in the emphasis placed on various aspects of the duties, the essence of the task was clearly described and a sound basis for the organisation of personnel work was provided. A later circular HSC(IS)57, described the policy and organisation for training services, setting out the role and scope of training and identifying the elements of the task, including the establishment of training need, the design and provision of training and the different roles envisaged for training officers at area, regional and national levels.

Organisation of personnel services after 1974

In the event, while all RHAs appointed personnel officers and all AHAs initially made such an appointment, in one or two instances AHAs have subsequently varied their arrangements in order to economise on their management structures. Within districts a very different picture emerged. By 1977 only two-thirds of the districts in England and Wales had a recognised personnel officer. In the remaining districts, the function was undertaken by a member of the general administration with more junior officers carrying out much of the routine work. In Scotland all but the very small boards appointed personnel officers, and posts were also created in many districts.

The pattern of organisation was varied in different parts of England and Wales. Some authorities placed considerable emphasis on the function, establishing relatively well-staffed departments, in some cases including a post of education and training officer, while others allocated smaller resources. Overall statistics of numbers of personnel officers to total staff employed are not a particularly useful measure without a detailed appraisal of the way in which personnel work is distributed between line managers and the personnel discipline within an organisation.

Within the DHSS the organisation of personnel and training is the responsibility of the deputy secretary in charge of the NHS personnel group. To him report four under secretaries responsible respectively for medical and dental terms and conditions of service in the widest sense; for matters relating to professional and technical, administrative and clerical and ancillary staff and the General Whitley Council; for terms and conditions of nurses, general practice dentists, opticians and pharmacists; and finally for the general personnel group covering overall personnel policies, training including the servicing of the National Staff Committees and the National Training Council and manpower planning. In addition the specialist divisions of the Department contribute to the formulation of personnel and training policies as well as negotiations on terms and conditions of service.

Bargaining over rates of pay and terms and conditions of service is centralised upon the General Whitley Council and functional councils covering the various staff groups. More will be said about Whitley Councils and their operation later but in essence they provide a national forum within which management and staff sides come together to resolve matters of pay and conditions of service. They do not cover other questions which might be considered to be of legitimate joint interest at the national level, such matters being dealt with separately between management at the DHSS and the senior officials of trade unions. Two groups of staff stand outside the Whitley Council mechanism for their pay negotiations: doctors' and dentists' pay is determined by an independent review body; NHS maintenance staff pay is allied to craft rates outside the service and is dealt with by direct negotiation between the DHSS and the trade unions concerned.

While many aspects of personnel policy flow from legislation or Whitley agreements, particularly the agreements of the General Whitley Council, the NHS also has a National Training Council and five National Staff Committees charged with the responsibility of advising the Secretary of State on recruitment, training and development of staff for different functional groups of NHS staff in England and Wales. These bodies are specifically precluded from infringing the responsibilities of the professional or statutory bodies such as the General Medical Council, the General Nursing Council or the Council for the Professions Supplementary to Medicine which control professional education and training for the relevant staff groups. There are five staff committees covering administrative and clerical staff, nurses and midwives, ambulance staff, accommodation, catering and other support services staff and works staff. The constitution of the committees consists of one-third management representatives from within the service, one-third external 'experts' and one-third staff-side representatives. Their recommendations are made to the Secretary of State who commends them, as appropriate, to NHS employing authorities.

The National Training Council is responsible for recommending to the Secretary of State training policies and practices common to all groups of staff. It has no formal relationship with the National Staff Committees, but includes within its remit matters such as management education and training and training for industrial relations. Contact with the National Staff Committees is maintained at the administrative level within the Department.

In Scotland the Common Services Agency has a division for management education and training, and in Northern Ireland there is a Staffs Council for the Health and Social Services.

In the field of manpower planning, the most comprehensive arrangements within the NHS are those relating to doctors and dentists. Over the years there have been a number of official studies and reports and the service provides to the DHSS detailed manpower statistics. The intake of medical schools in the country is closely regulated and the number of training and consultant posts available to doctors in the hospital field is controlled centrally in attempts to rectify staffing imbalances which exist nationally — the south-east of England and Scotland are well provided with doctors in relation to most of the rest of England and Wales. Within hospitals generally, training posts in certain specialties, e.g. general medicine, general surgery, are over subscribed in relation to consultant vacancies, whilst others, such as radiology and geriatrics, are by no means such popular career choices for junior staff.

Manpower information is less developed for other groups of staff. The output of trained nurses is determined by the intakes to schools of nursing within individual health authorities whose decisions are conditioned largely by their own needs and budgets, though they have to conform to the requirements of the General Nursing Councils and, in England, to the guidance of regional nurse training committees. Training provision for many paramedical staff can be determined only on a national basis. In these and other staff groups the present data is scanty and in some cases unreliable since there is no comprehensive capture of anything other than the most basic statistics.

Personnel policies

Although the relevant Secretaries of State are directly accountable to Parliament for the provision of the NHS staff working within the NHS are not civil servants. They are employees of the various health authorities which themselves are given the status of bodies corporate under the NHS Acts.

In general terms the personnel policies followed by the NHS are similar to those followed by other public sector employees. Thus, recruitment to the service is largely by means of advertisement. Terms and conditions of service are negotiated centrally through collective bargaining and apply to all members of the particular group of staff covered. Social policies enacted by successive governments, e.g. the provisions of the Equal Pay Act 1970, are automatically applied.

There is, however, no statement of policy within which is encompassed the general direction and intent of government or DHSS policy in relation to staff in the NHS. For the student who wishes to determine the intentions of management it is necessary either to look towards the policy statements produced by a number of individual health authorities in relation to their own staff or to glean such indications as he can from the various Whitley Council agreements, from ministerial statements and from explicit statements relating to individual staff groups. The reports and recommendations of the National Staff Committees for instance often contain useful pointers towards the sorts of personnel policies which the Secretary of State, on the advice of the committees, finds appropriate to commend to authorities. The Department's manpower policy on specific staff groups is made known to the service through a variety of means such as health circulars or operational and strategic planning guidelines.

Employment services

A basic component of the personnel function is the maintenance and development of employment services, covering the recruitment, selection, appraisal, training, career development and health and welfare of staff.

The National Staff Committees for administrative and clerical, accommodation, catering and other support services, and nursing and midwifery staff have all produced guidelines for the recruitment process, which are formally set out in official circulars. Recruitment and selection of consultant medical staff is regulated by statute. RHAs employ such staff for non-teaching AHAs in their region while AHA(T)s, the preserved boards of governors and the Welsh and Scottish authorities employ their own consultant staff directly.

Within the NHS the normal method of recruitment is through the advertisement of vacant posts and the competitive selection interview. Individual employing authorities use these basic procedures in differing ways according to their own needs and according to the resources they wish to deploy. In some authorities it will be common practice for the personnel officer to undertake the recruitment process for most grades of staff employed, although he will rarely undertake selection without the active participation of the manager concerned. In others, the personnel officer may handle some or all of the paperwork, leaving the individual manager to recruit from the applications received, whilst elsewhere, line managers may undertake the whole of the recruitment and selection process themselves. Nurse management, in particular, is often still isolated from the mainstream personnel function in respect of the recruitment and selection process, although there have been moves in many authorities in recent years to ensure an integrated approach to the practice of personnel management. With more senior appointments it is usual to find that the employing authority itself or a sub-committee of its members is involved at the stage of shortlisting and interviewing for selection. At such appointments, whether undertaken by a committee of members or a committee of officers, external assessors from another authority are normally co-opted to the selection panel to advise the employing authority on the suitability of candidates presenting for the post.

For appointments at consultant level the regulations lay down precisely the composition of advisory appointments committees involving assessors nominated by the appropriate college or colleges and representatives of the employing authority, the authority in whose area the consultant will work and a university with a medical school within the region.

Selection tests are used in relatively few cases. Certain aptitude tests are used in selecting craft apprentices for training in the building and engineering trades and similar tests are used in a small number of instances for other posts, notably in the ambulance service. Psychological or IQ testing is rarely undertaken, although the General Nursing Council prescribes a general test for candidates for nurse training who do not already possess the relevant GCE qualfications. The use of external agencies such as recruitment consultants or the Professional and Executive Register in helping to find candidates is rare, although in some urban centres the use of agencies to provide temporary staff is quite extensive in certain fields, e.g. secretarial staff and locum junior medical staff.

From time to time in the last decade the trade unions have attempted, sometimes successfully, to influence certain recruitment policies. In the field of maintenance staff, for example, tacit closed shop arrangements may exist, although there are very few examples of overt closed shop agreements. In certain other fields, notably the ambulance service, trade unions have made concerted attempts to enforce a closed shop. In the majority of professions the possession of an appropriate certificate of registration is a prerequisite for appointment to a post, but trade unions have not made strenuous attempts to enforce comprehensively a pattern of closed shop arrangements for all groups of staff.

The contract of employment has assumed an increasing significance in the relationship between employer and employee in recent years, partly because of legislation in the field of labour law which has resulted in the contract becoming more explicit, as to the terms and conditions of employment, and more complex. The contract has also become increasingly important as a document because staff have become more inclined to challenge managerial initiatives. Staff and their representatives are more ready to examine the small print than was formerly the case and to challenge managerial prerogative through interpretation of the contract.

Once within the health service, the needs of the employee for education and training are met in a variety of ways. It is commonly suggested that the service is a poor provider of training for its staff and many people in both general management and the personnel and training disciplines feel that the service needs the application of the stimulus provided by the industrial training boards elsewhere in the economy. The true picture, however, is one of great contrasts. While there are members of staff in ancillary and other junior posts for whom training may be no more than the traditional 'sitting next to Nellie' arrangement, in other fields of employment the service educates and trains extensively. A medical student, for instance, spends seven years in medical school before qualifying, though he is not at that time an NHS employee. If he chooses to make a career in hospital work, he may spend the next 10 to 15 years in a series of training posts with various examination hurdles to leap before he is sufficiently qualified to apply for a consultant post. Nurses training for the register of the General Nursing Council have a minimum of three years' education and training before qualifying and many will undergo further training, whether for a particular aspect of nursing or for nursing management, in the years to come. Similarly, staff in the professional and technical fields need good educational qualifications in order to train for the basic work of their professions and in many cases will need further qualifications before being able to advance their careers. The organisation of basic education and training rests with a variety of agencies. The General Medical Council regulates the framework of education provided by medical schools associated with universities and the different Royal Colleges prescribe the standards of postgraduate training for doctors proceeding to higher qualification in their particular specialty. The General Nursing Councils oversee the arrangements under which health authorities maintain nurse training schools and set syllabus requirements as well as the examination.

Some of the professions supplementary to medicine either have schools maintained by the NHS in health service premises or have educational facilities provided in local colleges of education. The regulation of education and training arrangements is the responsibility of the Council for the Professions Supplementary to Medicine and its appropriate board. In the scientific or technical professions, basic salaries or moves on promotion are dependent on the attainment of the specific qualification prescribed by Whitley Council agreements for which the course of study may be general, e.g. a physics degree at a university, or more particular, e.g. an HNC in medical laboratory science.

Training for professional administrators is provided through a variety of means. A national training scheme has been in existence for over 20 years recruiting both university graduates and promising candidates from inside the service who follow a prescribed pattern of training attachments within the service and attend courses at national education centres. The passing of the Institute of Health Service Administrators examination is regarded as the basic career qualification for the professional administrator whether he has been recruited to the national training scheme or not.

The responsibility for ensuring that appropriate training is provided, whether through attendance at college courses or through in-service training, lies with the employing authority in these cases. Some authorities employ a training officer in the personnel department whose job is concerned with the examination of training needs and the organisation of the appropriate training. On the staff of each RHA a regional education and training officer has the responsiblity of promoting training provision, although he may have little contact with the professional training of doctors, nurses and some of the other professions. The training organisations which exist within AHAs and RHAs, however, regularly have responsibility for the organisation of specialised postgraduate training for some of the professions and will be heavily involved in the organisation and provision of management training. At the level of supervisory management, local colleges are usually linked to a particular AHA or group of authorities to provide this training. At middle management level, again, local colleges may be used on a directly commissioned basis or the regional training organisation itself will run its own courses. At more senior levels management training is provided by a number of college or university departments specialising in health services studies and provision is made for a number of candidates from the health service to attend appropriate courses at business schools. More recently arrangements have been made for a small number of senior managers to have the opportunity of undertaking work for a master's degree at designated national centres of education.

A basic element in the definition of training need for middle and senior management was lost at the time of reorganisation. By 1974 staff in the administrative and clerical grades and in nursing and midwifery posts were subject to formalised appraisal systems. At the time of reorganisation, these systems were discontinued. Sadly, the administrative and clerical scheme, which was redrafted after 1974 by the National Staff Committee, has not yet been re-established.

Traditionally in the NHS training has been seen as a means of preparing the individual for the job he has to undertake and in some cases, such as management training, providing him with the knowledge and skills required to enable him to advance to a higher level post. The use of training as a method of developing the organisation or resolving organisational problems has been attempted on relatively few occasions. At the time of reorganisation the services of management consultants were made available to a number of teams of officers to assist in implementing the new style of consensus management and the consequent adjustment in roles and relationships. More usually, however, training activities are limited to the objectives of imparting increased knowledge, improved skills and a broader appreciation of the organisation and its activities.

In the field of health, safety and welfare, once again the NHS presents a curious kaleidoscope of contrasting development. A service that provides for the health of the population as a whole, often makes minimal provision for the health of its own staff. Thus, in many establishments, occupational health is limited to the provision of first aid boxes and an arrangement with the casualty department whereby staff who are unwell may see a doctor at short notice. In other places, health authorities have developed occupational health services, which screen the health of new employees, advise staff and managers on health precautions, initiate vaccination programmes, review staff with long term sickness and generally provide, from a relatively independent standpoint, a health and welfare service. While the Royal Commission recommended that the NHS should set up an occupational health service, there is little prospect of such a development generally for some years.

In the field of safety, while recent legislation has provided an impetus towards formalising a consultative relationship between management and staff on the subject, safe practices and procedures have received considerable attention over the years in certain departments. A comprehensive and well developed code for the protection of persons against ionising radiation has been in operation since 1957 in radiological and physics departments. Pathology laboratories, pharmacies, operating theatres and renal dialysis units have all been the subject of official reports recommending improved procedures. While no doubt the extent to which precautions are observed will vary from department to department, there is usually genuine awareness of the need for safe working and concern to improve standards in these areas. For some years the DHSS has operated a warning system in relation to both medicines and equipment which enables the health service as a whole to be alerted to defects discovered in a product in one part of the service. Certain parts of hospital premises are covered by the Factories Acts and although Crown exemption applies, the government accepts that the provisions of the Offices, Shops and Railway Premises Acts should normally apply to office accommodation.

Despite existing precautions, the health service has been apprehensive about the effect that the obligations under the Health and Safety at Work etc. Act 1974 will lay upon it. Safety precautions in many parts of the service are believed to be inadequate, although it is too early as yet to judge the reaction of the Health and Safety Executive to the conditions they find on their initial inspections of whole hospital premises. Recent events in laboratories have led to the belief that this is the area where attention should be concentrated initially. The whole question of safety, however, is one that has not perhaps received the priority it should have done prior to the passing of the Act, apart from those situations that were known to be frankly dangerous and that were already covered by reasonably stringent precautions. The effect of the new Act in requiring authorities to re-examine all their arrangements for safety cannot but be beneficial.

The scope of welfare services again varies from authority to authority. Some authorities have inherited or established active programmes ~~with~~ flourishing sports and social facilities, creches for children whose mothers wish to return to work and reasonable standards of staff catering, rest room and changing accommodation. Sometimes one or more of these facilities will exist without others. In almost all cases staff catering is reasonably well provided for and changing accommodation is usually found where needed. Standards, however, vary depending on the priority accorded to the provision of such facilities for staff. In some cases, too, authorities provide assisted or subsidised transport facilities, particularly where there is considerable interchange of staff between establishments or where local public transport facilities are poor. Generally, however, subsidies towards travelling and catering are officially discouraged on the premise that, in a service which is publicly accountable, it is a misuse of funds to assist staff in this way.

The personnel function in all employing authorities will be involved in providing or contributing to the whole range of work associated with employment services. The extent to which personnel departments are comprehensively integrated with managers in all disciplines varies from authority to authority depending on such factors as the geographical distribution of services within the authority, the resources available to the personnel function, the amount of personnel work that line managers themselves are expected to undertake and the degree of interaction between the different management disciplines. Policies and standard procedures are normally agreed either at health authority level or between members of the relevant team of officers. The personnel officer, responsible to the administrator on each team, has a crucial part to play in organising the function's contribution towards establishment and maintenance of these basic procedures. His staff often handle much of the administrative routine involved with recruitment, selection and training and it is his responsibility to see that agreed procedures are observed. It is also his responsibility to ensure that standards of recruitment and selection are adequate and appropriate to the posts being filled and that the authority's methods are effective and economic. The interpretation of Whitley Council salary, wage and terms and conditions of service agreements largely rests with him. The content and format of the contract of employment is increasingly becoming standardised and here again he has a role to play. He is expected to advise the administrator or the management team when issues relating to employment services arise and to take the initiative in recommending the development of new policies or the adaptation of existing policies as circumstances change.

Negotiations of pay and conditions of service

It has already been indicated that salaries and wages and terms and conditions of service in the NHS are determined for most groups of staff by Whitley Councils. The essence of the system is that representative groups of management within the service, together with representatives of the central departments, form a management side while the staff side consists of representatives of staff associations and trade unions. The power to approve or reject agreements lies with the Secretary of State under the terms of a statutory instrument approved by Parliament under the National Health Service Acts. In practice the Secretary of State rarely rejects any agreement, preferring to exercise influence through the departmental membership on the management side.

Of the 11 Whitley Councils the General Council deals with conditions of service (other than remuneration) and similar matters of general application. Its agreements cover annual leave, leave for special purposes, travelling subsistence and removal expenses and various procedural arrangements relating to the conduct of industrial relations in the service such as appeals machinery for grievance matters and disciplinary purposes, consultation arrangements and redundancy payments. Medical and hospital dental staff are party to some of the agreements of the General Whitley Council but in other respects their terms and conditions of service are negotiated outside the Whitley system since their functional council has been largely inoperative for many years. Ancillary staffs also have slightly different agreements on certain matters from the main general Whitley Council agreements. Otherwise the General Council reaches agreements relating to the whole range of staff in the service. Its processes, however, are extremely prolonged partly because staff-side membership is so wide ranging and contains within it organisations with widely differing objectives. In some areas too its scope is limited by individual Whitley Councils insisting on their own right to negotiate particular agreements. The result inevitably is that differing staff groups enjoy different terms and conditions on the same subject, for instance standby payments or sick leave agreements.

The functional Whitley Councils cover the administrative and clerical, ancillary, medical and (hospital) dental, nurses and midwives, optical, pharmaceutical, professional and technical (two councils) and ambulance staff. What was the dental (local authorities) council is now known as the joint negotiating forum for community dental services. Management-side membership consists of members or officers from health authorities in England, Wales and Scotland and officers of the Departments from the three countries. Recent changes designed to make management sides more representative are referred to later in this section.

Staff-side membership has remained largely unchanged since Whitley Councils were first established at the inception of the NHS. There are over 40 organisations representing staff in the NHS that have seats on the staff side of one or more councils or that negotiate directly with DHSS. Staff organisations differ in both type and size. Large public sector trade unions such as NALGO and COHSE sit with professional organisations both small and large and with unions concerned largely in the commercial sector such as USDAW and ASTMS. Full details can be found in *The Hospitals and Health Services Year Book*.

The extent to which staff organisations are representative of NHS employees is not accurately known. It is estimated that over 80 per cent of the work force now belongs to a professional association or trade union but precise figures are almost impossible to obtain, partly because many staff are in dual membership of a professional organisation and a trade union. The distribution of seats on the staff sides of the various Whitley Councils is thought to be disproportionate to the membership represented, possibly more so than in the early years of the councils. On the Ancillary Staffs Council for instance the four unions NUPE, COHSE, GMWU and TGWU each have four seats despite the fact that the first two of them have the greatest number of ancillary staff members in the NHS.

The secretariat of the management side of the full Whitley Council is provided by civil servants seconded from the DHSS. In practice, the civil servants concerned work in the Department alongside other departmental colleagues. To the service as a whole the distinction between their responsibilities to the management side whom they serve and their responsibilities to the DHSS seems a fine one. In recent years there has been much discussion on the desirability of establishing a management-side secretariat independent of the DHSS, leaving the Department to exercise its influence through its member on the management side. It is argued that the detailed composition of Whitley agreements often does not pay proper regard to the operational requirements of the service and that this is partly due to the secretariat's dual responsibility; a secretariat in some sense owned by the service, it is felt, would lead to agreements more sensitive to service needs. While the issue is not yet dead, the idea of an independent secretariat was rejected by Lord McCarthy in his report discussed later in this section. It would increase costs but more seriously, in his view, the proposal avoided the real issue, which was the need to develop a corporate spirit and sense of corporate identity within the management side. Without that an independent secretariat would be independent not only of the Departments but of everybody else as well. Since then there have been Whitley agreements that the service has found very difficult to implement though it can be argued that they are a consequence of difficult bargaining when money is tight rather than of defects in the machinery.

The secretariat of the staff side is provided by permanent officials of the major staff organisations. In almost every case the staff side of individual Whitley Councils is composed of representatives from different staff organisations and the choice of chairman and secretary of the staff side rests with the constituent organisations. The servicing of the full council is invariably undertaken by the management-side secretary.

The normal pattern of working for the councils is for a series of meetings to be held at regular intervals through the year. Each side meets separately prior to a joint meeting, with *ad hoc* meetings being arranged as necessary around the time of the annual settlement date. In some cases, negotiating meetings on pay settlements take place at full meetings of the two sides of the council and in other councils a negotiating sub-committee undertakes the bulk of the detailed negotiation. In all councils the management-side and staff-side secretaries have much informal contact between formal meetings and on occasion undertake jointly the major part of the detailed negotiations in accordance with the mandates given to them by their respective sides.

In the last decade, successive pay codes have underlined the extent to which management sides are constrained by government economic policies. While this has always been the case and no doubt will continue, it became particularly evident during the winter of 1978-9 that the real negotiations over national pay scales for ancillary staffs and ambulancemen were taking place between trade union officers and cabinet ministers with the management side being informed after the event of the sort of settlement which might be acceptable to the government.

In a number of councils the principles determining the settlement have become established by traditionally linking pay agreements to the pay of other groups within the economy. Thus, ancillary staff normally follow approximately the level and kind of settlement reached in local government; administrative and clerical staff, pharmacists and scientists and technicians of various classes have links established with particular settlements reached within the civil service. In the case of nurses, however, and certain of the paramedical staff, there are no such links with the apparently inevitable result that from time to time a parity, established some years earlier, gradually becomes eroded. There normally follows a special review which has to be carried out to satisfy staff-side claims that salaries have been allowed to fall behind salaries of other groups with whom comparisons are normally made, although such comparisons do not normally determine the level of annual settlement. The whole principle of comparability both between the public sector and other parts of the economy and within the public sector itself has in fact become the battleground on which pay bargaining has been conducted in recent years.

The form of pay agreements again varies from council to council. Generally speaking, in the salaried grades, rates of pay are fixed for particular job definitions, e.g. a laboratory technician with a defined level of qualification controlling a defined number of staff in a laboratory will be paid at the rate for a particular grade; if the staff increase beyond a certain number he may be paid at the rate for the next higher grade. In many cases, however, grading definitions are relatively imprecise with the result that there is room for both managerial flexibility in the structuring of jobs and grading conflict at the local level. Salaried posts are usually agreed on an incremental scale so that an officer starting at the minimum of the scale will progress automatically to the top of that scale over a period of years. Beyond that, his hope of pay improvement apart from the annual negotiations to improve all pay scales must rest either with promotion or with the expansion of his job to achieve the next grade above. In certain instances, additional payments are possible for the recognition of particular qualifications, e.g. shorthand and typewriting qualifications carry special allowances for secretarial posts. In most cases, however, where qualifications are a prerequisite for a particular grade, they do not bring with them additional allowances and it is rare for pay agreements to allow for any recognition of personal merit. Indeed, with the exception of consultants, whose position is discussed below, the only instances of personal merit being treated as a factor in pay relate to a small group of scientific and technical posts. (Incentive bonus schemes, which are discussed below, might possibly be described as a recognition of group merit.)

Internal pay relativities between the Whitley Councils are a fruitful bargaining area for staff sides. There is no common pay spine for health service staff as a whole. As a result, the relative position between, say, domestic assistants at ward level and staff nurses on the ward may vary over time, following successive pay agreements reached in the Ancillary Staffs and Nurses and Midwives Whitley Councils. It is argued by some that while the existence of a pay spine would not in itself remove this potential area of conflict, it would at least focus the minds of both management and staff sides on the problem of relativities within the NHS with the object of avoiding some of the worst anomalies.

Relativities within Whitley Council groupings of staff are dealt with in different ways according to the council concerned. In the Ancillary Staffs Council, for instance, it has been the practice for almost a decade to rely on a system of job evaluation to assist in determining the relative pay levels of jobs covered by the council. Attempts have been made in the last few years to introduce systems of job evaluation into both the Administrative and Clerical Staffs Council and the Nurses and Midwives Council but in both instances little progress has been achieved so far. Differentials, however, on those and other councils have become a matter for disagreement between the two sides and have caused some problems in recent years with the relatively strict application of government pay codes which in themselves have had the effect of narrowing differentials.

Doctors' and dentists' pay and conditions of service are examined by an independent review body reporting direct to the government. The health departments, on behalf of NHS management, and the doctors' and dentists' staff organisations both make detailed representations to the review body, which also carries out its own independent investigations. Its conclusions are reported to the government, which normally accepts them. Implementation of the recommendations and terms and conditions of service are subject to negotiation between the health departments and the profession but in essence the major elements of pay are settled by the review body. The settlements cover both the salaries, etc. of hospital medical and dental staff, community medicine staff and other directly employed staff and the fees and allowances that constitute the remuneration of general practitioners.

Rates of pay for the majority of salaried medical and dental staff used to consist of a relatively straightforward incremental scale settlement but junior doctors have now negotiated arrangements that reward work undertaken outside normal working hours. There were also negotiations for a consultants' contract that would provide additions to pay in return for specific elements of the job performed, but this was abandoned. A new contract became operative from the beginning of 1980, the main effect of which was to increase the scope for NHS consultants to undertake private practice, this even being permitted, within limits, to consultants on whole-time contracts.

A further element in the pay of consultants lies in the distinction award system, which was adopted at the outset of the NHS. It provides a financial incentive to consultants, many of whom reach the consultant grade in their thirties, and to some extent reflects the wider variations in medical earnings which would exist outside a salaried system. The awards, based on recommendations of a mainly professional advisory committee, are in four categories, ranging from C to A+. In 1979 there were 5,392 award holders in Great Britain, the largest number holding C awards and 135 holding the A+ which in value approached the maximum of a consultant's basic salary. About half of all consultants receive an award during their careers. The system has been criticised partly because the names of holders are not published and partly because awards tend to go to consultants in teaching hospitals and in the 'glamorous' specialties, which reflects the fact that they are based on clinical distinction. In future meritorious service to the NHS will also be a criterion, and a broader distribution of B and C awards will be sought across regions and specialties. Some critics argue that the money would be better spent on long-service increments, or on providing incentives to attract people to the less popular specialties and regions.

Reference has already been made to the introduction of productivity bargaining in the NHS. Since 1967 progress towards the introduction of incentive payments for ancillary staff has been patchy. In some regions almost the whole of the ancillary work force (approximately 20-25 per cent of total staff employed) has moved towards bonus payments. In others, progress has been much slower and overall only 30 to 40 per cent of ancillary staff are in receipt of bonus payments. The schemes in use vary from straightforward productivity arrangements whereby a 10 per cent saving in labour costs is rewarded by a 10 per cent bonus payment to measured day-work systems introduced following normal work study procedures to an agreed national framework. A detailed account is given in Chapter 12. Many managements are unhappy with these systems of payment. Quite apart from the pressure to divert scarce work study resources to the introduction of bonus schemes, under the present arrangements relatively few staff can benefit, with the consequence that other staff become dissatisified with their own inability to receive such payments. In some cases for instance at the ward level, domestic staff in receipt of bonus can earn as much or more than qualified nursing staff. This distortion of differentials becomes a particular pressure point during periods when fixed incomes policies are operated by government since the incomes policies themselves have the effect of distorting differentials and often allow productivity bargaining as a legitimate device for relieving pressures on the system. Within the public sector incentive bonus schemes are required to be self-financing or financially viable. Local management often find themselves in situations where the framework for a bonus scheme is agreed nationally but it is difficult to meet the strict requirements of public sector accounting in order to demonstrate financial viability. Growth in the numbers of ancillary staff employed has, however, been slower than for many other groups and this improvement in productivity must be due in part to incentive schemes of payment. It is perhaps unfortunate that bonus schemes are viewed largely as a payment device with less than due regard to their influence on productivity. As a consequence, the productivity of other groups of staff may have received less attention than it deserves.

From time to time governments have resorted to *ad hoc* review bodies to re-establish the position of different groups of staff within the earnings league. Politically the device has the advantage of postponing an award the government is unwilling to concede, and may result in a smaller award than could be negotiated; the results should also be more systematic and objective than the outcome of negotiations conducted at a time of strong staff discontent. A fairly recent example is the committee under the chairmanship of the Earl of Halsbury which reported in 1975 on the pay of nurses and of the professions supplementary to medicine. While it succeeded initially in satisfying those groups of staff, its reports were soon followed by further high inflation and high settlements elsewhere, which resulted in demands for a further review over and above the normal bargaining round.

In March 1979 the then prime minister established the Standing Commission on Pay Comparability under the chairmanship of Professor H.A. Clegg. It was:

> to examine the terms and conditions of employment of particular groups of workers referred to it by the government in agreement with the employers and unions concerned, and to report in each case on the possibility of establishing acceptable bases of comparison with terms and conditions for other comparable work and of maintaining appropriate internal relativities.

In the NHS field the commission produced reports on ancillary staff, ambulancemen, nurses and midwives and the professions supplementary to medicine but it proved to be short-lived for the new government, believing that its recommendations had been excessively inflationary, wound it up the following year. It might in any case have ceased to function for its recommendations, if higher than the government thought reasonable, fell so far below staff expectations that the unions would have been reluctant to refer further disputes to it. The commission's report may nevertheless prove to be of more than passing interest since problems of comparability will continue to afflict the service and the reports are illuminating on the complications which comparisons entail. The commission did not favour comparability, i.e. linking pay to that of some other group, and thought that at best such links would not be valid for more than two or three years. Therefore when job-for-job comparison was not possible, as is often the case with health service staff, it used a system of factor analysis, comparing the jobs to be assessed with a suitable sample of different jobs outside.

At the time that the Halsbury Committee was established there was also more general dissatisfaction with the operation of the Whitley system and the Secretary of State appointed Lord McCarthy, an experienced arbitrator, to review it. His report, *Making Whitley Work,* was designed to be acceptable to both management and staff sides as well as to the Department, since change could be brought about only by agreement. He examined the scope and nature of the work of the Whitley Councils and the roles of the various participants, the DHSS, the management side and the staff side. Questions on the composition of the two sides of the councils, the extent to which the departmental members must be influenced by governmental policy, whether the staff sides were representative of their membership, arrangements for devolving bargaining to lower levels, the issue of joint consultation and the possibility of establishing an independent management-side secretariat were all areas that received consideration. The main effect of Lord McCarthy's recommendations has been that of bringing a greater awareness to management-side members, from within the NHS, of the potential of their role. In particular, membership of the management sides has been revised, to comprise one member from each region on each council and to provide a voice from each of the levels of region, area and district on the management side. While the briefing of management-side members is carried out largely by the secretariat at DHSS, Lord McCarthy recommended increased co-ordination between the secretariats to the different councils and a much more positive role for the service in the field in providing briefs for individual management-side members. Within each region there are now arrangements whereby management-side members can be appropriately briefed on issues being raised in the particular council. With regard to the staff side, the report suggested that the staff-side organisations should review the distribution of seats between them in order to establish a more representative council. It recommended that staff sides should consider amalgamating organisations or reaching agency agreements whereby one organisation would act for another. So far there has been disappointingly little progress towards changing the situation.

Management policies in relation to Whitley Council processes have traditionally been reactive. The normal process has been for the staff side to lodge a claim for improvement and for the management side then to consider how far it is prepared to meet the claim. While regard is undoubtedly paid by the management side to the effect on field operations of reaching particular agreements and while there has been some co-ordination between Whitley Councils, in general management side deliberations take place without any overall manpower policy in mind and without the necessity of applying common conditions to all groups of staff in appropriate subject areas. On the staff side national bargaining seems to have been traditionally aimed at securing improvements that would keep staff roughly in line with perceived comparators in other sectors of the economy. To some extent concessions achieved in one Whitley Council have been used to achieve similar improvements in others.

Bargaining on pay is relatively restricted at local level, being concerned either with incentive schemes or with the application and interpretation of particular terms and conditions of service, a matter on which it is common for health authorities to seek advice from either the management side secretariat or from the Department itself. Variations on pay agreements, interpretations of conditions of service and managerial authorisations to meet exceptional circumstances are all matters where health authorities seek assistance from the DHSS. The need for such variation or advice arises from particular local circumstances within the district or institutions inside a district. In most cases advice is sought by the personnel officer concerned, although salaries and wages departments are also involved, particularly in the interpretation of pay agreements. In this area above all the gap between management at the local level and the central bargaining system creates strains and pressures. As staff have become more used to bargaining locally, so their frustrations increase as they experience the length of time it often takes to resolve problems nationally or as they begin to appreciate their own lack of influence over the central bargaining institutions. Local managers and personnel officers equally find their efforts frustrated by the difficulty of working through the system. While McCarthy had suggested that the service should frame its Whitley agreements more flexibly and should formally establish some consultative or bargaining machinery at regional level, these proposals did not find favour with the service generally and the problem which he identified remains.

Industrial relations

In evidence submitted to the Royal Commission on the NHS, the Advisory Conciliation and Arbitration Service (ACAS) was heavily critical of the conduct of industrial relations. The new rights accruing to staff under the legislation, changing attitudes towards industrial action and an increase in trade union membership were not matched by relevant resource or expertise on the part of NHS management. Reorganisation had lengthened lines of communication. In a service where negotiation on pay and conditions of service took place nationally, there were increasing pressures on such systems as existed locally for consultation and bargaining. The distance in organisational terms, between the local scene and the central Whitley Councils was too often found to be a major impediment in allowing management and staff to work out adequate joint relationships locally.

A major development in the last decade has been the importation to the public sector of the use of industrial action to secure negotiating objectives. From the early 1970s onwards various staff groups have pursued different forms of industrial action including the strike. Response to such tactics by management has been uncertain in many cases with little effective national leadership and in time has resulted in local management becoming highly sceptical of the abilities or intentions of ministers. The most militant of the trade unions have made two significant attempts during the 1970s to establish an improved relative position for their members. In 1973 and again in 1979 major bouts of industrial action took place in connection with the annual negotiations over ancillary staff's and ambulancemen's pay. On the first occasion little long-term advantage accrued to the staff concerned. In 1979 the major direct achievement was the Comparability Commission. As we have seen, the ultimate pay settlement was disappointing to staff.

By 1974, the only procedural agreements that had been concluded by the Whitley Councils nationally related to the settlement of individual disputes over terms and conditions of service and agreements on facilities for shop stewards. It is true there was also an agreement on joint consultation which had been reached in the very early days of the service but by 1974 this agreement was under considerable attack for the inadequacy of its basic terms and many authorities felt the need to establish joint procedures with the staff organisations and trade unions which would enable both bargaining and consultative issues to be dealt with locally.

In the years since reorganisation, national agreement has been reached on an interim disciplinary procedure and on a statement of principle on equal opportunities. Negotiations have taken place on a range of other issues, a developed agreement on facilities, the operation of the Health and Safety at Work etc. Act, union membership agreements, a revision of the agreement on joint consultation and a procedure for settling local disputes. Several years after the introduction of major legislation which concentrated attention on these subjects, only one of the negotiations has reached finality and joint discussion at national level on at least two of them, health and safety, and union membership agreements, has been abandoned.

The reasons for this failure to make progress are often difficult to see. Undoubtedly, the change in emphasis in the role of management-side members and the difficulty of co-ordinating the staff-side view from the many and diverse organisations representing staff interests are both impediments to progress. The management side also finds it difficult enough to reach consensus views representing, as it does, over 100 area and regional health authorities in England and Wales and 15 health boards in Scotland. In time, however, it may be that the 1970s will be looked upon as the decade during which the NHS came to learn about the realities of industrial relations, almost for the first time. While there had often been disagreement previously in the Whitley Councils (for example, the disciplinary agreement had been under discussion from the early days of the service but negotiation had long since ceased when the Trade Union and Labour Relations Act of 1974 focused attention on the subject once again), there had rarely been disagreements and conflict to the extent that was seen from the early 1970s onwards. In a sense, therefore, the NHS represented a 'green field site' in industrial relations terms at the beginning of the decade and at times it failed to respond adequately to the pressures brought about by the factors identified by ACAS in their evidence to the Royal Commission. In the event, many authorities entered into agreements of their own with local representatives of staff organisations and trade unions in the years following the reorganisation. The quality and effectiveness of agreements varied from authority to authority. The response of staff to the new situation varied likewise. Some authorities insisted that such agreements could only be concluded by the General Whitley Council and therefore played a waiting game. Others went part way down the road of establishing jointly agreed procedures without covering the whole field. Yet others established comprehensive policies and agreements. Industrial relations conflict likewise varied from authority to authority and between districts or institutions within authorities. In some places the situation seemed one of permanent conflict while in others much more harmonious relationships existed. The only clear statement that perhaps can be made is that the effect on morale in the service generally of the lack of clear and consistent policies posed constant problems for local managements and genuine dilemmas for many staff who still identified very closely with the patient and who were reluctant to undertake courses of action which would damage that tradition, but who demonstrated their own lack of experience in industrial relations by some of their actions in times of conflict.

Partly because the service was inexperienced in the conduct of collective industrial relations, reliable information about what was happening was difficult to obtain. Before 1973 the number of disputes in any one year and the number of staff affected by disputes was relatively small. After the major industrial action by ancillary staff in 1973, the number of disputes and the number of staff affected again dropped dramatically until the winter of 1978-9 when industrial action was widespread. In all years other than 1973, indeed, the number of days lost to strike action per 1,000 staff employed was considerably less than the average for the country as a whole. The bare statistics, however, are unreliable in themselves and give only the crudest of impressions of events. Industrial action took many forms, including go-slow, demarcation disputes, a general refusal to accept without question everything that management asked of staff and open challenges to management prerogative. Strikes in themselves were not necessarily the clearest indication of conflict. Tactics, once a dispute had begun, became more sophisticated involving, in many cases, the withdrawal of small numbers of key staff whose action would have the greatest effect on other groups.

The more dramatic conflicts were reserved for national issues, usually related to pay negotiations. In due course, it became clear that, not only were manual staff willing to take industrial action, but professional staff too had become involved in the same process. Management's response to this situation, particularly when national negotiations were concerned, was often conditioned by short-term considerations of maintaining services by whatever means was possible. It was common for ministers to become involved at an early stage when such disputes occurred and the policy adopted by the Department was to advise or request field authorities to keep a low profile and concentrate on the maintenance of services while the dispute lasted. In local disputes, the management response was likely to be more varied, with greater likelihood of resisting strikers' tactics.

In December 1979 the DHSS issued a circular, HC(79)20, which offered guidance on handling industrial disputes, dealing with the options available to management in responding to industrial action, with the use of volunteers and with contingency planning. The guidance, if followed, is likely to increase management resistance in local disputes and possibly also in disputes over national issues, which it did not treat separately. 'Ministers want NHS management to know that, having issued this guidance, they would hope not to intervene in their decisions. It should always be borne in mind, however, that this guidance is nothing more than advice on options to be followed by authorities and that the responsibility in individual cases rests with them alone.' The circular stressed that most forms of industrial action are a breach of contract and that staff should not be paid for work which they have refused to carry out. While the circular recognised the need to maintain services to patients, and the need for staff to work together again once the industrial action is over, the emphasis on non-payment, on the use of volunteers and the importance of contingency planning, and the request that authorities should let all staff know the policy which they intended to follow in the event of industrial action, indicated that the Department expected management to take a firmer line with industrial action in future. There are some indications that this is happening, though at the time of writing the effectiveness of the advice has not been tested on a large scale.

Leaving aside the question of strike action, the management of industrial relations has changed considerably within this last decade. Procedures for handling dispute and conflict of one kind or another are more developed now than they were in 1970; they are understood better by both management and staff sides; and they are used more extensively than was ever the case previously. Health authorities and the Department have made considerable efforts to train managers in handling industrial relations and to increase their knowledge of the subject and improve their skills. Managements are, more than ever, aware of the need to take into account staff reactions as a consideration in the formulation of plans or proposals for change. Consultation takes place on a formalised basis in the majority of authorities and, in many cases, becomes bargaining, as well as consultation. The beginnings of regular monitoring of the existing arrangements has been seen in recent years. Much remains to be done, however, in crucial areas. At the centre of the stage lies the failure to reach agreement in the General Whitley Council on the subject of joint consultation. Here, the management side has problems of its own in that the present agreement, which is 30 years old, allows only for consultation and does not provide for negotiation at local level. While there is general agreement that such matters as rates of pay and basic terms and conditions of service must be reserved for national agreement, there are varying views amongst managements on the question of whether local joint arrangements should cover both consultation and negotiation. On the one hand, it is argued that the distinction between the two processes is extremely fine and they will inevitably merge together. Others, however, feel that consultation should be the channel through which management formally cements its relationship with representatives of the staff, leaving negotiation as a matter to be pursued on specific issues by shop stewards or trade union officers representing the particular group of staff involved. A complication on the staff side is that, in a minority of authorities, trade unions affiliated to the TUC refuse to take part in discussions conducted jointly with representatives of the staff organisations that are not affiliated to the TUC. In the meantime authorities are faced with the problem of how to cope with the legitimate demands of a large and diverse work force for effective and meaningful discussions with its senior management.

Closely associated with the issue of joint consultation, although distinct from it, has been the lack of adequate machinery for settling disputes, whether local or national. In January 1980 the General Whitley Council at last reached an agreement on a local disputes procedure. It is too early to judge whether it will overcome the difficulties previously experienced. At national level the problem is that, at the end of the day, it is the government that has to accept and approve agreements of the Whitley Councils, but the government itself is, and must be, a party to the negotiations through the departmental representatives on the management side. In these circumstances, the trade unions will almost inevitably see the government as being both prosecutor and judge. The suggestion of the Royal Commission that the TUC should take the initiative in seeking a solution to this difficulty is unlikely to be taken up, at least for the present.

In the field of industrial relations, members of health authorities are regularly involved. Besides their responsibility for framing and approving policies and procedures, they are often closely in touch with situations where conflict arises and are concerned formally in the hearing of appeals on grievances, differences over conditions of service and discipline. The normal practice is for a sub-committee of the authority to hear such appeals and either reach a conclusion itself or make a recommendation to the authority.

Some aspects of the difficulties health authorities have experienced in handling industrial relations have already been touched on earlier in this section. Another area which is a matter for dispute at both local and national levels deserves brief mention here, though it is also touched on in Chapter 15. It is the problem of relationships between doctors and other health care professionals that has arisen from the expanding role of some of the professions.

Of all aspects of personnel management within the service, industrial relations is the one where the most anxiety and the greatest pressures have been experienced in recent years. The Royal Commission said: 'we are in no doubt that industrial relations in the NHS are in need of improvement' and it would be premature to claim that there has been much improvement since the commission reported. The commission did not suppose that there was any single solution to the problem of industrial action and of the specific measures it supported, only the agreement on a local dispute procedure has so far been achieved. In the last ten years or so the numbers of shop stewards and the amount of trade union activity in the NHS have both increased markedly, and although the increase may not continue a diminution seems unlikely. The events of the last decade, and the attitudes they reflect, are at least as much a product of changes in society in general as of the particular circumstances of the NHS and to that extent are unlikely to change in the NHS alone. At least it can be said that although formal participative management schemes have not become established since 1974 the service has operated on a much more participative basis, however uncomfortably.

Manpower planning

It should not be necessary to emphasise the significance of manpower planning for a service as labour intensive as the NHS. Although it is the last topic discussed in this chapter, and possibly the last aspect of personnel management to which the service has given attention, it must be basic to the whole subject.

The need for staff is determined by the distribution of health services throughout the country, by the morbidity within the local populations served and by the range and complexity of the services provided. For a long time, though with limited success, major efforts have been made to control and deploy medical manpower to achieve better distribution, but for other staff no such national efforts seemed necessary. As far as professional staff directly concerned in patient care were concerned, health authorities simply wanted more. Financial resources increased annually, so that it appeared that the only problem was to find the trained staff to do the work. In most hospitals, for example, the approved nursing establishment was considerably higher than the numbers actually employed, and much effort was devoted to recruitment. Within the last decade, however, it has become clear that resources available for health care will at best increase much more slowly than in the past, with the result that the need for careful planning on the supply and deployment of professional staff becomes more important.

With other groups of staff there has for the most part been less of a sense of shortage, and recruitment has not therefore been such an overriding concern. Planning for supply has, however, often been confined to establishing a ceiling for the budget, although where pay has been related to productivity for ancillary staff further controls have been necessary. Many of these staff, such as ancillary and clerical, are recruited largely from the local market, as indeed are some nursing and other professional staff. When staff are recruited locally and only short training is provided, national long-term manpower planning is hardly appropriate. Medical staff are at the other extreme; training is very long and very expensive, it involves the universities, and the labour market is a national one, even though it appears that the location of the medical school has some bearing on where a doctor subsequently practises.

The key to the provision of medical services lies with the deployment of medical manpower, and for a long time detailed national statistics have been kept of the make-up of the medical and dental work force, the career progression of doctors and the likely future manpower needs and supply, specialty by specialty. With these professions, two themes constantly recur. The first has been uneven distribution, both geographical and by specialty. The second has been the great difficulty with hospital staff in balancing the relationship between the number of trainees and the number of consultant posts available. The issues involved are rehearsed in a 1978 DHSS discussion document entitled *Medical Manpower — the next twenty years* and also in a research paper commissioned by the Royal Commission.

The Department, in direct negotiation with representatives of the medical profession, controls the establishment both of new consultant posts and of supporting posts at registrar and senior registrar level. Within the regions, manpower committees representative of the profession are required to scrutinise and approve applications for additional posts before the Central Manpower Committee, a joint forum of the Department and the profession, will consider them. There are equivalent arrangements in Scotland and Northern Ireland. The junior posts are viewed almost entirely as training posts and the aim is to control the numbers available according to the numbers of consultant vacancies expected to materialise within the planning period. Although formally in training posts, registrars and senior registrars in fact meet a large proportion of the service needs for medical manpower. For many years a large number of these posts have been held by overseas doctors coming to the country for postgraduate training, and as most of them returned to their own countries on obtaining their higher qualification, in effect they have met the service needs of the NHS without there being the need to provide permanent consultant posts for them. Moreover they have tended to fill training posts in the less popular specialties. Current policy is to reduce the dependence on this source of manpower through the increased output of medical graduates from British universities. This development will increase the problems of relating training posts to consultant posts, for more trainees will expect a permanent post in the NHS. A solution sometimes advocated is the establishment of a permanent grade below consultant level, possibly with shorter training requirements, but it is most unlikely to be acceptable to the profession. The logical alternative is a substantial increase in the number of consultant posts, which would mean that a consultant would have much less assistance from trainee doctors than at present. A radical change of this sort would certainly be difficult, but whatever solution is eventually found it is likely to entail less dependence on trainees for medical staffing.

A reduction in the number of overseas doctors may also increase the difficulties in filling consultant posts in the less popular specialties such as anaesthetics, radiology, geriatrics and psychiatry. The problem is the more serious because the services that have official priority for development are on the whole those least attractive to consultants. One element in the popularity or otherwise of specialties appears to be financial. Consultants in all specialties are paid on the same scales and it is unlikely that the profession would welcome higher rates as an incentive to move into the less popular specialties. On the other hand these specialties offer little or no scope for additional earnings through private practice, and have hitherto received a relatively small proportion of distinction awards. Against this, career prospects are good and this may be an incentive at a time when there is fear of an over-supply of doctors. The other element in unpopularity, even more difficult to meet, appears to be a matter of interest, and of prestige within the profession. Some critics would say it is a consequence of the values of the medical schools and teaching hospitals as now constituted — and that the same factor accounts for the relatively low standing of general practice.

As we have already said, for many years the main effort in nursing was expended on increasing the supply and in fact, despite frequent complaints about shortages, numbers have steadily increased. If there has been a matter for concern it is perhaps the distribution of nurses between the different grades and categories rather than total numbers. Despite the emphasis on nurse recruitment, nurse managers have been concerned with the efficient deployment of nursing staff. At one time various studies were undertaken in an attempt to provide standard formulae for determining the 'right' level of staffing for particular types of care; measured studies of work done, however, were liable to result in a recommended establishment very like the numbers in post, since the work a nurse does depends on the number of nurses available. More recently, with the tightening of health service budgets, manpower planning has been directed towards a more exact balance between the numbers recruited into training or into employment and the needs of the services provided. In this sphere health authorities, through their nursing officers and area or district schools of nursing, have been largely responsible for their own manpower planning. Although the General Nursing Councils are concerned with the trainee recruitment, recruitment is for the most part fairly local and has not been the subject of national control. Departmental intervention has been largely aimed at influencing the development of nursing services in the long-stay institutions. Although it is no easier with these than with any other type of nursing to determine a 'right' staffing level and thus measure shortage, the general opinion has been that the longer-stay hospitals have been short of staff.

Mention should be made here of three manpower problems which particularly affect manpower planning for nurses, though they are also relevant to other groups of staff. The first is wastage. The proportion of student and pupil nurses not completing their training varies remarkably and is sometimes very high. Whether or not it is in general unreasonably high might be difficult to assess, but wastage rates have perplexed the profession and have certainly meant that considerably larger numbers have had to be recruited than the planned number of trained nurses. The second problem, or rather problems, relate to the fact that nursing is predominantly a female profession. A large proportion leave the profession on marriage soon after qualification. This means, much more than in a profession where most members practise until retirement, that total numbers are greatly dependent on numbers recruited in the last few years and therefore on the birthrate some 18 years earlier. It requires a greater willingness to employ married staff part time. And for long-term planning it requires an assessment of the likelihood of attracting nurses back to the profession after their children have grown. The third problem is hours of work. Practically all groups of staff work shorter hours than in 1948 — a fact which needs to be borne in mind when considering the growth of staff numbers. Hours of work very broadly follow those in the community at large; they are negotiated in Whitley Councils and are thus outside the control of manpower planning. While reduced working hours for any group of staff have manpower implications they are particularly important in nursing partly because nurses are the largest group of staff and partly because most nursing services have to be staffed 24 hours a day. A health authority may need to recruit a considerable number of extra nurses to meet a shorter working week.

Manpower issues for medical and nursing staffing, however complex, can at least be seen as a whole. The case is very different with the other caring professions. As Chapter 15 explains, methods of recruitment and training are varied, and there are numerous interested bodies. It is hardly surprising, therefore, that progress towards the establishment of more rational and appropriate recruitment and training arrangements moves very slowly.

With the groups of staff mentioned so far, the NHS is largely a monopoly employer. Thus questions of the supply of trained manpower become of crucial interest to the professions not only in relation to the standards of service provided but also to the bargaining position they can adopt over pay. Thus it is not surprising that although generally the professions urge governments to improve standards and numbers, they are at times more worried at the risks of over-supply.

For other groups of staff, supply problems tend to be relatively easier. In many cases health authorities are recruiting in a local labour market in the expectation of employing staff already trained or staff whose training needs may not be high. In those circumstances their success will depend on the availability of a pool of labour and on the competitiveness or otherwise of NHS rates of pay in relation to the prevailing rate for the occupation concerned. Other staff are drawn from professions and occupations whose scope is much wider than the NHS and whose training is not a responsibility of the service; examples are scientists, architects and computer staff. Here again recruitment tends to be easier though it will vary with the state of the national market and the competitiveness of NHS pay.

While there are certain problems about the recruitment, career planning and retention of administrative staff, on the whole the problems are small compared with those say of the distribution of medical manpower or the supply of trained staff in the professions supplementary to medicine. A development of the last ten years has been the increasing number of women entering administration, and this is bringing with it questions such as provision for return to work after family commitments, which have already been faced by some of the other professions.

The effects of the legislation on equal opportunities, particularly in relation to women, have brought attention to bear on the opportunity for trained married women to return to their careers. An increase in the number of women entering medical schools has resulted in the adoption of various policies designed to encourage married women doctors to retain their interest in the profession and their links with the service generally and to make it easier for them to return to work by the creation of training posts on a part-time basis to meet their special needs. Mention has already been made of the implications of marriage for the nursing profession, and the use of part-time staff.

In Whitley bargaining, staff organisations frequently stress the need for better pay and conditions of service as a means to improved recruitment. As we have mentioned above, rates of pay are relevant to the ability to recruit, but the relationship is not always clear and the same considerations do not necessarily apply to all groups of staff. Rates of pay are national and a rate which may be competitive for a form of labour in one part of the country may be quite uncompetitive elsewhere. To some extent it is possible to use grading structures to offset such difficulties, so that secretarial staff in central London and some other urban centres tend to be paid on higher grades than their counterparts elsewhere in the country, but this sort of flexibility is generally rare within the Whitley Council agreements. Lack of flexibility in this respect may be seen as the price the service has to pay for avoiding local bargaining.

Throughout the whole of the manpower planning process the service suffers a major drawback. Apart from medical staff, the information base on which manpower planning rests is extremely limited. While progress has been made in some health regions and in Scotland towards establishing a relatively developed system of obtaining information from computerised payrolls, many authorities still have quite inadequate information systems both for the day-to-day task of controlling labour costs and for the longer term task of planning manpower needs and deployment. Such information as is available often has to be extracted manually from employee files. Questions that require urgent answers at particular times often have to be answered through the mounting of *ad hoc* surveys. Much time and effort has already been devoted to the establishment of standardised computer systems for providing manpower information. Progress is disappointingly slow and even the most basic of information relating to an annual headcount of staff is still, in some regions, undertaken by manual methods. Information on wastage, on staff flows and the level of qualification is scanty while the simplest of information needed to monitor other employment policies, such as equal opportunities, is nonexistent. Herein lies the crucial problem for manpower planning. Until it is resolved the manpower element of the corporate planning system will always lag behind.

Since 1974 considerable effort has been made to develop a number of standardised computer systems for use in the NHS, so that common payroll, accounting and manpower planning processes can be applied throughout the service. The work of developing systems has been taken on by different regions and while there are problems of integrating programmes, it seems likely that a standard manpower planning system will be available within the early 1980s. In the meantime such manpower planning as can be done is carried out largely at Departmental or regional level. A national forum where manpower planners come together to discuss their results and progress their work has been in existence since reorganisation. Progress, however, varies between regions and there are considerable differences between those regions that have access to computerised information and are able to make use of it and those where only the minimum of manpower planning is possible. Within AHAs manpower planning is most usually linked to the strategic or operational planning systems or to the building of new hospitals or redevelopment of existing institutions.

One matter which has concerned many managers in the service relates to the development of staffing norms or ideal staffing levels to deliver particular levels of service. It has received some attention; professional bodies have recommended certain staffing levels as ideal for a particular situation, the Departments and official committees have suggested minimum staffing levels and work study teams will advise management on the hourly paid staff required to undertake a certain amount of work in connection with productivity deals. The fact remains that virtually none of the recommended norms is regarded as authoritative. Perhaps generally acceptable norms can be achieved in the future. The best guide for the moment is a compendium of staffing norms published by the DHSS which discusses the purpose of different kinds of norm and provides a reference point for information on numerous staff groups.

A reason for lack of progress has been the difficulty of the exercise. Mention has already been made of attempts to measure the number of nurses a hospital should need. An even more difficult exercise, with important manpower (though not, strictly speaking, staffing) implications is to determine the best size for a GP's list and hence how many GPs are needed. It is commonly assumed that the average size should be smaller than at present, but it has been argued that they could manage much larger lists, and attempts to relate the measurable aspects of GP activity to list size have been inconclusive. The only safe generalisation seems to be that the case for shorter lists has not been demonstrated.

Possibly another reason for lack of progress has been the difficulty of applying norms. Health authorities must make use of norms, however questionable, when planning or in determining the staffing of a new hospital, but ultimately a limit is set to staff numbers either by a shortage of staff or by a shortage of money to pay for them. Norms may on occasion indicate staffing levels lower than these practical limits, but they are at least as likely to suggest levels higher than can be achieved, in which case they are unhelpful and politically embarrassing.

The case of management staffing throws some interesting light on this. Since 1976 health authorities have been required to reduce their management costs, and further reductions will be required by 1984. The limits are set in terms of cost as a proportion of total expenditure, and thus permit some scope for variations in posts, grades and numbers within total costs. But there is no known 'right' figure for management costs and the limit is arbitrary, unrelated to the tasks that have to be performed, so that authorities will have to adjust tasks to what is possible within the permitted costs. To a greater or lesser extent the same approach is necessary for most types of staffing.

Conclusion

This chapter has outlined the present state of personnel management in the NHS — the way in which it operates, the key features of the system and the stage of development that it has reached. To some extent its future will be determined by the future shape of the service, but personnel management will exist irrespective of the shape or the policies of the organisation; whether more or less of the work is carried out by personnel specialists than at present, the service will still need policies for recruitment, industrial relations, training and so on.

The personnel discipline achieved its full recognition in the service only in 1974 and thus its history has coincided with a period of change and difficulty. Further changes are pending and continuing financial restraint will increase pressure for efficiency — which necessarily means chiefly the deployment of staff in the most economic way. The performance of personnel managers in relation to the basic elements of the job — the recruitment and selection procedures, the handling of individual problems and the maintenance of established procedures — will continue to be a matter of crucial concern to health authorities. Some of the key problems facing the service have already been discussed. The Whitley system needs improvement, not least by the provision of better information on the costs of potential wage and salary settlements. Improved information is equally essential for the development of manpower planning and, related to that, for the development of staff training and career development. If strikes cannot be predicted it at least seems certain that industrial relations will continue to present difficulties, and management handling of them must be improved. Here that elusive concept, management style, is important. So, no less, is consistency. These qualities are possibly particularly difficult to maintain with a system of team management, and the personnel officer's role can become critical.

In one respect the future is uncertain. Since 1964 there has been a sometimes gradual, sometimes marked change in the relationship between staff and management in the health service. Relationships have been uneasy and while that cannot necessarily be ascribed to the attitudes of particular governments it does more broadly reflect the political atmosphere. The parties disagree more than in earlier years about the service and, while political fashions have oscillated between devolution and centralisation of managerial control, political influence over and interest in the NHS has tended to increase. In personnel management as in other matters, therefore, the future of the service is subject to the uncertainties of politics. Increased political influence seems likely, whether explicity in such matters as labour legislation or indirectly in the overall climate of affairs created between management and managed.

Further reading

Statutory instruments and circulars

England and Wales

SI74/296. The NHS (Remuneration and Conditions of Service) Regulations 1974
SI74/361. The NHS (Appointment of Consultants) Regulations 1974
HRC(73)37. Operation and development of services: organisation for personnel management
HSC(IS)57. Policy and organisation for training services
HSC(IS)141, WHSC(IS)195. Filling management posts in the NHS
HC(77)23. Report by National Staff Committees for A & C Staff and for Accommodation, etc. Staff: scheme for staff development and performance review
HC(79)20, WHC(79)14. If industrial relations break down

Scotland

SI74/276. The NHS (Remuneration and Conditions of Service) (Scotland) Regulations 1974
SI76/1679. The NHS (Appointment of Consultants) (Scotland) Regulations 1976
HSR(73)C27. Personnel function

Official reports

DHSS. *Making Whitley Work: A review of the operation of the National*

Health Service Whitley Council System (McCarthy Report). HMSO 1976

DHSS. *Management Arrangements for the Reorganised National Health Service* (The Grey Book). HMSO 1972

DHSS. *Medical Manpower: the next twenty years.* HMSO 1978

DHSS. *Report of the Committee of Inquiry into the Pay and Related Conditions of Service of Nurses and Midwives* (Halsbury Report). HMSO 1974

National Board for Prices and Incomes. Report No 29: *The Pay and Conditions of Manual Workers in Local Authorities, the National Health Service, Gas and Water Supply.* HMSO 1971

National Staff Committee for A & C Staff. *The Recruitment and Career Development of Administrators.* 1979

Review Body on Doctors' and Dentists' Remuneration. *Tenth Report* (Cmnd 7903). HMSO 1980

Royal Commission on the National Health Service. *Report* (Cmnd 7615). HMSO 1979

Royal Commission on the National Health Service. Research Paper No. 4 *Doctor Manpower 1975-2000: alternative forecasts and their resource implications* (A. Maynard and A. Walker). HMSO 1978

Standing Commission on Pay Comparability. Reports. 1 *Local Authority and University Manual Workers; NHS Ancillary Staffs; and Ambulancemen* (Cmnd 7641). HMSO 1979. 3. *Nurses and Midwives* (Cmnd 7795). HMSO 1980. 4. *Professions Supplementary to Medicine* (Cmnd 7850). HMSO 1980

Other publications

Bosanquet, N. (Ed). *Industrial Relations in the NHS — the search for a system.* King's Fund 1979

Cuming, M.W. *Personnel Management in the National Health Service.* Heinemann 1978

Dimmock, D. and Harrison, S. (Eds). *Industrial Relations Training Manual.* Nuffield Centre for Health Service Studies, Leeds 1980

Dyson, R. *The Management of Pathology Laboratories.* Association of Clinical Pathologists 1977

Hawkins, K. *A Handbook of Industrial Relations Practice.* Kogan Page 1979

Health Services Manpower Review. Special Series — 'The McCarthy Report'. 1977

Long, A.F. and Mercer, G. (Ed). *Manpower Planning in the National Health Service.* Gower 1981

McLachlan, G. *et al.* (Eds). *Patterns for Uncertainty? Planning for the greater medical profession.* OUP for Nuffield Provincial Hospitals Trust 1979

Millard, G. *Personnel Management in Hospitals.* Institute of Personnel Management 1972

Pigors, P. and Myers, C.A. *Personnel Administration.* McGraw Hill 1969

14
The independent sector

The independent sector may be defined as those institutions and arrangements for providing personal health care outside the NHS or other state provision. It is not quite the same thing as the private sector because on the one hand the independent sector contains charitable bodies not normally described as private, and on the other hand there is private care within the NHS and not organisationally part of the independent sector. The latter, however, is discussed in this chapter because to some extent private care without or outside the NHS is an alternative, and cannot be considered separately from the NHS.

The independent sector as it exists today dates from the establishment of the NHS, but many of the independent hospitals are much older, and before 1948 were little if any different in character from the voluntary hospitals which were incorporated in the NHS. The National Health Service Act 1946, and the equivalents for Scotland and Northern Ireland, vested voluntary hospitals in the Minister but gave him powers to disclaim hospitals which in his opinion were not required for the purpose of providing hospital and specialist services as defined in the Act. Governing bodies of hospitals disclaimed were given the option of serving a notice on the Minister stating that they wished the hospital to be transferred within the terms of the Act. The hospitals ultimately disclaimed did not have a common character other than that in one way or another they were unlike the ordinary voluntary hospital; they included nearly all hospitals affiliated to a religious body (although a few such opted for inclusion in the NHS), homes founded after 1919 for ex-servicemen, hospitals and schools for epileptics, hospitals providing care under employment-linked contribution schemes, hospitals supported by freemasons and by trade unions, and a number of hospitals for the mentally ill. Convalescent homes, except those belonging to hospitals absorbed into the NHS, did not come within the scope of the Act. Neither did institutions in private ownership, whether by an individual or a limited company; this category included the great majority of nursing homes.

Thus the independent sector in 1948 comprised old-established institutions left out of the NHS. Their future would depend on finding a role in a society in which the NHS aimed to provide comprehensive care for all the population. Since then there have been a number of developments. Possibly the most important has been the development of provident schemes. Their expansion has enabled an increasing number of people to pay for private medical care. In 1957 the British United Provident Association (BUPA), the largest of the provident schemes, established a registered charity, the Nuffield Nursing Homes Trust (not to be confused with the Nuffield Provincial Hospitals Trust) to help in the provision of more good standard private beds. Admission to these Nuffield Hospitals (originally called Nursing Homes) is not restricted to members of BUPA but is open to all private patients however funded. By the end of 1979 30 of these hospitals had been opened.

The Nuffield Hospitals have provided small modern hospitals in most parts of the country where there has been adequate demand for private treatment. A different form of expansion took place in the 1970s, mainly but not exclusively, in London. London has the largest collection of leading consultants, and for long it has had a number of hospitals, not all operating for profit, where they treat private patients. The new development was the establishment of a number of new hospitals, operated by limited companies for profit and catering mainly for patients from overseas, particularly the Middle East.

A quite different development, and one in line with the tradition of the voluntary movement, has been the provision of hospices for the terminally ill. While hospices are not a new idea, the need for more attention to the care of the dying has been appreciated in recent years, thanks particularly to the work of Dame Cicely Saunders. St Christopher's Hospice in south London, with which she is associated, was opened in 1967. In the 1950s the Marie Curie Memorial Foundation was established and by the end of 1978 was providing care in 11 homes together with a nursing service in the homes of patients. Some of its homes are in the grounds of NHS hospitals.

The Abortion Act 1967 (which does not apply to Northern Ireland) placed a new demand on the independent sector. Nearly half the abortions performed on women resident in the UK are peformed in private clinics and nursing homes, as well as practically all on non-resident women — 28,015 in 1978. In that year there were 60 registered private nursing homes approved under the Abortion Act, of which 19 were regarded as specialising in abortions. There are considerable geographical differences; in the Northern Region only about 10 per cent of abortions are private, compared with 78 per cent in the West Midlands region.

An important event in the history of the independent sector was the Health Services Act 1976, which is described later in this chapter. That Act, while concerned with the independent sector, has as its main objective the phasing out of private beds in NHS hospitals, and this was expected to be accompanied by an increase in the supply of private beds outside it.

The size of the independent sector

In a paper for the Royal Commission Rudolf Klein said: 'Determining the scale, and nature, of private practice is far from easy. There are no routinely collected statistics and hardly any special studies, a fact which, in itself, suggests both low salience and small scale'. In their report the Royal Commission provided more information than had previously been available.

In 1977 the numbers of private hospitals and nursing homes registered, and the number of beds they contained were as shown in Table 1. About 73 per cent of the beds were for medical patients, a category including convalescent, rehabilitation and care of the chronically sick and elderly. Many were nursing homes and medical care was provided by GPs under the NHS in the same way as if the people had been living in their own homes. Another 15 per cent were for surgery: 117 hospitals, of which 31 were run by religious orders and 44 by other charitable or non-profit making organisations. About 11 per cent were for mental health, and 2 per cent for maternity.

Table 1. Numbers of private institutions and beds

	Institutions	Beds
England	1,110	30,457
Wales	45	986
Scotland	84	2,847
Northern Ireland	10	256
UK total	1,249	34,546

The hospitals were unevenly distributed throughout the country — in relation to population they were more numerous in England. There were 2,059 'acute' beds in private hospitals in London and the south east, half of them in the North West Thames region, and only 30 in the Northern region. There were nursing homes throughout the country, but there were concentrations in coastal areas such as Kent, Sussex, Devon and North Wales.

About 4,000 beds in the private sector are occupied by NHS patients under contractual arrangements made by health authorities.

One indication of the size of the independent sector is membership of provident schemes. Membership increased fourfold between 1955 and 1975, largely because of group schemes organised by employers for white-collar staff. In 1978 there were 1.12 million subscribers covering about 2.39 million people, or one in 25 of the population. This does not mean that over two million people have opted out of the NHS. In the first place, three-quarters of members belong because of their employment, not through personal choice, though employers would not arrange group schemes if they did not think them attractive to staff. In the second place, it is likely that the majority use the NHS for most purposes (family practitioner services, maternity care, emergency admissions, etc.) and use their membership for 'cold' surgery. Contributory schemes are used for paying for treatment both in the independent sector and in NHS pay beds.

About 50 per cent of private patients receiving acute treatment are covered by provident schemes, some of the rest are covered by other insurance arrangements.

In England about 2 per cent of all acute hospital beds and 6 per cent of all hospital beds are in private hospitals and nursing homes, and the proportions are lower in the rest of the UK. The total spent on private health care is not known, but the Royal Commission thought that in 1976 it was of the order of £200 million, compared with total NHS expenditure in that year of £6,249 million. That would mean that the private sector accounts for about 3 per cent of total expenditure on health care in the UK.

Doctors and other professionals

The independent sector would not exist without the co-operation and in many instances the initiative of doctors. The majority of the profession in fact regard the possibility of practice outside the NHS as essential to their professional freedom. Not many doctors, however, practise solely outside the NHS. While a number of the larger independent hospitals have full-time medical staff, most doctors practising in these hospitals also have an NHS appointment.

The arrangements are somewhat similar to — and a continuation of — arrangements in voluntary hospitals before 1948 when honorary consultants treated private patients either in the private wing of the hospital or in nursing homes. The extent to which NHS consultants undertake private practice is not exactly known, but a good indication can be found in the number who hold part-time rather than full-time NHS appointments, because the possibility of taking private patients is the usual though not the invariable reason for opting for less than full time. Following an agreement with the profession in 1948, health authorities may not insist on full-time contracts (which before 1980 did not permit private practice). The new consultants' contract which was introduced in 1980 has been seen as an encouragement to take on private practice but, as the Royal Commission pointed out, an increase depends not only on its attractiveness to doctors but also on the demand from patients.

In 1976 42.8 per cent of NHS consultants in the UK had part-time contracts, a considerable drop from the 56.9 per cent in 1965. The choice of contract depends on the opportunities for private practice. In 1978 in England and Wales 94 per cent of geriatricians and 85.3 per cent of pathologists were full time, but only 14.4 per cent of general surgeons and 15.5 per cent of ENT surgeons. In the circumstance of the UK, 'cold' surgery is the type of health care most likely to attract the private patient. Specialty is not the only factor determining the choice between full time and part-time contracts; the uneven distribution of facilities for private care is also relevant. In the North West Thames region only 29 per cent of all consultants were full time in 1978, whereas in the Northern region it was 68.9 per cent and in Scotland 82.2 per cent.

General practitioners are free to undertake any other work they wish, provided it does not interfere with their obligations under their NHS contracts. It is probable that they nearly all undertake some work, such as examination for insurance purposes, for which they charge fees, but while a few live entirely by private practice the majority have few or no private patients. In 1971-2 about 6 per cent of general practitioners' income was from private practice.

General dental practitioners are equally free to take private patients and more of them do so. In 1977 some 11 per cent of their time was spent on work other than that in the general dental service, probably mainly on private practice. Some patients receive both NHS and private treatment from the same dentists, and there are complaints from some parts of the country that most dentists will not carry out certain forms of treatment under the NHS.

Members of the other health care professions work in independent hospitals and there are members of some professions, such as nurses, physiotherapists and chiropodists, who live by private practice outside hospitals. There are employment agencies which supply nurses and other professionals to independent hospitals and private patients and sometimes also to NHS hospitals. Also in private practice are members of professions not employed in the NHS, such as osteopaths and chiropracters.

Organisation within the independent sector

Before 1948 the British Hospitals Association represented most voluntary hospitals, and was influential in such areas as recommending salary and wage rates, setting standards and the provision of information services. It was dissolved in 1948 when most of its members entered the NHS but those institutions which remained outside, many of which had belonged to the association, felt the need for a similar body which could co-ordinate their interests. Accordingly the Association of Independent Hospitals and Kindred Organisations was founded in 1949 as an association, mainly, but not entirely, of institutions which were registered charities. The objectives were basically to bring together members for their mutual benefit and to provide an information and advice service. The Association now organises seminars and courses, regular meetings of representatives, publishes a bi-monthly news letter and an annual yearbook and is able to procure advice on a wide variety of subjects for members. At the end of 1978 there were 174 hospitals and homes in membership, providing in all 12,245 beds.

In 1970 the Registered Nursing Home Association was formed and incorporated as a limited company. Its membership has grown rapidly and today the Association provides a forum for the exchange of ideas and a means for the dissemination of information through a network of local branches, a series of bulletins on a wide variety of matters, the holding of day conferences and the publication of an annual reference book of all hospitals and homes registered with health authorities. One of its main objectives is to foster high professional standards and no home is admitted to membership of the Association until it has been visited by a member of the council.

In 1975, in view of the imminence of the Bill to phase out private practice from the NHS, a third organisation was set up, the Independent Hospital Group (IHG). This consisted primarily of hospitals and homes providing acute care. Its initial function was to endeavour to secure favourable revision of some of the provisions of the Bill. After the Bill became the Health Services Act 1976 it continued in being and offers an advisory service to its members.

There have been discussions between these three bodies about the possibility of either a merger or the establishment of a co-ordinating body.

Nursing Homes Act

Nearly all independent hospitals in England and Wales are subject to the provisions of the Nursing Homes Act 1975. (In Scotland the relevant legislation is the Nursing Homes Registration (Scotland) Act 1938 and in Northern Ireland the Nursing Homes and Nursing Agencies Act (Northern Ireland) 1971.)

Nursing homes originally came under the provisions of the Public Health Act 1936, when local authorities were given responsibility for some control over these homes. A subsequent act in 1963 increased the controls and repaired some of the loopholes of the 1936 Act. The 1975 Act is mainly a consolidating act and the main regulations were made under the previous legislation. Area health authorities have replaced local authorities as the responsible bodies. Both the 1975 Act and the 1938 Scottish Act were amended by the Health Services Act 1980.

The 1975 Act as amended, defines 'nursing home' as 'any premises used, or intended to be used, for the reception of, and the providing of nursing for, persons suffering from any sickness, injury or infirmity' including a maternity home and any other premises used for surgical procedures, the termination of pregnancy, endoscopy or haemodialysis or peritoneal dialysis. It excludes any hospital maintained or controlled by a government department or local authority (including NHS hospitals) or a body constituted by a special act of parliament or incorporated by royal charter and various other premises such as first aid rooms and GP consulting rooms, which might otherwise come within its scope. The Act also covers mental nursing homes, which are similarly defined. The Secretary of State has power to exempt Christian Science nursing homes from its provisions.

It is an offence to carry on a nursing home or mental nursing home without being registered under the Act. Registration is by the Secretary of State, but application is made to the relevant AHA. Registration may be refused, or cancelled, on various grounds including the unsuitability of the applicant or the premises and the failure to have in charge a qualified doctor or nurse or midwife. Regulations require nursing homes to maintain registers of patients and various records; medical officers or authorised persons have power to inspect these. Other regulations concern the conduct of homes; they require adequate accommodation, staffing, equipment, etc. and empower a registration authority to limit the number of persons who may be received. There are additional provisions in relation to mental nursing homes.

Administration

With such a variety of institutions within the independent sector both in size and in type of care provided, it is not surprising to find equally varied forms of administration. In most of the registered charities there is a committee, not necessarily at local level, and/or a body of trustees who are the legal owners of the institution. Organisations operating a number of institutions may have local committees, usually with limited executive powers, or just the central committee structure. The ultimate responsibility for the working of the institution will fall on these committees which are also legally responsible and can sue or be sued. As in many voluntary hospitals before 1948, most of these committees are self-perpetuating in the sense that contested elections are rare and existing members suggest new members for election.

Day-to-day control of the nursing services, and in the case of smaller places all the services, is usually in the hands of a matron or director of nursing. Medical services are provided by visiting specialists and general practitioners aided in a few of the larger hospitals by resident medical staff.

The secretarial and administrative services are, where size justifies this, usually controlled by an administrator, sometimes part time. Occasionally the chairman of the committee will fulfil this role. In the larger hospitals a full administrative staff operates, covering finance, supplies and general administration. Sisters of the order often fill many of these posts in hospitals run by religious bodies. Many nursing homes are under individual ownership and the proprietors manage affairs. Some belong to limited companies or partnerships often with medical directors, and then managers are usually appointed. There is movement of nurses and administrators between the NHS and the independent sector in both directions.

Most institutions charge fees to patients, in the case of registered charities sufficient to cover costs, in other types of institutions at levels to show a profit on operations for shareholders or proprietors. Some homes and hospitals still do not have fixed fees, but patients are left to contribute or not, as they are able. Donations and subscriptions still form a valuable and necessary part of the income of many well-known charitable organisations.

In some places where no NHS provision exists, or where it is insufficient to meet needs, contractual arrangements are made by health authorities with independent institutions providing care for long-stay patients, such as geriatric and mental handicap. This can take the form of paying for a specific allocation of beds, or for certain types of patient or even meeting virtually the full cost of running the hospital. Some institutions are dependent on contractual arrangements for their financial stability. Often the cost per patient is less than in the NHS, especially in hospitals run by religious orders. Local authorities sometimes pay the cost of caring for some patients, such as epileptics or the heavily physically handicapped.

Unlike NHS hospitals which, as Crown property, are not bound by certain legislation (though it is normally official policy that they should conform), all institutions in the independent sector must conform to legal requirements in such areas as health and safety at work, fire precautions and catering regulations. In addition they need to cover by insurance all risks under which damages may be suffered or claimed, including the risk of actions for injury to, or wrongful treatment of, patients.

Independent hospitals do not have the statutory or other obligations to the public as do health authorities and their hospitals and their relations with the public are therefore different. Some serve a local community and draw support from it; others are oriented more towards a particular group, e.g. to people particularly concerned for epileptics, and will draw from them financial and other assistance. The religious foundations are related particularly to their own denomination. Local interest is often encouraged by leagues of friends or similar bodies. Many charitable institutions use traditional methods of publicising their activities and raising funds, while a number of independent hospitals use more modern public relations methods.

Private beds in the NHS

Since its inception the NHS has made beds available in NHS hospitals for private treatment; the health authority charges the patient for accommodation and services etc., while the consultant's fees are a matter between him and the patient. Provision for private beds was originally made in Section 5 of the 1946 Act for England and Wales and of the 1947 Act for Scotland, and subsequently in Section 1 of the Health Services and Public Health Act 1968, which made certain changes in the arrangements. This in turn has been replaced by the consolidating Acts of 1977 and 1978. There is also provision in the Acts for the treatment of non-resident patients.

In most hospitals the occupancy rates of private beds has been considerably lower than that of NHS beds. If it is true that in a market system rationing is by price whereas in a system with no charges at the time the use of rationing is by queue, the difference may not be surprising. Occupancy rates have in fact been sufficiently low for a considerable reduction in the total number of pay beds to have been made without apparently falling below demand. In England there were 5,723 authorised pay beds in 1956 and by 1976 this had fallen gradually to 4,150. In contrast the number of patients treated in pay beds has increased; the figure for England and Wales was 78,274 in 1950, rising to 101,696 in 1966 and to 113,221 in 1974, the peak year. By 1976 it was down to 94,323. Pay beds represent only a very small proportion of total beds in NHS hospitals. In England, where they were most numerous, they were 1.07 per cent in 1976; the figures for Wales and Scotland were 0.25 and 0.39 per cent respectively. Northern Ireland, with a total of 415, had proportionately more.

The Health Services Act 1976 was designed to bring an end to the provision of private beds in NHS hospitals in Great Britain. It did not apply to Northern Ireland, but the government followed the same policy there. Its objective was to be achieved in two ways. First, the Act itself reduced by 1,000 the total number of authorised pay beds. Secondly, it established the Health Services Board with the duty of making recommendations at six-monthly intervals for further withdrawals of authorisations of pay beds and also of provision for non-resident treatment. The recommendations had to be implemented by the Secretary of State. The Board comprised a chairman, who was a lawyer, two doctors and two trade union officials. It had Scottish and Welsh Committees. In making its recommendations the Board had to take into account whether there was a reasonable demand for private accommodation and facilities, and whether alternative provision existed, either in the NHS or privately. Where alternative provision did not exist pay beds might continue to be authorised, but only if reasonable steps were being taken to provide private facilities. The Board made several proposals for revocation of private facilities, and showed some disappointment that it was not able to achieve a greater reduction. At the beginning of January 1976 there were 4,444 private beds, of which a thousand ceased to be authorised with the passing of the Act, and by July 1979 the number was 2,770.

The Board was also given the task of making recommendations for common waiting lists for private and NHS patients in NHS hospitals.

With the coming into office of a new government, the Board practically ceased to function in the latter half of 1979 and was dissolved under Part II of the Health Services Act 1980, which also re-established the powers of Secretaries of State to make accommodation and services available for private patients.

Control of hospitals outside the NHS

The 1976 Act envisaged that the reduction of pay beds would be accompanied by an increased provision of beds in the private sector, and that in fact happened. However, the authors of the Act were not anxious to see any large expansion of the private sector, particularly as it was thought that that might increase the difficulties of staffing NHS hospitals. The task of controlling expansion was given to the Health Services Board.

Hitherto although, as we have seen, hospitals in the independent sector had been subject to various statutory controls, there had been no limit on their establishment or expansion provided they conformed with the legal requirements in other respects. The new control was limited to acute hospitals, or, more precisely, to hospitals providing one or more of the following facilities: carrying out surgical procedures under general anaesthesia, obstetrics, radiotherapy, renal dialysis or radiology or diagnostic pathology. Furthermore it applied only to hospitals providing 100 or more beds in the Greater London area or 75 beds elsewhere. The Health Services Board was to authorise developments unless they were satisfied that these would to a significant extent interfere with the performance by the Secretary of State of any duty imposed on him by the NHS Acts to provide accommodation or services of any kind or would to a significant extent operate to the disadvantage of persons seeking or afforded admission or access to any accommodation or services under the NHS. The Board held several public hearings of applications for development which were opposed by health authorities and other bodies. Other hospitals outside the NHS were required to notify the Board of proposed developments that required planning permission, but the Board had no control in these cases.

The 1980 Act amended these provisions in several respects. With the abolition of the Board, its responsibilities for control of hospital building outside the NHS was transferred to the Secretary of State. The minimum size for control was raised to 120 beds but the Secretary of State was given powers to designate areas in which all hospitals within the scope of the legislation, i.e. acute as defined above, were to be 'controlled premises'. This was intended to meet a weakness of the 1976 Act under which there was no means of limiting the expansions of small hospitals of less than 100 or 75 beds even though the consequences in a particular area might have justified the refusal of authorisation if all the beds had been in a single hospital.

NHS or private care?

The NHS is available to all residents of the country free of charge (with minor exceptions) at the time of use, and people contribute to the cost, through taxation, even when they opt for private treatment. Why then should the private sector continue to flourish, even on a small scale?

The explanation does not lie in any particular characteristic of independent hospitals as a group. The Royal Commission reported:

> We visited a number of private hospitals with acute beds, including one run commercially and by charitable organisations. We found that the disparities between one hospital and another in premises and facilities and in general atmosphere were at least as great as the variations to be found within the NHS. We were not able to judge the quality of medical and nursing care provided, but in some the standard of accommodation was higher than that normally provided by the NHS. Others seemed to offer no advantages over the NHS except a room to oneself, and in some cases not even that. There are of course substantial variations in the cost of private hospitals, but we did not always find that the most expensive hospitals offered the best facilities.

People coming to the UK from overseas for medical treatment must necessarily seek private treatment, whether in NHS hospitals or in the independent sector, since the NHS is not available to them (though it is to visitors who fall ill while here and need emergency treatment). The proportion of private patients from overseas is not known, but the Royal Commission thought that except in some of the larger private hospitals in London it is probably small.

Most of the rich, it may be assumed, automatically turn to the private sector whether for their general practitioner or for hospital treatment. Other people have a variety of reasons for seeking private care. For acute care, the main reasons, apart from past dissatisfaction with the NHS, or loyalty to a particular hospital, are: the privacy of a single room, the convenience of being able to book a specific date for admission, the avoidance of a long waiting time for an out-patient appointment or in-patient treatment, and to guarantee seeing a particular consultant. Another, which applies to general practitioners as well as consultants, is that more time is usually given to private consultations. The Royal Commission considered that it should not be necessary to seek private treatment for a single room or to book admission, and that NHS hospitals should do more to make the availability of amenity beds known.

Patients seeking abortion, the Royal Commission found, did not turn to the private sector because they preferred it but because in some places the NHS facilities were inadequate. It thought there should be more NHS provision.

Reasons for choosing private accommodation for other types of patients, such as geriatric or psychiatric, are usually dislike of NHS provision or inability to secure it in the area where the patient, or his relatives, lives. Patients cared for in such hospitals under contractual arrangements are to be regarded as NHS rather than private patients.

While some people choose private medical care, or feel that they have no choice but to use it, there are many people who believe that the choice should not be available. In its more moderate form, this is the belief that there should be no facilities for private patients in the NHS.

Private treatment, it is argued, is incompatible with the principles of the NHS and to provide for it within the service is therefore anomalous. Various more specific objections are raised: that it uses beds which otherwise would be available for NHS patients; that it diverts consultants from their proper task, which is the treatment of NHS patients; that it imposes on junior doctors, nurses and other staff extra work for which, unlike consultants, they are not paid. Allegations are also made that patients can obtain early admission to the NHS in-patient waiting list by paying for a private consultation rather than waiting their turn on the out-patient waiting list; inevitably, there is no evidence as to whether this abuse is common. The fact that admission to a private bed for non-urgent cases is often quicker than to an NHS bed for a patient with similar condition is also sometimes seen as an abuse, and the Health Services Act 1976 made provision for common waiting lists in an attempt to end it, although it might be thought a natural consequence of the different principle on which private treatment is based.

Private beds are an historical accident and their defenders minimise their supposed disadvantages rather than claim special merits for them. These beds, it is said, are so few in number that the effect on waiting lists of using them for NHS patients would be negligible. Another argument, and one which the Royal Commission thought the strongest in favour of retaining private beds, is that if consultants are allowed to treat private patients it is better that they should do so in an NHS hospital, where they are available when needed in an emergency, than that they should leave the hospital to treat patients elsewhere. It has also been argued that the existence of private beds in the NHS has discouraged their provision in greater numbers outside it.

On both sides of the argument there have been assertions about costs: on the one hand that the NHS subsidises private patients and on the other that it gains financially from their presence. The Royal Commission thought that charges did not contribute sufficiently to capital costs.

Some, though not all, opponents of private beds in the NHS argue that no private medical care at all should be allowed. The basic argument is that since a country's total resources devoted to health care are necessarily limited, it is unfair and inefficient that the allocation of even a part of them should depend on ability to pay rather than on need. Against this it is argued that even if it were true that a state monopoly of health care would achieve the most efficient and equitable use of resources — and believers in a market economy would not concede that — it is unacceptable in a liberal society that people should be forbidden from seeking health care outside the NHS if they wish to pay for it, or that health care professionals should be forbidden from offering treatment outside the service, but may seek a professional career only within the service.

Supporters of private medicine argue that there is a limit to what the taxpayer can afford or the government can allocate for NHS treatment, and that if people who can afford private treatment are encouraged to do so the NHS will be able to devote more of its resources to those who cannot opt out. On the other side it is argued that while there is a limit to what a country can afford to spend on health care it is unrealistic to suppose that the limit would be higher if only part rather than all were raised by taxation. Furthermore, it is said, experience in other countries does not support the view that a large private sector facilitates relatively more expenditure on the types of care, particularly long-stay, which must fall to the public sector; on the contrary they are more liable to be 'Cinderella' services than in the NHS.

A further argument against the private sector, though subsidiary to the arguments of principle, is that it is parasitic on the NHS in that it does not bear the cost of training the professional staff it employs. This argument stresses the very considerable cost to the NHS of training but does not take into account the service benefit of staff in training.

Among the other arguments in favour of the independent sector one of the strongest is that the NHS could not do without it. This is undoubtedly true at present of the provision of long-stay care, particularly geriatric care. Also the NHS does not provide enough facilities for abortions. Most of the strong feeling against private medicine is directed at acute care, which is the sector most profitable to practitioners and institutions, although the arguments of principle would apply equally to those other forms of private care which in fact make up the greater part of the independent sector.

After examining the various arguments the Royal Commission were unable to reach any conclusion about the overall balance of advantage or disadvantage to the NHS of the existence of a private sector, 'but it is clear whichever way it lies it is small as matters now stand'.

The main arguments for and against private health care reflect different views of society, and thus different political attitudes. Pay beds, although established by a Labour government in 1946, have always been disliked by many members of the party, and they were reduced in number in 1968, but it was not until the Labour government of 1974-9 that they were a matter of great political interest. Some of the health service unions then took action against private patients at a number of hospitals and the eventual outcome was the Health Services Act 1976 and the establishment of the Health Services Board, which represented a compromise between conflicting interests of the unions and the medical profession.

The Conservative administration which came into office in 1979 put an end to the board, and discontinued the phasing out of private beds. Furthermore the health ministers in this administration have shown an interest in the private sector unprecedented since 1948, and have declared their intention of encouraging its growth.

Since disagreement about private medical care has increased rather than diminished, and the supporters of neither view share the Royal Commission's view about its negligible impact on the NHS, changes of policy seem likely with future changes of government.

Further reading

Circulars

HC(80)5, WHC(80)6. Charges for private resident and non-resident patients

HC(80)10, WHC(80)14. Health Services Act 1980: private medical practice in health service hospitals and control of private hospital developments; amenity beds

HC(81)1, WHC(81)1. Contractual arrangements with independent hospitals and nursing homes and other forms of co-operation between the NHS and the independent medical sector

HC(81)8, WHC(81)6. Registration and inspection of private nursing homes and mental nursing homes (including hospitals)

NHS Circular 1980(GEN)10. Charges for private resident and non-resident patients

NHS Circular 1981(GEN)1. Health Services Act 1980: private medical practice in health service hospitals and control of private hospital developments; amenity beds

NHS Circular 1980(GEN)31. Registration and inspection of private nursing homes under the Nursing Homes Registration (Scotland) Act 1938

Official reports

Klein, R. and Buxton, M. *Allocating Health Resources, A commentary on the report of the Resource Allocation Working Party.* Research Paper No. 3. HMSO 1978

Royal Commission on the National Health Service. *Report,* Chapter 18 'The NHS and Private Practice' (Cmnd 7615). HMSO 1979

Other publications

Lee Donaldson Associates. *Provident Schemes Statistics.* Report for the DHSS. Annual

15
Health care and the professions

What is a profession? A hundred years ago the answer to this question would have been easy. The Church, law and medicine were the three careers accepted as warranting the description. In the public mind they were distinguished from those in trade or the army by their independence, learned qualifications, direct personal relationship to their clients and acceptance that theirs was a calling that required them to work the hours necessary to fulfil the task and to a standard in which the client could place confidence.

Today, that somewhat imprecise instrument of definition, the public mind, seems to have accepted that many more careers can be termed professions and it is more difficult to be clear about the criteria to apply. Certainly facets of the professional career have changed, notably the degree of independence, and the activities of professional organisations have altered. It is, for instance, often difficult to discern the difference between a trade union and a professional organisation.

There are, nevertheless, a number of key elements which seem still to be accepted as criteria for a profession. W.E. Wickenden (once president of the Institute of Electrical Engineers) is quoted as suggesting the following 'hallmarks':

— A body of knowledge or skill held as a common possession to be extended by united effort.
— An educational process based on this body of knowledge and skill, in ordering which the professional group has a recognised responsibility.
— A standard of qualification for admission to the professional group based on character, training and proved competence.
— A standard of conduct based on courtesy, honour and ethics which guides the practitioner in his relationships with clients, colleagues and the public.
— A more or less formal recognition of status by colleagues or by the State as a basis of good standing.
— Organisation of the professional group devoted to its common advancement and its social duty rather than the maintenance of an economic monopoly.

Such criteria tend not to be static and rightly so because a dynamic organisation such as the national health service may have within it an increasing number of staff groups who gradually develop professional status and standards. Indeed, one of the major developments of health care in the past hundred years has been the emergence of specialist groups claiming, correctly, to be separate professions. The object of this chapter is to outline the current situation and analyse some of the contributions made and problems created by the various professions in their relationship to the health service.

Taking the criteria listed above, it is important to recognise that the key element for any profession is to have an organisation that is publicly accepted as being allowed to control its own register of members. Cartwright has pointed out[2] that one of the significant points about the Hippocratic oath is that it is a promise to support members of the group, to confine teaching of the art (of medicine) to a close circle, and not to reveal the mysteries to anyone outside that circle. The history of the Royal Colleges of medicine during the eighteenth and early nineteenth centuries was a battle to establish themselves as publicly acceptable guardians of the register of members. The culmination of the battle was the establishment of the General Medical Council in 1859.

Since that time each emerging health profession has sought to develop its position in a broadly similar way by seeking exclusive control of membership and the right to determine training and entry requirements. Abel-Smith in his history of the nursing profession suggests that the founders of the British Nurses Association saw training as 'an apprenticeship, a period of trial, almost an initiation ritual, to test who was fit to bear the title. The greater the severity, the higher its intellectual demands, the longer its duration, the greater the status of the profession. The very fact that every woman thought she could nurse made it the more necessary to emphasise and exaggerate the training requirements'. Many professional groups in the health service and elsewhere have trodden similar paths because the prerequisite of the exclusive register and control of training requirements is the definition of a body of esoteric knowledge or skills which cannot be encompassed by another professional group. Thus, although the medical profession 'over'arches' nursing and the professions supplementary to medicine, the increasing volume of specialised knowledge and skills has, in practice, made it impossible for doctors to oversee the detailed performance of treatments which they prescribe. Staff groups have, therefore, developed within medicine with a discrete body of knowledge and skills which have eventually formed the basis for an exclusive profession.

The oversight of ethical standards is a factor that varies greatly between professions even in the health services. There are some that would see it as determining whether or not a group was 'truly professional'. In practice, however, groups of staff are accepted as members of a profession despite the fact that the body which controls their respective professional registers has no power to cause them to be disciplined for misconduct so long as they remain appropriately qualified. At one extreme, the medical profession, through the GMC can prevent a doctor practising as such on such grounds as alcoholism, drug addiction, or improper relationship with a patient. (It cannot, incidentally, stop such people, or unqualified practitioners, from treating patients outside the NHS so long as they do not pose as qualified doctors.) An architect or administrator, on the other hand, has no such control by his professional body so long as he performs his duties within the law. A study of scientists and engineers[3], for instance, concluded that the prime concern of their professional associations was with technical, study and educational activities, not with status or ethics. Their qualifications were certificates of competence which led in most instances to their becoming employees rather than 'independent practitioners' and did not even guarantee them a monopoly position for jobs.

In order for a professional body to achieve a position whereby it exercises oversight of the ethical standards of its members it seems necessary for there to be clear performance criteria which, if unfulfilled, might cause what Wilensky[4] described as 'manifest disaster'. He suggests this as the reason why 'lay hospital administrators have so far found it impossible to restrict entry to the trained, notwithstanding ... the fact that they have a quite long-standing professional institute'.

Between the two extremes, those professions whose members have a direct relationship to patients are subject to dismissal from the register if in view of their profession's disciplinary committee they are guilty of 'infamous conduct'. There is no definition of what constitutes such conduct but, for instance, the Orthoptists Board indicates that:

No registered Orthoptist should:

1. Undertake the examination or treatment of a patient unless that patient has been referred to her by a registered medical practitioner.
2. Advertise, or attempt to promote her personal gain in any unprofessional way. The Committee would not regard it as a breach of this requirement for an Orthoptist to write to registered medical practitioners in order to draw attention to her name, address and qualifications, and the fact that her services as an Orthoptist were available.
3. Accept commission on the sale of goods or in respect of any action arising out of the practice of her profession.

Professions in the health service may thus be categorised as those having a direct relationship to patients (the 'caring professions') even if, as in the case of many medical laboratory scientific officers, they do not have personal contact with patients, and those such as administrators, quantity surveyors, accountants who are regarded as professional but whose work does not require oversight of professional standards for the protection of the public though they may have their own professional norms.

The last of Wickenden's hallmarks relating to the professional group seeking common advancement and social duty rather than the maintenance of an economic monopoly is likely to cause some wry comment in an age when the monopoly position of a number of professions is being likened to the 'closed shop' achieved by some trade unions. Whatever the formal position, the fact is that membership of a profession which has a control of the numbers qualified to practise must be an important factor in a wide range of activity going beyond standards and status to include recruitment, postgraduate training, pay and conditions and manpower planning even if professional bodies do not involve themselves directly.

Those who wish to explore further the difficulty of defining why some groups currently are accepted as professional while others are not should find a useful starting point in the reading list. The most important point, however, is to recognise that the broad public acceptance as professions, of the various groups about to be examined in this chapter, cloaks great differences in status, power, required intellectual and ethical standards, and the degree of independent professional judgement allowed to individuals.

Description of the professions

The range and number of professions in the health service is such that it is impracticable to provide a detailed description for all of them. Nor is it easy to classify them neatly according to work undertaken, history or importance. The brief description which follows therefore broadly categorises the professions by Whitley Councils since this, at least, means that their salaries are negotiated by the same body in each case and the staff concerned may therefore be regarded as being in the same 'family'.

The Whitley Councils covering health service professional staff are:

Medical and dental
Nurses and midwives
Optical
Pharmaceutical
Professional and technical A dealing mainly with staff having direct contact with patients, e.g. radiographers
Professional and technical B dealing with staff such as biochemists and engineers who are professionally qualified but whose work does not necessarily involve a direct relationship with patients.
Administrative and Clerical

One important addition to the classification must be social workers. Until 1974 medical social workers were covered by the PTA Council. They are now employed by local authorities but have such a close relationship to the health service that they must be included among the health care professions.

Medicine and dentistry

Medicine is an old profession. In this country it can, through the physicians, trace its history to the mediaeval universities and, more imaginatively, to the ancient Greeks. History and tradition lend prestige to the profession, though until fairly recent times only the small elite of physicians had high social standing, and for many centuries people were as liable to turn to wise women, soothsayers, astrologers or the like as to members of any of the medical professions.

The key event in the modern history of the profession, as we said at the beginning of this book, was the 1858 Medical Act which established the General Medical Council. The aim was to protect the public by distinguishing between acceptably qualified practitioners and others. This was valuable at a time when many people were practising medicine without qualifications. The local authorities supported the move for registration as they were seeking to appoint medical officers of health and had no easy means of checking the qualifications of applicants. If registration protected the public, it was no less advantageous to the profession. In the first place it protected its members from competition from the unqualified. In the second place it gave the profession control over admission to the profession. A system of registration required a statute, and could not be achieved by a voluntary medical organisation such as the British Medical Association or even by the licensing powers enjoyed by the Royal Colleges and certain other bodies, but it was the profession, through members of the GMC, that decided which qualifications were acceptable; no one else was qualified to make that judgement. The point about qualifications should be stressed. It is the disciplinary activity of the GMC that has received most publicity but the main concern of the Council has always been with qualification for admission to the register, not removal from it, important though the latter is.

The arrangements achieved in 1858 were the outcome of the interplay of the various medical and other interests at the time and of the developments in medical education during the preceding fifty years. This should be obvious and would hardly be worth saying were it not that medicine has become a model profession. It is the profession with much the highest prestige within the health service, and has few equals outside it. It thus forms the natural model for the other health service professions, which aspire to achieve comparable standing and similar arrangements in a shorter time.

The allied profession of dentistry has a less distinguished history, though tooth-drawing is an ancient occupation and dentistry fell to the barber element in the United Company of Barber Surgeons chartered in 1540. Dentists remained outside the control of the GMC until 1878 when the Dentists Act empowered it to examine and register suitably qualified dentists, but did not forbid practice by the unqualified. The founding of the British Dental Association was an important stage in the development of the profession, but it was not until the Dentists Act 1921 that all practitioners were required to be trained at a school of dentistry recognised by a new Dental Board. The board acted within the aegis of the GMC until 1957, maintaining the register and investigating cases of alleged misconduct but was not empowered to exercise disciplinary action. From that date the General Dental Council has taken over the functions of the Dental Board and the GMC so far as dentists are concerned, although the two councils co-operate closely in matters of dental education and examination.

From the formal recognition of the trained registered profession has stemmed a machinery for controlling ethical standards, training and discipline which, as we have said, other professions have tried to emulate in various ways. It may be one of the accidents of history that the 1858 Act added to rather than simplified the organisation of the profession. Thus the royal colleges of England and Scotland retained important if rather different roles, and the universities with medical schools remained independent examining bodies. All these, together with the British Medical Association and a variety of other professional bodies can claim to speak in one way or another for the profession or part of it. So the profession has an elaborate and powerful organisation outside the structure of the NHS, with much overlapping of membership, and this is a major factor influencing the relationship between doctors and the NHS. Senior doctors in particular are in a constant state of negotiation with the central departments and with the NHS which employs them.

If registration and what it entails fully accounted for the power and independence accorded to the medical profession, other professions might well hope to emulate it. In fact there are also other reasons for the high standing of the profession (which is paralleled in all western countries). The tradition of a high standing is a contributary factor, as are high earnings, which reflect the high value society puts on good health and on people who should be able to restore it. But the crucial factor is the principle of clinical independence. It is simply that no one can tell a qualified doctor who has reached the position of principal in a firm of general practitioners, or consultant in a hospital, how to treat his patients. To do so would be to accept responsibility for the treatment. So only the GP or consultant has the right of prescription for treatment. A patient may seek a second opinion, and if the treatment goes wrong he may seek redress in the courts or by complaint to the General Medical Council or, in the case of a general practitioner, to the Medical Services Committee of the Family Practitioner Committee. Both of the latter bodies are predominantly medical and therefore able to pass judgement on the doctor's clinical decisions. Employing authorities cannot, although they can exercise the same disciplinary role in relation to doctors as to other staff in non-clinical matters.

A doctor's power of prescription is limited by what is practicable. In private practice the limit may be set by what the patient can afford. In the NHS a consultant's freedom to prescribe or to treat his patients in a certain way is constrained by the ability of the health authority to provide the necessary facilities. While this may rarely reach a stage of conflict, there is an inherent tension in the desire of the doctor to treat each patient in the best possible way and the authority's wider responsibility to stay within the budget and to secure the community's health needs even if this may tend to reduce the quality of care for a number of patients.

The General Medical Council remained broadly unchanged for over a hundred years and formed the pattern for the General Dental Council in 1957. Following widespread dissatisfaction within the medical profession the Committee of Inquiry into the Regulation of the Medical Profession under Dr A.W. (now Sir Alec) Merrison made, in 1975, a number of major recommendations most of which were accepted by the Government and in 1978 were incorporated into a new Medical Act. The Merrison Report, however, stressed that the registration body for doctors and dentists should be independent of the NHS and government. It had no doubt that 'the most effective safeguard of the public is the self-respect of the profession itself'. The changes which have come about since 1975, significant though they are, have not altered the fundamental relationship of the medical and dental professions to the health service.

From February 1979, the GMC consisted of 50 members elected by the profession, 34 members elected by the Royal Colleges or faculties (including 22 from universities with medical schools), and 10 or 11, not all of them doctors, nominated by the Privy Council. It has the power to register all medical practitioners in England, Scotland, Wales and Northern Ireland or to remove them from the register if it thinks fit. (The Irish Republic, hitherto covered by the Council, was now omitted.) It is financed largely from the annual retention fee paid by practitioners for continuing registration.

There are three stages of registration covering: practice under supervision; independent practice; practice carrying responsibility for patient care at a high specialist level.

The Council has the power to control general standards of education and training leading to registration, though the assessment of an individual's competence rests at each stage with an educational body, i.e. either university or royal college. In pursuance of its responsibilities it can, for instance, visit medical schools and develop informal methods of controlling undergraduate medical education.

While the GMC cannot control standards of training for overseas doctors it has to satisfy itself that those coming to this country to practise are qualified to the minimum standard required of a medical graduate in this country. The scale of that task can be illustrated by the 1978 figures for registration. In that year full registration was granted to 2,669 overseas qualified doctors, and those listed as temporarily registered fell from 5,982 to 4,339 during the year. Out of the 1,828 who took the compulsory professional and language tests 770 received temporary registration.

The responsibility to remove from the register anyone who is unfit to practise has been extended to include those who are temporarily or permanently incapacitated on health grounds from undertaking their proper responsibilities, in addition to those who have committed a criminal offence or serious professional misconduct. The need for this function and the importance of its being fulfilled in a compassionate way was stressed by the Merrison Report. An analysis of the cases of professional misconduct brought to the Council in 1978 appears strongly to confirm the views. Nearly half of the 94 cases considered were categorised as abuse of alcohol or abuse of drugs.

The disciplinary aspect of the GMC's work is a relatively small ingredient. The maintenance of professional standards is its major task and this largely means educational standards. For basic qualifications, this is provided by the universities and their medical schools with the undergraduate teaching hospitals, within the GMC's overall standards. For postgraduate or specialist training leading to higher qualification, the GMC relies upon the Royal Colleges not only to act as the examining bodies, but also to accredit training posts in hospitals and general practice. Operating through such bodies as the Postgraduate Training Committee for General Practice and the Joint Committee on Higher Training (for hospital posts), the colleges with other interested parties, such as representatives of the postgraduate deans, establish criteria for posts and inspect them, recommend patterns of appointments and list courses for attendance.

As most junior medical staff are in training, the extent to which a hospital's posts are accredited is of great importance to a health authority. Lack of accreditation can mean, for example, closure of accident and emergency departments because of lack of staff, or grave problems in obtaining staff of good calibre for a post.

The effect of the medical training activities on the service and the independence of the College representatives from health authorities reinforces the independent stance of the medical profession. Later in the chapter this will be examined in relation to the professional advisory machinery, the changing status of professions, and measuring performance. Before doing so, the position of other professions needs to be examined.

The nursing profession

Florence Nightingale wrote in 1886 that 'nursing has to nurse living bodies and spirits. It cannot be tested by public examination, though it may be tested by current supervision'. Thus she signified her opposition to the movement towards state registration for nurses, an opposition which probably delayed registration by twenty years.

In the meantime midwives achieved registration under the Midwives Act 1902. Midwives are a separate profession from nurses, although many nurses take midwifery training after qualification, and the great majority of midwives are also nurses. Current developments seem designed to bring the two professions even closer together.

Midwifery is a very old occupation, though one long based on traditional lore rather than medical science. The advent in the eighteenth century of doctors undertaking obstetrics brought competition for patients but did not oust the midwife. However in general the standing of the occupation was low, and 1881 saw the founding of the Midwives Institute, now the Royal College of Midwives. It was the first professional organisation to be founded for women employed in health care. The objective of the Institute was 'to improve the status of midwives and to petition Parliament for their recognition'.

The advent of midwives as a profession was by no means smooth, because of the conflict of interest with doctors. Although nurses were not faced with this particular difficulty their history was more stormy. It can be found in all its fascinating detail in Professor Abel-Smith's history of the profession. The doctors had shown the advantages of registration, and the point was reinforced in time by the midwives. Some nurses were opposed to registration either for Florence Nightingale's reasons or for fear that it would tend to be based upon the lowest common denominator of nursing standards and militate against the achievement of the most successful schools of nursing. Nevertheless the general feeling amongst senior nurses moved in favour of registration, and hospitals also increasingly favoured it. However, the supporters of registration were bitterly divided between those favouring a three-year training and those who favoured one year; it was roughly a division between those seeking high professional standing and those looking for an adequate supply of trained nurses. A Parliamentary Select Committee set up in 1904 reported in favour of registration but because of the conflicting interests and pressures it was not achieved until 1919 when an act of parliament established the General Nursing Council for England and Wales. (There is a separate General Nursing Council for Scotland, established in the same year. Midwifery had its own statutory body in Scotland from 1915, and Northern Ireland in 1922. In Northern Ireland there is now a Council for Nurses and Midwives.)

In view of the disagreements in the years leading to registration, it is not surprising that the early years of the General Nursing Council saw some bitter arguments. The majority of members argued that state registration should be achieved through a single 'portal' of entry and throughout the early 1920s the battles raged between those who were prepared to adopt a liberal attitude towards the registration of practising nurses and those who saw the need for stringent standards to ensure that the status of the profession was safeguarded. It is a judgement that every emerging profession has had to apply. At what stage does one cease to accept as members skilful and experienced practitioners, unqualified by formal examination? Within the GNC those who had battled hard to achieve professional standing seemed likely to achieve an immediate limiting of the register to those who were formally qualified. However, the weight of those authorities who employed the nurses was clearly in favour of a more liberal view, and first the Minister of Health and then parliament intervened to support that view. A similar battle was fought over the syllabus for training with the Minister of Health turning down a Council proposal to make the syllabus compulsory for all training schools.

State registration has in fact never represented a single discipline after the preliminary examination. From the first, the register had six parts, one for men and the other for State Registered Nurses (SRN), Registered Mental Nurses (RMN), Registered Nurses of Mental Defectives (RNMD), Registered Sick Children's Nurses (RSCN) and Registered Fever Nurses (RFN). From 1924 all were entitled to wear a standard uniform and badge approved by the GNC but the barriers between the different fields of nursing remained. As educational requirements have risen so the time and cost of retraining to obtain entry to another part of the register have increased. Only in recent years has the emphasis on post-registration training in so many professions, including nursing, made the divisions between the various parts of the register less significant.

It was typical of the battle over standards that the recommendation in the 1919 Act that the central body, four years after being formed, should report to the Privy Council on the desirability of 'a separate register of nurses whose training is of a lower standard than that laid down on the register of nurses', was not implemented for a further 24 years. Not until the late 1930s was the idea of 'assistant nurses' becoming acceptable and in 1943 the Nurses Act made the first major change to the arrangements for registration by providing for enrolment of assistant nurses by the GNC. Even so, the reluctance of medical staff in particular to accept enrolled nurses as an acceptable supplement to state registered nurses lasted at least until the 1960s.

After the storms of the 1920s the GNC grew in status and statesmanship but it has never enjoyed the same degree of independence or power as the General Medical Council. Despite an understanding in 1927 with the Ministry of Health, for instance, that GNC inspectors could visit and approve training schools, there was no formal agreement until 1939. The natural clash of interest between a service which is concerned with 'pairs of hands' and a professional body anxious to raise standards has continued. The Council does have powers to withhold approval of training schools but only by recommendations to ministers. It has had control over the syllabus of basic training but not the training of tutors, clinical teachers, midwives, health visitors or district nurses. These awards are made by different bodies, some statutory such as the Central Midwives Board and the Council for Education and Training of Health Visitors, and others with considerable experience in a specific field such as the Joint Board of Clinical Nursing Studies or the Ophthalmic Nursing Board.

The most recent attempt to integrate the various branches of the nursing profession is represented by the Briggs Report (1972). It recommended the formation of a single central body responsible for professional standards, education and discipline for both nursing and midwifery in Great Britain.

By this means, and by the provision of a basic 18 months course leading to a Certificate in Nursing Practice, Briggs sought to develop nurse training on a modular basis with all entrants taking the certificate and subsequently undertaking further courses leading to registration as a nurse or as a midwife, or to obtain specialist training in, for instance, paediatric nursing. It was envisaged that the numerous schools of nursing would be superseded by two or three hundred colleges of nursing and midwifery financed by Area Committees for Nursing and Midwifery Education in place of the Regional Nurse Training Committees.

Although Briggs recognised the continuing need for nurse training to be a mixture of clinical work and theory, the implications of the report tended towards nurses becoming much more akin to other students than hitherto in their relationship to practical work. The emphasis was on nurses as students rather than apprentices and on the colleges being more independent of health authorities than the existing nurse training schools.

By April 1979, the government had accepted the need for structural change in passing the Nurses, Midwives and Health Visitors Act. However, this concerned only the formation of a central council and national boards for the four parts of the United Kingdom. While it was envisaged that these would take over responsibility for registration and training from the GNC by autumn 1980, this did not commit the government to full implementation of the Briggs recommendations on the content of training, manpower problems or conditions of work for nurses. Although, for instance, the number of schools of nursing in England and Wales fell from 432 in 1973 to 188 in 1976 and the average number of learners in each increased from 200 to 500, the concept of independent area colleges had not been accepted. The GNC continued to make changes in the various syllabuses for nurse training within the spirit of the report, but, so far as the structure for education was concerned, it seemed likely that the impact of the reduced working hours for nurses and the need to conform to EEC directives about nurse training would absorb the energies of the departments, senior nurses and authorities, and any money available. By the time the Central Council was established these changes coupled with the increasingly serious financial state of the service militated against any radical changes.

The EEC directives for general nursing became compulsory in June 1979 and laid down criteria that must be met in terms of a minimum length of training and the type of experience which must be achieved before freedom of movement within the EEC member countries could occur. This inevitably meant the tightening of the framework of nurse training and, for some training schools, problems of providing the necessary experience. It therefore reduced still further the number of nurses available in wards and departments.

The Briggs Report also gave rise to a need to examine the care of the mentally handicapped population by the Jay Committee. This committee reported in 1979 and placed its emphasis on mental handicap staff being trained by the Central Council for Education and Training in Social Work rather than as nurses in the accepted sense. Quite apart from the strong protests by nursing organisations at this change, the cost of the proposals were so considerable that the government decided against implementation.

Finally, the proposals for restructuring the NHS in England, with their emphasis on district rather than area authorities, seemed likely to work against the idea of area nursing colleges, even though these had not been intended as part of an AHA's responsibility.

As nursing moves into the 1980s, the hopes raised by the publication of the Briggs Report seem likely to be dampened by other major changes. Although the Nurses, Midwives and Health Visitors Act has achieved an independent council, with the various branches of nursing included within it, the very title of the Act indicates that this intepretation may not in practice be easy to achieve. It must nevertheless be said that the progress made by the profession in the 60 years since the formation of the GNC has represented a major achievement. Despite the problems and uncertainties, it is certain that nursing is now established by all the criteria earlier discussed as a major profession and its status increases annually.

Other professions concerned with diagnosis and treatment of patients

The range and variety of the professions concerned with diagnosis and treatment of patients is so great that it is impracticable to discuss each one here. Instead a number of examples are taken to illustrate aspects of their development and current status.

Opticians

Spectacles were first used in Britain about the beginning of the fourteenth century. With the invention of printing and the growth in the number of people who could read and write, the demand for spectacles increased and the making of them developed into a recognised craft. In 1629 the Worshipful Company of Spectacle Makers was formed and granted a charter which gave it power to make reasonable laws for the control of the craft. For over two centuries the Company exercised these powers as virtually the sole authority in this field, while methods of testing vision and making lenses for spectacles developed gradually.

Then in 1895 the British Optical Association was formed with the object of encouraging the science of optics and the art of applying this science to the improvement of human vision, and of protecting the interests of those practising in the profession of optician. In 1896 the Association became the first body to institute examinations for opticians, and the Worshipful Company followed in 1898.

Today, there is a clear distinction between the work and training of ophthalmic opticians, who are qualified to test eyesight and supply spectacles, and dispensing opticians, who on principle do not test sight, and who confine themselves to the supply of spectacles and various other optical appliances. Under the Opticians Act of 1958 a general council was formed with responsibility for promoting high standards of professional education and conduct and for the compilation and maintenance of registers of opticians.

Pharmacists

Pharmacy is concerned with the collection, preparation and supply of substances used for diagnosis, prevention and treatment. When in 1815 the Society of Apothecaries which hitherto had encompassed those concerned with the practice of pharmacy became the examining body for doctors, the nature of the Society changed. It soon became clear that those who wished to specialise in pharmacy would have to develop a separate organisation. By 1841 the Pharmaceutical Society was formed. It received a Royal Charter in 1843.

Although there are a considerable number of pharmacists employed in industry, most pharmacists are either in general practice working in chemist shops, or in hospital pharmacy. Any person wishing to practise retail or hospital pharmacy must be a member of the Pharmaceutical Society. Registration depends upon successful completion of a three-year full-time course of professional training and a year's practical experience under supervision. The three-year course leads either to a degree or the Pharmaceutical Chemist Diploma of the Society.

While pharmacists in hospital and retail work must fulfil doctors' prescriptions, they are much more clearly independent of medical supervision of their work than are many health care professionals. This is partly because their knowledge and skills have outstripped those which a doctor can expect to acquire in the normal course of his work but also because they have a number of specific responsibilities for control of poisons and dangerous drugs. Besides, nearly 140 years as a professional body, with traditionally a high proportion of male practitioners, has enabled pharmacists to establish a status closer to partnership with the medical and dental professions than any other. The profession indeed claims a centuries-long tradition of independence from the medical professions. Even the development of pharmacology as a medical specialty has not created a supervisory role for the doctors. The degree of independence is, perhaps, illustrated by the fact that the NHS reorganisation in 1974 gave the regional and area pharmaceutical officers chief officer status.

Since 1970, the Pharmaceutical Society has required that candidates for registration should have passed a degree course in the subject and it has exercised in relation to the universities a similar oversight of the syllabus to that of the General Medical Council in relation to medicine. While the degree course in itself bestows status on a profession, such an arrangement reduces the direct control over course content by the professional body. The professional body that educates, examines and registers has the opportunity to maintain a closer control over the standards of entrance to the profession than those that rely upon university courses for the education. It is typical of graduate professions that many graduates subsequently question whether the degree courses are 'too academic' for the practical tasks that subseqently confront them within the service. Despite the strong position of the pharmacists' profession, this is the kind of issue that is currently exercising it.

Medical social workers

Since 1974 social work services have been the responsibility of local authorities. In practice, this has often meant the continuance of a staff of trained medical and psychiatric social workers 'outposted' to hospitals and working closely with medical and nursing staff in broadly the same way as before. Any outposting arrangement tends to be an uncomfortable one, but in the eyes of the majority of the social workers consulted in the early 1970s the present pattern was seen as the most acceptable of the options presenting. Despite a tradition of graduate training, social workers have probably suffered more than any other health care profession from a misunderstanding of their proper role and skills. By being employed as part of the local authority social services department they at least established themselves firmly as part of an independent professional group of social workers.

Medical social work grew out of the profession of almoner. The first lady almoner was appointed to the Royal Free Hospital in 1895, her primary task being to prevent the abuse of the hospital by those who could afford to pay. When, after 1918, voluntary hospitals asked patients to pay what they could afford, the task of dealing with this fell to almoners, along with various other administrative tasks. From the first, however, almoners were social workers, concerned to help the poor cope with their problems. Some patients admitted to hospital are faced with the sort of problems that need social work help and which may be highlighted or exacerbated by illness. For others, problems may be created by illness or by the need for admission to hospital, and there are yet others whose illness, whether manifested in physical or psychological symptoms, has been created by their problems. Thus the skills and advice of the social worker may make an important contribution to diagnosis and treatment as well as in arrangements for discharge and after-care. The need for such help exists in the case of mental as well as physical illness, and the separate profession of psychiatric social worker developed.

Following the publication of the Seebohm Report in 1968, local authority social services departments were set up separate from the medical officer of health who had hitherto normally been responsible. The principle of the new system was to provide a comprehensive service based on the concept of the 'generic' social worker instead of separately trained and organised professionals dealing with different client groups. The change was an important stage in the development of the social work profession as a whole but although the Seebohm Committee had mooted the idea of hospital medical and psychiatric social workers becoming part of the new social services departments, this was not to happen until 1974.

The prospect was not welcomed by most hospital workers. Although it would associate them more closely with a now much stronger profession, they were a small, highly qualified, very specialised group and feared that in a large organisation based on the 'generic' principle they might be expected to undertake work for which they had no experience, and that much of the medical social work would fall to staff with little understanding of the complexities. Moreover there were doubts about retaining a close working relationship with doctors and nurses when they were employed by an 'outside' organisation.

In practice it seems that these fears have in most places proved groundless and the closer links with local authorities have brought greater flexibility and sometimes a better range of staff without the feared loss of confidence between hospital (and now also community health) staff and social workers. The price for continuity may have been a retreat from the ideal of the generic social worker and an acceptance of the status quo in many places but if so it probably represents sensible judgements by maturing social services departments about the extent to which the ideal is achievable. While nowadays the training for the basic grade social worker is generic there are postqualifying courses for specialist skills needed in a number of settings including health care.

The recent rise of the social work profession is an interesting phenomenon. It was based on the Seebohm Report which represented the aspirations of the profession and the report was implemented, it has been said, because to those pressing for it it was the one vital issue whereas to its opponents — the medical profession — it was only one issue among many. It has given the profession higher status, higher salaries and a fuller control over its activities, but it appears to have made the profession less popular; there have been strong criticisms of 'bureaucratisation' and of high earnings, and more people seem to have questioned the achievements and values of social work. It is perhaps a coincidence that there have also been strikes by social workers.

Perhaps another factor in achieving independence is that the concept of 'over arching' medical control does not really fit social work. While some social work, particularly that of medical social workers, is with clients under medical care and is thus contrained by the doctor's right to prescribe for his patients, at the other end of the spectrum it is concerned with matters where there is no medical involvement at all.

There have been instances of disputes over such matters as the confidentiality of social workers' records, but it is now firmly accepted that these have the same status as medical records.

The professions supplementary to medicine

The twentieth century has seen a radical change in the staff needed for patient care. The discovery of X-rays in 1895 coincided with the formation of the Society of Trained Masseuses and may be taken as the year that heralded the start of the professions supplementary to medicine. During the next 25 years the range of treatments available increased substantially and so did the number of individuals, some trained, some untrained, who undertook the treatments.

By 1920 the Society of Physiotherapy received its Royal Charter and started to promote the idea of an official register. By 1928, the BMA, recognising the dangers of electricity and radiation in treatment, formally supported the idea of registration and in 1933 actually produced the first National Register of Medical Auxiliary Services.

In 1936 a Board of Registration of Medical Auxiliaries was incorporated under the Companies Act, and it became open to any association of medical auxiliaries to apply for recognition. Among the earliest were the Association of Dispensing Opticians, the British Dietetic Association, the British Orthoptic Society, the Chartered Society of Physiotherapy, the College of Speech Therapists, the Society of Chiropodists and the Society of Radiographers.

In 1951, the Cope 'Reports of the Committee on Medical Auxiliaries' recognised that the board, as a voluntary body, had no power to ensure the completeness of its registers. They recommended the establishment of statutory registers.

The Professions Supplementary to Medicine Act 1960 enshrined the views expressed by the Cope Reports and provided for the formation of a council and seven boards for: physiotherapists, dietitians, chiropodists, occupational therapists, medical laboratory technicians, radiographers and remedial gymnasts.

Speech therapists opted for exclusion but regulations recognise the College of Speech Therapists as the appropriate body to issue a qualifying certificate. In 1966 orthoptists were by regulation added to the list of professions covered by the Act. Medical laboratory technicians are now known as medical laboratory scientific officers. A change of title is not uncommon in an aspiring profession.

Although the Act formally arranged for registration by a series of boards, it did not entirely replace the Board of Registration of Medical Auxiliaries which continued to prepare registers for such staff as audiology technicians, and operating theatre technicians. Indeed, it seems only a matter of time before such staff as these, physicists, cardiology technicians and so on become registered in a similar way to the professions supplementary to medicine.

The eight existing registration boards cover the United Kingdom and are responsible for promoting high standards of professional education and conduct through maintaining registers and approving courses of training, qualifications and training institutions. Each board has a majority of elected members of the profession concerned. In practice, one professional body dominates each of the boards and can normally secure the election of all its professional members.

On major matters the boards require the assent of the Council of the Professions Supplementary to Medicine and the CPSM in turn the approval of the Privy Council. The CPSM is composed of representatives of the eight professions, eight medical and seven lay members.

While the introduction of statutory registration for those members of the eight professions wishing to practise within the NHS has undoubtedly helped to give those professions status and safeguarded the safety of patients, the arrangements have received the familiar criticisms of professional organisations, namely of conspiring to limit entry by raising standards and of inducing rigidity in staffing. These criticisms were considered by the Royal Commission on the NHS. It found little sign of the former with the possible exception of chiropody, the greater pressures generally being to increase the numbers in the various professions. It did, however, express concern about the lack of progress made towards integration of the professions, notably physiotherapists and remedial gymnasts, and rejected the idea of precise delineation of roles, quoting the Dentists Act 1957: 'For the purposes of this Act, the practice of dentistry shall be deemed to include the performances of any such operation and the giving of any such treatment advice or attendance as is usually performed or given by dentists' adding the dry comment that in other words 'dentistry is what dentists do'. It therefore emphasised that relationships between professions and the duties undertaken by them must not be allowed to ossify if patterns of care for patients were to develop appropriately.

The Royal Commission also explored inter-professional relationships in multidisciplinary clinical teams and in particular the question of leadership. It received evidence from the BMA that the doctor should not 'hand over his control of the clinical decisions concerning the treatment of his patients to anyone else or to a group or team' whereas other contributors pointed to the wide range of decisions affecting patients which meant that, in practice, social workers, nurses and others took the lead at various times. The Commission thought it pointless to rule on who should be 'leader' so long as each professional was able to contribute according to his own professional competence. It nevertheless recognised that while local disputes might be easily resolved there would be occasions when the health departments might need to arbitrate between the various professional bodies on a national level if agreement could not be reached.

The conflicting evidence to the Royal Commission typifies the medical concern about the risk of what is described as 'clinical autonomy' by the emergence of health care professions with inevitably a deeper knowledge and skills in a particular aspect of medicine than doctors are able to maintain. The Health Service Organisation Research Unit at Brunel University has studied this topic and has concluded that the components of clinical autonomy are independent practice, patient choice, prime responsibility and primacy. It argues that the doctor does have primacy because he is the only one in the health field who understands what all the others are doing and therefore has to take prime responsibility for the patient and ensure the co-ordination of other professions' efforts. Against that, a number of professionals work with patients independently of the doctor, particularly in the long-stay services. Social workers and clinical psychologists do so, for instance. A number are certainly seeking independent practice even if they concede primacy to doctors in the co-ordination of treatment.

The current issues of professional independence seem to revolve mainly around doctors' relationships to nurses, professions supplementary to medicine and clinical psychologists. Is a consultant pathologist 'head' of a laboratory in all respects when the majority of its staff are medical laboratory scientific officers with a better knowledge of the detail of the work undertaken than he has? Is he a 'laboratory manager' or has he simply prescribing authority over the laboratory staff in the same way that a clinician has over nurses on the ward? These questions are not yet clearly answered.

Nor must it be assumed that there is one simple answer applicable in all cases. The range and variety of health care and professions involved may mean a different answer in different circumstances. More particularly, it is not now a question of the doctors versus the rest. In its evidence to the Royal Commission the Royal College of Nursing suggested that nurses need to extend their clinical role to the extent of prescribing physiotherapy. And, indeed, nursing itself has become so specialised that the extent of supervision which can be exercised by the nursing hierarchy over highly specialised units must be a matter of doubt. These examples are not given because serious problems exist but in order to illustrate the increasing complexity of inter-professional relationships. These need dispassionate and flexible judgements to achieve the continuing adjustments that the Royal Commission rightly saw as necessary.

Inter-professional relationships have been discussed in this section because the professions supplementary to medicine provide the most significant recent development in the formal status of health care professions. The eight professions also represent an interesting variety of progress towards their aspirations. The manpower issues are discussed later but from the professions' point of view increase in status equates largely with improved calibre of individual practitioners. This in turn affects the esteem in which they are held by other health care professions and ultimately the public. Hence the pressures to raise entry standards, and to lengthen and improve the quality of training. Radiographers, for example, since 1978 have required 'A' levels for training and have sought, against some resistance from health authorities and many radiologists to extend their basic training period from two to two-and-a-half years. The likely outcome is, at least, an agreement on a postgraduate course after two years' basic study. Dietitians are trying to develop a fully graduate profession. Physiotherapists and occupational therapists are trying to promote courses at university to produce a small percentage of graduates in the profession in a similar way to nursing. Thus in a variety of ways the professional bodies, supported by their registration boards, are pressing to achieve improved standards, higher status and greater independence through establishing a body of esoteric knowledge and skills peculiar to their particular profession.

Despite the fact that the Council was established in 1960, and has in recent years devoted considerable energy to the study of manpower problems, a variety of training forms and qualifications exists to complicate the process of manpower planning. In all except dietetics and medical laboratory sciences, the qualifications recognised by the various boards are those of the corresponding professional bodies. Dietitians use university and CNAA degrees and diplomas and medical laboratory scientific officers Higher National Diplomas, Certificates or university degrees. In some professions such as orthoptics and radiography, education takes place in schools entirely within the NHS, in others, such as physiotherapy, some schools are associated with academic institutions while others are hospital based. Occupational therapists are still in some areas trained in private schools not part of the NHS though like the other professions they undertake their clinical work in NHS institutions.

Even the arrangements for payment of staff during training are not the same for all professions. Although the majority are direct employees of health authorities during training, others, notably occupational therapists, receive grants from local authorities.

It seems likely that sheer shortage of local authority education funds will soon force a pattern to evolve whereby health authorities are responsible for the employment and training costs of all the professions concerned.

One aspect of registration which affects some professions more seriously than others is the 'closed register'. Like the medical profession, the eight professions require registration to practise within the NHS, but so long as they do not claim qualifications which they do not possess, they do not need registration for private practice. For medical laboratory scientific officers this has little significance because the opportunities are small, but for physiotherapists and chiropodists private practice by unregistered and sometimes unqualified practitioners is seen as 'devaluing' the profession. It is mainly for this reason that despite the shortage of chiropodists, the Chiropodists Board has been reluctant to accept the use of unqualified 'foot aides' in the way that the use, for instance, of occupational therapy aides is now widely accepted as a valuable adjunct to professional skills.

In its evidence to the Royal Commission the Council suggested that it was well fitted to play a larger part in manpower planning for the eight professions. This suggestion was not supported by the boards, although they recognised the need for improvements in this sphere. From what has been said about the variety of arrangements currently applying, it is probably fair to say that the boards are not yet confident enough in the evolution of their own professions towards autonomy to accept a major move towards rationalisation, be it manpower planning or common care training.

Scientific staff

A large number of professional and technical staff have no statutory boards under the Professions Supplementary to Medicine Act though in terms of numbers, qualifications and status an extension of the formal recognition and protection provided by the boards would seem to be overdue. There does not, however, seem to be great demand for such arrangements and it may be that such people as biochemists, clinical psychologists, cardiology technicians and so on consider that they have sufficient control over their own profession by means of their existing organisations to make statutory arrangements unnecessary. The problems of independence, of standards and of status must apply in varying degrees to these groups in broadly the same way as the professions supplementary to medicine.

The largest scientific discipline, the medical laboratory scientific officers with 15,878 staff in Great Britain in 1977, are covered by the CPSM, but others which have grown enormously since 1960 are not. The staff statistics for 1977 detail 1,627 biochemists and physicists, 965 psychologists, 1,428 dark room technicians, 1,767 medical physics technicians and 2,149 physiological measurement technicians. It is likely that these have been less concerned with professional organisation than with the possible implementation of the report of the Committee on Hospital Scientific and Technical Services (Zuckerman). This was published in 1968 but has never been implemented.

The aim of the Zuckerman Report was to set up an integrated scientific service in support of medicine to ensure its orderly development and the creation of a career structure which would provide a broader training and better career opportunities for the specialised groups involved in the service. The idea of an integrated service met with considerable resistance from some groups of staff who saw themselves losing status and perhaps pay. The 1974 reorganisation with its emphasis on devolution overtook the idea of greater regional involvement in organising scientific services.

A DHSS study group reviewed the report in 1977. It suggested three main scientific services rather than one and the exclusion of a number of specialties such as pharmacy, psychology, dietetics, orthoptics, medical illustration and photography. Still no progress has been made towards implementation of the structure although the suggestions were in general commended by the Royal Commission, which also supported the Zuckerman proposal for a national scientific council to oversee education and professional standards in the same way as the Council for the Professions Supplementary to Medicine operates.

The Royal Commission did not accept the view pressed upon it by representations of pathologists that the head of the laboratory should always be medically qualified. It considered that possession of a medical qualification should not outweigh an individual's capacity as a scientist. This independent assessment is one with great significances for inter-professional relationships and for organisation of laboratory services though it must be emphasised that medical heads of laboratories do not accept responsibility for individual patients and do not therefore exercise the same right of clinical autonomy as most of their colleagues.

Works staff

Hitherto the discussion has concerned professions directly dealing with patients, but Professional and Technical B Whitley Council also represents an entirely different category of professional staff, those concerned with building and engineering. This chapter started with an engineer's definition of what constitutes a profession, and qualified architects, engineers and surveyors, the works professions employed in the NHS, fall into that category. Whereas most health care professionals are trained at least partly within the NHS and are largely employed by health authorities, the professional works staff are part of much wider professional fraternities. Only a small proportion of the profession will have worked within the health service while studying for the professional qualifications. Most will have worked elsewhere while training and simply applied for a post in a health authority in preference to one in private practice or industry. To state this is not to imply that their concern for the service is any less dedicated than that of the health care professions. It does, however, mean that their professional interests and scope for advancement will be different. Most obviously, their skills are those which cannot be 'over arched' by doctors and their independent professional status is, in that respect, more clear-cut, particularly as there is a public acceptance of that status for their counterparts outside the NHS.

Although salaries in the health service have to be broadly competitive with those for similar work outside, the position of a directly employed professional without the power that the concept of clinical autonomy implies is more circumscribed than in private practice. The consultant architect, for instance, may ultimately withdraw from a commission if his advice is not accepted. An architect employed by a regional health authority can in the same circumstances only resign. The difference is that the consultant architect may have many commissions whereas the employee has only one job.

Among the works professionals employed in the service, the constraints have been given added force by the introduction in 1974 of works officers to co-ordinate their contribution. Although works officers are professionally qualified in at least one of the disciplines they supervise, they cannot be qualified in all. From an authority's view point, to have one officer who 'understands' the works professions and can 'manage' them is obviously desirable. The professions themselves, however, would question whether a works officer who is a qualified engineer necessarily understands the architect's professional judgement, and whether questions of professional judgement should be subject to managerial decision short of the client organisation itself.

The problem is not dissimilar to that which faces specialists in community medicine who have responsibility for exercising their professional judgement over a certain sphere of community medicine and the right to report to the health authority. In their case, the area or regional medical officer co-ordinates their activities but does not manage them. The works officer more positively manages the works professionals. Even if the system were to change in detail, however, it would not alter the basic fact that an employee does not have in practice the same degree of professional independence as a consultant to a client.

Administrative staff

In a similar category to the works professional so far as their relationship to patients is concerned, the staff covered by the Administrative and Clerical Whitley Council include those dealing with personnel, work study, supplies, medical records and statistics, operational research, accountancy and general administration. While individuals may be very well qualified, the professional qualifications required for appointment to a particular post are at varying stages of development. It would now be very unusual for an administrator to reach chief officer status without being an Associate of the Institute of Health Service Administrators, or for a treasurer to do so without an accountancy qualification, usually that of the Chartered Institute of Public Finance Accountants.

As the National Staff Committee for Administrative and Clerical Staff has pointed out in its report on the recruitment and career development of administrators (1979) there is no absolute bar to promotion to those who lack appropriate professional qualification, but one of the minimum standards which authorities should set for all senior management posts is a relevant professional qualification. In practice, this is less easy than it sounds because it is difficult to compare the standards of the various specialist qualifications now offered by such bodies as the Institute of Personnel Officers, the Association of Medical Records Officers and so on. All that one can say is that the professional bodies awarding the qualifications are deeply concerned to make them relevant and of a standard to enhance the status of the individuals holding them and the professional group. In this, the various branches of administrators are little different from the many other professions in the NHS who see the development of their group standards as something that is important not merely to enhance the stature of the profession but because it will benefit the service. They, like so many other professional staff, have the increasing sense of identity and professional pride which is both a great strength for the service and a factor that increases its managerial complexity.

Professions and the organisation of health care

The range of the task

So far, this chapter has concentrated on the nature of professions in the health service, the way they pursue their prime role which for most is the health care of the public, and the way the various professional groups have developed over the years. The discussion has, therefore, largely been concerned with the professional viewpoint. It is important to consider the professions from a different perspective, as employees of a health service which is responsible for providing the vast bulk of that health care. While the issues surrounding private practice are of political significance, the number of patients treated in this way is not sufficient to be relevant to a discussion of any profession other than doctors.

Before examining the way in which the professions relate to NHS management it is important to recognise the variety of health service provision. The direct service to patients extends from preventive medicine through a wide range of community services for patients and their families to a variety of hospitals, covering acute, long-stay and various types of special care. The major division is, however, between the community services and the hospital services.

In the community much of the work is undertaken by independent contractors, and primary care is often a team effort involving both independent contractors and professions organised hierarchically. Thus a group practice of general practitioner doctors may have attached to it health visitors, district nurses and social workers who are all out-posted from the health authority and local authority. From day to day they are working for the doctors but they are also subject to control from their own profession in terms of discipline, career development and training. While in most places this split accountability causes no problems, it can on occasion provoke tensions between the various professions concerned. A doctor, for instance, may derive his patients from a wide geographical area which bears no relation to the social service districts or the convenient organisation of a district nursing service.

In practice, primary care teams are very clearly medically led and the other professionals, being trained staff, well away from the direct supervision of their own professional hierarchy, exercise considerable independence in fulfilling the doctors' instructions. Within the hospitals the balance changes. While the consultant medical staff are clearly in clinical charge of the patients they have their own hierarchy of junior medical staff below them who in practice, with the nursing staff, provide for the continuing care of the patients. The ratio of other professionals to doctors is much higher than in general practice; all the staff, whether doctors or other professions, are direct employees of health authorities; a high proportion of staff are in training and therefore subject to a considerable degree of supervision; and the care is provided within a relatively small number of institutions rather than over a wide geographical area — all this makes for a much more complex organisation and much more sophisticated management is needed if the complexity is not to reduce the effectiveness of the arrangements.

Although in hospital, as in community work, the other professionals very often are carrying out the prescriptions of doctors not only for drugs, but also, for instance, for nursing care or rehabilitation, they more clearly do so as part of their own professional hierarchy and are more directly controlled within that structure. We have already discussed the way in which professions have emerged from the 'over arching' control of doctors to assume a greater degree of independence. The use of sophisticated techniques now employed in hospitals by a variety of professions inevitably means that medical staff can no longer judge the competence of other professionals to carry out their instructions. Instead the senior members of the other professions must become involved in ensuring that standards are maintained. This need not be a matter of individual competence; it can very often be a question of assessing staff numbers and experience in relation to workload. A surgeon, for instance, may wish to undertake a heavy operating list when the nursing officer does not feel confident that the number of night staff available for post-operative care is sufficient. Alternatively, a diagnostic department such as X-ray or pathology may be unable to undertake the appropriate number of tests required by the clinicians for the treatment of a particular condition, and a judgement may have to be made between, perhaps, 'open access' for general practitioners' cases, and investigations for in-patients.

As a result of the conflicting demands there inevitably needs to be negotiation and a balanced assessment of the contribution that the various professions can make to the care of the patients, particularly at times of staffing difficulty in a wide range of services.

Professional advisory machinery

The primacy of the medical profession in patient care whether in the community or in hospital has inevitably been reflected in the way the various professions have related to the management of the NHS. From the inception of the service in 1948, there was a medical presence strongly established in the management of all sections. The various independent contractors, including doctors, were represented on the executive council. The local authority health services were in the charge of a medical officer of health who was directly accountable to the authority as a chief officer, and regional hospital boards, boards of governors and hospital management committees each had medical members appointed to them.

No other profession achieved such an influential position. Although the doctors serving on hospital authorities were not elected by the profession but were appointed by the Minister of Health or, in the case of hospital management committees, by regional hospital boards, they were nevertheless able to present a professional viewpoint. In hospitals, moreover, the authorities had to establish medical committees to ensure that they received professional advice on the development of medical services. Initially the other professions had no professional advisory machinery, nor had they representatives on the committees of hospitals. Such influence as they were able to bring to bear was through senior officers.

Administrators and treasurers were, of course, able to advise their authorities direct because they were entitled to attend all formal meetings. Nurses had no such representation and it required two sets of advice by the Minister of Health in 1949 and 1959 and finally a firm instruction in 1961 before a matron was allowed the right to attend formal meetings of authority committees on behalf of nurses. Subsequently similar advice was offered to hospital management committees in a circular in 1965 regarding the attendance of the group engineer when matters requiring his advice were to be discussed.

The pattern of professional advice to authorities other than through a medical advisory committee and individual senior officers varied greatly. Many authorities had nursing committees dealing with both nursing services and nursing education but few considered matters relating to the other professions except through the medical advisory committee.

The only other professional advisory bodies that were common to all regions were the area nurse training committees. These consisted mainly of senior nursing staff from regional hospital boards, boards of governors, the General Nursing Council, Central Midwives Board and local health authorities together with representatives of local education authorities and lay and medical representatives of hospital management committees. They examined local arrangements for training and could report to both the GNC and HMCs or boards of governors in the area that was responsible for the training schools. However, they had no part in inspecting training schools and had no power to grant or withhold approval for schools for training purposes. This remained with the GNC. Nor did they control the training allowances for student nurses. While influential with the profession, it is fair to say that area nurse training committees did not have a major impact on the management of the service. Their main managerial function was to guarantee a financial allocation independent of the normal authority budget.

The 1960s saw the development of awareness among the professions in the health service that they must reorganise their own profession in order to meet the management demands of the second half of the twentieth century and that to be effective they must establish the same kinds of links with the authorities as those which the medical profession had achieved. The medical profession itself meanwhile was deeply concerned to improve its own impact upon the service. It is possible to discern through a whole series of reports on the various professions an anxiety to develop an improved career structure but also a greater emphasis upon the management of the profession by the profession itself. This management was seen as involving control over manpower, training and budgets and therefore required participation in the higher echelons of management within the health service. The increasing expectation of change in the structure of the NHS gave impetus to these concerns but it was also a natural progression from the growing confidence of the professions in the importance of the service that they provided and the increasing anxiety that this importance should be reflected in the wider councils of the NHS.

The health care professions' increasing involvement in management

Despite its apparently strong position in the management of health services the medical profession has been deeply concerned since the start of the NHS to improve its power to control the organisation of the service, simply in order to protect the interests of the profession. The Porritt Report in 1962 suggested the formation of area health boards to replace the HMCs and boards of governors in the running of the service. It proposed that the health boards should integrate the health service into one management structure but gave doctors a very strong position in that structure. Nothing directly came of that report although it obviously influenced the first green paper of 1968. By that time work of greater significance was being carried out through the Godber Working Party on Medical Management. This working party produced a series of three reports in the late 1960s and early 1970s entitled *The Organisation of Medical Work in Hospitals*. The working party under the chairmanship of Sir George Godber, chief medical officer of the DHSS, had a membership which consisted half of members appointed by the profession and half of members appointed by the Secretary of State. The majority were doctors and their report suggested that there needed to be a revision of the medical advisory machinery in order to keep pace with the changed pattern of hospital medicine.

In place of the very cumbersome medical committees, some of which consisted of all consultant staff, maybe up to a hundred in all, the Godber working party suggested that clinicians needed to organise their work in divisions, each one covering a broad band of medical specialties. While the report emphasised the need for flexibility it indicated that there might be a division of psychiatry, a division of medicine covering also geriatrics, a division of surgery probably with a separate division for obstetrics and gynaecology, etc. The divisions should not consist only of consultants but should contain junior medical staff and other professions concerned with the specialty. It would be expected that the chairman of a division would be a doctor and that either he or another medical representative of a division should serve on a small medical executive committee under the chairmanship of a clinician with time in his contract for administrative duties. The latter would then be the chief medical spokesman for a hospital or group of hospitals. Besides being the channel of advice to the authority, the machinery was intended also to enable clinicians and others to examine critically the work performance of the specialty and to ensure the most effective deployment of clinical resources. The main emphasis therefore was on management and peer review rather than advice on broad policies. It was strongly a participative system which involved doctors and others in the management of their own affairs and sought also to involve doctors and related professions in a more positive control of the budget for patient care.

Because of the need to interrelate the work of the various divisions and of the medical executive machinery with the management of the hospitals in other spheres, the front cover of the first Godber Report depicted a series of cogwheels and the report and its successors therefore became known as the 'Cogwheel Reports'.

HM(68)67 recommended hospital authorities to develop the organisation of hospital medical staff along the lines of the first Cogwheel Report and in the years between 1968 and the reorganisation of the health service in 1974 considerable progress was made in adopting principles behind the reports, even though the detailed arrangements varied considerably between authorities. This variation was not a matter that was of concern to the working party, for it essentially saw itself as pursuing a theme rather than a set pattern of management for doctors. Although some doctors undoubtedly would have seen it as a move towards medical audit and some administrators as a move towards a takeover of management by the medical profession, it is fair to say that neither was intended nor have the results justified those fears. What the Cogwheel Reports have achieved is a start towards the medical profession itself reviewing its performance in a way that does not introduce the threat of external medical audit on the lines of the hospitals in the USA, which safeguard their independence by allowing themselves and their medical staffs to be subjected to intense scrutiny through systems of peer review. Doctors have remained, under the Cogwheel arrangements, professionally independent although employed by health authorities. Their clinical autonomy has remained unaffected in that no chairman of a division or chairman of an executive committee has powers to instruct any other consultant in the way that a patient may or may not be treated or resources used, but they have in a number of instances taken the first steps towards examining the way in which they themselves handle resources within divisions and to that extent started on the process of a peer review.

The processes started by the Cogwheel Report have been uneven in their application and many of the medical profession itself consider that doctors, who by their actions control so much of the health services resources, are still not as concerned as they should be in ensuring that those resources are used effectively.

Partly as a result of the role suggested for the chairman of the Cogwheel Executive Committee, the importance of the medical advisory machinery and its chairmen increased in relation to that of the medical members of authorities. The chairmen saw themselves as more positively representing the views of the profession to the HMC or board of governors and with the secretary and the chief nursing officer, there developed a triumvirate of senior officers who by the early

1970s were attending the formal meetings of the committees and seeking to reach agreement among themselves about recommendations to authorities.

In the psychiatric hospitals in particular experiments were taking place in 'multidisciplinary' management teams which sought to formalise the relationship between the group secretary, the chief nursing officer and chairman of the medical executive committee.

Developments in nursing management

The publication of the Salmon Committee Report on senior nursing staff structure in the hospital service in 1966 and the similar Mayston Report on local authority nursing services marked the first major change in nursing management since 1948. So far as local authority services were concerned the main result was to create the post of chief nursing officer, in charge of the nursing staff working in the community, who would be directly accountable to the authority itself rather than through the medical officer of health. When coupled with the Seebohm Report on social work it was a clear indication of the changing relationship between professions which was leading to the other professions emerging from under the direct supervision of the doctor.

The Salmon Report had more radical implications for nursing in hospitals. There had already been, during the first 18 years of the health service, a reduction in the amount of supervision exercised by senior nursing staff over other services. The days when the matron controlled not only nurses but also the professions supplementary to medicine and the catering and domestic services, had already, in most places, disappeared. The emphasis following the publication of a report on the pattern of the in-patient's day was to remove from nurses all non-nursing duties and this chimed in well with the concern of other staff to manage their own professional responsibilities. The Salmon Report firmly underlined this change of pattern and stressed that senior nursing staff should concentrate on the management of the nursing services rather than retaining responsibility for supervising nurses' homes and other duties which did not strictly require the skills and experience of a nurse.

The major theme of the report was to combine the functions of teaching, general nursing and midwifery under one chief officer in each hospital or hospital group and to organise the nursing service largely on functional lines. It suggested three principal nursing officers accountable to the chief nursing officer, one for teaching and one for midwifery and the other for the general nursing service. Under the principal nursing officer for general nursing there might be a senior nursing officer responsible for the nursing in surgical wards and departments and between him/her and the charge nurse/ward sister level a number of nursing officers responsible for groups of wards or departments.

It was emphasised that the senior nursing officers and above should be regarded as managers and nursing officers and below should be clinically oriented. Senior nursing staff should be concerned with policy, middle managers with programming and first line management, the ward sisters and charge nurses with execution of policy. It was considered that the route to the post of chief nursing officer could be through any of the disciplines within nursing provided that the individual had the necessary managerial ability. In order to achieve the appropriate management education and training for senior nurse managers a systematic programme was proposed, organised through a national staff committee with regional nursing staff committees accountable to it.

Like the Cogwheel Report the proposals in the Salmon Report were not universally adopted through a Departmental circular, but a number of pilot schemes were developed in the late 1960s, and with the setting up of the national and regional nursing staff committees, the main proposals in the report were pursued progressively through the service. By 1974 a high proportion of authorities had adopted the Salmon structure in some form and thus had a chief nursing officer or principal nursing officer accountable to the authority for the nursing service and for advice on nursing matters.

One result of the introduction of the Salmon arrangements was the diminution in the number of nursing committees. Instead the nursing profession was emphasising the importance of managers taking decisions using informal consultative techniques rather than formal reports to a professional committee.

The pursuit of improved management by nurses following the Salmon Report has not been without its critics. It is not easy for a large profession to change direction so radically and the very enthusiasm with which nurses have embraced the idea of improving their management skills through formal training has caused colleagues in other professions to question whether in practice the nurses are any better managers than they were before such attention was paid to management training. Doctors in particular have related what they see as being a diminution in the relative status of charge nurses and ward sisters with what they regard as being the large numbers of middle managers in the senior nursing officer and nursing officer grades. It would be surprising so soon after implementation of the Salmon Report in many places if these criticisms were totally to lack substance. Many senior nurses would now welcome flexibility in the use of the middle grades but they would also stress the value of the Salmon approach to nursing management and the importance in terms of supervision and training of the much criticised nursing officer posts. They point out that with the changing social factors of shorter working hours, younger charge nurses, high turn over of staff and the need for nurses to absorb increasingly sophisticated techniques, the nursing officer appointment is an extremely important one for the clinical services and it would be a pity if inadequate performance in the post by a number of individuals were to reduce acceptability of the concept.

Developments in the management for other professions

The increasing awareness in the late 1960s of impending reorganisation for the health service lent significance to a number of studies undertaken at national level into management aspects of the service and the organisation of professions. Comment has already been made about the Zuckerman Report on scientific services which has never been implemented. The same is broadly true of the Trethowan Report on the work of psychologists. During the late 1960s and early 1970s however a number of other professions did undergo significant changes in their work as a result of a national examination of certain problems. For administrators the Lycett Green Report had led to a systematic approach to recruitment, training and career development working through a national staff committee and regional staff committees which pre-dated the Salmon proposals for nurses by three years. The administrative staff committees supervised the national administrative training schemes but also sought in a variety of ways to develop the performance of all branches of administration.

In 1966 the Farquharson-Lang Report examined the administrative practice of hospitals boards in Scotland and concluded that there should be much greater delegation to officers than had hitherto been the case. Its major proposal that a post of chief executive should be established was never accepted but the report undoubtedly influenced thinking about the way the service might develop if it were reorganised.

Also in 1966 the Hunt Report on hospital supplies organisation in England and Wales was circulated with HM(66)69, and area supplies departments were established. The arrangements are described in Chapter 11.

In 1970 the Noel Hall Report on the hospital pharmaceutical service similarly proposed that those services should be organised on a scale large enough to ensure that pharmacists were fully occupied on duties requiring their professional and managerial ability, to provide scope for the optimum use of technicians and other supporting staff and to create the conditions needed for a satisfactory career structure — it is described in Chapter 6. The Noel Hall Report was largely implemented before the 1974 reorganisation, at least so far as its structure was concerned, and posts of regional pharmacist were also created. In general the RHBs designated one of the hospital authorities within a pharmaceutical area to provide pharmaceutical services on behalf of all hospital authorities with an area pharmaceutical officer in professional and managerial charge though reporting like the area supplies officer through the administrator of the 'host' authority in matters of day-to-day management.

Also in 1970 the Woodbine Parish Report on hospital building maintenance commented on the need for the introduction of a comprehensive system of planning, financial control and cost comparison of building maintenance work in hospitals. It stressed the need for planned inspection and a formal report on a more detailed survey of the building maintenance requirement of the hospital group at regional level and the full implementation of the general principles of estate management modified to meet the needs of the hospital service. Although the implementation of the Woodbine Parish Report was not achieved before reorganisation the emphasis upon the importance of building maintenance in the health service was carried forward into the thinking about the need for regional and area works officers.

Finally, in 1972 just before the reorganisation the Hunter Report on medical administrators outlined proposals for community medicine in a unified health service. It foresaw the need for community medicine specialists who would have a special role to play in securing the most effective use of the AHAs' resources. It suggested that those specialists should be concerned with the provision of health information, with health planning and management services plus the provision of advice and assistance to local authorities, especially in such matters as environmental hygiene and communicable disease control. Thus, very late in the day, the report identified the need for a new specialty of community physician and those practising in that field opted for consultant status rather than administrative status for their function. This in turn affected not only their conditions of service and remuneration as consultants but also their position vis-à-vis the new authorities — the emphasis of their tasks became increasingly on epidemiology rather than administration.

The 1974 reorganisation

Although the management arrangements for the reorganised service set out in the 'Grey Book' appeared new, and were certainly more systematic and comprehensive, they derived a considerable amount from the activities within the service during the preceding ten years. Thus, district management teams formalised the kind of informal multidisciplinary group that had worked together in managing the hospitals for several years previously. More importantly the new arrangement sought to provide for the professions a career structure that provided for the profession to manage itself and have a senior representative either on or available to advise the management team. The 'Grey Book' for instance suggested that one of the district professional heads for each paramedical discipline might be appointed by the new AHA as area convenor to monitor the services and ensure that professional and technical standards were being maintained. Although Whitley Councils did not necessarily provide for a grade of district therapist in the various paramedical professions, the pattern of the new service strongly emphasised the importance of professional leadership and a number of professions working together in teams of officers to reach consensus management decisions about the way the service should develop. Indeed, the 'Grey Book' emphasised the desirability that the health care professions should be integrally involved in planning and management at all levels, that this involvement must be achieved without infringing the clinical autonomy of medical and dental consultants and general practitioners and without interfering with the professional standards of the health care professions or inhibiting the exercise of professional judgement by members of those professions.

The arrangements envisaged that the new health authorities should not have sub-committees but should have a series of professional advisory committees selected by members of the profession themselves rather than by the authorities. There are four such committees: medical, dental, nursing and midwifery, and pharmaceutical. In practice the performance of those committees in advising the new authorities has not had a major impact. On the other hand the involvement of a number of professions in the formal management teams and the creation of district and area posts as heads of the various professions has had a major influence upon the way the service has developed and has enabled the professions to exercise considerable influence.

It is, of course, impossible to generalise across such a wide field and while, for instance, it has been said that the nurses and treasurers have developed their sphere of influence considerably by membership of teams, the same cannot necessarily be said of the works professions who are represented on the regional team but not on teams at area or district levels. Moreoever, the creation of areas has been a mixed blessing to supplies officers and pharmaceutical officers who hitherto were relatively independent of the local management. The areas for their services have had to come under the control of the area health authority and they have become accountable in the case of the supplies officer to the area administrator and in the case of the pharmaceutical officer to the area authority. They might therefore be deemed to have lost a certain amount of independence as professions because of the reorganisation, though they have gained a greater identity with the organisation and easier communications.

Faced with a variety of pressures for professional independence, the reorganised service adopted a variety of solutions. Team membership probably constitutes the strongest position but in addition there are a number of officers who as head of their professions are directly accountable to their authorities although they are not members of the management team. Currently these are dental officers, pharmaceutical officers and at area level works officers. A number of other officers such as specialists in community medicine at area and regional levels and scientific officers enjoy a professional independence but can only report to the authority through the regional or area medical officer.

One of the problems of the formal professional advisory machinery is that it operates at area and regional levels whereas the prime interest of most professionals rests within the district or even individual hospital or community service. The management arrangements for the reorganised service recognised a need for representative machinery at district level for the medical profession though not for those professions which are hierarchically organised. Even here, however, the district medical committees, which in a single-district area also perform the functions of an area medical advisory committee, have often been regarded as too remote. Although they comprise both consultants and general practitioners many districts are larger than the previous management units for the health service, and the medical executive machinery proposed by Cogwheel has, for instance, often been continued as a further medical advisory and executive machine.

Research Paper No. 1 published by the Royal Commission in 1978 outlined considerable criticisms of the advisory committee structure. The general feeling was one of quite meagre impact and of additional burden on the consultative process. Advisory committees did not seem to have found ways of engaging the active interest of staff. While welcoming advisory committees' support, professional chief officers also saw little need for the function to be carried out by committees, whose views might be particularistic. Combining, for instance, independent contractors or retail pharmacists with hospital pharmacists did not necessarily make for composite views on the pharmaceutical service, so regional and area pharmaceutical officers might still be left with the task of proferring their own advice without support from one element of the profession. The problem is that the professions concerned tend to be ambivalent about committee work. On the one hand they attach importance to the opportunity to discuss major issues and advise authorities, on the other hand they do not wish to become involved with committees that are too far from their main interest and they resent the time given up to committee work.

Chief officers too vary in their attitudes. Most medical officers would accept the need for some form of representative machinery to enable the medical profession to give its views; indeed the need is obvious, and the problem is to get a medical consensus view. Nursing officers however naturally tend to see the advice from the nursing and midwifery committees as competing with that which should probably come from the nursing management structure. It may be that professional advisory machinery is incompatible with the hierarchical organisation of a profession when the members of the advisory committee are accountable to the chief officer.

The Royal Commission considered that the principle that the professionals should be involved in the running of the NHS through advisory committees was right but that in practice the process of consultation had proliferated unduly, particularly in the medical profession.

The apparent failure of much of the professional advisory machinery must be set against the apparent success of team working by officers although there are exceptions to the rule. In general the teams of officers at region, area and district levels have worked well together and have produced an acceptable forum for making major decisions, though there have been frequent criticisms of delay in making decisions and it is said that too many decisions are taken by the team which could more appropriately be made by an individual in consultation with individual colleagues. It is important to note a particular problem of district teams in England and Wales. Other team members are officers accountable to the authority, but the consultant and general practitioner members of district management teams are elected and can only be accountable to their colleagues who elected them. Given the natural tension that this arrangement produces it is surprising that teams have worked so effectively. There have been instances where decisions taken by the team with the support of the individual clinicians on it have then been heavily criticised by the medical profession within the district, and it should not be assumed that the marriage in one team of hierarchically organised professions and representatives of doctors can necessarily continue to achieve a high level of consensus decision making. Second tier officers and chief officers not represented on the teams who commented to the Royal Commission were less enthusiastic. While the right to attend team meetings or authority meetings when matters affecting one's profession are to be discussed seems to be satisfactory, in practice those who are not privy to the continuing discussions of the team or the authority inevitably have less impact upon the shaping of the service than do full team members. Although professional representation is much stronger therefore in management at all levels than it was before 1974, a number of professions still feel that their impact is much less than it should be.

Another way in which professions might hope to make an impact is through membership of authorities, though in practice it is open only to doctors and to a lesser extent nurses. It has been argued that staff representation on authorities is inappropriate and unnecessary but, at least for doctors, it has been normal practice since 1948 and was formalised in 1974; authorities invariably have a consultant, a general practitioner and a nurse member. In theory membership has never been representational; once appointed a member serves as an individual not as a delegate or representative of any particular interest. In practice the professions have not always seen it in that light. However, the greater emphasis upon delegation to officers and the potential for confusion, with, for instance, a nursing advisory committee, a nursing officer and a nurse member of the authority all discussing an item, have tended to make the membership of an authority by a particular profession much less valuable to the professional interest than in the past. There are nevertheless occasions when other professions may feel that their interests are less likely to be brought to the attention of the authority than if they had a member of the profession on it.

Professional involvement in family practitioner committees

As so often, the contractual services must be excluded here from what has been said about management arrangements. The four sets of independent contractors are very resistant to any idea of becoming part of a larger organisation. Although lay members are in a majority on family practitioner committees and on the services committees which deal with complaints, the local medical committee exerts very strong influence on the way in which the FPC pursues its role and has generally ensured that the FPC is essentially a regulatory mechanism rather than one which plays an active part in trying to raise standards. Thus although the professions probably have even greater influence in the family practitioner services than in other parts of the NHS, it cannot be said that they are collectively involved in advising on or participating in management in the way they are in the directly managed parts of the service. Although it is generally agreed that a good deal needs to be done to even up the standards of general practice, and although many people, including the Royal Commission, have questioned the need for a separate FPC, no radical change is in prospect.

The training relationship

Reference has already been made to the training requirements for the various professions, but it is important to stress the role of the health service management in partnership with the professions for providing the facilities for training within the service. While a number of outside institutions do provide training for health care professions, for many the complete organisation and financing of training is achieved through the NHS. This is true for the basic training of the largest staff group — the nurses — and it is perhaps a question for the future whether the nurse management structure, which must follow the health authority structure, will continue to provide a satisfactory pattern for nurse education. The Briggs Committee envisaged that area colleges of nursing and midwifery would be very clearly distinct from the health authorities. If that happened it would constitute a radical change of emphasis.

Clinical facilities for the training of doctors and dentists have been provided within hospitals for many years to supplement the pre-clinical work of the universities. It is important to note the impact this has on teaching hospitals' priorities and expenditure. At one extreme, dental hospitals would not be needed if it were not for the need to provide for the training of dentists. Small dental departments within general hospitals would be sufficient to allow appropriate hospital treatment of patients requiring dental care. More generally, the range of facilities needed for teaching, the importance of attracting high calibre professorial and other teaching staff and the need for teaching to be allied to research, require teaching hospitals to invest more heavily in manpower, equipment and special facilities than those required for non-teaching hospitals. This has been recognised in the way in which the resource allocation formulae have been developed but it also imposes a more complex task on health service managers in dealing with the university and with the various staff engaged in clinical teaching. To balance the health needs of the population at large for health services with the different priorities that are required for providing appropriate facilities for teaching is something which requires considerable judgement and negotiation.

Since the early 1960s the postgraduate education of doctors has been more systematically pursued in many places through the creation of postgraduate medical centres within hospitals and by formal appointments for postgraduate deans and clinical tutors. It is probably fair to say that the public and indeed health service staff in general have failed to recognise the great importance of this work in maintaining and improving clinical standards within hospitals and in general practice as well as forming the focus for better relationships and collaboration between hospital and community services.

The medical profession has achieved a national agreement which allows for a set period of time off in any three years for its members to pursue postgraduate education. Although a number of other individual instances of statutory refresher training exist, for instance for midwives and ambulance staff, there is a great variation between professions in the arrangements for postgraduate training of all sorts. Each staff side of the appropriate Whitley Council has negotiated provision for its own professions but all have had to be met in terms of finance from the normal budget of the health service authorities. In this, of course, they are no different from arrangements for much basic training whether it is allowances for student nurses, day release for medical laboratory scientific officers or grants for radiography or physiotherapy training. At times of financial difficulty all these discretionary elements in training are liable to be the subject of close scrutiny and reduction by authorities. This is one reason why so many professions are stressing the importance of manpower planning to avoid short-term financial considerations spoiling the prospects of developing the service in the future.

Statutory bodies, professional associations and staff organisations

It is important to recognise that there are several types of organisation involved in the conduct of affairs on behalf of the professionals, and individuals may participate in each type. First there are the statutory bodies such as the General Medical Council, the General Nursing Councils, the Council for the Professions Supplementary to Medicine and now the UK Central Council for Nursing, Midwifery and Health Visiting set up by parliament to order the proper conduct of the professions.

Also established under statutory powers, often under the National Health Service Acts, are other bodies concerned with professional matters, including the Standing Advisory Committees which reported to the Central Health Services Council until its abolition, the National Staff Committees, the National Training Council and the Joint Board of Clinical Nursing Studies.

Completely independent of parliamentary or government initiative there have evolved, for the most part before the establishment of the NHS, such bodies as the Royal College of Surgeons, the Royal College of Nursing, the Institute of Health Service Administrators, the Pharmaceutical Society and the Society of Radiographers. Constitutionally they vary, some existing by Royal Charter, some being limited companies, and so on, but they are subject to parliamentary control only in the sense that they are subject to the general laws affecting limited companies and so on. They are all voluntary bodies managed by and on behalf of their members. Their concerns for the development of their profession in terms of education, training and status have already been outlined. Within all the larger professions, and particularly in medicine, there are associations and societies concerned with a particular professional or occupational interest, such as occupational medicine, theatre nurses or unit and sector administrators. Generally they are complementary to the main professional bodies rather than potential rivals.

Increasingly professional concerns have become related to pay and conditions of service, and in a number of instances the organisation which is pursuing the professional objectives of its members has also become involved through Whitley Councils and with local health authorities in pursuing activities which are the proper interests of staff organisations such as trade unions. The picture is confusing because whereas the Pharmaceutical Society would not regard itself as a trade union and would expect its members to negotiate terms and conditions of service through such bodies as the Association of Scientific Technical and Managerial Staffs or the Confederation of Health Service Employees, the Royal College of Midwives and the Royal College of Nursing act both as professional bodies and as staff organisations.

The proposed legislation on the registration of staff-side organisations in the mid-1970s forced professional associations to consider their position very carefully. It seemed likely that they would have to choose between losing a number of their members or registering as trade unions and taking on the tasks that that entailed. The legislation has not come about but the Institute of Health Service Administrators, for instance, has decided to discontinue direct participation in Whitley matters accepting that NALGO, the trade union which represents a very high proportion of the Institute's membership in any case, should do so and allow the Institute to concentrate on purely professional matters. While such a decision makes the status of a professional association clear and tends to enhance its ability to claim a disinterested view of professional issues, not being represented on Whitley Councils does reduce the power of organisations to pursue issues with local management. On the other hand, retaining both professional and staff organisation interests causes difficulties within the organisation and considerable pressure to subjugate the professional interests to issues related to conditions of service.

The increasing pace of change in industrial relations means that relationships between staff organisations and professional associations are by no means settled. In a number of authorities the trade unions affiliated to the TUC have refused to take part in consultative committees that contain staff organisations which are not so affiliated. This clearly puts pressure on management to negotiate with the larger trade unions and on staff to join a trade union in addition to a professional association. Professional associations, however, would not wish to withdraw from staff consultation at either national or local level and they know that if they did so they would lose a number of their members who would not wish to pay subscriptions to both trade unions and professional organisations. For the most part, therefore, professional and staff organisations have an uneasy alliance in dealing with management on matters of common concern.

Research work and the professions

It is to be expected that any educational body involved in developing its profession should be interested in promoting research. In practice it is surprising how little research is undertaken outside the clinical field. The medical profession is naturally firmly entrenched as a major contributor to research activity.

For over 40 years the Medical Research Council at national level has been a dominant vehicle for regulating medical research. Additionally, considerable medical research is funded by the University Grants Committee within universities. The Social Science Research Council is partly involved in health services research. The pharmaceutical industry spends large sums on research related to health care and there are contributions to research from a number of voluntary bodies. Besides acting as the major arbiter of research activity and the channel for funds for this purpose, the MRC also has about 60 research units, mainly attached to hospitals and university departments.

At local level the Department used, until 1977, to allocate funds to each region for use in small schemes of locally organised research. Each region now uses its own funds for this purpose and has continued its research committee for locally organised research. Although the funds may be used for the work of other professions than medicine it is rare for a professional other than a doctor to obtain funds for research under this scheme or for other professionals to serve as members of the committee.

If the other professions are to achieve greater status and independence, research activity is something which is important to them. This is so, not only for doctors, scientists and pharmacists, but for nurses and the professions supplementary to medicine. In the last ten years nurses have begun to make an impact in this sphere but there is so far little evidence that the other professions have been as yet effective in obtaining the necessary funds or devoting the necessary skilled research effort to this important work.

Manpower planning

With 70 per cent of the health service budget being devoted to staff and about two-thirds of those staff being members of professional groups, the future needs for professional manpower of various sorts must be an important topic. It is, however, considered in Chapter 13 so it is only necessary to make some points about the specific interests of the professions here.

The recent concentration on a systematic approach to planning has revealed the paucity of knowledge about the likely pattern of staffing for the future. The only attempt to introduce effective manpower planning has, until recently, been for the medical profession and that has had an unfortunate history with the action taken on the Willink Committee's views causing a shortage of doctors and successive attempts to balance the interests of the profession and the interests of the NHS against the imponderables of forecasting seeming to be unsuccessful. As the Royal Commission commented, 'role flexibility and resource implications of alternative forecasts were not considered and the data base was inadequate'.

Coincident with NHS management's concern with manpower planning, the individual professions have also recently sought to extend their activities in this sphere. In its evidence to the Royal Commission the Council for Professions Supplementary to Medicine sought to obtain responsibility for manpower planning of the professions which it regulates. Interestingly it emphasised the importance of:

1. ensuring that professional standards and judgements are brought to bear appropriately in circumstances where the particular interests of employers and employees might otherwise prevail,
2. providing more precise regulation or adjustment of the processes of supply, demand and need for professional manpower in the interest of adequate health services.

The views of the CPSM are interesting as an example of the differing interest in manpower planning. It obviously saw itself as the mediating force between the conflicting and narrower interests of individual employing authorities and their staff. Others would say that the professional bodies also have special interests though these tend to work in two ways. There is a natural wish to expand the profession but at certain times at least a concern to keep numbers down in order to maintain standards or even perhaps to create 'scarcity value'.

At this early stage in the attempts to plan the main need is not for either professional bodies or NHS authorities to be defensive but to recognise the lack of a data base and to seek jointly to develop systems which will allow rational decisions to be made about the future, whether the problems are of over-provision or shortage.

The future

The problems of manpower planning in the professions illustrate the dangers of forecasting by extrapolation. Yet one can perceive trends which are likely to continue at least in the short term.

In its evidence to the Royal Commission, the CPSM suggested that many specialisms and skills which have been called ancillary or supplementary to medicine are now so complex that a number of professions should now be called 'complementary to medicine'. The existing evolution of health care professions in this way seems inevitable and it will be essential for the medical and other professions and the NHS itself to adjust to the new pattern.

Despite financial constraints, the demand for more advanced qualifications in all professions is likely to be pursued with a concomitant use of lesser qualified 'aides' to enable the range of professions to increase within reasonable financial limits.

The third factor which one can confidently predict is more balance between the sexes. Those professions such as nursing and physiotherapy which have traditionally had a small minority of men will increase their number while medicine, administration, and engineering will recruit more women.

It is far more difficult to be confident about the state of the labour market. This depends so much on a range of social factors such as pay and conditions in the NHS compared with those in other jobs, availability of nursery education, extent of reciprocity with other countries in the EEC, the state of private practice and, not least, the ability of the NHS to pay for professionals it would wish to employ. Certainly, the NHS has not yet shown itself able to judge its future use of the many professions it employs.

Amidst the uncertainties, it is clear that the NHS will continue to be dominated by professionals. This is not a bad thing so long as it is recognised that,however well motivated, their judgement of the public's interests is limited by their professional background. It is important, therefore, to have a system which counterbalances the professional view and enables the differing concerns of the various professions to be heard. It is not a recipe for tranquillity, but so long as the prime concern is for the welfare of the patients the controversies, which will undoubtedly arise, should be fruitful in developing a service that is appropriate to need rather than any individual profession's narrow ambitions.

References

[1] Baly, Monica. *Nursing and Social Changes.* Heinemann 1973

[2] Cartwright, F.F. *A Social History of Medicine.* Longman 1977

[3] Prandy, K. *Professional Employees: a study of scientists and engineers.* Faber 1965

[4] Wilensky, H.L. 'The dynamics of professionalism: the case of hospital administration' *Hospital Administration* Vol. 7 No. 2, 1962

Further reading

Statutory instruments and circulars

England and Wales

SI74/361. The NHS (Appointment of Consultants) Regulations 1974
SI74/455. The NHS (Service Committees and Tribunal) Regulations 1974 (as amended)
SI74/494. The NHS (Professions Supplementary to Medicine) Regulations 1974
SI74/495. The NHS (Speech Therapists) Regulations 1974
HSC(IS)4, WHSC(IS)6. Area nurse training committees: changes consequent on reorganisation
HSC(IS)16, WHSC(IS)27. Organisation of scientific and technical services
HSC(IS)101, WHSC(IS)100. The remedical professions and linked therapies
HSC(IS)148. NHS locally organised research scheme
HC(FP)(77)1. General Practitioners Vocational Training Act 1976
HC(77)33, WHC(77)40. Relationship between the medical and remedial professions
HC(78)10. Devolution of the locally organised research scheme
HC(79)19. Management of the remedial professions in the NHS

Scotland

SI74/504. The NHS (Service Committees and Tribunal) (Scotland) Regulations 1974
SI74/549. The NHS (Professions Supplementary to Medicine) (Scotland) Regulations 1974
SI74/667. The NHS (Speech Therapists) (Scotland) Regulations 1974
SI76/1679. The NHS (Appointment of Consultants) (Scotland) Regulations 1976

Official reports

Committee of Inquiry into the Medical Profession. *Report* (Merrison Report). (Cmnd 6018). HMSO 1975
Committee on Nursing. *Report* (Briggs Report). (Cmnd 5115) HMSO 1972
DHSS. *Management Arrangements for the Reorganised National Health Service* (The Grey Book) HMSO 1972
DHSS. *Report of the Working Party on Medical Administrators* (Hunter Report). HMSO 1972
DHSS, SHHD, Welsh Office. *Hospital Building Maintenance* (Woodbine Parish Report). HMSO 1970
DHSS, SHHD, Welsh Office. *The Hospital Pharmaceutical Services* (Noel Hall Report). HMSO 1970
Ministry of Health. *Report of the Inquiry into the Recruitment, Training and Promotion of Administrative and Clerical Staff in the National Health Service*

(Lycett Green Report). HMSO 1963

Ministry of Health. *First Report of the Joint Working Party on the Organisation of Medical Work in Hospitals* (Cogwheel Report). HMSO 1967

Ministry of Health and SHHD. *Hospital Scientific and Technical Services* (Zuckerman Report). HMSO 1968

Ministry of Health and SHHS. *Senior Nursing Staff Structure* (Salmon Report). HMSO 1966

Royal Commission on Medical Education 1965-68. *Report* (Cmnd 3569). HMSO 1968

Royal Commission on the National Health Service. *Report* (Cmnd 7615). HMSO 1979

SHHD. *The Organisation of a Medical Advisory Structure.* HMSO 1973

Other publications

Abel-Smith, B. *A History of the Nursing Profession.* Heinemann 1960

Baly, M. *Professional Responsibility in the Community Health Services.* HM&M 1975

Bendall, E. and Raybould, E. *A History of the General Nursing Council for England and Wales 1919-1969.* H.K. Lewis 1969

Council for Professions Supplementary to Medicine. *Submission to the Royal Commission on the National Health Service.* 1977

Etzioni, A. *Semiprofessions and their Organisation.* Oxford Centre for Management Studies. 1969

Forsyth, G. *Doctors and State Medicine: A Study of the British Health Service.* Pitman 1966

Jaques, E. *et al. Health Services, their nature and organisation.* Brunel Institute of Organisation and Social Studies. Heinemann 1978

McLaughlan G. *et al.* (Eds). *Patterns for Uncertainty? Planning for the greater medical profession.* OUP for Nuffield Provincial Hospitals Trust 1979

Nokes, P. *Professions and Vocation in Welfare Practice.* Routledge 1967

Parry, N. and Parry, J. *The Rise of the Medical Professions.* Croom Helm 1976

Rowbottom, R. *et al. Hospital Organisation.* Brunel Institute of Organisation and Social Studies. Heinemann 1973

Rowbottom, R. *et al. Professionals in the Health and Social Services Organisations.* Brunel Institute of Organisation and Social Studies. 1978

Shaw, Jane. *Landmarks on the Road: a study of developing health professions.* MPhil thesis for Brunel University

White, R. *Social Change and the Development of the Nursing Profession.* Kimpton 1978

16
Health care and the public

The members of the Royal Commission placed great confidence in the value of the public being closely involved in health care matters. In their report, when considering the problems of determining priorities, they said:

> ... we believe it is important that the lay public should be involved in the process. The discussion should not be left solely to health professionals and administrators, though we recognise that policies and priorities must be realistic and reflect what can be achieved, and must therefore take account of the views of professional and management staff in the NHS on their feasibility and likely consequences ... we recommend that more of the professional advice on which policies and priorities are based should be made public. This would strengthen the authority of the advice issued and lead to its readier acceptance in the field as well as promoting public discussion.

In 1972, two years after he ceased to be Secretary of State for Social Services, Richard Crossman gave a lecture on 'A Politician's View of Health Service Planning' in which he argued that until the public is made to face the problems of choice arising from decisions about who benefits from the use of scarce resources the decisions will be muffled and hidden: 'Either a man is given a renal dialysis or he is not. If he's not, he dies. There will always be a shortage, and so there will always be a choice of those condemned to death, just as there will always be a choice between the health preservation services ... and the life preservation services ...' Questions of real choices about life and death led him to conclude: 'It is only with a public which has allowed itself to face these problems clearly and openly that you can have the kind of rational planning of resources which I believe to be essential.'[1]

This chapter sets out to describe the varied approaches and responses to this view that, somehow, the public has a crucial part to play in decisions concerning the resource allocation, organisation and delivery of health care.

Before 1974

During the second reading of the National Health Service Bill in 1946 the member of parliament for South Tottenham had no doubts about the way in which the public should be represented in the new service:[2]

> The public, in the final analysis, have a certain amount of horse sense in the people they choose. That is why I am here. When the public elect a local authority and it throws up certain failures, they do not get re-elected. At any rate, that is the responsibility of the public. On the elective principle, the patient has some check on administration, whereas accountability, under this Bill, is only to the Minister and Parliament through the Minister.

Here is a statement of the widely held conviction that successful submission to the electoral process confers democratic authority. The public expresses its preferences by voting, and so transmits to its elected representatives powers to call to account the actions of the executive. This is the form of accountability on which the House of Commons and local authorities are based, and it applies of course to the national health service at the national level.

The use of selection rather than election as a means of representing the public was set out by the parliamentary secretary to the Minister of Health later on in the same debate:

> Every hospital or group of hospitals so related as to form a hospital unit is to have its own committee of management, and the members of that committee will not be black-hearted, black-hatted bureaucrats from Whitehall. They are to be appointed, not, mark you, by the Minister, but by the regional board of the area concerned, and after consultation with a number of local authorities. These local authorities include the local health authority, the local executive committee in charge of the practitioner service, the existing voluntary hospitals and the senior professional staff in the hospitals themselves. You can hardly have a more local body than that. Why should these local citizens, with greater means at their disposal, and greater opportunities for development, do less than their predecessors have done? I am convinced that they will do more. With the growing sense of social responsibility which is so evident in our people today, greater interest, greater initiative and greater participation in the development of our social service will become more potent than ever before.

Here we have a defence of the appointment and selection system which was adopted for the new NHS. Consultation with elected bodies and the use of professional expertise are two of the devices used to try to ensure that the people appointed to represent the public have a 'sense of social responsibility'. Election normally entails voting according to the party allegiance, and the adoption of appointment instead, for many years helped to create a spurious sense of a health service that was apolitical.

With nearly 380 hospital management committees set up in England and Wales in 1948 and 85 boards of management in Scotland, each having a membership of between 16 and 20, the potential for public awareness seemed to be a reasonable assumption as far as the hospital service was concerned. The assumption was less likely with the executive councils responsible for primary care, partly because of the nature of their activities, which were contractual rather than managerial, and partly because of the nature of the membership. These bodies too were appointed rather than elected, but there was less emphasis on public representation; half the members were appointed by the professions and two-thirds of the remainder by the local health authority, and the rest by the minister. The various services provided by local health authorities fell within the normal local authority pattern of accountability through election, but the wide range of local authority responsibilities made it unlikely that their activities in the health field would be a particular centre of public interest and scrutiny.

The 'nationalisation' of hospitals did not see a complete break with the public's former attitude to voluntary hospitals. The new hospital authorities were not allowed to appeal for funds, and in the early years appeals on their behalf were discouraged, but such bodies as leagues of hospital friends have flourished, and successful appeals in recent years for funds for hospices and whole body scanners suggest that if anything the willingness of the public to give money for health care has grown. As a proportion of health service expenditure, voluntary contributions have been very small, but they have been valuable in providing amenities, and sometimes special facilties which could not be financed from public funds. Section 5 of the Health Services Act 1980 empowered health authorities (and, in Scotland, local health councils) to engage in activities to raise money by appeals, collections and so on for health purposes. This new departure reflected the government's belief in the importance of voluntary contributions. Also it was hoped that allowing authorities to participate in appeals would help prevent appeals to the public for things the service did not want or could not afford, such as capital investments which would entail heavy revenue expenditure from public funds.

Giving money is not the only way in which the public has shown a direct interest in hospitals. Voluntary organisations and individual volunteers have helped in hospitals by befriending patients, helping in occupational therapy and in providing specific services like canteens, libraries and trolley shops. An early lack of enthusiasm in the health departments has been followed by an increasing appreciation of the value of volunteers in hospitals, particularly perhaps in long-stay hospitals isolated from the community, and in 1972 circular HM(72)5 encouraged the appointment of staff to organise volunteers. The use of volunteers is potentially delicate in that the health service unions naturally object if there is any suspicion that they are replacing paid workers. Fortunately they have been in general used to supplement rather than replace staff.

Fund raising and voluntary work were and remain an indication of the public's strong interest in hospitals; their function was to assist hospitals — and incidentally they served as a useful source of recruitment for membership of hospital authorities. They did not contribute much towards the public's involvement in the organisation and delivery of health care. A greater contribution might have been found in the house committees established in the 1950s for most individual hospitals, some or all their members being drawn from outside the membership of the HMC or board of governors. Originally the value of these bodies was seen to lie in overseeing the daily conduct of hospitals and the welfare of patients, and this remit included making recommendations to the governing body. Specifically they were identified as a link between the local community and the hospital, and as a suitable training ground for membership of HMCs and boards of governors. In 1954 the Bradbeer Report of the Central Health Services Council on the internal administration of hospitals discussed these committees and agreed with the Ministry of Health's view that it was unsound in principle to give them direct power to expend Exchequer money, although they were seen as valuable for the help they could give to medical staff, nurses and administrators in helping to solve immediate problems.

Some 12 years later, in 1966, the Farquharson-Lang Report on the administrative practice of hospital boards in Scotland also looked at house committees and was not in favour of them, with or without powers. This was not a difference between countries; it was rather that in the period subsequent to the Bradbeer Report the climate had changed. The mid-1960s was the period when management was often seen as a panacea for society in general and the use of managerial language became common in the health service. The committee felt that house committees encourage members to intervene in day-to-day management decisions which it considered should be left to officers. It did not agree that house committees were necessary to maintain a lively local interest in hospitals and as an encouragement to voluntary bodies in the raising of funds, etc. It saw the co-ordination of the efforts of various voluntary bodies as the primary responsibility of officers, although it thought that authorities might wish to designate individual members or groups of members to liaise between the boards and voluntary bodies. For this and other reasons, it recommended that house committees should be dispensed with and that their functions should be reallocated between members and officers on the basis of a reappraisal of their respective responsibilities.

The years between the Bradbeer and Farquharson-Lang Reports saw not only the development of managerial attitudes but also a new impetus towards consumer participation in NHS affairs. A straw in the wind was a Penguin Special *What's Wrong with Hospitals?* by Gerda Cohen, published in 1964.[3] It was a journalistic investigation originating in an unfortunate experience in hospital, and the author came to the conclusion that patients did not appear to count, even at the most praiseworthy hospitals. She had this to say about the bridge between the service and the consumer:

> The whole system, however, holds an inherent defect: Regional Boards select both members and chairmen of the committees from nominees put forward by various bodies on invitation from the Boards; this selection is crucial, enabling the Regional Board to manipulate management 'plans' as thought desirable. Thus the system can be either a tool for patronage and playing safe, or a genuine method of ensuring that go-ahead, public-spirited citizens contribute toward the Service but in no case can the system be truly democratic, on a level with local government democracy, because committees are never elected by the customers, the patients ... On the whole, though, conflict within managements seems submerged by a general tendency to identify *with* the hospital, *against* the non-hospital, outside world.

The book discussed maternity services, the environment within hospitals, caring for the mentally ill, and care for those at the end of their lives. The chapter on children in hospital illuminates the growth of consumer representation which can be subsumed under the general heading of pressure groups.

In 1959 the Central Health Services Council published the report of a committee chaired by Sir Harry Platt on the arrangements made in hospitals for the welfare of sick children. The Platt Report became a charter for various groups which had begun to question the wisdom of hospital regimes and out-patient activities when concerned with the young. Mrs Cohen had this to say: 'Whole paragraphs of the Platt Report are quoted at cocktail parties by women whose normal contact with Government publications is confined to the telephone directory'. Among the activities she reported was that of a parents' league entitled 'Mothercare for Children in Hospital'. A survey by parents of the existing practice regarding the care of children who were in-patients was undertaken by this league and soon blossomed into some 32 groups covering England and Scotland.

> The Mothercare groups hold meetings in draughty church halls to evangelise women who don't read the highbrow papers; they invite recalcitrant paediatricians to a chat over digestive biscuits; they back up mothers who want to accompany patients under school age. Once the hospital managements have bitten back their suspicion of 'nosey, under-employed neurotics' joint talks are held in an atmosphere of astonished calm.

From these early beginnings followed the work of bodies such as the National Association for the Welfare of Children in Hospital which must stand as a representative example of the way in which patients' consumer interests began to become significant in the health service of the 1960s. Knowledge is power, and the ability to quote official guidance, say, on good practice concerning visting hours for childrens' wards, could raise problems for medical, administrative and nursing staff which were unexpected and, in some cases, unsolvable. It has been said that dissatisfaction with the machinery of justice expressed by the middle-class press first arose when members of the middle class began to have experience of the courts through motoring offences. The greater exposure of middle-class patients to a state service might well have been a significant factor in the growth of general dissatisfaction with the NHS expressed through the media. It is not that the middle classes received a poorer service than others; if anything, the contrary is true. Nor is it necessarily true that they were more dissatisfied than members of the other social classes, though evidence on that subject is not clear. It is rather that their views are more likely to find expression in the middle-class newspapers read by politicians, health authority members and senior staff, and that they more generally have the attitudes and skills necessary for changing the services they use.

Another feature of the sixties was the incidence of specific 'scandals' revealed to exist within the NHS. As was mentioned in Chapter 1, they were heralded by the book of a voluntary association published in 1967: *Sans Everything: A Case to Answer.*[4] After accounts of conditions in various hospitals, the latter part of the book suggested some answers. Professor Brian Abel-Smith contributed a chapter entitled 'Administrative Solution: A Hospital Commissioner?'. After reviewing how the evidence of cruelty and neglect surfaced, the conclusion he came to was that there was need for an officer, independent of the Ministry of Health, with power to examine complaints requiring investigation:

> What is needed is an inspectorate service on the lines of Her Majesty's Inspectors who visit schools. A hospital inspectorate was envisaged in the first draft of the scheme for the health service, but it was dropped by the time the 1946 Bill was introduced. The scheme urgently needs to be revived — however unpopular it may be with the medical profession.

A number of large-scale official enquiries has since been made into individual hospitals. Of particular significance is the 1969 report on Ely Hospital, Cardiff, by a committee chaired by Sir Geoffrey Howe, which prompted the then Secretary of State, Richard Crossman, to establish the Hospital Advisory Service. The report talked about the several conflicting responsibilities of a hospital management committee:[5]

> As the representative of the consumer it must see that complaints are brought forward and investigated. As an employer it must see that its staff are protected from unjustified attack. As manager and purveyor of service it must make appropriate management decisions in the light of a complaint — and at the same time defend itself against unjust attack. And it must discharge and appear to discharge, all these functions with a proper sense of justice.

In general the various 'scandal' reports showed that hospital authorities faced with allegations of mistreatment were too inclined to defend the reputation and morale of their staff and insufficiently inclined to investigate allogations thoroughly. The difficulties of reconciling the managerial responsibilities of members with their role as representatives of the public was to have an important consequence for the 1974 NHS reorganisation.

Parliament, the NHS and the public

It was in parliament that the NHS was formally created in 1946 and reorganised in 1974 and in the House of Commons the elected representatives of the public have always discussed matters concerning the service; not only national issues but also issues of strictly local interest. Parliamentary questions are probably the best-known method of publicly bringing attention to bear on particular issues. There can be as many as 3,000 questions relating to the health service in a session; some receive oral answers, but most only written answers in Hansard. In addition MPs frequently write to ministers on matters raised by their constituents, and many members of the public write to ministers direct. The then Minister of State told the members of the Three Chairmen's committee that he answered personally up to about 1,600 enquiries a month from MPs and members of the public. Drafting answers to parliamentary questions and letters to ministers is an important task of the health departments, and on most topics they have to rely on health authorities to provide the information.

MPs can use adjournment debates on urgent matters of public interest as a way of drawing attention to a particular grievance and these are sometimes well reported in the press and other media, particularly in the constituency concerned. Ministers make statements in the House to announce important decisions. Thus in 1969 Richard Crossman made a statement in the House about the Ely Hospital report and his decision to establish a Hospital Advisory Service, and in 1980 Mr Patrick Jenkin announced his decisions on the restructuring of the service in the same way.

Some of the most influential work in parliament is done in the various standing or select committees which form an integral part of the legislative machinery. The two main committees, already mentioned in Chapter 9, are the Public Accounts Committee and the Select Committee on Social Services. The former, concerned more with financial rectitude and economy than with representing the views of the public, has over the years issued critical reports on various matters with a general application to health service management beyond the particular matter under examination. The Select Committee on Social Services, one of a series of committees concerned with the various government departments, was established in 1980, having been preceded first by a sub-committee of the estimates committee and then by a sub-committee of the expenditure committee. It has a small staff and is able to appoint specialist advisers. Both the PAC and the Select Committee examine ministers and senior civil servants, and their reports include verbatim reports of the examinations.

One of the reports produced by the Select Committee in its first year, on the government's white papers on public expenditure on the social services, contained a comment relevant to this chapter:[6]

> We share the Department's anxiety to devolve managerial responsibility and to avoid collecting unnecessary information. But the NHS — unlike education or the personal social services — is a central government responsibility. We would greatly deplore any change which would limit the ability of individual MPs to ask questions or of Parliament collectively to inquire into the operations of the NHS.

The committee was pressing for a comprehensive information system which would permit the committee and the public to assess the effects of changes in expenditure levels or patterns on the quality and scope of services. In a press statement about the report the Secretary of State for Social Services expressed a contrary view which has considerable implications for parliamentary oversight of the NHS:

> Perhaps the most disturbing aspect of this Report is its assumption that everything should be managed at Whitehall level and that Ministry should preside over every detailed decision. I reject that view. It is the Government's firm policy that detailed planning and management of resources are best left to those on the spot who know local needs and priorities.

The Health Service Commissioner

The office of Parliamentary Commissioner for Administration, or 'Ombudsman', was established in 1967 to make independent investigations of complaints against government authorities. His responsibilities did not extend to the NHS but those forces which had led to the establishment of the office — the consumer movement, a certain distrust of official authorities and so on — were also at work among people concerned with the NHS and in response to them the government decided that provision for an ombudsman should be made in the reorganised service. Accordingly the 1973 and 1972 Acts made provision for the three separate offices of Health Service Commissioner for England, for Wales and for Scotland. (There is no such provision in Northern Ireland.) The three offices have so far always been held by the same man, who has also held the office of Parliamentary Commissioner. Until the appointment of C. Clothier in 1979 the commissioner had always been a senior civil servant and in fact the first Health Service Commissioner had earlier been permanent secretary at the DHSS. The commissioner is not accountable to any minister or government department, and he reports to parliament.

The commissioner may investigate allegations of a failure to provide a service by a body whose function it is to provide that service, allegations of failure in a service which has been provided, and allegations of maladministration in any other action taken by or on behalf of a body subject to his investigations. While he can examine the way in which a decision has been reached, he may not examine the merits of the decision itself if it were properly taken. Such a limitation is normal in all countries with ombudsmen; investigations are not intended to be used as a means of replacing the properly-reached decisions of ministers, departments and other lawfully constituted authorities.

There are a number of limitations to this apparently wide remit, and in 1979, a typical year, the commissioner had to reject three-quarters of the complaints made to him as falling outside his jurisdiction. He may not examine actions taken solely in the exercise of clinical judgement, though he does examine matters surrounding clinical judgement, e.g. whether there has been a proper review of waiting lists. He may not examine complaints that have not been made to the health authority involved; his role is only to deal with grievances that an authority has not been able to resolve satisfactorily. He may not examine actions of GPs, dentists, etc. in contract with FPCs (or with health boards in Scotland) or complaints that have already been the subject of consideration by a Service

Committee or Tribunal. The administrative actions of FPCs, such as the handling of complaints, are however subject to investigation. Commercial, contractual and personnel matters are excluded, and there is a time bar. The commissioner is not expected to examine matters where the complainant has or could have a legal remedy though in this, and in several other exclusions, the commissioner has discretion. Complaints must come from an individual or body personally aggrieved by the action complained of and able to claim that he has suffered some injustice or hardship. Complaints by an individual or body on behalf of the aggrieved person are examined, so that, for example, a CHC might complain on someone's behalf, but the complaint of a CHC itself, or of any other publicly funded body, about the conduct of a health authority could not be investigated. Nor may the commissioner initiate an investigation himself in the absence of a complaint from an aggrieved person.

When a complaint is accepted as falling within the jurisdiction a detailed investigation is carried out. On the health side of his office the commissioner has a staff of about 30, drawn partly from the civil service and partly from the health service, under a deputy commissioner. There are wide powers to obtain documents and subpoena witnesses. Ultimately a report is produced and copies are sent to the complainant, the health authority concerned, the authority on the next tier of the organisation and to any member of staff named in the complaint. Investigation is an expensive and laborious procedure and since in the end a considerable proportion of the complaints are rejected, or are upheld only in minor aspects, it may seem in retrospect an unduly expensive procedure. There is, however, no way of assessing whether a complaint merits detailed examination without carrying out the investigation.

The remedies available are limited. Where there is a failure in administrative procedures or in the provision of services, authorities may be asked to look into their arrangements, but so far as an aggrieved individual is concerned normally the only direct remedy is an apology by the authority found to be at fault.

The commissioner issues an annual report which analyses the complaints received and those examined, the regions from which complaints come, the subjects complained of and which complaints were upheld. The report also discusses the general nature of complaints received and gives an account of some which are particularly interesting. Concerning the publication of full reports of individual investigations practice has varied, but either all or selected cases are published at intervals.

The type of complaint most commonly upheld concerns not the subject of original complaints but health authorities' handling of them. This is not surprising in that only complaints in which an authority has not satisfied the complainant can be examined by the commissioner. Nevertheless there are a disturbing number of cases in which an authority delays answering letters, or sends replies which do not adequately answer the complaints. Apart from this the most common complaints are allegations of lack of or incomplete information, failures in nursing care — particularly in connection with elderly patients, and failures in or lack of services. While most complaints are about shortcomings in the care and treatment of individual patients, with the same types of shortcoming alleged in many cases, there are a number concerned with a surprising variety of more administrative matters.

The House of Commons has a Select Committee on the Parliamentary Commissioner for Administration, to which the commissioner reports. In 1978 the Select Committee recommended that complaints arising from the exercise of clinical judgement should be within the jurisdiction of the Health Service Commissioner, and this recommendation was supported by the Royal Commission. Generally the medical profession is opposed to such a change, and no decision has yet been made. Doctors argue that matters concerning clinical treatment should be pursued through the courts, and that they should not also be subject to investigation by the commissioner. The counter argument is that a complaints procedure that excludes matters that patients are most likely to want to complain about is inadequate and that most patients with a complaint about treatment are not looking for damages, which they might obtain through the courts, but only for a full explanation of what happened and an assurance that it will not happen to other people. Most advocates of extending the commissioner's powers would accept that an investigation by him into clinical matters should not be used as a preliminary to a court action.

The Health Service Commissioner's role has been described here because it forms part of the parliamentary and public oversight of the NHS. It is, however, a sort of court of appeal from the main method of dealing with complaints in the service, which is described in Chapter 7.

Community Health Councils

Although the findings of the Health Service Commissioner may occasionally have a general application, his investigations are essentially concerned with grievances of individual members of the public. To give the public in general a voice on the organisation and delivery of health care below the parliamentary level the 1974 reorganisation introduced other arrangements: the community health councils and local health councils. The rationale was explained by Rudolf Klein and Janet Lewis in a study published in 1976.

> The political problem, therefore, was how best to square the circle of elitism and populism: how to reconcile the emphasis on centralised planning with the currently fashionable rhetoric of local participation. The answer was to invent the Community Health Councils: to add, as it were, a Gothic Folly to the Palladian Mansion — but to do so in a way which would not destroy the basic symmetry (as much intellectual as architectural) of the main building. 'The idea suggested itself', in the words of one of the Ministers involved, 'as soon as we had decided to go for unrepresentative AHAs'.

Although the councils were in this sense incidental to the main purpose of reorganisation they received a disproportionate amount of attention in the debates on the 1973 Bill and as a result of debates in the House of Lords it was provided that in England CHCs should be appointed by RHAs rather than by AHAs as originally envisaged.

Section 9 of the 1973 Act required the Secretary of State to set up community health councils in England and Wales to represent the interests of the public in the health service. The necessary regulations were issued, and in circular HRC(74)4 the DHSS gave guidance on the role of councils and on how RHAs should establish them. The purpose of councils was described as follows:

> Community Health Councils will provide a new means of representing the local community's interests in the health services to those responsible for managing

them. In the reorganised National Health Service management of the Service and representation of local opinion will be distinct but complementary functions, entrusted to separate bodies but working in close relationship. Successful administration of the Service will depend on a continuing and constructive exchange of ideas between Area Health Authorities and the Community Health Councils; the AHA will then be aware of local opinion on needs and deficiencies in the Service and the community, through the CHC, will know of the actions and intentions of the AHA and of the problems and constraints with which it is faced. To be effective, this relationship will call for positive effort and goodwill on both sides. The Secretary of State believes that this system will be seen to be mutually beneficial to those who operate and plan services and to those who use them. Membership of the Councils will give a worthwhile and satisfying role to many of the public-spirited people who take a particular interest in the quality of their local Health Service.

This introduction is very similar to the relevant passage in the 1971 consultative document. In contrast to the previous system, the role of representing local opinion was disentangled or distanced from direct managerial responsibilities.

RHAs were made responsible for the establishment of CHCs in their regions, and for the initial determination of the number of councils in the region. It was taken as a general rule that there would be a CHC for every district, and only very exceptionally was more than one council appointed in one district. When, subsequently, a number of multi-district areas were converted to single-district areas the usual practice was to retain the previous CHCs.

The regulations placed no upper or lower limit on the membership of CHCs, but it was expected, and proved to be the case, that the great majority of councils would have between 20 and 30 members. Appointments in the first place were for either two or four years, and there is a limit of two terms. Once regions had determined the total number of members to be appointed to each of its councils, the local authorities were approached to appoint at least 50 per cent of the total membership; where there was an odd number of members, local authority appointees would account for more, as opposed to less, than 50 per cent. Local authorities appoint directly to councils, and merely notify regions of the names of their appointees. They normally appoint councillors, but it is open to them to appoint non-councillors.

Any voluntary organisation active in a CHC district, and having a particular interest wholly or mainly in health matters, or which provided a service for NHS patients, or which had a special interest in a particular institution or institutions in a district could apply for a place on the CHC. As the number of voluntary organisations far exceeded the number of places available the selection procedure usually adopted was to invite all the applicants to confer together in order to decide amongst themselves how, in the initial period, their share of places on CHCs should be allocated. This exercise highlighted how many voluntary organisations saw themselves as fulfilling the criteria. In the Yorkshire region, over 1,000 responses were received for a total of about 140 places available.

The remaining places, as near as possible one sixth of total membership, were to be filled by the RHA, again after consultation with appropriate local authorities and other organisations. This gave scope for appointing representatives or bodies, such as women's organisations, trades unions, the churches, and youth and immigrant bodies that might not always obtain a place through the other appointing methods. In the early days many of these places were filled by former hospital authority members.

Most councils in England and Wales were set up during the period May-July 1974. They found that their responsibilities for representing the views of the public were very undefined. The matters to which their attention was directed by HRC(74)4 covered amongst other things: the effectiveness of services being provided in the health district; the planning of services, including criticism and comment on AHAs' plans; changes in services, e.g. closure or provision of new services; an assessment of the extent to which district health facilities conformed to standards set by DHSS norms; particular regard to facilities for patients, e.g. hospital visiting, waiting times, hospital amenities, the quality of catering in institutions within the district; and monitoring the volume and type of complaints received about a particular service or institution. It was made clear that individual complaints were a matter for the health authority and its staff but CHCs were enjoined, without prejudicing the merits of individual complaints or seeking out the facts, to give advice on request on how and where to lodge a complaint and to act as 'patient's friend' when needed. They were also required to bring any potential general causes of local complaint to the notice of the AHA. Apart from the duty of councils to represent the interests of the public in the health service of each district, the only other specified duty was that they should prepare and publish annual reports on matters which had arisen concerning health services in their districts. AHAs were required to make a public response. Apart from these annual reports, CHCs could, if they wished, publish at any time reports or statements as they saw fit. (Over the years a number of councils have published reports on a variety of topics, such as the results of a public opinion survey or the study of the needs of a particular group of patients. Some have produced guides to local health facilities, either in their annual reports or as separate documents; others consider that that work should be undertaken by health authorities.) In their responses to the annual reports, AHAs were required to include a statement of the action taken on issues raised. Under the Reorganisation Act, the Public Bodies (Admission to Meetings) Act 1960 applied to CHCs so that the public, including the press, would normally be admitted to meetings of the council.

In Scotland the creation of local health councils took place about a year later than in England and Wales. The legislation and departmental guidance were much the same as for England and Wales but there were significant differences. NHS Circular 1974(GEN)38 dealt with the preparation of schemes and 1974(GEN)90 with the function of councils. Amongst the eligibility-for-membership criteria there were certain differences from those set out in England. Local authorities were to appoint one-third of the total number of members for each council. As in England, they could appoint councillors or non-councillors, but their attention was drawn to the fact that they needed to ensure that all the members of an LHC could claim to represent the 'consumer' in the area of the LHC. The appointment of members of voluntary and other organisations rested with the health boards — consulting with voluntary bodies to obtain a comparable number to those appointed by local authorities — and also the boards had to obtain nominations from trade unions. In councils of up to 20 members, two would be trade union nominees and, in councils of 21 members or more, three would be such nominees. This reflects the close relations that existed between the Scottish TUC and the SHHD, and was a feature of preferred membership that the English authorities only came to later on. The remaining members were appointed from former members of boards of management, executive councils and regional boards.

Both the English and the Scottish circulars had a hospital bias built into them, both the Departments having had most of their pre-reorganisation dealings with that element of the service. As is usually the case in administrative matters in Scotland, the fundings and staffings of LHCs were considerably smaller in scale than in England, and below those obtaining in Wales. Part-time staff appointments and small budgets were the rule. The early guidance and advice to LHCs pointed towards their task being seen as more of a public relations role than was the case in England and Wales.

In Northern Ireland there are 17 district committees, one for each health and social service district, representing local consumer interests on the same lines as CHCs and LHCs.

The democracy papers

Even as CHCs came into existence they were confronted by the English and Welsh consultative papers on democracy in the NHS issued by the new government, which rejected the distinction between management and representation on which reorganisation had been based:

> The Government do not accept that it is possible or desirable to make such a clear-cut distinction between management of public services and representation of consumer interests and views. Our whole national democratic process as it has evolved over the years is a complex interweave of management and representation. While there are at times considerable advantages in the close definition of responsibility and even the separation of functions, to embark on total separation is to challenge in a fundamental way the essence of democratic control.

This radically different approach did not lead to such radical proposals for change as it might seem to entail; it did not for example produce any suggestion that health authorities could adequately perform both the management and representational functions, and that CHCs would be unnecessary. On the contrary, the government liked the CHC concept. 'The task now is to develop the CHCs into a powerful forum where consumer views can influence the NHS and where local participation in the running of the NHS can become a reality.'

The other proposals of the democracy papers have been described in earlier chapters, and only those involving CHCs are mentioned here. It was proposed that CHCs should nominate some of their members to be members of the AHA responsible for their district and that legislation should be introduced to allow concurrent membership of AHA and CHC. The proposal was dropped after it was found that the balance of opinion in CHCs was strongly against this attempt to fuse representation and management. The paper, although partly a consultative document, announced a number of decisions already taken to strengthen the role of CHCs. One or more spokesmen of the DMT should attend CHC meetings when invited, and answer questions in open session. CHCs should be among the bodies consulted by RHAs in making appointments to AHAs and in future appointing bodies should not feel inhibited from inviting NHS employees or family practitioners to serve as members of CHCs. In future, when a CHC accepted the proposal of a health authority to close a hospital, the specific authorisation of the Secretary of State would not be required. If a CHC wished to object to closure then it would be expected to make a detailed and consultative counter-proposal, with full regard for the factors, including restraints on resources, which had led the authority to propose closure.

The paper also said that the government considered that there should be a national council, with a budget drawn from central government funds, to advise and assist CHCs, and in fact there was provision for such a body in the 1973 Act. However, the steering committee charged with exploring the proposal found considerable distrust among councils of the type of national council envisaged by the government and in some even a feeling that a national organisation was not necessary for what were essentially local bodies. The Association of Community Health Councils for England and Wales (ACHCEW), which emerged from the consultations, proved more akin to the various associations of health authorities which have existed from early days of the NHS than to the sort of council envisaged in the democracy paper. It has been careful to avoid trespassing on the rights or duties of councils or trying to curtail the activities of individual CHCs. Most but not quite all CHCs have joined it. For the most part its income is drawn from members' subscriptions, i.e. public money, but not directly from central government funds. However, the DHSS does make a grant for two activities which are also available to non-members: the provision of informations services and the publication of a news bulletin, *CHC News*. Welsh councils have their own group within the association. There is a separate Association of Scottish Local Health Councils.

CHCs at work

In a study of the early days of councils in the north of England, *CHCs in Action,* Jack Hallas wrote that the differences between councils 'are often sharp enough to make the observer despair of finding any common denominators'. With the passage of time, and an increasing knowledge of each others' activities, the differences may have decreased a little, but CHCs are still more varied than any other health service bodies, and generalisations about them are difficult. One council sees itself as leading a campaign of the community and health service staff against cuts, while another earns local unpopularity by exercising its own judgement on proposals for hospital closures rather than automatically supporting local protest. To some extent the differences reflect differences in communities; it is not surprising that in some deprived inner city areas some councils inclined to the protest politics of the seventies and that in some rural areas they shared the general anger at reduced facilities and ever increasing isolation. However, this does not explain all the differences, for even neighbouring councils have shown quite different approaches to their work. The explanation probably lies in the different reaction of members and secretaries to the somewhat vague guidance on their role, and the lack of example.

Soon after councils were appointed Rudolf Klein and Janet Lewis sent them questionnaires which produced some interesting information about members. They found that members recruited to CHCs in the early days did not, on taking up the task, look at their functions in an aggressively critical way, though they found that younger members were more critical in their general assessment of local services and also more likely to perceive urgent problems in specific areas of provision. They found that CHC members overwhelmingly considered the services to be either good or adequate and this suggested to them that if CHCs became more critical of the NHS as a collectivity, it would come about because of what they learnt about the service from the inside rather than because of prejudices or biases they brought to their task in the first place.

The book raised questions about the quality and quantity of representatives in relation to social classes. Could predominantly middle-class councils hope to represent adequately the consumer views of social classes 4 and 5, who are the people standing most in need of the NHS? CHC members are indeed not a typical cross section either of the general public or of NHS users; in age, sex, social class and so on they are very similar to health authority members. However, neither parliament nor elected councils is representative in the cross-sectional sense and it is not to be expected that they should be, and it would be a mistake to criticise CHCs on these grounds. It does remain valid to ask whether CHC members fully understand and appreciate the needs and attitudes of social classes 4 and 5 (and a similar question might be asked of doctors and other NHS staff).

In their early days many councils publicly expressed their doubts about their ability to represent the users of the NHS, and their first task was to seek out their publics. A frequent theme in annual reports has been the need for more publicity, and despite limited budgets and generally a cautious approach to spending public money various methods have been used, including the distribution of leaflets and posters, the use of local radio and the local press and talks to local organisations. Full council meetings are seldom attended by members of the public, and not always by the press, although a few councils have succeeded in involving members of the public in these meetings. There has been more success in attracting the public to meetings on specific topics of general interest. Resistance to the closure or change of use of a hospital where local feelings were strong has sometimes been an effective way of making a council known. Although there are still complaints, both from councils and from outside, that CHCs are not sufficiently known, they have certainly established much closer relations with their publics than they had in 1974.

The second main task of councils was to establish relations with the health authorities. Jack Hallas reported that, as might have been expected, in the first two years they tended to keep their distance from AHAs; the initial annual meetings between AHAs and CHCs were more often than not fumbling sessions between two newly-appointed bodies with ill-defined responsibilities. In these early days the CHCs built up a somewhat easier relationship with the NHS at regional level. Since then relations with NHS bodies have been mixed; this is in fact one of the most striking ways in which councils differ. Some report cordial relations with AHA, DMT and so on, while others in their annual reports are outspokenly critical of these bodies. Some councils have had the satisfaction of seeing their suggestions welcomed by authorities, while others have felt they have had no influence at a time when the authorities were making wrong decisions.

Circular HSC(IS)194, which announced the decisions on the democracy paper, said that in future councils should be entitled to send one of their members to attend meetings of the AHA. This representative would have the right to speak but not to vote, and should not normally be excluded from the private part of the meeting. Councils have welcomed this arrangement, but have not been altogether successful in achieving extensions of it. FPCs have been urged but not required by the DHSS to allow CHC representatives to attend their meetings, but only some have done so. Most health authorities have welcomed CHC participation in health care planning teams, but others have considered it inappropriate. This is an example of the dilemma of the council's role. It is undoubtedly difficult in a short time, and without having been involved in the discussions, to produce informed criticism of an authority's plans; also criticism might be more acceptable and effective if made during rather than after the formulation of plans. On the other hand, involvement in the planning process may inhibit them in their role as critics. In this connection it is interesting to note an article that appeared in *CHC News* in 1976 in which the author pointed out how easy it was for councils to fall into managerial attitudes[7]. She set out how easily council members could be 'taken in' by the system, and urged them to remember that their job was not to understand and explain the service but to maintain a sense of independence, coupled with a realisation of the difficulties, but essentially remaining patient-centred. This is not an easy recipe, for councils need to be effective and they are not likely to persuade authorities or DMTs if their attitude is one of constant opposition.

Apart from producing an annual report there are few positive duties laid on councils, and accordingly they have varied in how they organise their work and what they take an interest in. While all important issues are discussed at full council meetings, many councils have centred their activities on the work of special interest groups, working parties, functional groups, etc. The services most frequently examined by working groups mirror the 'deprived groups' identified by health care planning teams: elderly, mentally ill, mentally handicapped, mothers and children. Most councils have about four or five members allotted to groups, so that nearly all members are involved. The acute services are usually grouped together and some councils have groups in the field of preventive medicine and health education. Most councils also exercise their right to visit hospitals and other health establishments. These activities make considerable demands on members' time and it was found from the early days that many local authority members attended infrequently because local authority activities had a prior claim on their time. The attendance record of this category of member has remained poor, though there are many exceptions.

Some of the matters on which councils have spent much of their time have been national issues, either the application in the local context of national recommendations, e.g. whether to support fluoridation of the water supply, or on national policy, such as possible changes in the abortion law, or the recommendations of 'Patients First'. Local councils as well as the national council are among the bodies consulted by the DHSS on policy matters.

For the most part councils are concerned with matters of local interest, and what they are depends on local problems and what the DMT or AHA consults them about. Some of these local issues are common to much of the country; for example, annual reports frequently mention the shortage of chiropody services for the elderly. Authorities are required to consult CHCs about their strategic and operational plans and also about their proposals for the closure or change of use of hospitals or other premises. Because closures are often contentious, and because of the particular responsibility given to councils in this matter by the democracy paper, they have been a prominent aspect of CHC activities. Closures and change of use have been more frequent in recent years as a consequence of the building programme, a more active approach to health service planning and, sometimes, financial stringency. Closure proposals frequently led to a local 'save our hospital' campaign long before CHCs were thought of, and the advent of councils has not displaced these *ad hoc* protest movements. More often than not CHCs have approved proposals for closure or change of use, but they have also led campaigns against proposals and have sometimes been successful. Councils have sometimes complained that it is unreasonable to require them to produce counter proposals since their resources are limited and they depend for information on the authority whose proposals they are challenging. The case for the requirement is that if money were no object practically any hospital or service would be worth retaining but since money will always be limited arguments for retention are not enough; a proposal must be considered in the light of the resources available and alternative ways of using them.

Most activities of councils are generated by the activities of the health authority, members' own interests and knowledge of local services, consultation by the central departments and approaches from both national and local pressure groups. They are also approached by patients and other members of the public, sometimes for information and sometimes with complaints. It is for health authorities to investigate complaints, but CHCs can give information, and act as the 'patient's friend'. The Royal Commission suggested that their role in complaints procedures should be a more active one, though not at the expense of other aspects of their work, and that there should be experiments with 'patient advocates' who would be paid employees of councils. It may be questioned whether the level of patient dissatisfaction or the present involvement of CHCs in complaints is enough to justify such a development.

It is understandable that, despite their initial doubts, and their continual worries about their effectiveness, CHCs should generally feel that their existence has been justified. It has even been claimed that they are the one success of the 1974 reorganisation. The Royal Commission was more cautious. 'It is almost impossible to determine from the available evidence whether or not CHCs are fulfilling their functions of representing consumers and channelling local opinions to health authorities, and five years is not long enough for any new institution to realise its full potential'. Nevertheless it considered that CHCs had been an experiment that should be supported and it made specific recommendations which are noted in Chapter 17. One of these — that councils needed additional resources — might be thought to undermine their present character. Councils have limited funds and their only staff are normally a secretary and an assistant. This undoubtedly puts a limit to what they can do but it could be argued that it also means that to be effective councils must depend on the active involvement of their members, and that to increase their resources would encourage dependence on paid officers and thus the creation of a counter-bureaucracy in place of the direct involvement of the representatives of the public.

As is explained in the next chapter, the report of the Royal Commission was followed by the government's proposals for restructuring the service. After their endorsement by the Royal Commission, it came as a shock to councils to find the government putting their future in question, and they energetically set about making the case for their retention. They were not alone in making their case, and the balance of opinion amongst all the interests consulted was heavily in favour of their retention. There was a minority strongly in favour of abolishing them and while the existence of this point of view is not necessarily a criticism of CHCs it might suggest that they have not always set about their tasks in the most effective way.

Conclusion

As the history outlined in this chapter shows, there are various possible ways of providing the public with an effective say in the management of the NHS, and none of them is without difficulties. There is another method of ensuring that the public gets the health care provision that it wants, though a method ruled out by the very principles of the NHS. If care is provided under a market economy the public will get what it wants enough to pay for, and facilities will not be provided simply because it is thought that they are what the public needs. The practical application of such a principle would be at least as difficult as any other, and there does not appear to be any example of a health service entirely based on the market.

Within the NHS context there are other approaches supplementary to those discussed in this chapter. Public opinion surveys may give a more accurate picture of what the public wants than pressure from interested groups. Surveys of this sort were carried out for the Royal Commission, and on a small scale they have been used in hospitals to assess patients' opinion on facilities. A number of CHCs have also conducted surveys. The technique is, however, no substitute for public representation because the initiative lies with whoever organises the surveys; it cannot originate a demand or grievance and it does not reflect the political pressures to which the service is subject. Another approach, in which the initiative is entirely with management, is the use of public relations techniques, and the importance of this has been increasingly realised in the service. While it is open to the objection that it is an attempt to manipulate rather than respond to public opinion, public relations is now a normal part of management. The health departments and health authorities have a duty to explain their policies and decisions, and the need is all the greater because on the whole CHCs have not seen it as part of their role.

In the UK the normally accepted way of providing for the public voice in public bodies is by election to the governing body. It is the most easily recognised way of achieving legitimacy although, as both central and local government show, it does not always produce public satisfaction and does not preclude the need for ombudsmen or for supplementary ways of ascertaining public opinion, particularly as these bodies become larger and more complex and the actual management falls on professionals rather than elected representatives. From this point of view, the public would be best served by putting the health services under local government. Such an arrangement has always been rejected on other grounds. Members of local authorities sometimes claim that, as democratically elected representatives of the community, they are also the legitimate spokesmen on matters of health care. That is a much more questionable point of view.

An alternative to local government control would be elected bodies responsible for health care. Although no longer an accepted approach in the UK, it has nineteenth century precedents in the poor law and education. There appear to be two reasons for rejecting this approach. First, the turn-out for local government elections is low, and would probably be even lower for separate health authorities; the result would hardly represent the public and the effective electorate might be little more than the staff organisations and pressure groups particularly interested in the service. Second, the nineteenth century *ad hoc* elected bodies had powers to levy rates, but the NHS is centrally financed and health authorities are the minister's agents. Independently elected local bodies seem incompatible with central finance and responsibility.

Appointed public bodies are no less traditional than elected, and the Labour government's 1974 democracy paper was right in saying that traditionally the management and representational functions of appointed members have not been kept separate. The clear distinction drawn in the 1974 reorganisation was based on difficulties when the roles were not distinct but, as we have seen, there have been different opinions on whether the distinction can, or should, be maintained. A study in Humberside shortly after reorganisation found that both AHA and CHC members described their main jobs as safeguarding patients and guiding developments, and the majority of CHC members questioned 'thought the CHCs should have executive responsibilities for district services and felt that the consumer was not adequately represented in the new service'.[8] However, that was early in the history of the reorganised service, and members may have become clearer about their roles since then.

Ironically, the Conservative government's 1980 proposals for restructuring are, in principle if not application, in some ways nearer to the ideas of the Labour government's democracy paper than to the Conservative government's reorganisation which that paper criticised. Although CHCs are to be retained for the time being, the Secretary of State has adhered to his view that they may not be needed because members of district authorities will be less remote from local services and more closely in touch with the needs of the community.

References

[1] Crossman, R.H.S. *A Politician's View of Health Service Planning*. A Maurice Block Lecture. University of Glasgow Press 1972

[2] Parliamentary Debates (Hansard), House of Commons, 30 April 1946. HMSO.

[3] Cohen, G.L. *What's Wrong with Hospitals?* Penguin 1964

[4] Robb, B *et al. Sans Everything — A Case to Answer.* AEGIS. Nelson 1967

[5] *Report of the Committee of Inquiry into Allegations of Ill-Treatment of Patients and other Irregularities at the Ely Hospital, Cardiff* (Cmnd 3975). HMSO 1969

[6] *The Government's White Papers on Public Expenditure: The Social Services.* Third Report from the Social Services Committee Session 1979-80. HC 702. HMSO 1980

[7] Williamson, C. 'Managerial Attitudes'. *CHC News* December 1976

[8] *New Bottles, Old Wine?* Institute for Health Studies, University of Hull 1975

Further reading

Regulations and circulars

England and Wales

SI73/2217. The NHS (Community Health Councils) Regulations 1973 (as amended)

HRC(74)4, WHRC(74)3. Community health councils

WHSC(IS)32. Establishment and membership of community health councils in Wales

HSC(IS)194, WHC(IS)188. Democracy in the national health service

Scotland

SI74/2177. The NHS (Local Health Councils) (Scotland) Regulations 1974
NHS Circular 1974(GEN)38. Local health councils — preparation of schemes
NHS Circular 1974(GEN)90. Local health councils

Official reports

Health Service Commissioner. *Annual Report*. HMSO
First Report from the Select Committee on the Parliamentary Commissioner for Administration. *Independent Review of Hospital Complaints in the National Health Service*. HMSO 1977

Other publications

Hallas, J. *CHCs in Action*. Nuffield Provincial Hospitals Trust 1976
Klein, R. and Lewis, J. *The Politics of Consumer Representation: A study of Community Health Councils*. Centre for Studies in Social Policy 1976
Levitt, Ruth. *The People's Voice in the NHS*. King's Fund 1980

17
The Royal Commission and after

The report of the Royal Commission on the NHS, published in July 1979, was a substantial document of nearly 500 pages. With the aim of reaching a wider audience, the chapter of conclusions and recommendations was also published separately. The commission had commissioned a number of research studies and the resulting research papers were published before the report, and in time for the commission to get the reaction of others to them. In 1980 the King's Fund Centre began publishing a series of project papers based on the working papers of the commission.

The commission had been asked to consider, in the interests both of the patients and of those who work in the NHS, the best use and management of the financial and manpower resources of the service. It interpreted these loose terms of reference in the widest way rather than in a narrow financial and administrative context. The result was a broad survey of the NHS in the UK that was achieved, as the commission recognised, at the cost of dealing only cursorily, and sometimes perhaps even superficially, with important topics. Thus, for example, while it discussed dental services at length, on such different topics as child health, nursing and supplies it relied for the most part on recently published reports.

The commission made 117 specific recommendations, ranging in character from radical to minor changes, which have to be seen in the context in which the topics were discussed. On balance the recommendations would increase the cost of the NHS, 'but our judgement is that these additional resources will be justified by the benefits which will flow from them'.

The objectives of the NHS

The principles and objectives of the NHS are defined, very broadly, in the duties laid on the Secretary of State in the National Health Service Act 1977 and the equivalent legislation for Scotland and Northern Ireland. The commission proposed rather more specific objectives. It believed that the NHS should:

— encourage and assist individuals to remain healthy;
— provide equality of entitlement to health services;
— provide a broad range of services of a high standard;
— provide equality of access to these services;
— provide a service free at the time of use;
— satisfy the reasonable expectations of its users;
— remain a national service responsive to local needs.

It recognised that some of these objectives lacked precision and some were controversial. Some, it added, were unattainable, but that did not make them less important as objectives.

An assessment of the service

What people think about the NHS is important because unless it is broadly acceptable to the public, to patients and to staff its effective working will be hampered. Moreover, a service little affected by the type of consumer reaction found in a market economy needs opinion about specific services and shortcomings as a guide to where improvement is needed.

As we saw in Chapter 1, for most of its history the NHS has on the whole stood high in public opinion and if staff have been more critical they too have for the most part endorsed its aims and been proud of its achievement. However, the appointment of the Royal Commission was a response to a widespread opinion after 1974, found most strongly but not only in the medical profession, that the service was suffering from serious shortcomings, particularly an unnecessarily cumbersome administrative structure and a serious shortage of finance.

Much of the evidence submitted to the commission was in turn the expression of opinion, to a greater or lesser degree well informed, and the commission commented on this: 'A good deal of the evidence presented to us, and a good deal of our own work, might be termed anecdotal or subjective. We have not regarded it as less instructive or valuable on that account and, indeed, given the difficulties of quantitative work in this field and the infinite variety of human behaviour, it is hard to see that we could have done otherwise'. However, this type of evidence was supplemented by the research studies mentioned above.

The report summarised the evidence that had been received about the administrative structure and finance, and the remedies that had been proposed. It noted the result of the research study on patient opinion, which confirmed previous findings of general high level of satisfaction, although patients found defects in some services. Staff on the other hand were critical: 'if patients give too rosy a picture of the state of the NHS, health workers paint one that is too gloomy'. After looking at some of the statistics for mortality and NHS expenditure, which indicate marked geographical and socio-economic class differences, and a short and inconclusive look at international comparisons, the commission gave its own verdict on the service:

> In the course of our work we have seen things we have liked and admired, and things we have not liked at all. But our general view is that we need not feel ashamed of our health service and that there are many aspects of it of which we can be justly proud.
>
> As we have seen in this chapter, social and geographical inequalities in health and health care remain. The NHS by itself cannot overcome this problem, but it must remain a cause for concern, and an area in which the performance of the NHS can be improved. There are problems in measuring efficiency in health care, but apart from improvements which may be achieved through the use of more resources, we are convinced that the NHS can provide a better service by making better use of the resources now available to it.

Elsewhere the commission at the same time sum up their own work and their views on the NHS:

> We are all too conscious that our report will be disappointing to those who have been looking to us for some blinding revelation which would transform the NHS. Leaving to one side our own capacity for revelation of this kind, we must say as clearly as we can that the NHS is not suffering from a mortal disease susceptible only to heroic surgery. Already the NHS has achieved a great deal and embodies aspirations and ideals of great value. The advances to be

made and which undoubtedly will be made will be brought about by constant application and vigilance.

Services to patients

The section of the report on services to patients, which contained half the total recommendations, began with a chapter on good health which discussed prevention, self-care, health education, environmental health and occupational health and safety, and made various recommendations under these heads.

The discussion then turned to priorities. As the demand for health care was always likely to outstrip supply and the capacity of health services to absorb resources was almost unlimited, choices had to be made about the use of available funds and priorities had to be set. The absence of objective criteria for setting priorities meant that decisions were for the most part a matter of judgement, and it was important to recognise that national priorities emerged from a variety of conflicting views and pressures expressed in parliament, by the health professions and various patient or client pressure groups among others. The commission thought that so far as possible discussion which led to the establishment of priorities should be conducted in public and illuminated by fact. The health departments should make public more of the professional advice on which policies and priorities were based. It thought that the current national priorities — services for the elderly, the mentally ill and mentally handicapped and children, with the emphasis on community care — were broadly correct, though they were not the only choices. The problems of implementing priorities were noted. 'It remains to be seen how far the NHS planning system introduced after reorganisation will turn out to be an effective mechanism for this purpose.'

After surveying the general practitioner, nursing and related services in the community, the commission concluded:

> These services are generally provided to a good standard but improvements are needed in a number of directions. The development so far of the primary health care team has been encouraging, but there is a continuing need to encourage closer working relationships between the professions who provide care for the community. District nurses and health visitors have a particularly important part of play. There have been a number of promising developments which have enhanced the quality of general practice, but more should be done to improve our training and continuing education of GPs. Improvement of the standard of existing premises is required and so are more health centres. Better training is needed for receptionists, and deputising services should be brought under closer control. More research should be undertaken into a number of aspects of community services.

To control prescribing costs, the commission suggested, the health departments should introduce a limited list of drugs and take further steps to encourage generic prescribing. The major challenge to community services was the provision of services in inner London and other declining urban areas, and a much more flexible and innovative approach was needed.

The report briefly surveyed the pharmaceutical, ophthalmic and chiropody services, and then discussed dentistry in considerable detail.

A chapter on hospital services discussed many of the main issues of the last ten years or more, yet made very few specific recommendations. It noted that most patients were satisfied with the overall service provided in hospital, though there were frequent criticisms about the inadequacy of information on treatment, and about early waking. Little was said by patients about waiting lists and the commission thought the significance of these had been exaggerated. It endorsed the district general hospital approach to providing specialist services and thought the nucleus hospital idea sensible. On the other hand there was still dispute over the best use of small hospitals not forming part of the DGH and the community hospital approach had been much criticised; the commission was relieved that the DHSS was rethinking its policy. Since 1962 policy in England and Wales had been gradually to close the mental illness hospitals. The commission thought that such a policy was no longer practical or desirable and that the Department's recent statements on revising the policy had been ambiguous. The uncertainty was bad for staff morale and it should be made clear that these hospitals would be required throughout the remainder of the century and for as long ahead as it was possible to plan. Much evidence had been received about the age and inadequacy of many hospital buildings and the commission recommended that:

> the government should find extra funds to permit much more rapid replacement of hospitals buildings than has so far been possible; and, more important, they should stick to their plans. The constant delays and shifts of policy so that a hospital promised is long delayed and then has to be modified or scrapped or cannot be opened because of lack of resources, inevitably leads to staff and public becoming bitter.

A planned programme of replacement and upgrading was needed over the next 15 years.

A chapter on the NHS and the public discussed three topics, the first being community health councils. They had made an important contribution towards ensuring that local public opinion was represented to health service management but they needed additional resources, and also further guidance from the health departments on their role. They should have right of access to FPC meetings and to their equivalent in Scotland and Northern Ireland. On suggestions and complaints procedures the commission generally endorsed a 1978 DHSS consultative paper on arrangements in the family practitioner services and the views of the Davies Committee and the Select Committee on the Parliamentary Commissioner for Administration on hospitals. It supported the view that the Health Service Commissioner should be allowed to accept cases involving clinical matters, and suggested that the CHC's role in complaints procedures could be more active. Finally, it discussed the contribution made by the public, voluntary bodies and volunteers. This was of major benefit to the service, and should be encouraged.

The NHS and its workers

The first part of the section on staff discussed a number of important general topics. The commission did not believe the people who told it that the NHS was about to collapse because of low staff morale but acknowledged that low morale was prevalent, even if its distribution was 'curiously patchy' both geographically and among different groups of workers. Low morale, it thought, was a symptom of other difficulties and would respond to action on them; it did not in itself require specific recommendations.

In view of the history of the preceding years it is not surprising that the commission was 'in no doubt that industrial relations in the NHS are in need of improvement' It accepted the analysis of industrial relations at local level prepared for it by the Advisory Conciliation and Arbitration Service and welcomed the proposals for dealing with local disputes which had been put to the General Whitley Council. Since industrial disputes at the national level turn on Whitley agreements, the report then discussed the Whitley machinery, though only briefly because the McCarthy report had examined it in detail. The commission found that procedures were sometimes cumbersome and hoped that Lord McCarthy's review would lead to improvements. It thought it essential that a procedure should be worked out for resolving national disputes about pay, and looked to the TUC to take the lead. Although aware of the difficulties of achieving an agreement to rule out strikes in the NHS, the commission did not dismiss the possibility.

Under the heading of 'Roles and Relationships' a number of important topics were discussed: flexibility, aides and unqualified staff, inter-professional relationships, and measuring and controlling quality. The main specific recommendation was that a planned programme for the introduction of audit or peer review of standards of care and treatment should be set up for the health professions by their professional bodies and progress monitored by the health departments. A discussion of manpower planning concluded that the needs and resources of different parts of the UK varied so greatly that centralised planning for all NHS staff would be wholly impracticable. Recruitment decisions should, for the most part, be made locally in the light of local needs within an overall policy. An exception to this was medical and dental manpower, because of the long time needed to expand training facilities, and the extent of the involvement of the universities. Finally, on general staff matters the commission recommended that the NHS should assume the same responsibility as any other employer for the health and safety of its staff and set up an occupational health service.

Turning to specific groups of staff, the report looked first at nurses, midwives and health visitors. While a number of recommendations were made on particular aspects, the main thrust was to press for the early implementation of the recommendations of the Briggs Committee. The chapter on doctors had more contentious matters to discuss. As the commission said, the question of how many doctors should be trained is an extremely complex matter. It concluded that it would be a mistake to cut back the planned output of medical graduates from UK universities at a time when there were shortages in some specialties and many places and more doctors were likely to be needed in future. It thought that the combined pressures of controls exercised by the central manpower machinery and the redistributive effects of RAWP and equivalents would lead to a greater geographical equality of medical manpower, and that the health departments should show more determination in enforcing their priorities in the shortage specialties, if necessary by blocking expansion of other specialties. It gave special attention to certain groups of doctors with special problems: doctors qualified overseas, women doctors and community physicians. The specialty of community medicine would have to be supported in the next few years if it was to survive. The commission did not like the new consultants' contract then under discussion and its criticisms would apply equally to the contract as it was agreed in 1980

The contract, the commission thought, would be most likely to benefit the surgical specialties and be injurious to the shortage specialties; like the junior doctors' contract already agreed, it was a step away from the traditional, flexible way that doctors and dentists had been employed in hospitals and undermined the traditional role of a doctor in assuming total care of his patients. Nor did the commission like the prospect of a GP contract extending items of service payments. It considered a good deal of evidence for and against the independent contractor status of family practitioners and, while not finding the arguments in favour of the system altogether compelling, it was not persuaded that there would be substantial benefits to outweigh the considerable difficulties of introducing a salaried service; and 'if the general practitioner service were to provide the same kind of cover as it does at present, then it seems to us likely that GPs would continue to be very much their own masters'. The farthest the commission would go was to recommend that the option of a salary should be open to any GP who preferred it; the option might help the staffing of health centres in deprived inner city areas. 'One of the few subjects on which our evidence seemed to be unanimous was the need for improvement in the hospital career structure for doctors. Unfortunately there was no such unanimity on methods of putting right what was wrong.' The commission did not make a recommendation but set out a possible alternative career structure as a contribution to the debate. The commission endorsed the principle of distinction awards.

A single chapter discussed other staff: ambulance, ancillary, professional, scientific and technical, works and maintenance. Two of the recommendations may be noted. There should be an independent review of the machinery set up by the Professions Supplementary to Medicine Act 1960 and in one or two instances the accident and emergency ambulance service should be organised experimentally on a regional basis with 'community transport services' being provided by the lower tier NHS authorities, the results being closely monitored.

The NHS and other institutions

Some criticisms had been received of the relationships between the NHS and local authorities, and it was clear from the evidence that relationships ranged from indifferent to excellent. While eventually the integration of these services might be possible, the commission argued, there was little in the present administrative arrangements to prevent or even hamper collaboration, though its success depended on the attitudes of the parties to it. If there was determination on both sides to work together, many of the problems could be solved. If, however, authorities or professions were at loggerheads, coterminous boundaries, overlapping membership and joint committees would be ineffective. The commission was not persuaded by arguments that local authorities should take over control of the NHS, or that the NHS should absorb the social work services, though joint administration of health and local authority services might become feasible if regional government were introduced in England.

Reviewing relationships between the NHS and the universities and research, the commission noted that arrangements for consultation with the universities had been disturbed by NHS reorganisation and it was likely that the teaching hospitals would have found themselves under financial pressure even if there had been no reorganisation. While the teaching hospitals were having a difficult time, in the long run they would gain through their closer integration into the NHS.

This chapter recommended that an independent enquiry should be set up to consider the special health service problems of London. Some of the problems it should consider arose from the large number of teaching hospitals in London: the pending University of London report on the future of the medical and dental schools, the future administration of the postgraduate teaching hospitals and whether the RAWP formula required some special adjustment. There were also other matters, such as whether London needed four RHAs, and measures to deal with the special difficulties of providing primary care services and joint planning in London. Another recommendation was that an Institute of Health Services Research should be established for England and Wales to encourage systematic research into health care issues, and its activities and output should be carefully evaluated.

The commission's views on the relationships between the NHS and private practice were discussed in Chapter 14.

Management

When it came to discuss management and finance, the commission looked first at parliament, health ministers and their departments, whose roles, and relationships with the NHS, stemmed from the way the service is financed. 'In principle health ministers and their departments are expected to have detailed knowledge of and influence over the NHS. In practice, however, this is neither possible nor desirable and detailed ministerial accountability for the NHS is largely a constitutional fiction.' It was clear that there was a gap between the formal, detailed accountability that a minister and his chief official carried for all that went on in the NHS and every penny spent on it, and the realities of the situation. It was not surprising that difficulties occurred.

So far as parliamentary control is concerned, the commission limited itself to recommending the establishment of a select committee on the NHS. It had a good deal more to say about the functions of the Secretary of State for Social Services, his permanent secretary and the DHSS. It was unhappy about the present size and structure of the DHSS and with the way it controls the NHS.

> The two main functions of the Secretary of State for Social Services are to give general directions and policy guidance to the NHS. We consider that wherever he gives guidance to the NHS which has financial consequences he must provide the resources necessary to follow his guidance. Again, if he feels that savings can be made the Secretary of State should indicate what he expects these savings to be. To do less than this is to raise expectations on the part of the public which the NHS is unable to fulfil.

The fact that the Secretary of State and his chief official were answerable for the NHS in detail distorted the relationship between the DHSS and health authorities, encouraging central involvement in matters which would be better left to the authorities. The essential functions of the DHSS were to:

— obtain, allocate and distribute funds for the NHS;
— set objectives, formulate policies and identify priorities;
— monitor the performance of health authorities;
— undertake national manpower planning;
— deal at a national level with pay and conditions of service for NHS staff;
— advise on legislation;

— liaise with other government departments on matters relating to the NHS;
— take a lead in promoting policies designed to improve the health of the nation and prevent ill-health;
— promote experiment, evaluation and the exchange of ideas on health questions.

There would also be departmental involvement in such matters as capital planning, supplies and international health. Some of the criticisms of the DHSS applied to the other health departments, but to a much lesser extent because their scale of operation was smaller.

Given the problems caused by the DHSS role, the commission looked for alternative arrangements. It had already rejected the suggestion that the NHS should be transferred to local government. Another approach sometimes advocated was the establishment of an independent health commission. Such an arrangement had its attractions, but the NHS would remain dependent on the willingness of parliament to vote funds and the effect might therefore be to duplicate functions at present carried out, however unsatisfactorily, by the health department and the top tier of health authorities. The proposal was therefore ruled out, at any rate until it became clear that improvements could not be achieved within the present framework. Having rejected two radical approaches, the commission recommended instead that in England formal responsibility, including accountability to parliament, for the delivery of services should be transferred to RHAs. Another approach, complementary rather than alternative, was to strengthen the arrangements for monitoring the quality of services, which was at present not adequately carried out by the DHSS and the Welsh Office or by some of the health authorities in England and Wales. While an independent special health authority might be established for the purpose, the commission hoped that the structural changes it proposed for the NHS would lead to better monitoring.

Dissatisfaction with the new health authorities and their organisation was one of the main reasons why a Royal Commission had been appointed, so that it is not surprising that a good deal of criticism was received under this head. The commission's approach was to try to help the NHS to help itself rather than produce a detailed blueprint. It thought that management arrangements had tended to be inflexible, and to follow too closely the guidance issued by the health departments. Flexibility was desirable and the commission continued to believe, as it had at the beginning of its investigations, 'that large organisations are most efficient when problems are solved and decisions taken at the lowest effective point'.

It was found that one of the innovations of 1974 — consensus management — was widely supported and the commission accepted the principle but, in view of various problems, recommended further guidance from the health departments on the role of team members. The co-ordinating role of the administrator was important. Another important feature of reorganisation had been the provision of strong professional advisory machinery and here, though accepting the principle, the commission was unhappy at the proliferation of committees that had resulted. It recommended that the health departments should urgently consider with the professions concerned the best way of simplifying the structure.

A lot of the evidence received had criticised administrators, both their increase in number and their performance, and early in its report the commission noted that administrators were often blamed for what had gone wrong with the NHS since reorganisation. 'For the most part we think this blame unfair. Administrators have perhaps been seen as the personification of new and unpopular management arrangements.' It continued: 'It is impossible to assess the quality of NHS administration with precision, but we have been impressed by the many able administrators we have met, the products either of in-service training or the national graduate trainee schemes, who are performing highly responsible tasks with distinction'. Nevertheless the commission believed that reorganisation had led to a decline in the quality of administration at hospital level; and that the role of the hospital administrator at unit or sector level should be expanded. One of the difficulties about hospital administration had been the expansion of functional management. Staff who were part of a functional hierarchy in hospital, while remaining professionally answerable for their services, should be responsible to the administrator in charge for their day-to-day work, and there should be a review of the number of functional managers above unit level. Hospital management should be the responsibility of an executive team of administrator, nurse and doctor. The commission, as we have said, wanted to strengthen the role of the administrator, and it had no criticism of nursing management arrangements, which followed the Salmon Committee recommendations, but it was concerned at the inadequacy of arrangements for medical representation. The clinical division system had not been developed effectively, particulary in large district general hospitals, and this should receive the serious attention of the health departments and the profession, for there did not seem to be a satisfactory alternative to making the system work. These various recommendations about hospital administration applied to all hospitals, but psychiatric hospitals had particular problems. 'Instead of the strong administration they need there has been sometimes almost an administrative vacuum. Psychiatric hospitals particularly need administrative staff of good quality.' The commission noted that the DHSS had set up a working group on organisational and management problems of mental illness hospitals. The group's report was subsequently published by the Department in January 1980.

There was general agreement in evidence to the commission that the structure of the NHS needed slimming, particularly but not only in England, though there was no such agreement about which tier should go. Although some people seemed to see the abolition of a tier as the universal solution to management problems, the commission did not agree. 'There are many reasons for the present difficulties in the NHS and structure is only one of them.' Talking simply of abolishing a tier was not necessarily helpful and it was better to think in terms of levels of functions: the planning of services and their delivery to the patient. Despite these reservations, the commission concluded that there was one tier too many in most places. In England RHAs should continue to be principally responsible for planning and for the major functions they carried at present. Below region in England, and elsewhere in the UK below health department, except in a minority of cases one management level only should carry operational responsibility for services and for effective collaboration with local government. These authorities would be formed from existing single-district areas, by merging existing districts, or by dividing areas. They need not be self-sufficient in all facilities. Since the commission was not offering a universal panacea and was against uniform solutions, it set out the broad ideas behind its recommendations:

— it is convenient, and will lead to better administration, to think of the

management of the NHS as made up of a planning level and a service level;
- each of these levels will have authorities composed largely of laymen; that is to say, not employed by the NHS and so able to represent patients easily;
- only rarely will it be administratively useful and in the interest of the patient to interpose a layer between the two levels we describe;
- the authorities at the service level should be of a size to encourage natural and easy discourse between authority members, patients and health service workers; and to link effectively with other services;
- we would encourage a flexible and imaginative approach to management arrangements at both the planning and service levels and to interaction between them.

Additionally the commission recommended that FPCs in England and Wales should be abolished and their functions assumed by health authorities as a step towards integration. Experience in Scotland and Northern Ireland suggested that the various objections to such a change were not conclusive.

The commission considered that a health authority should not normally exceed 20 members, though multi-district authorities might require slightly more. Membership should continue to be by nomination rather than election.

Finance

Only in its last chapter did the commission discuss directly that essential part of its terms of reference, the best use and management of the financial resources of the NHS. It asked first what should be spent on the NHS. Many of those giving evidence considered that the present level of expenditure was nothing like enough (and there were few suggestions for economies). The commission gave little support to this attitude and did not in fact offer an answer to its question. 'There is no objective or universally acceptable method of establishing what the ''right'' level of expenditure on the NHS should be.' The resources the nation devoted to health care must stand in competition with other claimants on the public and private purse, and they did not have any evidence that the NHS had fared badly in this competition. Nevertheless the commission was not satisfied with the nation's present level of expenditure and its recommendations would, if adopted, add significantly to expenditure. The nation's income was growing, if relatively slowly, and it was right that, as it did, more resources should be devoted to the care of the nation's health. Having said that, the commission issued two cautions. More expenditure would not make the nation proportionately healthier or longer lived, though it might improve the comfort and quality of life of patients or the pay and conditions of staff. And whatever the level of expenditure, demand was likely to rise to meet and exceed it.

Some of the people who advocate higher expenditure believe that it can be achieved by some system of financing other than through exchequer funds. The commission discussed the various methods that have been canvassed: insurance financing, supplementing existing funds with charges or such methods as a state lottery or local voluntary funding, and hypothecation, i.e. setting aside the proceeds of a particular tax for the health service. On all these it thought that the disadvantages would outweight the advantages, or that significant funds could not be raised. On charges it not only rejected suggestions for such things as hotel charges for in-patients and consultation charges for visits to the GP, but also argued that there was a firm case for the gradual but complete extinction of existing charges. Besides pointing out the difficulties of the various arrangements that had been canvassed, the commission made a general point:

> It must be understood that there is no escaping government supervision of health service expenditure whatever system of raising funds is adopted. Some advocates of an insurance system evidently see it as a mechanism for automatically increasing expenditure on the NHS as costs rise. They delude themselves if they do. The rising cost of health care is a major concern in most developed countries, and measures to control it may be, and are, introduced whatever the method of financing health services.

Whatever amount of money may be available for the NHS, the question arises of how it should be distributed. The commission considered that the RAWP approach was sound in principle but that the health departments should prosecute the research necessary for improvement of the resource allocation formulae. It went on to tackle an issue which has been avoided by the development of different formulae in the four countries: 'there is no explicit formula for the distribution of funds to the four parts of the UK, though there are marked differences in the resources provided' and the Commission said that there should be an explicit formula for the distribution of funds to the health service in the four parts of the UK.

Finally on finance the commission rather briefly discussed financial management, touching on equipment and supplies, budgets and incentives, clinicians and resource management, information, the family practitioner services, and capital. In summing up it said: 'The system of financial management in the NHS does not sufficiently encourage efficient resource use. Much of the information required for effective management is not produced, or is inaccurate, or too late to be of value. Those held responsible for expenditure are often not in a position to control it.' It based this assessment on the research study by Professor Perrin and his colleagues at Warwick University, the most substantial of the studies prepared for the commission, which it commended to the health departments.

Reception of the report

It is too soon to assess the long-term impact of the Royal Commission's report. In the short term it was much less than had been expected. In a statement in the House of Commons on the day of publication, the Secretary of State for Social Services said:

> This report has been made to the Government, and it is now up to the Government to respond with our own proposals. On the major issues of structure and management we shall put forward proposals in a document in the autumn, and will invite early comment on that document from the interests affected. Subject to this consultation, it is our view that early progress is essential to simplify the structure of the health service and to devolve management authority to the lowest effective level. A number of the commission's more detailed recommendations will be studied by the Health Departments through the ordinary machinery.

Subsequently the Scottish Home and Health Department said that there would be no consultation on proposals which would involve increased expenditure.

It is normal practice for health ministers to consult health authorities and other interested parties on the recommendations of official reports, and it had been widely assumed that the practice would be followed in the case of the Royal Commission. The ministers' decision to omit such consultation reflected their reluctance in the unfavourable economic climate to discuss recommendations involving increased public expenditure, their anxiety to put change in hand as soon as possible and the fact they already had firm ideas of their own on what changes were needed. Their analysis of the problems of structure and management, and their proposals for change, proved on publication to be broadly in line with the views of the Royal Commission, but they were also very much in line with what the ministers had been saying in opposition, before the views of the commission were known.

Health Services Act 1980

The first formal step towards restructuring the service was the introduction of the Health Services Bill early in December 1979, which became law in August 1980.

The Health Services Act 1980 deals with a number of miscellaneous matters. The provisions concerning finance are described in Chapter 9, and those concerning private practice in Chapter 14. It also contains certain provisions on the General Practice Finance Corporation and pharmaceutical services, and it dissolves the Central Health Services Council. The provisions relating to administration are sections 1 and 2; unlike most of the Act they are concerned only with England and Wales, because the changes contemplated for Scotland do not require legislation.

Both sections are enabling powers, so that formally speaking their inclusion in the Bill did not pre-empt the government's consultation on management arrangements. They permit but do not oblige the Secretary of State to make certain changes in the structure of the NHS and allow the changes to be made gradually rather than all together at a specific date. The effect of section 1 is that English regions and Wales need not consist wholly of areas having AHAs or AHA(T)s and that instead District Health Authorities or District Health Authorities (Teaching) may be established. Section 2 provides that the Secretary of State may direct an AHA or a District Health Authority not to establish a family practitioner committee as it would otherwise be required to do under section 19 of the 1977 Act, but to join with one or more other authorities in establishing one. The purpose of this provision is to avoid the breaking up of existing FPCs which would otherwise follow from the breaking up of the AHAs which established them.

Consultative documents

Shortly after the publication of the Bill, the health departments published consultative papers on structure and management. Specific proposals for the four countries differed considerably, as was to be expected from the differences in existing arrangements, but all were based on the same principles. Thus the explanation given in 'Patients First', the paper for England and Wales, applies equally to the others.

The Royal Commission had summed up the criticism of the 1974 changes as too many tiers, too many administrators in all disciplines, failure to take quick decisions and money wasted, and the government was in no doubt that these criticisms were well-founded. It agreed with the Royal Commission that some changes were necessary but was determined to avoid wholesale upheaval. Its approach was to propose only those adjustments to the present structure that experience suggested were needed to achieve better services to patients. Its proposals had four main elements:

1. the strengthening of management arrangements at the local level with greater delegation of responsibility to those in the hospital and community services;
2. simplification of the structure in England by the removal of the area tier in most of the country and the establishment of district health authorities;
3. simplification of the professional advisory machinery so that the views of clinical doctors, nurses and of the other professionals will be better heard by health authorities;
4. simplification of the planning system in a way which will ensure that regional plans are fully sensitive to district needs.

England

'Patients First' rejected the recommendation of the Royal Commission that RHAs should become accountable to parliament; this was considered inconsistent with the statutory responsibility and accountability to parliament which the Secretary of State must retain. It also rejected suggestions that the NHS might be transferred to local government, or responsibility for social services transferred to the NHS; although there were arguments for both, neither would command general support.

The government rejected the proposition that each authority should appoint a chief executive; the new district health authorities should have teams with the same composition as existing area management teams. There should be maximum delegation of responsibility to hospital and community services level. For each major hospital, or group of hospitals, and associated community services, there should be an administrator and nurse of appropriate seniority to discharge an individual responsibility in conjunction with the medical staff. There should not be a managerial tier between hospital and community services level and district headquarters and the senior administrator and nurse at the former level should wherever possible be directly responsible to the district administrator and nursing officer respectively. Wherever possible staff working within hospitals in non-clinical support functions should be accountable to the hospital administrator rather than to district level managers, and in general there should be no line management hierarchy above hospital level.

The government considered that the need in England was for a pattern of operational authorities throughout the service similar in the main to the present single-district areas. An ideal district health authority would be responsible for a locality which was 'natural' in terms of social geography and health care, large enough to justify the range of specialties normally found in a DGH, but not so large as to make members remote from services and staff, and coterminous with the boundaries of social services, housing and education authorities. Whilst some existing areas and districts came near to this idea, in many cases a balance would have to be struck between the various criteria: social geography, the catchment areas of major hospitals, size and range of facilities (with most districts having a population of 200,000 or over and very few more than 500,000) and coterminosity with local authorities. Existing single-district areas should not be changed unless there would be very substantial advantages. All multi-district areas should be restructured and there was much to be said for retaining existing district boundaries, although sometimes changes would be necessary. If, very exceptionally, a multi-district area were not restructured it should nevertheless be managed on the lines of the new district authorities, with a single team of officers. It was recognised that there might be difficulties in accommodating all the needs of a medical school within a small teaching district and it was hoped that the universities would continue the present trend of forging links with more than one authority.

District health authorities would be responsible for the planning, development and management of health services within national and regional guidelines, and there was therefore a strong case that all these authorities, not only teaching districts, should be responsible for holding the contracts of consultants as well as other staff. A strong advisory role would be needed at regional level.

The splitting up of multi-district areas would have implications for area-based non-clinical services. The paper divided these into two categories: the ambulance service and other services including supplies, works, certain scientific and technical services and the provision of nurse education. It recognised that it could be inefficient and costly to break these up and suggested that there were various possible arrangements on which the new district authorities and RHAs might agree, but it made no positive recommendations.

The new district authorities would consist of a chairman, appointed by the Secretary of State, and about 20 members. Of the latter, four would be local authority representatives, including members from both county and district authorities and London boroughs where appropriate. The practice of having a consultant, a GP, a nurse, a university representative and a trade union nominee on each authority should be continued. The government did not consider it appropriate to have formally elected staff representatives on authorities because employee participation was best achieved through joint consultative machinery. The consultant, GP and nurse representatives should continue to be appointed for their personal qualities and should not be elected representatives. The balance of members should be appointed by RHAs for the individual contribution they could make.

Effective collaboration between health and local authorities would continue to be necessary and the present statutory requirement for the establishment of joint consultative committees would be retained.

As already indicated by the provisions of the Bill, the government rejected the recommendation of the Royal Commission that family practitioner committees should be abolished. It did not believe that there was any major advantage that would justify upsetting the present system. Consultation was promised on the membership, funding and staffing of FPCs which would relate to two or more districts.

The paper, while acknowledging support given to CHCs by the Royal Commission, suggested that in future authority members would be less remote from local services and more closely in touch with the needs of the community and that the need for separate consumer representation in these circumstances was less clear. The government would therefore welcome views on whether CHCs should be retrained.

Two of the four main elements in the government's proposals were remitted for action by the DHSS. On the simplification of the professional advisory machinery, a working party had been established under the chairmanship of the Chief Medical Officer. The discipline of planning in both the Department and the NHS had demonstrated its value and was to be retained. A simpler system was being worked out and would be discussed with the service.

While the saving of money was not the main purpose of these proposals, the government did aim to reduce management costs and believed that after the transitional costs had been met the proposals, together with the general drive in the NHS for greater efficiency, should enable management costs to be reduced by up to 10 per cent. It had therefore been decided to retain central oversight of management costs.

One of the longest sections of the paper discussed the implementation of the proposals (including the effects on staff and consultation with staff interests). A distinction was drawn between structural change and change in management arrangements within districts, which need not be handled together. It was envisaged that much of the restructuring could be completed by mid-1982 and the aim was that all should have taken effect by the end of 1983. There was no reason why change throughout the country, or within a region, should all take place at the same time. An important decision announced in the paper was that the government rejected the recommendation of the Royal Commission that there should be an enquiry into the problems of the health service in London. Decisions about London should be taken in the light of reports already in hand and changes in the structure of the NHS in London should correspond to, and so far as possible should be implemented on the same timetable as, those in the rest of the country.

The paper envisaged that RHAs would have the task of initiating and overseeing changes in the structure of the NHS at area/district level and in the longer term they would be responsible for co-ordinating strategic plans, including medical manpower and service planning, for the allocation of resources and for ensuring that strategic plans were implemented. However, they must stand back from the operational activities of the districts and it might be necessary to adopt changes in the arrangements for exercising the regional role. RHAs must retain responsibility for financial control and for monitoring the implementation of district plans, but it was less clear that it would be necessary for them to have a broader monitoring role. The paper cast doubts on the role of region as a provider of many non-clinical support services for areas and districts, and favoured the level of these services being determined by the authorities using them, often on the basis of payments. Finally, it asked for views on whether in the longer term RHA members should be composed partly or wholly of district representatives.

Wales

Proposals for Wales were set out in two paragraphs of 'Patients First'. In the absence of a regional tier, and with most districts too small to satisfy the criteria for the new English districts, no general change in structure was proposed. It was, however, proposed to treat the Welsh health authorities as though they were like the new district authorities; there should be an early review of their management structures with the elimination of the formal district structure. While there was emphasis on the need for sensitivity to the needs of the various localities and on not producing an inflexible pattern, the aim was the same sort of delegation of decision-making as was envisaged for England.

Scotland

The Scottish consultative paper discussed the ways in which it was possible to implement the Royal Commission recommendation that below health department only one management level should carry operational responsibility for services. The health board was the authority on which the whole organisation hinged and any change at that level would have the widest repercussions. Such a change would not be justified, and there was not a good case for changing the numbers of boundaries of existing boards. Nor was any change proposed in the size of membership, which ranged from 14 to 22.

Instead, simplification was sought by the abolition of districts. The ten boards with multi-district areas were asked to review their administrative arrangements to this end. It was recognised that in a few cases that might be difficult, though even then it was hoped that the number of districts could be reduced. The paper suggested various measures which might follow from the abolition of districts: increased management responsibilities at unit and sector management levels, an increase in the number of sectors, the appointment of staff in some professional fields with supervisory responsibilities in part of an area, and even on occasion some strengthening of staff at area level. However, in line with the government's general approach, the main development would be to transfer responsibility down to local level rather than up to area. As was to be expected, no regional organisation was proposed but the paper saw a need to improve collaboration between boards and suggested joint planning committees for those parts of the country that look to Glasgow and Edinburgh to provide specialised services.

The paper simply sought views on how to simplify the professional advisory structure and on the value of the work done by local health councils. If LHCs were to be retained, it suggested, it might be possible to reduce their number.

As in the other parts of the UK, it was stressed that as many decisions as possible about the day-to-day running of the service should take place locally at unit or sector level and, again in line with the rest of the UK, the paper accepted the Royal Commission view that functional managers at unit and sector should be responsible to the administrator for their day-to-day work. It stressed that strong unit or sector administration required for its success that medical and nursing responsibilities at that level of management should be clearly identified. While there was no problem with nursing, arrangements in the medical profession were not always clear, and the profession was asked to discuss its arrangements.

Northern Ireland

The Northern Ireland consultative paper exemplified the same general approach applied to the particular circumstances of the province, including a continuation of the integrated system of health and social care. The main elements were very similar to those set out in 'Patients First', but the introduction of a straight-forward planning system replaced the simplification of an existing system, and an additional element was the clarification of the relationship between the DHSS and the health and social service boards.

In connection with the last element the paper rejected suggestions for the establishment of a regional authority either independent of or in an agency relationship with the DHSS. Instead, various measures were proposed: the introduction of a planning system, discussions with the four boards, the Central Services Agency, the Staffs Council and the Health and Social Services Council on the simplification of consultative machinery between the Department and these bodies, a renewed emphasis on delegation within the structure and a review of the medical advisory machinery.

The criteria of social geography, catchment areas, size and range of facilities and the requirements of teaching hospitals, it was argued, all told against replacing the existing four boards by a larger number of district authorities. The Eastern Board was much larger than the others and faced more complex problems, but nothing would be gained by its division. The government would like to see the membership of boards reduced below the present 25 – 34 while making allowance for the inclusion of personal social services, but reduction might be possible only at the expense of making less provision to reflect broadly the interests of communities. Boards were asked to review their committee structures, with a view to simplification. Views were invited on whether finance officers should become full members of the executive team and on whether clinical members would be needed on teams after the review of the professional advisory machinery.

As in Wales and Scotland, simplification was sought by the abolition of districts and by maximum delegation to local management. Application of this approach was thought reasonably straightforward for three of the four boards, but not for the Eastern. Three possible models for revised management arrangements were suggested for discussion, one of them retaining districts, though reduced in number.

Consultation and after

The proposals in the consultative documents were no more successful than previous versions from 1969 onwards in obtaining the full support of all those consulted, and that was only to be expected. The functions of the NHS are so many and complex that no rearrangement is likely to be equally suitable for all purposes and therefore equally welcome to all interests. Moreover, any proposed changes are likely to appear to benefit certain authorities, interests and professional groups and work to the disadvantage of others. Thus the proposals for functional management were generally welcomed by administrators but disliked by functional managers, and in England the staff of health districts generally favoured the proposals for restructuring but some if not all multi-district areas did not. Two general criticisms may be mentioned. It was argued that the emphasis on a more local management, based on districts, though right for some purposes, discounted the value of large scale for such services as supplies and ambulances, and for planning; and that the inevitable consequence, despite the intentions, would be to increase the role of regional authorities in England. The other argument was that the thinking behind the proposals was based too much on problems of hospital management and that they would work against the integration of hospital and community services, which had been one of the intentions of 1974. There was also widespread scepticism as to whether the savings in management costs, put by ministers at around £30 million a year in England, would be achieved. Nevertheless, the DHSS was able to claim that the broad thrust of comments received supported the aims set out in 'Patients First' and this was not surprising as the proposals broadly reflected the recommendations of the Royal Commission which in turn had broadly reflected the evidence presented to it.

The government's decisions for England were announced in July 1980 and set out in circular HC(80)8. For the most part they were a confirmation of the proposals in 'Patients First'. In one respect there was a change. The weight of comment had been strongly in favour of community health councils and it was decided that for the time being these should be retained, with one council for each district health authority. The government would issue a consultative paper seeking views on the membership and role of CHCs and later on the position would be looked at again to see whether these bodies were needed alongside the new health authorities. No decision was announced on the proposal that consultant contracts should be with the district authorities; comment from the profession had been generally hostile and the matter was deferred for further discussion between the DHSS, the profession and the NHS.

All AHAs and health districts would be replaced by one or more district health authorities (DHAs) responsible for planning, development and management of health services in its district within national and regional strategic guidelines. Only exceptionally would a district have a population below 150,000 or above 500,000. RHAs were to make recommendations to the Secretary of State about the future pattern of DHAs and it was hoped that most of the new authorities could be brought into formal existence on or before 1 April 1982. The process should in any case be completed by 1 April 1983, though there might be unavoidable exceptions. London was expected to conform to this timetable despite the particular difficulties there, which were set out in an appendix by the recently appointed London Advisory Group. Membership of authorities was to be as envisaged in 'Patients First' but with only 16 members plus the chairman. It would be for the new DHAs to decide on arrangements for services and functions covering more than one district. They should be guided by a presumption in favour of dividing them into district components unless there were strong arguments, for example of effectiveness and economy, against doing so. The Supply Council would give guidance on the organisation of supplies and the DHSS on ambulance services.

Each DHA was to have wide discretion in determining its management arrangements; in deliberate contrast to 1974 the government refrained from specifying what posts should be created. There were only two exceptions to this. Each authority was to appoint a district management team with the same composition and functions as existing area management teams, and should arrange their services into units of management, directly accountable to the district administrator and district nursing officer respectively. There should be maximum delegation to units, and wherever possible functional staff working in units should be accountable to the unit administrator.

The circular did not in general describe the roles of managers, but it did set out the co-ordinating role of the district administrator:

> In a service as complex as the NHS and comprising so many different independent disciplines and functions there must be clear arrangements for

> administrative co-ordination, which are understood and accepted by all. This will be a responsibility of the district administrator. This does not give him any managerial authority over other chief officers, but it does impose on him a responsibility to see that an account is provided to the authority on how its policies and priorities are being implemented. He will also be responsible for ensuring that individual responsibility is identified for each piece of action which the authority requires to be carried out. He will be the secretary of the authority and thus will be required to act as the official channel of communication on behalf of the authority with public authorities, the press and the public, obtaining reports from other officers as necessary for circulation to the authority.

The unit administrator was to carry responsibility for administrative co-ordination at that level on the same principle. The central control of management costs would continue, with a target 10 per cent below the March 1980 figure.

At the time of writing, measures were being taken to implement these decisions. By the end of July 1981 ministers had announced their decisions on the recommendations of RHAs for districts. There were to be 193 DHAs. Their populations were generally within the range envisaged in HC(80)8, but extended from 86,000 (Rugby) to 836,000 (Leicestershire). Some would be designated teaching districts, with additional university representation among the membership, but legislation would be sought to permit the omission of 'Teaching' from their titles. New membership regulations were made (SI81/933). The Health Service Supply Council issued its guidance on the supply function in circular SCC(81)2. The general effect was to enhance greatly the regional role.

Consultative papers had been issued on a number of topics, but final decisions had not been announced. Matters being considered included professional advisory machinery, the role and membership of CHCs and arrangements for the administration of family practitioner services.

One other publication should be noted. *Care in Action* was described in the sub-title as 'a handbook of policies and priorities for the health and personal social services in England'. It replaced the earlier priorities documents discussed in this book. Like most of the present government's publications it was shorter and less detailed than earlier documents. It was addressed to the chairmen and members of DHAs and social services committees.

For Wales 1980 saw no firm decisions comparable with those of HC(80)8. Instead, in July the Secretary of State issued a full consultative paper to replace the Welsh section of 'Patients First'. It announced certain decisions, such as the retention of FPCs and CHCs, and was clear about the intention to introduce local units of management on the English model, but its main purpose was to meet three objections raised in the original consultations. First, there had been a strong feeling in favour of basing the new structure on existing districts rather than areas. The paper argued that the Welsh districts were not comparable in size or standing with English districts and that the desired emphasis on local management would be achieved by delegation to strong units of management. Secondly, strong arguments had been particularly made for the division of two areas — Dyfed and Mid Glamorgan. The paper argued against division, particularly of Dyfed, but left the final decision until further comments were received. Thirdly, there had been criticisms that the NHS in Wales was insufficiently co-ordinated. The paper dicussed the role of the Welsh Office in achieving this co-ordination, and looked for further delegation of responsibilities to AHAs, but rejected the solution of a 'regional' authority for Wales. Instead it proposed an advisory council, which might be called the Welsh Health Council. Decisions were announced in June 1981. The Dyfed AHA would be divided, a new authority being formed for the former county of Pembrokeshire. Districts would go, and would be replaced by units of management, ranging in number from three to seven. The pattern of units varied; some were entirely geographical, but most authorities had some area-wide units, particularly for psychiatric services and community services. A Welsh Health Council would not be established. To ensure that region-wide issues received a sufficient public airing there would be a series of formal meetings under the chairmanship of the Secretary of State or the parliamentary under-secretary.

In Scotland the outcome of consultations has been inconclusive. At the end of July 1980 the Secretary of State announced that there had been considerable broad agreement that the administrative structure could be simplified and that no changes were needed in the number or areas of health boards. He proposed to ask those boards making use of services provided in Edinburgh and Glasgow to form joint consultative committees. Three boards had agreed that they could dispense with districts and he would encourage them to do so. The seven other boards with districts preferred to retain them and he intended to pursue the matter further with them. Boards had generally agreed about the need to delegate as much as possible to the unit or sector level and he would ask them to make the necessary arrangements. There had also been general agreement on the need to simplify the professional advisory structure, and further discussions would be held. There had been a marked division of opinion on local health councils; he was not persuaded that they need be a permanent feature of the NHS in Scotland and he would decide whether or not to propose their abolition when there was a prospect of new health service legislation. A year later decisions had still not been announced.

Early consultations in Northern Ireland proved even less conclusive and a statement by the Minister of State in June 1980 was mainly about arrangements for further consultation. Certain decisions were announced a year later. The basic structure of the four health and social services boards and the Central Services Agency and the Staffs Council would be retained; weaknesses should be remedied within the existing structure. There must be greater delegation of authority to local units of management within boards; the regional support services provided by the Department, the CSA and the Staffs Council needed to be matched much more closely to the requirements of the user boards; the planning, funding and monitoring of the specialist hospital services provided on a regional basis required greater attention, and the GP services needed to be more closely involved in the planning and delivery of care in the community. The further reviews and studies required for these purposes were to be completed by the end of the year, and changes would be phased in over the year beginning 1 April 1982. Meanwhile, boards had been given guidance on the organisation of units of management to replace districts. Each unit of management should have a unit management group comprising as appropriate an administrator, a nurse and a social services officer with executive authority together with, as equal participants, a representative of the hospital consultants and of GPs. The group would not operate corporately unless the board so directed. Ministers decided against the establishment of a separate regional authority or a contractors' committee for the family practitioner services. It was also decided not to divide the Eastern Board, despite the problems caused by its size.

Conclusion

The story told in this chapter stops almost in mid-sentence. It will have evolved further between going to press and publication, and further again before the reader gets to this page. Whether the story will actually have an ending remains to be seen. Whilst most people would agree that 'we cannot afford to get it wrong this time', the story since 1969 has been of the interplay between pressures from within the NHS and national politics, and the future cannot be predicted simply within a health service context. Even if the story does have an ending in the sense of a long respite from widespread structural change it is certain that changes will be made from time to time, as they have been ever since 1948, to meet changing circumstances and problems. An ability to change in response to need is essential if the service is to continue to function well.

This book is not the place for predictions. However, from the standpoint of mid-1981 two things can be said with certainty about the future. The first is that the implementation of the proposed changes will involve difficulties for the service. While the government hopes to avoid repeating the drastic upheavals of 1974, the changes it requires are widespread and sometimes radical, and some of the strains of the earlier reorganisation will be felt again. At a time when the personal future of nearly all senior managers is in question they will have to maintain continuities and financial control while establishing new roles and relationships and at the same time keep within lower management costs. During the transitional period some of the problems of the service may not receive the management attention they need. The other certainty is that in the longer term the changes will make a considerable difference to the management of the service, even if they achieve only half of what the government expects of them and even if some of the consequences are not what ministers expect. Nevertheless they will not transform the NHS; it will remain recognisably the service as it has existed since the 1974 reorganisation.

The story of structures and management arrangements is not the story of health service management. These things exist as a means — or sometimes a hindrance — to the purpose of management. The task of management will remain what it has been in the past: to make the best use of resources, to pursue efficiency and effectiveness, to establish priorities, to plan developments and to carry them out. If some of this terminology dates only from the last ten years or so, the task is older than that and will remain basically the same even if, as can be expected, new terminologies and concepts are adopted. The performance of the task will continue to depend on administrative techniques, financial management, personnel management and so on. There is very little in this book which will be out-dated by the forthcoming changes even though some of it will have to be applied in a changed context.

Health service management cannot in fact be presented as a story at all, for it does not have a beginning, shape and ending. At its weakest it can be accused of being no more than reaction to an unending series of events. At its most effective it is still the interplay of the planned and the contingent. Possibly even more than in other forms of management, the results of health service management are difficult to assess. A fairly common criticism of the NHS is that it measures its performance in terms of inputs, and knows very little about its outputs. Where management can be measured it is in terms of inputs: whether cash allocations were spent but not overspent, whether staff were recruited as planned, whether a hospital was completed on time and within the cost limits, and so on. Less is known about the outputs in terms of cures, treatment and care provided, and very little indeed about how these activities relate to the overall task of improving the nation's health. The conceptual difficulties of measuring these things are very great.

In any case the responsibility for this 'output' lies not with management but with the doctors, nurses and other caring professions. Management is only a facilitating process, made necessary by the complexities of health care and the large resources that it requires. Managers are sometimes accused of empire building and of doing things simply for administrative convenience. Although these accusations may occasionally be justified, health service managers are acutely aware that theirs is a facilitating role and that they are not in control of the essential activities of the service even though in some respects they are responsible for its overall performance. Their role remains a vital one, and the fact is acknowledged in a curiously negative way. When a service is lacking, or breaks down, the blame is put on the politicians or on the managers or on both. By the same reasoning they should receive the credit when, far more often, services are provided and do not break down, though the credit is less frequently given.

Further reading

Circular

England

HC(80)8. Health Service Development: Structure and Management

Official reports

DHSS, Northern Ireland. *Consultative Paper on the Structure and Management of Health and Personal Social Services in Northern Ireland.* HMSO Belfast 1979

DHSS and Welsh Office. *Patients First: Consultative paper on the structure and management of the National Health Service in England and Wales.* HMSO 1979

Royal Commission on the National Health Service. *Report* (Cmnd 7615). HMSO 1979

Royal Commission on the National Health Service. *A Service for Patients: Conclusions and Recommendations of the Royal Commission's Report.* HMSO 1979

Royal Commission on the National Health Service. Research Papers No. 1 *The Working of the NHS.* 1978. No. 2 *The Management of Finance in the NHS.* 1978. No. 3 *Allocating Health Resources. A commentary on the Report of the Resource Allocation Working Party.* 1978. No. 4 *Doctor Manpower 1975-2000: alternative forecasts and their resource implications.* 1978. No. 5 *Patients' attitudes to the Hospital Service.* 1979. No. 6 *Access to Primary Care.*

1979. HMSO

SHHD. *Structure and Management of the NHS in Scotland.* HMSO Edinburgh 1979

Welsh Office. *The Structure and Management of the National Health Service in Wales.* HMSO Cardiff 1980

Other publications

King's Fund Centre. Project papers based on working paper of the Royal Commission on the NHS. 1980

Abbreviations

The use of abbreviations and acronyms in the health service greatly increased with the reorganisation of the service in 1974. The following list consists mainly of those used in management since then but also a number of pre-1974 abbreviations, some of the main professional bodies and trade unions and a few other abbreviations in common use. It does not include professional qualifications or medical terms, or the initials used by the health departments for their various series of circulars.

AA	Area Administrator
ACAS	Advisory Conciliation and Arbitration Service
ACHCEW	Association of Community Health Councils for England and Wales
A&E	Accident and Emergency
ADO	Area Dental Officer
AEG	Area Executive Group
AHA	Area Health Authority
AHA(T)	Area Health Authority (Teaching)
AMO	Area Medical Officer
AMT	Area Management Team
ANO	Area Nursing Officer
APO	Area Personnel Officer
APhO	Area Pharmaceutical Officer
ASO	Area Supplies Officer
ASTMS	Association of Scientific, Technical and Managerial Staffs
AT	Area Treasurer
ATO	Area Team of Officers
BG	Board of Governors
BMA	British Medical Association
BoM	Board of Management
CADO	Chief Administrative Dental Officer
CAMO	Chief Administrative Medical Officer
CANO	Chief Administrative Nursing Officer
CAPO	Chief Administrative Phamaceutical Officer
CCU	Coronary Care Unit
CHC	Community Health Council
CHSC	Central Health Services Council
CMO	Chief Medical Officer
CMS	Community Medicine Specialist
COHSE	Confederation of Health Service Employees
CPSM	Council for Professions Supplementary to Medicine
CSA	Common Services Agency
CSSD	Central Sterile Supply Department
DA	District Administrator
DCP	District Community Physician
DDO	District Dental Officer
DEG	District Executive Group
DFO	District Finance Officer
DGH	District General Hospital

DHA	District Health Authority
DHSS	Department of Health and Social Security
DHSS-NI	Department of Health and Social Security (Northern Ireland)
DivNO	Divisional Nursing Officer
DMC	District Medical Committee
DMT	District Management Team
DNE	Director of Nurse Education
DNO	District Nursing Officer
DPhO	District Pharmaceutical Officer
DPO	District Personnel Officer
DRO	Disablement Resettlement Officer
FIS	Financial Information System
FPC	Family Practitioner Committee
FPS	Family Practitioner Services
GMC	General Medical Council
GMWU	General and Municipal Workers' Union
GNC	General Nursing Council
GP	General Practitioner
HAA	Hospital Activity Analysis
HAS	Health (*formerly* Hospital) Advisory Service
HB	Health Board
HCPT	Health Care Planning Team
HIPE	Hospital In-Patient Enquiry
HMC	Hospital Management Committee
HPSS	Health and Personal Social Services
HSSB	Health Service Supply Branch
ICD	International Classification of Diseases (International Statistical Classification of Diseases, Injuries and Causes of Death)
IHSA	Institute of Health Service Administrators
IPS	Institute of Purchasing and Supply
JCC	Joint Consultative Committee
JCPT	Joint Care Planning Team
LHC	Local Health Council
LMC	Local Medical Committee
LRC	Local Representative Committee
MEC	Medical Executive Committee
MPC	Medical Practices Committee
MRC	Medical Research Council
NAHA	National Association of Health Authorities
NALGO	National and Local Government Officers Association
NAWCH	National Association for the Welfare of Children
NHS	National Health Service
NO	Nursing Officer
NSC	National Staff Committee
NUPE	National Union of Public Employees
O & M	Organisation and Methods
OPCS	Office of Population Censuses and Surveys
OPD	Out-patient Department
PAA	Principal Administrative Assistant
PAC	Public Accounts Committee

PARR	Proposals for the Allocation of Revenue Resources
PHLS	Public Health Laboratory Service
PNO	Principal Nursing Officer
PPA	Prescription Pricing Authority
PPM	Planned Preventive Maintenance
PSS	Personal Social Services
RA	Regional Administrator
RAO	Regional Ambulance Officer
RAWP	Resource Allocation Working Party
RCCS	Revenue Consequences of Capital Schemes
Rcn	Royal College of Nursing
RDO	Regional Dental Officer
RHA	Regional Health Authority
RHB	Regional Hospital Board
RMO	Regional Medical Officer
RMSO	Regional Management Services Officer
RNO	Regional Nursing Officer
RPhO	Regional Pharmaceutical Officer
RSO	Regional Supplies Officer
RT	Regional Treasurer
RTO	Regional Team of Officers
RWO	Regional Works Officer
SAS	Standard Accounting System
SHARE	Scottish Health Authorities Revenue Equalisation
SHDO	Senior Hospital Dental Officer
SHHD	Scottish Home and Health Department
SHMO	Senior Hospital Medical Officer
SHSPC	Scottish Health Service Planning Council
SIFT	Service Increment for Teaching
SMR	Standard Mortality Ratio
SNO	Senior Nursing Officer
SPS	Standard Payroll System
STAMP	Standard Manpower Planning System
TGWU	Transport and General Workers' Union
TSSU	Theatre Sterile Supply Unit
WHTSO	Welsh Health Technical Services Organisation
WO	Welsh Office

Index

Reports are indexed as, e.g. 'Trethowan Report'; full details will be found in the lists of references at the end of the relevant chapter. Organisations, etc. are indexed by their full title; for abbreviations see page 487.